R. E. LEE

ROBERT EDWARD LEE IN THE DRESS UNIFORM OF A LIEUTENANT
OF ENGINEERS

After a portrait painted in 1838 by William E. West

Winner of the 1935 Pulitzer Prize

R. E. Lee

A Biography

Volume 1

Douglas Southall Freeman

Simon Publications

2001

First published in June 1935 by Ch. Scribner's Sons

Library of Congress Card Number: 38034421

ISBN: 1-931313-36-9

Published by Simon Publications, Safety Harbor, FL

TO
I. G. F.
WHO NEVER DOUBTED

FOREWORD

AFTER I had accepted the invitation Charles Scribner's Sons extended me in 1915 to write a biography of General Robert E. Lee, I was surprised to find that much the larger part of the source material had never been consulted. The records of the Bureau of Engineers and of the United States Military Academy had not been explored for information on Lee's professional career. Few collections of manuscripts belonging to Southern families had been searched for his letters. No effort apparently had been made to determine his state of mind in the winter of 1860–61 by examining the correspondence and memoirs of those who had been with him in Texas. His own unpublished military papers had never been assembled. Of his labors as a military administrator, and of the perplexities he faced in the perennial reorganization of an army that suffered ceaselessly from attrition, virtually nothing was known. Thousands of pages there were on the details of his battles, but surprisingly little concerning the development of his strategy. The wealth of illustrative incident had not been sifted from the lesser-known personal narratives of the War between the States. Even the files of Washington and Lee University, covering the years when he was laboring to save the South from becoming a second Poland, had been in great measure neglected by biographers.

For these reasons it became necessary to conduct a long research. As this brought new facts to light, a work projected for one volume grew to four. Had not the world war demonstrated the importance of the careful study of the campaigns of great strategists, I should feel disposed to apologize for such elaborate presentation. It is, however, indisputable that the British in that struggle certainly were the gainers for their close reading of Henderson's *Jackson,* and Foch for his familiarity with Napoleon. The professional soldier who will follow, step by step, the unfolding of Lee's strategic plans, will, I think, learn much and perhaps equally from the leader of the Army of Northern Virginia.

FOREWORD

Should this biography facilitate that study, I shall not feel that I have trespassed too much on the time of military men. I hope the general reader, especially if he already has some knowledge of Lee, will find in this book enough of fresh incident to justify his labor in turning so many pages.

Prolonged as my investigation has been, and puzzling as some of its problems have appeared to be, I have been fully repaid by being privileged to live, as it were, for more than a decade in the company of a great gentleman. A biographer can ask no richer compensation. Second only to that has been the satisfaction of meeting many grateful inheritors of the Lee tradition. In the dark period after the War between the States, the most glamorous memory of the South was that of the Confederate cause, whose finest figure was Lee. In his military achievement, Southern people saw the flowering of their racial stock; in his social graces they beheld their ideals embodied; in the honors paid his memory, every one of Lee's former soldiers felt that he had himself received the accolade. An old veteran, after meeting "Marse Robert" only once on the road, in the midst of some hurried military movement, would speak of him with a reverence no less marked than that of Colonel Talcott or Colonel Taylor, who had seen Lee daily and in all the revealing cross-lights of victory and of disaster. Nearly all those who gave me their personal recollections of General Lee are dead now, but their sons and their daughters have like devotion to his name. It has been profoundly gratifying to search out these men and women, to gather their family stories of Lee, and to copy those of his letters that they have saved from destruction. These individuals form a company so numerous and so helpful that I have thought it proper to list them, and others to whom I am indebted, in a special appendix of acknowledgments, which will be found at the end of the last volume of this work. I should like to add that in all my research I encountered only three individuals, one historical society, and one private library possessing Lee papers that did not cheerfully permit their use.

For the periods of Lee's life before and subsequent to the War between the States, my principal task was the interesting but comparatively easy one of bringing material together from many

viii

scattered sources. Once these documents revealed Lee as in all respects a man of normal impulses and of simple soul, presentation was not difficult. There were no "secrets" and no scandals to be exposed or explained. His quiet life, as engineer and as educator, did not lend itself to the "new" biography which is already becoming conventionalized. Neither was there any occasion to attempt an "interpretation" of a man who was his own clear interpreter.

Portrayal of Lee the soldier was, from the very nature of war, a more complex undertaking. For military biography, like military history in general, may fail to be instructive because, paradoxically, it is too informative. On occasion I have tried to master some narrative of a campaign, written by an author who manifestly knew the facts, but I have found my guide hustling me from one opposing line to the other and back again so often that he hopelessly confused me and wholly dissipated the "fog of war." The existence of that "fog" is, however, in military history as in actual hostilities, one of the prime realities. Every soldier's strategy must be judged, *inter alia,* by the efforts he makes to get information, by the nature and extent of the information he collects, and by the skill with which he analyzes it. Military biography written without regard for the scope and limitations of this intelligence cannot be accurate. To avoid an unscientific method, which is more often recognized than remedied, I have endeavored to give the reader no information beyond that which Lee possessed at a particular moment regarding the strength, movements and plans of his adversary. Except in one or two instances, as when he follows Pickett's charge at Gettysburg, the reader remains at Confederate G. H. Q. throughout the war and receives the intelligence reports only as they arrive. Even happenings in the Army of Northern Virginia are not mentioned until they are announced to Lee, though this sometimes has necessitated the lengthy employment of the awkward past-perfect tense. When explanation must be made of Federal operations that were unknown to the Confederate high command, this has usually been done in footnotes.

Whether to include or to exclude military matters not directly related to Lee's strategy and battles was a second puzzling question. He was constantly hampered because the authority of the Richmond administration was restricted and because the individualism of many of its supporters could not be bent, even in the fire of war, to reasonable co-operation. A revolutionary government was daily brought nearer to death by striving to live constitutionally. Professional soldiers, accustomed to the co-operation of a trained staff, shared responsible command with lawyers, planters, and politicians. Certain men whose names are now forgotten and whose generalship did not rise above mediocrity were figures so powerful at the moment that Lee had to take their peculiarities into account and sometimes had to entrust them with important operations. The necessities of war required the imposition of a strict discipline on an army which, in the words of one of its brilliant survivors, regarded itself at the outset as a "voluntary association of gentlemen, organized to drive out the enemy." There could be no cold impersonality in directing such a force. Moreover, from the late summer of 1862, the subsistence of the army was a major factor in determining when and where Lee could give battle. The decline in the horse supply progressively decreased the mobility of his forces.

Were these things properly to be explained in a biography of Lee or should they be dismissed with mere mention? And if they were to be treated extensively, how were they to be kept from encumbering and perhaps obscuring the account of field-operations? All these factors, I concluded, were as truly a part of the biography of Lee as his defense of Richmond in 1862 or his march into Pennsylvania. I decided that the simplest way to discuss subjects of a collateral character was to place them in the chapters devoted to winter quarters or in those covering the occasional long pauses in the fighting. This method, I hope, saves the narrative from being loaded with extraneous detail.

The continuity and close relationship of the campaigns on all the Confederate fronts had likewise to be made plain. Never was the government at Richmond able to consider the supply or the reinforcement of the Army of Northern Virginia in the absolute terms of that army's requirements. Always Lee's operations were bound up with those in Tennessee, in the Gulf States or along the seaboard. Similarly, the times were very few when Lee could regard any campaign on his front as definitely ended. After June 1, 1862, a new operation was dictated, in almost every instance, by the one that had preceded it. The losses in one limited the possibilities of the next. From Mechanicsville to Appomattox, Lee's strategy formed a continuous whole not readily broken into chapters or divided into periods. Looking backwards, it is obvious, of course, that the reduction of the food supply, the death of Jackson, the defeat at Gettysburg, the virtual starvation of the horses in the winter of 1863–64, the inability of Lee to force Grant back across the Rappahannock after the battle of the Wilderness, and the failure of conscription in the summer of 1864 marked definite stages in the approach of defeat that may have been inevitable from the first. None of this was plain at the time, and even if it had been apparent to the rest of the world, it would not have been admitted by the majority of Southerners. Lee saw clearly and without illusion, but most men hoped that the experience of Washington's continentals would be repeated and that a final Yorktown would redeem disaster. This state of mind was a ponderable factor in the war in Virginia. Any formal grouping of campaigns might, therefore, dispose the reader to attribute to the Confederates a sense of approaching defeat that was never theirs until the winter of 1864–65. I consequently have not essayed to divide Lee's operations into periods.

In respect to military terminology, I have applied that of Hardee's *Tactics* to all manœuvres covered by that standard work, which both armies used. For strategical description, I have, as a rule, adhered to the terms used in the reports of the period I have treated; but where those terms have a different meaning today, or where force and clarity seemed to require it, I have not hesitated to adopt the language of modern war. I have, for example, often referred to a "sector," and I have changed the familiar phrase "corps of observation" to "column of observation," because "corps" had at that time another and a more generally employed meaning.

Direct quotation, always a vexing question in historical writing, is doubly so in the case of Lee, who wrote thousands of letters over a period of nearly forty years There is opportunity, of course, of presenting the "man entire" by the liberal use of his correspondence, but the advantage of this is more than offset, I think, by the fact that a letter which begins with one subject may cover a dozen others and thereby divert attention from the main theme. Those who wish to see Lee as his own biographer, in his writings to his family and friends, will do well to consult Captain Robert E. Lee's delightful *Recollections and Letters of General Lee* and the two works on Lee by Reverend J. William Jones. It has seemed to me desirable to avoid long quotations and, instead, to weave into the narrative those brief sentences in which, with characteristic directness, General Lee epitomized his opinions. It has been necessary, however, to publish many letters hitherto unknown and to reprint *in extenso* a few that have heretofore appeared. In some of these latter cases, the failings of Doctor Jones as a copyist have prompted me to refer directly to the originals. Instances will be given where sharp and critical passages in some of the best-known letters of General Lee were deleted by Jones without any notice to the reader of an omission.

It will be found that I have retained many direct quotations of Lee's conversation. As these often are embodied in reminiscences written after the occurrence, they present possibilities of misinterpretation at the same time that they may help to create an atmosphere of reality. The canons of criticism that I have applied in accepting or rejecting direct quotation of this character are familiar and simple. I can only hope they have been rigidly applied. The nearer the quotation is to the event, of course, the more reliable it is apt to be. Remarks made by Lee to young soldiers or students, and to those who met him infrequently were, as a rule, more accurately remembered than those addressed to old generals or to staff officers who saw him often and might easily confuse two or more interviews. Exchanges of small moment, thought typical of the man, are less overdrawn than those cited by partisans in historical disputes. Several cases are mentioned in the footnotes where Lee's plain words have been expanded and glossed until he is made to deliver orations—which he never did. The alleged quotations that are most justly subject to suspicion are those that occur in publications prepared late in life by professional lecturers or *raconteurs*. In the very few instances where I have accepted direct quotations of this sort I have given in footnotes my reasons for doing so.

A propos of footnotes, it should perhaps be explained that while this biography has been written from the primary sources, some of the early works on Lee are in a classification midway between first and second-hand testimony. A very good illustration is the *Life of General Robert E. Lee* by John Esten Cooke. Its author was one of General Jeb Stuart's staff officers and was frequently with Lee. When he and others who enjoyed a like advantage are cited, it will be understood that, unless otherwise indicated, the references are to their direct evidence on events they witnessed. If secondary sources are quoted on incidents in the career of Lee or of his army, it is because the authors of those works appear to have had access to valid material which, in the the absence of specific reference on their part, it is impossible to identify. For the general background of the narrative, in matters not directly concerning Lee or his forces, I have not attempted to duplicate work of reliable historians but have freely and gratefully availed myself of their findings.

It may be that I shall irritate some readers by restraint and disappoint others by failing to answer some of Lee's detractors. On the one point, it seems to me that the fame of no man is promoted by extravagant utterance. Truth is not furthered thereby. Seventy years after the event, assertive rhetoric has no place in historical narrative. Comparison of Lee with other great soldiers falls, I think, into much the same category, for, as I have stated in the general review of his achievements as a soldier, in Volume IV, military circumstance is incommensurable. Lee, like every other leader, is to be judged by what he accomplished, where he was, with what he had at his command. Except to call attention to divergent opinion or to conflicts of testimony, I have purposely avoided historical controversy. I have tried to state the facts and to interpret them when it has seemed proper to do so.

FOREWORD

If other writers have a different interpretation, it is for the reader, and not for me, to sit in judgment.

A biographer, like a dramatist, has no place on the stage. When he has made his bow to his audience and has spoken his prologue, telling what he will try to exhibit, it is his duty to retire to the wings, to raise the curtain and to leave the play to the actors. Before I do this, I have one confession to make. For more than twenty years the study of military history has been my chief avocation. Whether the operations have been those of 1914–18, on which I happened to be a daily commentator, or those of the conflict between the states, each new inquiry has made the monstrous horror of war more unintelligible to me. It has seemed incredible that human beings, endowed with any of the powers of reason, should hypnotize themselves with doctrines of "national honor" or "sacred right" and pursue mass murder to exhaustion or to ruin. I subscribe with my whole heart to the view of General Lee that had "forbearance and wisdom been practised on both sides," the great national tragedy of 1861 might have been prevented. If, in this opinion, I have let my abhorrence of war appear in my description of Malvern Hill after the battle, and in a few indignant adjectives elsewhere, I trust the reader will understand that in these instances I have momentarily stepped back on the stage only because I am not willing to have this study of a man who loved peace interpreted as glorification of war.

D. S. F.

WILLIAM BYRD PARK,
RICHMOND, VIRGINIA.
Aug. 7, 1934.

CONTENTS

CONTENTS

ILLUSTRATIONS

Between Pages 300 and 301

ILLUSTRATIONS

MAPS

R. E. LEE

CHAPTER I

A Carriage Goes to Alexandria

THEY had come so often, those sombre men from the sheriff. Always they were polite and always they seemed embarrassed, but they asked so insistently of the General's whereabouts and they talked of court papers with strange Latin names. Sometimes they lingered about as if they believed Henry Lee were in hiding, and more than once they had tried to force their way into the house. That was why Ann Carter Lee's husband had placed those chains there on the doors in the great hall at Stratford. The horses had been taken, the furniture had been "attached"—whatever that meant—and tract after tract had been sold off to cancel obligations. Faithful friends still visited, of course, and whenever the General rode to Montross or to Fredericksburg the old soldiers saluted him and told their young children that he was "Light-Horse Harry" Lee, but she knew that people whispered that he had twice been in jail because he could not pay his debts. Of course, he wanted to pay, but how could he? She could not help him, because her father had put her inheritance in trust. Robert Morris, poor man, had died without returning a penny of the $40,000 he owed Mr. Lee, and that fine plan for building a town at the Great Falls of the Potomac had never been carried out, because they could not settle the quitrents. If General Lee had been able to do that or to get the money on that claim he had bought in England, all would be well. As it was, they could not go on there at Stratford, where the house was falling to pieces and everything was in confusion. Besides, Stratford was not theirs. Matilda Lee had owned it and she had left it to young Henry and he was now of age. So, the only thing to do was to leave and go to Alexandria, where they could live in a simple home and send Charles Carter to the free school and find a doctor for the baby that was to come in February.

That was why they had Smith and three-year-old Robert in the carriage, with their few belongings, and were driving away from the ancestral home of the Lees. Perhaps it was well that Robert was so young: he would have no memories of those hard, wretched years that had passed since the General had started speculating—would not know, perhaps, that the long drive up the Northern Neck, that summer day in 1810, marked the dénouement in the life drama of his brilliant, lovable, and unfortunate father.[1]

Fairer prospects than those of Henry Lee in 1781 no young American revolutionary had. Born in 1756, at Leesylvania, Prince William County, Va., he was the eldest son of Henry Lee and his wife, Lucy Grymes. From boyhood he had the high intelligence of his father's distinguished forebears and the physical charm of his beautiful mother. He won a great name at Princeton, where he had been graduated in 1773. But for the coming of the war he would have gone to England to study law. Instead, before he was twenty-one, he entered the army as a captain in the cavalry regiment commanded by his kinsman, Theodoric Bland. Behind him had been all the influence of a family which included at that time three of the outstanding men of the Revolution, his cousins Richard Henry Lee, Arthur Lee, and William Lee.

His achievements thereafter were in keeping with his opportunities, for he seemed, as General Charles Lee put it, "to have come out of his mother's womb a soldier." A vigorous man, five feet nine inches in height,[2] he had strength and endurance for the most arduous of Washington's campaigns. He made himself the talk of the army by beating off a surprise attack at Spread Eagle Tavern in January, 1778. Offered a post as aide to Washington, he was promoted major when he expressed a preference for field service; he stormed Paulus Hook on the lower Hudson with so much skill and valor that Washington praised him in unstinted terms and Congress voted him thanks and a medal; he was privileged to address his dispatches directly and privately to Washington, whose admiring confidence he possessed; he was given a mixed command of infantry and cavalry which was

---

[1] The whole course of Henry Lee's speculations and financial distresses is traced in Thomas Boyd: *Light Horse Harry Lee* (cited hereafter as *Boyd*), 180 *ff.*, 277 *ff.*
[2] *National Portrait Gallery*, vol. 3.

officially designated as Lee's partisan corps; when he wearied of inaction in the North he was transferred to the Southern department in October, 1780, with the rank of lieutenant colonel. Although he was just twenty-five when he joined General Nathanael Greene in January, 1781, "Light-Horse Harry" Lee was already one of the most renowned of American soldiers.

With not more than 280 men, Lee took the field in the Carolinas. The stalwart, dependable Greene was friendly and ready to take counsel. His theatre of operations was wide, the British posts were scattered. Surprises and forays invited the adventuresome commander. Marion and Sumter were worthy rivals. In Wade Hampton and Peter Johnston, father of Joseph E. Johnston, Lee found loyal comrades. Dazzling months opened before him. He was in the raid on Georgetown and won new honors at Guilford Courthouse. At least as much as any other officer, he was responsible for the decision of General Greene to abandon the march after Cornwallis and to turn southward instead, a decision that changed the whole course of the war in that area and brought about the liberation of Georgia and the Carolinas. Rejoining Marion on April 14, 1781, Lee co-operated with him in capturing Fort Watson and Fort Motte, and then advanced with only his own command to Fort Granby, which he bluffed into surrender, though not without starting some murmurs that he allowed overgenerous terms in order that he might receive the capitulation before the arrival of General Sumter. From Fort Granby, Lee swung again to the south. Marching more than seventy-five miles in three days, he reduced Fort Galphin, and had a large part in the capture of Fort Cornwallis at Augusta. His was the most spectacular part in the most successful campaign the American army fought, and his reputation rose accordingly. In the remaining operations of the year he was less successful, though he had the good fortune to be sent with dispatches from Greene to Washington in time to witness the surrender of Cornwallis at Yorktown.[3]

Then something happened to Lee. In a strange change of

[3] For the dates of Lee's commissions and for the augmentation of his command, see *Congressional Directory, 1774–1911*, p. 801, *Washington Papers*, 597; E. J. Lee, *Lee of Virginia* (cited hereafter as *E. J. Lee*), 331–32; 8 *Ford's Washington*, 489; H. Lee, *Campaign of 1781 in the Carolinas* (cited hereafter as *H. Lee's Carolinas*), 67 ff., 70; *Washington Papers*, 531, 532. For the offer of post as aide to Washington, see *Washington*

mental outlook, the tragedy of his life began. As soon as the fighting was over he became sensitive, resentful, and imperious. He felt that Greene had slighted him, that merited promotion had been withheld from him, and that his brother officers were envious and hostile. A curious conflict took place in his mind between two obscure impulses. One apparently was a desire to be master of himself and to remain in the profession for which he seems to have known he was best fitted. The other impulse was to quit the camps of contention for the quiet of civil life, there to win riches and the eminence he felt had been unjustly denied him in the army.

This inward battle may have had its origin in the restlessness of a soldier whose campaigning was over. Exhaustion and ill-health may have caused a temporary warp of mind. Resentment may have been at the bottom of it, the resentment that is so easily aroused in the heart of a young man whom praise has spoiled. More particularly, a love-affair then developing doubtless made Henry Lee discontented with his life. The mental conflict, in any case, was one that Lee felt himself unable to win by the exercise of will or of judgment, though he looked upon it as objectively as if it had been the struggle of another man. "I wish from motives of self," he wrote General Greene, "to make my way easy and comfortable. This, if ever attainable, is to be got only in an obscure retreat." And again: "I am candid to acknowledge my imbecility of mind, and hope time and absence may alter my feelings. At present, my fervent wish is, for the most hidden obscurity; I want not private or public applause. My happiness

---

Papers, 589. For the authorization to address his letters to Washington "private," see George Washington to Henry Lee, *MS.*, Oct. 7, 1779; *Washington MS. Papers*, Library of Congress, vol. 118. The Paulus Hook affair is set forth in Henry Lee: *Memoirs of the War in the Southern Department of the United States* (edition of 1869, cited hereafter as *Henry Lee's Memoirs*), 23–24; *E. J. Lee*, 332; 8 *Ford's Washington*, 27, 33; *Washington Papers*, 1119, 1120, 1128. Lee's restlessness in 1780 is reflected in *Washington Papers*, 1297, 1302, 1305, 1307, 1337; Henry Lee to George Washington, *MS.*, July 25, 1780; *Washington MS. Papers*, Library of Congress, vol. 143; Henry Lee to Thos. Sim Lee, *MS.*, Sept. 10, 1780, New York Public Library. The details of Lee's operations in the South are fully set forth in his *Memoirs*, 223–25; 331–47; 350–52; 361 ff.; 371 ff.; 389 ff.; 473; 528. See William Johnson: *Sketches of the Life and Correspondence of Nathanael Greene* (cited hereafter as *Johnson's Greene*), vol. 2, 121–23, for the charge that Lee hurried the capitulation of Fort Granby. For his presence at Yorktown, see *Washington Papers*, 1965; *Henry Lee's Memoirs*, 507 ff.; H. Lee: *Observations on the Writings of Thomas Jefferson* (second edition, cited hereafter as *H. Lee's Observations*), 153. To distinguish the writings of General Henry Lee from those of his son Major Henry Lee, the former is cited as Henry Lee, and the latter as H. Lee.

will depend on myself; and if I have but fortitude to persevere in my intention, it will not be in the power of malice, outrage or envy to affect me. Heaven knows the issue. I wish I could bend my mind to other decisions. I have tried much, but the sores of my wounds are only irritated afresh by my efforts." [4]

In this spirit Henry Lee debated—and chose wrongly. Early in 1782 he resigned from the army. He took with him Greene's acknowledgment that he was "more indebted to this officer than to any other for the advantages gained over the enemy, in the operations of the last campaign," [5] but he left behind him the one vocation that ever held his sustained interest.

For a while all appeared to go well with him. He seemed to make his way "easy and comfortable," as he had planned, by a prompt marriage with his cousin, Matilda Lee, who had been left mistress of the great estate of Stratford, on the Potomac, by the death of her father, Philip Ludwell Lee, eldest of the famous, brilliant sons of Thomas Lee. Their marriage was a happy one, and within five years, four children were born. Two of them survived the ills of early life, the daughter, Lucy Grymes, and the third son, Henry Lee, fourth of that name. [6]

Following the custom of his family, Henry Lee became a candidate in 1785 for the house of delegates of Virginia. He was duly chosen and was promptly named by his colleagues to the Continental Congress, which he entered under the favorable introduction of his powerful kinsman, Richard Henry Lee. In that office he continued, with one interruption and sundry leaves of absence, almost until the dissolution of the Congress of the Confederation. [7] To the ratification of the new Constitution he gave his warmest support as spokesman for Westmoreland in the

[4] 2 *Johnson's Greene*, 321 ff.; *Henry Lee's Memoirs*, 38–40, 550. For Johnson's charge and H. Lee's denial that Henry Lee had quarrelled with Marion and Sumter, and that his resentment grew out of his subordination to Laurens in the operations against John's Island, see 2 *Johnson's Greene*, 121–23, 129, 328; *H. Lee's Carolinas*, 328.

[5] *Garden's Anecdotes*, 66.

[6] Lucy was born in 1785 and Henry, May 28, 1787 (*E. J. Lee*, 165–67, 340, 403). The date of Henry Lee's marriage is not known, but it was prior to April 30, 1782 (*E. J. Lee*, 340 n.). Lucy Grymes Lee married Bernard Carter, brother of Ann Hill Carter, second wife of Henry Lee.

[7] The general assembly of 1786 failed to re-elect him, much to the humiliation of Lee and to the distress of George Washington and James Madison, but when a vacancy occurred soon thereafter, Lee was returned (2 *Hunt's Madison*, 284–85, 286–88; 11 *Ford's Washington*, 88 and note). For Richard Henry Lee's introduction, see 2 *Letters of Richard Henry Lee*, 406.

5

Virginia convention of 1788, where he challenged the thunders of Patrick Henry, leader of the opposition.[8] Quick to urge Washington to accept the presidency, he it was who composed the farewell address on behalf of his neighbors when Washington started to New York to be inaugurated.[9] The next year Lee was again a member of the house of delegates, and in 1791 he was chosen Governor of Virginia, which honorific position he held for three terms of one year each. Laws were passed during his administration for reorganizing the militia, for reforming the courts, and for adjusting the state's public policy in many ways. Some dreams of improved internal navigation were cherished but could not be attained.[10]

In the achievements of these years Lee was distinguished but not zealous. His public service was all too plainly the by-product of a mind preoccupied. For the chief weakness of his character now showed itself, and the curious impulse with which he had battled before he resigned from the army took form in a wild mania for speculation. No dealer he in idle farm lands, no petty gambler in crossroads ordinaries. His every scheme was grandiose, and his profits ran to millions in his mind.

He plunged deeply, and always unprofitably. Financially distressed as early as 1783–85, he put £8000 of hard money into some magnificent and foolish venture in the Mississippi country.[11] Losing there, he sought to recoup by purchasing 500 acres of land at the Great Falls of the Potomac, where he hoped to sell off innumerable lots to those who were to build a great city at the turning-basins of the canal. This project must have had real possibilities, for it won Washington's approval and it interested James Madison. Despite an attempt to finance it in Europe, the enterprise fell through.[12] Before Lee had abandoned all hope of

[8] 3 *Elliott's Debates*, 42, 187, 272, 333, 405.
[9] Henry Lee to George Washington, *MS.*, Sept. 13, 1788; *Washington MS. Papers,* Library of Congress, vol. 241; 5 *Marshall's Washington*, 154.
[10] 13 *Hening's Statutes at Large of Virginia*, 340, 357, 411, 427; James Madison to Henry Lee, Jan. 21, 1792, *Henry Lee's Memoirs*, 44.
[11] Henry Lee to John Fitzgerald of Alexandria, *MS.*, Aug. 3, 1783; Henry Lee to unnamed correspondent, *MS.*, Jan. 28, 1785, *Morgan Collection*, New York Public Library; R. H. Lee to William Shippen, May 8, 1785, 2 *Letters of Richard Henry Lee*, 355–56; 3 *Elliott's Debates*, 182.
[12] Henry Lee to James Madison, *MS.*, Oct. 29, Nov. 19, Dec. 8, 1788, *Madison MS. Papers*, Library of Congress, vol. 16; same to same, *MS.*, March 8, March 14, 1789, Aug. 6, 1791; Madison to Lee, *MS.*, Jan. 8, 1792, *Madison MS. Papers*, loc. cit., vol. 18; 3

succeeding with this scheme, he had pondered the possibilities of getting inside information on the financial plans of the new Federal Government, presumably in order that he might buy up the old currency and make a fortune by exchanging it for the new issues. In November, 1789, he presumed on his friendship with Alexander Hamilton to attempt to procure from the Secretary of the Treasury a confidential statement of the administration's policy. Hamilton affectionately but firmly refused to tell him anything, whereupon this, also, had to be added to Henry Lee's futile dreams.[13] A little later Lee was involved in transactions that prompted Washington to declare downrightly that Lee had not paid him what was due.[14]

By this time, though there never was anything vicious in his character or dishonest in his purposes, Henry Lee had impaired his reputation as a man of business and was beginning to draw heavy drafts on the confidence of his friends. His own father, who died in 1789, passed over him in choosing an executor, while leaving him large landed property.[15] Matilda Lee, who had been in bad health since 1788, put her estate in trust for her children in 1790, probably to protect their rights against her husband's creditors. Soon afterwards she died, followed quickly by her oldest son, Philip Ludwell Lee, a lad of about seven.

Desperate in his grief, and conscious at last that he had made the wrong decision when he had left the army, Lee now wanted to return to a military life. He sought to get command of the forces that were to be sent to the Northwest to redeem the Saint Clair disaster. When he was passed over for reasons that he did not understand, he was more than disappointed. "It is better," he wrote Madison, "to till the soil with your own hands than to serve a government which distrusts your due attachment—even in the higher stations."[16] For a time, he became antagonistic to the fiscal

---

Madison's Writings, 436; George Washington to James Madison, MS., Nov. 17, 1788, Washington's Letterbook No. 9, Library of Congress; Madison Calendar, 458, 459, 460; 5 Hunt's Madison, 306; James Madison to Henry Lee, Dec. 18, 1791, 6 Hunt's Madison, 69–70.

[13] Henry Lee to Alexander Hamilton, Nov. 16, 1789; Hamilton to Lee, Dec. 1, 1789; MS. copies, New York Public Library.

[14] George Washington to Henry Lee, MS., Sept. 8, 1791, New York Public Library; Boyd, 246 ff.

[15] See will of Henry Lee the second in E. J. Lee, 295–97.

[16] Henry Lee to James Madison, MS., April 4, 1792, Writings to Madison, Library of Congress, vol. 18. Washington decided against giving Lee the command because he was

policy of the administration of his old commander and was sympathetic with the bitterest foe of the Federalists in the American press, Philip Freneau. He might formally have gone over to the opposition had he not been rebuffed when he made overtures to Jefferson, who seems instinctively to have distrusted him.[17]

If he could not wear again the uniform of his own country there was an alternative, to which Lee turned in the wildest of all his dreams. He was head of an American state, but he would resign, go to France and get a commission in the army of the revolutionaries! First inquiries led him to believe he would be accepted and be given the rank of major-general, but he had some misgivings about the ability of the French to victual and maintain their troops. Before setting out for Paris he decided to take counsel with Washington. "Bred to arms," he confided to his old commander, then President, "I have always since my domestic calamity wished for a return to my profession, as the best resort for my mind in its affliction." Washington, of course, warned him to stay away from a conflict that was leading to chaos. The veteran diplomatist, William Lee, his cousin, volunteered like counsel.[18]

Despite his reverence for Washington, Henry Lee might have placed his sword at the disposal of the French terrorists had not his mind been turned to a softer subject: Like many another widower he found consolation for a lost love in a new. Visiting Shirley, the James River plantation of Charles Carter, who was then probably the richest man in Virginia except George Washington, he became attached to Ann Hill Carter, then twenty, Charles Carter's daughter by his second wife, Anne Moore.[19] Lee was seventeen years her senior but he must have appealed to her from the first. Was he not a Revolutionary hero, a gentleman of impeccable manners and flashing conversation, and was he not Governor of Virginia withal? Besides, there was the romance of

convinced that officers who had been Lee's seniors in the Revolution would not serve under him in this expedition (see 1 *Madison's Writings*, 547, 551, 553; *Henry Lee's Memoirs*, 44–45; 2 *Letters of Richard Henry Lee*, 549; 12 *Ford's Washington*, 137 ff., 514).

[17] 6 *Hunt's Madison*, 82 ff., 84 n.; *Madison Calendar*, 459, 460; H. Lee's *Observations*, 121.

[18] 12 *Ford's Washington*, 287–88, 288 n.; *Henry Lee's Memoirs*, 48.

[19] There seems to be no foundation for the story (F. and C. Hutchins, *Virginia*, 275–76) that Lee fell in love with Ann Carter when he saw her about to drop a bowl of strawberries. Anne was born Mch. 26, 1773.

his chivalrous purpose to offer his sword to republican France, the distressed land of his comrade Lafayette.

Charles Carter did not look at Lee through his daughter's eyes. As a father and a man of affairs, he would not permit Ann to marry a Virginian foolish enough to throw in his lot with the madmen of Paris. There were parleys and exchanges that ended finally in Lee's decision to abandon his French adventure. Carter at once softened and gave his consent to a union which he was considerate enough to say he had opposed on no other grounds. So, on June 30, 1793, when Robespierre was filling the tumbrels with the victims of the law of the 22d Prairial, the two were joined in the marriage of which Robert E. Lee was born.[20]

For a time after his second marriage, Henry Lee seemed to be stabilized. Returning to his former political support of his adored Washington, he received the confidences of the President in the delicate matter of French neutrality, and he supported the executive in a much-applauded proclamation.[21] When the "Whiskey Boys' Rebellion" broke out the next year he forgot his former grievance and gladly led the expedition sent to crush the rising, though his absence almost cost him his office as governor.[22] Meantime, he became vehemently critical of Jefferson.[23]

Retiring, as was then customary in Virginia, on the expiration of his third term as governor, Lee was enough in the public eye to be mentioned as a possible successor to Washington.[24] Instead of climbing onward to that office, however, all that remained to him were a few years of service in the general assembly, a temporary commission as major-general at the time of the threatened war with France, and a single term in Congress, where he eulogized his dead chieftain, as "first in war, first in peace, and first in the hearts of his countrymen."[25] Thereafter he held no

[20] Charles Carter to Henry Lee, May 20, 1793, *Henry Lee's Memoirs*, 48-49.
[21] 12 *Ford's Washington*, 308 ff.; *Journal of the House of Delegates of Virginia, 1793*, pp. 31, 69.
[22] *H. Lee's Observations*, 13 n.; *Henry Lee's Memoirs*, 47; 12 *Ford's Washington*, 480; *Journal of the House of Delegates of Virginia, 1794*, pp. 23, 24, 28, 29. Lee was already the commander of one of the divisions of Virginia militia and had undertaken to organize it (*Journal of the House of Delegates of Virginia, 1793*, p. 104; divisional order of June 30, 1794, MS., New York Public Library, 7975).
[23] Henry Lee to George Washington, Aug. 17, 1794, *H. Lee's Observations*, 13 n.; George Washington to Henry Lee, 12 *Ford's Washington*, 458.
[24] 2 *Madison's Writings*, 83.
[25] He was in the general assemblies of 1795, 1796, 1797-98 and 1798-99. At the last of these sessions he opposed the famous "Virginia resolutions" on the alien and sedi-

political office of importance and probably could have gained none.

The reason was that his old passion for wild speculation returned. Already it had entailed grief, loss, and the estrangement of friends. Now, everything was subordinated to his desperate efforts to make a fortune—his peace of mind, his family's comfort, his standing in the eyes of old comrades. His own son, Henry, who idolized his father, had to write of him: "He entered into a course of sanguine and visionary speculations, endeavoring to acquire wealth, not by rational and productive industry, but by a combination of bargains which could hardly benefit one party without injury to the other, and which were often mutually detrimental. To the task of making one yield what others failed to return, he devoted no little of misapplied talent and activity— in bearing the weight of distress and ruin which they finally entailed, he wasted a degree of fortitude which, however inglorious the struggle, could not be witnessed without admiration."[26]

Lee became involved with the Marshalls in the purchase of a part of the vast Fairfax estates in the Northern Neck and endeavored to finance it through Robert Morris, but, in the end, advanced Morris $40,000, which the old Philadelphian could not repay. Next Lee, it would seem, was entrusted by some of his friends with the sale of Western lands in 1797. In expectation of early payment, certain of these men made loans or assumed obligations they were unable to meet when the settlement was delayed. Lee worked feverishly to raise the funds through his attorney and agent, William Sullivan of Boston. He was harassed "by those distressed individuals who are all about me now," as he wrote Sullivan, and he had the humiliation of having one of his creditors, "poor Glassel," thrown into jail, presumably for debt.[27]

Undeterred, he was lured by the mysterious Western adventure of Aaron Burr, for whom he voted in 1801. He was not in Burr's

tion laws (*Virginia Report of 1799–1800*, Randolph Edition, 108–9. *Cf. ibid.*, 150, 155, 158). For his election to Congress, see *H. Lee's Observations*, 121, 193.

[26] *H. Lee's Observations*, 179.

[27] Henry Lee to William Sullivan, MS., July 14, Oct. 1, Nov. 12, Dec. 10, 1797, New York Public Library; *Boyd*, 245.

counseis, but his interest in the attempt to create a new empire was so great that it was reported he had left Staunton, Va., to join Burr.[28] It was at this stage of his speculative mania, when he was dreaming of a fortune that was to be won by the conquest of a new frontier, that his son Robert was conceived. At the time when the expectancy of the mother kept Henry Lee at home, in January, 1807, he was busy on a scheme to wipe out all his debts and to enjoy affluence once more by prevailing upon the British Lord Chancellor to order a final distribution of an estate which had been contested for sixty years. Lee had no claim to the property through kinship, but he and two others had bought up certain claims to it as a speculation. The letter that bears a closer date to that of Robert's birth than any of Henry Lee's extant correspondence is one in which he asked the help of James Monroe, then minister to England, in this chimerical enterprise.[29]

Ann Lee's pregnancy was not happy. Too many shadows hung over it. During the early years at Stratford, though her husband had forever been spurring restlessly about, she had been content. In the year when Henry Lee had been thundering against the Virginia resolutions, she had written the wife of her brother-in-law: "I do not find [my life] in the slightest degree tiresome: my hours pass too nimbly away. When in company, if agreeable company, I greatly enjoy it: when alone my husband and Child excepted, I am not sensible of the want of society. In them I have enough to make me cheerful and happy." She had then been from home for only one night in seven months.[30] But sickness after 1800 had brought suffering and many weeks of invalidism.[31] Henry Lee had been more and more frequently absent for long periods; the pinch of poverty had taken from her the comforts she had known in girlhood; she had lost even her carriage;[32] life had grown gray on the narrowed, untilled acres of Stratford. While the child was in her womb, she had gone to Shirley after

---

[28] Thomas Jefferson to H. Lee, Feb. 1, 1807; 19 *Writings of Thomas Jefferson* (Memorial Edition), 158.

[29] Henry Lee to James Monroe, *MS.*, Jan. 10, 1807; New York Public Library.

[30] Ann Lee to Mrs. Richard Bland Lee, *MS.*, Feb. 18, 1799, *Richard Bland Lee Papers*, Library of Congress.

[31] Same to same, *MS.*, Oct. 14, 1800, May 10, 1803, May 3, 1804; *loc. cit.*, Ann Lee to Doctor Robert Carter, Oct. 1, 1805, *Carter MSS*.

[32] Ann Lee to Mrs. Richard Bland Lee, *MS.*, Nov. 2, 1806, *loc. cit.*

the death of her father and had found it a house of mourning.[33] On her return home at the end of December, 1806, she had been forced to ride in an open carriage and had caught a cold from which she was suffering as the time for the delivery of her child approached. Eight days before the pains of labor came upon her she wrote Mrs. Richard Bland Lee, who also was *enceinte,* "You have my best wishes for your success[,] my dear, and *truest assurances,* that I do not envy your prospects nor wish to *share in them.*"[34]

On January 19, 1807, Ann Carter Lee's fourth child was born, an unblemished boy, who was named Robert Edward, after two of his mother's brothers, Robert and Edward Carter. His first cry was in the east chamber on the main floor of the old house,[35] the room nearest the garden, the very chamber in which, according to tradition, Richard Henry and Francis Lightfoot Lee, signers of the Declaration of Independence, had seen the light.

When Robert was sixteen months old, his half-brother Henry passed out of his minority and came into possession of Stratford. After that "Light-Horse Harry" and his family by his second marriage could only remain on the estate as the guests of the young master. With this prospect before him and his financial plight daily worse, the old soldier could see no alternative to beating a retreat. He must leave the country, if he could, and find shelter in some foreign land, where his creditors could not pursue him. Contemplating this, and presenting Mrs. Lee's ill-health as a reason, he solicited a government appointment to Brazil or to the West Indies.[36]

For the time, it was all to no purpose. There were no vacancies to be filled, and no new appointments to be made. Credit was gone, reputation was almost gone, civil judgments against him multiplied with the months. During the spring of 1809, when Robert was receiving his first impressions of Stratford as a place

[33] *Ibid.* and *Boyd,* 284.
[34] Ann Lee to Mrs. Richard Bland Lee, *MS.,* Jan. 11, 1807, *loc. cit.* Mrs. R. B. Lee, *née* Elizabeth Collins of Philadelphia, must have lost her baby, as it is not listed in *E. J. Lee.*
[35] On the right as one faces the front of the building, which looks south.
[36] Henry Lee to James Madison, Feb. 10, March 21, Dec. 17, 1808, *Madison Calendar,* 461.

of beauty and of glory, his father came to the last humiliation: Odds and ends of real estate that had been left to him after nearly thirty years of wild trading had to be deeded away. Of everything that could be sold, he was stripped bare. And even this did not save him. On April 11, 1809, he was arrested for a debt of some 5400 Spanish dollars, with accrued interest for nearly seven years, and was confined to jail at the county seat of Westmoreland. Later in the year he was imprisoned for the same reason in Spotsylvania. Not until the spring of 1810 was he at liberty, and then he had nothing left him except some lands he could not market.[37] While incarcerated, he had written a large part of his *Memoirs of the War in the Southern Department of the United States*. With a shadow of his old optimism, he flattered himself this book would enjoy a great run;[38] but that, of course, was almost as much a gamble as any of those on which he had lost his fortune.

At home again, writing furiously on his book, but with no immediate income, he decided on the move to Alexandria. Henry was twenty-four and could not be expected to supply food and shelter indefinitely. There was no money with which to employ a tutor for the three children, who were now requiring instruction. Everything left to Mrs. Lee and her young brood was the return from a trust that had been set up for her benefit under the will of her father. When the estate was settled, the revenue from this fund, which Henry Lee could not dissipate, would provide shelter, food, and clothing but nothing besides.

The little caravan from Stratford ended its journey at a small, but trim and comfortable brick house on Cameron Street in Alexandria, close to the Episcopal church. Life was easier there than in the sprawling Stratford mansion, but cares increased. During the winter, after the family settled in town, the new baby, a girl, was born to the burdened mother.[39] There were now five

---

[37] Boyd, 297 *ff.*; *H. Lee's Observations*, 180–81; *Orderbook of the Court of Spotsylvania County, Virginia*, 1805–7, p. 308; 1807–10, pp. 199, 208, 252, 262, 267, 268, 277, 288, 296, 300, 305; 1810–11, p. 35.

[38] Henry Lee to Colonel Rhea, Trenton, N. J., *MS.*, March 16, 1811, New York Public Library.

[39] Catharine Mildred Lee, known in the family as Mildred, born Feb. 27, 1811.

13

children, ranging from the new-born infant to a boy of thirteen, and one of the quintet, Ann, was sickly. Before the infant had ceased to be an hourly charge, and when Robert was five and a half, the final blow came.

Henry Lee's strong Federalism had led him to oppose a second war with Great Britain. Seeing no grievance that he did not believe could be corrected in amity, he had written repeatedly to Madison, over a period of five years, in the interest of peace.[40] When hostilities opened in June, 1812, Lee was unreconciled to the conflict and quick to sympathize with those who became the victims of war's passions. Among these sufferers was the young editor of *The Baltimore Federal Republican,* Alexander C. Hanson, whose plant, press, and building were wrecked by a mob which an antiwar editorial in his paper had inflamed. Hanson was no coward, and though he left Baltimore temporarily and came to Georgetown, not far up the Potomac from Alexandria, he determined to return to the city and to resume the circulation of his journal.

Hearing some whisper of Hanson's plan, Lee was aroused. On July 20, he wrote the editor how to conduct a defense in a barricaded house, though he advised him to call on the authorities for assistance and not to provoke the mob again. Lee apparently was not privy to Hanson's movements, but he either had business in Baltimore about the time of the expected return of the editor, or else he made business an excuse for going there to see what befell the courageous critic of Madison's war policy.

On July 27, 1812, Hanson issued in Baltimore a paper which had been printed in Georgetown. Henry Lee had paid two visits to Hanson after he had reached Baltimore, and when he observed the sensation created by the paper, he hastened to him again. He found the editor and a few friends assembled in a house that Hanson was using as a combined office and residence. Soon after Lee arrived, idlers in the street were swollen into a wrathful mob that threatened an assault. As an experienced soldier, Lee was asked to assist in protecting the premises. Undertaking this task with his war-time alacrity, he sent out for additional arms, barricaded the place, and disposed the little garrison. Firing soon

[40] *Madison Calendar,* 461–62.

broke out. One man was killed in the street and another was wounded. Maddened by these casualties, the mob would doubtless have attacked the building and would have slain the volunteer garrison then and there, had not the militia arrived and taken position in the street.

After a night of excitement, negotiations were opened between the troops and the friends of Hanson. Finally the twenty-three occupants of the house submitted themselves to the officers of the law, who escorted them to a large cell in the jail as the safest place in which they could remain until the passions of the hour had cooled. But the rioters were not so easily shaken off. All day of the 28th, the mob spirit spread through the town. After nightfall, a crowd of armed men gathered before the jail, intent on murder. Through negligence or connivance, the troops were not called out again. The jailer was helpless. An entrance was soon forced. The hallway was immediately packed with wild ruffians. Death seemed so certain that Lee proposed to his companions that they should take the few weapons they had and shoot one another rather than let themselves be torn to pieces by the mob. But better judgment prevailed, and when the door of the cell was beaten down, the defenders made a sally. Instantly there was a confused mêlée. When it was over, half of Hanson's friends had escaped, but one of them had been killed and eleven others had been frightfully beaten. Eight were thought to be dead and were piled together in front of the building, where they were subjected to continued mutilation.

Henry Lee was among this number. Drunken brutes thrust penknives into his flesh, and waited to see whether there was a flicker when hot candle grease was poured into his eyes. One fiend tried to cut off his nose. After a while, by asserting that they merely wished to give him decent burial, some of the town physicians succeeded in carrying him to a hospital. His condition was so desperate that his death was reported in Washington, but his great physical strength sufficed to keep him alive, and good nursing made it possible for him to return home later in the summer. But he was weak, crippled, and disfigured, doomed to invalidism for the remaining six years of his life, wholly dependent on the income of his wife, and of course incapable of accepting the military command that would almost certainly have been given him when the first tide of the war in Canada turned against the United States.[41]

Hope was dead now in the heart of Henry Lee. He dreamed no more of the fortune that was to be made in his very next venture. His one ambition was to leave the country, both for his health and for his peace of mind. In pressing for the means of escape, he did not even attempt to conceal his poverty. "As to my change of clime," he wrote Monroe, "without money, as I am, it will be difficult to execute my object even with your promised aid."[42] It was doubly difficult because Lee wished to go to a British island, inasmuch as he spoke neither French nor Spanish. The consent of the British admiral had to be procured if he was to pass the blockading squadrons and land unhindered. But Monroe was as good as his word, and after some months he arranged for Lee to go to the Barbadoes.

So, one day in the early summer of 1813,[43] Robert must have shed tears with the rest, as he shared the final embraces of his father. Behind him, in his own household, "Light-Horse Harry" left only sorrow. For, with all his financial follies, he had never lost the respect, much less the affection, of his family. Fully conscious of his failings, which they pitied, they still were awed by his dignity and fascinated by his conversation. On the youthful mind of Robert, his father's vices made no impress, but always in his memory the picture of his sire was glamorous with charm.

But Henry Lee could not have been greatly comforted, as he went down the Potomac, by the knowledge that he was still king of his fireside. He had received Congress's medal and had enjoyed

---

[41] *Niles Register*, Aug. 8, 1812; *National Intelligencer*, Aug. 1, 1812; *A Correct Account of the Conduct of the Baltimore Mob*, by General Henry Lee, One of the Sufferers; Published by a Particular Friend, C. B.; To which is Prefixed an Introductory Detail of the Circumstance, Substantiated by many Concurrent Evidences; Winchester, Va., July, 1814. See also *An Exact and Authentic Narrative of the Events which Took Place in Baltimore on the 27th and 28th of July last . . .* (n. p.) 1812. *Cf. Boyd*, 309 ff. It was believed in the Lee family that despite his injuries, General Henry Lee was given a commission of Major General during the War of 1812. See *Henry Lee's Memoirs*, 53, where President Monroe is cited as authority for this statement. No record of any such commission, however, is to be found in the office of the Adjutant-General of the United States army.

[42] Henry Lee to James Monroe, *MS.*, Jan. 13, 1813, New York Public Library. *Cf.* Henry Lee to James Madison, April 24, 1814, *Madison Calendar*, 462.

[43] He was in the Barbadoes by Aug. 4, 1813, according to the *Madison Calendar*, 462. In reaching his destination he owed much to the kindness of Admiral Sir John Warren.

the *entrée* to the commander-in-chief; his name had been on every patriot's tongue; he had told General Greene that he wished to put himself where it would not be "in the power of malice, outrage or envy" to affect him. And now he was sailing away from the state he had governed, from the creditors he could never pay, from a family he might not see again, and he knew he was passing over the gray horizon of failure.

CHAPTER II

A Background of Great Traditions

THE city that Henry Lee left behind him, the city of Robert Lee's widening consciousness, was a pleasant place of 7500 people, situated on the west bank of the Potomac River, six miles below the fields where the capital of the republic was rising. Organized in 1749, Alexandria had been peopled in part by Scotch of good station, but had later received Pennsylvania Quakers and native Virginia colonials in such numbers that by 1815 it differed little from the other towns of the Old Dominion.

Despite war, smallpox, building booms, and fires, the kindred plagues of most early American cities, Alexandria had grown. Ships of many flags tied up at its ample wharves. Fishermen brought thither their weighty catches from the lower stretches of the river. Hundreds of hogsheads of tobacco rolled in from nearby plantations and disappeared in the deep holds of ships bound for England. Thirty-four tavern keepers and more than 260 merchants competed sharply for the trade of sailor, farmer, traveller, and resident. Episcopal, Presbyterian, Methodist, Quaker, Baptist, and Roman Catholic churches all offered the comforts of religion to the pious, or held the threat of hell above the profligate's head. Justice sat with dignity, for Alexandria had become a part of the District of Columbia in 1791 and was under exclusive federal jurisdiction. A town hall Alexandria boasted, a market place, a library even, and a jail atop whose chimneys stood grim pikes where once the town had set in lasting warning the heads of slaves who had preached insurrection. In her prosperity the city abandoned wooden dwellings for enduring brick, but in her thrift she allowed herself few gardens. At some of her corners deep wells rewarded with clear water those who would tug at the complaining windlass. Buried cannon, placed there before the Revolution, marked other crossings. There were oil lamps on the streets, and in each ward the town paid a watchman to go the rounds every night, to cry the hours, and to make the drowsy burgher glad of his shelter by telling him in loud tones how hard the wind was biting. And if fire broke out, was not the Friendship Company ready to race to the flames with its engine? Did not each member of the Sun Company hasten with his two leather buckets and with his two-bushel Osnaburg bag, in which to store salvaged valuables?

To boys a trifle older than Robert, the town held high charm, even though a harsh ordinance of the unyielding city fathers forbade all bandy, ball, and kite-flying in the streets. Down on the waterfront were Jones's Point and the lighthouse, the ships and the flotsam, the landings and the loitering sailors. Northeast of the town were "King George's Meadows," a marshy place of adventure that got its odd name, tradition said, because his Majesty of colonial times had most ungraciously withheld his consent from a prudential bill of the Virginia burgesses for the draining of the flats. The streams were full of fish, and the tall grass sheltered unreckoned rabbits, providentially placed there, as it seemed, for disporting boys.

For elders who scorned the diversions that allured youth, the town had a social life of some dignity. Nearby were Abingdon and Preston, homes of the Alexanders who had given their name to the town. Mount Ida was the seat of Charles Alexander, Jr., who in 1813 claimed the title of Earl of Stirling. Up the river was a new mansion on a commanding hill, with heavy Greek columns on its high portico. Its builder had styled it Arlington, but neither he nor any who visited the hospitable place divined what connotations of sorrow and of strife that name was to have. Down the river was Mount Vernon and, four miles farther on, Gunston Hall, the home of George Mason, the Plato of the Revolution. In the town itself, surrounded by less imposing residences, rose the handsome Carlyle house, built in 1752 and long owned by the family whose patronymic it bore. Its prospective owner, George William Carlyle, had been killed while fighting under "Light-Horse Harry" Lee at Eutaw Springs.

Ties of blood or of common service joined the Lees to this

society. Cousins uncounted lived in Alexandria.[1] One of Henry Lee's brothers, Edmund Jennings Lee, was a luminary of the town. Their sister Mary had married Philip R. Fendall, a local lawyer of much social charm. Out at Ravensworth, in Fairfax County, lived William H. Fitzhugh, distant kinsman but close friend, the broad door of whose ample home was always open to Mrs. Lee and her children. For counsel or for assistance of any sort, Mrs. Lee always turned to Fitzhugh, who admired her both for her character and for her success in keeping up her home on her scant income.[2]

Twenty members of Lee's Legion had enlisted from Alexandria and nearly all of them affectionately remembered their unfortunate commander. Military titles were to be heard every hour on the street. There one might meet Colonel Charles Simms, the mayor, General Daniel Roberdeau, who always wore tight leather breeches, Colonel George Gilpin, the postmaster, Colonel Philip Marsteller, and Colonel Charles Little, who rode in from Denbigh in Fairfax County. Judge Cranch, whose name is familiar to all constitutional lawyers, presided over the United States court and lived on Washington Street.

At intervals that were all too far apart on the calendar of impatient lovers, the socially elect of the town gathered at Gadsby's City Tavern for formal "assemblies." The brilliance of these events was somewhat eclipsed, now that Washington was dead, but the memory of his presence on many a festive evening still lifted the gatherings above the commonplace and helped to draw to them, across the new Potomac "Long Bridge," the families of patrician congressmen, glad enough to escape the mud of the capital's streets and the monotony of its bad boarding-houses.

Somewhat less formal, but written large on the social calendar of the town, were the Masonic celebrations on the two Saint-John's days of the year. The fellowcraft then assembled for a

---

[1] The first recorded incident of Robert Lee's life is a trivial happening in connection with a visit by Mrs. Lee to the Alexandria home of Mrs. Hodgeson, who had married a Lee and lived on Oronoko Street. Mrs. Lee took Robert along to play with Portia Hodgeson, who was of about the same mature age of four. As ill-fortune would have it, Portia was asleep and could not entertain her guest. Robert doubtless was disappointed, and as the conversation of the ladies proved rather boring to a young gentleman of different tastes and interests, Robert philosophically crawled under Portia's crib and went to sleep (Mary G. Powell: *History of Old Alexandria*, cited hereafter as *Mrs. Powell*, 177).
[2] See Fitzhugh's letter, *infra*, p. 39.

sermon at the Presbyterian church and thereafter marched to John Wise's tavern, where they banqueted fraternally and later threw open their doors for a dance. Rarely was there lack of mirth, for the town did not frown on the spirituous refreshment its many taverns abundantly offered. In fact, if the worst must be told, when the worthy vestry of the Episcopal church supped together at their regular meetings, the wine flowed so freely that it produced a merriment most shocking to the religious sensibilities of the pious new rector, Reverend William Meade. He did not rest him from his protests till he broke up that brotherly supping, to the lasting loss of fellowship, if to the gain of temperance.

None of these things meant so much to the town as did its associations with George Washington. He had been dead more than ten years when the Lee coach brought the family up from Stratford. By the time Robert was old enough to understand something of the spirit of the Father of his Country, Washington had been twenty years in his tomb at Mount Vernon. But he was alive in the hearts of old Alexandrians. Reminders of him were everywhere. In the market place he had drilled his Virginia rangers ere he had set out with Braddock. In the City Tavern hardby he had kept his headquarters and had written out his reports in his swift, neat autograph. To the post office he had often come in person. Many still lived to tell, in Robert's time, how majestically the General had ridden by, and with what gracious dignity he had acknowledged their salutes. In the Masonic Hall he had repeated the ancient responses of the order. The very water of the town was a memorial, for it had been at Washington's instance, while he was a trustee of Alexandria, that the wells at the street-corners had been dug. Doctor James Craik, who had been Washington's physician and his closest friend in Alexandria, might have been seen by Robert, at seven years of age, when the old gentleman was driven in from Vaucluse.[3]

---

[3] This description of Alexandria is based on Mrs. Powell's book and on Colonel Charles Deneale's MS. *Sketch of Alexandria* (c. 1816), graciously copied for the writer by Mrs. Powell. A few useful references will be found in F. L. Brockett and Geo. W. Rock: *A Concise History of the City of Alexandria*, and in A. J. Wedderburn: *Souvenir Virginia Tercentennial of Historic Alexandria, Va., Past and Present.*

Amid these surroundings, Washington was a part of the life of Robert Lee from earliest childhood. Doubtless his mother remembered and perhaps preserved the letter in which Washington had written Henry Lee his congratulations upon the marriage: "As we are told that you have exchanged the rugged and dangerous field of Mars for the soft and pleasurable bed of Venus," Washington had written, "I do in this as I shall in everything you may pursue like unto it, good and laudable, wish you all imaginable success and happiness."[4] Henry Lee, who had the temerity to jest on one occasion with the *pater patriæ*,[5] had spoken often and reverently of him before he had sailed away. Pride in the friendship of the first citizen of the country had been the consolation of "Light-Horse Harry's" blackest days, and from his exile he was to write of "the great Washington," and was to repeat his old commander's words for the admonition of his son, Charles Carter.[6] The family held fast to this reverence. In the home where Robert was trained, God came first and then Washington.

In Robert's young eyes, of course, the centre of the town and of all its traditions was the home on Cameron Street. Over it presided his mother, charged for the rest of her days with the entire care of her five children, their finances, their religious training, and their education. Physically it overtaxed her, but spiritually she was equal to it. Ann Carter Lee was thirty-seven when they moved to Alexandria, and forty when Henry Lee went to the West Indies. Her sister Mildred had died not long after her father and had left her some property that supplemented the income from the trust fund Charles Carter had set up,[7] but the contrast between the rich ease of her girlhood and the adversity of her married life was sharp. Yet it did not embitter her. She continued to love the author of her misfortune. And he, for all his distresses, kept his devotion to her and his high respect for her. In his exile he remembered the anniversary of their marriage, and he sprinkled his letters to Charles Carter Lee with references to her.[8] But she had taken Henry's tragedy to heart,

[4] George Washington to Henry Lee, July 21, 1793; 12 *Ford's Washington*, 311.
[5] 4 *Washington Irving's Washington*, 440.
[6] G. W. P. Custis, quoted in *Henry Lee's Memoirs*, 53; Henry Lee to Charles Carter Lee, Sept. 30, 1816; Sept. 3, 1817; *E. J. Lee*, 346, 356.
[7] *Boyd*, 287.
[8] *Henry Lee's Memoirs*, 71; *E. J. Lee*, 347, 348, 349, 350, 353, 354.

and the reasons for his fall, and she was determined that his grim cycle of promise, overconfidence, recklessness, disaster, and ruin should not be rounded in the lives of her children. Self-denial, self-control, and the strictest economy in all financial matters were part of the code of honor she taught them from infancy.[9] These qualities which were the precise reverse of those his brilliant father had displayed, were inculcated in Robert so early and so deeply by his mother that they became fundamentals of his character. He probably never knew a time when they were not held up before him as great axioms of conduct. Thanks to Ann Lee, the weakness of the sire became the strength of the son. No wonder he was accustomed to say in later life that he "owed everything" to his mother.[10]

Although Robert lived among the Lees, the atmosphere of his home was that of the Carters. His mother corresponded with them, talked of them, and at least once a year endeavored to take her younger children with her on a visit to Shirley, her old home on James River.[11] It was a gracious place. Built early in the eighteenth century, it had been adorned by each generation of Hills and of Carters, as though they owed it a debt they were eager to discharge with generous interest. The parlors contained rich old furniture, on which the presentments of approving ancestors looked down from gilt frames. In the great hall was a majestic hanging stair; in the dining-room was Charles W. Peale's full-length picture of Washington, a portrait in which one could see the lines that Valley Forge had cut on a face still young, and all the misgiving that a doubtful war had put in honest, anxious eyes. Outside, to the south, was the turbid, silent river. Across the lawn lay the garden with ancient walks and dreamy odors.

---

[9] Emily V. Mason, *Popular Life of General Robert Edward Lee* (cited hereafter as *Mason*), 22. On matters of training and domestic life, Miss Mason is the most authoritative of the biographers of Lee by reason of her intimacy with Mrs. Robert E. Lee.

[10] *Personal Reminiscences, Anecdotes, and Letters of Gen. Robert E. Lee*, by Rev. J. William Jones, . . . New York, 1874, p. 366. This indispensable early work, containing material from which every other biographer has drawn freely, is cited hundreds of times in the pages that follow as *Jones*. It is to be distinguished from his later book, *Life and Letters of Robert Edward Lee, Soldier and Man* (Washington, 1906), cited as Jones, *L. and L.*

[11] These visits may have been discontinued during the years 1806–16, for Robert Carter, heir to Shirley, died in 1805, before his father, whose end came the next year. Shirley then passed to Robert Carter's son, Hill Carter, a minor (b. 1796). Hill Carter went to school in England, then entered the navy, and did not return to Shirley until about 1816. During the decade 1806–16, the place probably was in the care of overseers.

Here, on successive visits, as he grew older, Robert heard how John Carter had come to Virginia, had acquired much land, had outlived three wives[12] and had died in 1669, leaving a son Robert who had reaped richly where his father had sown. So wealthy did this Robert Carter become, and so widely did his acres spread that he was known as "King" Carter and lived with a dignified luxury befitting his estate. Around the door of the church which he built and furnished at his own expense, the admiring neighbors would wait on the Sabbath until his outriders had arrived and the great coach had rumbled up, and "King" Carter and his family had entered the house of prayer. Then the simpler folks would stamp after, glad enough to bow the knee on the same floor with so fine a gentleman.

Of the twelve children born to "King" Carter while he lived in splendor at Corotoman, his son John inherited perhaps the largest share of the property. He continued to reside at Corotoman and added as much again to his estate by marrying Elizabeth Hill, heiress to the Shirley plantation on James River. Their wealthy son, Charles Carter, Robert Lee's grandfather, was reared at Corotoman and brought his first wife there. After her death, Charles Carter married Anne Butler Moore, daughter of Augustine Moore and a descendant of Alexander Spotswood, perhaps the most popular and renowned of the colonial governors of Virginia.[13] With her Charles Carter moved to Shirley, which had become his property. His household was large, for he had eight children by his first marriage, and by his second, thirteen, among them Ann, Robert Lee's mother.[14]

Young Robert had a friendly multitude of close Carter cousins, for hundreds, literally, were descended from the twelve children of "King" Carter. Charles Carter's record of twenty-one by two wives was rivalled by that of his first cousin, Robert, or "Coun-

---

[12] One authority stated that five wives predeceased John Carter (*E. J. Lee*, 356, 357 n.).

[13] She was probably descended from John Moore, who settled in Virginia prior to 1625, and, according to tradition, was of the issue of Sir Thomas More. Several confused generations of Augustine Moores followed the original John. The last of them married Elizabeth Todd, the widow Seaton, and had a son, Bernard Moore, of Chelsea, Prince William County. Bernard Moore married Anne Catherine Spotswood, daughter of Governor Alexander Spotswood. The daughter of Bernard and Anne Spotswood Moore was this Anne Butler Moore (1 *Spotswood Letters*, ix, xiv; 25 *Va. Mag. of History and Biography; Richmond Standard*, Sept. 3, 10, 17, 1881).

[14] Her name is usually spelled *Anne*, but all the autographs now extant give it *Ann*.

cillor" Carter, whose single marriage yielded the sixteen children that appear in the charming *Journal* of their blue-stockinged tutor, Philip Fithian. Kinsmen were joined in marriage until the lines are at some points confused. The prime family characteristic of geniality and friendliness seemed to be accentuated with each new generation. The size and endogamy of the Carter tribe made it socially self-contained. Every true Carter liked everybody, but most of all he liked his kinspeople. Often and joyfully they visited one another. Of journeying and letter-writing and the exchange of family news, the years brought no end. It was at Shirley, amid the infectious laughter and the kindly chatter of his cousins, that the youthful Robert developed early the fondness for the company of his kin that was so marked in his maturity.

While Robert instinctively adopted the social attitude of the Carters, he was too young to observe in childhood—if, indeed, he ever realized—this most remarkable fact about his mother's family: The males of the Carter stock did not often aspire to public life or shine in it, but the women of the blood of "King" Carter, when they married into other lines, became the mothers and grandmothers of a most extraordinary number of distinguished men.

Robert Carter the first, "King" Carter, had five daughters.

The eldest of the five, Elizabeth, had a daughter of the same name who married William Nelson, president of the council of Virginia.[15] Their son, Thomas Nelson, was a signer of the Declaration and a man of high patriotism. By a second marriage, this granddaughter of Robert Carter became the wife of George Nicholas and was mother of a treasurer of Virginia and grandmother of a governor, Edmund Randolph.

Judith, the second daughter of Robert Carter, married Mann Page of Gloucester. Among the descendants of this union were a governor and many men of station.

Still another of Robert Carter's daughters, Anne, married Benjamin Harrison and was mother of a son of the same name, Governor of Virginia and signer of the Declaration of Independence. Another of her sons was a brigadier-general in the

[15] The council combined, in some sense, the functions of an upper legislative chamber with those of executive advisers to the colonial governor.

Revolutionary army, and a third was president of the state senate. This same Anne Carter Harrison was grandmother of one President of the United States, William Henry Harrison, and great-great-grandmother of another President, Benjamin Harrison.

Mary, fourth daughter of Robert Carter, chose George Braxton as her husband. Their son was Carter Braxton, publicist and signer of the Declaration.

The fifth daughter of "King" Carter was Lucy, who became the wife of Henry Fitzhugh, progenitor of distinguished Virginians not a few.

The families into which these daughters and granddaughters of "King" Carter were married in the eighteenth century were among those, to be sure, from which the leaders of an aristocratic society would naturally spring. But that society was fairly large by the time of the Revolution. It is hard to believe that pure chance should have made the five daughters of Carter the ancestresses of three signers, three governors, and two Presidents. Again, although the families with which the blood of the daughters of the Carter stock was blended, by these various marriages, were socially of equal distinction, this fact can be established: outside the branches that formed the Carter connection, none of them produced more than the average number of men of superior intellect and achievement. Inexplicable as it may seem in the present limited knowledge of genetics, one is almost forced to conclude that there was something in the stock of the Carters that bred greatness through the female side, or else that something in the dealings of the Carter mothers with their sons inspired successive generations to high endeavor. The Alexandria boy who played on the lawn of Shirley, during his mother's visits, was wholly unconscious of it but his possession of his mother's blood, in descent from Robert Carter, was the best endowment for greatness that he could have had in the Virginia of his day. In some subtle way, he was advantaged in the contests of men because his mother was of the Carters of Corotoman.

By those same Carters at Shirley, as by his mother in his own home, Robert saw exemplified a very simple, straightforward loyalty to family, to church, and to God. This was traditional with the Carters, though only one of them, it seems, could ever have been called a religious fanatic.[16] In the daily walk of Charles Carter, Robert's grandfather, revealed religion and *noblesse oblige* were blended without any thought of creed or system. Owning perhaps 25,000 acres of land and a multitude of servants, Charles Carter rode in a great coach with postillions, but he abhorred waste, and in his will he wrote, "I earnestly request my family and friends that they do not go into mourning or wear black clothes, and this whim I expect they will gratify me in, as I always thought the custom absurd and extravagant answering no good purpose that I know of." In the belief that his second wife would outlive him, he stated that he considered the £3000 due her under her marriage settlement as "too small a pittance for so valuable a woman she having been every moment of her life a most agreeable, dutiful, and affectionate wife." He accordingly left her a life-interest in Shirley and the nearby estates.[17]

If crops were a failure on James River, when the season had been favorable on his Rappahannock plantations, he hauled great caravans of corn across the peninsulas and sold it at the normal price to those who needed it. His agent in England had standing orders to give to the hungry of London a certain percentage of the proceeds of the Carter tobacco, because he held that there were not enough poor people in Virginia to call forth the measure of charity he felt he should dispense.[18] One of his many farms he placed at the disposal of a clergyman to whom he was attached, stipulating at the last that the minister's widow should remain undisturbed on the land during her lifetime. Similarly, he enjoined his executors not to foreclose a mortgage he held on the farm of friends at Malvern Hills—a name destined to suggest something not akin to kindness in the life of his grandson.[19] "From the mansion of hospitality," read one obituary published not long after Charles Carter's death on June 28, 1806, "his immense wealth flowed like the silent stream, enlivening and re-

---

[16] Councillor Robert Carter had been in turn Episcopalian, Baptist, Swedenborgian, and Catholic.

[17] Will of Charles Carter; *Carter MSS.*, for access to which the writer is indebted to the characteristic kindness of Spencer L. Carter of Richmond, Va.

[18] *Henry Lee's Memoirs*, 49.   [19] Will of Charles Carter, *loc. cit.*

freshing every object around." [20] Another friend wrote: "In him the poor have lost their best friend, and of him it might be truly said that he was a father to the fatherless and a husband to the widow—the appeal of the wretched always was *effectually* attended to by him." [21]

The same spirit showed itself in Robert's godfather, Robert Carter. Having abandoned agriculture because of his dislike of slavery, Robert Carter became interested in medicine while nursing one of his sons who had sustained a physical injury. His religion and his art were as one. Both were illuminated in a letter of advice he wrote his children in October, 1803, when he was about to sail for Europe to further his medical education. In intimate, affectionate terms, he exhorted his boys and girls to heed the word of God, to obey the ten commandments, to believe the New Testament, to avoid strong drink, and to be kind to their servants, of whom it was not likely they could be rid.[22] Robert Carter's religion was of the sort that lives and thrives in friendly, family talk. The extant letter addressed him by Robert E. Lee's mother displays characteristically both the love and the unfeigned faith of the Carters:[23]

Stratford October 1st—1805—

I hope my dearest Brother has not supposed that his illness has caused me less affliction than his other friends from my not having expressed it to him, for I must ever believe my regret to be more poignant than any other persons, our Parents excepted—

But having been so often an invalid, I imagine myself adequate to judging the feelings of those in a similar situation, and nothing at those periods excited more painful sensations than letters of condolence from affectionate friends.

Your return to America was one of the events I anticipated the greatest happiness from. That happiness is destroyed by your ill health, but I hope my beloved Brother it will soon be realized by your complete recovery.

I wish so anxiously to see you, that trifling difficulties shall not prevent my being gratified as soon after Mr. Lee's return from the upper Country, as we can make arrangements for the journey,

---

[20] Quoted in *Henry Lee's Memoirs*, 49.
[21] *Richmond Enquirer*, July 22, 1806.   [22] *Carter MSS.*   [23] *Carter MSS.*

and I implore my Heavenly Father, that I may find you, my best beloved Brother daily progressing in health! ANN LEE.[24]

DR. ROBERT CARTER
    Shirley
Via City Point.

As in this letter, so in every other expression of her religious life, Ann Lee was typically a Carter. Henry Lee himself held to no creed but he paid tribute to the nobility of his wife's faith: "Your dearest mother," he wrote to one of his sons, "is singularly pious from love to Almighty God and love of virtue, which are synonymous; not from fear of hell—a base, low influence."[25] At home there were prayers, and on Sunday attendance on the Episcopal church of Alexandria, later known as Christ Church, where the solemn words of Holy Writ were made the more impressive because they were read from George Washington's own Bible, within the walls where his pew still stood intact.[26]

When Robert was seven the war that his father had opposed before his departure for the West Indies had been in progress nearly two years. Robert's half-brother Henry was commissioned major of the 36th Infantry and was ordered to the Canadian border.[27] Ere long, the boy's ears caught the report of artillery— the first time that baleful sound had ever reached him. He was told that the town was celebrating because word had come from Lake Erie that Lieutenant Perry had "met the enemy and they are ours." The next year the rumble of guns had a more ominous pitch. This time the people did not smile. Instead, they blanched, for British ships were in the Potomac and were fighting with the forts below Alexandria. On August 28, 1814, Admiral Cockburn's squadron appeared off the unarmed, undefended town. Immediately surrendered by her mayor, Alexandria was put under heavy contribution before the war-vessels sailed down the river

[24] *Carter MSS.*
[25] Henry Lee to Charles Carter Lee, Feb. 9, 1817, *Henry Lee's Memoirs,* 63. See also E. J. *Lee,* 350, 354, for expressions of Henry Lee's own faith.
[26] The back of the pew was cut down in Lee's youth, and the space was divided, but subsequently the pew was restored to its first form.
[27] E. J. *Lee,* 403.

again.[28] It is likely that Robert was kept indoors or was sent into the country while the redcoats were in the city streets, but during that same humiliating campaign, if he had looked, he might have seen the smoke rising from the capitol which the British had set afire in Washington. A grim early memory it was for a soldier's son, destined to be a soldier himself!

Before the war was over, the time had come for Robert to begin his formal education. His first books doubtless were opened to him by his mother, who had instructed him thus far in everything else. A little later he was sufficiently advanced in the rudiments to be sent away to the family school. For the Carters were so numerous and so intimate that they maintained two schools for their children, one for girls at Shirley and one for boys at Eastern View, Fauquier County, the home of Mrs. Henry Lee's sister, Elizabeth Carter, who had married Robert Randolph. It is not known when Robert went to Eastern View, or how long he stayed there. The setting was among the rolling, grass-covered hills where the Robin Hood of the Confederacy, John S. Mosby, was to execute Lee's orders in later years. Robert's schoolmates were boy-cousins of his own age. The sons of Robert and Elizabeth Carter Randolph—Beverley, Robert, and Charles Carter—were too old for the instruction given at Eastern View.

Not all of Robert's first reactions to school were favorable. Character, the essential quality of the man, was discernible already in the boy. From his self-imposed exile, his father wrote of him, "Robert was always good, and will be confirmed in his happy turn of mind by his ever-watchful and affectionate mother. Does he strengthen his native tendency?" [29] But at Eastern View, away from the daily discipline of his mother, he became a trifle headstrong, after the manner of the imperious Lees. When he came home, perhaps for a holiday, this was observed by his careful mother, who mentioned it with sisterly frankness to Mrs. Randolph when she wrote to thank her for her kindness to the lad. Mrs. Randolph replied that she had always found Robert "a most engaging child," not difficult to handle, but that if he had become

---

[28] *Mrs. Powell*, 252–53; the seizures made by the British are listed in Brockett and Rock, *op. cit.*, 22. It is possible that Mrs. Henry Lee and her children were at Shirley during these operations, but there is no evidence of this.

[29] Henry Lee to Charles Carter Lee, Feb. 9, 1817; *E. J. Lee*, 349.

so, the only advice she could give was that which she applied with her own boys—to "whip and pray, and pray and whip." [30]

The life of the family changed somewhat during the years Robert probably was at Eastern View. For a time the finances of Mrs. Lee had been less strained. In 1813 she had been able to visit Long Branch and had purchased a new carriage.[31] By 1816, and perhaps a little earlier, the family had moved from Cameron Street to a house on Washington Street at the corner of Princess. From this home, in 1816, the oldest of Ann Carter Lee's children, Charles Carter Lee, started for Harvard, which his father for some reason preferred at the time to his own alma mater, Princeton, and to William and Mary, where Henry had been a student. Carter remained at Cambridge three years and graduated second in the class of 1819.[32] Apparently he was supported while there by an allowance from his mother.[33] Not long after Carter left, the elder Henry Lee's letters told of his plans to return home. Ill or better, he was determined to come back to his own state. But months passed, and no ship was available. Finally, Lee wrote that he would sail for Savannah, Ga., and would attempt to procure passage thence to Virginia. The next news was that Robert's father had been stricken mortally on the voyage and had been put ashore at Dungeness, Cumberland Island, Ga., the property of the daughter of his old commander, General Greene. He had refused to be operated upon when the physician had urged it as a means of saving his life. "My dear sir," he had said, "were the great Washington alive, and here, and joining you in advocating it, I would still resist." Babbling something about his son Carter, he had died at Dungeness, March 25, 1818. The details of his passing were not known to the family until the next autumn.[34]

---

[30] This correspondence, which contained the earliest known written references to Robert, except those in his father's letters, was lost with many other Randolph papers in the demolition and looting of Eastern View during the War between the States. The tradition, however, is well authenticated, and the quoted language is remembered by Miss Annie Minor, of Richmond, whose mother had seen the letter.

[31] Ann Lee to Zachæus [sic] Collins, MS., Sept. 20, 1813, *Richard Bland Lee Papers, loc. cit.*

[32] *E. J. Lee*, 404–5; Henry Lee to Charles Carter Lee, June 26, 1815, *Henry Lee's Memoirs*, 57.

[33] Henry Lee to Carter Lee, June 18, 1817; *Henry Lee's Memoirs*, 72.

[34] Henry Lee to Charles Carter Lee, Dec. 1, 1816, and letters following in *Henry Lee's Memoirs*, 63 ff. For the details of his death, see *Ibid.*, 78–79. There is a tradition in Alexandria that Robert was playing in the garden of the house at Washington and Princess Street when the news of his father's death arrived (*Mrs. Powell*, 176).

The death of Henry Lee meant financial relief, rather than otherwise for his family, but it was not mourned the less on that account. Despite his failure to practise all that he preached, his sons honored his memory and cherished his sayings. Perhaps certain of the qualities of Robert Lee may have been strengthened by the exhortations his father addressed to Carter in letters the family took care to preserve:

"I would rather see you unlettered and unnoticed, if virtuous in practice as well as theory, than see you the equal in glory to the great Washington." [35]

"Fame in arms or art, however conspicuous, is naught, unless bottomed on virtue." [36]

"It is hard to say whether too much eating or too much drinking most undermines the constitution." [37]

"Cleanliness of person is not only comely to all beholders, but is indispensable to sanctity of body. Trained by the best of mothers to value it, you will never lose sight of it." [38]

"Many lads . . . fall into another habit which hurts only themselves and which certainly stupefies the senses—immoderate sleeping." [39]

"You know my abhorrence of lying, and you have been often told by me that it led to every vice and cancelled every tendency to virtue. Never forget this truth and disdain this mean and infamous practice." [40]

"Self command . . . is the pivot upon which the character, fame and independence of us mortals hang." [41]

"Avoid debt, the sink of mental power and the subversion of independence, which draws into debasement even virtue, in appearance, certainly, if not in reality. 'A man ought not only to be virtuous in reality, but he must always appear so,' thus said to me the great Washington." [42]

". . . Avoid all frivolous authors, such as novel writers, and all skeptical authors, whether religious, philosophic, or moral." [43]

"The rank of men, as established by the concurrent judgment of ages stands thus: heroes, legislators, orators, and poets. The most useful and, in my opinion, the most honorable is the legislator,

[35] E. J. Lee, 346. [36] Ibid., 348. [37] Ibid., 348.
[38] Ibid., 348. [39] Ibid., 349. [40] Ibid., 347.
[41] Ibid., 353. [42] Ibid., 356. [43] Ibid., 346.

which so far from being incompatible with the profession of law, is congenial to it. Generally, mankind admire most the hero; of all, the most useless, except when the safety of a nation demands his saving arm." [44]

These pathetic admonitions were rendered the more impressive on Robert's mind when he was old enough to realize that Henry Lee had written them, from his sorrowful exile, in the spirit of Wolsey's "Mark but my fall and that that ruined me."

Although Robert was only eleven when his father died, responsibility was soon to fall heavily on his straight young shoulders. His sister Ann, to whom he showed special devotion, continued sickly and sometimes required medical attention in Philadelphia.[45] Mrs. Lee was slowly slipping into chronic invalidism. Carter returned from Cambridge in 1819 but opened his law office in Washington, and was not much at home to aid in the management of the household.[46] The next year President Monroe gave a midshipman's commission in the navy to Smith, who went to sea.[47] The duties of an only son and of a daughter as well fell on Robert. Besides attending to the horses, he "carried the keys," in a now-forgotten Virginia phrase, and apportioned the food-supplies of the family. When free from his lessons he often accompanied his mother if she drove out during the afternoon. In case she was in low spirits, he admonished her that the drive would not do her good unless she were cheerful. On cold days, when the chill from the Potomac crept into the

---

[44] *Henry Lee's Memoirs*, 66. While in the West Indies, during 1813–14, Henry Lee had advocated a peace-settlement and at one time had hoped that he might be the means of effecting it through indirect negotiations. His letters of this period show that his health and his hopes fluctuated greatly from time to time (Henry Lee to James Monroe, MS., Nov. 13, 1813; Feb. 23, June 8, 1814; New York Public Library).

[45] A. L. Long: *Memoirs of Robert E. Lee* (cited hereafter as *Long*), 30; R. A. Brock, ed.: *General Robert Edward Lee* (cited hereafter as *Brock*), 146. Mrs. Powell, in a personal letter to the writer, recorded a tradition in Alexandria that Ann's ill-health originated in a bone injury that she received one day when she was sitting at a table with Robert, showing him a book. She had her hand extended, palm-down, on the table, while Robert's elbow rested on it. Before she realized it, the pressure of the joint had injured the muscle-casing.

[46] Carter Lee must, however, have been frequently in Alexandria while practising law, because he is listed in 1821 as one of the founders of the Periclean Society, a debating organization among the young men of the city (*Mrs. Powell*, 286). For Carter's career, see *E. J. Lee*, 404–5.

[47] See Henry Lee's letter, *infra*, p. 43. It is persistently and erroneously stated in virtually all the sketches of Sidney Smith Lee that he attended the naval academy. Actually, of course, there was no naval academy at the time.

vehicle, he sometimes pulled out his jackknife and pretended to keep out the wind by stuffing paper into the cracks.[48]

This attendance upon his mother continued until Robert left Alexandria. More than anything else, perhaps, his filial attention to her was the prime obligation of his youth, precisely as care for an invalid wife was to be one of the chief duties of his mature years. The man who was to order Pickett's charge at Gettysburg got part of his preparation for war by nursing sick women. The self-command that his mother had inculcated from his babyhood was confirmed at the bedside. Yet his association with his mother did not make the boy effeminate, though it gave him a love for the company of women. He stayed at home uncomplainingly when his mother required his attendance, but when he· was free he delighted to swim in the Potomac, to share in the sports of the neighborhood boys, with his cousin and playmate, Cassius Lee, or to follow the chase all day in the rolling country behind Alexandria.[49]

If Robert had a longer holiday he spent it at Chatham,[50] or at Ravensworth with the Fitzhughs, or at Stratford with his brother Henry, who, about the time Robert was ten, married Anne McCarty of Westmoreland County. The dates of his visits to the old home of the Lees are not known, but he must have gone there not infrequently, because in later life he cherished clear memories of a place of which he could have had only the vaguest impressions before the family moved to Alexandria.

The great brick mansion-house, Stratford Hall, had been built about 1730, in the form of a large H. Below was a half-cellar with small windows. The principal apartments were on the floor above, reached by long steps. Over all was a high attic under a shingle roof. From the two wings, corridors ran to a central hall, some thirty feet square, with bookcases in panelled walls. Here were the portraits of the earlier Lees.

---

[48] *Mason*, 22–23.

[49] *Mason*, 23. Robert must have found interest in the happenings of the growing town of Alexandria. Down on Royal Street, near Sharpskin Alley, the city built a market house, with a clock and a tower, very much like Bow Bells in London, the travelled Alexandrians affirmed. On the upper floor of this edifice a museum was opened, to which wondering youth had access, chiefly on Saturday mornings, for twelve and one-half cents, cash in hand. A little later, to the admiration of all the city's boys, a tower, a steeple, and a bell were put on Christ Church (*Mrs. Powell*, 58, 87, 90, 234–35).

[50] D. H. Maury: *Recollections of a Virginian* (cited hereafter as *D. H. Maury*), p. 3.

Robert not only explored every corner of the house, but heard all the myths that were told him about the greater glories of an earlier Stratford—how it had boasted a hundred chambers, with four outbuildings of fifteen rooms each, how its stables had stalls for five score horses, how it had been burned in the days of Thomas Lee, how the East India Company had rebuilt it in tribute to that worthy, and how from the privy purse Queen Caroline herself had made a gift for reconstruction. None of this was true except that George II probably granted the distressed proprietor a few hundred pounds.[51] The house the boy visited was, in reality, the only one that ever stood on the site, but the fanciful stories formed a respected tradition, real in every detail to Robert. As he sat in the hall, he must have seen the ghosts of his ancestors. When he walked along the winding way that led through the vast, affrighting garret to promenades framed on the roof around the central chimneys, he must surely have heard the scraping of the fiddles in the band that the builder of Stratford was reputed to have kept at the call of his daughters, while they took the air or danced with their suitors in the hall.

In front of the mansion-house, where the none-too-fertile fields of Westmoreland stretched away, the widespreading lawn was dotted with oaks and poplars. On one side of the greensward was a grove of sugar-maples, past which a driveway curved up to the entrance. Flanking the central building was the garden. Toward the Potomac were open fields and then woodland, through which a lane led to a high bluff, whence there was a long sweep of shining waters. Set off from each corner of the residence were four smaller brick structures, to which Robert Edward Lee must have been a frequent visitor, especially the kitchen, with a fireplace like a dragon's mouth, hot and steaming, but with the lure of sweet odors. Beyond the outhouses, to the left as one approached the mansion from the highway, were the large brick stables, where horses were forever stamping, and hens were always scratching and clucking. It was a realm of endless marvels for a boy of ten.[52]

[51] *Boyd*, 19.
[52] *Henry Lee's Memoirs*, 41; *Mason*, 15; *E. J. Lee*, 70, 74, 116, 118, 119, 576; *Long*, 19; Lucinda Lee: *Journal of a Young Lady of Virginia*, edited by Emily V. Mason, 23. E. J. Lee, *op. cit.*, 117 *ff.*, cited several letters from Thomas Lee Shippen, who visited the Lees and spent some hours at Stratford in 1790.

The young master of Stratford at that time could have had little in common with his half-brother Robert. Henry Lee the fourth was later called "Black-Horse Harry" or "Black Harry," both to describe his conduct and to distinguish him from "Light-Horse Harry," his father. Born the year the Philadelphia convention met, he was twenty years older than Robert. He had been to the College of William and Mary in 1808, though there is no record of his graduation.[53] His father's facility for composition, somewhat accentuated, he had inherited, and he was developing a deep, partisan interest in politics. As the rich member of the family, he must have seemed an awesome person to Robert, but he had about him then little to suggest the passionate tragedy that was to wreck his career.[54]

As visits and pleasure were interspersed with hard work for Robert, he developed rapidly in physique and in character, and by the time he was thirteen he had learned all that could conveniently be taught him at home and at Eastern View. Accordingly, by 1820, possibly before that year, Robert entered the Alexandria academy. This had been established about 1785, and had been privileged to list Washington as one of its first trustees. Occupying a one-story brick house on the east side of Washington Street, between Duke and Wolfe, the school was made free to all Alexandria boys after January, 1821. Here Robert met at their desks the boys with whom he had played in the fields, and here he came under the tutelage of William B. Leary, an Irishman for whom young Lee acquired enduring respect.[55]

For approximately three years Robert studied the rudiments of a classical education under Mr. Leary. He read Homer and Longinus in Greek. From Tacitus and Cicero he became so well-grounded in Latin that he never quite forgot the language, though he did not study it after he was seventeen. Late in life, he expressed deep regret that he had not pursued his classical course further.[56] In mathematics he shone, for his mind was already of

---

[53] According to Doctor E. G. Swem, librarian of the College of William and Mary.

[54] E. J. Lee, 403.

[55] Mrs. Powell, 152–53, 154, 155; Mason, 23–24; R. E. Lee, Jr.: Recollections and Letters of General Robert E. Lee, first edition (cited hereafter as R. E. Lee, Jr.), 417.

[56] Edward S. Joynes in Robert E. Lee: Centennial Celebration of His Birth—University of South Carolina (cited hereafter as Cent. U. S. C.), 29.

the type that delighted in the precise reasoning of algebra and geometry.[57]

By the end of 1823, and perhaps earlier, he had completed the course of study at the Alexandria academy. What should he do next? It was a question not easily answered. He could not continue to follow cultural study and settle down as a country-gentleman, after the manner of his ancestors, because he did not have money for the education, much less the land on which to live in leisure. He possessed no aptitude for public utterance and no taste for the law. Although a moral, high-minded boy and an attendant upon Christ Church, deeply if indirectly influenced by Reverend William Meade, he had never presented himself for confirmation and he probably never gave a thought to the ministry. There is no record that he ever debated the possibilities of a medical career, despite his contact with the sick and his growing skill in nursing. What, then, should he do?

While this question was being debated, Henry Lee wrote a book that may have contributed in an unexpected way to the answer. In 1822, Judge William Johnson of the Supreme Court of the United States published in two volumes his *Sketches of the Life and Correspondence of Nathanael Greene,*[58] a work in which he pointed out various errors and exposed what he regarded as false claims in "Light-Horse Harry" Lee's *Memoirs of the War in the Southern Department.*[59] There probably was no animus on Johnson's part toward Lee, but some of his criticisms were severe. Henry Lee the younger felt that his father's honor and military reputation had been assailed, and he wrote in reply a book of more than 500 pages under the title *The Campaign of 1781 in the Carolinas; with Remarks Historical and Critical on Johnson's Life of Greene.*[60] It is more than likely that Johnson's charges and the preparation of Henry Lee's reply were both discussed in Alexandria, and that an hereditary fondness for a career of arms was thereby strengthened in Robert. His brother Smith had gone into the navy: why should not Robert go to the United States Military Academy at West Point and be a soldier? His love of

---

[57] See certificate of W. B. Leary, *infra*, p. 40.   [58] Published at Charleston, S. C.
[59] *Johnson's Greene*, vol. 1, pp. 406, 412, 424, 439, 457; vol. 2, pp. 20, 33, 72–73, 100, 105, 131, 142, 168, 174, 221, 279, 296, 327–28 and "Postscript."
[60] Philadelphia, 1824; copyrighted Feb. 13, 1824.

mathematics would help; his education would cost him nothing. By this process of reasoning, it would appear, Robert E. Lee decided to become a soldier.[61] He lived to see the time when he considered that decision the greatest mistake of his life, though he then had behind him all his military achievements from Vera Cruz to Petersburg.[62]

The age-limits for admission to West Point were fourteen to twenty years, for boys who were at least four feet, nine inches, free of physical defects, able to read and write well, familiar with arithmetic, and willing to sign articles to remain five years in the army, including the four years of cadetship.[63] Robert could meet all these requirements, if he could have the good fortune to be named one of the 250 cadets for whom the government made provision. The appointments were at the pleasure of the President, on the nomination of the Secretary of War, who at that time followed no rule respecting their geographical distribution.[64] Nine Virginians had been appointed in 1822. Six more had been named in 1823, but thirty-six applications had then been rejected.[65] In an effort to satisfy as many as he might, the secretary, John C. Calhoun, was lavishly anticipating nominations, beyond Monroe's term of office; but the number did not suffice even then, and the scramble was keen. Robert's age and his mother's circumstances were such that he could not afford to wait on a chance appointment. He must either begin soon as a soldier, or turn immediately to something else. It consequently was decided in the family-circle that he should make personal application to the Secretary of War. But who would introduce him to that august personage? The duty fell to the family's counsellor, William H. Fitzhugh of Ravensworth, whose kindness had not weakened in all the years of the Lees' residence in Alexandria. He wrote Secretary Calhoun as follows:[66]

[61] This statement is qualified and is in part conjectural. It rests solely on the letter of William H. Fitzhugh, printed *infra*, p. 39, and on the tradition that both Smith and Robert chose their professions because the navy and the army offered careers without a heavy financial outlay, which Mrs. Lee was unable to make.

[62] See *infra*, Volume IV.

[63] Act of April 29, 1812, quoted in Boynton's *History of West Point* (cited hereafter as *Boynton*), 344; *Military Academy Regulations*, pp. 4–5; §§ 1337–39, see *infra*, pp. 44–45.

[64] *Centennial of the United States Military Academy* (cited hereafter as *Cent. U. S. M. A.*), Vol. I, 226.

[65] *American State Papers, Military Affairs*, vol. 3, 220; 4, 343, 344.

[66] MS., U. S. War Department.

My dear Sir,   Ravensworth Feb 7th 1824.

I cannot permit the young gentleman, who will hand you this letter, to make his intended application, without carrying with him, such testimony in his behalf, as a long & an intimate acquaintance both with himself and his family, justify me in giving. He is the son of Genl. Henry Lee, with whose history, you are, of course, acquainted; and who (whatever may have been the misfortune of his latter years) had certainly established, by his revolutionary services, a strong claim to the gratitude of his country. He is the son also of one of the finest women, the State of Virginia has ever produced. Possessed, in a very eminent degree, of all those qualities, which peculiarly belong to the female character of the South, she is rendered doubly interesting by her meritorious & successful exertions to support, in comfort, a large family, and to give to all her children excellent educations.

The young gentleman, whom I have now the pleasure of introducing to you, as a candidate for West-point, is her youngest son. An intimate acquaintance, & a constant intercourse with him, almost from his infancy, authorize me to speak in the most unqualified terms of his amiable disposition, & his correct and gentlemanly habits. He is disposed to devote himself to the profession of arms. But his final determination on this subject, must, of course, depend on the result of his present application, and you will find him prepared to acquiesce in whatever decision, circumstances may require you to make in his case. Next, however, to promising him the commission, which he asks, the greatest favor you can do him will be to tell him promptly if you think the obstacles to his success are insurmountable. His own age (eighteen I believe) and the situation of his mother require that he should lose no time in selecting the employment to which his future life is to be devoted.

Accept my dear Sir the assurance of the very great respect with which

I am

Yo^r &c   W. H. FITZHUGH

39

Robert presented this letter in person. A strange interview it must have been between the man who was soon to be the "father of nullification" and the boy who, in maturity, was to carry the burden of the bloody struggle that was, in a sense, the unescapable consequence of the application of that doctrine. Calhoun could not have failed to be impressed by young Lee and probably told him that if he produced suitable recommendations, they would be considered. The boy promptly filed an endorsement from Wm. B. Leary, his teacher, but as this was clothed in rather general terms, Robert presented another and more specific statement to this effect.[67]

"Robert Lee was formerly a pupil of mine. While under my care I can vouch for his correct and gentlemanly deportment. In the various branches, to which his attention has been applied, I flatter myself that his information will be found adequate to the most sanguine expectations of his friends. With me he has read all the minor classics in addition to Homer & Longinus, Tacitus & Cicero. He is well versed in arithmetic, Algebra & Euclid. In regard to what he has read with me I am certain that when examined he will neither disappoint me or his friends.

W B LEARY"

Robert must also have had an intimation from some source that his chances would be better if he had the backing of some members of Congress. As a resident of the District of Columbia he had, of course, no representation, but the Lees were traditionally of Westmoreland and had never formally quit the county. Robert, or some member of the family, accordingly invoked the help of Congressman R. S. Garnett, who wrote Calhoun as follows:[68]

Washington City
Feb 16 1824

Sir

I beg leave to recommend to your favorable attention, Master Robert Lee who is desirous to be placed in the Military academy as a cadet. He is a son of the late General Henry Lee and has

[67] *MS.*, U. S. War Department.   [68] *MS.*, U. S. War Department.

strong hereditary claims on the country. I am not able to state what proficiency he has made in his studies, but testimonials will be exhibited by him in relation to this subject, that I presume will prove satisfactory. He is about 18 years of age, and of excellent disposition. If he can obtain the appointment he desires, I have no doubt that he will justify the expectations which his recommendations would authorize

Very respectfully

Yr serv^t

R S GARNETT

C. F. Mercer, congressman from a part of Virginia immediately adjacent to the district, also wrote a general letter of endorsement which Henry Lee, or some interested friend, took the trouble to circulate among senators and members of the House of Representatives. This was dated from the Senate, as though it had originated there. Of its signers, George Tucker, like Mercer and Garnett, was a member of the House from Virginia. James Barbour was senator from Virginia and was to succeed Calhoun as Secretary of War. Richard M. Johnson, then senator from Kentucky, later became Vice-President under Van Buren. Henry Johnson, senator from Louisiana, soon resigned to become Governor of that state. The junior Alabama senator, Wm. Kelly, likewise signed, as did David Holmes, a native of Virginia, and spokesman for Mississippi in the upper house. Their joint letter read:[69]

Senate Chamber

Feb. 23d 1824

Sir

We beg leave to recommend to your favorable consideration Mr Robert Edward Lee, a son of the late Genl. Henry Lee of Virginia as an applicant for admission to the military academy at West Point.

The assurances which we have received of the talents and attainments of this young gentleman apart from the regard we feel for the military services of his deceased father, induces us to

[69] *MS.*, U. S. War Department.

hope that the gratification of his wishes may prove compatible with the rules which you have deemed it proper to establish for the admission of cadets into the academy.

We are, Sir

Very respectfully

Your Ob^t. Servt

C. F. Mercer

George Tucker

R. S. Garnett

James Barbour

Rh. M. Johnson

H. Johnson

David Holmes

Wm Kelly

Endorsement by five senators and three representatives was certain to be weighty, especially when given the son of a Revolutionary officer, who had fought in Secretary Calhoun's native South Carolina.

This helpful paper was supplemented by a letter of a more personal character from Robert's older brother Charles Carter in these terms:[70]

"Sir,

"I enclose you a letter from my youngest brother, who is an applicant, as you know, for a place at the Military Academy. Permit me to add, by way of a supplement to his statement,[71] what it would have been unbecoming in him to have averred, but what I hope I may be excused for alledging, [sic] viz: that his intellect seems to be a good one, that he appears to be sufficiently inclined to study, that his disposition is amiable, & his morals irreproachable. I can adduce no other merits on which to rest his claims to the preferment he seeks at your hands, unless perhaps the revolutionary services of the father should obtain some favour for the son.

---

[70] *MS.*, U. S. War Department.
[71] Robert's letter has disappeared from the records. It probably was a statement of the scope of his previous studies.

"I had rather have taken any other opportunity than the present
.o assure you of the sincere respect & esteem of Sir,
Your most obedient & humble servant
C. C. Lee.

Alex^a. Feby. 28th 1824
To J. C. Calhoun Esqr."

Henry Lee added his influence in behalf of Robert with a longer
letter, in which the claims of the boy were based in large part on
his father's military service:[72]

"Sir,
"My brother Robert E Lee has applied to you for the appointment of a Cadet
"I know of no principle of *rational* selection, that should exempt
him from the hazards of a fair competition upon the ground of
personal advantages and mental qualifications, (for which he is
well prepared) but the just and admitted one of refering to the
services of the Father in estimating the claims of the Son. In the
case of the late Genl. Lee it was confessed by M^r. Monroe, that
the title of his offspring to national patronage *ceteris paribus* was
emminently strong; and on the principle here suggested, he
appointed my brother Smith a Midshipman in 1820, against a
force of competition and a weight of previous application, as
great at least as those which now exist.
"On this principle I beg leave to rest the claims of Robert. To
a person of your enlarged sentiments, and accurate knowledge of
our national history it would be unnecessary to enumerate the
exertions of my father in the cause of this country, or to trace
the grand and beautiful process of morality, by which the orphans
of publick benefactors, become the children of the State.
I have the honour to be
with perfect respect Sir,
Your very ob^t. & very humble Servant
H. Lee

Fredericksburg, Va.
6th March 1824."

Calhoun had before him numerous applications from Virginia
and was being importuned in behalf of new candidates every

[72] *MS.*, U. S. War Department.

few weeks.[74] Robert could only wait and hope, because he had now brought to bear all the influence his family could exert. Finally there came notice from the War Department: As of March 11, Robert was appointed to West Point, but owing to the long list of applicants, he could not be admitted until July 1, 1825.[75] That entailed a year's delay but it meant opportunity then!

Doubtless there was much excitement in the mind of the boy, and doubtless, too, he made several drafts before he concluded his letter of acceptance which, for all his care, did not escape one error of spelling. It is the earliest letter in his autograph now extant.[76]

"Sir

"I hereby accept the appointment to the station of a Cadet in the service of the United States, with which I have been honnoured by the President.

"The above is the declaration of consent which my letter of appointment instructs me should accompany my acceptance.

"I remain with the highest respect, Sir
 Your most obliged & most obedient Servant
                                               R. E. LEE

Alex^a. April 1st 1824
To
 The Honble J. C. Calhoun"

Mrs. Lee's consent, in the simple terms of the army regulations, was written at the top of her son's letter in this language:

"Sir

"As the surviving Parent of Robert E. Lee I consent to his

---

[74] He rejected twenty-five applications from Virginia in 1824 (*American State Papers, Military Affairs*, 4, 346).

[75] For the date of the appointment, see *American State Papers, Military Affairs*, 3, 220.

[76] *MS.*, U. S. War Department. It has long been believed that Mrs. Lawrence Lewis, *née* Nellie Custis, an aunt of the future Mrs. Robert E. Lee, took Robert to Washington "and introduced him to Genl. Jackson, who was so much pleased with him that he got him the appointment" (*Long*, 28). This cannot be established but it is quite possible that at Henry Lee's instance, or that of Mrs. Lewis, Jackson interested himself in Lee's application. If it be a fact that Washington's adopted daughter was responsible for the appointment of Robert E. Lee, it adds to the strong Washington tradition and influence that helped to shape Lee's life.

signing articles, binding himself to serve as a Cadet five years, to be computed from the time of his joining the Military Academy.

ANN H. LEE"

It is a singular fact that the next appointee of Calhoun, after the date on which Lee and one other boy were named, should have been Joseph E. Johnston.[77] Oddly enough, also, the first letter of Jefferson Davis that has survived the years is one in which he, like Lee, acknowledged and accepted an appointment from Calhoun to the military academy.[78]

The very atmosphere of Alexandria seemed to lend itself to martial affairs after Robert learned that he would be admitted to the military academy. Greece was struggling for liberty, and all the intellectuals of the Potomac were much interested in the contest.[79] Soon they had promise of a sensation closer at hand: Lafayette was coming! "America's Friend," now an old man, was revisiting the scenes of his greatest adventure. He was, of course, to make a pilgrimage to Mount Vernon and would walk the streets of Washington's city. All that the little town could offer, of hospitality and display, was put forth for the venerable marquis when he arrived in October, 1824. On Washington Street, which is 100 feet wide, the city erected a triple arch, north of King Street. The central span over the roadway was sixty-eight feet. Each sidewalk had a lesser arch of eighteen feet. In the direction of Lafayette's approach, this greeting was blazoned: "Welcome LaFayette! A Nation's Gratitude Thy Due." On the opposite face of the main arch was a quotation from one of his speeches: "For a Nation to Be Free, It is Sufficient That She Wills It." Atop the arch, as a crowning touch of realism, Colonel Mountford, father of the Alexandria Museum, placed a live eagle from the city's collection. On the great day, the bird obligingly spread its wings just at the moment the city's guest was passing beneath. At least it was so reported.[80]

For no family in the town was Lafayette's visit more interesting than for the Lees. The marquis had not forgotten the brilliant

---

[77] *American State Papers, Military Affairs*, 3, 220.
[78] Dunbar Rowland, editor: *Jefferson Davis Constitutionalist* (cited hereafter as *Rowland*), 1, p. 1.
[79] *Mrs. Powell*, 291.
[80] *Autobiography of Benjamin Hallowell* (cited hereafter as *Hallowell*), 100–101.

cavalryman of Washington's army, who was only a year and a half his senior. Hearing that the widow of his comrade was residing in Alexandria, he made a call on the morning of October 14, 1824,[81] when Robert doubtless saw him. That contact of his youth was one of the many that bound the boy in spirit to the Revolution.

The day before Lafayette called, a young Quaker named Benjamin Hallowell had brought his bride to Oronoko Street, where he proposed to open a boys' school in the house adjoining that of the Lees. For a while he had no pupils. Then it was discovered that he was a man of unusual ability and of much skill in teaching. About January 1, 1825, Robert Lee's chum, Cassius, son of Edmund Jennings Lee, was sent by his father to Mr. Hallowell.

Perhaps it was on the basis of Cassius's report that the family began to talk of giving Robert a few months under the new dominie. The boy had not been in school for a season; he naturally was "getting rusty" on his mathematics. Would it not be well to have him refurbish that subject and prepare himself somewhat ahead on the more advanced mathematics he was to study at West Point? Robert entered in February, 1825, and remained with Mr. Hallowell until he was ready to set out for West Point.[82] The charges were $10 a quarter, no small item to a widow who had to count costs carefully, but the expense was justified. Hallowell was ambitious and as his students were still few in number, he was able to give the boy intimate and close instruction. Robert responded to Hallowell's full satisfaction. "He was a most exemplary pupil in every respect," Hallowell wrote long after. "He was never behind time at his studies; never failed in a single recitation; was perfectly observant of the rules and regulations of the institution; was gentlemanly, unobtrusive, and respectful in all his deportment to teacher and his fellow-students. His specialty was *finishing up*. He imparted a finish and a neatness, as he proceeded, to everything he undertook. One of the branches of mathematics he studied with me was Conic Sections, in which some of the diagrams are very complicated. He drew the dia-

---

[81] *Hallowell,* 100.
[82] *Hallowell,* 103; *Mrs. Powell,* 157; *Mason,* 25. The crude sketch of Hallowell's school that appears in Wedderburn, *op. cit.,* is not of the building used during the time Robert Lee was a student.

grams on a slate; and although he well knew that the one he was drawing would have to be removed to make room for another, he drew each one with as much accuracy and finish, lettering and all, as if it were to be engraved and printed."[83] The early, earnest lessons in self-control were yielding results.

On March 17, 1825, unknown to him, Robert's name was read out at the military academy as a member of the incoming class.[84] Soon thereafter he must have started to acquire the leather trunk and all the clothing and equipment called for in the precise regulations of West Point—from "2 prs. of Monroe shoes" to "1 foul-clothes' bag, made of ticken."[85] When June came, all was ready, but his mother was bewildered: "How can I live without Robert?" she asked, "he is both son and daughter to me." Loath he was to leave her, but he was then past eighteen, very well grown, and anxious to try the reputed hard classes and stern discipline of the military academy. He set out while Abraham Lincoln was battling for the rudiments of an education in the Indiana backwoods. Three-year-old Ulysses Grant was then toddling about his father's farm in Clermont County, Ohio.

[83] Letter of Benjamin Hallowell, quoted in *Mason*, 25.
[84] *MS. Diary of Cadet S. P. Heintzelman*, March 17, 1825 (cited hereafter as *Heintzelman's MS. Diary*).
[85] *Article 78* ("*Military Academy*"), *Army Regulations*, § 1395. This is an undated pamphlet in the Library of Congress but presumably of about 1823. It is cited hereafter as *M. A. Regs.* and contains substantially the same regulations that were reprinted (as of 1824) in *American State Papers, Military Affairs*, 2.

CHAPTER III

First Impressions of West Point

By steamer and stage, Robert Lee journeyed toward West Point in June, 1825. At New York City, which was then a bewildering Babel of at least 200,000 people, Robert doubtless took the Hudson River steamboat. In a few hours he was deposited in a skiff off his landing place, for the vessel disdained to stop at the nascent academy.[1] He reported to the superintendent, and then to the adjutant, who assigned him to quarters.

The institution that Robert saw at dawn the next day, as he watched the cadets muster for roll-call, has one of the loveliest sites in America. West Point is situated thirty-seven miles north of New York, on the west bank of the Hudson, at a point where the river bends from east to south. The high hills that close in on the stream are here brought down to a lofty plain, as if some giant had toppled the heights into the river, and then had smoothed out a bit of land in order to give favored mortals a vantage point from which to view the Hudson. At the tip of the point was old Fort Clinton. Above the plain the ramparts of Fort Putnam were already weathering. Beyond them were piled up the wooded hills and the unmarred mountains.

The military academy was then twenty-three years old, though its corps of cadets had been small until 1817, eight years before Robert's arrival. Its buildings, which were few and unimpressive, had been erected to the west of Fort Clinton and not far from the river. The largest structures were two stone dormitories of approximately the same graceless age, set at right angles to each other and known as the North and South Barracks. The North were of four stories, and the South of three, with a most unattractive piazza. West of the South Barracks was the two-

---

[1] This was the experience of F. H. Smith who went to the Academy in 1829, and it probably was the usual method of landing. See F. H. Smith: *West Point Fifty Years Ago* (cited hereafter as *F. H. Smith*), p. 2

story Academy, or academic building, which made some languid pretenses at architectural dignity. Beyond the Academy was the long mess-hall, also of two stories, a forlorn place, used as a hotel by the mess contractor, William B. Cozzens, who nightly crowded into its ten rooms most of those who came to the Point to visit friends. These buildings were all that were used at that time by the students. To all four of them stucco had been applied with generous hand and with much success in adding to their natural ugliness.

Not far off were the wooden "Long Barracks" put up during the Revolution and formerly occupied by cadets. Overlooking the north crest of the plain was one double stone building, while a solitary brick residence defaced the western side of the plain. The house that had been Washington's headquarters was to the north of the Point, about a quarter of a mile away. To the south, as steep and narrow a path as ever the righteous walked led up from the cottage where Kosciuszko had lived. On the east were a howitzer, a couple of mortars and the ten cannon of the academy, two of which had been sent over with the French during the 1770's and bore the somewhat undemocratic inscription, *Ultima Ratio Regum*. More conspicuous than barracks or battery—a warning to all newcomers that the soldier's life was not one of ease—was the well-trampled field where the cadets did their drilling. Out of bounds were a few houses of unhappy aspect and of reputation not uniformly of the best.[2] Chief among them was North's Tavern, at which, as a sorrowing board of visitors not long before had affirmed, the cadets individually were spending an average of $50 per annum. It was all unfamiliar to Robert, and doubtless most impressive, but the landscape could not have seemed altogether alien to him. There was something about it that suggested the upper stretches of the Potomac, near the falls where his luckless father had fashioned in fancy a great metropolis.[3]

[2] *Cent. U. S. M. A.*, 1, 243; 2, 83; *Reminiscences of West Point in the Olden Time* (Anonymous, East Saginaw, Mich., 1886), p. 28; H. D. Gilpin: *A Northern Tour; Being a Guide to Saratoga* (cited hereafter as *Northern Tour*), 31; *Boynton*, 254, 255, 256, 264. Boynton printed pictures of the barracks and of the academy.

[3] A view of West Point, as of 1824, appears in Wall's *Hudson River Portfolio*. Reference to various other contemporary pictures of the school will be found in *Cent. U. S. M. A.*, 2, 31.

The worst thing at the academy was among the first to which the new cadets were introduced—the food. At seven o'clock they were marched to the mess-hall where they could not fail to get an unpleasant opinion of the hospitality of Mr. Cozzens. One of the boys who was received at the same time with Robert found the diet of indescribable badness. The soup was unpalatable at dinner time, the molasses was inedible, and the pudding was untouchable.[4]

Not long after his arrival, Robert was summoned before the academic board for his preliminary examination. There at the head of a table, where a number of officers and professors sat in inquisition, he saw at closer range the gentleman to whom he had reported when he reached West Point, Sylvanus Thayer, brevet lieutenant-colonel of engineers and superintendent of the military academy. Then forty years of age, with clean-cut features and the bearing of an aristocrat, Thayer was flawlessly apparelled in uniform, with the white drilling trousers that he never put aside till frost. He was an austere man in his official relations and steadfastly repelled any appeal to sentiment or emotion. An instructor at West Point prior to the War of 1812, he had been an engineer during that struggle. In 1815 he had been sent to Europe to study the allied operations in front of Paris and to report on military schools and works. After two years, he was called to the weak academy at West Point. As superintendent there, he had greatly raised the standards of instruction and had placed the school under a stern and exacting discipline. Robert Lee was to find that while thoughtful people recognized Thayer's service to his country in training young soldiers, the cadets disliked him and accused him of constant espionage. No matter how venal or disreputable the source, Thayer would always give ear to every accusation against any member of the corps.[5]

Robert's examination was oral and easy,[6] and after it had been completed, he and his fellow-newcomers were assigned tents on the plain, Camp Adams, as it was styled in honor of the new

---

[4] F. A. Mitchell: *Ormsby MacKnight Mitchel* (cited hereafter as *F. A. Mitchel*), 20.

[5] For Thayer's rank, etc., see *American State Papers, Military Affairs*, 4, 833. See also *F. H. Smith*, 4; Leonidas Polk to his father, undated, in W. M. Polk: *Leonidas Polk* (cited hereafter as *Polk*), 1, 61.

[6] The entrance examinations are described briefly in *Cent. U. S. M. A.*, 1, 220.

President, John Quincy Adams.[7] No announcement of the board's decision as to which of the applicants would be admitted to the academy was made until June 28. At 8 P.M. that day, the applicants were ordered to form in front of the barracks. When they were in line and at attention, they were told that an alphabetical list of those who had passed the examination would be read, and that as each man's name was called he was to advance four paces.

Down the roll, through an interminable list of "H's" the adjutant went—"Charles W. Hackley, Archibald Hall, James W. Hamilton, William Hoffman, Theophilus H. Holmes, Chileab S. Howe, Franklin E. Hunt, Hampton Hunter." Next into the "J's": "Peter Johnson, Joseph E. Johnston, Fayette Jones."

The "K's" followed:

> "John L. Keffer
> Miner Knowlton"

Then—"Robert E. Lee—"

The boy stepped forward four paces, and became Cadet Lee.[8]

Together with his future room-mates, Lee now proceeded to purchase the Spartan requirements for their joint toilet—a looking-glass, a wash-stand and basin, a pitcher, a tin pail, a broom, and a scrubbing brush.[9] He bought, also, a regulation gray uniform, four pair of white trousers, a blue fatigue jacket and trousers, two silk stocks, and that crowning adornment of the cadet, a cap. This was of black leather, bell crowned, seven inches high, with a polished leather visor, a diamond-shaped yellow plate, an eight-inch black plume for dress parade, and, for less formal use,

---

[7] The old cadets had gone into camp on June 24 (*Heintzelman's MS. Diary*).

[8] *F. A. Mitchel*, 21. Twenty of the youths who had reported for admission failed to pass the entrance examination. It was not until Sept. 25 that Lee and his classmates signed the oath, which then read as follows: "I, Robert E. Lee, a cadet born in the State of Virginia, aged 18 years and nine months, do hereby acknowledge to have this day voluntarily engaged with the consent of my mother to serve in the Army of the United States for the period of five years, unless sooner discharged by proper authority. And I do promise upon honor that I will observe and obey the orders of the officers appointed over me, the rules and articles of war, and the regulations which have been or may hereafter be established for the government of the Military Academy" (*Heintzelman's MS. Diary;* statement of Major James C. R. Schwenck, U. S. A., Department of Law, U. S. Military Academy, prepared April 1, 1921, at the instance of A. R. Lawton of Savannah, Ga., who has kindly placed the paper at the writer's disposal). When registering, Lee gave Westmoreland County, Virginia, as his place of residence, and Colonel Henry Lee, his half-brother, as his guardian.

[9] *M. A. Regs.*, § 1396.

a leather cockade, to say nothing of the eagle and the yellow scales that could be fastened in front or under the chin.[10] In procuring this equipment young Lee had his first acquaintance with his account-book, on which all purchases were entered, to be charged against his pay of $16 a month or against his subsistence allowance of $12 a month.[11] He needed all his shining new array almost as soon as he got it, for on July 2 there was much pomp and a formal review in honor of Lafayette, who paid the academy a visit.[12] Robert doubtless saw the marquis again, but hardly at so close range as when the old veteran had visited Mrs. Lee in Alexandria.

Lee's duties while the corps was under canvas consisted of four hours' drill each day, much of it, at the outset, directed by an upperclassman. In addition, he probably had instruction in the mysteries of the dance, which had become compulsory at West Point for third and fourth classmen.[13] There were, however, no classes during July and August, and many of the men who had just completed their second year at the academy were away on leave. It was a period of extreme heat, followed by a long succession of rainy days.[14]

The boy had ample time to prepare for the work of the coming winter and to learn the "Thou-shalt-nots" that constituted a large part of life at West Point. No cadet could drink or play cards, or use tobacco, or bring the weed on the grounds or keep it on his person. He might not have in his room any cooking utensils, any games, any novel, any romance or any play. With the consent of the superintendent, he might subscribe to one periodical, but to only one. Too much reading was accounted bad for a soldier: the library was open only two hours a week—on Saturday afternoons. If the cadet possessed any musical instrument, he might not perform on it except during the hour of recreation. Societies and meetings were forbidden without the consent of the superintendent. No visitors might call on Sunday, in study hours, or

---

[10] For a description of the uniform, see *Condition of the Military Academy, 1824, American State Papers, Military Affairs*, 2, 653–64 (cited hereafter as *Cond. M. A.*).
[11] *M. A. Regs.*, §§ 1328–32, 1399–1403; for the pay regulations, see *American State Papers, Military Affairs*, 2, 66.
[12] *Heintzelman's MS. Diary.*
[13] *American State Papers, Military Affairs*, 3, 381; *Cent. U. S. M. A.*, 1, 908. The dancing master arrived on July 25 (*Heintzelman's MS. Diary*).
[14] *Heintzelman's MS. Diary.*

in the evenings. A cadet was forbidden to go beyond designated limits, or to drop in at North's, or to loiter a bit around the public wharf, or even to bathe in the river without the permission of constituted authority. As for the favorite pranks of academicians, woe to him who slyly dropped a bucket of waste-water on a fellow cadet passing under the window. And a double woe to him who answered for another at roll-call or reviled a sentinel. Any compact on the part of old cadets to haze the "plebes" by refusing to speak to them carried with it the threat of instant dismissal. Fist fights and their far more foolish counterpart, the *duello,* were forbidden in all forms and in all circumstances. A cadet might not sign any statement regarding any fellow-cadet's behavior or grievance in an affair of honor, and if he heard of any challenge in the making or of any rendezvous with pistols at dawn, he was supposed to report it. And so for a still longer list of things that a gentleman and soldier should not do—if Colonel Thayer knew it.[15] If a student were aggrieved, he had an appeal to the superintendent, who was required to investigate forthwith, and if the verdict of the superintendent did not satisfy the complainant, he could formally address the Secretary of War.[16] Such were the regulations; the practice fell far short of this stern assumption of the perfectibility of youth. There was drunkenness and fighting and abstention from parade and occasional visits after taps to North's, where supper and strong drink were to be had. Cadets were caught often and not infrequently were court-martialled but were rarely dismissed.[17]

While in camp that first summer, Robert was directly under the charge of the commandant of cadets, whose rule only Colonel Thayer himself could dispute during the two months when classes were not held.[18] The commandant was Major William J. Worth, whom Lee was to know better in the years that lay ahead. Although only thirty-one at that time, Worth had behind him already a record of service in the War of 1812. Tall, handsome, and a splendid horseman, he was physically the ideal soldier. To the irreverent cadets, who admired him but saw his weaknesses

---

[15] *M. A. Regs.,* §§ 1408–13; *Cond. M. A.,* 655, 657.
[16] *M. A. Regs.,* § 1431.
[17] Heintzelman's diary set all this forth with naïveté.
[18] *M. A. Regs.,* § 1316 and p. 12.

with the clear eye of youth, he was known as "Old Hant," [19] perhaps because he "haunted" the barracks at hours when the boys thought he might well have been in his own quarters.

The first-classmen stood only a little lower than the officers themselves in the estimation of a new "plebe" like Lee. The outstanding cadet among the boys who had just become first-classmen was a youth of twenty-two, of superb physique and magnificent head. All his fellow-cadets looked up to him and expected him to become a leader of men. His name was Albert Sidney Johnston.[20] At the head of that class stood William H. C. Bartlett, a mathematician of high promise, already designated as acting assistant professor of mathematics. Midway this new first class stood a lad who was writing a diary every night and was occasionally playing a flute, unaware that he was to make a far louder noise in the world—Samuel P. Heintzelman. And near the bottom of the class, well liked by his comrades but by no means brilliant in his studies, was a youngster fated to be remembered whenever the battle of Seven Pines was mentioned—Silas Casey.

Of these lordlings of the institution, "Plebe" Lee saw little that first summer. Somewhat less awesome, but still of a dignity not to be presumed upon, were the new second-classmen, most of whom were then absent on summer leave, after two years of hard work. When they returned, Lee discovered that some of them were brilliant students, but that few of them had outstanding soldierly qualities. Among them was a versatile young Virginian named Philip Saint George Cooke. He was to become the father of a girl who years afterwards married a gay young soldier, then unborn, whose triple initials prompted every one to call him "Jeb" Stuart. Then there was a lad with a great head and luminous eyes, Leonidas Polk of Louisiana. Close to Polk in the standing of the class was Gabriel J. Rains, who was to develop inventive ability. High on the roll was Napoleon B. Buford.

The third class, that summer of 1825, consisted of the boys who had just been promoted from the lowly rank of the "plebes" and who, in consequence, like most new gentry, were exceedingly jealous of their prerogatives and scornfully superior to the lads who had come to the academy only the week before. Intellec-

[19] *F. H. Smith*, 13.   [20] W. P. Johnston's *Albert Sidney Johnston*, 11.

tually, the leader of this class was a lovable, genial youth, Albert
E. Church, by name, who shone in mathematics. The boy who
cut the largest and the most tragic figure in life, among all the
class of 1828, was a tall youngster of sharp, clean-cut features.
It is not known when Lee first saw him, or how he came to hear
his name, but it is certain the newcomer learned on August 29
that a military court had been appointed to try Cadet Jefferson
Davis, who was in an exceedingly embarrassed plight. He had
gone out of bounds to a place where liquor had been sold—both
acts strictly forbidden by the regulations. Not only so, but he had
imbibed personally. The evidence was conclusive, and on September 3 the court-martial found him guilty, with a sentence of
dismissal. Clemency was recommended, however, in view of
Davis's previous good record, and he was allowed to remain at the
academy.[21]

Of Lee's own classmates, the boy destined to be his chief rival
for honors was a New Yorker of studious habits and uncommon
ability, Charles Mason. Another who was to contest academic
leadership was William H. Harford, a Georgian, keen-minded
and diligent. A third boy who displayed promise from the outset
was Ormsby MacK. Mitchel, later a famed astronomer. The lad
to whom Lee was to be most drawn was Jack Mackay of Georgia.
Next to him, perhaps, was to come Joseph E. Johnston, a Virginian whose father had fought with "Light-Horse Harry" Lee
in the Carolinas.[22]

By the time Lee had become acquainted with the corps and
had learned the rudiments of drill, August 27 arrived, the encampment ended and the corps went back to barracks. The
cadets had formed four companies while in camp; now they were
only two, one in the North Barracks, four men to a room, the
other in the South, with three men bunked together.[23] Every boy
in turn was room-orderly for a week, and if he failed to keep the
quarters in condition to pass daily inspection, he served an additional week. Saturday afternoon, he had the pleasure of scrubbing

[21] *Cent. U. S. M. A.*, 2, 86; *MS. Court Martial Proceedings*, U. S. Military Academy;
Heintzelman's MS. Diary.

[22] See *supra*, p. 3. For the maturity of Mason, see Jefferson Davis in 150 *North
American Review*, 55.

[23] Boynton, 223; *Cond. M. A.*, 654; *Northern Tour*, 26. Some of the bedchambers had
a study adjoining in which the cadets worked and kept their arms.

the room-floors, preparatory to turning over his duties to his successor on Sunday morning.[24]

It was a full and instant routine on which Robert entered when recitations were resumed on September 1. At dawn of day, reveille was sounded, and the cadets had to dress immediately and answer roll-call. Quarters had then to be put in order and arms and accoutrements had to be cleaned. Half an hour after reveille, the cadet officers made their rounds of the barracks. From the firing of the sunrise gun until seven o'clock, the first-classmen studied mathematics. Then they formed squads in front of the South Barracks and marched to the commons. Each squad was composed of the men who sat at the same table, and each was in charge of the "carver," a gentleman-cadet who had little meat to cut, but that of the toughest. Within the mess-hall, all had their regular places and might neither indulge in promiscuous conversation nor summon the slow-footed serving-man. Only the "carver" could enjoy that measure of intimacy with the waiter.[25]

Thirty minutes for breakfast, then came guard-mount at 7:30, and at eight class parade. Following this each section of the class in mathematics formed on the parade-ground, or, if the weather was bad, in the lower hall of the North Barracks. There was another roll-call, and a brisk march to the academy, for Colonel Thayer fulfilled to the letter the army regulation that the cadets spend not less than nine, nor more than ten hours a day, at their studies.[26]

The academic building to which Lee and his classmates tramped at eight o'clock each week-day morning had the chapel in the centre on the ground level, with the library above. To the west of the chapel was the chemical laboratory, over which was the "philosophical room," or physics laboratory. East of the chapel was the engineering department and, on the second story, the adjutant's office.[27] In the room where mathematics was taught, blackboards covered the walls. All the "academies," as the separate classrooms were styled, had sand on the floor.[28]

[24] *Cond. M. A.*, 656.
[25] Hallard's *George Ticknor*, 1, 374; *Cond. M. A.*, 655, 656; *M. A. Regs.*, § 1356.
[26] *M. A. Regs.*, § 1355; *Cond. M. A.*, 655.   [27] *Reminiscences of West Point*, 27
[28] *American State Papers, Military Affairs*, 3, 812.

Robert found very exact regulations in force for reporting the absentees from class, with a strict record of those who stayed away, and stiff penalties for those who shirked.[29] Once the class in mathematics was in place, instruction began. Three men were called to the blackboards and were given problems to demonstrate. Questions were answered. Difficulties were eased. Till the minute-hand went thrice around the clock the work went on, as the teacher sought to make sure that every student knew the assignment for the day.

At eleven o'clock the class was dismissed, and the cadets went back to their rooms, where they spent an hour, presumably reviewing the lesson in mathematics and preparing for the next day. When noon came, the boys forsook Euclid for *Gil Blas* and kept the company of that delectable until dinner, which was at one o'clock. From the time they finished the meal until two o'clock the cadets were free, and might even indulge in music, within the limits laid down by Colonel Thayer. At two, there was formation, and then two hours of study and recitation of French.

From four o'clock to sunset or later was the time given over to military exercises, which for fourth-classmen consisted only of the school of the soldier, and of the evolutions of the line. At sunset came dress parade and roll-call, with supper immediately thereafter. When the meal was done, the signal was given to retire to quarters, where the cadet was to wrestle once more and until 9:30 with mathematics. Tattoo and roll-call ended the day—ended it, that is, except for a precautionary inspection of quarters just before ten o'clock, when lights were extinguished.[30]

It was a long day, regulated overmuch, and with too little time for recreation. In winter, the cold, the bad food, and the lack of exercise—for drill had virtually to be suspended—made it too hard a schedule for boys who were not of the most robust.[31] Robert was equal to it physically, and he found it academically

---

[29] *M. A. Regs.*, §§ 1434, 1438.

[30] *M. A. Regs.*, § 1356; for the military instruction, see *Ibid.*, §§ 1350, 1357; *American State Papers, Military Affairs*, 3, 381.

[31] For comments on the appearance of the corps in 1832, with special reference to the lack of exercise in winter, see J. E. Alexander: *Transatlantic Sketches* (London, 1833), 2, 277. Heintzelman noted in his *Diary* on Feb. 5, 1826, that 163 of the cadets had to be excused from duty because of illness.

easy. He had gone further in mathematics before he came to West Point than the curriculum carried him during the whole of the first year. Probably he found nothing to balk him in Farrar's translation of the *Treatise on Plane and Spherical Trigonometry*, and on the *Application of Algebra to Geometry*, by Lacroix and Bezout. Legendre's *Geometry* may have been the very text he had used at home. Lacroix's *Elements of Algebra* and his *Complement* were not unduly difficult.[32] Lee accordingly found himself very soon enrolled in the first of the several sections into which the fourth-year class in mathematics was divided.[33] This placed him under the tutelage of Professor Charles Davies, the good-natured and capable head of the department, then a young man of only twenty-five, but already preparing to publish a book on descriptive geometry. Davies illustrated his lectures with many apposite anecdotes, and had unfailing patience and good humor in clearing away his students' misconceptions, but he had no mercy on the cadet who failed to prepare himself. His familiar name, in the Who's Who of irreverent youth, was "Old Tush." [34] The first assistant professor, Lieutenant Edward C. Ross, was an oddity. When he first put an exercise on the blackboard, and tried to explain it to the section, he would twist and wriggle, pulling at his long whiskers and spitting much tobacco-juice. He often ended for the day in making the problem more confusing than at the start. But at the next session of the class, when a cadet started the demonstration, Ross would begin a series of questions so searching and so logical that they brought out everything in the problem. One of his students, who subsequently became an educator of distinction, declared Ross the best teacher he had ever seen.[35] Ross's orderly approach probably had larger influence on some of his pupils' methods of reasoning than they realized.

Lee's only other academic study that winter was French, to which two hours of study and one hour of recitation were given daily, with the class divided into sections of not more than twenty

---

[32] For the list of textbooks, see *M. A. Regs.*, Form D.

[33] For the division of the classes into sections, see *M. A. Regs.*, §§ 1370–71, 1375; for the scope of the course, see *Ibid.*, § 1347.

[34] *F. H. Smith*, 7; G. W. Cullum, *Biographical Register . . . of the U. S. Mil. Acad.*, third edition, Boston, 1891 (cited hereafter as *Cullum*), 3, 151.

[35] *F. H. Smith*, 9. In addition to Ross, Professor Davies had three young assistants—Alexander Bache, George S. Greene, and Alexander Bowman—who were later to win high reputation. Lee, however, probably had no classes under any of these.

men each.[36] In theory, the course was designed to cover translating French into English, and English into French, and "pronouncing the language tolerably."[37] As a matter of academic fact, the instruction did not carry the boys much beyond the point where they could read their French texts with reasonable ease. Conversational French was not taught,[38] which probably accounts for the fact that in all Lee's recorded conversation there are few French words not solely related to military affairs. The reason for this shortcoming was the institution's emphasis on mathematics, rather than any lack of equipment on the part of the professor of French. For Claudius Bérard, the "first teacher" of French, was a fine scholar of good taste, with an excellent knowledge of English, much diligence, and some sense of humor. It seems not to have been held against him that he, an instructor in a stern academy of military art, had employed a substitute in Napoleon's army and had subsequently fled from France, lest he be again called to the colors, after his substitute had been killed in the Spanish campaign.[39] The books with which the cadets began their study of French were Bérard's own—his *French Grammar* and his *Lecteur Français*. The survey of French literature during the first year did not progress beyond *"le tome premier"* of *Gil Blas*.[40]

Military instruction was limited in Robert's first year to what a private soldier would have received at an active army post under a good company-officer. Drill, however, ate up the little time that French and mathematics left. When the weather was good, there were few hours for outside study.[41] Fortunately for the larger culture of the cadets, there came to the academy that year a man who taught the boys some things not set down in Colonel Thayer's tables of instruction and some they might not have sought out for themselves. This man was Reverend Charles P. McIlvaine, chaplain and professor of geography, history, and ethics. He was then twenty-six, tall and majestic in bearing, with a voice of much richness, and a moving eloquence. Cadets who came to hear him,

---

[36] *M. A. Regs.*, §§ 1342, 1351, 1372.   [37] *M. A. Regs.*, § 1342.   [38] 1 *Polk*, 55.
[39] 1 *Appletons' Cyclopædia of American Biography*, 243; F. H. Smith, 12.
[40] *M. A. Regs.*, Form D.
[41] *Cf.* Leonidas Polk, Nov. 16, 1823: "Our time is so wholly engrossed in our academic duties that it is impossible to devote any to *literary attainments* privately." 1 *Polk*, 55.

in the expectation of nodding or reading during his sermon, were entranced by his oratory and enthralled by his earnestness, even though his sermons sometimes consumed two hours.[42] The spiritual life of the school was improved somewhat by McIlvaine's coming, and Cadet Leonidas Polk was inspired by the chaplain to decide on the ministry as a life-calling.[43] It was perhaps well for Lee, as for many another young man at West Point, that the zealous ministry of McIlvaine entered his life so soon after he left home.

The first six months at the school were probationary. The instructors made daily notes of individual proficiency and filed weekly reports, in all classes supplemented by examinations in January. Not until these tests had been passed by a cadet did he receive his warrant and become a regular member of the corps.[44] After November 1, when bad weather forced even Colonel Thayer to suspend most of the field exercises,[45] Robert had longer hours in which to prepare for the coming test. French he found somewhat difficult because he was unfamiliar with its idioms, but through the stern, early winter he applied himself to it.

On January 2, 1826, the semi-annual examinations began. The confident and the fearful alike were subjected to an hour's quizzing. Robert Lee came out well, though he discovered that some of his classmates had been working as hard as he had, and were possessed of keen minds. Charles Mason, Catharinus L. Buckingham, and William H. Harford were tied with him in mathematics, and as his patronymic was alphabetically the third of the quartet, he got that rating. In French, he was fifth. On conduct he was third, but had no offenses recorded against him. He received his warrant, and settled down to a hard battle to improve his showing in the June examination.[46]

---

[42] *Heintzelman's MS. Diary*, Sept. 18, 1825.   [43] 1 *Cullum*, 45; 1 *Polk*, 71.

[44] *M. A. Regs.*, p. 2, and §§ 1361–65, 1383–84; *Cent. U. S. M. A.*, 1, 230.

[45] *American State Papers, Military Affairs*, 4, 24.

[46] *Heintzelman's MS. Diary; M. A. Regs.*, § 1340; *MS. U. S. Military Academy Records*, made available through the kindness of Captain R. R. Neyland, former acting adjutant, and Major E. E. Farman, U. S. A., Librarian of West Point.

CHAPTER IV

The Education of a Cadet

WITH the return of spring, the corps' field exercises were less interrupted by bad weather, and there were fewer extra hours for study, but Robert made the most of them, despite an assignment in April, 1826, to special duty.[1] Meantime, he was developing a military bearing, and by his friendliness and good humor was winning friends in the corps.

June came, and with it the board of visitors. This board consisted of five men of distinction, named by the Secretary of War to attend the academy, to supervise examinations and to report on the needs and condition of the institution. The new head of the War Department, James Barbour of Virginia, who had been one of those to recommend Robert for appointment, was interested in the academy and availed himself of a clause in the regulations which authorized him to invite to the examination, along with the board, such other "literary and scientific gentlemen" as he pleased.[2] Jared Sparks, George Ticknor, Lieutenant-Colonel J. G. Totten, and General Samuel Houston were among those he named that year. From their presence, in his regular turn, Robert emerged the third man in his class. Charles Mason led and William Harford was second. Pressing close behind Lee were William Boylan and James Barnes. Neither Lee, Mason, nor Barnes had received a demerit during the year, but Harford had seven and Boylan thirty-five, which made the standing of Boylan all the more remarkable.[3] In mathematics Lee was fourth, and received a credit of 197 of a possible 200. In French he was fifth, and was rated 98¼ of a possible 100. On the roll of general merit,

---

[1] The West Point muster roll does not give the nature of this special duty.
[2] M. A. Regs., §§ 1326–27; 1361–64.
[3] Official Register . . . of United States Military Academy for 1826, "Roll of Cadets According to Merit in Conduct," p. 3.

he was put at the sum of these two ratings—295¼ of a gross 300.[4]

This was a good showing and it brought immediate rewards. For it was a part of the code of Colonel Thayer to honor the diligent while punishing the wayward and dismissing the slothful. Robert was placed on the list of "distinguished cadets"—the first five in each class—whose names were certified to the Secretary of War for inclusion in the army register. His first appearance in that document was in the edition of 1826 when he was credited with special proficiency in mathematics and in French.[5]

Another honor awaited him. Under the rules of the corps, the best soldiers of good standing acted as officers. From the boys who had just completed their first year's work were chosen the corporals. The second class previously had furnished the sergeants, and the first the lieutenants, the captains, and the most-sought-after post of all, that of adjutant. During the winter of 1825–26, the regulations had been so changed that the sergeancies did not all go to the second class.[6] Robert had done so well in his drill, and had already developed such good military bearing that on June 23, when the appointments were read out, he was named staff sergeant, as high a position as any to which a man just finishing his first year at the academy could then aspire.[7]

A week later, on July 1, 1826, a great date was set on the calendar: Robert and his fellow-toilers ceased to be "plebes" and overnight became "upper-classmen," fit to hold fellowship with the lofty souls of the class of 1828, and permitted to look without apology on the faces of those who were now the first class.[8] On the same day, the annual encampment on the plain began. Lee, with his comrades, had the monotony of infantry drill broken for

---

[4] This seems the simplest way of describing his standing. The technical method of determining general merit was to credit the top man in the class with the full allowance for that study, 100, 200, or 300 as the case might be, while the bottom man was credited with one-third of that maximum. The men between top and bottom had their general merit determined by the "common difference." This was arrived at by subtracting the standing of the last man from that of the first, and dividing this by a number one less than the number of men in the class. This "common difference" was then subtracted as many times as the individual stood from the head of his class. *Cent. U. S. M. A.*, 1, 232–33. For the merit basis, see *M. A. Regs.*, §§ 1366–68. Lee's rating is in the *MS. U. S. Military Academy Records.*

[5] *American State Papers, Military Affairs*, 3, 575; for the order authorizing a list of distinguished cadets, see Boynton, 219; *M. A. Regs.*, § 1368.

[6] *Heintzelman's MS. Diary*, Nov. 19, 1825.

[7] *West Point MS. Orderbook*, June 23, 1826. For the usage in such appointments, see *American State Papers, Military Affairs*, 2, 655.

[8] *M. A. Regs.*, §§ 1359–60.

the first time by their introduction to artillery. For about nine weeks they had two hours daily with their muskets and four with artillery; work enough for warm days when the woods called and the river lured the boys who were sweating under canvas.[9]

With the return to barracks on September 1, 1826, Lee and his class plunged into more advanced mathematics—calculus, analytical and descriptive geometry and difficult conic sections, with instruction chiefly by Professor Davies. A course in perspective, shades and shadows was included with the mathematics.[10] French was continued, with *Gil Blas* the text, followed late in the session by Voltaire's *Histoire de Charles XII,* as suited for the education of a soldier.[11] The one added academic study was free-hand drawing of the human figure. This was under the tutelage of Thomas Gimbrede, an amiable Frenchman, a good miniaturist, and a competent engraver, who was not altogether without the blessed quality of humor. It was Mr. Gimbrede's custom to give each class of beginners an introductory lecture, in the course of which he endeavored to prove to unbelieving third-classmen that every one could learn to draw. His proof was: "There are only two lines in drawing, the straight line and the curve line. Every one can draw a straight line and every one can draw a curve line —therefore, every one can draw." [12] Gimbrede was Lee's only new teacher that winter, though there were eleven changes in the academic staff.[13] No material difference was made in the schedule, except that drawing alternated in the afternoons with the study and recitation of French.[14] Infantry drill continued, in the school of the company, with instruction in the duties of corporals.[15] Two hours every second afternoon during the academic term were devoted to artillery, under the direction of Lieutenant Z. J. D. Kinsley, a West Pointer of the class of 1819.[16]

This was a busy routine, but Robert was now so well-grounded

[9] For the drill requirements, see *M. A. Regs.,* § 1350; *American State Papers, Military Affairs,* 3, 381.
[10] The text-books were Lacroix's *Traité du Calcul Différential et Intégral;* Biot's *Essai de Géométrie Analytique Appliquée aux Courbes et aux Surfaces du Second Ordre;* Crozet's *Treatise on Perspective, Shades and Shadows;* Crozet's *Treatise on Descriptive Geometry and Conic Sections* (*M. A. Regs.,* Form D).
[11] *M. A. Regs.,* Form D.
[12] 1 *Cullum,* 38; *F. H. Smith,* 12; for the scope of the course, see *M. A. Regs.,* § 1342.
[13] *Register . . . of the United States Military Academy,* 1827.
[14] *M. A. Regs.,* § 1356.
[15] *American State Papers. Military Affairs,* 3, 381.   [16] 1 *Cullum,* 211.

that he felt he could indulge himself in a little outside reading. For his first study, he borrowed from the library the second volume on Montholon's *Memoirs of Napoleon* and during October and November he seems to have steeped himself in the early operations of the Corsican, notably in the Italian campaign of 1796, and the advance on Moscow.[17] To this same study he was to turn again, twenty-six years thereafter.

In addition to his reading, Robert essayed some teaching. The regulations authorized the appointment of a number of "senior cadets" to serve as acting assistant professors of mathematics, with a compensation of $10 a month and the assurance—as if in apology for the smallness of the pay—that the post was in the nature of an honorary distinction. Generally, the words "senior cadets" were interpreted to mean members of the first class. This year, however, either because of their own proficiency, or else because a large number of new cadets were backward in their mathematics, Lee and the three others members of his class who had stood first in that subject were made acting assistant professors.[18] The duties of the position were largely tutorial, and they consumed hours that Lee must have wished he could have given to other subjects, but they were helpful. His mother was greatly pleased at the distinction and was delighted that he received compensation for it.[19] He must have been encouraged as he faced the tests of the second year, already staff sergeant and an acting assistant professor of mathematics.

But Robert's outside activities proved too much for him. On the semi-annual examination in January, 1827, his rating reflected the loss of the time he had devoted to reading and to teaching. In mathematics he was fourth, in French he was fifth, and in drawing fifth. He still had no demerits, and his drill-record was clean.[20] William Boylan, who had stood next after Lee at the end of their first year, was no longer at the academy, but Catharinus P. Buckingham, No. 9 in June, 1826, was pushing ahead.

[17] The books he borrowed in the fall of 1826 were: Montholon: *op. cit.*, vol. 2 (October 14 and 28); Light: *Histoire de Napoléon* (October 28); Ségur: *Expéditions de Russie*, vol. 1 (November 11); Montholon: *op. cit.*, vol. 3 (November 11); Montholon: *op. cit.*, vol. 1 (December 9). For a full list of Lee's borrowings from the library during his cadetship, the writer is indebted to Major E. A. Farman, Librarian of West Point.
[18] *M. A. Regs.*, § 1317; *MS. Muster Rolls, U. S. Military Academy*, October, 1826.
[19] Ann Carter Lee to Smith Lee, April 10, [1827]; *Lee MSS.*
[20] *MS. U. S. Military Academy Records.*

Charles Mason and William Harford continued to do admirably. Warned by their progress, Robert forthwith abandoned most of his extra reading and buckled down to his classes.

But there was one historical work he probably could not resist. That was the new edition of his father's *Memoirs of the War in the Southern Department* This had been prepared by his half-brother, Henry Lee, at the instance and expense of Colonel John R. Fenwick, who had been interested in the book both as a South Carolinian and as a soldier. The work was in a single volume, and though poorly printed by Peter Force, it contained some useful notes and addenda.[21] Robert doubtless had read the first edition in boyhood, but now he could bring to bear on the book something of the understanding of a soldier, and could appreciate more fully the military qualities of his father.

"Light-Horse Harry" Lee, it will be remembered, had written late in life that "mankind admire most the hero; of all, the most useless, except when the safety of a nation demands his saving arm." [22] Yet it was plain to Robert that his father had loved military life and had possessed high ability in it. Washington had thought so. After the Paulus Hook affair he had praised Henry Lee for displaying "a remarkable degree of prudence, address, enterprise, and bravery." [23] Greene often mentioned Lee in orders. "Everybody knows I have the highest opinion of you as an officer," he told Lee in the correspondence preceding Lee's resignation from the army in 1782.[24]

What were the military qualities, then, that Robert Lee discovered in his father when he read the new edition of his *Memoirs?* The answer could not be without some effect on the education of the son as a soldier.

Skill in reconnaissance Henry Lee undoubtedly possessed,[25] and with it a positive military logic, and a definite strategic sense, well

[21] *Memoirs of the War in the Southern Department of the United States, by Henry Lee . . .; a New Edition, with corrections left by the Author, and with Notes and Additions* by H. Lee, the Author of *The Campaign of '81;* Washington, Printed by Peter Force, 1827 (copyright entry, Feb. 26, 1827).

[22] Henry Lee to Charles Carter Lee, April 19, 1817; *Henry Lee's Memoirs,* 66.

[23] 8 *Ford's Washington,* 27; *cf.* his commendation of Marion and Lee for the capture of Fort Watson, 9 *Ford's Washington,* 265.

[24] 2 *Johnson's Greene,* 322.

[25] *Cf.* George Washington to Anthony Wayne, July 14, 1779; 7 *Ford's Washington,* 493.

illustrated in his advocacy of operations in South Carolina after Cornwallis had started into Virginia. Perhaps the most notable quality of Henry Lee, the soldier, as revealed again in his book, was his ability in creating and maintaining an *esprit de corps*. His command, the biographer of Greene admitted, "was, perhaps, the finest . . . that made its appearance on the arena of the Revolutionary War."[26] The first mention of his troopers in "Light-Horse Harry" Lee's extant correspondence shows him planning to have them make a good appearance. "How happy would I be," he wrote his colonel, "if it was possible for my men to be furnished with caps and boots, prior to my appearance at headquarters. You know, my dear Colonel, that, justly, an officer's reputation depends not only on the discipline, but appearance of his men."[27] Months later, when he took a British fort, he created much murmuring by appropriating the available stores, and supplying his men with new uniforms, in which he proudly paraded them next morning. Each member of the corps in time acquired a Potter's sword, "the weapon most highly estimated for service, taken in personal conflict with the enemy," according to one of Lee's officers.[28]

As he read his father's *Memoirs* Robert discovered, also, that "Light-Horse Harry" was stern in his discipline. Immediate death had been threatened any soldier who did not observe absolute silence during the advance on Paulus Hook.[29] When desertion began to spread, that same summer of 1779, he captured a man who had gone over to the enemy, hanged him, then cut off his head, with the rope still around the neck, and sent head and rope to Washington's headquarters, much to the horror of the commander-in-chief.[30] Desertion, however, ended that day.

On the other hand, when his men behaved with bravery, "Light-Horse Harry" saw to it that they were rewarded. After some of his dragoons had helped him and his brother officers beat off the attack at Spread Eagle Tavern, he assured the soldiers,

[26] 1 *Johnson's Greene*, 354.
[27] Henry Lee to Theodoric Bland, April 13, 1777; *E. J. Lee*, 330.
[28] *Garden's Anecdotes*, 67.
[29] See the order in *Henry Lee's Memoirs*, 22–23.
[30] *H. Lee's Observations*, 150; Lee to Washington, July 11, 1779, *Washington Papers*, 1074. Robert E. Lee, in recounting this in his edition of his father's *Memoirs*, p. 21, considerably omitted the grisly details.

in the words of one of his admirers, "that he should consider their future establishment in life as his peculiar care, and he honorably kept his word. They were all in turn commissioned. . . ." [81] He was careful not to expose them or himself needlessly, and was always so vigilant that after the episode at the tavern, he was never surprised. The animals of his command received almost as much attention at his hands as did the men.[32] If his command deserved credit, he saw that they got it. "No officer," said Johnson, "was ever more devoted to the interests of his own corps or his own fame." [33]

The effect upon Robert of the probable reading of this edition of his father's *Memoirs* does not show in any of his letters but it must have confirmed him in his determination to follow the career of a soldier. In ways that neither biographer nor psychologist may fathom, it is possible, also, that Robert's admiration for his father led him to magnify and to copy the military virtues of the sire. The morale of the Army of Northern Virginia may have been inspired in 1781, though it was not until 1862 that the army itself was created.

Much closer to Robert in the winter of 1826–27 than any dream of emulating his father in military achievement, was the daily round of his study. He adjusted his hours to his teaching duties and began to form plans to win a furlough in July. No cadet could leave, except for serious illness, until he had been two years at the academy, and even then, only those could go home who had received the written consent of their parents and stood well on Colonel Thayer's records.[34] Robert procured Mrs. Lee's written approval of his application; the money he was earning would suffice to pay his expenses; the rest depended chiefly on his own efforts. April arrived at last, and field exercises were resumed. May drew on, and the students settled to their special preparation for the June ordeal. Finally the examinations were over, and the results were announced. In mathematics Robert was fourth in his class and had earned 286 of a possible 300. His acquaintance with

[81] *Garden's Anecdotes*, 67.
[32] 2 *Johnson's Greene*, 323; *Garden's Anecdotes*, 62. *Cf.* Henry Lee to C. C. Lee, Feb. 9, 1817: "You know I am almost an Egyptian in my love for the cow and ox . . ." (E. J. Lee, 348).
[33] 2 *Johnson's Greene*, 123.
[94] *M. A. Regs.*, §§ 1392–94; *American State Papers, Military Affairs*, 2, 656.

Gil Blas and his mental marching with Charles XII left him fifth in French, receiving 98½ of a maximum 100. Among those whom Mr. Gimbrede was trying to convince they could draw, he was fourth, being credited with 46 of a possible 50. Leading in not a single class, he had not fallen far behind the pace-makers in any of them. His total on the roll of general merit was 430½, and this put him second in the class. Charles Mason continued first. Robert remained staff sergeant, kept on the list of "distinguished cadets," and, of course, won his furlough.[35]

This began on June 30,[36] in time to permit him to reach northern Virginia when sociable kinspeople of his name were starting their summer visits to one another. He found his mother residing in Georgetown, deeper in her invalidism, old at fifty-four by reason of disease and the burdens she had borne. He was able, however, to take her with him on at least one journey to the home of some of her Carter cousins. As her escort, dressed in his gray cadet uniform, with its white bullet buttons, his looks and his manners called forth admiring comment from the girls of his stock.[37] He was becoming by this time an exceedingly handsome young man, with manners in keeping. At the academy he was already styled the "Marble Model."[38] A fellow-cadet testified years afterward, "His personal appearance surpassed in manly beauty that of any cadet in the corps. Though firm in his position and perfectly erect, he had none of the stiffness so often assumed by men who affect to be very strict in their ideas of what is military. His limbs, beautiful and symmetrical, looked as though they had come from the turning lathe, his step was elastic as if he spurned the ground upon which he trod."[39]

Shortly after his return to the academy on August 28, 1827, just as the encampment was about to end, Lee resumed his work as acting assistant professor of mathematics. Simultaneously he entered on scientific studies that were entirely new to him. Mathe-

[35] *MS. U. S. Military Academy Records; Register of . . . the United States Military Academy, 1827.* Mason and Lee were the only men on the list of distinguished cadets of the third class who were credited with excelling in all three of the subjects of the year's study.

[36] *MS. Muster Rolls, U. S. Military Academy.*

[37] Long, *op. cit.,* 30, quoted a letter from a cousin who saw Robert at the time.

[38] General L. L. Lomax, quoted in Walter Watson's *Notes on Southside Virginia,* 245.

[39] "An Old Dragoon," evidently a fellow-cadet, quoted in *The Lexington* (Va.) *Gazette,* July 24, 1867.

matics was dropped. Drawing was continued and was given a higher credit. It called for two hours' work each week-day afternoon and included landscape and topography. Chemistry and "natural philosophy"—physics in modern academic terminology —became his major studies for the year.[40]

The course in "natural philosophy," had a valuation of 300 on the merit-roll, three times as much as the year's work in chemistry. Taught only to men of the second class, it covered the elements of mechanics, experimental physics, light, heat, magnetism, electricity, and astronomy.[41] The cadets on the upper half of the merit-roll were instructed by the professor, Jared Mansfield; those on the lower half were in the care of the assistant professors, S. Stanhope Smith and Thomas S. Twiss.[42] Mansfield had been one of the pioneer physicists of the country, had also served as lieutenant colonel of engineers before the War of 1812, and had been a teacher at the academy for fifteen years when Robert entered his class. He was then sixty-nine and about to retire. Smith, the senior assistant, was a young man of promise but was destined to die within a year. Twiss, who had stood No. 2 in the class of 1826, did not remain long at the academy.[43] Twiss's predecessor was a very interesting man who, in 1826, had turned from physics to mathematics and was then teaching that subject as an assistant professor. Lee probably saw something of him in his own rôle as an instructor of the mathematical dullards. He was Robert Parker Parrott, later the inventor of the "Parrott gun" that roared in so many battles of the War between the States.

Physics was taught every week-day from 8 to 11, and was supposed to command the study of second classmen from sunrise to 7 A.M. and from half an hour after sunset until 9:30.[44] The texts were Newton's *Principia,* Gregory's *Treatise on Mechanics,* and Enfield's *Institutes of Natural Philosophy.*[45] The subject interested Robert. It dealt with material, practical things that always appealed to him; it was an approach to engineering, which was the goal of nearly all ambitious cadets; and it meant much in

[40] M. A. Regs., § 1367. [41] M. A. Regs., § 1348.
[42] M. A. Regs., §§ 1373, 1375.
[43] For Mansfield, see *Appletons' Cyclopedia of American Biography,* 5, 194; for his resignation, March 31, 1828, see *Cent. U. S. M. A.,* 2, 88; for Smith and Twiss, see 2 *Cullum,* 186-87, 365.
[44] M. A. Regs., §§ 1351, 1356. [45] M. A. Regs., Form D.

determining a cadet's standing. Lee seems to have concentrated on it his best energies during his third year at West Point.

The work in chemistry was the first half of a two-year course designed to cover the theory of the science, "chemical philosophy," as it was styled, and the application of chemistry to certain of the arts. The text was Henry's *Chemistry,* and the time allotted to the subject was one hour daily for study and one hour for recitation.[46] The professor in charge was Doctor John Torrey, who subsequently became a botanist of repute. The assistant was Lieutenant Nicholas Tillinghast, of the class of 1824.

In military study, Lee's class passed that year through the school of the battalion, learned the duties of sergeants, and was drilled in the exercise and manœuvres of artillery pieces. A new assistant professor of tactics had come to the academy that autumn, in the person of Lieutenant John H. Winder, destined to have charge of many Federal prisoners, first at Richmond and then at Andersonville. Lee probably saw little of him, as most of the second class's instruction was in artillery, with Lieutenant Kinsley again in charge.

Corps activities took a certain amount of Lee's time that winter. Kosciuszko was in those days the patron saint of West Point. He had designed the Revolutionary forts, Clinton and Putnam, and had resided in the little cottage that had been preserved.[47] For some years, the corps had been contributing twenty-five cents monthly per man toward the construction of a monument in honor of the Lithuanian supporter of American independence. Lee was one of the committeemen entrusted with completing the fund. Their progress was such in 1827–28 that the formal preparation of a model was begun by the designated artist, John H. B. Latrobe. He was a former cadet, who became more famous as the inventor of the stove that bears his name than as a maker of monuments.[48] It was the plan of the committee to raise a total of $5000 and to unveil the shaft within the ramparts that Kosciuszko had laid out.

While the cadets were preparing to add a memorial of the struggle for independence, one possessed by West Point was de-

---

[46] M. A. Regs., §§ 1346, 1356, and Form D.   [47] See *supra*, p. 49.
[48] The design for the monument had been approved Feb. 26, 1825—*Heintzelman's M.S. Diary.* See also *Reminiscences of West Point,* 29; *Cent. U. S. M. A.,* 2, 88. The com-

stroyed; on December 26, 1827, the "Long Barracks" were burned. This two-story building, which was near the site of the hotel, had been constructed during the first war with England, as already noted, for the use of the garrison, and from the establishment of the academy until the erection of the South Barracks, had housed the cadets.[49] The weathered old structure had been the largest and, except for the forts, the most familiar of man's work at West Point to remind the country's prospective soldiers that they were in a literal sense sons of the Revolution.

The winter of 1827 brought a lesser sensation—but perhaps a deeper sorrow. It was not often that changes in the academic staff were made during the term, for the vigilant Colonel Thayer saw to it that such upsetting things occurred while the cadets were encamped and had no classes. Now came news that Chaplain McIlvaine had received a call to Saint Ann's Church, Brooklyn, and had accepted. At the end of 1827, to the vast regret of the corps, he left West Point, and on January 1, his successor, Reverend Thomas Warner, took up his duties, as chaplain and professor of moral and political philosophy. He was an elderly man of fine appearance, somewhat resembling Andrew Jackson. A strong logician, he lacked the brilliant appeal of the eloquent McIlvaine, and in his lectures, he usually disported himself intellectually in waters beyond the depth of the cadets. Fear lest he would make Sunday chapel the ordeal it had been before the coming of McIlvaine was removed by the pleasing discovery on the part of the boys that the reverend gentleman seldom preached longer than ten minutes.[50]

At Mr. Warner's coming there was little time for an appraisal of his qualities, for the cadets were groaning over their extra study for the semi-annual examinations. On January 7, the solemn academic board met, the blackboards were put in place, and the troubled cadets were commanded to give evidence of the knowledge that was in them. Robert Lee came out from the inquisition with an excellent showing. The wisdom of his concentrated attack on natural philosophy was rewarded by a standing of No. 2

mittee, besides Lee, were Charles Mason, John Mackay, Charles Petigru, and William E. Basinger, the last-named being of the class of 1830. Basinger was latter an officer of Dade's command and fell in the battle of Dec. 28, 1835, with the Seminole Indians (1 *Cullum*, 448).

[49] *Boynton*, 253; *Cent. U. S. M. A.*, 2, 88.   [50] *F. H. Smith*, 13.

in that subject. He was third in chemistry, and in drawing fourth.[51]

Encouraged by this showing and relieved after April 1 of his mathematical teaching, Robert had more time for independent reading during the late winter and early spring of 1828 than in any other period of his cadetship. Between January 26 and May 24, he drew fifty-two books from the library. They covered a wide field—navigation, travel, strategy, biography, and history. His principal interest seems to have been in seamanship and in the works of Alexander Hamilton, for he borrowed Atkinson's *Navigation* seven times, and the second volume of Hamilton's *Works* no less than nine times during this period. This volume contains *The Federalist,* which Lee must have read very thoroughly. He indulged himself, moreover, in a reading of a French edition of Rousseau's *Confessions.*[52]

The whole list for these months has interest and is as follows:

Jan. 26, 1828: *Museum of Foreign Literature,* vols. 5 and 6.
Feb. 2: The same, vol. 6.
Feb. 2: Martin's *Optics.*
Feb. 9: *Westminster Review,* vols. 1 and 2.
Feb. 16: Rousseau, vol 23.
Feb. 23: The same, vol. 24.
Feb. 23: Leslie's *Geometry,* vol. 2.
Feb. 23: Atkinson's *Navigation.*
Feb. 23: Machiavelli's *Art of War.*
March 1: Chartekkun's *Travels,* etc.
March 1: *North American Review,* vol. 2.
March 1: Rousseau, vols. 24, 25.
March 1: Leslie's *Geometry,* vol. 2.
March 1: Atkinson's *Navigation.*
March 8: Rousseau, vol. 26.
March 15: *North American Review,* vol. 18.
March 22: Hamilton's *Works,* vol. 2.
March 29: The same.

[51] *MS. U. S. Military Academy Records.*
[52] The edition he used was *Œuvres Complètes de J. J. Rousseau,* nouvelle édition, classée par ordre de matières, et ornée de quatre-vingt-dix gravures (Paris, 1788–1803), 40 vols. For this information the writer is indebted to M. L. Samson, assistant librarian of West Point.

March 29: Atkinson's *Navigation.*
March 29: *Edinburgh Review,* vols. 33, 34.
April 5: Hamilton's *Works,* vol. 2.
April 5: Atkinson's *Navigation.*
April 5: *Retrospective Review,* vols. 6 and 7.
April 5: Drean's *Military Dictionary.*
April 12: Hamilton's *Works,* vols. 1 and 2.
April 12: Atkinson's *Navigation.*
April 12: *Retrospective Review,* vol. 2.
April 26: Hamilton's *Works,* vol. 2.
April 26: Wamery's *Anecdotes.*
April 26: *Life of Paul Jones.*
April 26: Bonnyearth's *Algebra.*
April 26: *Retrospective Review,* vols. 5 and 6.
May 3: The same, vol. 3.
May 3: Atkinson's *Navigation.*
May 3: Hamilton's *Works,* vol. 2.
May 3: Sempriere's *Biographical Dictionary,* vols. 1 and 2.
May 10: Atkinson's *Navigation.*
May 10: Hamilton's *Works,* vol. 2.
May 10: Ferguson's *Astronomy,* vol. 4.
May 10: Arrowsmith's *Atlas.*
May 24: Hamilton's *Works,* vol. 2.
May 24: Ferguson's *Astronomy,* vols. 1 and 2.

Robert's reading did not interfere that spring with his studies or with his military duty. He went into the annual oral test with the comforting assurance that his record in drill and in conduct was clean. Under the rules of the academy, however, the advantage from these things in the examinations of the second classmen was moral only. The credits for tactics, for artillery, and for conduct were deferred until the final computation of standing at the end of the fourth year. When the examinations were over, about June 19, 1828, Robert had not headed Charles Mason but he was immediately below him on the roll of general merit. He was credited with 295 of a possible 300 in physics and was second in that subject. He stood No. 3 in chemistry, with 99 of the allowable 100. In drawing, he was third, higher than he had ever stood in Mr. Gimbrede's course, which now yielded him 97 of a maximum 100 points. His general merit for the year was very high—491.[53]

The academic mortality in the class, however, had been heavy. Of the eighty-seven who had started in July, 1825, seventeen had fallen by the way at the end of the first session. Several had dropped out during 1826–27, and three more had failed by July, 1827. Now eight men went down, and others were despairing.[54] Of the four Virginians who had entered together in 1825 only half were left, Lee and Joe Johnston, nicknamed "The Colonel." These two were drawn closer together when they realized they were the sole representatives of their state, and they spurred themselves to new effort in order that Virginia might not be discredited.[55] "We had the same intimate associates, who thought as I did," Johnston wrote years afterwards, "that no other youth or man so united the qualities that win warm friendship and command high respect. For he was full of sympathy and kindness, genial and fond of gay conversation, and even of fun, while his correctness of demeanor and attention to all duties, personal and official, and a dignity as much a part of himself as the elegance of his person, gave him a superiority that every one acknowledged in his heart. He was the only one of all the men I have known that could laugh at the faults and follies of his friends in such a manner as to make them ashamed without touching their affection for him, and to confirm their respect and sense of his superiority." [56]

These qualities and his high standing made Lee a contender in the mind of every cadet for that most coveted of West Point honors, the office of corps adjutant, which was awarded about July 1, when a class entered its final year. The appointment usually was awarded the first-classman of good standing who had the finest military bearing and the best record on the drill ground. Would it go now to Charles Mason, who had been No. 1 since the first examination, or would the post be awarded some other

[53] MS. U. S. Military Academy Records.
[54] Register of . . . the United States Military Academy, 1826, 1827, 1828.
[55] R. M. Hughes, J. E. Johnston, 15–16.
[56] Joseph E. Johnston, quoted in Long, 71.

cadet high on the honor roll? The answer came positively and promptly, as was the way with the decisions of Colonel Thayer and of Major Worth: The adjutant of the corps for 1828–29 was to be Robert E. Lee of Virginia.

The award was popular and made Lee the most prominent cadet in the corps, though some of the young men thought that his Southern birth had something to do with the selection.[57] He was again certified to the War Department as a "distinguished cadet." Mason, Buckingham, and himself had this recognition on all three subjects of their study; Harford and Barnes had it on natural philosophy and chemistry.[58] Temporarily, in June and in August, Lee resumed duty as acting assistant professor of mathematics, for a reason that does not appear from the records. It probably was to coach backward cadets.[59]

Now began the term for which all else was preparatory, the term into which was crowded all the technical military training, together with a second course in chemistry and a hurried, superficial survey of geography, history, ethics, and moral philosophy. Lee put aside all extra reading and concentrated his efforts. His day began, as previously, at dawn. From sunrise until seven o'clock, he studied engineering and the science of war. After breakfast and class parade he went to the academy and spent three hours daily in drafting and in recitation of the subjects on which he had just prepared himself. Then came rhetoric and moral philosophy, with lectures and study periods alternating until one o'clock daily. At 2 P.M., as in previous years, military instruction began for all cadets and continued until sunset. Following supper, Lee worked over his engineering until 9:30.

In this subject he found especial satisfaction. His mind was scientific in its interests. As among the sciences, the applied meant more to him than the theoretical, though his devotion to mathematics was always high. When he began engineering he may have felt, also, that this more fully than anything else represented the profession he had chosen. He gave to it, in any case, high interest and warm enthusiasm.

[57] E. D. Keyes: *Fifty Years' Observation of Men and Events* . . . (cited hereafter as Keyes), 212; John N. Macomb in *Long*, 28.
[58] *American State Papers, Military Affairs*, 4, 80.
[59] *MS. Muster Rolls, U. S. Military Academy.*

The course was comprehensive, considering the limitations of time, and was divided into five parts—field fortification, permanent fortification, the science of artillery, grand tactics, and civil and military architecture. The instruction in field fortification covered the description and analysis of various systems of fortified lines, the building of batteries and redoubts, calculation of the labor, time, and materials for the construction of different kinds of field works, military bridges, the defense of posts, and field defilement. All of these, as far as possible, were taught "on the ground." Permanent fortification included the attack and defense of fortified places, analysis of the systems of Vauban, Cohorn, Cormontaigne, and of the later improvements, the construction of mines and *fougasses* and their use in attack and defense, the erection of works, the art of defilement, and the armament of fortresses. The "science of artillery" covered a technical study of the various types of guns and projectiles, followed by instruction in the principles of gunnery, as far as range-finding and ballistics were understood at the time. "Grand tactics" comprised strategy as well as tactics—the organization of armies, the conduct of marches, the preparation of orders of battle, combat, the review of the general maxims of war deducted from the most important operations of history, and the study of castramentation, or the art of laying out a camp. Civic and military architecture dealt with the elementary parts of buildings and their construction, the orders of architecture, the design of buildings and arches, canals, bridges, and other public works, a description of the machines used for them, and the execution of drawings to illustrate the course.[60]

The principal textbook for these studies was S. F. Gay de Vernon's *Treatise on the Science of War and Fortification,* which had been translated in two volumes, with a separate atlas, by Captain J. M. O'Connor.[61] Cadets who did not remember much that was contained in the work rarely forgot that it cost twenty dollars—more than a month's pay.[62] It was, however, perhaps

[60] *M. A. Regs.,* § 1349.
[61] The full French title was: *Traité élémentaire de l'art militaire et de fortification, à l'usage des élèves de l'Ecole polytechnique, et des élèves des écoles militaires* (2 vols.; Paris, 1805). For a note on Gay de Vernon (1760–1822), see *Nouveau Larousse Illustré,* 4, 793.
[62] *F. H. Smith,* 5.

the best book then available on the subject, for Baron Gay de Vernon had been eminent in his sphere and had served as professor of engineering in the French *Ecole Polytechnique*. O'Connor added to his translation "A summary of the principles of grand tactics and operations," taken largely from Jomini, who, said O'Connor, "transcended all writers on war, and . . . exhibited the most extraordinary powers of analyzing and combining military operations."[63] The gunnery book was Lallemand's *Treatise on Artillery,* and the work on mechanics was Hackett's untranslated *Traité des Machines.* For architecture, the text was Szannin's *Programme d'un Cours de Construction.*[64]

Under the regulations of the academy the section that stood first on the merit roll received personal instruction from the professor of engineering.[65] This put Lee directly under the eye of David B. Douglass, head of the department of engineering. Douglass was then thirty-eight and a man of great versatility. A Master of Arts of Yale, he had served brilliantly as a young engineer in the War of 1812, and among other feats he had repaired Fort Erie under the guns of the enemy. Ordered to West Point, he had first been assistant in physics, then professor of mathematics, and, after May, 1823, professor of engineering. His summer vacations were given over to special professional work, chiefly as consulting engineer for the state of Pennsylvania. His reputation was of the highest, and his standards of instruction and performance probably as good as any in the United States at the time.[66] Douglass's assistant professors were Lieutenant W. H. C. Bartlett, who subsequently turned to physics, teaching that subject at West Point for thirty-seven years, and Lieutenant William Bryant, a Virginian, later a clergyman. Bryant assisted in engineering only for the session of 1828-29.[67]

In chemistry and mineralogy the work was a continuance of what had gone before. The other course for the graduating class, was supposed to cover geography, history and ethics.[68] In the

[63] Eben Swift: "The Military Education of Robert E. Lee," 35 *Va. Mag. of History and Biography,* 101.

[64] *M. A. Regs.,* Form D.   [65] *M. A. Regs.,* § 1374.

[66] 1 *Cullum,* 35; 2 *Appletons' Cyclopædia of American History,* 216. After he resigned, in 1831, Douglass had a varied career as engineer and professor. He it was who demonstrated to New York City how the flow of Croton River could be used for its water supply.

[67] 1 *Cullum,* 364-65.   [68] *M. A. Regs.,* § 1351.

first-named subject the text was Morse's *Geography*. History, according to the regulations, was to "comprise a general summary of universal history, with a view, more particularly, of the history and political relations of the United States,"[69] but the only text, so far as is known, was Tytler's *Elements of General History*. Ethics was taught from Paley's *Principles of Moral Philosophy*, and was to "include moral philosophy, and the elements of national and political law."[70] Vattel was the authority on international law.[71]

This course was an *omnium gatherum* of the subjects a soldier should know but could not learn in the other departments. It was so crowded and instruction was of necessity so hurried that the board of visitors in 1826 had recommended that it be "broken up."[72] Under Chaplain McIlvaine, who was a man of wide reading and varied interests, the curriculum was changed from year to year. During the term of 1825–26, a course on American constitutional law was given. The textbook was Rawle's *On the Constitution*, in which the right of secession by the states was plainly and repeatedly set forth, though the exercise of that right, in other than extreme cases, was reprobated.[73]

It has been assumed that Rawle was a text in subsequent years, also, and that Jefferson Davis, Robert Lee, and other Southern leaders got their views of secession from Rawle, or had their Southern opinions on the subject confirmed by the book officially used in the military academy of their country.[74] In the case of Davis, it is probable that if he had been brought to trial after the War between the States he would have sought to vindicate the constitutionality of secession by reference to the use of Rawle at West Point.[75] But Davis himself is authority for the statement that though Rawle had been used by preceding classes, he was

---

[69] *M. A. Regs.*, § 1344.   [70] *M. A. Regs.*, § 1345.   [71] *M. A. Regs.*, Form D.
[72] Quoted in E. S. Dudley: "Was 'Secession' Taught at West Point"? *Century Magazine*, Aug., 1909, p. 632.
[73] The impressive passages from Rawle are quoted in Robert Bingham's *Sectional Misunderstandings*. This appeared originally in the *North American Review*, Sept., 1904, but was republished as a pamphlet (Asheville, N. C., n.d.) with Colonel Bingham's authorities for his statement that Rawle had been a text at West Point. The paragraphs in which Rawle deplores recourse to secession are printed conveniently in Dudley, *loc. cit.*, 634. The conclusive evidence that Rawle was used in 1825–26 is found in four references in *Heintzelman's MS. Diary*, Feb. 21, 23, March 27, and June 7, 1826. For these references the writer is indebted to Judge Edgar J. Rich of Boston, Mass.
[74] Bingham, *op. cit.*, 10.   [75] Bingham, *op. cit.*, 4, quoting Reverend L. W. Bacon.

himself taught Kent's *Commentaries.*[76] As for Lee, there is no first-hand evidence that he was instructed in Rawle, or that he ever read the book. The course during his last year at West Point covered geography, rhetoric, and moral philosophy, with nothing in the records to indicate that constitutional law was included.[77] Lee's individual accounts at West Point do not show that he purchased Rawle. Moreover, Mr. McIlvaine, who previously had adventured with Rawle and various other authors, was no longer at West Point. In his place was an older man, not so well furnished for instruction in new subjects and interested primarily in "moral philosophy." It is hardly probable that the Reverend Mr. Warner in the first year of his service as chaplain would have gone beyond the regular curriculum. Warner may have used Rawle in 1831–32, for B. S. Ewell, who graduated at the end of that session, owned a copy;[78] but even this instruction is not certain. A little later, when constitutional law is known to have been taught again, the textbook was not Rawle, but Kent, which had been employed in 1827–28. Kent was used for many years thereafter and was the textbook during Lee's own superintendency.[79] The only evidence of any consequence, as distinguished from tradition, in support of the view that Lee was taught Rawle at West Point, is a letter of Joseph Wilmer, in which he said: "I have a distinct recollection of my father's [Bishop Wilmer's] statement that General Lee told him that 'Rawle' was a textbook during his cadetship at West Point."[80] This, it will be noted, is not direct affirmation that Lee himself was instructed in the theories of that author.

Whether Rawle was among his textbooks or not, Lee spent a winter that was devoid of sensation, and full of crowded work. Seven changes in the academic staff had been made that autumn, but none of these affected the departments in which Lee was

---

[76] *Southern Historical Society Papers* (cited hereafter as *S. H. S. P.*), vol. 22, p. 83.

[77] *MS. Records of Cadets' Examinations at West Point.* These show the subjects taught. Colonel Dudley (*loc. cit.*, p. 633) apparently overlooked the "G" (Geography) in the records, and consequently he stated that only rhetoric and moral philosophy were taught in 1828–29.

[78] *Tyler's Magazine*, October, 1930, p. 87.

[79] Dudley, *loc. cit.*, 633; *infra*, p. 347, n. 47. In *Ex. Docs.*, 2d sess., 26th Cong., vol. 1, p. 152, is a protest by the Democratic majority of the board of visitors of 1840 against the use of Kent's *Commentaries* and Bayard's *Exposition*.

[80] Bingham, *op. cit.*, 2.

studying.[81] In November, however, it became known that on January 1, 1829, the commandant, Major Worth, was to be transferred. Robert had been under Worth during the whole of his cadetship and esteemed him greatly. To him, perhaps more than to any one else, Lee owed the military bearing that was to distinguish him throughout his military career. Other cadets felt as Lee did toward Worth, and they united in a petition that they might present the departing commandant with a sword. The request was duly forwarded to Washington, but for reasons that were hidden in the always curious logic of the executive mind, it was disallowed by the President.[82] Worth went to other duty, much lamented, and on March 13, 1829, Captain Ethan A. Hitchcock, an able man, well-equipped and earnest, assumed charge cf the cadets. In less than twenty years thereafter the new commandant and the young cadet who formed the battalion and presented it to him on parade were to be serving together on Scott's staff, battering their way to Mexico City.

Before Hitchcock took command, the critical semi-annual examinations of Lee's final year were held. Robert must have thought himself weak on his geology, for, thrifty as he was, he paid for special coaching on that subject,[83] with the result that he was second in chemistry and mineralogy. He had like rating in rhetoric and moral philosophy. In engineering he was tied with Buckingham at the head of the class, and for the first time in any subject he stood ahead of the invincible Charles Mason.[84] After the examinations, with even greater energy, he turned to the work of the final half term. On April 1 he procured relief as adjutant of the corps,[85] got permission to board at Cozzen's Hotel,[86] and thereafter, for two months, he concentrated on his studies.

Quickly enough the finals approached, and the board of visitors arrived. The new president of that august company was General

[81] Including the coming of Edward H. Courtenay as professor of natural philosophy, in succession to Jared Mansfield (cf. Register, 1828 and 1829). Among the other newcomers was Captain J. L. Gardner, of the 4th Artillery, assistant quartermaster, who preceded Major Robert Anderson in command at Fort Moultrie.

[82] Cent. U. S. M. A., 2, 88.

[83] MS. Accounts, U. S. Military Academy, made available through the kindness of Major E. A. Farman, Librarian of West Point.

[84] MS. U. S. Military Academy Records.

[85] MS. Muster Rolls, U. S. Military Academy.   [86] MS. Accounts, loc. cit.

THE EDUCATION OF A CADET

Pierre van Cortlandt of Peekskill, N. Y., grandson of Stephenus van Cortlandt and great-grandson of the redoubtable Oloff Stevense van Cortlandt, one of the pioneers of New Amsterdam. General Pierre van Cortlandt's title had been won in the militia, not in the country's wars, but he had his distinctions, for he had studied law under Alexander Hamilton, and while at the head of the Westchester levies he had named James Fenimore Cooper as one of his aides. Another member of the board was Major Worth, now Lieutenant Colonel Worth, who so recently himself had been subject to successive visitors. Still another of the fifteen members of the board was Doctor Robert Archer, then an assistant surgeon, stationed at Fort Monroe, a man of great ingenuity, who subsequently worked with his son-in-law, Joseph R. Anderson, in developing the Tredegar Iron Works in Richmond, where many of Lee's cannon of the 'sixties were cast.[87]

Beginning June 1 the visitors and the academic board met jointly every day for a fortnight. It was a ceremonious test. In the examination room, at the head of one table, sat Colonel Thayer in full uniform, with the professors around the board. At the other table were General Van Cortlandt and the visitors. In front of this awesome group, three large blackboards were placed on easels. Six cadets were called in at a time, two for each board. While one demonstrated orally, the others prepared their problems. In this setting, Robert made his appearance when his name was called, and for five separate grillings of an hour each he explained what he knew of engineering, of strategy, and of the other subjects of the year's work.[88]

At last it was done; all forty-six members of the class were examined; the credits were all computed. Lee's consistent good conduct and soldierly bearing now found their reward in these entries on the roll of general merit:

Mathematics (maximum 300) 286
French (maximum 100) 98½
Natural Philosophy (maximum 300) 295

[87] *F. H. Smith*, 1. *Cf.* Kathleen Bruce: *Economic Factors in the Manufacture of Confederate Ordnance* (*Army Ordnance*, vol. 6, Nos. 33 and 34).

[88] This account of the final examinations is taken from a letter written by George Ticknor, while he was a member of the board of visitors in 1825. It appears in Hillard's *George Ticknor*, 1, 374. There is no reason to believe the method of holding the examinations was changed between 1825 and 1829.

Drawing (maximum 100) 97

Engineering (maximum 300) 292

Chemistry and Mineralogy (maximum 100) 99

Geography, Rhetoric and Moral Philosophy (maximum 200) 199

Tactics (maximum 200) 200

Artillery (maximum 100) 100

Conduct (maximum 300) 300

General Merit (maximum 2000) ....1966½[89]

These credits put him at the head of the class in artillery and tactics and gave him equal place in conduct with Barnes, Burbank, Harford, Kennedy, and Mason, who had received no demerits during the whole of their four years at the academy.[90] In final class standing Mason was No. 1; Lee was No. 2; Harford, Joseph A. Smith, and James Barnes followed in order.[91] Lee finished his fourth year, as he had all the others, with a place on the list of "distinguished cadets."[92]

Exercising the right accorded the class-leaders of selecting the arm of the service in which they desired to be commissioned, he asked to be assigned to the Engineer Corps. This was the usual choice of those who stood highest on the merit roll and it conformed to Lee's own inclination. No subject of study at the academy had enthralled him so much as that which he now made the basis of his professional work in the army.

Commencement at West Point a century ago was not the great event it is today. There was usually a valedictory address and sometimes a speech by the Secretary of War or some other dignitary, but that was all. Each graduate received a formal diploma, signed by the superintendent and academic board.[93] Likewise, each was granted a two-months furlough and to each was given whatever balance of pay and allowances his account book showed was due him. In Lee's case this amounted to $103.58, for while

[89] MS. U. S. Military Academy Records.
[90] But because his initial "L" was fifth among those of the men who had received no demerit during the whole of their cadetship, he appears as No. 5 on the Conduct Roll of 1829 (Register . . . of the United States Military Academy, 1829, p. 19).
[91] Ibid., 1829.   [92] American State Papers, Military Affairs, 4, 251.
[93] M. A. Regs., §§ 1385-88.

he had spent as much as the average cadet with the tailor, and something more than the average for postage, he had been most economical in all his other personal expenditures.[94]

The tragedy of commencement was the separation of boys who had spent four years together in close and revealing companionship. Death was to claim seventeen of Robert's forty-five classmates and nine were to quit the service prior to the War between the States. Of the 323 who were with him at the academy and graduated in the classes of 1826–32, inclusive, 119 came to their end before 1861. Seventy resigned and, so far as is known, did not return to the service when North and South took up arms.[95] Robert's intimates and his rivals for academic honors found varying fortune. Jack Mackay, who was perhaps his closest friend, served in the Artillery and in the Engineers, chiefly in and near his native Georgia, until 1846, when protracted illness forced him to procure sick leave. He died in 1848, aged forty-two.[96] William Harford left the Army in 1833 and lived only three years thereafter.[97] Charles Mason remained at the academy for two years, as principal assistant professor of engineering, then practised law in New York and served as temporary editor of *The Evening Post* until 1836, when he went to Wisconsin. He later had a civil career of some eminence in Iowa, living to be seventy-seven.[98] Mason, however, was by no means the last survivor of his class: Joseph B. Smith, No. 7, defied time until he was ninety-three.[99]

The only men of '29 with whom Lee was closely associated in 1861–65 were Joseph E. Johnston and Theophilus H. Holmes, but eleven of the cadets who were at "the Point" during his four years were to become general officers in the Confederacy, and one was to be president. Lee's future chief of artillery, W. N. Pendleton, was in the class of 1830. L. B. Northrop, the commissary general who was to cause Lee many an agonizing hour, graduated

[94] *MS. Accounts, U. S. Military Academy.*

[95] These figures are checked from *Cullum* and from the registers of the different classes. Men who entered the academy but failed to graduate are not included.

[96] 1 *Cullum*, 425.   [97] 1 *Cullum*, 421.

[98] 1 *Cullum*, 419–20; *Annals of Iowa*, 2, 163, 168–73; 3, 203–4; 4, 595; 5, 268; 7, 28.

[99] *Cent. U. S. M. A.*, 2, 359. Smith was graduated as Jos. Smith Bryce (1 *Cullum*, 424–25).

in 1831, and Abraham C. Myers, quartermaster general of the South until 1863, was an humble "plebe" in Lee's last year.[100]

Two of Lee's classmates, James Barnes, who was No. 5, and Sidney Burbank, No. 17, were later to face him in Virginia, though not as commanding generals. Silas Casey, of the class of 1826, as already noted, was to stand stubbornly on the doubtful field of Seven Pines. Samuel P. Heintzelman, also of 1826, served with the Army of the Potomac, as division and corps commander, until October, 1863. W. H. Emory, a third classman in Lee's last year, came, in time, to command the Nineteenth Federal Corps in the Shenandoah Valley, in the campaign against Early. Erasmus D. Keyes, of the class of 1832, served with the Federals in the Peninsular campaign, as did Philip Saint George Cooke of '27. Randolph B. Marcy, a graduate of 1832, later acted as chief of staff to his son-in-law, George B. McClellan, who was a child of three years when Lee quit West Point. George W. Turner, a second classman, was to appear in the grisly tragedy of the John Brown raid, and was to be killed by the insurrectionaries whom Lee put under arrest at Harpers Ferry.[101] Others of the corps were to fight in the west for the Union. A boy of the second class in Lee's final year, A. A. Humphreys, at the head of a famous corps, was to oppose Longstreet on the last day of all Lee's warring. In the main, however, cadets who were with Robert Lee at West Point were not those with whom or against whom he was to fight. Such pre-war knowledge of his opponents as he was to use effectually in the 'sixties he acquired in the Mexican campaigns, or in his later service, and not during the years that came to a close, that June day, 1829, when he shook hands and said good-bye to some, and climbed aboard the steamship with others to go down the Hudson, on the way home.

As the ship churned southward, Robert Lee doubtless looked back to get his last glimpse of West Point. He was then twenty-two and a half, full grown to his height of five feet, ten and a half inches, with brown eyes that sometimes seemed black. His hair was ebon and abundant, with a wave that a woman might

---

[100] The other general officers of the Confederacy were: Albert Sidney Johnston, class of 1826; Leonidas Polk and Gabriel J. Rains of 1827; Thomas Drayton of 1828; Albert G. Blanchard of 1829; John B. Magruder of 1830; and Humphrey Marshall of 1832.
[101] 1 Cullum, 473–74. For Turner's death, see O. G. Villard: John Brown, 440–41.

have envied. There was dignity in his open bearing, and his manners were considerate and ingratiating. He had candor, tact, and good humor. The self-control he had learned from his mother was his in larger measure. The habit of "finishing up" that Hallowell had observed in him at Alexandria had been strengthened by the fine discipline and precise instruction of the academy. Already his character was formed and his personality was developed. It was easy for him to win and to hold the friendship of other people. His professional interest was fixed in engineering and thereafter it never wavered until disappointment over slow promotion led him to accept a cavalry commission. He was not, of course, a finished, or even an accomplished soldier. For him, as for all other cadets of his day, drill had been needlessly prolonged at the academy, and the technical instruction in war had been crowded into too brief a period. But the training he had received was the best his country could give. The rest lay with him.

CHAPTER V

Sorrow and Scandal Come to the Lees

In holiday seasons, Robert and Smith Lee sometimes arranged to have their furloughs run simultaneously, and they would join their elder brother, Carter, in mirthful journeyings to the homes of their kinspeople. There would be laughter, teasing, sprightly anecdote, and much harmless gallantry. When liquor was passed, Robert and Smith would decline but Carter was agreeable. "I have always told these boys," he would say, "that I would drink their share of wine, provided they would keep me generously supplied." Carter was the centre of amusement at these parties, for his social gifts were of the highest and his humor keener than that of either of his brothers.[1] Robert's most favorable impression was made by the dignity of his fine person and by his gracious, considerate manners.

On one of his visits, his manners and his regard for his elders brought him no little embarrassment. In the company there chanced to be a bibulous old gentleman who was much pleased with the clean, high-minded cadet. The night before Robert left, this worthy came to the boy's room. To quote a feminine biographer who did not fail to point the moral, the veteran of many a drinking-bout "lamented the idle and useless life into which he had fallen, excusing himself upon the score of loneliness, and the sorrow which weighed upon him in the loss of those most dear. In the most impressive manner he besought his young guest to be warned by his example; prayed him to cherish the good habits he had already acquired, and promised to listen to his entreaties that he would change his own life, and thereby secure more entirely his respect and affection."[2] So runs the story; sober history suggests that the gentleman had been to the shrine of Bacchus before he staggered to the confessional. It probably

---

[1] Fitz Lee: *General Lee* (cited hereafter as *Fitz Lee*), 17.
[2] *Mason*, 24–25. This incident may have occurred during Robert's furlough of 1827.

took all of Robert's tact to dispose of the penitent and to get him out of the room.

Barring a repetition of such a scene, the summer after his graduation should have been for Robert the happiest of all these seasons of care-free visiting, but it was, instead, one of the saddest periods of his life. The joy of home-coming was ruined by the illness of his mother. Her health had been bad during the winter, though there had been some signs of improvement with the spring.[3] When Robert arrived, she was at Ravensworth in a worse condition than ever, and was ready to die. Charles Carter was developing his practice; Smith was progressing in the navy; Ann in 1826[4] had married William Louis Marshall, a minister who later became an attorney of station; Mildred, in her nineteenth year, was in friendly hands. And now Robert was embarking on a career of high promise. Ann Carter Lee had seen it through, but the struggle had cost her all her vitality. She could fight for nothing further.

Robert immediately resumed his old duties as a nurse. He mixed her medicines, administered them, and watched by her bed almost continuously. When he left her room, her gaze followed him, and she would look steadily at the door until he entered again.[5] It was not a long siege this time. On July 10, Robert saw the light leave her eye and the last faint breath fail her. He turned from the bed in a grief that he never forgot.[6] She was buried at Ravensworth, and there her ashes remained until they were moved to rest in a vault at Lexington, Va., near those of her son, whither also, in 1913,[7] the bones of Henry Lee were brought from Cumberland Island.

Ann Carter Lee was fifty-six when she died. She had been a mother for thirty-one years and a widow for eleven. Nearly all her married life of two decades and a half had been clouded with financial worry. For at least seventeen years before her death, she had carried the burden of maintaining the family on her personal income. Of all that she thought and planned and suffered

[3] G. C. Lee to Hill Carter, *MS.*, March 11, 1829; *Carter MSS.*
[4] Ann Carter Lee to Smith Lee, *MS.*, April 10, [1827] *Lee MSS., infra.*
[5] An anonymous cousin, quoted in *Long, 26.*
[6] *R. E. Lee, Jr.,* 363; see infra, p. 89.
[7] *Report of the Committee Appointed . . . for the Purpose of Reinterring the Remains of General Henry Lee . . . at Lexington, Virginia* (Richmond, Va. [1913]).

during those years, hardly an echo has survived the indifferent roar of a hurrying century. The scant score of letters in her autograph that now remain and the few references to her in the extant correspondence of her kinspeople and friends do not suffice to give more than the most shadowy outlines of her personality. She had patience in misfortune; she used wisely the little that she possessed; she served a God who was very real to her; she kept her friends and she loved her kin; she had the wisdom and skill with which to vitalize for her children the virtue of self-control; she made their interests her own; she must have had much of the Carter interest in life and some of the Carter sense of humor; she had high, uncomplaining courage in facing continued adversity. This much is known. But in what manner she dealt with a spend-thrift husband seventeen years her senior, and what she thought of the life she had left at Shirley or of the life she had led among the Lees, and how she went about the rearing of Robert, and whether she believed he would become a great man, she does not tell us. None of her letters to Robert is known to be in existence, and only two of those to Smith are left. The earlier of these exhibits her devotion to her children and to her kinspeople. It follows:

My dear Son.   Georgetown April 10, [1827][8]

I believe my last letter to you was conveyed by Mr. Dulany. I thank God I have been spared to write to you again, for my health has declined very much in the last two years, and I never calculate on living longer than from season to another. Am very happy to learn from Mr. Dulany that the North Carolina will return home as soon as the vessel reaches the Mediteranian I hope to see both of my dear boys home in June Robert will then have been absent two years. He is much pleased with his situation at West Point, has advanced rapidly, never having recieved a mark or demerit an assistant Professor of Mathematics which appointment gives him $10.00 per month in addition to his monthly allowance. The Captain (as Robt calls Carter) is driving on at law. . . . He was admitted to the bar of the supreme court during the last session, so I hope in time he will be in a more

[8] *Lee MSS.*, placed at the writer's disposal by the late Mrs. C. P. Cardwell, acting for all the generous descendants of Captain Smith Lee.

prosperous situation. I think when I last wrote you I informed you of Ann's intended marriage which was solemnized on the 22nd of June. This is the 8th day since the birth of her daughter who lived only a few hours, and you can readly imagine from Ann's disposition how much she deplored the event. Mildred has grown since you were here, and I hope you will find her improved in some respects, she is as fond of books as the Captain, and both do very little else but read, so you will know how the family affairs are conducted, when you condsider that I am too much of an inviled to take part in the management of them that I formerly did. Alas, Alas, I wish I had my little boys Smith and Robt living with me again. My brother Bernard's three elder daughters and Capt Henry spent the last four months with us. They are accomplish pretty girls, Mildred is quite a beauty, Charles is also a handsome man, very honorable and correct. They left us this day week to go to "Shirley." They were accompanied by your Uncle Williams, Shirley, John Hill Carter, and Carter Lee. They will return to Phil. the latter part of this month to await the return of their Father from England they returned from America last June after an absence of five years. Your relations generally are going on as much as when you knew them, I believe all living that you left last, excepting your Uncle Randolph, dear Blanton Carter and your uncle R. B. Lee who died a few weeks ago Poor Alexandria has suffered much by fire this winter. Mr. Dulany will give you the particulars, it has lost some of its old inhabitants too. Capt Dangerfield, Mr. Irvin, dear Dr. Dick, and Sam Thompson. My dear Smith I have told you everything I thought interesting to you and now have arrived at the disagreeable point in my letter, the obligation I feel to chide you for never writing to your Mother more especially as her health is so impaired that you cannot calculate on ever seeing her again, but exclusive of my desire to hear from you I lament your dislike of writing because it will be such a disadvantage to you through life. A man that cannot write a good letter on business or on the subject of familiar letters will make an awkward figure in every situation and will find himself greatly at a loss on any occasion. Indeed I cannot imagine how he could pass through life with satisfaction and respectability should you arrive at any eminence in your proffession my dear Smith it will be essential to your reputation to write a good letter, the knowledge of which cannot be acquired in after life. You must write often now in the days of your youth, and form a good style let me entreat you my dear son to write often to me if your letters are not well written at first you will improve after while, and I promise no eye shall see but mine. I must again mention my hopes of seeing you in June My disease is an unconquerable one but the symptoms at present are such as do not threaten a speedy death, but as all things are uncertain in this world nothing so precarious as our hold on life I must beg you my dear child always to know how anxious I am about your welfare neither of which can be attained without exertion on your part. You must repel every evil and allow yourself to indulge in such habits only as are consistent with religion and morality. Oh that I could impart to you the knowledge gained from the experience of 54 years, then would you be convinced of the vanity of every pursuit not under the control of the most inflexible virtue. I wish the powers of my mind were equal to the affections of my heart then could I give you such precepts as would influence your conduct through life but as the advantage has been denied me I must entreat you my dear son to reflect often on your poor Mothers solicitude for you, let it stimulate you to require the best habits and indulge not one that you could not remember on your death bed with satisfaction Keep my letters that you may read them when I can write no more They will awaken your Mother's great fondness for you and perhaps prove incentive to the cultivation of these virtues she was most desirous you should possess Join your prayers with mine my dear son that God may bless you and impart to your mind every good gift and best of all the peace which passeth all understanding—Your devoted Mother   ANN H. LEE

The second letter was written not long before her end, and it showed how the long fight wore on her nerves. It reads:

"Georgetown March 24th 1829.[9]

"I thought when I parted with you dear Smith, that your contemplated voyage was not objected to, in as much as you would

[9] Lee MSS., loc. cit.

be absent but a short time and it would probably prevent your being sent out soon again, but I have been uneasy all day from reading the papers last night that the pirates were sometimes secreted in part of the Island into which ships of war could not go, and that boats were sent to apprehend them. Now my dear Smith these expeditions in boats must be attend with great danger and I trust in God you will avoid as much as possible placing yourself in such perilous situations. I entreat you to write to me from New York and let me know all the plans respecting your cruise as far as you have been made acquainted with them. You left us Saturday and this is Tuesday evening. So that I can not have much to tell you. Nannie and Matilda visited us on last Sunday after church to console with us on your loss. They say they are truly sorry they shall have no more sleigh rides, no more pretty flowers, no more music presented them, no kind beau to escort them in the walks this spring, but insist on your coming back here when you return from Cuba and positively forbid you going to Colombia with the new minister. Catherine Mason came yesterday to beg for your profile and Carter insists on being allowed to carry her one this evening which he will sell for a high price. He wishes he had thought of it before you went, he says, and he would have made Master Ranks cut many and would have sold them to your favorites, by the way of getting a little money. My dear Smith I am very unhappy about you since I read that paragraph in the paper respecting the pirates. If you can, give me some comfort on the subject. Ann wept often in the course of the day you left us, and is still grieved about you. I beg you will not go to Colombia without coming home first. I pray to God to protect and bless you my dear son. Ann H. Lee

Mildred is down stairs and does not know I am writing to you or would beg to be tenderly presented to you. Ann sends more love than my paper could hold. God bless you God bless you."

These letters are the only picture of herself that she has left. Much that a curious world would like to know about the mother of her son can never be established.[10]

[10] A dress of Ann Lee, preserved in Richmond, would indicate that she was a woman of about 5 feet 6 inches and of middle weight.

For a time after her death, Robert apparently was in George-town,[11] engaged no doubt in helping to settle his mother's estate. She had prepared a will not long before her death, so there was little difficulty in executing her wishes. To Ann Marshall, she left her maid and the Negress's child, together with three slaves that were then with Mrs. Marshall. To her also went the white tea china, the wardrobe, two of the mother's tablecloths—she had but four—and half the napkins and wearing apparel. Mildred received the old family servant Nat, the carriage and horses, the piano, the other two good tablecloths, and an equal share of the napkins and wearing apparel. Each daughter was given, in ad-dition, $10,000 of the principal of the trust-fund which had been prudently invested in bank stock. The rest of her property Mrs. Lee directed her executor to sell, and to divide the proceeds among her three sons. The size of the bond given when the will was probated in Fairfax County would indicate that the amount allotted the boys was hardly more than $3000 each.[12]

It was sad, sad business breaking up the home in Georgetown and dividing the treasures to which Ann Lee had clung through her darkest days. Robert doubtless was relieved when he was able to return to Virginia about August 1 and sojourn with relatives. But, with the buoyancy of youth, he quickly recovered from the immediate grief of his mother's death and, as one of his cousins remembered, was "as full of life, fun and particularly of teasing, as any of us." [13] He visited much at Eastern View, the Randolph home in Fauquier, but there was another mansion to which his interest and his horse were turning very frequently. This was Arlington, the home of George Washington Parke Custis, on the hills above Alexandria, overlooking the country's capital. Custis was the grandson of Mrs. George Washington and was the adopted son of Washington. Having resided at Mount Vernon from 1782, when he was an infant, until the end of his grand-

---

11 His first official letter to the chief of engineers, Charles Gratiot, notifying that of-ficer where he was in case he was called to duty before the expiration of his furlough, was written from Georgetown July 31, 1829; *U. S. War Dept. MSS.* Engineers, File 137. These *MSS.* are the letters from officers of engineers, and are filed by date and by the letter of the sender's last name. Those of Lee, therefore, appear under the letter *L*, and are cited hereafter as *Eng MSS.*, with the date and file number.

12 Will of Ann H. Lee, *Will Book 1, P., Fairfax County, Va.* The bond, $60,000, was, under Virginia law, twice the estimated value of the estate.

13 *Long,* 30.

mother's life in 1802, he had observed Washington closely during the general's last years. His temperament was such that he delighted in the sentimental appellation, "The child of Mount Vernon," which clung to him all his days, though he measured out his full seventy years and more.[14] Arlington had been built by him after the death of his grandmother, when Mount Vernon had reverted to the Washington family. The house, which was named after an old Custis home on the Eastern Shore of Virginia, was distinguished more for its site and for the impressive columnated portico, with Doric capitals, than for interior beauty or convenience. Its rooms, though large, were few and gloomy; the heavy columns dwarfed the mansion. It gives the impression of being built to be looked at, rather than to be lived in.

To Arlington, in 1806, Custis brought as his bride Mary Lee Fitzhugh, daughter of Colonel and Mrs. William Fitzhugh of Chatham, opposite Fredericksburg on the Rappahannock. She was eighteen at the time and he was twenty-five, and they had ahead of them forty-seven years of married life. Of their four children, only one survived infancy. She was a girl, Mary Anne Randolph Custis, born October 1, 1808, and reared in the amplest luxury. Twenty-one years of age when Robert came home from West Point, she had known him almost all her life, for the families were distantly related through the Lee ancestry of the Randolphs and they visited one another frequently.[15] She was something of a toast in the Lee family, as much admired by Robert's brother Carter, as by the boys nearer her own age. "I heard of dear Miss Custis yesterday," Carter had written not long before Robert's return from New York, "and that she was much afflicted with a cold."[16] She was a frail, blonde girl. Her features were aristocratic but they were not beautiful. The nose was a trifle too long and the chin a bit too sharp, but she had freshness,

[14] *Brock*, 155 *ff*. Mrs. Washington, it will be remembered, was born Martha Dandridge and had first married John Daniel Parke Custis, by whom she had four children, among them John Parke Custis. In 1773, while still a very young man, John Parke Custis married Eleanor Calvert of Mount Airy, Prince George County, Md., a granddaughter of the sixth Lord Baltimore. George Washington Parke Custis was their son. In 1781 John Parke Custis died, presumably of the hardships sustained during the campaign of that year, when he served as aide to Washington. His daughter Nellie and the boy then came to Mount Vernon to reside.

[15] *Cf. Long*, 30. For the kinship of the two families and for the ancestry of the Fitzhughs, see *E. J. Lee*, 82, 89.

[16] Charles Carter Lee to Hill Carter, *MS.*, March 11, 1829; *Carter MSS.*

bright eyes, a ready smile, and quick, sympathetic interest. If Robert did not actually love her from boyhood, he certainly put her in a place by herself. She it was who drew him to Arlington. When he went away, it was to come again, always with deepening delight in her company.

While Robert was visiting at Arlington and at Eastern View, one legacy left to Mildred by his mother required his care. This was Nat, the Negro coachman and house-servant. Nat was typical of a rather large element among Virginia slaves. He had helped to rear the children; he had served long and loyally; he had shared in all the struggles of the family. None of the Lees ever regarded him otherwise than as a member of the family. And now Nat was sick, with some slow, devitalizing malady. What should be done to provide for him? The carriage would creak no more over the Georgetown streets as Mrs. Lee went out to take the air. The household was broken up. How could he be assured good nursing? While this question was being debated, Robert's orders came. They read as follows:

Engineer Order No. 8.
Washington, D. C., Aug. 11, 1829
Brevet Second Lieut. Robert E. Lee . . . will, by the middle of November next, report to Major Samuel Babcock of the corps of Engineers for duty at Cockspur Island, in the Savannah River, Georgia.
C. GRATIOT,
Brig. Gen. Comndg.[17]

Cockspur Island! A God-forsaken spot by all accounts, re-deemed only by the fact that it was near Savannah, where lived the family of Lee's chum, Jack Mackay. But orders were orders, and besides, as the climate there was mild, Nat's health might be improved. So, when Robert said farewell to all his kinspeople and to the young mistress of Arlington, Nat accompanied him on the long sea-journey to Savannah. It was a curious companionship for the beginning of active duty in an army which Lee was to

<hr>

[17] Photostat, Virginia State Library, *Records Adjutant General's Office, U. S. Army*, Adjutant General's Office, General orders No. 50 and orders of Aug. 5, 1829; Lee to Gratiot, *Eng. MSS.*, 140; *R. E. Lee, Jr.* (2d ed.), 446.

leave, more than thirty years afterwards in order, his enemies alleged, to fight for the perpetuation of slavery.[18]

The town at which the young lieutenant and the old Negro arrived by packet, about November 1, 1829, was a place of some 7300 people, the largest city and the principal port in a state that had been settled less than one hundred years and then counted no more than 300,000 whites in a population of 516,000. Savannah had history, for it had been occupied by the British in 1778, and in October of the following year, it had been besieged by the American and French forces. These operations, which were unsuccessful, had cost the life of Count Pulaski. With that part of the story of the town, Robert was of course familiar from his father's memoirs, for "Light-Horse Harry" had fought farther up the river on which his son was now to labor as an engineer. The same tide that flooded Savannah, swept Cumberland Island, where Henry Lee had ended his days. Socially, the town was attractive and cultured. The Mackays, who welcomed Lee with open doors, were among the most distinguished of Savannah families, with daughters who were interesting even at first sight. In a few days Lee was introduced to all the civilians who were accounted worth knowing. As for the army, Savannah boasted a small garrison of United States artillery, among whom were several officers with whom Lee became friendly. Jack Mackay had been assigned to this garrison.[19] Another of its officers was Lieutenant James A. Chambers of the Second Artillery, who may have been distantly connected with Lee.[20]

The post was by no means so pleasant as the town. It was, in fact, as drab and desolate as its reputation. Cockspur Island lies twelve miles down-stream from Savannah and is the easternmost islet of a number of flats in Tybee Roads, as the mouth of the river is styled. The island is about a mile in length and about two-thirds as wide. Very little of it was above normal tide level at the time of Lee's arrival, and most of it was marsh-land, flooded daily and completely covered in heavy storms. Up the river was a string of similar swampy islands. Northward, across nearly two miles of water, were Turtle Island and a tangle of flats on the

---

[18] Nat died at Cockspur Island or nearby. The date is not known (*Mason*, 23).
[19] 1 *Cullum*, 425. [20] *Cf. E. J. Lee*, 101.

mainland, broken by winding estuaries and untouched by man's labor. To the south of Cockspur Island and separated from it by a narrow channel were other swamps, even more confusing and inhospitable. Eastward the open sea was spread. In summer, Cockspur had virtually to be abandoned because of mosquitoes, heat, and fever. It was, however, a training-school for Lee in the practical problems of military engineering and in the management of labor. He came to his duty there at a most advantageous period. Congress had recently begun its first extensive programme of coast defenses, which the engineers had the satisfaction of locating, designing, and constructing. Promotion was very slow, and the jealousy of some high functionaries was pronounced; but there probably was never a time of peace in the history of the corps when it held out so many opportunities, or gave young officers so much responsibility, as it did when Lee joined it.

Lee's orders had indicated that his commanding officer at Cockspur Island was to be Major Samuel Babcock of Massachusetts, one of the earliest graduates of the United States Military Academy. Babcock had been in the army more than twenty years when Robert was graduated and his health was becoming impaired by his exertions. For that reason, the load of his youthful subordinate was heavy from the very outset. Aside from the engineering duties, Lee had to discharge those of acting assistant commissary of subsistence. It was the only time in his life that he labored in that most thankless of army services.[21]

His engineering work was not always interesting but it usually was troublesome. The project at Cockspur Island was to locate and subsequently to construct a heavy fort on an island that afforded at best, a doubtful foundation.[22] After the site was chosen, embankments had to be reared to keep out the tide. Then a canal had to be constructed, and when this had drained the site, the fort was to be laid out. Into the first stages of this hard work, Robert put all he had learned at West Point and all the strength of his staunch physique. He spent so many days in mud and water, up to his arm-pits, that a certain interested young woman,

---

[21] Samuel Babcock to George Gibson, commissary-general, Feb. 1, 1830; *R. E. Lee, Jr.* (2d ed.), 447.

[22] The defenses do not appear officially as "Fort Pulaski" until 1833. (*Cf. report of the chief engineer of the army*, 1832–33; *Ex. Docs., 1st sess., 23d Cong.*, vol. 1, p. 53.)

up in Virginia, wondered how he ever survived it, and to the end of her days she never ceased to marvel at it.

Finding friends in Savannah whenever he could go there, and occupying his leisure hours in letter-writing and in sketching,[23] Lee passed the winter of 1829-30. Such social life as he could have in Savannah must have been less pleasant than it would normally have been to a young man of his temperament because the proud name of the Lee family had become involved in a humiliating public scandal in the very circles where it had stood highest. In 1817, Henry Lee, Robert's half-brother, son of "Light-Horse Harry" by his union to Matilda Lee of Stratford, had married a young woman of means in Westmoreland County.[24] Living as a country gentleman, first at Stratford and then at Fredericksburg, Major Lee had dabbled in letters, much to the neglect of his estate, and had served as assistant postmaster general under J. Q. Adams.[25] In 1827, Henry Lee's affairs had become so much involved that a judgment of $9000 was procured against him by Henry Storke. As Lee could not meet this, Stratford had been sold for $11,000 and, on June 30, 1828, had formally passed out of the Lee family.[26] Impoverished and embittered, Henry Lee had tried to make a living by writing. By inheritance he was a Federalist, but he had become a protagonist of Andrew Jackson. He had resided at "The Hermitage" after the sale of Stratford, had been engaged in arranging Jackson's military papers,[27] and had written several polemics in behalf of "Old Hickory." Jackson found these last to be indited in a temper that matched his own and he felt much gratitude to Lee. When he became President, he named his defender United States consul to Morocco. It was a vacation appointment, which Lee was very glad to accept. He left the country for his post, only to find that he left a storm behind him. His wife had a younger sister, co-heiress to her father's estate. In some

---

[23] Two of his sketches, the only examples known to be in existence, are reproduced in *R. E. Lee, Jr.* (2d ed.), 449. Lee gave them to Miss Sarah Anna Minis of Savannah.
[24] *E. J. Lee,* 403. [25] J. S. Bassett: *Correspondence of Andrew Jackson,* 3, 291.
[26] *Westmoreland County MS. Deed Book* 26, p. 78. The next conveyance of Stratford, Dec. 13, 1843, was from Henry Storke to his widow, Elizabeth (*Ibid., Deed Book* 31, p. 473), by whom it was bequeathed, in 1865, to her grandnephews, Charles E. and Richard H. Stuart (*Ibid., Deed Book* 41, p. 412). On Nov. 5, 1919, Richard H. Stuart deeded the property to Charles E. Stuart (*Ibid., Deed Book* 83, p. 500), from whom it was purchased by the Lee Memorial Foundation.
[27] Henry A. Wise met him there, Oct. 9, 1828; B. H. Wise: *Life of Henry A. Wise,*
28.

way, Henry Lee became enamoured of her and had been guilty of misconduct with her. The ugly facts apparently had been whispered about, and perhaps had caused Henry Lee to be socially ostracized, but they had led to no public reprisals. Now, when Jackson submitted his name for confirmation by the Senate on February 3, 1830,[28] an open fight was made on him. As he had already admitted some items of the charge, no defense was made. Every senator who cast a ballot voted against him, among them his long-time friend and college-mate, John Tyler.[29] The whole of the scandal became common knowledge in March, 1830. Henry Lee had to leave his post, and after a stay in Italy, removed to Paris, where he was to live until his death, seven years later.[30]

This affair must have been an intense humiliation to Lieutenant Lee. Much as he had cherished the memory of his father, he could not have been ignorant of "Light-Horse Harry's" financial reputation, and now to have his father's name disgraced by the son who bore it was to add the blush of shame to the ruddy complexion of the young engineer. So far as is known, he never referred in later life to his half-brother, though he possessed and doubtless studied the one volume that "Black Harry" issued in 1837 of a projected life of Napoleon.[31] Significantly, Robert Lee failed, in later years, to name any one of his three sons Henry, perhaps in the belief that to do so would be to revive the scandal. Doubtless as he read by the candle of his crude quarters on Cockspur Island the story of his brother's misdeeds, he was strengthened in his resolution to efface by his own conduct the blot on the proud scutcheon of the Lees. Such things in a man's life are not to be proved by citation or confirmed by footnotes, but there is every reason to believe that the stern morality of Robert Lee was stiffened by the warning of his brother's fall. In exactly the same way, the rigid exactness of the son in all money-matters, small and large, was a reaction from his father's laxness.

[28] *Journal of the United States Senate*, 1830, Appendix, 408.

[29] *Journal of the United States Senate*, 1830, Appendix, 423; Bassett, *op. cit.*, 3, 291.

[30] James Parton: *Life of Andrew Jackson*, vol. 3, pp. 274 and 297–98, quoting letter of March 11, 1830, from Major W. B. Lewis to Colonel L. C. Stanbaugh. There is in the Library of Congress a *MS.* letter, Aug. 24, 1833, from Henry Lee to Richard T. Brown, confessing his misdeed but arguing, in a singularly callous strain, that his conduct was no worse than that of Thomas Jefferson, whom he accused of attempting to betray the wife of a friend.

[31] H. Lee, *The Life of Napoleon Bonaparte Down to the Peace of Tolentino and the Close of the First Campaign in Italy* (London and Paris, 1837).

CHAPTER VI

MARRIAGE

By the time summer and mosquitoes came in 1830, the embankment at Cockspur Island had been thrown over part of the island, and the drainage canal had been dug.[1] Because of the weather and the insect pests, the work was then suspended, and most of the force left the island. Lee went home; that is, he went to visit among friends who lived close enough to Arlington for him to go there often to see Mary Custis. He found Mrs. Custis not unsympathetic. She was his kinswoman, she was young enough to be interested in romance, of which she read much, and she was one of those rare persons in whose presence every honest man felt at ease.[2] Mr. Custis, however, was not pleased at the frequent appearance of the same horseman in the park at Arlington.

To be sure, Mr. Custis had nothing against Robert Lee personally, but he knew the financial tragedy of the Lee family and was aware that his daughter's admirer had very little beyond his pay as second lieutenant. He did not welcome the idea that his only child was interested in a man who could not support her as she was accustomed to live.

If Lee knew of Custis's opposition, he did not let it deter him. When Mary journeyed down to Chatham, her mother's former home on the Rappahannock, Robert appeared there also, and while sitting with her under a great tree on the lawn he talked to her of those gentle themes that make any suitor eloquent. Below him stretched the Rappahannock; across it were the spires of the sturdy little town of Fredericksburg, and beyond the town a line of hills, one of them forest-covered, another crowned with a mansion in the style of the Grecian revival. Soldier though he

[1] Lee to Gratiot, Nov. 11, 1830; *Eng. MSS.*, 186.
[2] Thomas J. Packard, ed.: Joseph Packard: *Recollections of a Long Life* (cited hereafter as *Packard*), 157.

was, he would have shuddered to think that a day would come, when he would stand atop one of those distant hills, and, through the battle-smoke, search with his field-glasses for a glimpse of that very tree.[3]

In company so delightful, with so absorbing a siege to engross him, the summer of 1830 passed far too rapidly for Lieutenant Lee of the Engineers, and the call to return to Cockspur Island came all too soon. He left New York on the packet for Savannah and arrived at his station on the night of November 10. He found a situation from which a timid young man would have been glad to run away. Major Babcock had not arrived. Lee was the only engineer on the ground. A recent gale had broken the embankment erected during the previous winter and spring. Across the mouth of the canal that drained the ditches on the site of the fort, the embankment had been entirely swept away. The canal itself was choked. The wharf was in such condition that repair seemed impossible. It was Lee's duty to take hold at once and to resume the work with the help of the few men who had remained on the island during the summer.[4]

By the first of December, Lee had replaced enough of the embankment to keep the water off that part of the island on which the fort was to be erected, but he proceeded to strengthen this barrier so that the next storm would not beat it down or breach it. When this was completed he planned to clean out the canal leading to the ditches.[5] About a month later word came that Major Babcock had resigned.[6] In his place, as superintendent, Lieutenant J. K. F. Mansfield was sent to Cockspur. He was a man four years Lee's senior, had graduated No. 2 in the class of 1822, and already had to his credit some solid service in the construction of Fort Hamilton, New York harbor. The assignment of Mansfield to Cockspur Island was almost in the nature of a life-sentence, for he continued in charge, with temporary duty on various other engineering projects, until 1846.[7]

Young Mansfield was a pleasant companion, but, of course, he could not enliven Cockspur Island. So, as often as he could, Lee

[3] See *infra*, Volume II, p. 461.
[4] Lee to Gratiot, Nov. 11, 1830; *Eng. MSS.*, 186; *R. E. Lee, Jr.* (2d. ed.), 447–48.
[5] Lee to Gratiot, Dec. 1, 1830; *Eng. MSS.*, 188; *R. E. Lee, Jr.* (2d ed.), 448.
[6] Doubtless because of ill-health; he died June 26, 1831 (1 *Cullum*, 81).
[7] 1 *Cullum*, 276.

slipped up the river to Savannah and enjoyed the gay company of his friends. The family of Isaac Minis gave him cordial welcome, made the more delightful by the presence of two daughters, Sarah and Phillipa.[8] Jack Mackay had been sent to a post in Alabama,[9] and, needless to say, was greatly missed, but the fine old house on Broughton Street[10] was hardly less attractive on that account. Margaret Mackay, as charming as her name, had married Ralph E. Elliot, but there remained Catherine and Eliza. And Eliza was captivating, so captivating that the young lieutenant from Cockspur found some consolation in her presence for his long separation from the blonde girl at Arlington.

Joseph Mansfield had not long been on duty when he concluded that the original plan was not adapted to the site and that a new design would have to be prepared.[11] Captain Delafield was summoned as consultant on the changes and arrived in April, 1831.[12] Before that date, however, it was apparent that the work would have virtually to be suspended for a season. This, of course, would involve the partial idleness of Lee, and that was no light matter to the bureau. The Corps of Engineers then had more contracts at other locations than the limited personnel could supervise. Although the chief engineer had often appealed for the enlargement of his force, Congress had failed to act, and the different enterprises had been divided, as far as practicable, among the officers. In only four instances did the supervising engineer have another officer of the corps as his assistant. On the other projects the assistants were civilians.[13] In these circumstances, needless to say, a lieutenant could not be kept unemployed at Cockspur Island. Lee had been expecting an assignment to Old Point, Va.,[14] and sometime before April 13, he received orders directing him to proceed thither.[15] He would have been altogether delighted but

[8] Later, respectively, Mrs. Isaac Hayes of Philadelphia and Mrs. Edward Etting of the same city (Letter of J. F. Minis to the writer, Sept. 30, 1930).

[9] 1 Cullum, 425.

[10] Between Abercorn and Lincoln Streets (May Wood Cain in Savannah Press, Jan. 19, 1929, copy of which was kindly supplied by Oliver Orr, Esq., of Macon).

[11] Rept. Chf. Eng. Army, 1830–31; Ex. Docs., 1st sess., 22d Cong., vol. 1, p. 77.

[12] R. E. Lee to Eliza A. Mackay. MS., "Wednesday, 13," but, by the internal evidence, dated April 13, 1831, graciously loaned the writer by Mrs. Frank Screven of Savannah, Ga.

[13] Rept. Chf. Eng. Army, 1830–31, loc. cit., 89.

[14] Charles Gratiot to J. K. F. Mansfield, MS., March 26, 1831; MS. U. S. War Dept.

[15] Lee to Eliza A. Mackay, loc. cit.

for the prospect of separation from the friends in Broughton Street. He was not in love with Eliza Mackay and she had suitors enough and to spare; but he was much her cavalier and perhaps he flirted a bit with her. When no letters came from her, he professed himself afflicted.[16] When he should go away . . . well, he gallantly and teasingly wrote of her missives, "I don't know what I shall do for them at Old Point. But you will send me some sometimes, will you not, Sweet ——? How I shall besiege the P. Office." [17] He was sorry that he might be denied a farewell to the family, which at the time was visiting near Beaufort, S. C. "Perhaps," he wrote Eliza, "Owing to Capt. D[elafield]'s arrival I shall be obliged to stay longer. Perhaps I can get to Beaufort. Perhaps your two weeks will be *out* next Tuesday. Perhaps I shall be taken sick." [18] But no desired malady added to his jest. His moving orders were acknowledged on April 21,[19] and he had to say *au revoir*. He remained for the whole of his life a close friend of the Mackays and their children. Mansfield he was to meet again on numerous occasions and, at the last, was to face him at Sharpsburg, where Mansfield fell at the head of his corps of infantry, attempting to storm Lee's position.

When Lee reported at Hampton Roads on May 7, 1831,[20] much of the labor on Fort Monroe itself had been completed, and the place was occupied by a garrison, but the outworks and the approaches had not been constructed. His was the necessary but uninspiring task of computing costs, ordering supplies, and directing men in hauling earth, in grading, and in excavating the ditch that was to surround the fort. A little later he had to supervise the masons who erected a wall on the outer side, or counterscarp, of the ditch, which was exposed to the tide from the nearby waters of Mill Creek.[21]

Out in Hampton Roads, less than a mile offshore from Old Point, was Fort Calhoun, later known as Fort Wool. This work had been started on rip-raps, or stones placed in deep waters to serve as a foundation. The walls were rising to the level of the

---

[16] Lee to Eliza A. Mackay, *loc. cit.*: "It did grieve me to see the Boats coming down, one after another, without any of the *little comforts* which are now so *necessary* to me."
[17] *Ibid.*   [18] *Ibid.*
[19] Mansfield to Gratiot, *MS.*, April 21, 1831, *U. S. War Dept.*
[20] Andrew Talcott to Gratiot, *MS.*, May 11, 1831, *U. S. War Dept.*
[21] See the report on Fort Monroe in the *Rept. Chief Eng. Army, 1830–31; Ex. Docs., 1st sess., 22d Cong.*, vol. 1, p. 76.

second battery not long after Lee's arrival, but there was a dangerous subsidence, which showed the futility of immediate attempts to build higher. Thereafter, and for the whole of Lee's stay in Hampton Roads, when any work at all was done at Fort Calhoun, it was that of unloading and distributing stone, so as to bring to bear on the foundations as great a weight as they would have to carry when the walls were completed.[22]

Life at Fort Monroe, from the very outset, was mixed pleasure and controversy. The commander of the fort was Brevet-Colonel Abram Eustis, who was then forty-four, a native Virginian, well-schooled at Harvard. He and the engineers were not friendly. Lee's immediate superior was Captain Andrew Talcott, who was in charge of the construction at both forts. Talcott was a native of Connecticut, ten years older than Lee,[23] and had graduated No. 2 in the class of 1818 at West Point. Nearly the whole of his professional career, up to the time Lee joined him, had been spent in building fortifications. He was capable, careful, and considerate of his subordinate, and he speedily won the fullest respect of his new assistant.

The year after Lee came to Fort Monroe,[24] Talcott married Harriet Randolph Hackley, a lovely Virginia girl of high blood, with a fine coloring, brown eyes, a graceful figure, and a manner of much attractiveness. Her picture in oils, by Thomas Sully, is one of the finest of early American portraits. Lee, who was only three years her senior, admired Mrs. Talcott most extravagantly, both for herself and also because she was a cousin of the young mistress of Arlington. He played faithful courtier to her, with much gaiety and jest.[25] The Talcotts continued to be Lee's closest friends at Fort Monroe and they brightened the life of the post for him.

There were, in addition, thirty-one artillery officers on the station, for Fort Monroe was the Artillery School of the army, and at that time had six companies of gunners in garrison.[26]

[22] *Rept. Chief Eng. Army, 1830–31, op. cit.,* vol. 1, p. 77.
[23] Born April 22, 1797. [24] April, 1832, according to the Talcott genealogy.
[25] She was born June 26, 1810. Her mother, Harriet Randolph (1783–1859) who married Richard S. Hackley, was the twelfth child of Thomas Mann Randolph of Tuckahoe (1741–93). His wife was Anne Cary (1745–89). Thomas Mann Randolph of Tuckahoe was the great-grandson of William Randolph of Turkey Island. Thanks are due Miss Harriet Talcott of Richmond for this information.
[26] *Rept. Adjt. Genl. Army, 1829–30; Ex. Docs., 2d sess., 21st Congress,* vol. 1, pp. 55, 89.

Among these officers, Lee found three of the men with whom he had been at West Point—John Kennedy of his own class, Dick Tilghman of the class of 1828, and James H. Prentiss, who had graduated the year after Lee had left. With these he was on easy terms, and with the others he quickly had *camaraderie.* His social charm, his abounding physical cheer, and his consideration of others made this easy. It was noticed that he never had anything disparaging to say of his fellow-officers, a habit that was as attractive as it was unusual among soldiers who had overmuch leisure.[27]

Already Lieutenant Lee was a devotee of military promptness. If he must lay siege to a heart, he would do it with as little delay as he would countenance in investing a city. So, very soon after he returned from Georgia, and perhaps before he reported for duty at Fort Monroe, he took steamer up the Potomac to visit Miss Custis, who was much more interested in him than a young lady of her generation in Virginia would ever let a gentleman know. Mrs. Custis watched with sympathy, though the master of Arlington still frowned. One day soon after his arrival, he was in the hall of Arlington house, reading aloud to Mary and to Mrs. Custis from a new novel of Sir Walter Scott's. The interest of the narrative and of the audience was such that Robert kept on until his weariness must have been apparent to Mrs. Custis.

"Mary," she said, at a pause in the reading, "Robert must be tired and hungry; go into the dining-room and get him some lunch."

Miss Custis obediently rose, and Robert, excusing himself, followed her. At the sideboard, she stooped to get her guest a piece of fruit cake. Robert leaned forward too, and then and there the question was put and answered.[28] If he ate his fruit cake, it was with a happy heart.

Mr. Custis reluctantly gave his consent to a marriage his daughter was old enough to contract on her own account. The nuptials were set for June 30, and the place, of course, was to be Arlington, with bridesmaids and groomsmen in a number becoming so important an event. Robert was to get a furlough for as long a time

[27] Statement of James Eveleth, clerk at Fort Monroe, quoted in *Long,* 35.
[28] Sally Nelson Robins, quoting the family tradition, in *Brock,* 323. It is impossible to fix the date of the proposal with certainty.

as he could, and when the festivities were over and the furlough had expired, the two were to live at Fort Monroe—live on his pay, as other young couples did, without any help from Mr. Custis. Mary was determined on that.

There followed many gay preparations, not least of which was Mary's choice of six bridesmaids, among her cousins. Robert called upon a corresponding number of his friends, to support him in the hour when the bravest man trembles. The desired furlough was procured through the friendly help of Captain Talcott. Arlington, which usually wore a somewhat neglected look, was put in order for the great day. The attendants arrived early and, of course, were all housed at the bride's home. Catharine Mason, a neighborhood friend of Mary's since childhood, was the counterpart of the present-day maid of honor, though a more courteous age gave equal honor to all. Her escort, Robert's best man, was naturally his brother Smith, who was almost as handsome as Robert and of fine, cordial manners. Next was Mary Goldsborough, a cousin of the bride's on the Custis side. With her stood Lieutenant John P. Kennedy, Robert's classmate and now a lieutenant of the 1st Artillery, stationed at Old Point. Miss Marietta Turner had as her cavalier, Lieutenant James A. Chambers, somewhat older than the rest of the bridal party, and a friend of Robert's days at Cockspur Island. Miss Angela Lewis, still another cousin of the Custis stock, was entrusted to Lieutenant Richard Tilghman, familiarly "Dick" to all West Pointers and to all the officers at Fort Monroe. Miss Julia Calvert, who was of the Lord Baltimore stock of G. W. P. Custis's mother, was in the chivalrous care of Lieutenant James H. Prentiss, who had come up with the others from Old Point to hearten his comrade. The other bridesmaid was Mary's cousin, Britannia Peter, of Georgetown across the Potomac—a kinswoman who was to prove her love and loyalty to the Lees at a time when the very name of Arlington connoted woe. Her gallant was Thomas Turner, cousin of the groom's on his mother's side.[29]

While the guests were assembling on June 30, 1831, a heavy downpour of rain swept over the country around Arlington.

[29] This list has been reconstructed from that given originally by Long (*op. cit.*, p. 32) and copied by other biographers. The internal evidence suggests that the list probably was supplied from memory by Mrs. Lee, late in life, for the names of all the girls are

Through it, at length, Reverend Reuel Keith, the officiating clergyman,[30] arrived on horseback, drenched and dripping, in no condition assuredly to stand on the floor of the drawing-room at Arlington, amid young officers in full-dress uniform, much less in the presence of young women apparelled in all the glory of two states, and of the District of Columbia, besides. There was nothing to do except to provide Mr. Keith with dry clothes. But whose could they be? The soldiers had only their uniforms; Mr. Custis was the sole civilian on the place with an extra pair of breeches available. And Mr. Custis was short and of unequal proportions, whereas the reverend gentleman was as tall as a grenadier and as thin as an anchorite. Into Mr. Custis's clothes, however, the clergyman had to step, to the high amusement of those who aided him in effecting the change. The other guests were cheated of the sight of an angular parson in the garb of a small aristocrat, because when Mr. Keith put on a cassock and surplice, they hid the folds and concealed the shortness of his garments.[31]

All was ready. The bridal party marched into the drawing-room, which is the chamber on the right as one enters Arlington from the portico. Mary was nervous; Robert was pale but noted mentally that he was not so excited as he thought he should have been. He felt very much as if he were at the blackboard at West Point waiting to recite a problem. The minister, Lee confided later to his friend Captain Talcott, "had few words to say, though he dwelt upon them as if he had been reading my Death warrant, and there was a tremulousness in the hand I held that made me anxious for him to end." [32]

given with precision, while those of the groomsmen are vague or incorrect. There was no "Lieutenant Thomas Kennedy" in the army at that time, but as Lee's classmate John P. Kennedy (1 *Cullum*, 429) was then at Fort Monroe, he is almost certainly the man. "Lt. Chambers" could hardly have been any one else than the James A. Chambers (1 *Cullum*, 250), who was at Savannah while Lee was working at Cockspur Island. "Mr. Tillman" may be identified with less certainty as Lieutenant Dick Tilghman (1 *Cullum*, 406). "Lieutenant Turner" of Long's list is shown in Mrs. M. M. Andrews' *Scraps of Paper*, 202–3, to have borne the given name of Thomas. He belonged to the navy (Avery Craven, ed.: *To Markie, the Letters of Robert E. Lee to Martha Custis Williams*, cited hereafter as *Markie Letters*, p. 38).

[30] Mr. Keith had come to Alexandria in 1823 as principal of the newly established Episcopal Theological Seminary and for several years was rector of Christ Church as well.
[31] *Long*, 32; *Packard*, 157, Mrs. M. M. Andrews, *op. cit.*, 202–3.
[32] R. E. Lee to Andrew Talcott, *MS.*, July 13, 1831 (*Talcott MSS.* (F)), printed in full in Freeman: "Lee and the Ladies," *Scribner's Magazine*, Oct., 1925, pp. 342–43. The

The wedding party remained at Arlington in festivity and merriment[33] until the following Tuesday, July 5, when the young officers, their leaves ending or their endurance failing, were forced to say good-bye. Some of the bridesmaids, being of more durable social fibre, lingered until the end of the week. Then the young lovers were left alone for a day or two, with no company save that of Mr. and Mrs. Custis. But it was not for long. Robert rode over to Washington on Monday, July 11, got all the news of the engineering office, and on his way probably stopped at Alexandria, in order to make some purchases for the quarters at Fortress Monroe. The next day, or the day after, he and his bride, accompanied by Mrs. Custis, went to Ravensworth, on the first leg of a journey to visit Randolph and Lewis kin in Fauquier and Loudoun Counties.

As he appeared on his honeymoon, Robert was blissfully happy, and seemed already to bear unconsciously the air of a man destined to achievement. "I looked up," a cousin wrote of his appearance that fall, "and my eye fell upon his face in perfect repose, and the thought at once flashed through my mind: 'You certainly look more like a great man than any one I have ever seen.' "[34] In love and merriment, with much jest and teasing, the days ran rapidly on, but he did not forget his duties at Fort Monroe. He was to return early in August, and to the letter which he wrote Captain Talcott about the wedding he added this postscript: "They are talking around me at such a rate that I hardly know what I have written and despair of reading it. But please send the boat out for me, the first trip the [steamboat] P[otomac] makes in August."[35]

Lee's marriage to Mary Custis was one of the major influences that shaped his career. Although she was not often able to travel

---

Talcott papers, cited hereafter as *Talcott MSS.*, are divided into two approximately equal parts. One part belongs to the Virginia Historical Society; the other is the property of the writer, to whom it was graciously presented by Mr. and Mrs. John Stewart Bryan. For convenience of reference, those Talcott letters belonging to the society are designated as "(*VHS*)" and those of the writer "(*F*)."

[33] The printed notice of Lee's marriage read simply: "Married, June 30, 1831, at Arlington House, by the Reverend Mr. Keith, Lieutenant Robert E. Lee, of the United States Corps of Engineers, to Miss Mary A. R. Custis, only daughter of G. W. P. Custis, Esq." (*Fitz Lee*, 26).

[34] Quoted in *Long*, 30; Mrs. M. M. Andrews, *op. cit.*, 199.

[35] Lee to Talcott, *MS.*, July 13, 1831, *Talcott MSS.* (*F*). The vessel is identified by a reference in a later letter from Lee to Talcott.

far or to share the hardships of an engineer's life on a frontier
project, she bore him seven children in fourteen years. Ahead of
her lay invalidism more nearly complete and more pitiful than
that of Lee's mother. Like her father she was careless in her
personal apparel to the point of untidiness, until, late in life, she
found a maid who took pride in dressing her attractively. Rising
from one illness she found her hair in such a tangle that she im-
pulsively took the scissors and cut it off. Her domestic management was complimented when it was termed no worse than
negligent. In her engagements she was forgetful and habitually
late,[36] an aggravating contrast to the minute-promptness of her
husband. Once when her husband was expecting guests, a few
years after their marriage, he apologized frankly in advance. "Tell
the ladies," he wrote, "that they are aware that Mrs. L. is somewhat addicted to laziness and forgetfulness in her Housekeeping.
But they may be certain she does her best, Or in her Mother's
words 'The Spirit is willing but the flesh is weak.' "[37]

Despite these early shortcomings and later a nervous whimsi-
cality that sometimes puzzled him, she held the love of Robert
Lee through life. His fondness for the company of pretty women,
which was always strong, never led him away from her or involved him in any sort of scandal. Ministering, rather than
ministered unto, his first thought always was of her. She accepted
this as her due from "Mr. Lee" as she called him, and even after
the War between the States, when he was a demigod in the eyes
of the South, she ordered him about. Yet rarely was a woman
more fully a part of her husband's life. This, fundamentally, was
because of his simplicity and her fineness of spirit. She was interested in people and in their happiness. A keen, if uncritical,
interest in public affairs she retained all her days, nor did she
hesitate to differ from Lee and to voice a fiery opinion in plain-
spoken terms, when his sense of justice and his reserve alike
disposed him to say little. She loved wildflowers and old gardens
and evening skies. Religion she had, of the same sort as that
which her husband developed. They talked to each other of
religion as neither talked on that subject to others, and she kept

[36] *R. E. Lee, Jr.*, 11.   [37] Lee to Talcott, April 10, 1834; *Talcott MSS.* (F).

her faith in the triumph of the things in which she believed. A certain quick and understanding sympathy was shown in her kindling eye and ready smile. Her alertness made friends and brought admiring attention. She was wholly without personal ambition, beyond that of sharing in the experiences and confidences of her friends.

Although she was never awed by his presence, she had for his character a respect that became in time a positive reverence. It is futile to speculate on whether she ever shared what some are fond of terming "the inmost secrets of a great man's heart." He had no such secrets, for in age as in youth he was always objective in mind. Loving her, he saw her best qualities, not her worst. Next after binding him to her in deepest spiritual love, perhaps her greatest influence on him was that she strengthened his self-control, because, as her health became impaired, she required much care at his hands. They needed all the love and all the faith and all the self-mastery they could develop, for they were to endure more of tragedy than is measured out to most mortals. It was fortunate they could not see ahead in that dreamy summer of 1831, when there were kisses and confidences and the happy freedom of youth.

When Lee married Mary Custis, he married Arlington as well, and that, too, was to have a profound influence upon him. The estate was to bring much harassment of spirit, but it was to deepen his reverence for the Washington tradition. Mr. Custis himself was, of course, the nearest link with the first President. Many of the Washington relics were at Arlington—the portraits, the lantern from the hall of Mount Vernon, the china presented by the Society of the Cincinnati, which probably had been ordered by Lee's own father, Washington's bookcase, his camp equipment, even some of the clothes he had worn, and the bed on which he had died.[38] Mrs. Washington's Negro maid, Caroline Branham, who had been in the room on the December night when the great spirit of the nation's founder had passed, was among the servants at Arlington at the time of Mary Custis's wedding.[39] To come into the atmosphere of Arlington was to Robert Lee almost like

[38] *Mason*, 28–29.   [39] *Mrs. Powell*, 244.

living in the presence of his foremost hero, his father's old com
mander. "This marriage," wrote a kinsman-biographer, "in the
eyes of the world, made Robert Lee the representative of the
family of the founder of American liberty." [40]

[40] Edward Lee Childe: *The Life and Campaigns of Gen. Lee . . . Translated from
the French . . . by George Litting . . .* (cited hereafter as *Childe*), p. 24.

CHAPTER VII

The Ancient War of Staff and Line

EARLY in August, 1831, and doubtless on the "first boat," as promised, Lee and his wife reached Fort Monroe. Their plain quarters in the fort had been set in order by the friendly Talcott. The furnishings were simple, with no feather beds or luxuries, for Mrs. Lee brought with her no independent fortune and accepted no financial help from her father.

Within a few weeks of their arrival at Old Point occurred the most exciting incident of their three years' residence there. On August 23, Colonel Abram Eustis, the commanding officer of the fort, received word from the mayor of Norfolk that a menacing insurrection of slaves had broken out in Southampton County, forty miles from the city, and that the Negroes had procured arms and were mustering in large numbers. Help was needed. Eustis at once prepared three of his five companies of artillery for the field. The warships *Warren* and *Natchez*, then in Hampton Roads, also supplied detachments. Setting out the next morning, and using water transportation for a part of the distance, the force was able to cover sixty miles in twenty-four hours. It found, most fortunately, that the rising had been put down and that the Negroes had been scattered.[1] Nearly sixty white people, however, had been slain.

As a staff officer, Lee did not go to Southampton, but he was, of course, profoundly concerned over the outburst, and believed, on the basis of what he heard, that only the Negroes' misunderstanding of the date of the rising prevented "much mischief." He wrote Mrs. Custis: "It is ascertained that they used their religious assemblies, which ought to have been devoted to better purposes, for forming and maturing their plans, and that their preachers

---

[1] *Report of the Major-General of the Army, 1830–31; Ex. Docs., 1st sess., 22d Cong.,* vol. 1, p. 55. Nat Turner, the Negro who inspired the rising, was not captured until Oct. 30 (W. S. Drewry: *The Southampton Insurrection*, 91).

were the leading men. . . . The whole number of blacks taken and killed did not amount to the number of whites murdered by them." [2]

The insurrection had a thousand repercussions. Apprehension spread throughout the South. In Richmond the concern was so acute that Major Worth, Lee's old commandant at West Point, who was then in garrison at Fort Monroe, was sent on a special journey to Bellona Arsenal to see that the arms stored there were secure against seizure.[3] At Old Point, as a measure of precaution, Colonel Eustis put into effect a series of regulations for the exclusion of Negroes from the post. This greatly embarrassed the engineers and increased the long-developing friction that was to lead to a "post war" between them and the colonel.[4] The temper of some of the Negroes in the tidewater section of Virginia was considered so menacing that five additional companies of artillery, three of the 3d Regiment and two of the 4th, were brought to Fort Monroe and put on duty. This gave the fort a garrison of 680 men, no small part of the army of the United States.[5]

The troops were not needed to suppress any further insurrection, but the presence of their officers added to the social life of the fort. To none was their advent more welcome than to Lee, for among the lieutenants who came with the artillery was his companion of West Point days, Joseph E. Johnston. The two took up where they had left off at the academy and seemingly were having a joyous time when their fellowship was interrupted by the Christmas holidays. The Lees went up the James River, probably to visit the Carters of Shirley, and then journeyed to Arlington via Baltimore, where they spent some snowy days with Mrs. Marshall. Soon after they got to Arlington they received a belated invitation to the wedding of the fair Eliza Mackay to William H. Stiles, a Georgian of distinction. Lee sat down to write his good wishes and congratulations in a letter which was broken off

---

[2] Quoted *in extenso* in *Fitz Lee*, 27–28.

[3] Lee to Talcott, *MS.*, Sept. 14, 1831, *Talcott MSS.* (F). Bellona Arsenal was on the south side of James River, above Richmond.

[4] Eustis's order No. 101, Nov. 13, 1831; Lee to Eustis, Nov. 16, 1831; Lee to Gratiot, Nov. 16, 1831, *Eng. MSS.*, 221; Gratiot to Lee, Nov. 18, 1831, *MS. Letters to Officers of Engineers*, vol. 4, p. 225.

[5] *Report of the Sec. of War, 1830–31, Ex. Docs., 1st sess., 22d Congress*. vol. 1, pp. 55, 66, 67.

more than once by the comings and goings of guests. He began the letter on her wedding day:

"How I should like to say 'Mr. and Mrs. Lee have the honour to accept Mrs. Mackay's kind invitation for Wednesday night.' But this cannot be Miss Eliza (My Sweetheart) because it only arrived here last night, by this token that I have been in tears ever since at the thought of losing you. Oh Me! Gilderoy you are a lucky fellow to have got so bright a New Year's gift this January 1832. Why Man, it is better for you than the gift of life. . . .

"But Miss E. how do you feel about this time? Say 12 o'clock of the day, as you see the shadows commence to fall towards the East and know that at *last* the sun will set? Though you may not be frightened I 'spect you are most marvellously alarmed. . . . Well I do wish I could be there. It would do me so much good to be with you all again and see you so happy. I wonder it has never entered the dull heads of Congress that I ought to be there and that they ought to make special provision for the occasion. But the wretches take no care of 'us youth.' And through their negligence you are deprived of my presence and I of your sweet company. If I could but drop in this morning and tell you what a powerful fine thing it is to stand up before the Parson with all eyes bent on you (except one pair) he mournful and solemn as if he were reading your funeral service. A man feels of so much, and I am sure, he could not add to the stillness of the scene though he were dead. Would not this revive you Miss E."

When he picked up the letter four days later, he was in the same merry mood.

". . . And how did you disport yourself My child? Did you go off well, like a torpedo cracker on Christmas morning. . . . Oh Mercy Are you really married Mrs. Stiles. The idea of it is as great a damper to a man's spirit as that of the cholera. But it must feel mighty funny to you. And I suppose you are so busy that you will not have time to read this scrawl so I must think about bringing it to an end. . . ."

After which he trailed off into chatter about mutual acquaintances in the army. Mrs. Lee added her congratulations in a
postscript that presents most charmingly the contrast between her
temperament and Lee's:

"You see what a small space is left me my dear Miss Eliza to
offer my congratulations and to wish that your pathway in life
may be as bright as our beneficent Creator and Father sees best
for you. I still indulge a hope, though it may seem a vain one,
that we may one day meet with a friend to us both so dear. I am
now a wanderer on the face of the earth and know not where we
are going next and hope it will be East. I suppose you remain in
Savannah near your Mother? What happiness! I am with mine
now—the past and the future disregarded. I offer my love and
congratulations to you and the family on the late joyous occasion.
We should have been delighted to participate in it—So farewell
Your sincere and Affectionate
M. LEE."[6]

Apparently Mrs. Lee remained at Arlington after the Christmas
holidays, and Lee went back to Old Point. He and Joe Johnston
had a merry season. Johnston, still "The Colonel" to his intimates, was impregnable in his self-discipline. Lee neither drank
nor swore nor gambled. But if the pair walked not in the counsel
of the ungodly, they had no compunctions about standing in the
way of sinners, at least to see what the sinners were doing. When
good man Eustis was safe behind the door of his quarters, quiet
for the night, Lee and Johnston would prowl about, visiting the
just and the unjust, with observant eye. On one call they found
a friend, as Lee wrote Jack Mackay, "in the middle of the floor,
trying to get off his uniform. We had to assist his lendings, or
Borrowings rather, for there was nothing his own but his pants,
and he had slept in the Colo's uniform."

There was no reproach in this, no shocked sensibilities. It was
always so with Lee in his youth. He did not share in the excesses
of his comrades but he did not wear a sombre face. When hard
duty was given them, Lee shared their distress and understood

[6] R. E. and Mary C. Lee to Mrs. E. A. Stiles, *MS.*, Jan. 4, 1832, a copy of which Mrs.
Frank Screven has kindly given the writer.

how they might seek solace in their cups. "The poor devils of Subs," Lee confided to Mackay, "are drilled off their feet." This may have been the reason that one of the young officers kept as "his constant companion . . . that phial of Texas whiskey, hermetically sealed to celebrate his meeting with Dick T[ilghman] whenever that should take place." As for Tilghman himself, companion of West Point, he "left yesterday for Baltimore, cursing the whole concern."[7] Subsequently, Lee had to report that Johnston "from occasionally acompanying me over the river, is in some danger of being caught by a pair of black eyes."[8]

Mrs. Lee returned with milder weather; the nightly visitation of quarters by the engineer and the artillerist became less frequent; the scare of a slave rebellion subsided; most of the officers slipped back into the leisurely routine of life at an army post. But for Lee and his brothers, there opened a new and a strange warfare, a warfare that brought all the sons of "Light-Horse Harry" closer together. Even the exiled and disgraced "Black-Horse Harry" emerged from the shadows as a defender of the family name.

The circumstances were odd: Except for one period of wavering, "Light-Horse Harry" Lee had been consistently opposed to Jeffersonian ideas. Charles Lee, his brother, had been Attorney General under Washington, and of counsel in the famous case of Marbury *vs.* Madison. The whole politics of the family was anti-Jefferson, though Jefferson was their distant kinsman through the Randolphs.[9] Because of Henry Lee's part in procuring from his pen a statement regarding the character of a lady to whom Jefferson was alleged to have made improper advances, the Lees had long felt a certain contempt for the third President.[10] There had been no open hostilities, however, until the appearance in 1829 of T. J. Randolph's four-volume edition of Jefferson's correspondence.[11] This contained two unpleasant references to "Light-

---

[7] Lee to Mackay, MS., Nov. 3, 1831; *Elliott MSS.; Long,* 35, quoting Lee's clerk; B. T. Johnson's *Joseph E. Johnston,* 7.

[8] Lee to Mackay, MS., Feb. 18, 1833; *Elliott MSS.*

[9] Emory Speer: *Lincoln, Lee, Grant,* 47.

[10] Henry Lee to Thomas Jefferson, MS., Sept. 8, 1806; Colonel —— to Henry Lee, MS., n. d., 1805, Library of Congress.

[11] *Memoir, Correspondence, and Miscellanies, from the Papers of Thomas Jefferson.* edited by Thomas Jefferson Randolph; Charlottesville, Va., 1829.

Horse Harry." One was the statement in a letter of 1815 from Jefferson to Monroe, asserting that although the legislature of Virginia had absolved Jefferson of all blame for the seizure of public arms by the British at Richmond in January, 1781, "Gen. Lee has put all these imputations among the romances of his historical novel,"—Lee's *Memoirs of the War in the Southern Department*—"for the amusement of credulous and uninquisitive readers."[12] The other reference was in a letter to Washington, written at the time of the neutrality agitation. In this Jefferson branded Lee for repeating to Washington a tale that Jefferson had insinuated Washington was under British influence. It was, said he, "The slander of an intriguer, dirtily employed in sifting the conversations of my table, where alone he could hear of me; and seeking to atone for sins against another who had never done him any other injury than that of declining his confidence." Lee, the talebearer, he concluded, was a "miserable tergiversator, who ought indeed to have been of more truth, or less trusted by his country."[13]

These references greatly incensed the Lees. The younger Henry had been at Monticello, at the invitation of its master, only three days before Jefferson's death, to examine papers which Jefferson held were absolution of any charge of mismanagement of Virginia's affairs in 1781,[14] and now Henry Lee took up the charges in his exile and wrote a tedious but terrific indictment of Jefferson under the title *Observations on the Writings of Thomas Jefferson, With Particular Reference to the Attack They Contain on the Memory of the Late General Henry Lee.*[15] This appeared in 1832.

The thesis of the book was that Jefferson had been guilty of the duplicity that Lee had charged against him. The conduct of the two men during and after the Revolution was compared, in an effort to show how much better Lee had behaved than Jefferson. The author attempted to prove that Jefferson had maligned others

[12] Jefferson to James Monroe, Jan. 1, 1815; 17 *Jefferson* (Memorial edition), 11; Randolph edition, 4, 246.
[13] Thomas Jefferson to George Washington, June 19, 1796; H. Lee's *Observations* (2d ed.), p. 6; Randolph editions, *supra*, 3, 330–32.
[14] Henry Lee to Andrew Jackson, July 1, 1826; J. S. Bassett; *Correspondence of Andrew Jackson*, 3, 305.
[15] There is no copy of the first edition of this in the Library of Congress, but there is one at Harvard and another in the New York Public Library.

—Washington, Hamilton, Knox, Marshall, and Jay—as he had maligned Lee. It was a savage, bitter, and wordy book, but it showed the intensity of the family's devotion to the memory of "Light-Horse Harry." In reaction, Lee and his brothers became more confirmed in their opposition to the party of Jefferson. By inheritance, Robert Lee was a Federalist; by circumstance he became a Whig, wholly out of sympathy with the party that controlled the government during the greater part of his service in the United States army.[16] Carter Lee was as bitter against Jefferson as Henry was, and in 1839 he issued a second and even more elaborate edition of the *Observations,* with new criticism of his father's assailant.[17] The whole ran to 262 closely printed pages. Robert's temperament was not one to indulge in vendettas, and his name does not appear in the controversy, but he was as zealous as any of his brothers in upholding the public record of his father, and then, as always, he regarded his father as a hero who had fallen on misfortune.

Despite this affair, Robert Lee's spirits were high during most of 1832, and his new domestic life was most happy. Mrs. Lee was sick part of the time, and was often away, but she bore him a fine baby on September 16, 1832. The youngster was named George Washington Custis Lee, after his grandfather, and he throve despite childish ills.[18] Lee joked with the mother on occasion— "Mercy, what gets into women's heads"—[19] but he told Mackay, "I would not be unmarried for all you could offer me." [20] As for the baby, he confessed in due course, "Master Custis is the most darling boy in the world." [21]

Now that he was *pater familias,* the company of the wives of the officers at Old Point interested him vastly. "I am left to console them," he said of the women whose husbands were sent

[16] *Cf.* Cassius F. Lee to Robert E. Lee, *MS.,* Sept. 8, 1838: "I am sorry you Whigs did not do your duty better, but O, the love of treasury pap, be it gold or paper!" (*Lee MSS., VHS*).
[17] Philadelphia; Thomas Cowperthwait & Co.; Carey & Hart.
[18] Mrs. Lee was sick in September, 1831, and in March, 1834, and was away from Old Point in December, 1832, July, 1833, and November, 1833 (Lee to Talcott, *MS.,* Sept. 14, 1831, Dec. 6, 1832, July 3, 1833, Nov. 22, 1833, March 27, 1834; *Talcott MSS.* (*F and VHS*)). For the birth of Custis Lee, see *Brock,* 163, and *E. J. Lee,* 455; Lee to Talcott, *MS.,* July 2, 1834; *Talcott MSS* (*F*).
[19] Lee to Talcott, *MS.,* March 24, 1834; *Talcott MSS.* (*VHS*).
[20] Lee to Mackay, *MS.,* Feb. 3, 1834; *Elliott MSS.*
[21] Lee to Talcott, *MS.,* Nov. 1, 1834; *Talcott MSS.* (*VHS*).

South in the Seminole War, "and am in the right position to sympathize with them, as Mrs. Lee and her little limb are at Arlington." [22] And again, "As for the daughters of Eve in this country, they are formed in the very poetry of nature, and would make your lips water and fingers tingle. They are beginning to assemble to put their beautiful limbs into this salt water." [23] The news of expectancy and of birth found in him an amused and enthusiastic chronicler. "The population of the Point," he announced to Mackay, "has been increased by the little Huger boy, and I take it upon myself to predict the arrival of a small French." [24] The coming of a new Talcott baby drew from him congratulations and avowals—the first of numerous such messages that he was to send: "I was sincerely delighted yesterday to learn by your note, of the *magnificent* present offered you by Mrs. T. and had some thought of taking the Barge this morning and presenting my congratulations to Mrs. T. in person. Do offer them in my stead in the kindest manner. We have been waiting for the event to decide upon the sex of our next and now determine it shall be a girl in order to retain the connection in the family." [25] The joke was made the more pointed by the fact that the "next" was begotten soon thereafter and, sure enough, was a girl.

For the company he kept, Lee's inclination and his disciplined neatness disposed him to wear handsome, well-cut clothing. He got himself a dress-uniform coat, made by the fashionable tailor at the military academy, and he thriftily calculated the difference in cost between purchasing a new chapeau and buying new trimmings for his old one.[26] "We shall be a grand set of fellows with our gold and silver," he said, "and if I could only catch some of the grandiloquence of my neighbor Fabius [Whiting], I might hope to rise in the world." [27] It probably was about this time, or perhaps in 1831, that Lee sat for the first of his portraits. Reproduced in this volume, it shows him in the full-dress uniform of his corps, with the side-whisker that was the *dernier cri* of

[22] Lee to Mackey, *MS.*, Nov. 28, 1833; *Elliott MSS.*
[23] Lee to Mackay, *MS.*, June 26, 1834; *Elliott MSS.*   [24] *Ibid.*
[25] Lee to Talcott, *MS.*, March 1, 1834; *Talcott MSS.* (*F*).
[26] Lee to Talcott, *MS.*, Dec. 6, 1832; *Talcott MSS.* (*VHS*); Lee to Talcott, *MS.*, May 23, 1834; *Talcott MSS.* (*F*).
[27] Lee to Talcott, *MS.*, May 23, 1834; *Talcott MSS.* (*F*).

fashion.[28] Then, as in later life, he preferred the company of women to that of men, but even when Talcott was away from Old Point, Lee had a number of able men besides Johnston with whom to consort. Benjamin Huger, West Pointer of 1824, James Barnes of his own class, Robert Parrott, who had been an assistant professor while Lee was at the academy, and Albert E. Church of the class of 1828, all of them brilliant, were at Old Point during Lee's service there.[29] So was Doctor Robert Archer, who had been on the board of visitors in the year of Lee's graduation. These friends sufficed. Beyond the social life of the fort, Lee had little diversion at Old Point and seemingly craved none. He kept up a rather extensive correspondence,[30] he played some chess,[31] and, for the first time, became interested in his Lee ancestry and coat of arms.[32]

In the better mastery of his profession, these years were a busy and a most important period with Lee. He came as an assistant of limited experience; he was to leave fully qualified to direct a large engineering project. Talcott was absent on other duty for part of the building season of 1832, and for virtually all the seasons of 1833 and 1834. The daily burden of the work rested on Lee. At Fort Monroe the counterscarp wall was finished, the scarp wall was pointed, and a considerable part of the casemated covert-way was arched by August, 1832, when cholera broke out and forced Talcott, who was then on duty, to suspend operations. Slave owners became alarmed for the safety of their servants and would not hire them in adequate numbers.[33] The arches, however, were finished before the season ended.[34] Labor continued scarce during 1833, despite an increase of 15 per cent in wages. Some painting and a good deal of carpenter work was done, but

---

[28] This portrait, attributed to Benj. West, Jr., was the property of General Custis Lee after his mother's death. It was long at Washington and Lee University and subsequently passed into the hands of the widow of Colonel Robert E. Lee, son of General W. H. F. Lee.

[29] Lee to Talcott, *MS.,* Oct. 21, 1833; *Talcott MSS.* (F).

[30] Lee's autograph began to change in 1833, especially when he wrote with a pencil. A letter to Talcott of Oct. 21, 1833, contains a pencilled postscript that shows almost the handwriting of the war period. Prior to that time, except for the letter "c" his autograph would hardly be recognized by those familiar with his chirography in the eighteen-sixties.

[31] Lee to Talcott, *MS.,* Oct. 21, Dec. 1, 1833; *Talcott MSS.* (F).

[32] Lee to Talcott, *MS.,* Dec. 1, 1833; *Talcott MSS.* (F).

[33] *Rept. Chief Eng. Army, 1831–32, Ex. Docs., 2d sess., 22d Cong.,* vol. 1, p. 86.

[34] Lee to Talcott, *MS.,* Dec. 6, 1832; *Talcott MSS.* (VHS).

progress was not so rapid as had been hoped.[35] It was nearly December before enough workers were at hand to resume labor on the ramparts, and thereafter they had to be laid off in a little more than two weeks because of the damage done by a heavy storm.[36]

At the beginning of the season of 1834 Lee left Arlington before the Potomac was opened and rode overland to Fort Monroe—"up to my ears in mud and alone."[37] He went to work as soon as he could assemble his force of laborers and, undeterred by another heavy storm that wrecked several vessels in Hampton Roads, he got an extensive season's programme under way.[38] When the project was nearing completion, uncertainty concerning further appropriations threatened to force a discharge of the laborers, but this was averted for the time. Very little work was undertaken at Fort Calhoun, despite President Jackson's desire to have it completed before the expiration of his term. The unobliging foundations continued to sink at the rate of three inches a year. All that could be done was to continue to pile up stone in the hope that the substratum would be so compressed that it would carry the weight of the walls.[39]

Lee bore these responsibilities heavily,[40] but he continued to learn. He did some designing of buildings, wharves, and fortifi-

---

[35] *Rept. Chief Eng. Army, 1832–33, Ex. Docs., 1st sess., 23d Cong.*, vol. 1, p. 32; Lee to Talcott, MS., March 27, 1833; *Talcott MSS. (VHS)*; Lee to Talcott, MS., Nov. 22, 1833; *Talcott MSS. (F)*.

[36] Lee to Talcott, MS., Dec. 1 and Dec. 16, 1833; *Talcott MSS. (F)*; Lee to Engineer's office, MS., Dec. 24, 1833; Eng. MSS., 332.

[37] Lee to Mackay, MS., Feb. 3, 1834; *Elliott MSS.*

[38] Lee to Talcott, MS., April 7, 1834; *Talcott MSS. (F)*. Two vessels carrying stone went on Hampton bar and one of them split open. Two ran aground near the mouth of Mill creek but were gotten off that night. One large schooner was lost at the head of the bar and a child, two women, and a man with a broken thigh were rescued while she was sinking.

[39] Lee to Engineer's office, MS., June 6, 1834, *Eng. MSS.*, 353, Gratiot to Lee, MS., June 9, 1834. *MS. Letters to Engineers*, vol. 5, p. 27; *Repts. Chief Eng. Army, 1831–32 to 1833–34, inclusive; Ex. Docs., 2d sess., 22d Cong.*, vol. 1, pp. 86–87; *Ibid., 1st sess., 23d Cong.*, vol. 1, p. 52; *Ibid., 2d sess., 23d Cong.*, vol. 1, p. 101. Jackson in the summer of 1833 visited the Rip-Raps, as Fort Calhoun was usually called, and not only said the fort must be finished in two years but also ordered changes in design. "The President," Lee wrote Talcott, "has played the Devil with the plan of Fort Calhoun" (Lee to Talcott, MS., Sept. 12, 1833; *Talcott MSS. (F)*).

[40] *Cf.* Lee to Talcott, MS., Feb. 25, 1834: "I shall be in a fever till the arrival of the lime" (*Talcott MSS. (F)*); *Cf.* also Lee to Talcott, MS., Dec. 16, 1833, following a very severe storm: "I will do all in my power to repair damages but you had better come down" (*Talcott MSS. (F)*). *Cf.*, further, Lee to Talcott, MS., Sept. 12, 1833: "The Engr. Dept. here is but so so, and I fear badly represented" (*Talcott MSS. (F)*).

cations;[41] he supervised the preparation of accounts and of monthly and annual reports;[42] he faced some of the problems of sanitation, with which the science of his day was quite unable to cope;[43] he had a large experience in estimating construction costs;[44] he acquired a further knowledge of the working of the commissary;[45] he was inducted into the mysteries of banking and departmental finance.[46] The art of dealing with labor he acquired so successfully that after an emergency in April, 1834, when all hands had been called out to build a barricade in a blinding blow of sand, hail, and rain, he had been able to say with pride, "I never saw men work better." [47] He learned, also, how to combine initiative with deference, and in nearly all his personal letters to Talcott there was a tactful line asking, if that officer thought him in error, to forward further instructions.[48] Most particularly did he shine in applying to public works the principles of economy he had been taught at home. He bargained closely for schooner hire, and was uneasy when he thought the vessels did not carry so much as they should.[49] His inspections of material were critical;[50] his disposition was to seek the most favorable time for awarding contracts. When additional stone was needed at Fort Monroe he figured he could take the rough hewings at Fort Calhoun and dress them for not much more than half what the material would cost elsewhere.[51]

[41] Lee to Gratiot, MS., Nov. 9, 1831, Eng. MSS., 220; Lee to Gratiot, MS., April 16, 1832, Eng. MSS., 242; Lee to Gratiot, MS., Nov. 20, 1832, Eng. MSS., 270.

[42] Lee to Engineer's office, MS., Oct. 19, 1832, Eng. MSS., 266; July 9, 1834, Ibid., 364; Lee to Gratiot, MS., Nov. 2, 1832, Ibid., 267; Lee to Engineer's office, MS., July 22, 1833; Ibid., 309; Lee to Engineer's office, MS., May 1, 1834, Ibid., 349; Lee to Engineer's office, MS., Sept. 8, 1834; Ibid., 376; Lee to Engineer's office, MS., Oct. 8, 1834, Ibid., 379.

[43] Lee to Engineer's office, MS., July 18, 1834, on standing water, Eng. MSS., 367.

[44] Lee to Engineer's office, MS., Nov. 23, 1832, Eng. MSS., 271; Lee to Engineer's office, MS., April 19, 1833, Ibid., 293; Lee to Engineer's office, MS., Aug. 19, 1833, Ibid., 314; Lee to Engineer's office, MS., Dec. 9, 1833, Ibid., 327; Lee to Engineer's office, MS., July 9, 1834, Ibid., 365; Lee to Engineer's office, MS., Oct. 3, 1834, Ibid., 378; Lee to Engineer's office, MS., Oct. 15, 1834, Ibid., 380.

[45] Lee to Engineer's office, MS., Dec. 6, 1832, Eng. MS., 272; Lee to Talcott, MS., Aug. 31, 1834, Talcott MSS. (VHS).

[46] Lee to Engineer's office, MS., Oct. 21, 1833, Eng. MSS., 323; Lee to Engineer's office, MS., July 9, 1834, Ibid., File 363; Engineer's office to Lee, MS., Sept. 13, 1834, Letters to officers of Engineers, vol. 5, p. 108; Engineer's office to Lee, MS., Oct. 9, 1834, Ibid., vol. 5, p. 124.

[47] Lee to Talcott, MS., April 7, 1834; Talcott MSS. (F).

[48] E.g., Lee to Talcott, MS., Aug. 2, 1833; Talcott MSS. (F).

[49] Lee to Talcott, MS., Oct. 21, 1833, April 9, 1834; Talcott MSS (F).

[50] Lee to Talcott, MS., Oct. 23, Nov. 22, 1833; Talcott MSS. (F).

[51] Lee to Talcott, MS., Dec. 4, 1833, Feb. 13, 1834; Talcott MSS. (F).

Lee liked the location of Fort Monroe[52] and the companionship of many of the officers, and he felt that he would not readily find another such chief as Talcott.[53] Vexations there were, however, some of them so galling that in 1833 he contemplated resignation from the army. "Know, my friend," he wrote Mackay, "that it is a situation full of pains, and one from which I shall modestly retire on the first fitting opportunity. . . . My opinion on these matters has been formed, from the little experience I have had of a Garrison life in time of peace, where I have seen minds formed for use and ornament, degenerate into sluggishness and inactivity, requiring the stimulus of brandy or cards to rouse them to action, and apparently a burden to the possessors and perhaps an injury to their companions."[54] The drinking in which some of the officers indulged in their idleness ceased to be taken as a matter of course and came to puzzle him. "He is a fine looking young man," he said of a lieutenant who had been arrested for being drunk on parade. "Graduated very well in 1832 and appears to be intelligent But his propensity, it is impossible for me to comprehend."[55] He kept up with politics, yet he wearied of its perpetual discussion: "Congress is doing nothing but hammering on the tariff and makes no mention of promoting modest merit in the persons of you and I."[56] And again: "There is nothing new here or in these parts. Nullification! Nullification!! Nullification!!!"[57] Besides all, promotion in the Engineers Corps was incredibly slow: it had been 1832 before he had passed from brevet to regular rank as second lieutenant.[58]

But all these things were less of a burden to him than the constant jealousies and conflicts of authority between the staff and

[52] "Fort Monroe is a post by no means to be despised" (Lee to Mackay, *MS.*, Feb. 27, 1834; *Elliott MSS.*).

[53] "As much as I like the *Location* of Old Point and as fond as I am of the company of some of the Offrs. and of some persons in the neighborhood and notwithstanding the great partiality I have for my comdg. Offr. (I mean no flattery) and my belief I shall not meet with such another. . . ." Lee to Talcott, *MS.*, June 4, 1834; *Talcott MSS.* (F).

[54] Lee to Mackay, *MS.*, Feb. 18, 1833; *Elliott MSS.*

[55] Lee to Talcott, *MS.*, Nov. 22, 1833; *Talcott MSS.* (F).

[56] Lee to Mackay, *MS.*, Jan. 23, 1833; *Elliott MSS.*

[57] Lee to Talcott, *MS.*, Dec. 7, 1832; *Talcott MSS.* (VHS). He referred to politics in his letter of Feb. 21, 1833, to Talcott (*Talcott MSS.* (F)), and in his letters of Feb. 27 and July 22 to Mackay; *Elliott MSS.*

[58] In the *Army Register* of 1832 (*American State Papers, Military Affairs*, 4, 833) he had been listed as brevet second lieutenant. His promotion to regular rank was announced in special order No. 62, A. G. O. (*War Dept. MS.*), July 19, 1832, to rank as of July 1, 1829, the date of his first commission.

the line, between the engineers on one side and, on the other, the commandant at Fort Monroe. The line officers disliked the large liberty the engineers had to make contracts and to disburse public funds. Following the clash with Colonel Eustis in 1831 over the orders for the exclusion of Negroes from the fort,[59] there had been several squabbles,[60] and in one instance a controversy of some seriousness over the discharge of Lee's principal overseer because of a quarrel with a captain at the post.[61] In this instance, junior officer though he was, Lee did not hesitate to express to headquarters his sympathy with the discharged man, who, he said, had been zealous and faithful in the discharge of his duties.[62] Lee's differences, however, were incidental to a continuing feud between Captain Talcott and the line. This quarrel was over the engineers' use of quarters within the fort, and, more hotly, over the direction by the engineers of the remaining work at Fort Monroe. Talcott thought the engineers should complete the whole enterprise. The officers of the garrison wished it finished by the troops and laborers at the fort.[63] Each side suspected the other of plotting against it.

Early in 1834 the Artillery School of Practice at Fort Monroe was broken up and its officers and batteries were ordered to different stations. The engineers regarded this as a victory, though they had no part in compassing it. Lee rejoiced that "the Cincinnati," as he put it, were called "from their ploughs to their swords." [64] The number of idlers, in the eyes of the busy engineers, was graciously reduced. Of course, this involved separation from Joe Johnston, and that was lamentable, especially in the circumstances. For when the artillery officers were ordered from Old Point they were put aboard the *Alabama,* and there they remained—indefinitely, as it seemed. Having nothing to do, and

<hr/>

[59] See *supra,* p. 112.

[60] Lee to Talcott, *MS.,* March 1, 1834; *Talcott MSS. (F)*; Lee to Talcott, *MS.,* May 13, 1834; *Talcott MSS. (F)*; Lee to Engineer's office, *MS.,* June 23, 1834; *Eng. MSS.*

[61] Lee to Engineer's office, with enclosures, *MS.,* July 6, July 17, 1833, and June 6, 1834; *Eng. MSS.,* 306, 307, 354.

[62] Letter of June 6, 1834, *supra,* and Lee to Talcott, *MS.,* June 6, 1834 (*Talcott MSS. (F)*). Lee had the support of the Engineer's office in these differences, but when he violated regulations inadvertently by forwarding directly a furlough application that should have gone through Talcott, he was promptly reprimanded (Engineer's office to Lee, *MS.,* Dec. 15, 1831, *MS. Letters to Officers of Engrs.,* vol. 4, p. 234).

[63] Lee to Talcott, *MS.,* April 23, 1834; *Talcott MSS. (F).*

[64] Lee to Talcott, *MS.,* April 23, 1834; *Talcott MSS. (F).*

never having had any work, as Lee maintained, the bored artillerists arranged a grand party. They did not invite the wives of the officers of the garrison or the young aristocrats of Hampton Roads. Instead, they summoned to the ship the ladies of easy virtue in the neighborhood. If they had to be caged in that confounded ship, forever rolling and pitching in the wintry sea, the gunners would at least have one great evening, with merriment unrestrained. High preparations were made in galley and in cabin; eagerly the young officers awaited the arrival of the Circes. They came not. At last, when an explanation was had, it was distressful: In order to tune themselves up for the evening the expected guests had indulged themselves in a little spirits and, most deplorably, had become too drunk for the journey.[65] Johnston had no part in this, except perhaps as a spectator aboard the ship, but it was a flat anticlimax to the residence at Old Point of officers who had given gaiety to day and noise to night.

If the engineers rejoiced when the disappointed artillerists at last sailed away, their satisfaction was brief. Congress adjourned during the last week of June, and, among its final acts, confirmed all the *brevet* commissions in the army as regular grades. The exultation of the artillerists who remained at Fort Monroe aroused Lee's amusement and almost his disgust.[66] Then, on July 18, though the regular inspection had already been made, Major General Alexander Macomb, the commanding officer of the army, came to Fort Monroe with the Secretary of War and examined the work being done at Old Point and at the Rip-Raps. He said little about his findings but went back to Washington and filed a report. Of its contents Talcott and Lee knew nothing at the time, though they attributed to Macomb the general hostility that line officers were supposed to feel toward the staff. Six days later the inspector general of the army, Colonel John E. Wool, arrived at the fort to examine the works. Talcott happened to be absent in Norfolk at the time, so Lee had to do the honors. When he waited on Wool for that purpose, the colonel asked if it were not a fact that General Macomb had recently made an inspection. As Lee confirmed this without comment, Wool said that he saw

[65] Lee to Mackay, *MS.*, Feb. 3, 1834; *Elliott MSS.*
[66] Lee to Talcott, *MS.*, July 2, 1834; *Talcott MSS. (F).*

no reason for going over details of the work, but that, for his own information, he would like to see Fort Calhoun. Lee took him out to the Rip-Raps immediately. It was blistering hot, but Lee was determined, as he jestingly wrote Talcott, that the three inspections "might complete our measure of Glory for this work." On the way, Wool "propounded several wise *querries,* and among them, whether there were not quarters for us outside, which," said Lee, "I take for a premonitory symptom." Wool did nothing further that day and on the following morning merely walked on the ramparts with Lee for a time before breakfast.

That was all there was to inspection number three,[67] but by no means all the story. On July 31 the adjutant general issued "Order No. 54 . . . received from the War Department." This stated that "on the report of the Major General Commanding the Army" the engineer department in Hampton Roads should be transferred to the Rip-Raps and that the commandant at Fort Monroe should be charged with the completion of the works at Old Point Comfort, "under directions and instructions from General Head Quarters." Only one officer of engineers was to be left at Hampton Roads and he was to take up his quarters at the Rip-Raps, with all his force, by August 31, "or earlier if convenient." As a special concession, so to speak, the engineers were to be allowed to get their water from the cisterns at Fort Monroe. The order concluded with a statement that it was understood no further appropriations were to be asked for Fort Monroe. It was hoped by a judicious application of unexpended balances, and funds made available through the sale of surplus engineering property, "that Fort Monroe may be placed in a respectable condition both as to defence and appearance."[68]

When this order was received by Talcott, on August 5, he considered it a direct censure of his management of the work in Hampton Roads, and he believed every one else at Old Point so regarded it. He accordingly demanded a court of inquiry.[69] Gratiot promptly concurred in this demand, though he toned it down to a "request" in his covering letter to the Secretary of

[67] Lee to Talcott, *MS.,* July 26, 1834, Nov. 1, 1834; *Talcott MSS. (VHS).*
[68] *U. S. War Dept. MSS.,* Orderly Book No. 3, Eng. Dept.
[69] Talcott to Gratiot, *MS.,* Aug. 5, Sept. 1, 1834, in Gratiot to Acting Sec. of War, Aug. 9, 1839; *U. S. War Dept. MSS.*

War.[70] Macomb, however, did not approve of an investigation. "For my part," he wrote, "I cannot see that any censure is either expressed or implied in any part of the order from the War Department, and I am sure none was intended in the report on which it is founded." [71] Macomb was justified in this statement, because the report did not contain any criticism of Talcott. It was simply a statement that the work remaining to be done at Fort Monroe was comparatively unimportant in character and in extent and could easily be done by the garrison. The report stated wrongly that Talcott favored this arrangement, but Macomb gave the engineers full credit for the construction they had directed. The report, in a word, was unexceptionable, whatever the feeling that prompted it. The trouble was with the blunt, explicit language of the order from the adjutant general's office.[72]

Not realizing this, Lee went to Washington to see what lay behind the report and the order. Through the kindness of one of the assistant engineers, a West Pointer of his own day, Lee got a look at the correspondence, and learned that a modification of the offending order was in prospect, with high compliments to Talcott. The engineer's workmen, however, were to go to the Rip-Raps, with Lee in charge, and Talcott was to be sent to the Hudson River, to supervise improvements in contemplation there. "It was all as you supposed got up by General M.," Lee reported grimly to Talcott.[73] A little later, Lee suspected that some other influence had been at work, though that did not lessen his resentment at what he considered to be the mistreatment of Talcott by Macomb. "But now I think of it," he asked Talcott, "is there no way of cooking Macomb up and that the scullions be so arranged that I could have one stir in the pot? He is a most precious 'v——n' surely and obeys his instructions as well as another. Something must be done with him, but what can?" [74]

The sentiments of the captain and of the lieutenant, as positive

[70] Ibid.

[71] A. Macomb to John Forsyth, Acting Sec. of War, MS., Aug. 11, 1834 (U. S. War Dept. MSS.).

[72] Macomb to Acting Secretary of War, MS., July 30, 1834; U. S. War Dept. MSS.

[73] Lee to Talcott, MS., Aug. 22, 1834. This letter is docketed July 22, but must have been written a month later.

[74] Lee to Talcott, MS., Oct. 1, 1834; Talcott MSS. (VHS).

as insubordinate, did not reduce the immediate authority of the major general. Nor could the juniors foresee that in a little more than a year the offending order would be revoked and the authority of the engineers restored.[75] For the time the work was ended. Talcott received instructions to set out for the Hudson, and Lee moved over to the poorly equipped Rip-Raps. He went there so much in advance of the designed 31st of August that he wrote Talcott on that day he might "be considered an old inhabitant."[76]

Despite his indignation at the political aspect of the matter, Lee did not regard the change at Fort Monroe as a reflection on himself or Talcott, or on their work, which he knew was creditable to them. For some time he had wished to get away from Old Point because of the bickering,[77] and now that the line had triumphed over the staff, he philosophically viewed it as the triumph of animosity. "I was heartily sick of it," he confided to Mackay, "and am rejoiced that it is at an end. . . . The jealousy that existed concerning the contract exercised by the Engineers was a continual thorn in my side."[78]

That the chief engineer did not consider the transfer of Talcott as a discredit to Lee was soon evident. At the Rip-Raps, Lee's task was simply that of supervising the piling up of stone on the foundations, which still continued to sink just enough to make construction of the fort impossible.[79] It was no work for a young and active man whose ability his chief in Washington had already discovered. About October 25, 1834, when he had been at the Rip-Raps only some two months, Lee received an invitation from General Gratiot to come to Washington. On his arrival Gratiot told him that he was contemplating the transfer of Lieutenant Bartlett, an assistant in the office, and was considering Lee for the place. Lee, of course, was as anxious for his family to be near Arlington as he was to get away from Hampton Roads, but he

---

[75] Lee to Talcott, MS., Nov. 17, 1835; *Talcott MSS. (VHS).*
[76] Lee to Talcott, MS., Aug. 31, 1834; *Talcott MSS. (VHS).* For conditions at Fort Calhoun and for Talcott's transfer, see Talcott to Gratiot, MS., Aug. 11, Sept. 1, Sept. 8, 1834; Gratiot to the Sec. of War, Aug. 19, 1834; *U. S. War Dept. MSS.*
[77] "There are so many of the *desagremens* connected with the duty that I should like to get another Post." Lee to Talcott, MS., June 6, 1834; *Talcott MSS. (F).*
[78] Lee to Mackay, MS., Oct. 18, 1834; *Elliott MSS.*
[79] For the continued subsidence of the work, as late as 1835, see *Rept. Chief Eng. Army, 1834–35; Ex. Docs., 1st sess., 24th Cong.,* vol. 1, p. 102.

frankly said he had no desire for office work. Gratiot, however, was intent on having Lee, and he painted the prospect alluringly. Lee agreed, before he left, to try the work if Gratiot desired him to do so. Shortly thereafter he was relieved at Fort Calhoun by Captain W. A. Eliason and was ordered to report for service as assistant to the chief of engineers.[80]

[80] Lee to Talcott, *MS.*, Nov. 1, 1834; *Talcott MSS. (VHS).* For the transfer of Lee, see *Order Book of Engineers*, 3, 26. Other correspondence relating to the fort during Lee's supervision, Sept. 1, and Oct. 1, 1834, is extant in *Eng. MSS.*, 374 and 377.

CHAPTER VIII

LEE IS BROUGHT CLOSE TO FRUSTRATION

WHEN Lee took his wife and little son from Fort Monroe to Arlington, in November, 1834, he expected to rent a house in Washington, but as he could not find suitable quarters he decided to leave them at Arlington for the winter.[1] And there they remained, as their children increased, during the whole of Lee's service in the national capital. It was an arrangement physically taxing on Lee, who rode to and from his office every day except in the very worst weather. For his family it was the most pleasant of lives. Mary Custis's marriage did not make the least difference in her status at home: she remained the "young mistress," the heiress to the estate. Her children were a delight to her parents. Mrs. Custis, whose warm heart, piety, and kindliness impressed Lee more and more as he lived at Arlington, watched ceaselessly over her daughter and her grandchild.[2] Mary's father, George Washington Parke Custis, who very soon abandoned his antagonism to her marriage, was an easy-going, indolent man, then fifty years of age. "His features were sharp and irregular, his nose long and thin, his forehead low and receding, his hair was light and thin, and in after years his head was bald. A firmly set mouth and a well-rounded chin were his best features, and indicated a firmness of character which his light-blue and rather weak eyes seemed to contradict. His cheeks were slightly sunken and gave to his face a somewhat cadaverous appearance, which was hardly improved by the thin side-whiskers he wore. He was careless

---

[1] Lee to Talcott, *MS.*, Nov. 28, 1834; *Talcott MSS. (VHS)*. No members of Lee's immediate family were then residing in Alexandria. His sister Mildred had married Edward Vernon Childe in 1831 and had gone away. Most of her later life was spent in Paris.

[2] Bishop Meade wrote of her: "For good sense, prudence, sincerity, benevolence, unaffected piety, disinterested zeal in every good work, deep humility and retiring modesty, I never knew her superior" (*Brock*, 162).

with his dress, and the visitor to Arlington was often surprised at the shabby-appearing gentleman who appeared to welcome him to so splendid a mansion." [3]

Custis possessed considerable ability, and could both speak and write with fluency and power, but he was at heart a *dilettante*. He had never been compelled to work, but he dabbled at the writing of drama, at poetry, at playing the violin, and, later in life, at painting. He was a good student of sound reading and no small culture, but he preferred the society of men to the company of books. All comers were welcome to the Arlington estate, rich and poor alike. At a large spring on the property he subsequently erected a kitchen and other buildings, threw open that part of the grounds to the public, and even went so far as to arrange for a small steamer to bring over the populace of Washington for picnics and frolics. Usually he would come down from the mansion house to the spring, when a party was there, and would play with the children. As a planter Mr. Custis was not successful. Except for sheep raising, which he helped to promote in the United States, he had little interest in farming. He lived off the produce of properties that overseers or tenants operated, and his own Arlington he kept as a park.

His servants were numerous and were fond of him, but otherwise they seem to have been noted only for their laziness. The whole atmosphere of the place was friendly and leisured, but always slightly disordered and neglected. [4] Although Mr. Custis professed to be a *littérateur* at the time of his daughter's marriage, he made no pretense to being a saint. He loved the larger world in which he had all too little a part, and when Washington's theatres offered attraction Mr. Custis shook off his indolence and became an enthusiast. He was "amusing himself," Carter Lee had written in 1829, "with beholding and describing Madame Vestris dance. Her manner of saluting the audience particularly strikes him, and he expatiates upon the style with which she elevates her toe higher than her waist and points it deliberately at the spectators." [5] When there was jovial company at Arlington, Custis

[3] Karl Decker and Angus McSween: *Historic Arlington*, 36.

[4] *Ibid.*; B. J. Lossing: Arlington House, *Harper's Magazine*, September, 1853, p. 433, containing some interesting contemporary sketches of Arlington; recollections of Jim Parke, former slave, given E. A. Chase, *Washington Star*, Nov. 4, 1927, pt. 7.

[5] Carter Lee to Hill Carter, MS., March 11, 1829; *Carter MSS.*

threw himself most cheerfully into the entertainment—a little theatrically, perhaps, and with some self-consciousness, but hospitably and generously.[6] At bottom he was a sincere, kindly gentleman, and he soon had for Lee a respect and an affection that were cordially returned.

The Washington tradition seeped more deeply into the spirit of Lee as he lived among the Arlington relics and heard Mr. Custis talk of the Father of his Country. Across the river he found traditions of another sort and a routine of labor that was pleasant only because his commanding officer made it so. In origin, Charles Gratiot, chief engineer of the army, was French-Louisianan, of the highest social station, and had been one of the young men General Wilkinson had first selected as cadets at West Point, when he had been sent out to win the good-will of the people of Louisiana. With a brilliant career in the army Gratiot had received the thanks of Congress for his conduct during the War of 1812, and as chief engineer he had earned the reputation of being an indispensable officer—a model of the military virtues. "His manners," attested one admirer, "were as child-like, simple and unpretending as his talents were brilliant and cultivated."[7] Every project aroused his interest. The welfare of each officer of engineers was his particular charge. Shortcomings on the part of his subordinates he was ready to overlook; their interests he was quick to defend against the rivalries of the line and the neglect of Congress. He had the warm good-will of the corps and when Lee went to Washington he seemed fully entrenched in power, well able to care for himself. "It is useless to waste a man's good wishes on him inasmuch as he never requires them," Lee said, half admiringly, half in jest. He "will seemingly knock his way through life."[8]

Lee had brought with him from Old Point the clerk who had carried the burden of his accounts and official papers there,[9] and with this help he was able to dispose of the correspondence that

[6] *Cf.* the account of Smith Lee's wedding-party in *E. J. Lee*, 410; *cf.* Mrs. Powell, 243.
[7] J. F. Darby, *Personal Recollections* (cited hereafter as *Darby*), 226.
[8] Lee to Talcott, *MS.*, Oct. 1, 1834; *Talcott MSS. (VHS).* Lee in 1831 had joined with the rest of the corps in procuring a portrait of Gratiot for West Point (Lee to Talcott, *MS.*, Dec. 6, 1832; *Talcott MSS. (VHS)*).
[9] *Long*, 35.

Gratiot turned over to him. The assistance of this experienced clerk was the more important because Lee complained that his own memory was bad—bad, it would appear, because he could not remember indefinitely every detail of each financial transaction.[10] Besides correspondence, he was given some of the odd jobs of the office, the most important of them being the installation of a lithographic press.[11]

Although Lee usually hurried home in fair weather, he was quick to find his old friends and to enter again into their lives in the spirit of West Point or of Fort Monroe. Joe Johnston was on duty in Washington at the time and shared in Lee's social activities, with more restraint, however, than at Old Point. Under the shadow of the White House, Lee and Johnston had to be more circumspect than had been necessary when Colonel Eustis was in his quarters and the night was waning. One day Lee was riding along Pennsylvania Avenue when he hailed a brother officer on the sidewalk. "Come, get up with me," Lee cried cheerily, and as his comrade was willing, the two proceeded together on the back of the astonished horse. Still more astonished was the Secretary of the Navy when he chanced to see the spectacle. If he informed his brother of the War Department of the undignified behavior of two officers of the army, Lee heard nothing of it, despite numerous prophecies and much chaffing by his comrades.

On nights when the weather was too inclement for the journey home, or the roads were too heavy, Lee often joined a "mess" at Mrs. Ulrich's, a boarding house where Joe Johnston and James H. Prentiss and other army men resided, together with one or two Cabinet officers and a number of congressmen.[12] It was a more expensive life than Lee's thrifty nature approved, and when a change in the army regulations reduced the allowance for rations, he vainly sought a transfer to another post.[13]

Except for this expense and the dull duties assigned him, Lee enjoyed the life of Washington and of the Arlington neighbor-

[10] Lee to Talcott, MS., Nov. 28, 1834; Talcott MSS. (VHS) ". . . my memory is so bad that I could not trust to it." Cf. same to same, MS.. Nov. 9, 1835, loc. cit.: '. . . my memory, which you know is wretched."
[11] R. E. Lee to Engineer's office, MS., April 4, 1835; Eng. MSS., 405.
[12] Long, 36–37.
[13] Lee to Engineer's office, MS., March 18, 1835; Eng. MSS., 405.

hood. All his social impulses were aroused by it. "Your humble servant . . . ," he confided to Talcott, "has returned to a state of rejuvenesency . . . and has attended some weddings and parties in a manner that is uncommon. My brother Smith was married on the 5th inst. and the Bride I think looked more beautiful than usual. We kept agoing till Sunday and last night I attended a Bridal party in Alexandria. . . . I will only tell [Mrs. Talcott] that my Spirits were so buoyant last night, when relieved from the eyes of my Dame, that my Sister Nanie was trying to pass me off as her spouse, but I was not going to have my sport spoiled that way, undeceived the young ladies and told them I was her younger brother. Sweet, innocent things, they concluded I was single and I have not had such soft looks and tender pressure of the hand for many years." [14] Affairs of this nature were some compensation for a routine that made Lee exclaim—in the language of many a soldier of the same rank— "What a pity it is a man is a poor lieutenant." [15] Occasionally he gave a dinner, to which he invited some of his army friends. For one such affair, set at 4 P.M., he called five young officers. "There will be one room devoted to the gentlemen," he wrote John Macomb, "and those who can sleep three in a bed will find 'comfortable accommodations.' " [16]

The round of office work was pleasantly broken in the spring of 1835. The boundary between Ohio and the territory of Michigan was then in dispute. An armed clash between the two neighbors seemed not unlikely. Talcott had previously been employed in making a survey of the line in controversy, and in May, 1835, he was directed to make new observations to answer the rival contentions. "His old-time and able assistant, Lt. R. E. Lee of the Corps of Engineers"—in that gentleman's own bantering announcement to Mrs. Talcott—"will join him forthwith for same duty." The mission was not expected to take more than one month, but it occupied the entire summer. It involved a number of interesting calculations and it carried Lee to the Great Lakes,

[14] Lee to Talcott, MS., Feb. 10, 1835; Talcott MSS. (VHS); Lee to Mackay, MS., February, 1836; Elliott MSS.; cf. E. J. Lee, 409–10.

[15] Lee to Talcott, MS., May 8, 1835; Talcott MSS. (VHS).

[16] Lee to "John Macomb or Dick Tilghman," MS., Jan. 10, 1835, copy of which was generously given the writer by W. S. Carroll, Esq., of Memphis, Tenn.

which he had never seen before. The tour of duty added little, however, to his equipment for the duties that lay ahead.[17]

Early in October, Lee got back to Washington and hastened on to Ravensworth, where the family was visiting. He found Mrs. Lee ill in bed. Her second baby, a girl, who had been named Mary, had been born that year. The mother unfortunately got a pelvic infection of some sort, which the physicians attributed to overexertion on her part. Lee regarded her condition as serious and he removed her to Arlington the day after his return. She suffered acutely until two abscesses that had formed on her groin broke. Then she began to mend, though very slowly. It was the beginning of 1836 before she was able to walk about again.[18] The children got the whooping-cough as their mother grew better —"whooping, coughing, teething, etc. and sometimes all three together," in the language of the despairing father. Whereupon, Mrs. Lee, not to be outdone by her youngsters, contracted mumps.[19] As the summer of 1836 came on, her improvement was more rapid. Lee then took her to one of the mineral springs of Virginia, where she was able to resume her normal life except for a slight lameness. When he brought her back in the autumn he was himself much worn down by work and worry. "I never saw a man so changed and saddened," a cousin recorded.[20]

Lee's duties during these difficult months confined him closely to the office of the chief engineer, with no outside assignment except one inspection at Fort Washington.[21] He would have tried

[17] Talcott's orders were sent him May 16, 1835, Lee to Mrs. Talcott, *MS.*, May 16, 1835; *Talcott MSS.* (VHS); Lee to Talcott, *MS.*, May 16, 1835; *Talcott MSS.* (F). *Cf.* same to same, *MS.*, May 8, 1835; *Talcott MSS.* (VHS); Lee to Engineer's office, *MS.*, June 1, 1835, Albany, N. Y.; *Eng. MSS.*, 415. Talcott's report on the previous survey is in *Ex. Docs., 1st sess., 23d Cong.*, vol. 6, p. 497. The Ohio petition is in *Ibid.*, 4, 243. The chief engineer's report is in *Ibid., 2d sess., 23d Cong.*, 1, 111. The official correspondence of 1835, between the United States mediators and the parties to the quarrel was printed as *Ex. Doc. No. 6, 1st sess., 24th Cong.* On Nov. 25, 1835, Lee wrote Talcott congratulating him on the acceptance of his observations. An unhappy incident of Lee's experience on this survey was the accidental death of a Canadian lighthouse keeper "in a scuffle" over the use of his tower for running one of the survey lines. The only reference to this, so far as is known, is in Lee to G. W. Cullum, July 31, 1835 (*Freeman MSS*). A search of Canadian records yields no details.

[18] Her symptoms and progress are set forth at length in her *MS.* letter of Nov. 21, 1835, to Mrs. Talcott, and Lee to Talcott, *MS.*, Oct. 7, Oct. 12, Oct. 21, Oct. 24, Nov. 9, Nov. 17, Nov. 18, Nov. 25, Dec. 19, 1835; Feb. 13, May 5, May 23, June 22, 1836; *Talcott MSS.* (VHS). It was during this illness (Lee to Talcott, *MS.*, Nov. 25, 1835) that Mrs. Lee got her hair in such a tangle that she cut it off. See *supra*, p. 108.

[19] Lee to Talcott, *MS.*, May 23, June 22, 1836; *Talcott MSS.* (VHS).

[20] Quoted in *Long*, 31.

[21] Lee to Engineer's office, *MS.*, Jan. 4, 1836; *Eng. MSS.*, 438.

to escape from it, by prevailing on General Gratiot to give him a post elsewhere, had Mrs. Lee's condition permitted him to leave her.[22] Hearing all the department gossip[23] and witnessing many of the controversies among his superior officers,[24] he was drawn into the campaign to procure more consideration for the Engineers' Corps at the hands of Congress.[25] His efforts at lobbying, which were not very successful, deepened his dislike of politicians. "Oh! we have been horribly, shamefully treated," he wrote Jack Mackay. He was temporarily buoyed up a bit, later in the year, by interest in Texas's struggle for independence and by the promotion he tardily received on September 21, 1836, when he was made first lieutenant.[26] But the routine of the office continued to chafe him and made him restive. Talcott had quit the army for private engineering earlier in 1836 and Lee had almost been tempted to resign with him. If he should himself surrender his commission, he said, he would do so with less regret,[27] now that Talcott was out. In February, 1837, Lee wrote him:

"You ask what are my prospects in the Corps? Bad enough—unless it is increased and something done for us, and then perhaps they will be better. As to what I intend doing, it is rather hard to answer. There is one thing certain, I must get away from here, nor can I consent to stay any longer than the rising of Cong[ress].

"I should have made a desperate effort last spring, but Mary's health was so bad I could not have left her, and she could not have gone with me. I am waiting, looking and hoping for some good opportunity to bid an affectionate farewell to my dear Uncle Sam, and I seem to think that said opportunity is to drop in my lap like a ripe pear, for d——l a stir have I made in the matter and there again I am helped out by the talent [of procrastination] I before mentioned I possessed in so eminent a degree. You may think it remarkable that a man of my standing should not have been sought after by all these companies for internal improve-

22 Lee to Talcott, MS., Feb. 2, 1837; *Talcott MSS.* (VHS).
23 *Cf.* Lee to Talcott, MS., Oct. 12, 1835; *Talcott MSS.* (VHS).
24 *Cf.* Lee to Talcott. MS., Nov. 25, 1835; *Talcott MSS.* (VHS).
25 Lee to Talcott, MS., Feb. 13, 1836; *Talcott MSS.* (VHS).
26 U. S. A., Order No. 46, Nov. 1, 1836. For his interest in Texas, see Lee to Talcott, MS., May 23, 1836; *Talcott MSS.* (VHS).
27 Lee to Talcott, MS., Feb. 13, June 9, June 22, 1836; *Talcott MSS.* (VHS).

ments, but I assure you they have never even consulted me as to their best measures. Well if people are so negligent of their own interests, they can't blame me for it." [28]

There was ebb and flow in his spirits for the next few years. In one letter he would joke merrily; in the next there would be ill-concealed depression. A sense of frustration was slowly stealing over him, and as Mrs. Lee came back to health he took refuge in his home life. "The country looks very sweet now," he said in the spring of 1836, "and the hill at Arlington covered with verdure, and perfumed by the blossoms of the trees, the flowers of the garden, Honey-suckles, yellow jasmine, etc. is more to my taste than at any other season of the year. But the brightest flower there blooming is my daughter. Oh, she is a rare one, and if only sweet sixteen, I would wish myself a cannibal that I might eat her up. As it is, I have given all the young ladies a holyday, and hurry home to her every day." [29]

He carried on through the winter and spring of 1837 a somewhat grim joke with Talcott about the number of their respective children. With deliberate superiority he wrote: "As to those articles you mention in the form of blankets and India rubber cloth, they have served my purpose, and if they can now serve yours, I shall be satisfied." [30] Suspecting that the Talcott family had further promise of increase, he twitted Mrs. Talcott somewhat airily in his letters to her husband. He was anxious to review her progeny, he intimated, and wanted her to see her little cousins at Arlington. When she failed on one expected visit he put a reproachful paragraph in a long, gossipy letter to her spouse: "But Talcott, my Beauty, how could you have served your uncle so! I know the sight of his red nose looming above the W[ashington] wharf, would have been a grateful sight to you, and then your reception at A[rlington], would have been so warm, for it was afterwards ascertained that the servant in preparing your room had made up a large hickory fire, the thermometer then ranging to about eighty degrees." [31] At Fort Monroe he had play-

[28] Lee to Talcott, *MS.*, Feb. 2, 1837; *Talcott MSS.* (VHS).
[29] Lee to Talcott, *MS.*, May 5, 1836; *Talcott MSS.* (VHS).
[30] Lee to Talcott, *MS.*, Feb. 2, 1837; *Talcott MSS.* (VHS).
[31] Lee to Talcott, *MS.*, May 5, 1836; *Talcott MSS.* (VHS).

fully contracted to mate a Lee to every Talcott, but now that the captain's children numbered five—"You are aware that you must look out for connexions for three of them in some other families, for I had given up in despair some years ago the hope of supplying them, and now I doubt where there is any one family in Va. that can keep pace with their number. Having retired from the lists myself, I have engaged my sister Nanie [Smith Lee's wife] to enter the ring. She, however, is not sanguine, seeing that upon a trial of her speed, two for the same year was her only mark. The Secty. of the Navy thinks it is time for Smith to go to Sea. So your resources in that quarter are cut off." [32] All this he wrote with unqualified assurance, and in his next letter he said: "Tell my beautiful Talcott that we have been anxiously expecting the appearance of the new copy of her annual, which she has been editing so long for our gratification. Her rival in the other Hemisphere, the Countess of Blessington, can produce nothing equal to her. . . . I hope in the spring, before breaking ground, we may be able to get there for a short time, where besides the pleasure of seeing the authors, we can peruse at leisure each production and enjoy the sight of the masterpiece with the blue eyes." [33] On May 31, 1837, the joke was turned on the censor of Talcott's domesticity: Lee was presented with a third child, a boy whom he named after his own friend and his wife's uncle, William Henry Fitzhugh of Ravensworth.[34] Lee gamely welcomed the newcomer to the beloved circle of his family,[35] and he held patiently, if unhappily, to the routine of the engineer's office;[36] but he kept working to get away from Washington and back to active duty on some interesting project of engineering, even though he knew he would not be able to take his family with him.

His opportunity came at last. General Gratiot was a native of Missouri, very proud of the fact, and vastly interested in the development of the Mississippi. He had kept there one of his

[32] Lee to Talcott, MS., Jan. 14, 1837; *Talcott MSS.* (VHS).
[33] Lee to Talcott, MS., Feb. 2, 1837; *Talcott MSS.* (VHS). The same idea of an "annual" had been mentioned in Lee to Talcott, MS., Nov. 17, 1834; *loc. cit.*
[34] The date of the birth is given in *Brock*, 163.
[35] "I am the father of three children . . . so entwined around my heart that I feel them at every pulsation" (Lee to Mackay, MS., Oct. 12, 1837; *Elliott MSS.*).
[36] Lee mentioned in a letter he wrote Talcott, June 22, 1836, that he had only twice been absent from the office otherwise than from necessity; *Talcott MSS.* (VHS).

best officers, Captain Henry Shreve, in charge of the force that had been clearing snags from the bed of the river. Shreve had done very well,[37] but now a situation developed that called for further action: the ever-changing Mississippi was cutting a new channel on the Illinois side of the river and was throwing up a bar opposite Saint Louis. Another bar was forming in the stream from a point opposite the middle of the city as far down as its southern limits. The river commerce of Saint Louis was in danger of complete destruction. In 1836 Congress made an appropriation of $15,000, "with which to build a pier to give direction to the current of the river near St. Louis." Shreve thereupon drafted a plan for the pier but found that it was too late to begin work in 1836. He figured, also, that the appropriation would have to be increased by at least $50,000.[38] Congress voted this amount. As a further improvement on the upper Mississippi the lawmakers provided money with which to cut a shipway through the rapids of the Mississippi near the Iowa-Missouri boundary. Shreve was something of an expert on snag removal and was active, but he manifestly could not superintend work along the whole of the Mississippi, the Red River, and the Missouri. In 1836 the work at Saint Louis had to be delayed because Shreve was occupied elsewhere and no other engineer was available. Lee was familiar with all this in 1837, knew the difficulties of the work, and sensed the loneliness of life so far from his home. But he was disgusted with official Washington and the spirit that prevailed there. So, as he subsequently confided, "I volunteered my services . . . to get rid of the office in W[ashington] and the Genl. at last agreed to my going." . . . "I was cognizant of so much iniquity in more ways than one that I feared for my morality, at no time strong, and had been trying for two years to quit."[39] In his usual bantering style, he insisted to Mackay, a few months after he reached the West: "I will briefly tell you that they wanted a skillful engineer on the upper Mississippi and Missouri and sent me. You know I

---

[37] For a typical early report on his work and methods, see *Ex. Docs., 1st sess., 22d Cong.*, vol. 1, pp. 90–93.

[38] Stella M. Drumm: "Robert E. Lee and the Improvement of the Mississippi River," *Missouri Historical Society Collections*, vol. 6, No. 2, February, 1929, p. 159. The writer is indebted to Miss Drumm for many courtesies in helping him procure material on this period of Lee's career.

[39] Lee to Mackay, *MS.*, June 27, 1838; *Elliott, MSS.*

was heartily sick of the duties of the office and wished to get away. The Genl. has gratified me. I also had a desire to see this Country, so I was gratified again." [40]

The assignment of Lee for this enterprise was dated April 6, [41] and permission was given him to purchase the instruments necessary for the surveys, [42] but he was not immediately dispatched, probably because Mrs. Lee was expectant. While Lee waited, General Gratiot went to Saint Louis, and personally made an inspection of the work to be done there. Gratiot promised the mayor of the city, John F. Darby, to send him a competent engineer, but did not mention Lee's name. [43] By the end of June, 1837, when Gratiot returned to Washington, the Lees' third baby had been born and Lee was free to go. He was in high spirits at the prospect of a change in his drab, uninteresting duties and immeasurably relieved at the improvement in Mrs. Lee's health. His wife was very well, he reported to Talcott. "Her little limb is as ugly as ever, though she still thinks his nose is to subside, his mouth contract, eyes to open, hair to curl, etc. etc. and in fact to become a perfect beauty. I shall leave my family in the care of my eldest son [Custis, aged 5], who will take them over the mountains somewhere this summer, and his grandmother along with them." [44] A new and stimulating period of his life was about to open, and he sensed it.

[40] Lee to Mackay, *MS.,* Oct. 12, 1837; *Eliott MSS.* Miss Mason, *op. cit.,* 31, quoted Captain May as saying that Lee was assigned on the recommendation of General G. W. Jones and General Henry Dodge. It is possible that these gentlemen knew Lee through his work on the Ohio-Michigan boundary, but there is no confirmation of May's statement. Page (*Lee, Man and Soldier,* 21) is almost certainly wrong in saying General Winfield Scott recommended him. Scott had troubles enough of his own at that time, for he was facing a congressional inquiry into the failure of his Indian campaigns.
[41] Gratiot to Lee, *MS.,* April 6, 1837, *Letters to Officers of Engineers,* vol. 6, 233.
[42] Lee to Talcott, *MS.,* April 8, April 28, 1837; *Talcott MSS. (VHS).*
[43] *Darby,* 226-27.
[44] Lee to Talcott, *MS.,* June 29, 1837; *Talcott MSS. (VHS).*

CHAPTER IX

YOUTH CONSPIRES AGAINST A GIANT

DELAY in procuring some of the instruments forced Lee to postpone his start for the Mississippi in the summer of 1837. Despair-
ing finally of getting delivery, he left on two days' notice for
Philadelphia, to make the purchases there. Later he received
authorization, if he could not find what he wanted in the Quaker
City, to travel to New York.[1] He set out with Second Lieutenant
Montgomery C. Meigs, a young engineer of twenty-one, who
had graduated at West Point in the class of 1836. Meigs was a
Georgian by birth and later became quartermaster-general of the
United States army during the War between the States. He it
was, also, who superintended the erection of the capitol dome in
Washington.

The two went to Pittsburgh, where they were lucky enough to
find a new steamer bound for Saint Louis. Aboard this craft they
went down the Ohio to Louisville. There the vessel obligingly
waited while Lee looked over the equipment that Captain Shreve
had ordered for work on the rapids. Two "machine boats" for
raising stone were nearly complete, and a small steamer for tow-
ing them was almost ready. Lee directed that the vessels be
brought on to Saint Louis under a captain and crew whom he
engaged for that purpose. With the assurance that all work on
the boats would be finished in four or five days, and that they
would then follow him to the Mississippi, Lee set out from Louisville, counting himself fortunate, as he put it, to have "a clean
state room and clean boat the whole way." He arrived at Saint
Louis August 5, and, with introductions from General Gratiot,
soon made some desirable acquaintances.[2]

[1] MS. *Letters to Officers of Engineers,* vol. 6, pp. 291, 292, 295, 301, 307; Lee to Mackay, *MS.,* Oct. 12, 1837; *Elliott MSS.* Double rations were allowed him (*Engineers' Orderly Book,* July 10, 1837, vol. 3, p. 206).
[2] Lee to Talcott, *MS.,* Saint Louis, Aug. 15, 1837; *Talcott MSS. (VHS); Darby,* 227.

Saint Louis did not impress him at first. "It is," said he, "the dearest and dirtiest place I was ever in. Our daily expenses about equal our daily pay." [3] In a later letter he said: "I make an exception in favor of the pretty girls if there are any here, and I know there are, for I have met them in no place, in no garb, in no situation, that I did not feel my heart open to them like a flower to the sun." [4]

This closing note of gaiety was somewhat forced, for in his letters home there was constant thought of Mrs. Lee and of her heavy responsibility in rearing the children alone. He wrote her in the tones of a troubled and inexperienced father: "The improved condition of the children, which you mention, was a source of great comfort to me; and as I suppose, by this time, you have all returned to Arlington, you will be able to put them under a proper restraint, which you were probably obliged to relax while visiting among strangers, and which that indulgence will probably render more essential. Our dear little boy seems to have among his friends the reputation of being hard to manage —a distinction not at all desirable, as it indicates self-will and obstinacy. Perhaps these are qualities which he really possesses, and he may have a better right to them than I am willing to acknowledge; but it is our duty, if possible, to counteract them and assist him to bring them under his control. I have endeavored, in my intercourse with him, to require nothing but what was in my opinion necessary or proper, and to explain to him temperately its propriety, at a time when he could listen to my arguments, and not at the moment of his being vexed and his little faculties warped by passion. I have also tried to show him that I was firm in my demands, and constant in their enforcement, and that he must comply with them; and I let him see that I look to their execution, in order to relieve him as much as possible from the temptation to break them. Since my efforts have been so unsuccessful, I fear I have altogether failed in accomplishing my purpose, but I hope to be able to profit by my experience. You must assist me in my attempts, and we must endeavor to combine the mildness and forbearance of the mother with the sternness

[3] Lee to Talcott, *MS.*, Aug. 15, 1837; *Talcott MSS.* (*VHS*).
[4] Lee to Mackay, *MS.*, Oct. 12 1837; *Elliott MSS.*

and, perhaps, unreasonableness of their father. This is a subject on which I think much, though M—— may blame me for not reading more. I am ready to acknowledge the good advice contained in the text-books, and believe that I see the merit of their reasoning generally; but what I want to learn is to apply what I already know. I pray God to watch over and direct our efforts in guarding our dear little son, that we may bring him up in the way he should go. . . . Oh, what pleasure I lose in being separated from my children. Nothing can compensate me for that; still I must remain here, ready to perform what little service I can, and hope for the best." [5]

In a word, he was lonesome and homesick. He was exasperated, also, by the non-arrival of the boats from Louisville. "They are the greatest people for promising and not fulfilling, that I ever saw. Never hesitate to undertake anything, but completing, is another matter. So you will see instead of being nearly done with our examinations here, we have not commenced them." [6] When the boats at last reached Saint Louis, the river was still eight or ten feet above low water, but on the rapids it was reported to be at the lowest. So Lee packed off his force as soon as possible, intent on making a survey of the upper rapids, which were approximately 150 miles above Saint Louis.

Prior to this formal beginning of Lee's work on the Mississippi, the activities of the Federal Government for the improvement of navigation had been confined chiefly to the removal of snags, caused by trees, or parts of trees, that fell into the stream and became imbedded in its soft bottom. These were an endless danger to steamboats, for the vessels then in use were lightly planked and had no bulkheads. When one of them ran into submerged timber, it usually filled at once and sank in the channel. To be "snagged" had a definite and unhappy meaning on the river. Captain Shreve had devised a method of removing snags, and sometime prior to 1830 had invented a "snag boat" for this purpose. From that time onward, when the water was low enough to permit, Shreve and his assistants or substitutes scoured long stretches of the river searching for snags. In good seasons

[5] Lee to Mrs. Lee, Oct. 16, 1837; *Jones,* 368–69.
[6] Lee to Talcott, *MS.,* Aug. 15, 1837; *Talcott MSS. (VHS).*

one steam "snag boat" would remove more than 2000. In addition, axemen employed by the engineers worked on the banks of the Mississippi and felled trees on the banks that were doomed to be washed away by the current. The engineers and the people along the river were divided as to the wisdom of this. Some maintained that it simply added new material for snags. Where this feeling was strong, the engineers had sometimes to suspend their labor.[7] Beyond this, when Lee set out from Saint Louis for the rapids, little had been done for the improvement of the river. At Cumberland Island, on the Ohio, a dam had been constructed to save a situation somewhat similar to that at Saint Louis.[8] As for the Des Moines rapids and the mouth of Rock River, Captain Shreve had made examinations and had concluded that a perfect channel could be cut through both.[9] That was all.

Lee, therefore, was doing pioneer work on the river, and he had some of the experience of the pioneer. As the engineers and their helpers came to the lower rapids, near the mouth of the Des Moines River, their steamboat ran on the rocks, nor could they budge her at that stage of the water.[10] Instead, therefore, of examining the upper rapids first, they accepted circumstance and with their boat as a base made their surveys of three or four miles of the river. "Then," Lee explained later, "[we] found an empty log house in which we placed our men and eatables which so completely filled its single apartment that Meigs and myself took up our blankets and walked a short mile to the City of Des Moines composed of the worst kind of a small log cabin which contained the Proprietor and the entire population. Here we were kindly received and all accommodated with the softest Puncheon on the floor."

"How much I could tell you," Lee went on, "of this same city, its puncheons, dwellings and inhabitants, but I must look to my limits. In this way we progressed to the head [of the lower rapids] where we found plenty of house room at the Des Moines

[7] *Rept. Chief Eng. Army, Senate Docs.*, 2d sess., 21st Cong., p. 96; report of same officer, *Ex. Docs.*, 2d sess., 22 Cong., vol. 1, p. 114; *Ibid.*, 1st sess., 23d Cong., vol. 1, p. 102; *Ibid.*, 1st sess., 24th Cong., vol. 1, p. 163.

[8] *Rept. Chief Eng. Army, Ex. Docs.*, 2d sess., 23d Cong., vol. 1, p. 152 ff.

[9] Report of H. M. Shreve in *Rept. Chief Eng. Army, ibid.*, vol. 1, p. 297 ff.

[10] M. C. Meigs, quoted in *Long*, 41.

Garrison. We then moved to the Upper Rapids, being obliged to leave our steamboat behind[,] and commencing at its head, worked downwards in the same manner, but with more comfort, as we found a better class of people and better accommodations, besides having the whole range of an old steamboat or two sunk on the rocks, whose upper decks were out of the water. I assure you we were not modest, but fell without difficulty into the manners of the country, and helped ourselves to everything that came our way. And now I think of it, we were the only lawful squatters in that region, and perhaps alone had authority to be there. I need not tell you what a beautiful country it is and I think at some time, some future day, must be a great one. You would scarcely recognize it. Villages have sprung up everywhere and some quite pretty ones too. Stephenson, between Rock Island and the mouth of Rock River—Quincy, Burlington, etc. were the most thriving. Some ten years hence, many that I saw will be even smaller than they are now—while others will have grown into cities. If you can tell me which these last will be, I will make your fortune. The formation of a good channel through these rapids will be of immense advantage to the country, and great anxiety seems to be felt on the subject." [11]

The wrecked steamer was a somewhat unstable base, for the lower deck was submerged and great holes had been cut in the cabin floor for the removal of the engines, but the staterooms were dry and afforded much better quarters than were to be found ashore. The surveyors left her in the morning and, at the end of the day, came back to her, and if they were so minded, could sit on her deck and fish for blue catfish, with which to enlarge their menu.[12]

The survey of the upper rapids convinced Lee that a channel could be cut without great difficulty.[13] By the end of September the survey was completed and the party was able to descend to the lower rapids on a steamer bound that way. They found a great encampment of the Chippewa Indians at the Des Moines rapids, awaiting the usual distribution of gifts. Lee did not tarry, for an

[11] Lee to Talcott, MS., Oct. 11, 1837; Talcott MSS. (VHS).
[12] Meigs in Long, 41–43.
[13] Cf. William Salter: Life of James W. Grimes, 320–21.

unexpected rise in the river had floated their own steamer, the one that had gone ashore when they first ascended the stream. With all his men and equipment Lee went back to Saint Louis, easy in his mind as to the upper rapids but puzzling over the engineering problem presented at the lower rapids. He was in Saint Louis by October 11, somewhat lonesome and anxious for the company of his wife and children, but better pleased with the city and ready to make his examination of the sand bars that threatened the complete ruin of the harbor of Saint Louis.[14]

The main current of the Mississippi, strengthened by the waters of the Missouri, at that time flowed rapidly along the Illinois shore for several miles below the juncture of the two rivers. Then the main current was deflected toward the Missouri side and ran to the west of Cascarot Island, which was a little more than four miles above the upper end of Saint Louis. Below Cascarot Island, the stream narrowed into a gorge and was as deep as fifty-three feet. Southward the river spread out again until it was about 1500 yards wide, at a point about two miles above the city. Here the current began to divide. Part of it continued along the Missouri shore; part was thrown against the opposite Illinois shore, where it wore away the bank. The tendency of the current on the Missouri side was to diminish and on the Illinois side to deepen. Between the two shores an island had been thrown up in the middle of the river, years before Lee came West. This island was about 500 yards across and about a mile long. Above it a long shoal was gradually extending itself upstream. The lower end of the island extended downstream until it was nearly opposite the centre of Saint Louis. It was covered in 1837 with a thick growth of flourishing cottonwood trees and was known as Bloody Island, because it was the ground usually chosen for duels.

There was fear that as the current wore away the Illinois shore beyond Bloody Island, the stream on the Saint Louis side would become so shallow that the harbor would be ruined. Bloody

---

[14] Meigs in *Long*, 42; Lee to Talcott, *MS.*, Oct. 11, 1837 (*loc. cit.*). Meigs stated that Lee returned "about the end of October" to the lower rapids, but the date of the letter to Talcott, which was written from Saint Louis, indicates an error of approximately one month. For Lee's more favorable view of life as an army engineer in Saint Louis, see Mrs. Lee to Mrs. F. D. [Mary Archer] Goodwin, *MS.*, Nov. 2, [1837], copy of which was generously given the writer by Miss Mary F. Goodwin of Williamsburg, Va.

Island, however, was not so serious in itself as in the condition
it helped to create. The old channel of the Mississippi, below the
city, had kept to the Missouri bank, but for a number of reasons
—chiefly, perhaps, because of the diversion of water by Bloody
Island—this channel had slowly filled in after about 1818, and a
large shoal had formed opposite the lower end of the town. This
shoal crowded in toward the Missouri side, narrowed the channel,
and choked the entrance to it at the downstream end. At length
it became known as Duncan's Island, and its area of some 200
acres was covered, like Bloody Island, with cottonwood trees. The
current seemed to be adding new shoals below Duncan's Island.

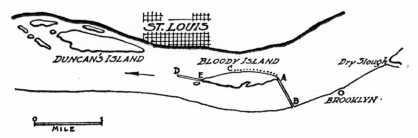

Simultaneously, the island itself was increasing in area. At the
time of Lee's arrival it was nearly a mile in length and almost
half as wide. From the upper end of this island the water was
getting more and more shallow in the direction of Bloody Island.
The prospect was that Saint Louis, having lost the old channel
by the encroachment of Duncan's Island on the Missouri side,
would be cut off altogether from deep water by the formation of
a bar that would join the two islands. Graphically, the situation
was about as shown above,[15] disregarding, for the moment, the
dykes marked with the letters *A, B,* etc.

What could be done to save the harbor? That was the question
to which Lee now devoted himself. The first essential was an
accurate map. Getting the finances of his enterprise in hand, and
organizing his forces,[16] he rented the second floor of a warehouse
on the levee as his office and sent out parties on either side of the
river to make the surveys and to do the triangulations. The actual

---

[15] Detailed map in Lee's report, *Doc. 298, Ex. Docs., 2d sess., 25th Cong.*
[16] MS. *Letters to Officers of Engineers,* vol. 6, pp. 320, 327, 328, 332, 354, 369;
Darby, 228.

drafting of the map he put under the direction of Meigs. The surveying he handled in person, with the assistance of J. S. More-head, his steamboat captain, and Henry Kayser of Saint Louis, employed for the purpose.[17] As the survey revealed the depth of the water and showed what the current was doing, Lee developed his plan for utilizing the current to wash away Duncan's Island and the other sand bars. Shreve had previously devised a scheme, in part, and Gratiot himself had studied the problem closely.[18]

Lee's solution, which was quickly reached, was an adaptation of what both Gratiot and Shreve had proposed.[19] The whole plan, as presented in a formal report to General Gratiot, on December 6, 1837,[20] was very simple: From the Illinois shore, a long dyke was to be run to the head of Bloody Island, with the object of diverting the waters of the river to the western, or Saint Louis side of the island. The line of this dyke is marked *A–B* on the sketch printed above. The face of the island beyond the dyke was to be revetted (*A–C*), so that it would not be washed away by the force of the current. At the foot of Bloody Island another dyke was to be made (*D–E*) in order to throw the full force of the current against the head of Duncan's Island and against the shoals that were forming between that and Bloody Island. Lee confessed that the construction of these dykes would be "attended with great difficulty." The total cost was estimated at $158,554.[21] He wanted to talk over the whole project with Talcott and he was debating in his mind whether he was right in proposing to start the dyke at the head of Bloody Island. However, he was satisfied that the obstacles to navigation could be removed, and that the work was well worth while in order to stimulate the growing commerce of Saint Louis, in which he was now much interested.[22]

By the time this report was finished in 1837, it was too late to attempt to do anything in execution of the plan that winter. Lee accordingly procured permission to return to Washington, disbanded his party, laid up the steamboat on the Ohio, made contract for building another, for the next year, ordered four new

---

[17] Meigs in *Long*, 42; names on the map, *loc. cit.*
[18] *Drumm, loc. cit.*, 159; *Darby*, 226.
[19] *Professional Memoirs, Corps of Engineers*, vol. 9, No. 46, p. 362.
[20] Doc. *298, loc. cit.*
[21] Lee's report, quoted in Saint Louis *Missouri Republican*, June 23, 1838.
[22] *Doc. 298, loc. cit.*, p. 4; Lee to Talcott, Nov. 18, 1837; Oct. 3, 1838.

flatboats, and with Meigs started eastward over the Cumberland Road, via Wheeling. At Frederick, they struck the new Baltimore and Ohio Railroad, though the cars had to be drawn by horses for a part of the distance. It was Lee's first journey by train, his first contact with the transportation that was to play so weighty a part in the strategy of his campaigns.[23] He probably got home about Christmas.

Lee parted from Meigs when they reached Washington and was not again fortunate enough to have him as an assistant, but he was always affectionately remembered by the younger man, even when war divided them. Lee was then, Meigs wrote long after, "in the vigor of youthful strength, with a noble and commanding presence, and an admirable, graceful and athletic figure. He was one with whom nobody ever wished or ventured to take a liberty, though kind and generous to all his subordinates, admired by all women, and respected by all men. He was the model of a soldier and the beau ideal of a Christian man."[24]

Lee spent the rest of the winter of 1837–38 partly on leave at Arlington and partly on duty in the engineer's office in Washington.[25] Early in the spring he began to make arrangements and to assemble his supplies. For experience had shown him that at Saint Louis he could procure little beyond labor and raw material, and that even in Washington some of the things that he needed were unprocurable. He had to order drawing instruments from Europe to take the place of Talcott's, which he had borrowed the previous year. Tracing paper had to be sent him from Washington when he required it, later in the season.[26] Domestic preparations had to be made, also, because this time Mrs. Lee and the three children were to accompany him.[27]

Shortly after March 25,[28] the family set out for Pittsburgh. Arriving there, they had to wait for a week to get a steamboat down the Ohio to Louisville. A week was quite enough. "I must

[23] Long, 42; MS. Letters to Officers of Engineers, Dec. 6, 1837; vol. 6, p. 387; Jan. 3, 1838, vol. 6, p. 398; March 19, 1838; vol. 6, p. 419.
[24] Meigs in Long, 44.
[25] Lee to Mackay, MS., June 27, 1838; Elliott MSS.; Lee to chief engineer, Feb. 28, 1838, Eng. MSS., 12.
[26] Lee to chief engineer, MS., Jan. 15, 1838; Eng. MSS., 3; Lee to Talcott, MS., March 29, 1838; Talcott MSS. (VHS); MS. Letters to Officers of Engineers, vol. 6, 442.
[27] Lee to Talcott, MS., March 17, 1838; N. Y. Historical Society.
[28] Lee to Engineer's office, MS., March 25, 1838; Eng. MSS., 16.

say," Lee had to confess, "that [Pittsburgh] is the darkest, blackest place I ever put foot in. Even the snow, milk and everything intended by nature to be white, not excepting the rosy cheeks of the pretty girls, partake of its dingy nature, and I am afraid my complexion is ruined." [29] From Pittsburgh the family descended the Ohio on a steamer. There had been intermittent rain and snow over the whole journey thus far and it continued till Louisville was reached. "Our journey," Lee chronicled, "was as pleasant as could be expected in a country of this sort. . . . The boys stood it manfully and indeed, improved on it, and my Dame, taking advantage of frequent opportunities for a nap, and refreshed as often by the good viands of the West (it would make your mouth water if I was to dilate upon the little roast pigs and sausages) defied the crowding, squeezing and scrambling. You know these little disagreements are to be met with at all times and in all countries, and are not worth mentioning, but as they form in part the pleasure of the trip." [30]

At Louisville, where they stopped, they were most kindly received, being invited to a wedding and enjoying much hospitality. In Cincinnati, Lee made some purchases of furniture, which was put aboard the steamboat *Moselle* for shipment to Saint Louis. Luckily, the family did not embark on the same craft, for it was blown up in a disastrous accident, and Lee's belongings, as he put it, took "a very different course from the one projected." [31] On May 1, Mrs. Lee and the children got their first view of Saint Louis, but as they found the rooms Lee had engaged for them had been otherwise disposed of, it was June 1 before they were finally placed in comfortable quarters, with meals at the home of Doctor William Beaumont, an army surgeon and the leading professional man of the town. The Beaumonts had three young children who gleefully joined the little Lees in play suited to the great river. "As drumming was the mania at Old Point, riding and driving at Arlington, so, steamboating is all the rage here. They convert themselves even into steamboats, ring their bells, raise their steam (high pressure), and put off. They fire up so frequently, and keep on so heavy a pressure of steam"—as Lee

---

[29] Lee to Mrs. Andrew Talcott, *MS.,* May 29, 1838; *Talcott MSS.* (*VHS*).
[30] Lee to Mrs. Talcott, *MS.,* May 29, 1838, *loc. cit.*   [31] *Ibid.*

himself veraciously reported—"that I am constantly fearing they will burst their boilers." [32]

Lee was very happy to have his family so pleasantly situated, as he expected his work up the Mississippi would require his absence from Saint Louis often and for long periods. Instead, he remained for the most of the season in the city, for reasons that did not spell satisfaction. On May 14 there arrived at Saint Louis Lieutenant Horace Bliss, who was to be Lee's assistant for the year. With him Bliss brought from Louisville the steamer and the flatboats that Lee had ordered the previous winter.[33] Lee planned to put Bliss in immediate charge at the Des Moines rapids, and dispatched him up the river on May 19 with some of the boats and a force of men. These were to be reinforced as soon as the river was low enough for work to begin. At that time the Mississippi was five feet above low water and was falling, but it went down so slowly that Bliss and his men spent weeks in waiting. Toward the end of July the gauge was so low that Lee believed blasting could be undertaken in a few days, and he sent up additional men from Saint Louis—only to be faced by a swift and unexplained rise that carried the stream to twelve feet and more above low water. Lee held his force at the rapids until the lateness of the season and the slow decline of the waters convinced him that nothing could be done. He therefore laid off his men and was about to abandon the project for the year—when the river fell as rapidly as it had risen. It was enough to make a man damn the Mississippi and all its vagaries! Calling up a small improvised personnel, Lee set it to work on September 20 cutting out rock at a particularly troublesome point on the west side of the Illinois chute of the lower rapids.[34] The drills showed a flint surface of an inch or two in thickness. Below this were eighteen to twenty inches of limestone, and then a decayed siliceous or slaty stone which eroded very rapidly when exposed to the current. The men blasted the rock away in great blocks weighing a ton or more and then removed it on their flatboats, but they had scarcely cleared away the point they had attacked—some 408

[32] Lee to Mrs. Talcott, MS., May 29, 1838; Talcott MSS. (VHS).

[33] Lee to Engineer's office, MS., May 18, 1838; Eng. MSS., 27.

[34] Lee's report for 1838 on the improvement of the Mississippi, Ex. Docs., 3d sess. 25th Cong., vol. 1, p. 233 ff.; Lee to Talcott, MS., Oct. 3, 1838; Talcott MSS. (VHS).

perches of stone—when cold weather came, on October 10. Lee once again reduced force and tried to carry on with the hardiest of the men, whose wages he more than doubled. The weather was too severe even for them. On the night of October 16 there was a quarter of an inch of ice, and the next day it snowed. The men simply could not endure the chilly water. Reluctantly Lee had to close the year's activities, with only twenty working days to his credit. What had been done during that time had not improved navigation perceptibly but it had convinced Lee, more than ever, that a good channel through the rapids could be made.[85]

Lee made several journeys to the falls during the season and he personally directed the last attempt, but most of his time he spent on the Saint Louis project.[86] Keeping the complicated finances of the undertaking well in hand,[87] he made war on the sand bars. With the money available he could not construct both the dykes during 1838, so he started the one intended to relieve the worst situation, directly in the harbor of the town. He reasoned that the dyke he proposed to build from the foot of Bloody Island would throw the heaviest current against the head of Duncan's Island, and would deepen both the old channel next the Missouri shore and the sand-choked channel between Bloody Island and Duncan's Island, as will appear from an examination of the map on p. 146.

In accordance with this plan, before the end of June, the river being then eleven feet above low water, Lee started the dyke close to the downstream end of Bloody Island, on the side nearest Saint Louis. Two rows of piles were driven from twelve to seventeen feet into the bed of the river, with a space of forty feet between the rows. This space was filled with sand and small stone, raised well above the water level. On both the outer faces of the dyke, brush was dumped into the river until it extended thirty to forty feet beyond the piles, with an exterior slope of three to one. The brush was then anchored with stone, in the expectation that sand would soon fill in all the open spaces.

Although the river continued high until September, Lee pushed

---

[85] Lee's report for 1838, *loc. cit.*; Lee to Mackay, MS., Oct. 19, 1838; *Elliott MSS.*
[86] The proposed improvement of the Missouri he was glad to turn over to Captain Shreve, MS. *Letters to Officers of Engineers*, July 16, 1838, vol. 6, p. 460.
[87] MS. *Letters to Officers of Engineers*, vol. 6, pp. 425, 434, 446, 467, 469, 477, 492, 493, 494, 495, 503, 508, 514, 517, 520, 523, 531, 534, 540, 544; vol. 7, pp. 14, 21.

the construction of the dyke, and before the season was over he had run it so far downstream that the lower end was opposite Market Street, a distance of approximately 2500 feet, or virtually the whole length contemplated under the plan of 1837.

As the dyke was lengthened Lee anxiously watched to see if it would have the effect he anticipated. It was the first large design he had ever undertaken, and into it he had put all the reasoning of which he was capable, and all the knowledge he had been able to acquire. Daily he studied the force of the current; almost hourly he turned his eyes to Duncan's Island. The current, as if repenting its whimsicalities, rushed obligingly down. The mud of the island, expecting no such onslaught, began to wash rapidly away. By the end of the construction season, 700 feet of the island had disappeared. Not only so, but the channel across the bar between Bloody Island and Duncan's Island, below the foot of the dyke, had been deepened seven feet. The old channel had been much improved, and on the Illinois side the eighteen-foot channel had been filled in until it was only eight feet deep. When boats once more could reach the lower part of the city there was as much rejoicing among the merchants as there was in the heart of the young engineer. The confidence of Saint Louis people was restored, and a building boom began. In his annual report Lee wrote with modest conservatism of what had been accomplished, but in his private correspondence he showed himself convinced that the harbor could be saved and all the problems solved if the height of the lower end of the dyke were increased and the projected dyke above Bloody Island were constructed.[38]

To that upper dyke, though he did not know when he would have sufficient funds for constructing it, Lee gave much thought. During the previous winter the shoal above the head of Bloody Island had stopped the ice, which thereupon formed a barrier across the head of the island. This in turn had thrown both water and late ice to the east of the island. The channel on the Illinois side had accordingly been deepened still farther, and more stream-flow had been diverted from the Missouri side. The proposed dyke at the head of the island was more necessary than

---

[38] Lee's report for 1838, *loc. cit.*, pp. 236–38; Lee to Talcott, *MS.*, Oct. 3, 1838; *Talcott MSS. (VHS).*

ever. But how could the dyke withstand the pressure of the winter's ice if the barrier were drawn on a straight line from the Illinois shore to the head of Bloody Island? Lee had foreseen this difficulty the previous year, but the alternative was the expensive one of starting the dyke much higher upstream, near an old dry slough, so as to present a slanting face to the ice. The cost of this had made Lee hesitate in 1837. Now he saw the necessity in sharper terms. As he studied his problem he reasoned that the longer slanting dyke would run through shallow water,

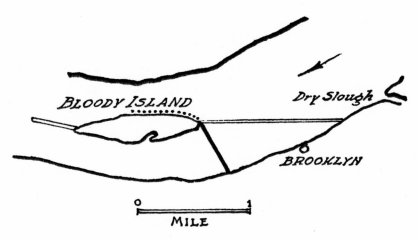

whereas the dyke he had originally planned perpendicular to the Illinois shore had to cross a twenty-two-foot channel. The expense of the longer dyke would not, therefore, be greater than the first estimates, if proper economy were shown in its construction. Lee accordingly proposed the change in his annual report, frankly stating that the dyke designed the previous year might not be permanent.[39] He proceeded also to procure drawings and to award a contract for a steam pile-driver.[40] The old and the new proposals for dykes stood in the relation to each other shown in the plan on this page. The single line represents the first and the double line the second proposed dyke.[41]

The season continued favorable, and the interest of Saint Louis

[39] Lee's report for 1838, *loc. cit.*; Lee to Talcott, *MS.*, Oct. 3, 1838, *loc. cit.*
[40] *MS. Letters to Engineers*, vol. 6, 441, 537; *Eng. MSS.*, 59.
[41] The location of the upper end of the projected slanting dyke is only approximate.

in the project remained high. As Congress had delayed appropriations for harbor improvement, citizens of the town had advanced $15,000 to prevent a suspension of the enterprise. When Congress adjourned on July 9, 1838, without allowing any money for Saint Louis, the mayor and the citizens authorized Lee to spend the balance of the fund they had raised. This action, as might have been expected in any municipality at any time, became an issue in local politics. Lee found himself, for the first time, the subject of contention between factions and in the press. The Whig newspaper, *The Missouri Republican,* charged that the state's Democratic congressmen had been negligent in seeking an allotment from Congress for the improvement of the river. *The Argus* replied that Lee himself had stated that enough was available to complete the programme for the year. *The Republican* replied with some skepticism. Controversy developed, during which Lee very carefully avoided taking sides. "The character of the Superintendent," *The Republican* admitted, "forbids the idea that he would make such a declaration for electioneering purposes, in fact, we believe he deported himself throughout our election as every government officer should, but as very few at this day do, taking no part in the contest." [42]

Lee's interest in his work, and the success of his labors won much praise. "Since the commencement of the work in May last," one informed correspondent said in *The Republican,* "it has been prosecuted with great activity, and with unexpected dispatch, when the character of the locality, the scarcity of laborers, and other difficulties are considered. I have been much gratified by a personal inspection of the works; and during my visit I observed the ingenious manner in which the Superintendent had taken advantage of the late rise of the river, which, though it caused a suspension of operations for three weeks, yet in consequence of dispositions previously made, it has caused a deposit of much alluvion about the dyke, to the manifest saving of many thousand cords of stone." [43] At a "public improvement meeting" on September 29, Montgomery Blair moved a resolution endorsing Lee's "energy and skill," urging appropriations by Congress and rec-

[42] *Missouri Republican,* July 23, Oct. 2, 1838.
[43] "Viator" in *Missouri Republican,* Sept. 13, 1838.

ommending, if the Federal Government did nothing, that the municipality act.[44]

Acting on the authorization given by the city and approved by General Gratiot, Lee made the most of the remainder of the city's fund and began construction of the upper end of the slanting dyke[45] that was to run from the Illinois shore to the head of Bloody Island. Two rows of piles were industriously driven for a part of the way down this dyke, but cold weather came early in November and the river was so filled with running ice that it was not possible to fill all the space between the rows with stone.[46]

During the months of this active work at Saint Louis, Lee's sense of frustration was diminished by the consciousness that he was achieving something. He found continuing delight in his children and unfailing interest in the country.[47] The election excitement was a novelty to him.[48] He was even amused by the manner in which he grew thin from his exertions: "I am fast wasting away," he gaily admitted, "and there is but little left now but nose and teeth." [49] The strain of the work, however, must have been severe, and if there was less of frustration in his heart, there was less of the old exuberance of spirit and more of resentment. At least once during the summer he broke out—partly because of the obstacles he had to overcome in performing his work and partly because of an injustice that had been done his friend, Jack Mackay. He wrote:

"The manner in which the army is considered and treated by the country and those whose business it is to nourish and take care of it, is enough to disgust every one with the service, and has the effect of driving every good soldier from it, and rendering those who remain discontented, careless and negligent. The instance that you mention in your own person of the authorities at W[ashington] listening to the miserable slander of dirty tergiva-

[44] *Missouri Republican*, Oct. 1, 1838.
[45] This structure is indifferently styled "dyke," "pier," and "dam" in the contemporary reports.
[46] *Rept. Chief Eng. Army 1838–39; Ex. Docs., 1st sess., 26th Cong.*, 1, 199–201.
[47] Lee to Mrs. H. Hackley, *MS.*, Aug. 7, 1838; *Talcott MSS.* (VHS): "My little Milly can walk across the floor alone."
[48] *Ibid. Cf.* R. E. Lee to C. F. Lee, Aug. 20, 1838; Jones, *L. and L.,* 33.
[49] Lee to Mrs. H. Hackley, *MS., loc. cit.*

sators[50] and then acting on such filthy ex-parte evidence, is an insult to the Army, and shows in what light its feelings are estimated, and its rights sacrificed at the shrine of popularity. . . .

"I wish all [the work] were done and I was back in Virginia. . . ."[51]

He was in this state of mind when he received notice that he had been commissioned captain of engineers, as of August 7, 1838.[52] Lee was gratified, of course, but not quite sure the outcome would be for the best. "I do not know," said he, "whether I ought to rejoice or not . . . as in all my schemes of happiness I look forward to returning to some quiet corner among the hills of Virginia where I can indulge my natural propensities without interruption, and I suppose the more comfortably I am fixed in the Army, the less likely I shall be to leave it. As, however, one great cause of my not putting these schemes in execution arises from want of money, I shall in the meantime handle with pleasure the small addition arising from what the Genl. calls 'the tardy promotion.' "[53] As promotion went in those days of a small army, his new rank was not "tardy," certainly as compared with his former advancement. He had been brevet second lieutenant from July 1, 1829, to July 19, 1832; he had been second lieutenant from that date until November 21, 1836; but he had been first lieutenant only one year and eight months. It was, however, to be more than eighteen years before he received further promotion, except by brevet.

Lee was well within the facts in saying he could "handle with pleasure" the additional pay of his new grade, for not long after he had completed most of his financial statements and had filed his reports on the season's work,[54] he was given an intimation

[50] It is curious that Lee here employed almost precisely the epithet Jefferson had used in speaking of Lee's father. See *supra*, p. 116.

[51] Lee to Mackay, MS., June 27, 1838; *Elliott MSS.*

[52] *A. G. O.*, G. O. 23, MS., July 12, 1838; *cf. A. G. O.*, Order 46, MS., Nov. 1, 1838, *U. S. War Dept. MSS.*

[53] Lee to Mrs. H. Hackley, MS., Aug. 7, 1838; *Talcott MSS. (VHS).*

[54] His first financial statements went off on Oct. 10, 1838 (Lee to Engineer's office, MS., Oct. 10, 1838; *Eng. MSS.*, 59). His reports were dated Oct. 24, 1838 (*loc. cit.*). He stated in his report on the improvement of the Missouri River (*Ex. Docs., 3d sess., 25th Cong.*, vol. 1, p. 235) that because of the delay in receiving instructions, two snag boats from the lower Mississippi could not be used on the Missouri, where the water was low, and that as only half the appropriation was available in 1838, work had been deferred until 1839. He wrote Talcott on Jan. 1, 1839, that only the "Island accounts" remained to be finished before the year's work was done (*Talcott MSS. (VHS)*).

that he might expect a fourth baby in the early summer of 1839. The prospect was not inviting: his family was increasing more rapidly than his income.

As his work lightened, his unhappiness diminished and his state of mind became easier, but late in December, 1838, he received one of the worst shocks of his whole life. Ever since his early years at Old Point he had enjoyed the affectionate encouragement of General Charles Gratiot, whom he regarded as a most capable officer and a gentleman of unchallengeable integrity. To Lee's bewilderment and to his profound distress there came news that Gratiot had been dismissed from the service of the United States for refusing to account for certain public funds. The General claimed that the money in dispute was due him as commissions and allowances; the Treasurer disputed this; the case went to the President, who decided against Gratiot. And when the engineer still refused to yield, the President ordered his name dropped from the roster of the army. The Secretary of War was not unfriendly to Gratiot. In clearing the General's books, the secretary ordered all his accounts opened anew and settled on the most liberal terms, and he directed that if Gratiot were found to owe the government money, suit for it should be entered against Gratiot in the Missouri courts. But that did not change the grim fact that the chief engineer was out of the service, disgraced. "It came upon me like a thunderclap," Lee said in acutest grief, "and I was as little prepared for such an event as I would have been for the annihilation of the city of Wash. by an earthquake, and indeed I now can scarcely realize it. . . . Nothing has distressed me so much [for] many years, and indeed, separated as I am from a knowledge of the facts, and all ability to extend relief or assistance, with rumor daily crying out the worst; I believe the news of his death would have been less painful to me. Nor when I call to mind his zeal and integrity in the discharge of his duties, with such of the circumstances as have come to my knowledge, and the indulgences shown to others having lesser claims, can I either comprehend or account for a result that has deprived the country of so valuable an officer, or the Army of so worthy a member." [55] Lee was not a man to desert a disgraced friend. He

[55] Lee to Talcott, *MS.*, Jan. 1, 1839; *Talcott MSS. (VHS).*

conferred with the General's brothers, who lived in Saint Louis, and later he attended the hearing of the government suit. On his next visit to Washington he collected papers and data the General desired in his defense, but it was to no purpose: Gratiot retained Lee's affection and good opinion, but he ended his days as a clerk in the general land office in Washington. Lee concluded that "from some cause either real or imaginary [Gratiot's] removal from the Bureau was determined on, and that the situation of his accounts was taken advantage of, as the means, and that the dismissal was upon the true issue." [56] In Gratiot's place, Colonel Joseph G. Totten was named,[57] an officer of whom Lee had seen little, and one who had no personal interest in the project Lee was directing. It was several years before Lee had the same intimate standing with Colonel Totten that he had enjoyed with General Gratiot.

While the Gratiot affair was still a fresh wound, Lee closed his accounts and formally ended his work for the year. He was free, then, to go home, but it was already January 5, 1839, and all navigation was closed on the river. His only means of getting back to Arlington would be to ride overland, and that, of course, was not practicable with three children, and with his wife in a delicate condition.[58] They were forced, therefore, to remain at Saint Louis. It was the first winter they had been away from Arlington since 1834.[59]

[56] Lee to Talcott, MS., May 18, 1839; cf. same to same, MS., April 15, 1839; Talcott MSS. (VHS).

[57] Cf. Letters to Officers of Engineers, Dec. 17, 1838; vol. 7, p. 13.

[58] Lee to Talcott, MS., Jan. 1, 1839; Talcott MSS. (VHS); chief engineer to Lee, MS., Jan. 18, 1839; Letters to Officers of Engineers, vol. 7, p. 42.

[59] Lieutenant J. M. Scarritt, who had worked with Lee during the year, was ordered to Florida, where peace had come in a war that Lee had reprobated because of the treatment of the natives. Lee had regarded the employment of Indians against the Seminoles as a "cruel and unwise policy." Lee to Engineer's office, MS., Dec. 19, 1838; Eng. MSS., 74; Lee to Mackay, MS., Oct. 12, 1837; Elliott MSS.

CHAPTER X

LEE STUDIES HIS ANCESTORS

FOR diversion during his months of idleness in the winter of 1838–39, when his own future seemed none too bright, Lee continued a study of his genealogy, a study he had begun in 1837. Then he had tried to get a correct copy of the family coat of arms in order that he might have a seal cut. He knew, of course, his general line of descent, and his degree of kinship with most of the other Lees of northern Virginia, but he had little information about the early generations of his family in the New World. He was so unfamiliar with his arms that he wrote down the motto as "Non Incautus Futurus" instead of "Futuri" ("Not unmindful of the future"), a mistake over which he would have blushed in the days when Mr. Leary had been teaching him his cases.[1] Captain Talcott, whom Lee consulted, was not satisfied with his former assistant's heraldry. A quest for correct data followed. "I once saw in the hands of Cousin Edmund, for the only time in my life," Lee explained to Cassius F. Lee, "our family tree, and as I begin in my old age"—he was then thirty-one—"to feel a little curiosity relative to my forefathers, their origin, whereabouts, etc., any information you can give me will increase the obligation."[2] Cassius Lee had a copy of the coat of arms, which, it developed, was not quite correctly drawn, and he also possessed a sketch of the family, made by William Lee, before the American Revolution. These were forwarded to Captain Lee. He did not, at the time, fathom all the heraldic mysteries, but before sending the papers to Captain Talcott, Lee read and perhaps copied the sketch.[3] It formed the basis of his knowledge of his forebears, and he believed its assertions to the day of his death.

[1] Lee to Talcott, MS., Aug. 17, 1837; *Talcott MSS. (VHS).*
[2] R. E. Lee to C. F. Lee, Aug. 20, 1838; Jones, *L. and L.,* 33.
[3] Cassius F. Lee to R. E. Lee, Sept. 8, 1838; R. E. Lee to Talcott, MS., Oct. 3, 1838, Jan. 1, 1839; *Talcott MSS. (VHS).*

Inasmuch as the Virginia Lees were bearing as early as 1659 the arms of one branch of the Lee family of Shropshire, it is quite probable that kinship existed between them. If so, the stock of Robert E. Lee was that of an upper-class English family of somewhat better than average intelligence, whose descent can be surmised from the end of the twelfth century and can be followed with some probability from the sixteenth. But every effort to establish definite connection between Robert E. Lee's American ancestors and any line of the English Lees has failed.[4] It does not matter. After reading his cousin William's manuscript, Robert E. Lee believed that he had in his veins the blood of conquerors, crusaders, and cavaliers. That belief contributed to his sense of *noblesse oblige,* and if it was based on fiction it was as influential with him as if it had been sustained by the adjuration of all the heralds of Europe.

The American ancestry of Robert E. Lee began with his great-great-great-grandfather, Richard Lee, who, as early as 1642, was residing in Virginia, and was patenting land as a married man. Before his death, in 1663 or 1664, he became one of the most considerable men of the colony. Owning some 16,000 acres of land, he must have lived in a style almost baronial.[5]

The son of the first Richard Lee bore the same name. He was born in 1647 and died March 12, 1714, "a gentleman," said Governor Alexander Spotswood, who knew him well, "of as fair character as any in the Country for his exact justice, honesty and unexceptionable loyalty." [6] Educated at Oxford, he was more interested in letters than in life, and more often to be found in his large library than on his wide plantations.[7] Robert E. Lee, who was his great-great-grandson, wrote of him, almost reproachfully, in later life, "Richard . . . spent his time in study, writing his notes in Greek, Latin, and Hebrew, and did not improve his paternal estate, which might have produced a princely revenue." [8]

---

[4] *E. J. Lee,* 2 *ff.* After Robert E. Lee became famous, one of his admirers, W. W. Fontaine, satisfied himself that he had proved the descent of Lee from Robert Bruce (9 *S. H. S. P.,* 193–206).

[5] *E. J. Lee,* 51 *ff.* Richard Lee is said by one contemporary to have produced tobacco worth £2000 annually (*ibid.,* 60), and on one return voyage from England to America he had with him 200 ounces of silver plate engraved with his arms (*ibid.,* 61).

[6] 1 *Spotswood Letters,* edited by R. A. Brock, 178.

[7] For his library, see *William and Mary Quarterly,* 2, 247.

[8] *Henry Lee's Memoirs,* 13.

By the third generation the Lee connection was becoming large. Henry Lee, General Lee's great-grandfather, was the fifth son of Richard Lee, the scholar, by his wife Letitia Corbin, herself a well-born woman of a prominent colonial family. This Henry Lee (1691–1747) lived at Lee Hall on the Potomac, adjoining the older Lee mansion, Mount Pleasant. While probably not so wealthy a man as his father or grandfather, Henry Lee the first was a planter of ample means. He married Mary Bland, daughter of Colonel Richard Bland, representative of a family of high station.

Henry Lee the first had a son Henry, who was born in 1729 and died in 1787. He was Robert E. Lee's grandfather and for convenience is styled Henry the second. Tradition has it that this Henry Lee and his wife were rather dull persons, so dull, indeed, that their phrase-making son "Light-Horse Harry" was wont to explain his own scintillation by saying "two negatives make an affirmative." [9] But the evidence now available does not bear out tradition: if Henry Lee the second was not a brilliant man, he had his share of mental endowment. And if his few remaining letters suggest that he might have been the better for a closer acquaintance with Doctor Johnson's dictionary, his spelling is no worse than that of a certain gentleman who resided up the Potomac at Mount Vernon. Many of his distinctive qualities, in surprising confirmation of current theories of eugenics, are plainly discernible in his grandson, Robert E. Lee.

"Grandfather" Henry Lee the second on December 1, 1753, married Lucy Grymes, who is supposed to have been the "Lowland Beauty" that won the heart of the youthful Washington.[10] Probably bettering himself financially by this union, Henry Lee developed the plantation known as "Leesylvania," which occupied

---

[9] Mrs. Roger A. Pryor, in *Brock*, 99.
[10] Her genealogy, admirably done by W. G. Stanard, is in 27 *Va. Mag.*, 185 *ff.*; 28 *Va. Mag.*, 90 *ff.* Reverend Charles Grymes settled in York County, Virginia, by 1644, and married a woman whose name is not now known. His son John (1660–1709), a justice, a colonel of militia, and a man of moderate fortune, married Alice Grymes (d. 1714). They had two sons. The elder was John Grymes the second (1691–1748), member of the house of burgesses, a councillor, auditor general and receiver general. The younger son of John and Alice Grymes was Charles Grymes the second (*c.* 1697–1743). This Charles, who was also a burgess, married Frances Jenings, daughter of Edmund Jenings, colonial governor. Lucy Grymes was their daughter. Bishop Beilby Porteus of London was her uncle (*Henry Lee's Memoirs*, 15; 2 *Spotswood Letters*, 54 n.; *Dictionary of National Biography*, vol. 46, p. 195).

a point of land extending into the Potomac, three miles north of the old town of Dumfries, in Prince William County.[11] There he raised tobacco that usually was of a superior quality,[12] and there he attained to measurable prosperity. He "was apparently a favorite in the community," according to his grandson,[13] and he served Prince William for many years as county lieutenant, burgess, member of the Revolutionary conventions, and justice of the peace. In 1773–74 he was among the Virginia negotiators of Indian treaties.[14] Although possessing no dominant qualities of leadership, he was heart and hand in the Revolutionary causes. "We are determined," he wrote in 1775, "on preserving our libertys if necessary at the Expense of our Blood, being resolved not to survive Slavery."[15] As might be expected, his letters show him proud of the achievements of "Light-Horse Harry" Lee. "Your brother's enterprise," he wrote another of his sons, "does him signal honour, and I flatter myself it will not be in the Power of his Enemies to Pluck from him those laurels they cannot acquire, and on his conduct being inquired into, his Military fame will be raised. I agree with you that the surprise of Paulus Hook casts a shade on Stony Point. . . ."[16]

Serving in the general assembly during the time his son and namesake was winning fame at arms, Henry Lee heard all the empty rumors of victory and disaster that come to a war-time capital. He took a coldly critical attitude towards these reports and in time developed a certain flair for analyzing them. This is amusingly illustrated in a letter he wrote from Williamsburg on June 12, 1779, to his son Charles, who was then studying law in Philadelphia. Two Frenchmen had come from Charleston, S. C., with a blood-stirring report of a great American victory. On their heels, a British deserter told how the Continentals were advancing on the English, who were cooped up on James Island and likely to share Burgoyne's fate unless their fleet arrived and relieved

---

[11] *Henry Lee's Memoirs*, 16.
[12] R. H. Lee to William Lee, June 28, 1773; 1 *Letters of Richard Henry Lee,*
[13] *Henry Lee's Memoirs*, 16; the quotation is from Robert E. Lee.
[14] *E. J. Lee*, 329.
[15] Henry Lee the second to William Lee, March 1, 1775; *E. J. Lee*, 293.
[16] Henry Lee to Charles Lee, *MS.*, Sept. 8, 1779; *E. J. Lee*, 292.

them. "The truth is I believe," Henry Lee concluded in disgust, "they have had some small skirmishing and we got the better."[17] His own grandson, contending with wild rumor as he studied the intelligence reports of the Army of Northern Virginia, might well have employed those very words.

System, thrift, and love of horses were three characteristics of Henry Lee the second, plainly observable from the few of his papers that have survived, and equally pronounced in Robert E. Lee. "I received your agreeable letter by post, but without date;" Henry told his student-son Charles in Philadelphia, "the best way is dating letters at the top, for fear of omitting in the hurry of conclusion"—a practice the grandson always followed.[18] In another letter Robert Lee's grandfather wrote: ". . . as soon as I get home shall endeavor to contrive you a remittance. The expenses of your Phila. Studies when had you taken my advice might in a great measure have been saved, had you applied yr. hours wasted in Idle pursuits of dissipation to Cooke, [sic] Blackstone, etc., having had a gen'l. knowledge of the System of Law tracts, Possessing the fundamental Principals, you might have been now employed in reading the reports and applying the Practical Cases and digesting the reasoning of the Pleaders and Judges on the applied maxims. . . ."[19] Despite this thrifty scolding, when Henry Lee came to die, he named Charles his executor, rather than his eldest son, "Light-Horse Harry," who never could keep money, and he provided that in case of Charles's death, his son Richard Bland Lee and his cousin Ludwell Lee should serve in that capacity. In his will he took pains, also, to list the horses "and the bay mare Famous," that were to be his wife's.[20] His letters to Charles, and his messages through him to Henry Lee, contain several references to the young men's animals. "Your mare," he wrote Charles, "is in good order at Whaley's and with foal by Megnanine; her colt is small but in good order, and a pretty Neat turned thing. I would not advise the sale of her."[21]

[17] E. J. Lee, 294.
[18] Henry Lee the second to Charles Lee, Sept. 8, 1779; E. J. Lee, 292.
[19] Henry Lee the second to Charles Lee, June 12, 1779; E. J. Lee, 294.
[20] E. J. Lee, 295–97.
[21] Henry Lee the second to Charles Lee, Sept. 8, 1779; E. J. Lee, 292–93.

There had thus been in succession two Richard Lees and three Henry Lees as follows:

Richard Lee the first (d. 1663 or 1664)—m. Anna [last name unknown]
|
Richard Lee the second (1647–1714)—m. Letitia Corbin.
|
Henry Lee the first (1691–1747)—m. Mary Bland.
|
Henry Lee the second (1729–1787)—m. Lucy Grymes.
|
Henry Lee the third (1758–1818)—m. Ann Hill Carter.
|
Robert E. Lee.

For these five generations, at least, the ancestors of Robert E. Lee had sustained their social position or had bettered it by advantageous marriages. For in those instances where the younger son inherited comparatively small property he increased it by winning the hand of some wealthy heiress. No misalliance marred the strain of Robert E. Lee's blood or lowered his inherited station as a gentleman. Eugenically, his career is perhaps, above all, a lesson in the cumulative effect of generations of wise marriages.

Along with this gentle blood, Lee inherited a tradition of public service and of leadership. The family record in this respect bears out the statement George Washington is reported to have made in 1777. Said he, "I know of no country that can produce a family all distinguished as clever men, as our Lees." [22]

The first Richard Lee was justice, burgess, secretary of state for the colony and a member of the council. To hold the office of councillor in Virginia was to have one's social status fixed above cavil. Richard Lee the second, despite his love of books, took time to be burgess, colonel of horse, and councillor. Henry Lee the first was lieutenant colonel of militia, but apparently held no other public office. Henry Lee the second was justice, long-time burgess, delegate to Revolutionary conventions, county lieutenant, and

[22] *Fitz Lee*, 6. The writer has been unable to find this remark in either Sparks's or Ford's edition of Washington's writings.

member of the state senate. The public record of "Light-Horse Harry" Lee has been given already. A great-granduncle of Robert E. Lee, Thomas Lee, brother of Henry Lee the first, was a member of the council and later was its president and acting governor of Virginia. His sons were the remarkable brothers, Thomas Ludwell Lee, Philip Ludwell Lee, Richard Henry Lee, Francis Lightfoot Lee, William Lee, and Arthur Lee, all of whom attained to definite distinction in the service of their state or of their country. Two of them were signers of the Declaration of Independence. Still another branch of the Stratford Lees, as they were called, went to Maryland, where it was long prominent in public life.

From Richard Lee, the immigrant, through the sixth generation, that of Robert E. Lee, fifty-four male members of the Stratford line are known to have lived to maturity. Five of them were professional men who did not hold office. Of the remaining forty-nine, thirty-seven had some record of public service. These thirty-seven included ten burgesses, ten members of the state legislature, six professional soldiers, three naval officers, six militia officers, six members of the colonial council, four members of Revolutionary conventions, three governors or acting governors, two signers of the Declaration of Independence, two diplomatists, three members of the Continental Congress, three members of the United States Congress, one member of the United States Cabinet, one secretary of the colony, one London alderman, one town mayor, one judge, five justices of the peace, two clerks and one deputy clerk of courts, and two prosecuting attorneys—a total of seventy-two offices.[23] The record is the more impressive when it is remembered that during the later years of Richard Lee the second the family was little in public life.[24]

Several of the families that had intermarried with the Lees had also contributed perceptibly to the life of Virginia, in some instances, perhaps, less because of special aptitude for politics than because their social position carried with it a certain right of

[23] This list has been compiled from E. J. Lee. Probably there are other offices that Doctor Lee did not mention. As divided, thirty-two of the seventy-two offices were legislative, six were judicial, fifteen were military, four were executive, and nine were administrative. The six members of the colonial council combined various of these functions.
[24] This is apparent from the *Spotswood Letters*, which seldom mention the Lees.

leadership in a society where the franchise was much restricted. The Corbins supplied two burgesses, one councillor, and one president of the council.[25] Of the Carters and Moores, including the Spotswood ancestors of the Moores, one was burgess, three were councillors, one was speaker of the burgesses, one was treasurer, one was acting governor, and one, Alexander Spotswood, was governor. The family of Robert E. Lee's paternal grandmother, Lucy Grymes, was connected with the Jenings stock. Among her forebears and family were one governor, two receivers general, one auditor general, two members of council, two burgesses, one militia officer, one justice, and one sheriff.[26] The Blands, the family of Robert E. Lee's paternal great-grandmother, were less numerous than the Lees, but they were brilliant people and, with the related Bennett stock, listed one governor, one speaker of the burgesses, four members of the council, two burgesses, one member of a Revolutionary convention, one member of the Continental Congress, one member of the Congress of the United States, one Revolutionary soldier, and one militia officer.[27] Robert E. Lee's remoter kinsmen held other posts almost as numerous and distinguished. Of Virginia's seven signers of the Declaration of Independence, he was connected with five. In eastern Virginia there were few families of the highest standing whose members Robert Lee did not call cousin.

These partial lists of the major lines of Robert E. Lee's inheritance show, in summary, that to and including his own generation, his ancestors and immediate kinsmen filled the following offices the indicated number of times:

OFFICE	NO. OF TIMES HELD	OFFICE	NO. OF TIMES HELD
Governor or acting governor	7	Colonial auditor general	1
President of council	1	Burgess	17
Speaker of the house of burgesses	2	Member state legislature	10
Secretary of the colony	2	Member Revolutionary conventions	5
Member of the council	16	Soldier	7
Colonial treasurer	1	Naval officer	3
Colonial receiver general	2	London alderman	1

[25] E. J. Lee, 85–86.
[26] Including, of course, the multiple offices held by one individual during the course of his career; E. J. Lee, 299–300.
[27] E. J. Lee, 137.

OFFICE	NO. OF TIMES HELD	OFFICE	NO. OF TIMES HELD
Militia command	8	Town mayor	1
Sheriff	1	Signer Declaration	2
Court clerk	2	Diplomatist	2
Deputy clerk	1	Member U. S. Cabinet	1
		Member Cont. Congress	3
Justice of the peace	6	Member U. S. Congress	4
Prosecuting attorney	2	Federal judge	1

In seeking and holding office, the earlier Lees displayed a degree of clan spirit. Robert E. Lee's grandfather, the second Henry Lee, announcing to William Lee in 1775 the death of William's brother Philip, said downrightly, "The vacancy I hope you will use your utmost efforts to fill up in council with your Brother Thomas or Francis . . . I could wish the honor of the family to be fixed at Stratford, as to your Bro. Col. Ric'd. Henry I would by no means have him out of the House of Burgesses, as there is at present the greatest reason to Expect he will succeed Mr. Randolph as Speaker, who is old and infirm." [28] Some years later Richard Henry Lee, William's brother, solicited Governor Patrick Henry to make Henry Lee commissioner for the estate of a "Mr. Paradise," a British sympathizer. [29] On one occasion, the Lees had to choose among their own kinspeople for the public weal. Richard Henry Lee, in Congress, wrote his brother Francis in 1787, urging him to prevail upon their eccentric cousin, Richard Lee, to resign from the Virginia legislature, or to stand aside so that "Light-Horse Harry" Lee might represent the County of Westmoreland. "I know," said he, "it is like persuading a man to sign his own death warrant, but upon my word the state of public affairs renders the sacrifice of place and vanity, necessary." [30] Always in the attitude of the Lees toward the offices they held, there was a conscious and sensitive regard for public opinion. The feeling of generations of the family was expressed by young Lucinda Lee, when she insisted, about 1787, in a journal kept for a girl friend: "I would not have you think from this that I pay no regard to the opinion of the world; far from it; next to that of a good conscience, the opinion of the world is to be regarded." [31]

[28] Henry Lee to William Lee, March 1, 1775; *E. J. Lee*, 293.
[29] 2 *Letters of Richard Henry Lee*, 380.   [30] 2 *Letters of Richard Henry Lee*, 425.
[31] *Journal of a Young Lady of Virginia*, ed. Mason, 11.

The Lees without exception were Revolutionaries in 1775. The sons of Thomas Lee, who were then the chief representatives of the family, were in the full vigor of their early forties or late thirties, and were among the leaders in the rising against England. Henry Lee the second was forty-seven, and though he was not so influential as his cousin Richard Henry, he was as ardent in his opposition to the policy of the crown. But in no other crisis of their one hundred and sixty years of residence in Virginia, prior to the birth of Robert E. Lee, had the sympathies of the Lees been with the younger government or with the apostles of change. Their older allegiance was their stronger.

It was so from the time of the first Richard Lee. His heart was with the Cavaliers, and when Charles I was executed, Lee "hired a Dutch vessel," according to an admiring contemporary's account, "freighted her himself, went to Brussels, surrendered up Sir William Barcklaie's [Berkeley's] old commission (for the Government of that province) and received a new one from his present majesty (a loyal action and deserving my commemoration)." [32]

Singularly enough, the second Richard Lee had to meet a like test on two occasions. He opposed Bacon's rising against Berkeley, and for his obduracy spent seven weeks in the rebels' prison, "at least 100 miles from his own home whereby he received great Prejudice in his health by hard usage, and very greatly in his whole Estate by his absence." [33] Little more than a decade later, after the flight of James II, when Parliament called for a new oath of allegiance to William and Mary, Richard Lee the second was unwilling to subscribe to it. He was a member of the council of Virginia at the time and quit that body rather than foreswear his fealty to the Stuarts. It must have been some years before he reconciled himself to the new régime and acknowledged the House of Orange. [34]

Three generations later, when the father of Robert E. Lee was governor of Virginia, James Madison inquired whether "Light-Horse Harry" was disposed to accept the command of the forces that might be sent to the Ohio to redeem Saint Clair's defeat at the

---

[32] John Gibbon, *Introductio ad Latinam Blasioniam*, 158; quoted in *Brock*, 75.
[33] Report of March 15, 1677–78, quoted in *E. J. Lee*, 76; cf. Neil: *Virginia Carolorum*, 365.
[34] 2 *Spotswood Letters*, 38.

hands of the Indians. Lee was pleased with the prospect, but as he wrote Madison, he did not like to abandon "my native country, to whose goodness I am so much indebted." He added, "No consideration on earth could induce me to act a part, however gratifying to me, which could be construed into disregard or forgetfulness of this commonwealth." [35] Henry Lee did not have to make a choice then between Virginia and the Union. Two years later, when called to lead a militia force to put down the "Whiskey Boys' Rebellion" he left his post of governor and thereby almost forfeited the office. But he held fast to his first allegiance to "his country," as he often called Virginia. In 1798, as a member of the house of delegates of his state, he defended the Federal alien and sedition laws against the resolutions of condemnation sponsored by the Jeffersonians. Exhausting argument and realizing that his was the losing side, he concluded his address with this language: "Should my efforts, Mr. Chairman, be unavailing, I shall lament my country's fate, and acquiesce in my country's will, and amidst the surrounding calamities, derive some consolation from recollecting my humble exertions to stop the mad career." [36]

Thus the Lees had the choice between the older and the newer allegiance presented to them six times in five generations, and in every instance except that of the American Revolution, their decision was to support the older government. That was a tradition that became a part of the inheritance of the greatest Lee of the sixth generation.

Robert Lee did not get all these data from the paper that William Lee had written and Cassius Lee, in 1838, had lent him. Some of the most interesting facts about his ancestors Robert Lee never knew, because they were not established until his own fame had made men curious to ascertain more precisely what was his background. Lee, however, was conscious that he had traditions of honor, of loyalty, and of public service. He set himself to be worthy of them, precisely as he had made Washington his model, almost without being conscious of it.

[35] James Madison to Henry Lee, Jan. 21, 1792; Henry Lee to James Madison, Jan. 29, 1792; *Henry Lee's Memoirs*, 44–45.
[36] *Va. Report of 1799–1800*, 108–9.

CHAPTER XI

AN ESTABLISHED PLACE IN THE CORPS

SOME dim hope had been cherished that Congress would appropriate money at the "short session" of December, 1838–March 4, 1839, for rivers and harbors. In the acute financial distress of the government, following the notorious "specie circular" this hope was not realized. Congress was hard put to provide revenues for the indispensable work of the departments, without undertaking projects that could wait. Not only so, but Lee was called upon to divide part of the money remaining from previous appropriations. Twenty thousand dollars of the balance left in his hands by his close economy were diverted to pay for the removal of snags from the Missouri River under the direction of Captain Shreve. Lee was told: "The Department is particularly desirous that, under the present state of political affairs, you should not be involved in the details of these civil works more than is absolutely necessary. It has no fears that you will consider this arrangement as indicating any purpose of lessening your trust or restricting your functions." He was further enjoined to keep "operations in such a condition that they may be transferred to other hands on the briefest notice." [1] This was discouraging to a man who was deeply interested in the completion of an improvement he believed to be of great value to the entire West. Moreover, through the whole of 1839, Lee's financial transactions with banks that held tightly to all available funds during a monetary crisis were tedious and difficult.[2]

Before he could begin work that year, with his scant balance, Lee had to take his wife home. She was expecting her fourth baby in June. Sentiment and prudence alike dictated that she

[1] MS. *Letters to Officers of Engineers,* March 14, 1839, vol. 7, p. 93; *cf. ibid.,* Feb. 11, 1839, vol. 7, p. 61.
[2] MS. *Letters to Officers of Engineers,* vol. 7, pp. 64, 72, 81, 100, 118, 135, 152, 154, 157, 163, 172, 179, 198, 232, 242, 262, 273, 283, 330, 332, 361, 362.

should be delivered at Arlington, rather than on the frontier. The children, of course, had to go with her. The family accordingly set out on May 1, reached Wheeling, Va., by steamboat on May 8, and took a private stage for Frederick, Md. They proceeded as leisurely as possible, for Mrs. Lee's comfort, but they had very hard travel on May 11, the last day of their journey. No ill-effect followed, however, and the mother and her brood were safely placed in Mrs. Custis's care late that night.[3] Lee was pleased that only eleven days had been consumed en route from Saint Louis to Washington. In communicating the news of that feat to his old-time comrade, Captain Talcott, he confided, with some adroitness, the reason that had brought him East. "We have six little Lees here now," he said, "and will then have seven, . . . three of whom belong to my brother, which I have borrowed for the occasion." The family, he explained, with the new accession, was to leave about August 1, for the mountains, not to return until the beginning of October.[4]

It was during his brief stay in Washington that Lee sought to ascertain the facts about the dismissal of General Gratiot, and procured for him certain papers that Gratiot believed would be helpful to him in the rehearing of his case. Investigation did not disclose much. Lee confessed, before he left, that he was "still in the dark," though satisfied that the condition of Gratiot's accounts was only a pretext for action that had previously been determined on.[5]

Leaving Arlington about May 25, 1839, Lee started out alone for the West and pursued a new route, via Staunton, Va., a journey that he was to remember twenty-two years thereafter, when he followed part of the same road at the beginning of a forlorn campaign to redeem disaster. He reached Guyandotte, on the Ohio, Sunday, June 2, and before he even alighted from the stage he had the good fortune to see a steamer coming downstream. He hailed her, got aboard, and went on to Cincinnati, which was her destination. Thence he voyaged to Louisville, where he arrived on the evening of June 4. His thoughts naturally

[3] Lee to Talcott, MS., May 18, 1839; *Talcott MSS.* (VHS). Lee applied for leave on March 29 and was allowed it on April 9 (MS. *Letters to Officers of Engineers*, April 9, 1839, vol. 7, p. 136).

[4] Lee to Talcott, MS., May 18, 1839; *Talcott MSS.* (VHS).

[5] *Ibid.*, and *supra*, pp. 157–58.

were of his growing family, and of the indulgent mother left to care for them. The familiar note of homesickness crept into the letter he wrote his wife the morning after he got to Louisville:

"You do not know how much I have missed you and the children, my dear Mary. To be alone in a crowd is very solitary. In the woods I feel sympathy with the trees and birds, in whose company I take delight, but experience no pleasure in a strange crowd.

"I hope you are all well and will continue so, and therefore must again urge you to be very prudent and careful of those dear children. If I could only get a squeeze at that little fellow turning up his sweet mouth to 'Keese babe!' You must not let them run wild in my absence, and will have to exercise firm authority over all of them. This will not require severity or even strictness, but constant attention and an unwavering course. Mildness and forbearance, tempered by firmness and judgment, will strengthen their affection for you, while it will maintain your control over them." [6]

Back in Saint Louis, Lee received word, about July 1, 1839, that he had a new daughter, who had arrived on June 18 and had been named Annie Carter Lee.[7] The father was philosophical about the event: "Do you know," he remarked in a letter to Mackay, "how many little Lees there are now? It is astonishing with what facility the precious creatures are dressed up for the return of their Papa! I am sure to be introduced to a new one every Christmas. They are the dearest annuals of the season. . . . I am informed that there is now at home a little long nosed fellow waiting for my first benediction, and my sis Nanie has a black headed duplicate to greet the arrival of my sailor brother from the West Indies. With what a bountiful hand are these little *responsibilities* distributed." [8]

His domestic affairs thus settled in the fashion of his fecund generation, Lee dispatched Lieutenant Bliss to begin the removal of rock from the Des Moines Rapids as soon as the stage of the

---

[6] Lee to Mrs. Lee, June 5, 1839; *Jones*, 369.
[7] For her name and the date of her birth, see *Brock*, 163.
[8] Lee to Mackay, *MS.*, Nov. n. d., 1839; *Elliott MSS.*

river permitted. For his own part he prepared to continue work on the dyke above Bloody Island, which had been somewhat damaged the previous winter by the accumulation of ice against the section that had not been strengthened with rock. To increase his funds for the enterprise Lee got permission from the bureau to sell the equipment he did not need for his reduced force.[9] He had, also, to abandon his revised plan for running the dyke, and under orders from the chief engineer returned to the original project of a dyke perpendicular to the Illinois pier. There was added to the design an intersecting dam, which was intended to secure the head of the dyke on the Illinois side.[10] Despite these discouragements Lee was cheerful, as he usually was when so busy that he had no time to think of his distant family or the uncertainties and disappointments of the public service. "We are just getting to work at the Rapids with a good prospect of success," he wrote his friend, Major E. A. Hitchcock on July 24. "The river here has not been very high this year. The bar has elongated from the foot of the B[loody] Is[lan]d, and the head of Duncan's Is[lan]d has been proportionately shortened. The river is falling quite rapidly and I am preparing to get to work here the 1st of next month." [11]

By August 12 the Mississippi was low enough for Lee to begin construction. It was undertaken with all his energy. "He went in person with the hands every morning about sunrise," the then mayor of Saint Louis wrote, "and worked day by day in the hot broiling sun,—the heat being greatly increased by the reflection of the river. He shared the hard task and common fare and rations furnished to the common laborers,—eating at the same table, in the cabin of the steamboat used in the prosecution of the work, but never on any occasion becoming too familiar with the men. He maintained and preserved under all circumstances his dignity and gentlemanly bearing, winning and commanding the esteem, regard, and respect of every one under him. He also slept in the cabin of the steamboat, moored to the bank near the

[9] MS. Letters to Officers of Engineers, May 3, 1839, Aug. 23, 1839, vol. 7, pp. 165 and 260.

[10] MS. Letters to Officers of Engineers, May 18, 1839, vol. 7, p. 182.

[11] Lee to E. A. Hitchcock, MS., July 24, 1839, graciously made available to the writer by Mrs. W A. Croffut, of Washington, D. C., daughter of General Hitchcock.

works. In the same place, Lieut. Lee,[12] with his assistant, Henry Kayser, Esq., worked at his drawings, plans and estimates every night till 11 o'clock." [13]

The driving of piles and the extension of the pier to the head of Bloody Island had been going on just two weeks when a man named Morris, a property holder on the Illinois shore, procured from the judge of the Second Illinois Circuit an injunction against the further prosecution of the work. Lee had procured the necessary permits from the owners of Bloody Island and from the owner of the land where the dyke left the Illinois shore, but he was restrained by the court because it was alleged that the harbor improvements would create a shoal on the Illinois side and would injure property values in Brooklyn, a "town" laid out on paper below the ferry that operated to Saint Louis. Lee regarded the argument as fallacious and the fears of the Illinois complainants as unfounded. He reported the proceedings to the United States district attorney for Illinois, and requested him to move to have the injunction vacated, but that was all he could do.[14] There was little probability that the case would be decided before the regular term of the court in February, 1840.

Work at Saint Louis, therefore, had to be suspended after August 27, despite many grumblings and some protests that Lee should go ahead in the face of the court order,[15] but the improvement in conditions on the river had been great. The dyke at the lower end of Bloody Island was holding fast and had given so much added strength to the current that a further section of Duncan's Island and a stretch of 1700 feet of the bar above the island had been swept away. Where the bar had previously been dry, when the river was still six feet above low water, a two-fathom channel now gave access to the wharves. The upper dyke, though still unfinished, had so contracted the sweep of the river that a new channel, a thousand feet wide, had been cut through what, as recently as 1838, had been a dry sand bar. Steamboats now had a straight course down the river. The results satisfied

[12] Darby always referred to Lee in his autobiography as "Lieutenant," the grade Lee held when he came to Saint Louis.

[13] Darby, 228.

[14] MS. Letters to Officers of Engineers, Sept. 18, 1839, vol. 7, p. 286; Missouri Republican, Sept. 7, 1839.

[15] Missouri Republican, Sept. 7, 25, 1839.

Lee, but when he came to sum them up he gave warning that the project had to be carried to completion if the improvement was to be permanent. A year's delay, he cautioned, might produce a wholly changed situation. The expenditures had only been some $57,000 of the estimated $158,000.[16]

For work on the upper Mississippi in 1839 Lee had proposed that a large party be organized, with ample machinery, and that the rocks in the river be attacked simultaneously at several points, so that if interruption came at one place progress could still be made elsewhere. Because of lack of funds this extensive plan had to be curtailed. With no money except the balance carried over from 1838 Lee was forced to confine his activities to the Des Moines Rapids. And in order that no charge of favoritism could be brought he was directed to divide his time and money between the bad "lower chain," opposite the modern Keokuk, and the still worse "English chain," slightly more than two miles upstream.[17]

Work began early and favorably, with Lieutenant Bliss in charge. The weather was mild. The river was low. Lee himself was at the rapids about the middle of July. He saw the redoubtable Dick Tilghman then, returning from Dubuque, where he had been to award a contract for a road. "General Brooke happened at Galena while we were there," Lee subsequently reported to Joe Johnston, "and besides the pleasure of meeting him again, we had much sport in fighting the battles of Old Point over again. But it was done temperately and in a temperance manner, for the general has foresworn strong potations, and our refreshments consisted of only soda-water and ice-cream, delicacies that had been untasted by the general for the last *nine* years, and four times a day did we pay our respects to the fountain and freezer. Dick . . . finding some spare days on his hands, 'accoutred as he was,' . . . plunged into a pleasure party for the Falls of St. Anthony that came along in fine spirits with music playing and colors flying."[18]

---

[16] Lee's report 1838–39, in *Ex. Docs., 1st sess., 26th Cong.,* vol. 1, pp. 199–201.

[17] These places are accurately located on Sheet No. 116 of the Mississippi River, published by the Mississippi River Commission, 1895, courteously supplied by the chief engineer of the United States army.

[18] Lee to J. E. Johnston, July 26, 1839, *Long,* 45–46. Some local references to Lee's quarters while on this or earlier expeditions to the rapids will be found in 2 *Wisconsin*

The upper "English chain" at the Des Moines Rapids was the best point at which to begin work. Going north through this chain the anxious navigator first encountered a detached bed of rock, and then entered a channel not more than thirty feet wide, obscurely marked and swept by a heavy current. This channel ran parallel to the Illinois shore for some 500 yards and then turned at right angles to the west and wound around a reef in a course that could hardly be followed at all when the water was low. From the pool reached at the end of these windings the channel passed through another detached bed of rock. Under Lee's plan the narrow thirty-foot channel at the lower end of the chain was widened to fifty to eighty feet, according to the position. The difficult windings above the right angle were cut to a straight channel eighty feet wide and four feet deep. Funds did not suffice for the removal of the beds of rock at the head and the foot of the channel.

From the "English chain" the whole force was moved down the river to attack the "lower chain." Here the great obstacle to navigation was a flat reef 200 feet long and upwards of 40 feet wide, with only a narrow chute on either side. As there was a bad cross-current through this chain, as well as a crooked channel and a shoal, navigation at low water was impossible. Bliss removed nearly all the reef during the period of operations at the "lower chain" and opened a passage fifty feet wide and nearly four feet deep. Before suspending work at the close of the season Lee set eight buoys, though he suspected that the ice would carry them away that winter.[19]

When the boats were brought back to Saint Louis from the rapids and the men were discharged in the fall of 1839, some 2000 tons of stone had been removed. Lee believed that "a tolerable season's work" had been done, "considering the lack of cash,"[20] but he was persuaded that sound economy called for the

Magazine of History, 229, 239. He is there said to have been at Fort Madison and at Montrose, but there are no specific references to these places in his extant correspondence. A few memorabilia, of no historical importance, appear in Lee's *MS. Letter-book* as president of Washington College, Feb. 11, and March 16, 1869. *The Iowa Journal of History*, 25, 646, stated that his map of the Des Moines Rapids was printed in *The Burlington Post*, June 18, 1927.

[19] Lee's report, *Ex. Docs., 1st sess., 26th Cong.*, vol. 1, p. 197 ff.; *MS. Letters to Officers of Engineers*, Nov. 7, 1839, vol. 7, p. 336.

[20] Lee to Mackay, *MS.*, Nov. n. d., 1839; *Elliott MSS.*

construction of boats and machinery capable of working a larger force of men. The decay of boats and the time spent in repairing them, he reported, consumed nearly half of the appropriations.[21]

He had few added opportunities to study costs and results that autumn, for after the injunction had halted operations in Saint Louis harbor, Colonel Totten, back in Washington, had shown no disposition to let Lee kick his heels idly off the side of the steamboat. Instead, Lee was sent to inspect improvement work on the Ohio, and then down the Mississippi, where he made a faithful count of snags. Lee was next ordered to the Missouri and again up the "Father of Waters" to "Lamallee's Chain," midway the Des Moines Rapids. Through this chain a very practicable channel was found that would admit of easy navigation simply by widening a narrow passage. In making these reports on the activities, particularly in that on the improvement of the Missouri River, Lee argued downrightly for internal improvements to help build up the West. A Whig politician would hardly have been more serious.[22]

Having no duties to perform during the winter season, either in the harbor or at the rapids, Lee procured leave of absence and made the long journey overland to Arlington. He had been gone more than seven months and he was overjoyed to be home. "I suppose you have heard of my escape from the West," he jubilantly wrote his cousin, Hill Carter of Shirley. ". . . You must not understand that I am displeased with the state of things in that country; on the contrary I think it is a great country and will one day be a grand one, all is life, animation and prosperity, but that it is far more pleasant for *me* to be here than there. I felt so elated when I again found myself within the confines of the Ancient Dominion that I nodded to all the old trees as I passed, chatted with the drivers and stable-boys, shook hands with the landlords, and in the fulness of my heart—don't tell Cousin Mary—wanted to kiss all the pretty girls I met." [23] His real re-

---

[21] Lee's report, *Ex. Docs., 1st sess., 26th Cong.,* vol. 1, p. 197 *ff.*

[22] Lee's report on the Missouri River, *Ex. Docs., 1st sess., 26th Cong.,* vol. 1, p. 202; Lee to chief engineer, *MS.,* Oct. 31, 1839; *Eng. MSS.,* 166; Lee's report on the lower Mississippi, *Ex. Docs., 2d sess., 26th Cong.,* vol. 1, p. 123; Lee's report on Lamelee's Chain, *ibid.,* 1, 135; *MS. Letters to Officers of Engineers,* vol. 7, p. 345.

[23] Lee to Hill Carter, *MS.,* Jan. 25, 1840; *Shirley MSS.,* placed at the disposal of the writer through the kindness of Mrs. Marian Carter Oliver of Shirley.

ward was not the greetings of wayside maidens, but the sight of his new baby, Annie. As he gathered his children about him he must have felt patriarchal for a man just thirty-three. His progeny now numbered four, a boy of eight and another approaching his fourth birthday, a girl in her sixth year and the newcomer in the cradle. It may have been at this time, during the winter of his return from the West, that the youthful Custis unwittingly impressed on Lee his ever increasing moral responsibility for this growing household. Lee took Custis out for a walk one snowy day, and when they had ploughed along together awhile, Custis dropped behind. After a few minutes Lee looked back and found that his little boy was behind him, imitating his every move and walking in the tracks the father had made in the snow. "When I saw this," Lee told one of his friends long afterwards, "I said to myself, 'it behooves me to walk very straight when this fellow is already following in my tracks.'"[24]

Lee was apprehensive that he would be sent to the Red River, but after four happy months of leave, approximately for the somewhat dull social season of January–April, 1840,[25] he was assigned to temporary duty in the office of the chief engineer, waiting for the decision of Congress on further appropriations for the Mississippi. Virtually all the money that had previously been voted for the work had been spent; there was no use going West again until he knew whether it would be to resume operations or to close the project, unfinished. On July 21 Congress adjourned without allowing a dollar for the enterprise. Not only so, but the temper of the lawmakers was such that Lee doubted whether Congress would resume internal improvements for years to come. Lee was convinced by the politicians' arguments, stoutly as he had advocated the work entrusted to him. "As far as I could learn, . . ." he said, "[congressmen] seem satisfied to leave the subject to the individual States, and I think the U. S. have done their part in commencing it."[26] Nothing remained except

[24] *Long*, 34.

[25] Lee to Hill Carter, *MS.*, Jan. 25, 1840; *Shirley MSS*. One of his brothers was ill during this time. Lee mentioned it as a "domestic calamity"; Lee to chief engineer, *MS.*, Dec. 16, [1839]; *Eng. MSS*.

[26] Lee to Mackay, *MS.*, July 23, 1840, copy of which, from the original in the possession of Mrs. Robert L. Mercer, the writer has gratefully received through Mrs. Frank Screven of Savannah, Ga.

to cover the long road once more and write "finis" to all the hopes of a completed Federal enterprise. "I anticipate no pleasure on the trip, I assure you, but altogether the reverse," Lee wrote in disgust to Captain Mackay. "The rivers are all low, weather hot and country sickly and I am afraid I shall have to go all the way over land." [27]

Receiving his orders on July 24,[28] Lee started west shortly thereafter, and on his arrival in Saint Louis began a survey of the effects of the ice and freshets on the piers he had constructed in 1838–39. The dyke from the Illinois shore to the head of Bloody Island continued to operate, as Lee had expected, in throwing the current west of the island, thereby deepening the channel on the Missouri side. The other dyke was still diverting the water and throwing it against the head of Duncan's Island, which was steadily being washed away. By this time the channel between Bloody Island and Duncan's Island was deep enough to pass the largest of the Mississippi steamboats to the Saint Louis wharves. If the Missouri side of Bloody Island were revetted with stone to protect it from a curious cross-current that had developed, the work, it appeared, would permanently serve its purpose, when finished. There was, also, a new small shoal near the foot of the lower pier and between it and the city. This gave Lee some temporary concern. Watching it closely, however, he concluded that it was gradually diminishing and that it consisted only of sand washed downstream from the vicinity of Bloody Island.[29] Up at the Des Moines Rapids, Lee found that the buoys he had placed the previous autumn had washed away. The new channels cut in 1839 were being used exclusively and had facilitated navigation. The improvement, however, was incomplete and failed to give to passing ships the depth of direct channel the growing commerce of the river required.[30]

Now that he was back in the West, he was not so philosophical about the abandonment of the project to the state and the city. It seemed a shame to have made so effective a beginning and not to finish it after so much labor. But orders were given to be obeyed! The maintenance of the equipment was so expensive

[27] *Ibid.*   [28] Lee to chief engineer, *MS.*, Oct. 10, 1840; *Eng. MSS.*, 263.
[29] Lee's report, *Ex. Docs., 2d sess., 26th Cong.*, vol. 1, p. 135.
[30] *Ibid.*, p. 134.

that it was uneconomical to retain some of the boats in the hope
they might be useful when and if Congress authorized resumption. Lee accordingly sold at public auction all the boats, the
machinery at Saint Louis and the greater part of that which had
been employed at the rapids. It was with a heavy heart that he did
this. "Lee expressed to me," the mayor of Saint Louis recorded,
"his chagrin and mortification at being compelled to discontinue
the work. It seemed as if it were a great personal misfortune to
stop, when the work was about half finished." [31] Lee's distress
was deepened by another attack of the homesickness that so often
beset him in the West. The very sight of children made him
yearn for his own. He wrote Mrs. Lee:

"A few evenings since, feeling lonesome, as the saying is, and
out of sorts, I got on a horse and took a ride. On returning
through the lower part of the town, I saw a number of little girls
all dressed up in their white frocks and pantalets, their hair
plaited and tied up with ribbons, running and chasing each other
in all directions. I counted twenty-three nearly the same size. As
I drew up my horse to admire the spectacle a man appeared at
the door with the twenty-fourth in his arms. 'My friend,' said I,
'are all these your children?' 'Yes,' he said, 'and there are nine
more in the house, and this is the youngest.' Upon further inquiry, however, I found that they were only temporarily his, and
that they were invited to a party at his house. He said, however,
he had been admiring them before I came up, and just wished
that he had a million of dollars and that they were all his in
reality. I do not think the eldest exceeded seven or eight years
old. It was the prettiest sight I have seen in the West, and perhaps
in my life." [32]

On October 6, Lee completed his last work at Saint Louis, the
writing of his reports. A few days later he started back home,[33]
where his presence was needed for the usual reason—the approach
of still another baby. Lee naturally was not anxious to have a
fifth child arrive while Annie was under two years of age, but, as
usual, he accepted the inevitable. "Among the things that then

[31] *Darby*, 230.   [32] Lee to Mrs. Lee, Sept. 4, 1840; *Fitz Lee*, 30.
[33] Lee to chief engineer, *MS.*, Oct. 10, 1840; *Eng. MSS.*, 263.

distracted my attention," Lee wrote in March, 1841, "was the arrival of another little Lee, whose approach, however long foreseen, I could have dispensed with for a year or two more. However, as she was in such haste to greet her Pa, I am now very glad to see her."[34]

Lee's return to Washington, several months before the advent of this impatient youngster, marked the end of his labor on the Mississippi. Covering roughly the thirty-first to the thirty-fourth years of his life, it was his initial independent detail as a responsible supervising engineer. It taught him little that he did not know already concerning the management of labor, the handling of accounts, and the award of contracts, but it did three things for him. First, it developed his ingenuity in the practice of his profession and it strengthened still further his quiet confidence in his ability to meet unexpected problems. There had been no cocksureness in his approach to the task of diverting the current of the Mississippi. He had sought and doubtless had received the counsel of Shreve, of Gratiot, and of Talcott, the last of whom had been studying a similar condition on the Hudson. In some of his proposals, Lee had been overridden by Gratiot.[35] Always deferring cheerfully, as well as officially, to the chief engineer, he had shown, on the other hand, no disposition to dodge his responsibility. He hesitated only once over the safe length of the pier from the Illinois shore to the head of Bloody Island, and then he chose the bolder alternative. As far as his method may be reconstructed, it was thoroughly scientific: He analyzed carefully the conditions he had to correct and he did not start construction until he was entirely satisfied that the solution he proposed was the one that gave the best promise of the desired result at a reasonable figure. As he left the West, he was more than ever convinced that study of a problem—detached and adequate study on the ground—was the engineer's first duty and his greatest pledge of success.

The Saint Louis enterprise brought him, in the second place, into close relations with municipal officers and a critical public.

[34] Lee to Mackay, MS., March 18, 1841; Elliott MSS. The Misses Lee were not accustomed to confide their age to their friends, nor do accessible records give the dates of the birth of all of them. Brock stated Eleanor Agnes Lee was born "about 1842." The actual date was sometime in January–March, 1841.
[35] Darby, 229.

He won the support of the officials, as he did of nearly all the men with whom he was closely associated. The people who had opposed the diversion of the current, because they believed the improvement would hurt their imaginary town of Brooklyn, failed to arouse any personal feeling in his heart. He reasoned with them candidly and in the light of all the facts, but he did not get angry. His experience in the injunction proceedings neither soured nor disgusted him. He met it with quiet poise as one of the vexations of his work. In this respect he had gained greatly since he left Fort Monroe. His letters show none of the spirit, half-jesting though it was, that had made him wish in 1834 he might have a hand in "stewing" Macomb for the General's treatment of Talcott.

Finally, Lee's two years and a half on the Saint Louis project established his professional standing. He went to Missouri a promising young officer; he returned an engineer of recognized reputation in his corps. A difficult task had been brilliantly performed, and the fullest praise for it had been accorded him. From that time onward, though his friend General Gratiot was no longer chief engineer, and he was not yet intimate with Colonel Totten, he had the highest esteem of his superiors. He did not realize it at the time, for sometimes that old intermittent spirit of frustration arose in his heart and the neglect of the army by Congress made him think he was working in a blind alley. Yet the fact remained: the opportunities that were to come to him in Mexico were created at Saint Louis.

The withdrawal of Federal aid did not prove the end of the Saint Louis project. What Congress refused to do, the city undertook on its own account. Henry Kayser, who had been one of Lee's civil assistants, was named to carry on the improvement at the expense of the municipality. He consulted Lee frequently about his difficulties and held to that officer's plan. Duncan's Island was washed completely away, and Bloody Island became, in time, a part of East Saint Louis.[36] The people of the city gave chief credit to Lee. "By his rich gift of genius and scientific knowledge," wrote Mayor Darby, "Lieut. Lee brought the Father of Waters under control. . . . I made known to Robert E. Lee, in

[36] Drumm, *op. cit.*, 169.

appropriate terms, the great obligations the authorities and citizens generally were under to him, for his skill and labor in preserving the harbor. . . . One of the most gifted and cultivated minds I had ever met with, he was as scrupulously conscientious and faithful in the discharge of his duties as he was modest and unpretending. He had none of that coddling, and petty, puerile planning and scheming which men of little minds and small intellectual calibre use to make and take care of their fame. The labors of Robert E. Lee can speak for themselves." [87]

[87] *Darby*, 229, 231, 231–32.

CHAPTER XII

FIVE DRAB YEARS END IN OPPORTUNITY

His record at Saint Louis entitled Robert E. Lee to a good assignment on his arrival in Washington, October 22, 1840, and he doubtless would have received it at once but for the fact that the very conditions that had forced him to leave the West, namely, the lack of government appropriations, prevailed equally in the East. The treasury was almost empty; Federal finances were in chaos. There was talk of a loan to meet current obligations. No construction was in progress except on the coast defenses, which Colonel Totten was anxious to complete speedily. Most of this work was under engineers whom it was not expedient to transfer. Nothing better could be given Lee, therefore, after a month in Washington, than a tour of inspection of three of the forts in the Carolinas, where the constant pounding of the waves was damaging the works or the breakwaters designed to protect them.

The first of the three to be visited by Lee was Fort Macon, situated close to Beaufort, Carteret County, N. C., and designed to cover one of the entrances to the sound that extends, under various names, along nearly the whole of the coast line of that state. Fort Macon was being built when Lee graduated from West Point, and it had received its garrison while he was working under Gratiot at Washington. The site had been continuously subject to encroachment by the sea, and during flood tides, a part of it was overflowed. Examination in 1840 had indicated that strong jetties were necessary on the sea side, and that a dyke would be required to halt the overflow.[1] Various repairs were needed, also, on leaky casemates, etc. Lee went to Beaufort about November 7, 1840, and made a close examination of the fort. This

---

[1] *Rept. Chief Eng. Army*, 1839–40, *Ex. Docs.*, *2d sess.*, *26th Cong.*, vol 1, p. 104. For earlier reports, see successive reports of the chief engineer in vol. 1, of the *Ex. Docs.*, *1st sess.*, *22d Cong.*, p. 77; *2d sess.*, *22d Cong.*, p. 87; *1st sess.*, *23d Cong.*, p. 52; *2d sess.*, *23d Cong.*, p. 109; *1st sess.*, *24th Cong.*, p. 102.

convinced him that it needed more protection from the battering Atlantic,[2] and he set about devising a method for providing this.

From Beaufort it is likely that Lee went southwestward along the coast for about 100 miles to the mouth of the Cape Fear River. There he was to make a similar inspection of the breakwaters at Fort Caswell, which had been virtually completed in 1834, but had been injured by the sea the very next year. Sundry repairs and improvements, subsequently made, had not altogether served their purpose. A further small appropriation for additions to the dykes had been authorized but had not become available at the time Lee planned to go there.[3]

The site of the fort was interesting. It stood on a point of land known as Oak Island, projecting eastward from the mainland, and overlooking the channel, which was entered from the south. Across the channel from Oak Island was Smith's Island, on the southern end of which was Cape Fear. Above Fort Caswell and Smith's Island was the long, wide mouth of the Cape Fear River, leading up to Wilmington. On a narrow spit between the river and the sea was ground that must have appealed to Lee's eye as an ideal location for a fortification to defend the stream. The time was to come when that site on the eastern spit was to figure much in Lee's mind, for there was to be located Fort Fisher, guardian of the Southern Confederacy's last open port on the Atlantic.

If Lee reached Fort Caswell he had scarcely begun his investigation there when the time came to go home for Christmas.[4] After the holidays he drew up his reports on Fort Macon, covering both the repair of the fort and the extension of the jetties. It was March 20 before the last of the drawings to accompany the reports and estimates had been finished.[5]

[2] Lee to the chief engineer; *MS.*, Beaufort, N. C., Dec. 9, 1840; *Eng. MSS.*, 273.

[3] *Rept. Chief Eng. Army*, 1839–40; *Ex. Docs.*, *2d sess.*, *26th Cong.*, vol. 1, p. 105. For earlier reports on Fort Caswell, see the report of the same officer in the first volume of the *Ex. Docs.*, *1st sess.*, *24th Cong.*, p. 102; *2d sess.*, *24th Cong.*, p. 190; *2d sess.*, *25th Cong.*, p. 310; *3d sess.*, *25th Cong.*, p. 182; *1st sess.*, *26th Cong.*, p. 166.

[4] Lee to Mackay, *MS.*, March 18, 1841; *Elliott MSS.* There are no letters by Lee from Fort Caswell and no reports on that work; consequently there is no certainty that he went there. In one of his letters from Fort Macon, however, he stated his intention of going on to Fort Caswell and to Fort Moultrie to examine the breakwaters. Available evidence does not show that he visited Fort Moultrie.

[5] Lee to chief engineer, *MS.*, Jan. 7, Jan. 22, Feb. 22, 1841; *Eng. MSS.*, 280, 286, 293; chief engineer to Lee, *MS.*, Jan. 9, Feb. 23, March 20, 1841; *MS. Letters to Officers of Engineers*, vol. 8, pp. 267, 296, 349.

By that time an alternative assignment was open, and Lee had a choice of going to New York harbor or returning soon to North Carolina to supervise the improvements on the two forts there. He had not been particularly happy in Carolina, and for that reason alone he doubtless would have elected to go to New York. In a larger sense, there was no comparison between the two posts. Both would involve much routine, but the Carolina forts were of relatively little importance at the time, whereas the works in New York harbor were the most vital of the country's coast defenses.[6] Lee quickly decided for New York, but he did not escape all responsibility for Fort Macon,[7] and, until June 14, 1842, he likewise remained in official charge of the Saint Louis improvements.[8]

Reaching New York on the night of April 10, 1841, in a period of very bad weather,[9] Lee soon discovered that his task was not as interesting as he had hoped it would be—that it was laborious but technically not difficult. His instructions were to institute somewhat elaborate repairs at Fort Lafayette, and to make various changes in Fort Hamilton, particularly in the parapet, so as to adapt it to barbette guns.[10] Both these forts were at "the Narrows," between the upper and the lower bays of New York harbor. Fort Hamilton was on the Brooklyn side, in a somewhat inaccessible location, with Fort Lafayette almost directly under its shadow, though separated from it by a channel. Before he had been in New York a week Lee received instructions to take over, in addition, Batteries Hudson and Morton, two fortifications formerly under state control on Staten Island,[11] that were to be modernized

6 Lee to Mackay, MS., March 18, 1841; Elliott MSS.
7 Chief engineer to Lee, MS., March 2, 1843; MS. Letters to Officers of Engineers, vol. 10, p. 188; same to same, March 22, 1843, ibid., vol. 10, p. 238.
8 Lee to chief engineer, MS., Feb. 11, 1841; Eng. MSS., 291; chief engineer to Lee, MS., Feb. 23, 1841, loc. cit., vol. 8, p. 295; chief engineer to Lee, MS., April 5, 1841, ibid., vol. 8, p. 392; same to same, MS., April 28, 1841, ibid., vol. 8, p. 421; same to same, MS., May 29, 1841, ibid., vol. 8, p. 458; same to same, MS., June 4, 1841, ibid., vol. 8, p. 465; same to same, MS., July 3, 1841, ibid., vol. 8, p. 496; same to same, MS., July 30, 1841, ibid., vol 8, p. 528; Jan. 18, 1842, ibid., vol. 9, p. 279; same to same, ibid., April 6, 1842, ibid., vol. 9, p. 409; ibid., June 14, 1842, ibid., vol. 9, p. 503; same to same, MS., Dec. 28, 1842, ibid., vol. 10, p. 119.
9 Lee to Talcott, MS., April 11, 1841; Talcott MSS. (VHS); Lee to chief engineer, MS., April 12, 1841; Eng. MSS., 310.
10 Lee's instructions, April 2, 1841; MS. Letters to Officers of Engineers, vol. 8, p. 373; cf. same to same, ibid., vol. 8, 396.
11 Chief engineer to Lee, April 12, 1841, loc. cit., vol. 8, p. 400; Lee to chief engineer; Eng. MSS.. 313.

and rearmed. Four projects were thus under his superintendence, on either side of the Narrows and in it.

Fort Hamilton had been completed in 1831 and had been a source of much pride at that time to the engineering corps, but it had lacked some essentials even then, and after ten years its condition was bad. Its casemates were damp and leaking. The sea wall had yielded in places to the pounding of the surf.[12] Fort Lafayette was also in ill repair, and part of it had virtually to be rebuilt. As no drawings of this fort could be found, either at Governor's Island or in the chief engineer's office in Washington, Lee had to spend a good part of the summer of 1841 in making measurements and in preparing a full set of tracings.[13]

Because the work at New York gave every promise of extending over a term of years, Lee brought his family to Fort Hamilton a month or so after he was ordered there. He established his wife and children in a house the government had acquired along with the site of Fort Hamilton, though the premises were in so wretched a condition that they had to be renovated before they were habitable.[14] The young Lees who descended on the fort now numbered five, for the new baby was of course brought along with the rest. She had been named Eleanor Agnes, but the "Eleanor" was dropped early and she was always known as Agnes.

Into his new duties Lee threw himself with the same energy he had displayed at Saint Louis. Employing a little boat known as the *Flash,* he regularly visited the four forts under repair and in a short time he was able to get results at each place. Much of the bookkeeping and virtually all the engineering he had to do in person, for he had only one clerk for the whole enterprise, and only one foreman at each fort. It was not until late in September that he felt justified in employing a draftsman to copy the drawings he had personally made of Fort Lafayette. Diligent as Lee was, the routine soon became deadening. The old sense of frus-

[12] For progress on Fort Hamilton, see *Rept. Chief Eng. Army* in the first volume of the *Ex. Docs.* of the following: *2d sess., 21st Cong.,* p. 92; *1st sess., 22d Cong.,* p. 76; *1st sess., 23d Cong.,* p. 51; *3d sess., 25th Cong.,* p. 181; *1st sess., 26th Cong.,* p. 162; *2d sess., 26th Cong.,* p. 102.

[13] Lee to chief engineer, *MS.,* April 30, 1841; *Eng. MSS.,* 317; chief engineer to Lee, *MS.,* May 3, 1841; *MS. Letters to Officers of Engineers,* vol. 8, p. 425; same to same, May 28, 1841, *ibid.,* vol. 8, p. 456; Lee's *MS.* monthly reports, May–August, 1841.

[14] Lee to chief engineer, *MS.,* Sept. 21, 1841; *Eng. MSS.,* 400.

tration besieged him. Days were so crowded with a multiple of construction details that he had little opportunity for correspondence. The high-spirited letters to Mackay and to Talcott became less frequent. Those that he wrote show youth vanishing and life becoming that of a hard-worked superintendent of indifferent labor. He seemed to be weighted down by the very stones of the forts. During that first summer he left his station only twice— once to visit the Connecticut quarries from which he was getting stone and once to confer in Washington with Colonel Totten.[15]

Before the end of August, 1841, the repairs were so much advanced that the War Department ordered troops to Fort Hamilton and to Fort Lafayette. The latter work was still much lumbered, and gave the soldiers little room, even when the mechanics who had previously been housed there were moved, at no little inconvenience, to the mainland. Lee himself had to vacate the house his family was using.[16] He would have preferred, of course, that the garrisoning of the places had been delayed, but after twelve years in the army he made the best of what he could not prevent and might not change. Having no quarters, he rented a house at $300 a year from James C. Church, having previously received the consent of the chief engineer.[17]

With the hardest of effort, Lee completed by September 30 the greater part of the work then planned for Fort Hamilton. He closed the open embrasures in the parapet wall, raised the wall, and prepared the terreplein for twenty-three guns. To find sufficient space for this number of guns he had to extend the terreplein seven feet into the parapets of the northwestern and southeastern faces of the fort. He also stopped the leaks in the casemates on the water front and renewed the floor and ceiling of the magazines. Meantime the drawings of Fort Lafayette had been completed, the trusses of the second floor of that fort had been placed, materials for the construction of the other trusses and for paving

---

[15] His visit to Connecticut was after April 20, and his trip to Washington was in June; Lee to chief engineer, *MS.*, May 7, June 12, June 15, 1841; *Eng. MSS.*, 320, 336; *MS. Letters to Officers of Engineers*, June 15, 1841, vol. 8, p. 475.

[16] Lee to chief engineer, *MS.*, Aug. 26, 1841 (two letters); *Eng. MSS.*, 379, 380; *MS. Letters to Officers of Engineers*, Aug. 30, 1842, vol. 9, p. 22.

[17] Lee to chief engineer, *MS.*, Sept. 9, 1842; *Eng. MSS.*, 531. Generous investigation of Brooklyn directories and tax returns by H. M. Lydenberg and other officials of the New York Public Library, and by the Municipal Reference Library, has failed to locate the house Lee rented.

one of the batteries had been assembled, and progress had been made in preparing the barbette battery for its armament. Battery Hudson and Battery Morton were completed except for the construction of a few magazines. Lee was much interested in Battery Hudson and believed that it would "prove more powerful in the defense of the passage than any other at the Narrows." He reasoned that it would afford the first fire on an approaching enemy, whom it would force within range of Fort Hamilton and Fort Lafayette. The extension of this battery Lee urged in strong terms on the War Department. Fifty guns, he said, ought to be put into the battery.[18]

Work continued on a diminished scale until January, 1842, and in March was resumed at all the forts.[19] Shot furnaces were provided for Batteries Hudson and Morton, and the former was extended, as Lee had suggested, with provision for thirteen additional guns.[20] Lee took up also an appeal that Colonel Totten had previously made for the acquisition of Fort Tompkins, a ruined old defense on Staten Island belonging to the state of New York. An enemy, he argued, could land beyond the range of the guns bearing on Staten Island and could seize Fort Tompkins, which completely dominated Batteries Hudson and Morton. Having reduced these batteries, the enemy might be able to pass his ships up the Narrows, undisturbed by the fortifications on the opposite side. The chief engineer repeated this plea in his next annual report, but he could not prevail upon Congress to act. All he could do at the time was to have Lee prepare a drawing of Fort Tompkins. The War Department, however, did not let the matter end here. The bureau of engineers was working under a well-considered plan of completing and maintaining a new system of fortifications, and of putting into condition for service such of the old works as could not be speedily superseded. The improvements Lee urged were an essential part of this plan.[21]

[18] Lee's MS. Annual Report for 1841 (dated Oct. 18, 1841); Eng. MSS., 413; MS. Report for 1842, loc. cit., and Ex. Docs., 3d sess., 27th Cong., vol. 1, pp. 239–40.
[19] Lee to chief engineer, MS., Dec. 7, 1841, Jan. 8, 1842; Eng. MSS., 434, 450; chief engineer to Lee, MS., Dec. 10, 1841, Jan. 13, 1842; MS. Letters to Officers of Engineers, vol. 9, pp. 204, 256.
[20] Lee to chief engineer, MS., Sept. 30, 1841, March 23, 1842, Aug. 10, 1842; Eng. MSS., 403, 473½, 523; MS. Letters to Officers of Engineers, April 6, 1842, vol. 9, p. 409.
[21] Chief engineer to Lee, MS., Jan. 3, 1843; MS. Letters to Officers of Engineers, vol. 9, p. 252; Lee to chief engineer, MS., Jan. 5, 1842; Eng. MSS., 448. Rept. Chief Eng. Army, 1841–42; Ex. Docs., 3d sess., 27th Cong., vol. 1, pp. 227, 240.

The work at Fort Hamilton and Fort Lafayette during 1842 consisted of a long list of repairs and minor improvements. They were not very difficult, though they called for close supervision. Not a little ingenuity had to be employed, also, in effecting some of the changes. Lee pressed all this as rapidly as he could, in the face of general orders from the chief engineer to reduce expenditures.[22] By fall he had Fort Lafayette in good condition and was satisfied with the water front at Fort Hamilton. On the land fronts, he saw much that needed to be done. He kept at the task all summer, with apparently only one absence. That was in April, when he went to Washington and reconciled the accounts of his Saint Louis work with those of the bank, prior to turning over that enterprise to John W. Russell.[23]

No work being practicable at the Narrows during the winter of 1842–43, Lee and his family spent that time at Arlington, but by March, 1843, he was back in New York, pushing the repairs as fast as he could in view of Congress's delay in making appropriations.[24] Mrs. Lee and the children returned to New York with him, but journeyed homeward again in the early autumn, in order that the sixth baby might be born under its grandparents' roof. The young gentleman made his appearance on October 27, 1843, and was named Robert Edward.[25] "He has a fine long nose like his father, but no whiskers," Lee reported to his friend Kayser, in Saint Louis.[26]

Together with Major J. S. Smith and Captain Henry Brewerton, Lee was sent to West Point during the summer to report on the best location and suitable dimensions of proposed new cadet barracks.[27] That pleasant break in the regular course of duty gave Lee his first close view of the changes that had been made

---

[22] Lee to chief engineer, MS., July 19, 1842; Eng. MSS., 513.

[23] Lee to chief engineer, MS., April 4, June 17, July 19, Oct. 7, 1842; Eng. MSS., 477, 503, 513, 545; Ex. Docs., 3d sess., 27th Cong., vol. 1, pp. 239–40. Lee had much difficulty in closing his accounts because the holders of some of his checks were slow in presenting them for payment. As late as March 19, 1843, he still had a balance, concerning the disposition of which he consulted the bureau (Lee to the chief engineer, Eng. MSS., 586).

[24] Lee to chief engineer, MS., Dec. 1, 1842, Jan. 15, Feb. 1, March 1, March 16, July 24, 1843; Eng. MSS., 558, 568, 573, 581, 584, 618; chief engineer to Lee, Jan. 7, 1843; MS. Letters to Officers of Engineers, vol. 10, p. 130.

[25] Brock, 164.

[26] Kayser MSS., quoted in Drumm, op. cit., 169.

[27] Chief engineer to Lee, MS., June 29, 1843; MS. Letters to Officers of Engineers, vol. 10, p. 447; Lee to chief engineer; Eng. MSS., 610.

at the academy since his own cadet days. The routine repair work of the year—painting and mounting guns at Fort Lafayette, restoring the advanced redoubt, raising walls, paving floors, and waterproofing at Fort Hamilton—was again interrupted, and not so pleasantly, on August 22, by a storm of unparalleled violence that caused several of the slopes at the forts to slide or to collapse. In asking for authority to repair this damage, Lee urged that the slopes be reduced and that they be resodded. Despite a régime of economy that had called for a curtailment of work in July, these changes had to be approved by the bureau, though the execution of some of them was of necessity deferred until the next season.[28]

Part of the winter of 1843-44 was spent in Washington and at Arlington on the unromantic task of verifying and tabulating the government's titles to the lands occupied by the public defenses. Lee came to the capital after January 10, 1844, and on April 15 was ordered back to Fort Hamilton.[29] The construction during the season that followed was the simplest and the easiest Lee had directed since he had been assigned to the Narrows. Batteries Hudson and Morton were fenced in and put in condition for service, except for mounting the guns; at Fort Lafayette nothing had to be done except to point up certain masonry and to undertake some painting; at Fort Hamilton work on the slopes was completed, larger waste pipes were installed, waterproofing was continued, and some decayed woodwork and furring were pulled out and replaced. That was all.[30] And a drab labor it was for a man whose whole impulse was to action.

For the first time in many summers Lee had a little leisure, which the vigilant chief engineer employed in the public service and to Lee's own gratification, by naming him one of the officers to attend the final examinations at West Point[31] in June, 1844. The board of visitors had been abolished in 1843, and special commissions of prominent men from the army, named by the President, acted in its stead.[32] This assignment lasted more than

[28] *Rept. Chief Eng. Army, 1842–43, Ex. Docs., 1st sess., 28th Cong.,* vol. 1, p. 99 *ff.;* Lee to chief engineer, *MS.,* Aug. 23, 1843; *Eng. MSS.,* 623; chief engineer to Lee, *MS.,* Aug. 30, 1843; *MS. Letters to Officers of Engineers,* vol. 11, p. 67.
[29] Chief engineer to Lee, *MS.,* Dec. 19, 1843, Jan. 10, 1844, April 15, 1844, *loc. cit.,* vol. 11, pp. 287, 337, 489.
[30] *Rept. Chief Eng. Army, Senate Docs., 2d sess., 28th Cong.,* vol. 1, p. 171.
[31] Lee to chief engineer, *MS.,* May 30, 1844; *Eng. MSS.,* 678.
[32] *Senate Docs., 1st sess., 29th Cong.,* vol. 1, p. 275.

two weeks, during which time most of the visiting soldiers lodged together, ate together, and became well acquainted with one another. On the board, which convened that year on June 10, were Lee's old cadet commandant, Major W. J. Worth, now a brevet brigadier general, much honored for his conduct of the Seminole campaign; a capable young captain of artillery, Erasmus D. Keyes, whom Lee learned to admire very highly; and above all—physically and in the vigor of his personality—Major General Winfield Scott, who had become the commanding general of the army on the death, two years before, of General Macomb.

This period of association with old "Fuss and Feathers," as he later became known, was a major event in the life of the tired, frustrated engineer. Lee doubtless had met Scott many times in Washington, for the General essayed to be a lion in the society of the capital, where Lee himself was not averse to bowing. The fortnight at West Point, however, was the first time the two ever sat down to a common task, where the intelligence and judgment of each was displayed at its real value, regardless of the differences in their military rank. Lee must have made a very deep impression on Scott, whose influence and good opinion were to become among the strongest forces in Lee's career. Lee did not win Scott's esteem, however, by any sort of sycophancy. On the contrary, Lee nominated and procured the appointment of Captain Keyes as instructor of artillery and cavalry, in the face of Scott's open advocacy of another man. Keyes was enduringly grateful, and even when he was leading a division against Lee's army, eighteen years thereafter, he had not forgotten the former kindness of his antagonist. The two had many frank talks on questions of the day, as they watched the ordeal of the cadets[33] that summer of 1844.

Lee meantime was making other Northern friends at his own station, among the garrison officers. John Sedgwick of Connecticut, a West Pointer of the class of 1837, had been on duty at Fort Hamilton as an artillerist in 1842–43 and had become one of Lee's stoutest admirers, though destined to fall in Spotsylvania County, May 10, 1864, before the rifle of one of his sharpshooters. Still another young soldier who became attached to Lee at this

[33] *Keyes,* 188–89.

period was a man of high promise, then a second lieutenant of artillery at Fort Hamilton, Henry J. Hunt by name. Lee was then, in Hunt's eyes, "as fine-looking a man as one would wish to see, of perfect figure and strikingly handsome. Quiet and dignified in manner, of cheerful disposition, always pleasant and considerate, he seemed to me the perfect type of a gentleman." [34]

Lee and Hunt found a ground of friendly understanding in the controversy that shook Saint John's, the little garrison church at Fort Hamilton, of which Lee was a vestryman, though he was not then a communicant. [35] The Episcopalians at the fort were much divided in their view of Puseyism, the high-church theology of the day, promulgated at Oxford by Edward Bouverie Pusey. As Lee was reticent during the time the discussion rose to an excited climax, every effort was made to trap him into a declaration, pro or con, on high church and the "real presence" in the Eucharist. Lee became amused at the feline character of the controversy. On a certain evening, when the argument was very catty, one of the disputants went even further than usual in trying to draw him into the debate. Lee turned to Lieutenant Hunt, with much assumed gravity: "I am glad," said he, "to see that you keep aloof from the dispute that is disturbing our little parish. That is right, and we must not get mixed up in it; we must support each other in that. But I must give you some advice about it, in order that we may understand each other: Beware of Pussyism! Pussyism is always bad, and may lead to unchristian feeling; therefore beware of Pussyism!" His warning and his inflection sharpened the point of his little pun: there was less discussion of Puseyism around the post and less pussyism. Lee's own views were never revealed to the curious amateur theologians of Fort Hamilton. [36] He was, however, in practice and in faith, definitely "low church" all his life.

With the approach of cold weather in the late months of 1844, Colonel Totten, the chief engineer, ordered Lee to Washington to act once more as office assistant. [37] It was, of course, pleasant to Lee to get back to Arlington with his family and no less

---

[34] Hunt in *Long*, 66–67.
[35] The Daughters of the Confederacy in 1922 placed a tablet in Lee's honor in this church. Richmond (Va.) *Evening Dispatch*, April 12, 1922; 30 *Confederate Veteran*, 163.
[36] Hunt in *Long*, 67–68.   [37] *Markie Letters*, 8.

pleasant to escape a winter of tempests in the harbor of New York. It was a thrifty arrangement, also, from the standpoint of Colonel Totten, for it helped him to utilize the slack season of at least two of his assistants. During the winter he could employ Lee in the office, and when it was warm enough for Lee to begin operations in New York it was beginning to get too torrid on the Gulf of Mexico for efficient work there. Totten accordingly could summon from Mobile a brilliant young lieutenant named George L. Welcker to take up the duties Lee laid down.[38]

Lee went to Washington about December 22, 1844, in time for the family to have Christmas at Arlington, but he soon found that the work assigned him under Colonel Totten's economical arrangement was much the same as that in which General Gratiot had first schooled him in the dark, restless months of 1834–35. Lee wrote wearily of it to his old friend, Jack Mackay: "Could you see my list of correspondents among whigs, democrats, congressmen and officers, you would [not] wonder at my horror at the sight of pen, ink and paper, and with what perfect disgust I pick up my hat between 4 and 5 P.M. with the firm determination of doing nothing until the next morning, except to go home, eat my dinner, play with the little Lees and rest. At 8 next morning I am again in the saddle to go through the same routine." [39]

It was so grim a battle with officialdom that Lee could not have been sorry when orders came on March 31, 1845, to return to Fort Hamilton. But his labors at the Narrows during the season of 1845 constituted, if possible, as dull a routine as that at engineering headquarters. No new work was undertaken at Batteries Hudson and Morton. Only a few guns had to be mounted at Fort Lafayette. The renovation of the magazines was deferred because of the possibility they might be needed in case of war with England over Oregon, or with Mexico over Texas. Even at Fort Hamilton, where some trouble arose with the contractor regarding the delivery of stone, nothing more exciting had to be done than to

---

[38] For Welcker, see Cullum, *op. cit.*, No. 842. See also chief engineer to Lee, *MS.*, Nov. 28, 1844; *Engineers' Orderly Book*, vol. 3, p. 393; Lee to chief engineer, *MS.*, Dec. 4, 1844; *Eng. MSS.* [file no. missing]; chief engineer to Lee, March 31, 1845; *MS. Letters to Officers of Engineers*, vol. 13, p. 51.
[39] Lee to John Mackay, *MS.*, March 18, 1845; *Elliott MSS.*

repair quarters, cut two posterns, excavate a ditch through the covert way, and the like.[40]

The gray round of this uninteresting life was brightened somewhat in September, 1845, by an appointment as a member of the board of engineers for the Atlantic coast defenses. This honor came to Lee in part because he had the leisure for the duties, and in part because of his general attainments as an engineer. His special knowledge of New York harbor made him a particularly desirable member of the board at a time when it was to make a special analysis of the fortification of that port, the improvement of which the Secretary of War regarded as the work most needed for the better defense of the country.[41] Without being relieved of his assignment at the Narrows, Lee was to join with his brother officers of the board in studying the best method of fortifying Sandy Hook, in examining the entire defensive system of New York, and in forming a project for occupying the site of old Forts Tompkins and Richmond. The board was, in addition, "to extend a reconnaissance over all the country which an enemy must cross in making an attack by land, and to indicate in a full report the position and nature of such land defenses (if any) as it would be desirable to erect in time of war."[42] This was a fascinating assignment, and the more so as it meant association with some of the best men of the corps of engineers—Colonel Thayer, Lee's old superintendent at West Point, Major John Lind Smith, a senior in the service, and Major Richard Delafield, who had just been relieved as head of the military academy.

Lee, as the junior officer, was made recording officer of the board, and, as it pursued its study, he filed frequent reports of its proceedings, which, of course, were confidential in character.[43] While his part in the deliberations probably was not predominant, it added to his equipment as an engineer. At Fort Pulaski, at

[40] Rept. Chief Eng. Army, Senate Docs., 1st sess., 29th Cong., vol. 1, pp. 245–46. For the stone contract, see Lee to chief engineer, MS., April 29, 1845; Eng. MSS., 753; chief engineer to Lee, May 3, 1845; MS. Letters to Officers of Engineers, vol. 13, p. 93; Lee to chief engineer, MS., May 24, May 28, 1845; Eng. MSS., 761 and 763. Lee visited the Connecticut quarries May 27.

[41] For the views of the Secretary of War on the importance of the New York defenses, see Senate Docs., 1st sess., 29th Cong., vol. 1, pp. 200–201.

[42] Engineers' Orderly Book, Sept. 8, 1845, vol. 3, pp. 408–9.

[43] Lee to chief engineer, MS., Nov. 2, 1845; Eng. MSS., 800; same to same MS., Aug. 6, 1846; Eng. MSS., 864; chief engineer to Lee, May 6, 1846; MS. Letters to Officers of Engineers, vol. 14, p. 195.

Fort Monroe, and at the Narrows, he had learned to build and to repair forts. Now he was to study how to locate them.

The winter of 1845–46 was the one period of Lee's service at Fort Hamilton, above all others, when he would most have wished, for personal reasons, to be at Arlington. Custis, who was now thirteen, was sent back to Virginia for his schooling.[44] Mrs. Lee was pregnant again and wanted to be with her mother and to have the baby born at home. Lee naturally desired to attend her in the ordeal. But it could not be arranged. He had to remain near New York to discharge his duties on the board of engineers.

During the last week of November, Mrs. Lee packed up, made ready to leave, and began her farewell visits to her friends. Her actual departure was delayed a short time because of an accident to the second boy, William Henry Fitzhugh, who already was nicknamed Rooney. This adventuresome young man, being of the mature age of eight, climbed into the hayloft in the absence of the family and succeeded in cutting off the tips of two of his fingers while experimenting with the chopping knife. For some days it was doubtful whether the ends of the digits would reknit where the doctor sewed them back. "He may probably lose his fingers and be maimed for life," Lee wrote Custis. "You cannot conceive what I suffer at the thought." For several nights the father sat by the lad's bedside lest Rooney should disturb the dressing or break the ligatures while tossing in his sleep.[45] As a man and as a parent, Lee was singularly sensitive to personal beauty and always seems to have had an inward shuddering at any deformity. Fortunately, in this case, Rooney's fingers were saved and he grew up to manhood physically as magnificent as his father. It pleased Lee, however, to pretend that this youngster was ugly. He described him to Henry Kayser as a "large heavy fellow," who required a "tight rein," a "big, two-fisted fellow with an appetite that does honor to his big mouth." [46] He never jested about the looks of his daughters, whom nature had slighted in that respect while favoring their brothers.

[44] As early as March, 1842, Lee had been debating where Custis should be schooled. Lee to Mrs. A. M. Fitzhugh, MS., March 5, 1842; Duke Univ. MSS.

[45] R. E. Lee to Custis Lee, Nov. 30, 1845; Jones, L. and L., 37–39; Lee to H. S. Kayser, Oct. 15, 1845; Kayser MSS., Drumm, loc. cit., 169; W. H. F. Lee to Custis Lee (with R. E. Lee as amanuensis), MS. copy, Dec. 18, 1845; Taylor MSS. For a note of these papers, see Bibliography.

[46] Kayser MSS., Drumm, loc. cit., 169.

When the family went to Arlington, after Rooney was well enough to travel, Lee was left for as lonesome a time as he had known since 1839 at Saint Louis. His distress, he wrote Mrs. Lee, had communicated itself to the servants. "I do not know," he said, "whether it was your departure or my sombre phiz which brought Miss Leary out on Sunday in a full suit of mourning. A black alpaca trimmed with crape and a thick row of jet buttons on each sleeve, from the shoulder to the wrist, and three rows on the skirt, diverging from the waist to the hem; it was, however, surmounted by a dashing cap with gay ribbons." [47] His chief companion was the family's little black-and-tan terrier Spec, son of Dart, whom Lee had picked up one day in the Narrows, where it was supposed she had fallen from a passing ship. Dart's tail and ears had been cropped, but Lee would not permit her puppy to be treated in this way. Spec was duly grateful and insisted on going regularly to church with the family. Now that his master was alone, he spent his time with Lee in the office,[48] whenever he could.

But Lee was not always in his office. He had to visit New York every day, probably to attend meetings of the board of engineers, and he chose to make the journey on horseback, alternating his mounts Jerry and Tom.[49] He found New York very cold in January, with sleighs in the place of wheeled vehicles. Among the sleighs was a large one named "Oregon," about which he wrote: "I did not learn how many passengers it carried. But they went 'the whole or none.' The girls returning from school were the prettiest sight; held on each others laps with their bags of books and smiling faces. Indeed there was no lack of customers at sixpence a ride, and you might be accommodated with a lady in your lap in the bargain. Think of a man of my forbidding countenance having such an offer. But I peeped under her veil before accepting and though I really could not find fault either with her appearance or age, after a little demurring preferred giving her my seat. I thought it would not sound well if repeated in the latitude of Washington, that I had ridden down

[47] R. E. Lee to Mrs. Lee, Jan. 14, 1846; *Fitz Lee*, 30.
[48] R. E. Lee to Mrs. Lee, Jan. 18, 1846; *R. E. Lee, Jr.*, 7.
[49] R. E. Lee to W. H. F. Lee, March 31, 1846; Jones, *L. and L.*, 39–40; *Jones*, 371.

B. D. [Broadway] with a strange woman in my lap." [50] He
showed like caution in all his dealings with the fair sex. It will
be recalled that he had assured Jack Mackay in 1834, "I would not
be unmarried for all you could offer me," [51] and he never changed
his mind or his morals. The dramatic skill of Fanny Kemble
had enchanted him as a young married man, [52] and when he was
around thirty-five he confided to Henry Kayser, "You are right in
my interest in pretty women—it is strange that I do not lose it
with age. But I perceive no diminution." [53] It was, however, no
more than "interest."

Early in the new year (1846) word came from Arlington that
the new baby had arrived—a girl, who was named Mildred
Childe, after Lee's younger sister in Paris. [54] She was the seventh
child, and the last, born when her father was thirty-nine and her
mother thirty-eight. Her coming made the girls of the family
number four. Custis, the oldest boy, was then in his fourteenth
year, Mary was eleven, Rooney was nearing nine (and very penitent about the chopping knife), Annie was six and a half, Agnes
was five, Robert was two and a half—and Mildred was in her
cradle. The brood had almost doubled since he had left Saint
Louis, and his responsibilities to it had increased even more,
because his children were growing older. Lee always considered
that his wife was lenient with the new generation, and though
harsh discipline was wholly contrary to his nature, he felt that he
must take a hand in the rearing of the youngsters, his boys particularly. It was about this time, when Custis was beginning to
do battle with algebra, that Lee started the long series of letters
in which he sought to give his sons guidance, help, admonition,
and counsel in their careers. For years his messages to his boys
were full of solemn preachments, adorned with monitory instances, and in one case with a story that the revered Horatio
Alger might have coveted for his pages. [55] "I do not think," he

[50] Lee to John Mackay, MS., Jan. 30, 1846; *Elliott MSS.*
[51] Lee to Jack Mackay, MS., Feb. 27, 1837; *Elliott MSS.;* see *supra*, p. 117.
[52] *Ibid.* and same to same, MS., Jan. 23, 1833; *Elliott MSS.*
[53] *Kayser MSS., loc. cit.*
[54] The date of her birth is not given in family records, but the time of Mrs. Lee's departure from Fort Hamilton and Lee's reference in his letter of March 31, 1846, to
"that little baby you have got to show me" (Jones, *L. and L.,* 39–40) fix the time as the
very end of 1845 or early in 1846.
[55] Among the earliest of these letters is that of Nov. 30, 1845, to Custis, and that of
March 31, 1846, to Rooney; Jones, *L. and L.,* 37–40.

said, "I ever told you of a fine boy I heard of in my travels this winter. He lived in the mountains of New Hampshire. He was just thirteen years of age, the age of Custis. His father was a farmer, and he used to assist him to work on the farm as much as he could. The snow there this winter was deeper than it has been for years, and one day he accompanied his father to the woods to get some wood. They went with their wood-sled, and, after cutting a load and loading the sled, this little boy, whose name was Harry, drove it home while his father cut another load. He had a fine team of horses and returned very quickly, when he found his father lying prostrate on the frozen snow under a large limb of a tree he had felled during his absence, which had caught him in its fall, and thrown him to the ground. He was cold and stiff, and little Harry, finding that he was not strong enough to relieve him from his position, seized his axe and cut off the limb and rolled it off of him. He then tried to raise him, but his father was dead and his feeble efforts were all in vain. Although he was out in the far woods by himself, and had never before seen a dead person, he was nothing daunted, but backed his sled close up to his father, and with great labor got the body on it, and, placing his head in his lap, drove home to his mother as fast as he could. The efforts of his mother to reanimate him were equally vain with his own, and the sorrowing neighbors came and dug him a grave under the cold snow, and laid him quietly to rest. His mother was greatly distressed at the loss of her husband, but she thanked God who had given her so good and brave a son. You and Custis must take great care of your kind mother and dear sisters when your father is dead. To do that you must learn to be good." [56] The choice of such a story as this for the admonition of a lad was itself a commentary on the simplicity of the sire. It was only when the boys became young men that Lee slowly dropped his moralizing and came to rely more on the effects of his personal comradeship with his sons.

Mildred made her appearance when Lee had been at the Narrows nearly five years. He had done much to improve the forts during that time, and had learned no little about the location of coast and harbor defenses. His logic had sharpened Colonel

---

[56] Lee to W. H. F. Lee, March 31, 1846; *Jones,* 370.

Totten's appeal for the better fortification of New York. A practical method had been suggested by him for procuring the sites of Forts Richmond and Tompkins, which were the property of the state of New York. The United States owned old Fort Gansevoort, far up the harbor. Buildings had sprung up around the fort. It was quite useless for defense; why not acquire Tompkins and Richmond by trading Fort Gansevoort, which New York could readily divide into lots and sell? This proposal, as far as is known, originated with Lee, and it was now about to be adopted by slow-moving congressmen, stirred by the reflection that New York might have been captured if the Oregon controversy had led to war with England.[57]

Superintending dull repair work at the Narrows, sharing in the plans of the board of engineers, and contributing a few suggestions for the better defense of New York were, when all was said, a scant return for five of the most valuable years of Lee's life. He was burdened, too, with the unpleasant details of much accounting, some of it especially obnoxious. Subscription to a newspaper had provoked correspondence. A mistake that led him to draw pay twice for May and June, 1845, was readily accepted by his superiors as no more than a mistake, but it distressed him profoundly. "It has caused me more mortification," he wrote the adjutant-general, "than any other act of my life, to find that I have been culpably negligent where the strictest accuracy is both necessary and required." [58]

Lee was settling down, in short, to another year of the formal-

---

[57] Appeals for fortifying Staten Island had been made by the chief engineer for several years. *Cf.* report for 1840–41; *Senate Docs.*, *2d sess.*, *27th Cong.*, vol. I, p. 120. The final summing up is in the report for 1845; *Senate Docs.*, *1st sess.*, *29th Cong.*, vol. I, p. 248. For Congress's authorization to acquire the Staten Island site under act of Aug. 8, 1846, see *Ex. Docs.*, *1st sess.*, *30th Cong.*, vol. I, p. 607. The first proposal by the chief engineer to exchange Fort Gansevoort for the forts on Staten Island appears in his report for 1841–42, *Ex. Docs.*, *3d sess.*, *27th Cong.*, vol. I, p. 241.

[58] N. Towson, paymaster-general, to R. Jones, adjutant-general, Feb. 12, 1846, with enclosures; *A. G. O. MS.*, File 32, T 46. For the correspondence over the newspaper subscription, see chief engineer to Lee, July 12, 1845, *loc. cit.*, vol. 13, p. 234; Lee to chief engineer, *MS.*, Aug. 6, 1845; *Eng. MSS.*, 780. For his monthly reports, quarterly reports (noted as *Q*) and returns, see Lee to chief engineer, May 1, 1841; *Eng. MSS.*, 319, June 2, 1841; *Eng. MSS.*, 330, July 5, 1841 (*Q*), 347; July 13, 1841, 355; July 13, 1841 (*Q*), 356; Aug. 9, 1841, 373; Sept. 10, 1841, 393; Oct. 11, 1841 (*Q*), 407; Nov. 11, 1841, 424; corrected *ibid.*, Nov. 19, 1841, No. 429; Nov. 2, 1841 (*Q*), 340; Dec. 9, 1841, 435; Jan. 10, 1842 (*Q*), 449; Jan. 28, 1842 (*Q*), 455; Feb. 4, 1842, 456; Feb. 28, 1842, 463; March 14, 1842, 468; April 2, 1842, 474½; April 22, 1842 (*Q*), 485; May 7, 1842, 491; June 9, 1842, 501; July 11, 1842 (*Q*), 508; July 22, 1842 (*Q*), 514; Aug. 5, 1842, 522; Sept. 8, 1842, 530; Oct. 14, 1842 (*Q*), 549; Nov. 4, 1842, 554; cor-

ized routine of an army engineer when word reached Washington on April 7, 1846, that the Mexican Government had again refused to receive the American minister, John Slidell, who was returning to the United States. On May 9 dispatches were received from Brevet Brigadier-General Zachary Taylor, announcing that his forces and the Mexicans had clashed on April 25, near the Rio Grande, in territory over which President Polk claimed a title. On May 11 Polk laid the facts before Congress, which declared war two days later. Meantime, unknown to the administration, Taylor had met a force of Mexicans at Palo Alto on May 8, and again at Resaca de la Palma on May 9, and had defeated it. Twenty thousand volunteers were soon called for from the Southern states. All the talk in Washington was of preparations, appointments, and expeditions. The line officers, of course, expected to be sent to Mexico as soon as a plan of operations was determined upon. But the engineers, especially those in charge of work at the forts—would they be given duty in the field? Nobody knew anything of any one's prospective assignments except that General Scott had overplayed his hand, was in disfavor, and had been forced to eat humble-pie in a letter which he had composed in answer to one from the Secretary of War, received, as Scott wrote, "at about 6 P.M. as I sat down to take a hasty plate of soup." Excited as the country was, it chuckled over that soup. Lee could only wait and, like all soldiers, hope for a part in the campaign the administration was feverishly, if unmethodically, planning.[59] If he were left at Fort Hamilton he might as well reconcile himself to the certainty that he would grow old, unregarded in a corps that would assuredly give preference to the engineers who distinguished themselves in war. They would have fame; he would have slippers and old age on the

rected *ibid.*, Nov. 12, 1842, 556; Dec. 1, 1842, 558; Jan. 2, 1843 (*Q*), 566; Feb. 1, 1843, 573; March 1, 1843, 581; April 4, 1843 (*Q*), 590; May 2, 1843, 597; June 5, 1843, 606; July 7, 1843 (*Q*), 613; Aug. 2, 1843 (*Q*), 621; Sept. 4, 1843, 627; Oct. 5, 1843 (*Q*), 632; Oct. 24, 1843 (*Q*), 647; Nov. 2, 1843, 650; Dec. 4, 1843, 654; Dec. 30, 1843 (*Q*), 658; May 1, 1844, 675; June 6, 1844, 681; July 11, 1844, 691; July 11, 1844 (*Q*), 692; July 30, 1844 (*Q*), 697; Aug. 6, 1844, 700; Aug. 21, 1844 (*Q*), 701; Sept. 12, 1844, 705; Oct. 12, 1844 (*Q*), 707; Nov. 2, 1844, 713; Jan. 1, 1845 (*Q*), 727; Feb. 1, 1845, 731; March 1, 1845; May 1, 1845, 754; May 6, 1845 (*Q*), 756; May 24, 1845, 761; June 3, 1845, 764; July 5, 1845 (*Q*), 772; Aug. 6, 1845, 780; Sept. 6, 1845, 784; Dec. 3, 1845, 803; Jan. 10, 1846 (*Q*), 808; Feb. 2, 1846, 814; April 7, 1846 (*Q*), 828; May 2, 1846, 832; May 25, 1846, 838; June 1, 1846, 843; Aug. 8, 1846, 864.

[59] An admirable account of these preliminaries of the Mexican War will be found in G. L. Rives: *The United States and Mexico*, vol. 2, p. 128 *ff.*, cited hereafter as *Rives*.

porch at Arlington, as merely another retired army officer. But if he were sent to Mexico and had a chance . . .

For three months after the declaration of war that "if" hung in his mind. Ruefully he went over to Governor's Island and wistfully he said farewell to the men bound for Mexico.[60] Returning, he found his work at the fort duller now than ever, because Kearny was advancing on Santa Fe, Taylor was gathering troops at Camargo for a march on Monterey, and Santa Anna had slipped through the blockade at Vera Cruz, inwardly mocking the Americans who connived at his entry in the belief that he would be willing to make a favorable peace. Then on August 19, 1846, Lee got the letter he was hoping to receive—orders from the chief engineer to turn over his work at the Narrows to Major Richard Delafield, to proceed, via Washington, to San Antonio de Bexar, Texas, and to report to Brigadier General John E. Wool for service in Mexico.[61] Twenty-one years after he had entered West Point, opportunity had come to Captain Lee of the engineers.

[60] His duties with the board of engineers had continued through the winter, but activities at Fort Hamilton, suspended during the cold months, were not resumed until May 19, owing to the fact that scarcely any of the appropriation had been left at the close of the previous year's operations (chief engineer to Lee, MS., May 6, 1846, MS. Letters to Officers of Engineers, vol. 14, p. 165; Lee to chief engineer, MS., May 19, 1846; Eng. MSS., 835; Rept. Chief Eng. Army, 1844–45, loc. cit., p. 247). With new funds provided under an act of May 21, Lee began a programme of the usual sort—repairs, remodelling, and waterproofing. He made still another journey into Connecticut to procure stone (chief engineer to Lee, MS., May 21, 1846, loc cit., vol. 14, p. 199; Lee to chief engineer, MS., July 9, 1846; Eng. MSS., 851; chief engineer to Lee, MS., July 11, 1846, loc. cit., vol. 14, p. 318; Lee to chief engineer, MS., Aug. 8, 1846; Eng. MSS., 864). For his farewell to the departing troops, see Markie Letters, 19–20.

[61] Chief engineer to Lee, MS., Aug. 17, 1846, loc. cit., vol. 14, p. 386; Orderly Book, vol. 3, p. 465; A. G. O., Aug. 25, 1846, S. O. 80. Lee was notified Aug. 21, 1846, that as his separation from the board of engineers was considered temporary, he should turn over to Major Delafield for the present the records of the board of engineers (chief engineer to Lee, loc. cit., vol. 14, p. 392). For Delafield, see Cullum, No. 180.

CHAPTER XIII

A CAMPAIGN WITHOUT A CANNON SHOT

MAKING up his statements as quickly as possible, Lee turned over the work at the Narrows to the capable Delafield, and hurried to Washington, where he filed his accounts on August 28, 1846. Three days later he made his will.[1] As he prepared his kit for field service his friends insisted on giving him presents for it —among them a bottle of much-praised whiskey, which politeness compelled him to accept and to take with him.[2] He had always moved promptly on receipt of orders, and now, under the spur of opportunity, he lost no time in adieux, even to the proud but anxious household at Arlington. On the first available steamer he travelled to New Orleans, where he was surprised to find, despite the flow of government funds in the purchase of supplies, that treasury notes were at a discount of 2½ per cent—a fact that grieved his thrifty soul.[3] From the busy Louisiana base he embarked for Port la Vaca, a Texas port town, on the bay of the same name, 120 miles down the coast of Texas from Galveston, through Pass Cavallo. Arriving there on September 13, 1846, he spent his first night on land at Sarassa[4] with a French family, M. and Mme. Monod. The next day he took horse for San Antonio, then styled San Antonio de Bexar, which he reached on September 21, a month and two days after he had been relieved of duty at Fort Hamilton.[5] It was a very rapid journey for the times.

[1] Lee to chief engineer, MS., Aug. 19, 1846, Aug. 28, 1846; Eng. MSS., 869–870. Will in Rockbridge County (Va.) Will Book, 1870. This document was never changed, even after the War between the States. It left all his property to Mrs. Lee for life and provided that after her death it should be distributed equally among his children unless Annie, who had received an injury to the eye, should need more than the others.
[2] Jones, 169.
[3] Lee to chief engineer, MS., Sept. 21, 1846; Eng. MSS., 882.
[4] The writer has been unable to locate this place. It is possible that the name was wrongly transcribed by Jones.
[5] Lee to chief engineer, MS., Sept. 13, 21, 1846; Eng. MSS., 877, 882; Lee to Mrs. Lee, March 27, 1857; Fitz Lee, 67.

The quaint border town had a civilian population of about 2000, chiefly farmers and herdsmen, many of them Mexicans.[6] It bore many marks of the war for Texas independence, and in its externals was still foreign. The old missions, the so-called "palaces," and the ruins of the Alamo, where the Texas garrison had been slaughtered ten years previously—all these were unlike anything Lee had ever seen before. The town's past, however, was engulfed in its present, and its quiet streets were swamped with soldiers. Two squadrons of regular cavalry were there, one battery of regular artillery, three companies of the Sixth Infantry, two regiments of Illinois infantry, and a sufficient sprinkling of other volunteers to raise the total to 3400 men.[7] The atmosphere was one of excited preparation, for it was known to every one that the troops were to start an advance into Mexico as soon as supplies were accumulated and equipment was complete. It was Lee's first contact, after twenty-one years of military service, with the contagious elation that pervades a camp when the talk is of a march "into the enemy's country." With that same spirit he was to become grimly familiar before he was to unbuckle his sword for the last time.

The commander of this expedition, the officer to whom Lee reported on arrival, was Brigadier General John E. Wool, the same Wool who had come to Fort Monroe for an inspection of the engineering work not long before General Macomb's order that had ended Lee's labors under Captain Andrew Talcott.[8] Wool had grizzled much since the hot day in July, 1834, when he had been rowed out to Fort Calhoun with Lieutenant Lee. He had received his promotion to the rank of brigadier in 1841, and in the years since Lee had been with him in Hampton Roads he had directed the transfer of the Cherokee Indians west of the Mississippi, but otherwise had been engaged in routine duties. He was now sixty-two, and although he had not heard a gun fired in action for thirty-one years, he was full of ardor and was organizing his forces with real skill.

Among the line officers at San Antonio, Lee probably found

[6] *Memoir Descriptive of the March of a Division of the United States Army, under the command of Brigadier-General John E. Wool from San Antonio . . . to Saltillo . . . by George W. Hughes . . .; Senate Doc. 32, 1st sess., 31st Cong.* (cited hereafter as *Hughes*), 9. The author was Wool's chief topographical engineer.
[7] *Hughes*, 5.   [8] See *supra*, pp. 124–25.

few whom he had met before, but on the staff were a number of West Pointers, some of whom served in his own corps or in the affiliated topographical engineers. To this latter service belonged a busy young second lieutenant named William B. Franklin, who was then making ready to set out on a reconnaissance. Sixteen years later, almost to the very day, that same Franklin was to be in command of some very troublesome troops at a place called Crampton's Gap, in South Mountain, Maryland. Another young man of whom Lee heard much talk at the time of his arrival was one of General Wool's aides-de-camp, Irvin McDowell, first lieutenant of artillery, then absent, none other than the McDowell whose threatened march on Richmond from the North had to be taken into account when Lee, on June 1, 1862, assumed command in front of the Confederate capital.

The officer with whom Lee had the closest official relations, from the very day he reached San Antonio, was Captain William D. Fraser of the corps of engineers, a New Yorker who had graduated from West Point at the head of the class of 1834. Fraser was seven years younger than Lee but had risen fast in the army and had been commissioned captain on the same day as Lee, who doubtless had met him before they came to Texas. Fraser had worked assiduously under Wool's orders and had well in hand most of the engineering arrangements for the expedition. General Wool, therefore, did not supersede him on the arrival of Captain Lee, but, it would appear, associated Lee with Fraser, more or less as a supplementary officer, not assigned to definite duty. Lee's first task was to assist in the collection of tools for use in road and bridge building. San Antonio had few artisans, prices were very high,[9] and neither Lee nor Fraser had any government funds with which to make purchases.[10] Progress accordingly was slow and results were discouraging.

Two days after Lee arrived, and while he and Captain Fraser were searching for picks and shovels, the topographical engineers set out to find the best road for General Wool's advance. The four officers who had this distinction must have been the envy of the whole camp as they rode off under Captain George W.

[9] *Hughes*, 9.
[10] Lee to chief engineer, *MS.*, Sept. 21, 1846; *Eng. MSS.*, 882. For Fraser, see *Cullum*, No. 750.

Hughes, with their guide and their interpreter, their wagons having gone ahead. Young Franklin was one of this quartet.[11]

The expedition had not long to wait after the topographical engineers started. On September 28 a column of some 1954 men moved out of San Antonio, toward the Rio Grande. The rear guard was to follow with delayed supplies. It was the first time that Lee, though he was not far from his fortieth birthday, had ever ridden with troops on a march against the enemy. Indeed, it may have been the first time since he left West Point that he had been with a column.

General Wool's advance was in accordance with the tentative and incomplete plan of campaign that had been slowly formulated after war had been declared. Mexico had conceded to Texas a boundary line no farther south than the river Nueces, which is approximately 130 miles north of the Rio Grande. President Polk claimed the territory running south to the Rio Grande and in March, 1846, had sent General Zachary Taylor forward to occupy it. Taylor had reached the river on March 28 at a point opposite the Mexican town of Matamoras, where he had entrenched himself in the works later known as Fort Brown. The efforts of the Mexicans to force him to abandon the line of the Rio Grande had led to the battles of Palo Alto and Resaca de la Palma. Following up his successes, Taylor had crossed the Rio Grande on May 18 and had occupied Matamoras, from which the enemy had fled. There he had remained until July 30, when he had started up the river to Camargo to undertake his part of the larger operations upon which the administration by that time had determined.

The plan was this: One small column was to be sent to seize New Mexico; another was to co-operate with the navy in upsetting the Mexican government of California. With these possessions taken from the enemy and held as war indemnity, General Taylor was to advance from the Rio Grande to Monterey, and General Wool, acting under Taylor's orders, was to go forward from the river to Chihuahua. These two advances were thus to be as shown on the opposite page.

The hope was that these operations and a strict blockade of the

11 *Hughes*, 12.

eastern coast would bring northern Mexico under American control.

Nothing beyond this had been decided. The administration knew little about the country that was to be entered. The general staff was not certain whether Wool could reach Chihuahua, whether it was really important that he should do so, or whether he and Taylor could subsist their troops on local supplies if they

were to attempt to move southward toward Mexico City after they had reached their first objectives. The strength of the Mexican forces in nearby districts was equally unknown. Washington waited on Taylor for a more definite plan; Taylor waited on Washington for more extensive orders.[12]

An uneventful march of 164 miles in eleven days brought Wool's first column to the Rio Grande, just east of the presidio named after the river. The rapidity of this advance was attributed by one observer to "the indefatigable exertions of those distinguished officers, Captains Lee and Frazier [Fraser]," who built a road and bridged the streams.[18] Being now on the boundary

[12] Taylor's correspondence with the War Department will be found in *House Doc. 60, 1st sess., 30th Cong.* The uncertainties of the plan of operations are well set forth in 2 *Rives*, 195 ff., 276 ff.

[18] Francis Baylies, *A Narrative of General Wool's Campaign in Mexico* (cited hereafter as *Baylies*), 12.

claimed by the United States, the army on its next advance would assume the offensive in Mexican territory. The ardor of every soldier was inflamed at the thought. "We have met with no resistance yet," Lee wrote his wife. "The Mexicans who were guarding the passage, retired on our approach. There has been a great whetting of knives, grinding of swords, and sharpening of bayonets, ever since we reached the river." [14] Invasion was not, however, easily begun. The few fords of the Rio Grande were deep, and the current was swift. It was necessary to camp on the American side of the river until the engineers could place a bridge with the pontoons Captain Fraser had built at San Antonio and had brought forward in the wagon train. Lee doubtless had a hand in this. He probably assisted, also, in choosing and running the lines of the field defenses that General Wool ordered the engineers to construct at the bridgeheads. It was the first earthwork he ever constructed of the general type that he, more than any one man, was to develop in utility.

On October 12, the bridge having been completed, the whole force passed over to the right bank of the Rio Grande. There, under a flag of truce, a Mexican officer, escorted by a contingent of lancers, was awaiting General Wool. He brought news that was more pleasant to the Americans than to the messenger: General Taylor had advanced to Monterey and after a battle there had forced the Mexican troops to withdraw. The articles of capitulation had provided that the Mexicans should march out of the town with their arms, and should retire beyond a designated line. The "forces of the United States," the sixth article of capitulation read, "will not advance beyond the line . . . before the expiration of eight weeks, or until the orders or instructions of the respective governments can be received." [15] This had been signed on September 24. The Mexican officer exhibited a copy of the paper and insisted that General Wool's advance directly contravened the agreement, which virtually declared an armistice. Wool, of course, was delighted at Taylor's success, of which he had previously received no definite information, and he did not consider that the first stages of the advance he had in contemplation were violative of the agreement. He accordingly sent back

[14] *Jones, 50.* [15] *Ex. Doc. 60, 1st sess., 30th Cong., 349–50.*

word that he would continue his march.[16] The Mexican withdrew as he had come.

In the hearts of inexperienced soldiers, ambitious for battle, this incident raised hope of early action. Anywhere, they reasoned, an enemy might be lurking; the very next day they might have opportunity of capturing a Monterey of their own. Expectancy tightened. But how, meantime, should the column proceed? Inquiry showed no direct western route to Chihuahua. The only way to reach that city was to move southward and take one of the few roads that ran northwestward from the general vicinity of Monclova, which was about 200 miles south of the American camp near the Rio Grande. That, then, must be the line of advance. With high heart the army followed a route the topographical engineers selected, and on October 30 reached the environs of Monclova.[17] Not an enemy was seen; not a gun was fired at a human mark; some of the enthusiasm of the army began to exhaust itself as the days passed in hard marches through a dull country. Nor was this uneventful march the only disappointment of the soldiers: General Wool considered that he had now reached a position where the Monterey armistice applied and that he could not go farther until it expired. This meant nearly three weeks around Monclova, a town of 8000, cleaner and more pleasant than most Mexican cities, but no place, surely, for a restive army to wait. General Wool kept the men occupied with drills, and exercised his talents for organization by establishing depots and a hospital. The spirit of the volunteers, however, did not respond to routine duties. Wool became doubtful of his ability to control them during a period of prolonged inaction, and he so notified General Taylor.[18]

While waiting for the expiration of the armistice, Wool continued to study the routes to Chihuahua. He concluded there was no practicable road for an army unless he moved almost to Saltillo and thence followed the route via Parras. This seemed so circuitous a way to an objective of such uncertain value that he proposed the abandonment of that expedition and requested

[16] *Hughes,* 19.
[17] Justin H. Smith: *The War with Mexico* (cited hereafter as *J. H. Smith*), 1, 270 *ff.*; *Baylies,* 13–15.
[18] 2 *Rives,* 290; *Hughes,* 26.

Taylor, instead, to permit him to move on Saltillo.[19] He asked, also, to be allowed to break up his old line of communications and to open a new and shorter line by way of Camargo, which was already being used as Taylor's principal depot.

Lee was fairly busy during this time. Captain Fraser had gone back during the march to Monclova[20] in order to conduct the rearguard, which had subsequently advanced from San Antonio under Colonel Sylvester Churchill. After Fraser came up with Churchill on November 6, the engineers examined Monclova and its vicinity with a view to its defense in the future. This was no easy task, for the town was commanded by hills. Nevertheless the two officers selected a site and made ready to build a redoubt.[21] Lee prepared, in addition, a rough map of the town and its environs.[22] He had, ere this, established himself in the good opinion of General Wool, and though he had thus far received no important independent assignments to duty, he was apprised of Wool's problems and plans.

The Monterey armistice expired on November 19, according to Wool's interpretation of its terms; so, on the 18th, he pushed his advance guard forward. That night he received an express from General Taylor. This directed him to maintain his position at Monclova, to abandon the plan of operations against Chihuahua, and to open the proposed new line of communications with Camargo.[23] A few days later he was authorized to move on Parras, whence he could join Taylor, or unite with Worth at Saltillo, or march on Chihuahua, if changed circumstances required.[24]

On November 24, leaving five companies of Illinois volunteers to guard Monclova, the column took up its southward march. A pioneer detachment that had been organized at Monclova from the Illinois troops was sent ahead under Fraser and Lee and

[19] 2 Rives, 290.

[20] Baylies, loc. cit., 13, said Fraser was left behind to build works on the Rio Grande at the crossing.

[21] Lee to chief engineer, MS., Dec. 5, 1846; Eng. MSS., 906.

[22] Original among the Lee Maps, Virginia Military Institute, Lexington, Va.

[23] Lee to chief engineer, MS., Dec. 5, 1846; Eng. MSS., 906; Taylor to A. G. O., Nov. 9, 1846; Ex. Doc. 60, 1st sess., 30th Cong., p. 361.

[24] Hughes, 27; Taylor to Secretary of War, Nov. 24, Ex. Doc. 60, loc. cit., 377. The reason for assuming this order came subsequently to that for abandoning the Chihuahua expedition is that in his letter of Dec. 5, 1846, summarizing the dispatch received on Nov. 18, Lee does not mention the order to move on Parras.

prepared the roads for the main army. Through the efforts of the quartermaster's department, tools for this work were at last available. The pioneers must have worked hard, for the march of the infantry was fast and uninterrupted, though some parts of the road, even when repaired, were rough and difficult for the artillery and wagons.

Seventy miles from Monclova, the troops left the Saltillo road and struck west for Parras. Northers, fast-changing temperature, dust, and heat taxed the endurance of the soldiers. But Wool kept them moving. Ten days after the start, the army halted near Parras, and on the following day it took position in a broad plain about two miles north of the city. The distance covered on the march was computed at from 165 to 181 miles.

The column was now about 365 miles within the enemy's country and had not seen a single Mexican soldier since bidding farewell to the officer and lancers who had met the vanguard at the crossing of the Rio Grande. Part of Taylor's army, under General W. J. Worth, was at Saltillo, about one hundred miles eastward, as the roads ran. Presumably there was an enemy in front of Worth, but here at Parras there was hospitality rather than hostility, a welcome rather than a battle. "Our camp," wrote the chronicler of the expedition, "was constantly crowded with the beauty and fashion of the town, who visited the tents of the officers without hesitation or restraint, and the most cordial feelings and intercourse were established between us." [25] It was a dull experience, however, despite the visits of the ladies, for men who had come to Mexico anticipating daily battles and hourly opportunity for feats of daring.

Nearly two weeks went by at Parras, with no alarms and no promise of excitement. Then, on December 17, there came a hurried messenger from General Worth. The Mexicans were preparing to attack Saltillo, Worth wrote, and he wanted Wool, if possible, to reinforce him. Wool immediately decided to do so, and determined to move at once and at top speed, because his only practicable road to Saltillo lay, in part, by the route the enemy would certainly take in moving on that city. If the Mexicans reached the hacienda of La Encantala, on the road from San Luis

[25] *Hughes*, 26 *ff.*, 33; Lee to chief engineer, *MS.*, Dec. 5, 1846, *loc. cit.*

Potosi to Saltillo, a junction between Worth and Wool would be impossible and both American forces might be wiped out.[26] Orders were given to break camp and to put the column in motion. Soon there was hustle and excitement everywhere, no man in the ranks knowing whether the enemy was a hundred miles away or just over the horizon.

Thanks to the good organization that Wool had set up, the head of the column moved within two hours after word had been given to break camp. For the next four days there was no rest for any one, except when men and horses became exhausted. Fearful that the threat against Worth might be serious, and that Saltillo might soon be attacked, Wool kept up a forced march.

Much of his line of advance lay through a valley and part of it through mountains from Patagalana to Castanuela. Here again the engineers had to improve the road to make it practicable for the wagon train and the guns. Progress on that part of the march was necessarily very slow, but on the better stretches of the road the infantry made thirty-five miles one day and almost as far another day. Not only so, but an officer who followed the troops reported that with the exception of the camp sites he saw no evidence that an army had passed. "Not a broken wagon, or a dead animal, or a straggler was to be seen." [27]

On the evening of December 20, being close to the positions the foe might be expected to occupy in an advance on Saltillo, Wool sent forward a reconnoitring party. It returned with a report that no enemy was to be found. The next day the little army moved forward again and encamped near Agua Nueva, some seventeen miles south of Saltillo. The troops had come more than one hundred miles in four days—a very good performance—but they were denied the battle they expected to fight upon arrival. For it developed that the reported advance of the enemy was a false alarm and that all Wool's haste had been to no purpose.[28] As he nursed his bruised and sore feet, the soldier in the ranks found small compensation in reflecting that the forced

---

[26] 2 *Rives*, 304.
[27] *Hughes*, 32 n., 61–62. *Cf.* Lee to chief engineer, *MS.*, Jan. 1, 1847; *Eng. MSS.*, 910. Hughes said the army made nearly forty miles a day on two days of the march, but Wool reported the distances here given.
[28] *Hughes*, 26; Lee to chief engineer, *MS.*, Jan. 1, 1847; *Eng. MSS.*, 910; Wool to R. Jones, *MS.*, Jan 17, 1847, Office of the Adjutant-General of the Army, File *Wool*, 116.

march had brought about a very desirable concentration of the United States troops in the zone where the enemy might most reasonably be expected to attack—whenever that might be.[29] Wool's long separation from the other forces had been a jest among the soldiers of Taylor, whose favorite gag was, "When did you hear from General Wool?"[30] But now that they had emerged from the wilderness the fine discipline of Wool's men evoked much praise.[31]

Lee now found himself with one division of what was immeasurably the largest body of troops he had ever seen, fully 6000 men! Once the reconnaissances were made and the camp was laid out he had no special duties until Christmas eve, when Captain Fraser received orders to report at Monterey.[32] This left Lee the senior engineer officer with Wool. For the time being, his new responsibilities were negligible. That evening his mind turned homeward, where he knew his children were preparing for Christmas. From his tent he wrote Custis and Rooney: "I hope good Santa Claus will fill my Rob's stocking tonight; that Mildred's, Agnes's and Annie's may break down with good things. I do not know what he may have for you and Mary, but if he only leaves for you one half of what I wish, you will want for nothing. I have frequently thought if I had one of you on each side of me riding on ponies, such as I could get you, I would be comparatively happy."[33]

Shortly after breakfast Christmas morning a hurried message from some of the subsistence officers was sent to headquarters: The enemy was coming! Great clouds of dust had been seen in the line of his advance. The alarm was sounded at once. The men were ordered to stand to their arms; General Butler was notified and was asked for orders. Lee immediately hurried out from camp and found a good point of observation. There he threw himself on the grass, his bridle rein over his arm, and focussed his telescope on the gap in the mountains through which the Mexi-

---

[29] Major General William O. Butler had also been marching, meantime, from Monterey to support Worth, and as he outranked both Worth and Wool, he assumed command (Taylor's orders, Dec. 22, 1846; *Ex. Doc. 60, 1st sess., 30th Cong.,* p. 515).
[30] J. R. Kenley: *Memoirs of a Maryland Volunteer* (cited hereafter as *Kenley*), 167. Taylor had accounted Wool's expedition an "entire failure" (*J. H. Smith,* I, 276).
[31] W. S. Henry: *Campaign Sketches of the War with Mexico,* 275.
[32] Lee to chief engineer, *MS.,* Jan. 1, 1847, *loc. cit.*
[33] Lee to G. W. C. and W. H. F. Lee, Dec. 24, 1846; *Fitz Lee,* 34.

cans would have to advance. Behind him the troops only awaited his report that the enemy had been sighted, for General Butler sent word that as soon as the Mexicans approached, Wool's little army was to fall back. "The Mexicans, however, did not make their appearance," Lee wrote his wife that night. "Many regrets were expressed at Santa Anna's having spoiled our Christmas dinner for which ample preparations had been made. The little roasters remained tied to the tent pins wondering at their deferred fate, and the headless turkeys retained their plumage unscathed. Finding the enemy did not come, preparations were again made for dinner." The feast did not awaken enthusiasm in Lee's heart. He found, instead, what comfort he could in writing Mrs. Lee. "We have had many happy, happy Christmasses together," he said. "It is the first time we have been entirely separated at this holy time since our marriage. I hope it does not interfere with your happiness, surrounded as you are by father, mother, children, and dear friends. I therefore trust you are well and happy, and that this is the last time I shall be absent from you during my life. May God preserve and bless you till then and forever is my constant prayer." [34] The language differed little from that which he was to employ in a letter written on a dark Christmas day, with far greater issues at stake, fifteen years thereafter.[35]

Investigation proved that the clouds of smoke seen by the subsistence officers had been raised by the Arkansas cavalry, which had been out reconnoitring,[36] but rumor and military logic still represented General Santa Anna as close at hand. On December 28 there came another false alarm, which caused General Butler to order General Wool to move his force back where it could have the support of the other troops. The site chosen by Butler, much to Wool's disgust, was Encantada, at the entrance to the valley that leads to Saltillo. It was a most uncomfortable place, where the command, in Wool's grumbling words, was "exposed to high winds and almost constant clouds of dust." [37]

Wool was getting skeptical, by this time, of all the false alarms of Mexican activity near at hand, and when a new report came one evening of a great force marching down on the Americans,

---

[34] Lee to Mrs. Lee, Dec. 25, 1846; *Fitz Lee*, 35.   [35] See *infra*, p. 620.
[36] R. S. Ripley: *The War with Mexico* (cited hereafter as *Ripley*), vol. 1, p. 328.
[37] Wool to R. Jones. MS., Jan. 17, 1847, *loc. cit*

he determined to ascertain the enemy's position. Lee happened to be with him at the time and volunteered to make the required scout. The general at once accepted Lee's offer, told him to procure a guide, and gave orders that a company of cavalry should meet him at the outer picket line and go with him. Lee found a young man, the son of a neighboring old Mexican, who knew the country, and he prevailed upon him to act as his guide. Before they set out Lee showed the Mexican his brace of pistols and gave him to understand that if he played him false he should have the contents of them.

In some way Lee missed the cavalry escort at the picket line. Rather than search for it and waste the hours of darkness, he determined to press on with no other companion than the unwilling native. They had not ridden many miles when they saw in the road, by the aid of a bright moon's full rays, the tracks of many wagons and mules. Lee examined these closely to see if he could discern whether artillery had been along. As he found no evidence of this, he reasoned that a wagon train had traversed the road after the guns had passed. The wagons, he concluded, evidently had been used for foraging or reconnoitring and were now returning to camp. This seemed strong evidence that the enemy was near at hand, but wishing to confirm it by closer reconnaissance, Lee decided to push on until he came to the Mexican picket line. A long ride brought him no sign of the enemy, and no challenge from picket or outpost, but a little later he saw the light of numerous camp fires on a hill not far away. This was enough for the Mexican guide, who doubtless decided that if he and the hard-riding American officer were captured he would be hanged as a spy and traitor. He besought Lee to turn back. There was a stream near the place where the lights were burning, he insisted; there could be no doubt that an army had chosen that site for its camp. They must return or they would be caught! Lee was not quite satisfied. He let the native stay where he was, and rode on alone. Presently he was rewarded by the sight of what seemed to be a large number of tents on the hillside. Some impulse carried him still farther, through a little sleeping town and down to the stream, across which he could hear loud talking and noise. He was now so close that he could see clearly—and could realize that the white objects he had taken for tents were a large flock of sheep, part of a caravan that was moving to market and had stopped by the road for the night. Undisturbed, Lee crossed the stream and, with the little Spanish he possessed, questioned the drovers. They were as much surprised by his appearance as he was at finding them to be peaceable herdsmen, and they told him the Mexican army was still on the other side of the mountains.

With many thanks and *adios,* Lee rejoined his guide and hurried back to camp, to find something of a hubbub over his failure to return sooner. General Wool, suspecting duplicity, had sent for the father of the guide and was holding him prisoner, with threats to hang him if Lee were not forthcoming. "The Mexican," said Lee, in recounting the story long afterwards, "was the most delighted man to see me." [38]

Lee had ridden forty miles, but with the information given him by the drovers he felt that he could speedily locate the Mexican forces. He rested three hours, changed mounts and started off again with a cavalry escort. This time he went much farther than during the night, and when he returned it was with fairly definite news of the position of the enemy.

Wool apparently believed that hard work was the best reward of men who had done it, and shortly after Lee's reconnaissance he named him acting inspector general without relieving him as engineer.[39] Scarcely had Lee assumed these duties than there came another wild report of Santa Anna's advance with a great force. This caused Butler to order Wool's withdrawal to Buena Vista, a place six miles from Saltillo and destined to have fame as the scene of a hard battle the following month.[40] The change

[38] The story of this reconnaissance was first printed in *Jones,* 288–90, and appears also in *Long* (49–51) and in *Brock* (168–69). It doubtless was told Jones by Lee at Lexington. Jones probably is in error in saying that on the second day of his adventure Lee brought back *precise* news of the enemy's position, for Wool wrote the adjutant general on Jan. 17 that it was almost impossible to get accurate news of the movements of Santa Anna. The date of this reconnaissance is not given by Jones, who simply says it was "not very long before the battle of Buena Vista" (p. 228). Inasmuch, however, as mention is made of the bright moonlight, the adventure must have occurred at the very end of December, 1846, or in the first week of January, 1847, as the moon was full on Jan. 1, 1847 (*American Almanac,* 1847, p. 10).
[39] Order No. 189, Jan. 10, 1847, Headquarters Centre Division; Orders and Special Orders Headquarters of the Army, War with Mexico, 1847–48, *MS.,* Office of the Adjutant-General of the Army.
[40] Wool to R. Jones, Jan. 17, 1847, *loc. cit.*

brought relief from the dust and drafts of Encantada, but it probably brought, also, several days of hard labor for Lee in locating a new camp and in making good its approaches.

Pleased as General Wool was at leaving Encantada, he was growing weary of continuous wild tales of Santa Anna's advance. General Taylor was even more disgusted at the endless reports of threatened attacks that never materialized. Lee chanced to be at Taylor's headquarters one day when an excited young officer announced that he had seen 20,000 Mexican troops moving up with 250 guns.

"Captain," asked Taylor, "do you say that you *saw* that force?"

"Yes, General," said the officer.

"Captain," answered the General, "if you say you saw it, of course I must believe you; but I would not have believed it if I had seen it myself."

The old General's critical attitude toward exaggerated reports of the enemy's strength made a deep impression on Lee. Sixteen years later, on the field of Chancellorsville, he was to meet a wild report of the Federals' movements and strength with a recountal of Taylor's answer that day at Buena Vista.[41]

It was not alone of Santa Anna's movements that rumor spread among the waiting troops. By the middle of January, 1847, it was whispered everywhere that another American army was mustering on the coast, and that a descent was to be made on Vera Cruz by General Scott.[42] For once, camp-fire gossip was right. The previous November, Scott had prepared a detailed plan for an attack on the principal Mexican Gulf port,[43] and while Lee was tracking the drovers' caravan, Scott was at Brazos de Santiago, off the mouth of the Rio Grande, gathering ships and supplies for what he expected would be the major operation of the war.[44] Campaigning without a cannon shot was about to end, for Captain Lee in particular.

[41] Charles Marshall: *Appomattox,* 4.
[42] *Kenley, op. cit.,* 301, heard this rumor for the first time on Jan. 14.
[43] *Ex. Doc. 60, 1st sess., 30th Cong.,* p. 1270 ff.
[44] Scott spelled the name of his base in various ways. Brassos san Iago was the most ponderous official form.

CHAPTER XIV

First Experiences Under Fire
(vera cruz)

When Captain Lee learned of the Vera Cruz expedition is uncertain. Nor is it known whether he exerted himself to procure a transfer to Scott's army. There is no evidence to bear out the tradition that Scott particularly requested that Lee be sent to him.[1] Scott's order book shows no such entry, and his correspondence with the War Department discloses few requests for the services of individual staff officers. He wrote General Butler: "I do not wish to ask, specifically, for the chief of any branch of the general staff now on duty under the orders of Major General Taylor."[2] It may have been that Scott requested Lee's services, in spite of the absence of any record to that effect; it is more probable that Lee's name was mentioned to Scott by Colonel Totten, who had been chosen chief engineer of the expedition that was to operate farther south. Totten was then fifty-nine, and though he possessed extraordinary physical endurance, he doubtless wished to associate with him the best of his young subordinates.

Whatever their inspiration, Lee received orders about January 16, 1847, to proceed to Brazos and there to join General Scott.[3] Lee was doubtless overjoyed to go, for he was not advantageously placed with General Wool. He was to show, very shortly, that he possessed the "strategic sense" that is indispensable at army headquarters, but with Wool, he had no opportunities of displaying it. In northern Mexico he could only have had a suitable opening at the headquarters of General Taylor, and thither he had small

---

[1] *Long,* 51.   [2] Jan. 8, 1847; *Ex. Doc. 56, 1st sess., 30th Cong.,* p. 44.
[3] Wool in his dispatch of Jan. 16, 1847, to R. Jones, *loc. cit.,* mentioned Lee's orders in a postscript, as though they had just been received. The orders for Lee certainly came between Jan. 10 and 17, 1847. Orders for the detachment of a large part of Wool's division had been revised on Jan. 12, 1847 (*Ibid.*).

chance of receiving a transfer, though he and Taylor were fourth cousins, whether they were aware of it or not.[4]

With hasty farewells and high hopes, Lee left Wool about. January 17, 1847, just before his fortieth birthday. Mounted on his mare Creole, he made a long ride of more than 250 miles. He probably was in the company of some of the troops sent from Taylor's army to Scott, much to the indignation of Taylor and his lieutenants. The journey was completed without mishap or hardship. Creole was in such good condition when Lee rode her into Brazos that she attracted no little attention.

Lee found General Scott immersed in preparations for the descent on Vera Cruz, fuming at every wasted hour and writing vigorous letters to all whom he accounted guilty of delaying the start of the expedition. The newly arrived captain of engineers was received as a member of the general staff attached to Scott's headquarters. He stepped overnight, as it were, from the execution of small operations to the planning of great enterprises, and although he did not know it, he had started up the ladder of fame. He found himself, too, in the company of friends, among them Major John L. Smith of the engineers and "Joe" Johnston, his sworn comrade of West Point and Fort Monroe. When the time came for quarters to be assigned on shipboard, Johnston and Lee were given a cabin together on the General's ship, the *Massachusetts.*

Creole and one of his other horses Lee left in the care of Jim Connally, his orderly,[5] for fear that if they were forwarded by the army hostlers they would be injured aboard ship. Even as it was, Lee was destined to worry over the rough handling his mounts might be forced to endure. "I hope they may both reach the shore again in safety," he wrote his sons, "but I fear they will have a hard time. They will first have to be put aboard a steamboat and carried to the ship that lies about two miles out at sea, then hoisted in, and how we shall get them ashore again, I do not know. Probably throw them overboard and let them swim there." [6]

---

[4] *Letters of Zachary Taylor* (Bixby Collection), p. viii.
[5] This man's first name is wrongly transcribed Jem in *Jones,* 372, and in the other biographies that copied Jones's version of Lee's letter of Feb. 27, 1847, to his sons.
[6] Lee to his sons, Feb. 27, 1847; *Jones,* 371–73.

On February 15, 1847, Scott raised his red pennant and led the way down the coast toward Tampico, where some 6000 American soldiers were awaiting transports. Three days later the convoy was off the mouth of the Panuco. Seen from the river, Tampico must have stirred the imagination of Lee and the other soldiers. It was built on the side of a hill rising on the right bank of the stream. A wide, well-paved market place stood between the wharves and the red and white houses of the principal citizens. But Tampico, like many another city, presented its best side to the visitor. Its back streets and its suburbs contained wretched rows of gloomy shacks, sheltering a population deep in poverty.[7]

The next morning, February 19, Lee went ashore in the suite of General Scott, whose known love of pomp and display was to be gratified to the fullest that day by the waiting regiments in Tampico. The troops had all been paid off on the 18th, and were in a humor to contribute to a holiday. As Scott and his staff approached, Lee saw the river bank lined with soldiers, while the heaviest guns barked a salute. At the landing below the market place, the artillery were drawn up, and large details of infantry kept back the multitude of Mexicans who were intent on seeing the leader of the hated *Llanquies,* as the worthy Tampicoans styled the "Yankees." When Scott stepped on land, the band from Governor's Island struck up a tune, and all the high officers then ashore came forward to pay their respects. They had a mount at hand for Scott, a fine gray horse with handsome trappings, but the General declined to ride. His great bulk rising above that of all the large men of his staff and escort, he strode across the market place and up the streets to the quarters that had been selected for him. All Tampico seemed to be looking out of the windows at him or gaping from the pavement.[8]

Scott was soon deep in conferences with the commanders, so Lee had some time for sight-seeing in the town. In the company of Major Smith he had a taste of the boasted Mexican chocolate, which greatly pleased his companion. He soon began to meet old acquaintances, among them Lieutenant William Barry, whom he had known at the Narrows in New York harbor. As a lover of

---

[7] *Autobiography of an English Soldier with the U. S. Army* (cited hereafter as *English Soldier*), 134, 137.

[8] *Kenley*, 238–39; Lee to his sons, Feb. 27, 1847, *loc. cit.*

animals, Lee kept an eye open, also, for the town's showing in horses, donkeys, and ponies, and when he wanted to have a look at the fortifications he procured a pony for the purpose.

Altogether it was a diverting and exciting day. For many of the men it ended in a disastrous conflict with the strong drink of Mexico. "Everybody talked, everybody knew what was just told him, everybody was delighted and everybody made a night of it, except the town-guard, and it had a night of it, for there was the sound of revelry on the banks of the Panuco. Drunken soldiers and drunken sailors fraternized, and the long bitter oath of the Western volunteer and teamster drowned the *caramba* of the Mexican. The full moon came up to lighten the scene, while the glowing fires and the fiery furnaces of the steamers in the river threw a lurid glare upon the heavy armaments bristling upon their decks." [9]

On February 20, Lee steamed southward again with Scott aboard the *Massachusetts*. This time their destination was the Island of Lobos, the rendezvous of the fleet, seventy miles south of Tampico and 200 miles up the Gulf coast from Vera Cruz. Part of the passage was rough and most discomforting to Joe Johnston, but it did not disturb Lee, who found what company he could with the officers who possessed sea legs, among them Lieutenant John Sedgwick, formerly at the Narrows. [10]

The *Massachusetts* arrived off Lobos on February 21, but did not discharge her passengers because of the heavy weather. [11] The place itself was so uninviting in appearance that the delay in landing could only have seemed a hardship to those who were still in the throes of *mal de mer*. Lobos was only a few feet above the surface of the sea, which broke in heavy surf. Barrenness was everywhere except for stunted shrubs. Even these had been cut away by the six regiments of American troops who had been landed and encamped there to prevent the spread of smallpox that had broken out aboard one of the ships. [12]

The day after Lee's arrival off Lobos the guns of the sloop *Saint Mary* and the cannon on shore fired a salute in honor of

[9] *Kenley*, 239.　　　　　　[10] Lee to his sons, Feb. 27, 1847, *loc. cit.*
[11] J. J. Oswandel: *Notes on the Mexican War* (cited hereafter as *Oswandel*), 59.
[12] *English Soldier*, 142–43; *Oswandel*, 58; Scott to Marcy, Feb. 28, 1847; *Exec. Doc. 60, 1st sess., 30th Cong.*, p. 87.

Washington's birthday. Most of the troops celebrated the anniversary with such dinners as could be provided from the scant stores, and not a few of them found the liquor with which to drink toasts to the success of their adventure.[13] Almost before rebellious stomachs had become quiet there came another storm that set the ships abobbing.

General Scott, meantime, was getting more and more restless. His transports, surfboats, and supplies had been held back, he wrote, "by no want of foresight, arrangement or energy on my part, as I dare affirm." The season was drawing on; if he did not capture Vera Cruz and get into a higher country before the beginning of April the yellow-fever would be fatal to the expedition.[14] On February 25 he was able to re-embark the troops on the island, as the smallpox was under control, but even then he had to fume nearly a week before he could give the order to make sail. During this period of waiting Lee may have had some hand in preparing the orders for the guidance of the engineers after their landing at Vera Cruz.[15] Otherwise, he was master of his own time. Some of his leisure he devoted to a long newsy letter to his older sons at home, a letter in which narrative was mingled with admonition in a somewhat emotional strain that he never employed except in addressing his boys. "I shall not feel my long separation from you," he said, "if I find that my absence has been of no injury to you, and that you have both grown in goodness and knowledge, as well as stature. But, ah! how much I will suffer on my return if the reverse has occurred! You enter all my thoughts, into all my prayers; and on you, in part, will depend whether I shall be happy or miserable, as you know how much I love you. You must do all in your power to save me pain."[16]

The end of riding the tides off Lobos came on March 3. By no means all of Scott's transport was then at the island, and half his surfboats had not arrived, but he felt that what he had at hand was sufficient for the first stage of his operations. The red pennant was accordingly raised once more and the fleet began to make its way down the coast, headed by the steam vessels. Scott himself walked the *Massachusetts* from bow to stern, watching

---

[13] *Oswandel*, 59.   [14] Scott to Marcy, Feb. 28, 1847, *loc. cit.*
[15] *Cf.* G. O. 33, Feb. 25, 1847, with *Eng. MSS.*, 993.
[16] R. E. Lee to his sons, Feb. 27, 1847, *loc. cit.*

the movement of the other ships. The soldiers on all the transports were cheering in high glee, and the sailors were singing:

"We are now bound for the shores of Mexico
And there Uncle Sam's soldiers we will land, hi, oh!"[17]

The weather was favorable as the fleet continued southward before the wind. Shortly after noon on March 5, following the little brig *Porpoise,* Lee saw Vera Cruz, with its castle, and a little later he sighted the American fleet that had been blockading the port for months. All around the *Massachusetts* and astern of her were transports, carrying their full canvas and manœuvring boldly, despite the reefs among the islands. As the incoming ships passed the men-of-war, the soldiers crowded the rail and sent up roars of greeting, to which the sailors instantly replied in kind. Some of the transports dropped anchor amid the warships to the lee of Isla Verde, directly off Vera Cruz; the others kept on eleven miles farther to the anchorage off Anton Lizardo, where many supply ships already were assembled. It must have been a day of many thrills for Captain Lee of the engineers.[18]

Commodore David Conner, senior officer of the navy in Mexican waters, had been in touch with Scott since December and had studied the coast carefully to determine where Scott's army could best effect a landing for the investment of Vera Cruz. A wise choice of a landing place was, of course, most important to the army, inasmuch as it was taken for granted that the Mexicans would offer the sternest resistance. The day after Scott's arrival, Conner invited the General, his principal officers, and his staff to make from the sea a reconnaissance of the landing places and of the town and fortress as well. Lee went with the rest aboard the steamer *Petrita,* and they ventured so close to the castle fort off Vera Cruz, San Juan d'Ulloa by name, that men on the other ships expected to see them blown out of the water. The castle opened on the *Petrita* when it was a mile and a half distant, but the fire went wild. It was the first hostile shot Captain Lee had ever heard as a soldier. A young lieutenant in the party, George

[17] *Oswandel,* 63.
[18] W. H. Parker: *Recollections of a Naval Officer* (cited hereafter as *Parker*), 82–83; Raphael Semmes, *Service Afloat and Ashore* (cited hereafter as *Semmes*), 124–25.

Gordon Meade, who was later to be one of Lee's chief opponents, thought that General Scott took needless risks in going so close inshore; a single hit might have disabled the little ship, and two or three rounds more might have broken up the expedition.[19]

This reconnaissance brought General Scott to the opinion Commodore Conner already had formed, namely, that the best available landing place was on a sandy beach about three miles southeast of the walls of Vera Cruz, opposite the little island of Sacrificios. Anchorage was afforded here, sheltered by the island and used by foreign ships. It was a rather small roadstead, but it offered a measure of protection against the frequent "northers" that were and are the curse of the sailor's life off the Mexican coast.

Immediately on his return from the reconnaissance Scott gave orders for a landing the following day at the selected beach. Hope and excitement both ran high. Dawn, however, brought rough weather and prompted postponement of the enterprise until the next morning. All the transports were sent down to Anton Lizardo, because Scott had determined to transfer the troops to the men-of-war, and thereby reduce the number of ships that had to be crowded into the Sacrificios anchorage.

March 9 was to Lee perhaps the most interesting day he had thus far spent as a soldier. Early in the morning the troops were placed in the surfboats and were rowed to the men-of-war, the decks of which were soon jammed with men, muskets, and equipment. When the soldiers had all been transferred, the bands struck up, and the steamers started northward between 10 and 11 o'clock, headed by Commodore Conner's flagship, the *Raritan,* behind which came the *Massachusetts.* In perfect weather, the fleet passed over nine miles of calm seas in two hours, and dropped anchor in assigned positions at Sacrificios. The light *Spitfire,* under Commander Tatnall, and the *Vixen,* Commander Sands, together with five armed schooners, were run in close ashore to cover the landing. Thus far, not a gun had been fired, though it was assumed that the Mexicans were in position behind the dunes and were merely biding their time. The crews of the

---

[19] George Meade: *Life and Letters of George Gordon Meade* (cited hereafter as *Meade*), 1, 187. Parker, *op. cit.,* 82, was manifestly in error in saying the vessel was not fired on.

three foreign men-of-war at Sacrificios, and the men of the merchant ships riding there, thronged rail and rigging to watch for the thunder to break as the Americans went ashore. "It put me in mind," wrote one humble soldier in his diary, "of seeing so many robins or black birds on a wild cherry tree, or crows on trees, watching the dead carcass lying beneath." [20]

The infantry were now returned to the surfboats, about fifty men in each, under a naval officer, with eight or ten sailors as oarsmen. The boats were then towed astern of the *Princeton,* which was anchored abreast of the landing place. At last all was ready and the great moment was at hand. Every spectator on every ship within sight of the landing place waited breathlessly. The distant walls of Vera Cruz and of the castle, plainly visible, were covered by a multitude of excited people. "It was just before sunset," one observer wrote, "an hour at which all the beauties of the Mexican coast are wont to stand out in bold and beautiful relief. The day had continued as clear as it had begun, and the breeze, as it died gradually away, had left behind it a glazed and unruffled sea. The magnificent mountain of Orizaba, with its snow-clad summit, which had been hid from view most of the day, suddenly revealed itself with startling distinctness and grandeur; the distant Cofre of Perote loomed up, also, in blue and mystic beauty, and the bold and rugged outline of the coast seemed more bold and rugged still. . . ." [21] None of this splendor was lost on Robert Lee, as he saw it from the poop-deck of the *Massachusetts.*

The division of Lee's old drillmaster, General Worth, contained most of the regular infantry in Scott's expedition, and naturally had been chosen as the van. General Worth himself was to head the landing party. When word came that the boats were all loaded, Worth stepped down into a swift gig and took his place. A gun boomed out from the flagship; the surfboats cast off from the *Princeton* and formed in line abreast. The sailors bent to their task, and the bands once more struck up. A few tense moments, and the men of the 6th Infantry, forging ahead of the others, sprang out on the beach. Not a shot greeted them. Quickly the contingents of the other leading boats joined them and made a

[20] *Oswandel,* 68.   [21] *Semmes,* 127.

rush for the crest of the nearby sandhills. In an instant this high ground was won, and the flag of the United States was planted in plain view of all the ships. Not until then did it dawn on every one that the landing was unopposed, through some unexplained miscalculation on the part of the Mexicans. In universal relief, a cheer rolled from the fleet and echoed on the sanddunes.[22]

With the landing of the Vera Cruz expedition began Lee's first real opportunity in the field. He had every advantage. General Scott had already formed a high opinion of Lee's ability and had included him in what he termed his "little cabinet," consisting of Lee's own chief, Colonel Totten, Lieutenant Colonel Ethan A. Hitchcock, acting inspector general, Lee, and General Scott's son-in-law, Henry Lee Scott, who was the commander's assistant adjutant general and chief of staff.[23] Lee was thus brought into close daily contact with Scott, who was a man quick to recognize merit and ready to take sound counsel, deferentially tendered, however pompous and dogmatic he seemed. Lee was, moreover, in the strongest branch of the general staff. Colonel Totten had seen to that. Directly under Totten was Major John L. Smith, next came Lee, and then a number of other officers of the highest promise, men who had stood at the very top of their respective classes at West Point. Among them was a youngster of twenty, Brevet Second Lieutenant George B. McClellan, who had been No. 2 in 1846 at the Military Academy. One step above him was First Lieutenant P. G. T. Beauregard, of the class of 1838. Another junior officer of fine abilities was Zebulon B. Tower of Massachusetts, a second lieutenant, and No. 1 in the class of 1841. In the affiliated corps of topographical engineers, besides Joe Johnston, was Lieutenant Gustavus W. Smith, whose ambitions were to cross the career of Lee fifteen years later.[24] George Gordon Meade was also in the topographical detachment

---

[22] *Semmes*, 128; *Parker*, 84; *Oswandel*, 69–70; 2 *Rives*, 382; MS. G. O. 34, Feb. 26, 1847, with Lee 993, *Eng. MSS.*; P. S. P. Conner: *The Home Squadron under Commodore Conner* . . . (cited hereafter as *Conner*), 57.

[23] *Memoirs of Lieut. General Scott*, written by himself (cited hereafter as *Scott*), 2, 423.

[24] All these men except Major John L. Smith are listed in *Cullum*. Totten mentioned all of them in his report on Vera Cruz, *Exec. Doc. No. 1, 1st sess., 30th Cong.*, 244–45. This document, which contains most of the important reports on Scott's campaign, is cited hereafter as *Mexican Reports*. For the organization, etc., of the engineer troops, see *Mexican Reports*, 67, 97, 627–28.

and watched with indignation the efforts of Colonel Totten to give the engineers the advantage. "I have been pretty much of a spectator for a week," young Meade confided to his wife, "the corps of engineers having performed all the engineering that has been done. This is attributable to the presence of Colonel Totten, who wishes to make as much capital for his own corps, and give us as little, as possible." [25]

Toward evening, on the 10th of March, General Scott and his staff came ashore. Establishing temporary headquarters in a few tents pitched close to the bowers that the soldiers had erected over night, Scott and his official family rode around the city. From the distance at which they saw it, Vera Cruz appeared strong and not unimposing. The hillocks of brush-covered sand gave place to level ground as the city was approached. The port was encircled by a curtain wall connecting a line of bastions and redans that seemed to be heavily armed. Prickly pear had been set out between the bastions and a system of *trous de loup*[26] had been dug in the shifting sand in front of the walls. Beyond the towers of the city, as seen from the land side, rose the castle San Juan d'Ulloa. It was about 1000 yards off shore, was protected on three sides by reefs, and had a formidable water battery. In 1838 the French had taken it, and a young American sailor who had watched the bombardment, David G. Farragut by name, had hastened to the fort and had studied its condition. He had concluded that it was vulnerable because shell easily shattered the coral-like limestone of which the place was built. Scott, however, had been told that the castle had been "greatly extended, almost rebuilt and its armament about doubled." He estimated that the garrison of the town numbered about 5000 and he anticipated no great trouble in taking it, but he was doubtful of his ability to reduce the castle with the siege train then available.[27]

Having completed his first reconnaissance, Scott gathered Lee and the other members of his "little cabinet" about him and raised

---

[25] 1 *Meade*, 192–93.

[26] A *trou de loup* is a conical hole in which is a sharpened stake, designed to impale any one who steps or falls into the trap.

[27] E. A. Hitchcock: *Fifty Years in Camp and Field*, edited by W. A. Croffut, p. 239 (cited hereafter as *Hitchcock*); *English Soldier*, 152; 2 *Scott*, 422–23; *Mexican Reports*, 221; *Parker*, 79; 2 *Ripley*, 19. For a map of the fortifications, see 2 *Ripley*, 31. The copy of the map in the Lee collection, doubtless one used in the siege, is very crude.

the question of whether Vera Cruz should be stormed or taken by siege. Descanting at length on the public's demand for a heavy "butcher's bill," he declared unequivocally for regular approaches. Somewhat to his surprise, Totten, Lee, and the rest agreed with him. The investment of the city was accordingly ordered, despite the difficulties imposed by lack of transportation for use on the sandy, broken ground. It was foreseen that all the heavy guns had to be dragged by hand from the landing place to the batteries.[28]

Owing to a succession of northers, March 12 arrived before the five miles of the line of investment had been taken up;[29] and it was March 17 before all the entrenching tools had been brought ashore.[30] The next day ground was broken for the batteries.[31] It was one of the busiest times Lee had ever experienced. He had a hand in most of the work of the engineers, who laid off the lines, located the batteries, and directed the preparation of the platforms for the heavy ordnance. With the others he studied the condition of the city walls for General Scott, in order to ascertain if they could be utilized for an attack on the castle.[32] This reconnoitring, which was very different from that which he had done under General Wool, sometimes carried him so close to the Mexicans that he was warned of their proximity by the barking of their dogs.[33] The northers blew as though they were the allies of the natives. The sand was insufferable, the food was poor. And then there were the fleas, the unrivalled fleas. "I have never seen anything like [them]," one officer wrote years afterwards. "If one were to stand ten minutes in the sand, the fleas would fall upon him in hundreds. How they live in that dry sand, no one knows. They don't live very high, for they are ever ready for a change of diet. The engineer officers, G. W. Smith, and McClellan, slept in canvas bags drawn tight about their necks, having previously greased themselves all over with salt pork." [34]

---

[28] 2 *Scott*, 423; *Mexican Reports*, 216.
[29] For the northers, see *Semmes*, 129; *Hitchcock*, 240; *Mexican Reports*, 217, 220. On March 15 Lee made a tour of inspection with Scott (*Oswandel*, 78; *Hitchcock*, 240).
[30] *Semmes*, 130.
[31] 2 *Scott*, 426; W. S. Myers, ed.: *The Mexican War Diary of George B. McClellan* (cited hereafter as *McClellan's Diary*), 61, 63.
[32] *Mexican Reports*, 220.
[33] *R. E. Lee, Jr.*, 8, quoting undated letter of R. E. Lee to G. W. C. Lee.
[34] D. H. Maury, 34.

On the 19th, Lee very narrowly escaped death. From the position of one of the working parties, he started back to the lines, accompanied by Lieutenant P. G. T. Beauregard, with whom he had to make his way along a narrow path cut through the brush. At a turn in this path, they suddenly saw the figure of an American soldier and heard his challenge, "Who goes there?"

"Friends," cried Lee.

"Officers!" Beauregard yelled in the same breath.

It was too late. The soldier, thinking that the Mexicans were upon him, blazed away with his pistol, straight at Lee, who had no time to dodge or to strike at the man's weapon. The bullet passed between his left arm and his body, singeing his uniform. A deviation of a fraction of an inch in the soldier's aim would have changed some very important chapters in the history of the United States. Naturally enough, word of Lee's close escape reached headquarters. He explained the facts and appealed for leniency toward the offender, but to no purpose. General Scott was furious over the recklessness of the sentinel and demanded that he be punished.[35]

General Scott was now ready to open the bombardment, but he had concluded that his army ordnance was not heavy enough, and he had asked the navy for the loan of six heavy pieces to be used against the walls. Lee was designated to locate these in battery. He picked a position within 700 yards of the Mexican defenses, and succeeded in masking it so completely that the enemy was unaware of what was being done. Using details from the various infantry regiments, together with the engineer troops, Lee started to construct a protecting work with sandbags, and at intervals of every two guns he erected a very thick traverse.[36]

On March 22 selected detachments of sailors began to drag the guns from the Sacrificios landing to the new "naval battery," as it was styled, a distance of about three miles. The guns weighed 6300 pounds each, and they had to be hauled along winding sandy trails and through a lagoon two feet deep and seventy yards wide. The sailors, however, were glad of an opportunity to share in the operations, and they contrived with the aid of some homely "trucks" to deliver the guns to Lee.

[35] Hitchcock, 243.　　　　[36] Parker, 96; McClellan's Diary, 68.

Scott, meantime, had grown impatient of delay and had decided
to begin the bombardment with the army ordnance. This fire continued for two days and caused much suffering in the city without breaching the walls or silencing the Mexican artillerists. The
naval battery would still be needed to deliver the decisive sledge
strokes. As the six guns had come from five different ships, each
vessel was permitted to supply a gun crew. These men, with the
officers, were sent ashore and were bivouacked in rear of the battery, itching for action. Among them was Lee's brother, Sidney
Smith Lee. He had been given the honor of heading the detachment from the *Mississippi,* which had contributed a 64-pound
shell-gun to the battery.

The naval battery having been ordered to open on the morning
of March 24, Lee pushed the construction as rapidly as he could
without disclosing the position to the enemy. On the evening of
the 23d so much work remained to be done that Lee exercised
the authority given him by Totten and called on the sailors to
help with the parapets.[37] The seamen, who had come from the
fleet in the expectation of having a fight, were much disgruntled
at the order, and though they went about filling the sandbags and
wielding the shovels, they growled so much that their commanding officer, probably Captain John H. Aulick, protested to Lee.
His men did not want to hide behind dirt, he said; all they asked
was that they be allowed to get at the enemy. It was an outrage
to employ them in digging ditches; when Lee finished them, the
men would not stay behind them. There was nothing left for
Lee to do but to show his orders and to keep the sailors at the
work despite their complaints.

By daylight on the 24th all the sandbags were filled, and soon
thereafter the last gun was in place. The sailors were sponging it
and were trying to get the sand out of it when well-directed shots
showed that the battery had been observed by the Mexicans.
Orders were at once given to unmask the pieces and to open on
the enemy. It was then 10 o'clock, and Captain Lee, who was

---

[37] This episode, which is given in Jones, *L. and L.,* 46, could not have occurred on
the night of the 24th, for Raphael Semmes was then in the rear of the battery and specifically stated the work of repair was done by engineer troops. It could not have been
on the night of the 25th, because the action the next morning was brief. All the evidence
fixes the night of the 23d as the time.

directing the fire, had his first experience in actual combat. He had been under fire aboard the *Petrita* on March 6, but until that moment he had never aimed a weapon at a foe in more than twenty-two years of military duty. His thought that morning was not of himself or of the novelty of his position. Objective-minded, then as always, he seemed unconscious of personal danger. "No matter where I turned," he recorded in a letter home, "my eyes reverted to [Smith Lee], and I stood by his gun whenever I was not wanted elsewhere. Oh, I felt awfully, and am at a loss what I should have done had he been cut down before me. I thank God that he was saved. He preserved his usual cheerfulness, and I could see his white teeth through all the smoke and din of the fire. . . . [The service from the American battery] was terrific, and the shells thrown from our battery were constant and regular discharges, so beautiful in their flight and so destructive in their fall. It was awful! My heart bled for the inhabitants. The soldiers I did not care so much for, but it was terrible to think of the women and children." [38]

The fire of all the nearby Mexican batteries was quickly concentrated on the sailors. They had all the fighting they cared for, and they were not at all unwilling to take advantage of the shelter they had been loath to provide the previous night. Some of them had the narrowest of escapes. "Just in rear of the guns," to quote a midshipman from the *Potomac*, "a trench had been dug for the powder-boys to jump into for shelter. They would run from the magazine a little farther back, and wait in the trench until the cartridge was wanted. A large shell happening to fall just back of the trench, the order was given to lie down. A powder-boy threw himself upon the ground very near the shell, and I saw him eye it anxiously. He then commenced rolling himself toward the trench, and there being a gentle inclination the disturbance of the loose ground caused the shell to roll after him. . . . Finally he rolled into the trench and the shell followed—fortunately not on top of him. No jack-in-the-box ever sprang up with more sprightliness than did that powder-monkey. After all the shell did not explode." [39]

[38] Undated letter quoted in *Fitz Lee*, 36–37.
[39] *Parker*, 97–98; R. E. Lee to Smith Lee, March 27, 1847; *Fitz Lee*, 37; *Hitchcock*, 245.

The sailors cut down the Mexican flag with a fair shot, and twice they silenced a heavy battery known as the Red Fort. They kept up their salvoes until 4 o'clock and then ceased only because their ammunition was exhausted. The Mexican counter-fire, which had been well-directed and stubborn, had meantime slackened. The effect of the battery's bombardment of the walls of the town was already apparent. Satisfied with their day's work, but loath to quit the scene of so much excitement, the sailors and their officers left the battery at sunset, and other contingents moved in. In the hurry of the relief, Lee was unable to say good-bye to his brother. Nor did he have opportunity of exchanging adieux with Captain Aulick, who had protested so hotly against his men being required to dig dirt the previous evening. The captain went back to his ship in order that another officer of the same rank might have the honor of commanding the battery for a day. Not long afterwards Lee met the captain, who seemed to feel that he owed an apology for expressing himself so vehemently against fortification. "Well," said he, "I reckon you were right. I suppose the dirt did save some of my boys from being killed or wounded. But I knew that we would have no use for dirt banks on shipboard—that there what we want is clear decks and an open sea. And the fact is, Captain, I don't like this land fighting, anyway. It ain't clean!" [40]

The men who came from the fleet on the evening of the 24th were as good as those who went back to the ships. One of the newcomers was Raphael Semmes, later the captain of the *Alabama* in her exploits against Federal shipping. Pondering the inhumanity of the bombardment, Semmes spent a sleepless night. In his *Service Afloat and Ashore* he left a very vivid account of the scene in the battery—"the engineers working away at our sand-bags, like so many specters, by the starlight, the sentinel, at a little distance, pacing his solitary round, and the sailors collected in small groups, discoursing, *sotto voce*." [41]

Before daylight on the 25th Lee had the damaged battery fully prepared for a renewal of the action. The boatswain's mate piped all hands to the guns, and the bombardment was resumed. The enemy responded with spirit. A small Mexican battery directly in

[40] Jones, *L. and L.*, 45–46.   [41] *Semmes*, 137.

front of the naval guns was handled with especial skill, while the castle San Juan d'Ulloa, partially aroused at last, sent over a few shells at intervals. One of these, from a thirteen-inch gun, struck the sand some five yards in rear of a naval gun. "At about this distance in the rear of each piece," Semmes recorded, "we had stationed a quarter-gunner, with a small copper tank, capable of holding eight or ten charges of powder—each charge weighing about ten pounds. The shell falling near one of these petty officers, he turned, upon hearing a noise behind him—he had not seen the shell fall—and finding a monstrous cannon ball there, as he thought, mechanically put his hand upon it. Finding it hot, it at once occurred to him what it was. It was too late to run, and in the consternation of the moment . . . he doubled himself up in a heap, and attempted to burrow himself, head foremost, in the sand, like an ostrich. All this occurred in the space of a second, and in a moment more the shell exploded, with the noise of a thousand pieces of artillery, shaking the battery like an earthquake, and covering the officers and men with clouds of dust and sand. Our fire was suspended for a moment, and when the smoke had cleared off sufficiently to enable us to distinguish objects, every officer looked around him in breathless anxiety, expecting to behold the blackened corpses, and mutilated bodies of half his comrades at least. Strange to say, not a soul was hurt." [42]

Not long after the guns opened for the third day's fire on the morning of March 26, a flag of truce was sent out by the Mexicans through the flying sand of another severe norther. [43] Soon word passed around that the enemy was preparing to surrender. Ere long firing ceased. It was renewed no more at Vera Cruz, for though the Mexicans rejected Scott's first terms, they resumed conference during the forenoon of March 27, and that night signed the capitulation. This provided that the Mexicans should march out with the honors of war, surrender their arms, and be paroled. The city and its armament were to pass into

[42] *Semmes,* 140.
[43] D. H. Maury stated (*op. cit.,* 35), that Lee and J. E. Johnston were the commissioners named by Scott to arrange the terms of surrender. This is incorrect, though it is possible that these two officers met the Mexican representatives and escorted them to headquarters. Colonel Hitchcock did this for one of the parties that came out under flag of truce.

the possession of the United States. The castle, its garrison and its guns were included in the surrender, much to the satisfaction of the Americans, who had not warmed to the prospect of besieging it with the ordnance then available.[44]

Released from duty with the naval battery, Lee took the first opportunity of riding again around the walls of the town to observe the effect of the bombardment. Some 2500 shells had been fired, 1800 of them from the long cannon of the sailors. The Mexican batteries had been almost demolished, a long stretch of city wall had been reduced to powder, and many houses in the poor district facing the American works had unfortunately been wrecked. Although Lee could not see it at the time, much damage had been done one of the churches, where a shell had penetrated the roof and had exploded among women and children who had taken refuge there.[45]

Next came the ceremonies attending the formal surrender of Vera Cruz, in which Lee had no conspicuous part, though he doubtless witnessed the march of the Mexicans on the morning of March 29 to the field where they laid down their arms. It was a smaller force than Scott had thought, for instead of numbering 5000 men in the city alone, the strength of the troops in Vera Cruz was 3360, and that of the castle garrison, 1030—a total of 4390. Some 600 of these had been killed or wounded, according to Mexican accounts, which may have been exaggerated. The American casualties, army and navy, were nineteen killed and fifty-seven wounded.[46]

In appreciation of the part the engineers had in this easy victory, General Scott entrusted his victory dispatch to Colonel Totten and commended him, after the manner of conquerors, "to the very favorable consideration of the department."[47] Before Colonel Totten left for Washington, he, in turn, wrote Scott in warm commendation of the other engineers who had been engaged in the siege. He listed them by seniority and by name, Lee second on the list.[48] Two days later Lee got his first mention in orders,

[44] *Hitchcock*, 246–47. For the articles of capitulation, see *Mexican Reports*, 237–38.
[45] *Semmes*, 140; *Kenley*, 268; R. E. Lee to S. S. Lee, March 27, 1847; *Fitz Lee*, 37; *Hitchcock*, 248.
[46] 2 *Rives*, 385, 388.
[47] Scott to Secretary of War, March 29, 1847; *Mexican Reports*, 229–30.
[48] Totten to Scott, March 28, 1847; *Mexican Reports*, 244–45.

when Scott included him among those who, in Scott's words, were "isolated by rank or position as well as by noble services." Lee was cited along with Joseph E. Johnston for having rendered "occasional aid" in staff work.[49] The distinction Lee gained at Vera Cruz was much greater, in reality, than the orders indicated. Scott's good opinion of him was confirmed.[50] On Totten's departure he became second ranking engineer officer of the army, and from the beginning of the subsequent operations he seems to have been consulted by the commanding general much more than was Major John L. Smith, the senior engineer, who was in ill-health.

There followed a few days of comparative inaction, during which Lee managed to prepare his financial statement for the engineer's office.[51] Similar reports were made quarterly during the whole of his service in Mexico, and sometimes they had to be prepared in the midst of action, but not one of them was delayed beyond the due date.

On Sunday, April 4, occurred one of the oddest incidents of the occupation. Although the articles of capitulation had guaranteed freedom of religious worship to the population of Vera Cruz, some of the local clergy hesitated to open their churches for fear that the American soldiers might profane them. Word of this having reached General Scott, he sent a message to the bishop, and asked if he might have the use of two churches, as he had some excellent chaplains in his army. The Mexicans took this to mean that the General desired religious exercises held, and they decided they had better officiate themselves than have the Americans do so. Services were accordingly resumed in all the churches. The "Catholic question" was a live one in the United States at that time, and even attendance on mass was something of a danger to a man with political ambitions such as Scott cherished; nonetheless he set an example by going to church the next Sunday, accompanied by his staff, all of them in full-dress uniforms. There were no seats in the church, which was situated

---

[49] G. O., 80, March 30, 1847; *Mexican Reports*, 239–40.

[50] *Cf.* Scott's mention of Lee in his Cerro Gordo report (*Mexican Reports*. 263): "This officer, greatly distinguished at the siege of Vera Cruz . . ."

[51] Lee to the chief engineer, MS., April 1, 1847; *Eng. MSS.*, 937; *Cf. ibid.*, July 1, 1847, 978.

close to one of the American batteries, but the ecclesiastics promptly placed a bench against the wall for the distinguished worshipers. Lee sat down with the General.

Noticing, in the crowd of soldiers around the door, his friend Lieutenant Henry J. Hunt, who had been in garrison at the Narrows with him, Lee motioned to him to come and take a seat by his side on the bench. After Hunt had joined him the acolytes cleared a way around the church for a procession. Then one of them brought down a large lighted candle from the altar and gave it to Scott. The General did not understand what was afoot, but he took the candle and passed it to his aid. The acolyte promptly returned with a smaller taper intended for the aid, and when he saw what had happened, he blew it out, retraced his steps and soon returned with another light, as large as the first, which he placed in the General's hand. This time Scott kept it, though he still did not realize what he was expected to do with it. In a few moments the other officers were supplied with candles, and all of them were requested to stand up. A side door opened, a company of prelates entered, and before they knew it Scott and his staff were marching in procession around the church. The probable candidate for the presidency of an anti-Catholic country not only was in a Catholic church, but was participating in a Catholic ceremony! It was too much for the risibles of officers who knew the extent both of Scott's ambitions and of the religious prejudices of many American voters. Lee walked as seriously as if he had been on parade at West Point, but soon he felt Hunt touch his elbow. Lee looked reprovingly at his companion, but when Hunt did the same thing again, Lee bent his head and whispered: "What is it?"

"Captain Lee," said Hunt.

"Well?"

"I really hope there is no *Pussyism* in all this," reviving the jest of the religious controversy at Fort Hamilton over the righteous Doctor Pusey.[52] Lee said nothing and continued his march; "but," said Hunt, "the corners of his eyes and mouth were twitching in the struggle to preserve his gravity."[53]

[52] See *supra*, p. 193.   [53] Hunt, quoted in *Long*, 69–70.

CHAPTER XV

A Day Under a Log Contributes to Victory
(CERRO GORDO)

Less than a week after General Scott's embarrassing experience at church, Lee saw Twiggs's division of regulars set out from Vera Cruz for the interior. Scott had planned from the first to find and to defeat the main army of the enemy, even if he had to march to Mexico City, and he had tarried at the coast solely because of the slow arrival of transportation. No certain news was available at the time concerning the strength, the movements, or the position of the enemy, though it was reported that General Santa Anna had hurried southward after his defeat at Buena Vista and had organized a new army with which to dispute the advance of the Americans towards his capital. To give Twiggs support in case these rumors proved true, other units of the army marched inland from day to day until April 12, when General Scott himself left Vera Cruz, accompanied by Lee and the rest of his staff. The division of Worth and a few detachments remained behind, but were to join the main army as soon as practicable. There still was no definite information of the enemy, but rumor had it that Santa Anna was already at Jalapa, sixty miles northwest of Vera Cruz.

Anticipating the advance, Lee took advantage of the final wait to bid farewell to his brother with the fleet. He had spent one night aboard the *Mississippi,* where the visit had not been altogether a success. "He was very well," Lee wrote of Smith, "but what a place a ship is to enjoy the company of one's brother." [1]

Without more ado he joined his commander. Travelling through rich plains, which delighted the heart of Lee, the cavalcade came on April 14 to the broad and swift, though shallow, Rio del Plan at a bridge leading to a village and a pleasant

[1] Letter quoted (without date) in *Fitz Lee,* 37.

meadow styled Plan del Rio. The village was deserted, but the surrounding fields were covered with bowers set up by the advance American column.[2] All the troops that had preceded Scott were there, with Major General Robert Patterson in command. The men received their general in chief with loud cheers; but much as he loved it, he had little time for their applause. His subordinates had grave news for him. The enemy had been located: in a grim mountain pass that rose above Rio del Plan, Santa Anna himself, with a force estimated at 12,000 or more, was awaiting the Americans. All the extensive mountain ridges commanding the pass were held by strong Mexican batteries. General Twiggs had wished to attack on the 13th, and had planned to do so on the 14th, but had been held back by General Patterson, who did not want an action opened against a position of such strength until Scott himself was on the ground with all his forces.

Scott at once ordered a full reconnaissance. Young engineers had been working on the right of the road that led through the pass, and they had some reason to believe that a practicable route for the army might be found there.[3] Lee was directed to press the reconnaissance and to ascertain whether the enemy's position could be turned. Going out on the morning of the 15th with his guide, John Fitzwalter, Lee found that Santa Anna had chosen his ground well. The right of the Mexicans overlooked the river, on bluffs so nearly perpendicular that it was manifestly futile to attempt a turning movement there. Back from the river the ground rose fast to three ridges that ran eastward and northeastward toward the position of the United States army. These ridges were crowned with well-sighted batteries. Just north of the ridge farthest from the river the so-called "National Road" mounted to the pass. On this thoroughfare, at a high point dominating it for nearly a mile, was still another battery. North of the road and northwest of the ridges rose a conical hill, known as Cerro Gordo. Guns had been placed here and a tower had been erected. North and west of Cerro Gordo the strength and position of the enemy, among the high hills and deep ravines that cut the landscape,

---

[2] *English Soldier*, 177; *Semmes*, 174.
[3] The honor of this initial reconnaissance is claimed both for Lieutenant W. T. H. Brooks and for Lieutenant P. G. T. Beauregard.

were not discoverable by the Americans. Even the course of the road from Cerro Gordo northwestward toward Jalapa had not been ascertained. Roughly sketched, the terrain was assumed to be about this:[4]

Manifestly, it was as foolish to deliver the main attack up the National Road as it was to undertake a turning movement along the river. The army's only hope lay in finding a practicable way through the ravines on the Mexican left that had been partially explored. Lee himself stated his problem thus: "The right of the Mexican line rested on the river at a perpendicular rock, unscalable by man or beast, and their left on impassable ravines; the main road was defended by field works containing thirty-five cannon; in their rear was the mountain of Cerro Gordo, surrounded by intrenchments in which were cannon and crowned by a tower overlooking all—it was around this army that it was intended to lead our troops." [5]

Slowly Lee worked his way up the ravines north of the river, on the Mexican left. The ground was very difficult, but to Lee it did not seem altogether impossible to construct a road over which troops might advance with proper caution. At last Lee stopped his stealthy movements to look about him. Near at hand was a spring, to which a path led from the south. This path must have been well-trampled, and the bushes around it must have been broken, for Lee at once concluded that he was in rear of the Mexican left flank. As he waited and studied the ground he heard voices and conversation in Spanish. Pausing only a moment he got a glimpse of a group of Mexican soldiers coming toward the spring. What should he do? How could he escape? There was only an instant for reflection, then silently he

[4] The best map is in *Mexican Reports*, opposite p. 250. The ground is described in *Hitchcock*, 251–52, and in *Semmes*, 175. The clearest account is in 2 *Rives*, 395–98.
[5] Lee to Mrs. Lee, April 25, 1847; Jones, *L. and L.*, 51.

dropped down behind a great log close to the water. Fortunately, the undergrowth was so thick by the side of the log that it formed a screen.

Louder the voices; louder, too, the sound of men making their way along the path. Soon the soldiers halted at the spring, drank deeply and paused in the shade to talk of the Yankees that were gathering under the ridge. If one of those Mexicans should chance to see the print of an American boot in the soft earth and should grow inquisitive, then it would be a quick death for Captain Lee and for Fitzwalter who was hidden nearby. There would be surprise at headquarters because of Lee's non-return, and, to end all, there would be weeping at Arlington when the news came that he had gone off on reconnaissance and had never been heard of again.

Quietly Lee lay under the log, not daring to move a muscle. Soon more soldiers arrived and some of those who had first come to the spring straggled back. Was it to be so all day? Was the spring the water supply for that wing of the army? If so, then there could be no hope of escaping detection. Some one surely would begin to poke about among the bushes. Down on the log sat a Mexican; down sat another. Their backs were not three feet from Lee. At last they got up and lazily went their way. But others came and still others and began to prowl around as they chattered one to another.

There was a momentary shadow and a Mexican stepped over the log—almost on Lee. Had he slipped he would have landed squarely on the flank of the engineer. There was no prospect that all of them would go away. Lee could only pray that they would not see him.

The shadows slipped and the drowsy afternoon came. Rigid and silent, scarcely daring to breathe, Lee hugged the damp bark of the fallen tree and let the insects crawl and bite unhindered. Hours passed, hours that seemed ages, while that endless procession of thirsty soldiers came and drank and loafed. At last the air grew cooler, the shade began to blur. It was twilight. The Mexicans were less numerous. Finally they ceased to come and the last loiterer shuffled off. Silence then and tropical blackness. Not another sound on the path, only the distant buzz of voices around far-off camp fires. Slowly Lee lifted his stiff joints from his refuge and slipped out. He was safe! Satan himself could not have seen in that blackness.

And now to find the way down that treacherous ravine back to the American lines. Well it was that Lee as a boy had prowled about King George's Meadows around quiet old Alexandria and had developed his sense of direction. Running now into a tree, slipping here down the side of the ravine, peering at every little watercourse to see which way it flowed and feeling at every step to discover the nature of the ground, he at last reached head-quarters.[6] He reported his findings, but he was by no means satisfied with them. Major Smith had also been out that day and had reached the same conclusion as Lee, but he, too, was still in some doubt whether the army could manœuvre around the Mexican left.[7] Scott directed them to continue the reconnaissance the next day and he placed at Lee's disposal a working party with which to cut a trail.[8] Lee accordingly went out on the 16th and before nightfall had pushed his reconnaissance much farther. He did not reach the Jalapa road, which the Americans must occupy if they were to cut off the Mexican retreat, but he was reasonably sure that he was close to it.[9] The new trail up the ravine was passable by the close of day, thanks to the efforts of the pioneer troops.

A decision had now to be reached: Either the army must remain in the valley, exposed to yellow-fever, which was expected to appear very soon, or else Scott had to attack at once; and if he attempted to drive the Mexicans from their perches he must deliver his main assault around the enemy's left flank, in the direction of Lee's and Smith's reconnaissance. There was no al-ternative. True, the route on the Mexican left was exposed at one point to the fire of the enemy; true, also, the distance to the Jalapa road, from the farthest point that Lee had reached, might be an upsetting factor. But Lee believed the Jalapa road was close to Cerro Gordo, and Scott thought the risks were justified. When Lee and the other engineers had reported, Scott decided to send Twiggs's division around Santa Anna's flank the next day, April

[6] Reconstructed from *Long*, 53, quoting John Fitzwalter; Jones, *L. and L.*, 51.
[7] *Cf*. 2 *J. H. Smith*, 50.
[8] *Hitchcock*, 250; 2 *Scott*, 432; Jones, *L. and L., loc. cit.*   [9] 2 *Scott*, 445

17, with Lee as guide. The battle was not to be opened until the second day following, April 18, as Scott desired to have the aid of Worth, who was nearing Plan del Rio with some 1600 men and a part of the siege train.[10]

As reveille was sounded for Twiggs's division, at 4:30 on the morning of April 17, there opened for Lee two days of the heaviest responsibility he had ever known. He left before Scott's order for the battle had been issued,[11] but he doubtless knew all that was contemplated. General Gideon Pillow was to make a demonstration on the 18th, along the left of the American line, opposite the three batteries on the ridges, though it was not considered likely that his volunteers could storm such formidable positions.[12] The troops in the centre, along the National Road, would have to wait until the flanking movement had forced the enemy from the commanding batteries; everything depended on Twiggs's division, which depended on Lee. If he led the troops into a slaughter pen in the mountains, the blame would be wholly his. The mission of Twiggs's division was explicit: that afternoon (April 17) it was to occupy the approaches to Cerro Gordo, particularly the hill Atalaya, which was somewhat lower than Cerro Gordo and lay about one-third of a mile northeast of it. This having been done, Twiggs's soldiers were to storm Cerro Gordo the next morning and were to press on until they blocked the Jalapa road. The other troops would then complete the envelopment of the Mexican forces.

With the greatest vigilance, Lee carried the men up the ravines that led around Santa Anna's left. "We . . . moved very slowly," one participant recorded, "every now and then halting half an hour or so, while the [Rifle Regiment], as skirmishers, cautiously felt the way through the chapparal in advance."[13] Lee was with the van; General Twiggs was close by. As the column approached the Mexican position absolute silence was enjoined on the men. Suddenly there was a thud and a rattle. Men stiffened themselves to the alert, only to discover that the commotion had been caused by a soldier who had slipped on a loose stone and, in trying to recover his balance, had struck his musket against his canteen.

[10] *Hitchcock,* 250.
[11] G. O. No. 111, April 17, 1847; *Mexican Reports,* 258–59.
[12] *Hitchcock,* 251.   [13] *English Soldier,* 179.

Instantly the man's captain was upon him, sword in hand: "You infernal scoundrel," he roared at the top of his lungs, "I'll run you through if you don't make less noise." The spectacle of the captain brandishing his blade and the poor example of silence that he gave his company set the column laughing. The tension of the toiling line was eased, and the advance continued.

About 11 o'clock, when the column was within 700 yards of the enemy, a company of the Seventh Infantry was sent up a hill separated by a ravine from the higher hill of Atalaya, in order to observe the movements of the Mexicans, prior to an attack against Atalaya itself. The infantrymen soon found that a Mexican force from the direction of Atalaya was advancing against them in greatly superior numbers. A clash followed in a few minutes, and as it was apparent that his movement was now discovered, Twiggs ordered two regiments forward to support the men of the Seventh Infantry and then to advance on Atalaya. Word was passed quickly. The excited soldiers formed line of battle. Just before the command was given them to go forward, one of the captains approached General Twiggs.

"I beg pardon, General," he said, "how far shall we charge them?"

"Charge them to hell," Twiggs stoutly replied.[14]

The First Artillery and the Rifle Regiment sprang up the hillside, quickly relieved the men of the Seventh Infantry, swept the Mexicans down the nearer hill, up Atalaya, over its crest, through a ravine—and had started up the sides of Cerro Gordo in hot pursuit before they heeded the recall. Then some of them found they could not return to their lines under the fire the Mexicans were pouring into the side of Atalaya from Cerro Gordo. There was danger, for the time being, that the vanguard would be taken prisoner by a Mexican counterattack, but this was prevented by the fire of some light guns, hurriedly pulled to the top of Atalaya.

After nightfall the venturesome vanguard returned to Atalaya, and such of the men as were not designated for special duty threw themselves on the ground and went to sleep. There was no rest for Lee, however. He felt that thus far all had gone flawlessly.

[14] *English Soldier,* 180.

The troops were in an advantageous position with only a few casualties. But as the attack on Cerro Gordo the next morning promised to be a more serious affair, Lee had two special duties to perform, first to locate a battery on Atalaya, and then to see that the heavy guns which were being painfully brought forward were in position and ready to open at sunrise. Fortunately, three volunteer regiments of Shields's brigade had arrived on Twiggs's line about 5 o'clock, and as these troops were much fresher than the regulars, they were at once put to work, under Lee's direction, hauling the heavy pieces up the hill and putting them in place. Before daylight on the 18th all was ready.[15]

Twiggs had consulted Lee freely on the 17th and had taken his advice with assurance. He doubtless sought Lee's counsel that night on the assignment of troops for the bloody task of the morrow. At Scott's suggestion it was decided that a part of the division was to assault Cerro Gordo as soon as the artillery opened. Simultaneously, Lee was to conduct the men of another brigade around the northern flank of Cerro Gordo and was to lead them to the supposed location of the Jalapa road, so that they could cut off the enemy's retreat, as provided in the general plan of action. Shields's brigade was to follow on this route with the same objective.

Early in the morning of the 18th Lee set out with Colonel Bennett Riley, commander of the Second Brigade, who was to be in charge of the turning movement. About the same time fire was opened by the three guns Lee had placed on the summit of Atalaya, and the direct assault on Cerro Gordo began under the eye of General Scott, who had ridden out to witness it. Lee saw little of this assault. The column he was conducting had not gone far before it came under raking gunfire from the northern and western sides of Cerro Gordo. Part of the command had to be turned to the left to protect that flank. With the remainder Lee kept on. As he ploughed his way through the fire his thoughts turned homeward to Custis and he found himself wondering where he could have put the boy, to insure his safety, if the lad had been with him.[16] Very soon General Shields was

---

[15] Reports of Twiggs and his subordinates, *Mexican Reports*, 275 ff. For the placing of the heavy guns, see report of Colonel E. D. Baker, *ibid.*, 298.
[16] Lee to Custis Lee, April 25, 1847; Jones, *L. and L.*, 53.

ordered to swing around and take position to the west of Riley's division. With the left regiment scrambling along the sides of Cerro Gordo, the united force turned south to meet the troops that had swept over the crest.

Riley's troops had become somewhat scattered during the advance, and while they were being reformed for a charge on a five-gun battery on the Jalapa road, southwest of Cerro Gordo, Lee paused to help collect the Mexican wounded. Close to a little hut he came upon a Mexican boy, a drummer or a bugler, lying with a shattered arm under a dying soldier. Nearby was a little girl, probably from the hut, who was tormented by the plight of the boy, but unable to help him. "Her large black eyes were streaming with tears," Lee remembered, "her hands crossed over her breast; her hair in one long plait behind reached her waist, her shoulders and arms bare, and without stockings or shoes. Her plaintive tone of 'Mille gracias, Señor,' as I had the dying man lifted off the boy and both carried to the hospital still lingers in my ear." [17]

Breaking his way toward Cerro Gordo through the chapparal, Lee mounted Creole and soon rejoined the infantrymen, who were now ready to attack the five-gun battery. They were met with only light fire as they dashed forward. A few minutes more, and the troops of Riley and Shields were across the Jalapa road, which was found as close to Cerro Gordo as Scott and Lee had expected it would be.[18] This turning movement can be seen at a glance from the sketch on the next page.

While this operation had been in progress, the attack on Cerro Gordo had been proceeding with equal success. The entire centre and left of the Mexican position was occupied, and the right of Santa Anna's army, near the river, was cut off from retreat, though General Pillow's attack along the Rio del Plan was a failure. The Mexicans on the right speedily surrendered, and Patterson's division in the centre, finding the pass clear, undertook to pursue the enemy up the Jalapa road. In this pursuit Twiggs's division and Shields's brigade also had a part. Before nightfall the remnants of the enemy were driven ten miles and were broken into small detachments. Approximately 3000 troops

[17] Lee to Custis Lee, April 25, 1847; *Fitz Lee*, 41.
[18] Riley's report, *Mexican Reports*, 287 *ff.*; Report of Colonel E. D. Baker, who took command of Shields's Brigade when that officer was wounded, *ibid.*, 298–99.

were captured, together with thousands of small arms and most of the Mexican artillery. Santa Anna himself barely escaped, on muleback, leaving his carriage, his headquarters equipment, his correspondence and his money chest to fall into the hands of the Americans. His forces, it subsequently developed, numbered

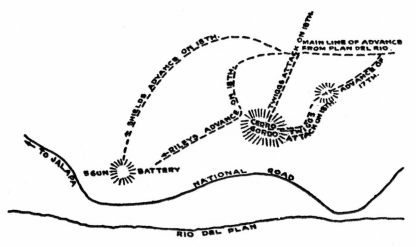

Sketch of turning movement, American Right Wing, Battle of Cerro Gordo, April 17–18, 1847.

about 8000, while Scott had 9000. The Mexican losses, which were never officially reported, must have run to hundreds. Those of the United States army, April 17–18, were 263 killed and 368 wounded.[19]

Lee came out of the action at Cerro Gordo, which was his first open engagement, with a new realization of the hideousness of war. He wrote Custis: "You have no idea what a horrible sight a field of battle is." [20] But if there could be glory for any individual in so much misery, it came to Lee from Cerro Gordo. He, a captain of engineers, had been one of the two officers to find the route on which the plan of battle had been based, and he had successfully led the turning-column on both days. His reasoning as to the position of the enemy and the location of the Jalapa road had been correct. He had disclosed a special aptitude for

[19] 2 *Rives*, 406.
[20] Lee to Custis Lee, April 25, 1847; Jones, L. and L., 53; *cf.* to Mrs. Lee, *ibid.*, 51.

reconnaissance, and by the possession of this quality he was commended anew to Scott, who leaned more and more heavily on him.

When the reports came in, Lee was mentioned in the warmest terms by each of the commanders under whom he had served. Colonel Riley said of him:

"Although not appropriately within the range of this report, yet coming under my immediate observation, I cannot refrain from bearing testimony to the intrepid coolness and gallantry exhibited by Captain Lee, United States engineers, when conducting the advance of my brigade under the heavy flank fire of the enemy." [21]

General Twiggs began a separate paragraph of his report to declare:

"Although whatever I may say may add little to the good reputation of Captain Lee, of the engineer corps, yet I may indulge in the pleasure of speaking of the invaluable services which he rendered me from the time I left the main road, until he conducted Colonel Riley's brigade to its position in rear of the enemy's strong work on the Jalapa road. I consulted him with confidence, and adopted his suggestions with entire assurance. His gallantry and good conduct on both days deserve the highest praise." [22]

General Scott mentioned Lee twice in the body of his report and outdid his lieutenants in this studied tribute:

"In expressing my indebtedness for able assistance to Lieutenant Colonel Hitchcock, acting inspector general, to Majors Smith and Trumbull, the respective chiefs of engineers and topographical engineers—to their assistants, Lieutenants Mason, Beauregard, Stevens, Tower, G. W. Smith, McClellan, engineers, and Lieutenants Derby and Hardcastle, topographical engineers—to Captain Allen, chief quartermaster, and Lieutenant Blair, chief commissary—and to Lieutenants Hagner and Laidley, ordnance—all actively employed—I am impelled to make special mention of the services of Captain R. E. Lee, engineers. This officer, greatly distinguished at the siege of Vera Cruz, was again indefatigable

[21] *Mexican Reports,* 289. [22] *Mexican Reports,* 277.

247

during these operations, in reconnaissance as daring as laborious, and of the utmost value. Nor was he less conspicuous in planting batteries, and in conducting columns to their stations under the heavy fire of the enemy." [23]

No other officer of the army received such high praise; none gained so much in prestige by the action. Captain Robert Anderson believed Lee to be the man best qualified by participation to write a history of the battle.[24] On August 24, though he did not get the news till much later, Lee was brevetted major, to date from April 18, 1847, "for gallant and meritorious conduct in the battle of Cerro Gordo." [25] Opportunity had come in his first battle; he had made the most of it.

[23] *Mexican Reports*, 263.
[24] *An Artillery Officer in the Mexican War*, 191.   [25] *A. G. O., G. O. 47.*

CHAPTER XVI

Laurels in a Lava Field
(Padierna and Churubusco)

WITH the vanguard of the troops that followed the defeated Mexicans, Lee entered the city of Jalapa on April 19. It was a pleasant place of some 5000 people and had an elevation of about 4500 feet.[1] From Jalapa he hurried on to Perote, which General Worth took without opposition. There Lee helped to verify an inventory of the arms and ammunition in the old castle.[2] It was a tedious task, though performed in an ancient building that greatly interested Lee. During the intervals of work he found opportunity for reflection and prayer: "I endeavored to give thanks to our Heavenly Father for all his mercies to me, for his preservation of me through all the dangers I have passed, and [for] all the blessings which he has bestowed upon me, for I know I fall far short of my obligations"—thus he wrote Mrs. Lee on the 25th, after attending a service in the courtyard.[3]

A few days later he rejoined Scott, who had established himself in the governor's palace at Jalapa. Despite the recent victory the atmosphere of headquarters was not happy. Transportation was still far below the army's needs; there was no news of the arrival of reinforcements at Vera Cruz; the term of several thousand of the volunteers was about to expire, and they showed no disposition to re-enlist; Scott's suspicious nature led him to believe that the administration was withholding support at a time when he was sure that he could lead, with negligible losses, a properly equipped army straight to Mexico City.[4] His apprehensions were intensified by the arrival early in May of Nicholas P. Trist, chief clerk of the State Department, who was sent to conduct preliminaries of peace, without previous intimation to Scott either of

---

[1] A pleasing description of Jalapa will be found in *Semmes*, 187 *ff*.
[2] *Mexican Reports*, 301–2.　　　　　　[3] Jones, *L. and L.*, 52.
[4] *Ex. Doc. 60, 1st sess., 30th Cong.*, 944 *ff.*, 954, 963; 2 *Rives*, 413–14, 427; *Hitchcock*, 257.

his coming or of the nature of his mission. Both Scott and Trist lost their temper in an undignified exchange of letters before they reached an understanding.[5]

While Scott and Trist were firing long letters at each other, old "Fuss and Feathers" sent Worth forward to Puebla, which was entered on May 15, after a brush the previous afternoon with the enemy's cavalry.[6] Puebla is about 120 miles southwest of Jalapa, by the route Worth followed, and was at that time the second city of Mexico in population. It lay 186 miles from Vera Cruz and 93 miles, as the roads then ran, from Mexico City. Santa Anna's failure to defend so important a place could only mean that since the battle of Cerro Gordo he had not been able to collect an army capable of putting up a fight. Scott accordingly moved his headquarters forward, and on May 28 entered Puebla with his staff, Lee among them.[7]

Here occurred another long period of delay and dark misgivings while Scott waited for reinforcements. He saw to it that his troops were occupied with hard drilling, and he held nightly levees to amuse and to instruct his officers. Touchy, pompous, and vainglorious though he might be, Scott none the less was the most scientific soldier at that time in America, and around his supper table he discussed for two or three hours with the heads of the various divisions of the general staff the particular problem that then confronted the army, whether of transport, supply, drill, gunfire, or march. If no military matter pressed, he talked of other things, for his reading was wide and his culture was real.[8] These evening conferences were a very material part of the military education of Robert Lee. Equally instructive was his special duty. For Scott directed him and Major William Turnbull, chief topographical engineer, to make separate studies of the approaches to the city of Mexico, and to prepare a map. Each collected what data he could from travellers and natives and pencilled these on his map. When this information was verified, it was "inked in." The result was a map of substantial accuracy, though faulty in many details.[9] Scott examined the engineers' progress almost

[5] 2 *Rives*, 418 ff.   [6] *Ex. Doc. 60, 1st sess., 30th Cong.*, 994–95.
[7] *Ibid.*, 993. There was an unfounded report in the army, while Lee was at Puebla, that he had been sent under a flag of truce on a mission to Mexico City. *An Artillery Officer in the Mexican War*, 247, 258.
[8] *Hitchcock*, 256.   [9] Copy in the *Lee Maps*, Virginia Military Institute.

daily and especially desired them to make full investigation of the roads leading into Mexico City from the south, beyond Lake Chalco, as it was soon apparent that a direct advance on the city from the east, by the main road, if not impracticable, would be very difficult.[10]

On August 7, Franklin Pierce arrived at Puebla with a second contingent of reinforcements, 2500 in number. The American force now numbered 10,738 officers and men,[11] organized as follows:

Harney's Cavalry Brigade: Detachments of the 1st, 2d, and 3d Dragoons.

First (Worth's) Division:

First (Garland's) Brigade: 2d and 3d Artillery (dismounted); 4th Infantry; Duncan's battery.

Second (Clarke's) Brigade: 5th, 6th, and 8th Infantry; one battery.

Second (Twiggs's) Division:

First (Smith's) Brigade: 1st Artillery (dismounted); 3d Infantry; rifle regiment; Taylor's battery.

Second (Riley's) Brigade: 4th Artillery (dismounted); 1st and 7th Infantry.

Third (Pillow's) Division:

First (Cadwalader's) Brigade: Voltigeur Regiment;[12] 11th and 14th Infantry; light battery.

Fourth (Quitman's) Division:

First (Shields's) Brigade: New York volunteers (one regiment); South Carolina volunteers (one regiment).

Second (Watson's) Brigade: detachment 2d Pennsylvania volunteers; detachment U. S. Marines.[13]

The size of this force led Scott to determine, with the greatest boldness, to abandon his line of communications and to undertake to live off the country while he pursued, found, and destroyed

---

[10] 2 *Ripley*, 184; Lee to Totten, *MS.*, Jan. 1, 1848; *Eng. MSS.*, 993; Hitchcock in *Senate Doc. 65, 1st sess., 30th Cong.*, 523, cited hereafter as *Pillow Inquiry*. This is the report of the court of inquiry called to investigate the charges made against General Gideon J. Pillow by General Scott.

[11] 2 *Rives*, 448–49; *Semmes*, 280–81; *Hitchcock*, 271, 2 *Scott*, 466.

[12] *Voltigeurs*, in the original French military application of the term, were "irregular riflemen," used as skirmishers or as sharpshooters; later the term meant simply riflemen.

[13] 2 *Scott*, 463–65.

his adversary. The very morning after Pierce reported, Scott put Twiggs's division on the road to Mexico City. It was his belief that Santa Anna must make a stand to save his capital, but where he would give battle, and in what strength, Scott did not pretend to know.

Slowly, on August 10, the army crawled up the Rio Frio range, the great natural barrier to an attack on Mexico City from the east. As the column started down the western slope Lee got his first glimpses of the great valley of Mexico, shining and verdant, spangled with white villages and girdled with mountains. Mexico City itself, with frowning walls and defiant towers, was plainly visible through glasses. "Recovering from the sublime trance," Scott wrote, "probably, not a man in the column failed to say to his neighbor or himself: *That splendid city soon shall be ours!*" [14] The sentiment of the average soldier, gazing downward on the plain, could not have been very different from that of Cortez and his *conquistadores,* three hundred and twenty-eight years earlier.

Some earthworks were found on the mountains, but these had been abandoned before they had been finished. No enemy was encountered until after the army had reached Ayotla, the last town on the road to Mexico. Here, on August 11, Scott established headquarters. To the west of Ayotla the road to Mexico, which was nineteen miles distant, was known to run on a narrow causeway through marshes, between Lake Texcoco on the north and Lakes Xochimilco and Chalco on the south. The most casual examination of this ground showed that it was as strongly occupied and fortified as Lee had been told it was when he was making his map at Puebla. Could the army assault the enemy's position or turn it successfully between the lakes? That was the question Lee was sent out on the 12th and 13th to answer. By evening on the second day he was able to report in some detail. His own description of the obstacles, written nine days later, was as follows:

"[The enemy's] principal defence was at El Peñon, commanding the causeway. . . . The hill of El Peñon is about 300 feet

[14] 2 *Scott,* 467.

252

high, having three plateaus, of different elevations. It stands in the waters of Lake Tezcuco [Texcoco]. Its base is surrounded by a dry trench, and its sides arranged with breastworks from its base to its crest. It was armed with thirty pieces of cannon, and defended by 7000 men under Santa Anna in person. The causeway passed directly by its base; the waters of the lake washing each side of the causeway for two miles in front, and the whole distance, seven miles, to the city. There was a battery on the causeway, and four hundred yards in advance of the Peñon; another by its side; a third a mile in front of the entrance to the city, and a fourth at the entrance. About two miles in front of the Peñon a road branched off to the left, and crossed the outlet of Lake Hochimillico [Xochimilco], at the village of Mexicalcingo, six miles from the main road. This village, surrounded by a marsh, was enveloped in batteries, and only approached over a paved causeway, a mile in length; beyond, the causeway continued through the marsh for two miles further, and opened upon terra firma at the village of Churubusco." [15]

Scott believed that he could storm the Peñon, but he knew it would cost him many lives and he wished to conserve his force for the major battle he felt sure he later would have to wage before he could enter Mexico. The route by Mexicalcingo, though difficult, was less so than the other. Scott accordingly decided tentatively to mask El Peñon and to turn the enemy's positions via Mexicalcingo.[16] Before this could be undertaken, word came from General Worth that some of his officers had returned from a reconnaissance made at Scott's order. They were convinced that the army could move around the lower end of Lake Chalco and could advance on Mexico from the south, avoiding all the works between the lakes. Scott had considered this line of approach while he was at Puebla, but had never reached a final decision regarding it. Now his problem, shown on page 254, was clearer.

The reconnaissance to the south of Chalco had not been complete and some of the inferences drawn from it were to prove

[15] Lee to Mrs. Jos. G. Totten, Aug. 22, 1847; *Pillow Inquiry*, 461.
[16] All this is controverted. The admirers of General Worth claimed that full credit for the choice of the route by way of Lake Chalco belonged to him. Colonel E. A. Hitchcock (*Pillow Inquiry*, 526) denied this, even going so far as to assert that the operations against El Peñon were a feint.

erroneous.[17] None the less, an advance in that direction offered
so much the better chance of avoiding heavy losses that Scott
promptly gave orders for the army to take the road around
Chalco, leaving one division temporarily in front of Ayotla to
delay the enemy.[18] The distance from Ayotla to San Augustin,

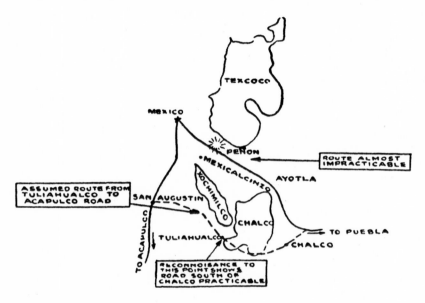

on the road from Acapulco to Mexico City, was estimated to be
twenty-seven miles.[19] While the army was slowly plodding
around the eastern shore of Lake Chalco—which was more a
marsh than a lake—Lee went ahead on the 17th and made a
reconnaissance of the roads to the south and west of Chalco. On
his return to Ochlomilco, where General Scott had stopped for the
night with Pillow's division, Lee reported the facts and confirmed Scott in his purpose to advance on San Augustin. However, Scott did not deceive himself. He knew he would not have
the element of surprise on his side, because he was sure the movements of his army had been observed and reported to Santa Anna.
Consequently, he expected to encounter the whole of the Mexican

---

[17] 2 *Ripley*, 189–90 and appendices Nos. 1 and 2, pp. 647–48. Appendix I contains
Lee's summary (Aug. 14) of the intelligence reports on the roads south of Lake Chalco.
    [18] Scott's report, *Mexican Reports*, 303.   [19] *Ibid.*, 304.

army in the vicinity of San Augustin. Advancing steadily on that village he met with no opposition, but when he arrived there on the morning of August 18, he received a message from General Twiggs that made him even more certain a battle was imminent. For Twiggs reported that as he had marched away from Ayotla on the 16th, with the rear division, he had encountered and had exchanged shots with a large force of Mexican cavalry, who must have discovered that the whole American army was moving to the south of Lake Chalco.

First reconnaissances showed singularly difficult terrain around San Augustin. The Acapulco road to Mexico City led northward to a hacienda known as San Antonio, distant about three miles. Although quite practicable for the wagon train and the artillery, this highway was swept for a long distance by gunfire from San Antonio, which was found to be heavily fortified. It was not possible to avoid this road by marching to the east of it, because there the ground was so soft that wheeled vehicles would be mired. Nor did it seem possible to turn San Antonio from the west, because the most conspicuous feature of the landscape was on that side—a great field of lava, more than five miles wide on its east-and-west axis and three miles long, from north to south, broken into great blocks and fissures—a hopeless barrier to the advance of the guns or the trains.[20] Such a tract of volcanic scoria was known locally as pedregal and bore an evil name. Furthermore, even if a way for the infantry could be found through the pedregal, so that they could turn San Antonio without artillery support, their advance would be halted in another two miles at the town and river Churubusco, which had not been reconnoitred but were believed to be heavily fortified.[21] In short, an advance up the Acapulco road seemed an almost hopeless undertaking.

What was to be done; what alternative offered? Only one: About two miles west of San Augustin, the "San Angel" road was known to run. This led in a northeasterly direction to Churubusco, where it joined the Acapulco-Mexico City highway. If a passage could be made from San Augustin to the San Angel road, then San Antonio could be turned and perhaps no battle would

[20] *Hitchcock*, 274–75; *Semmes*, 378; Scott in *Mexican Reports*, 304.
[21] The best brief description of the ground is in 2 *Rives*, 459 *ff*.

R. E. LEE

have to be fought till Churubusco was reached. The situation, graphically represented, was thus as shown on page 257.

Before he had been many hours at San Augustin, Scott did the sensible, obvious thing: he determined to ascertain by accurate reconnaissances whether the direct road northward toward Mexico City by San Antonio was as difficult as had been reported; and, secondly, whether a route could be opened across the pedregal to the San Angel road. On the first mission he sent Captain James L. Mason with an escort; to the important task of finding if there was a way over the pedregal he assigned Lee, accompanied by the 11th Infantry and two companies of dragoons. The latter were under command of Captain Phil Kearny, whose dead body Lee was one day to send across the lines in northern Virginia.

Lee soon found a road that led over some mounds to the west of San Augustin, and then followed the edge of the pedregal. It was no boulevard, to be sure, but it was passable for infantry and with some work it could be made practicable for artillery. For nearly three miles he made his way westward until he reached the side of an eminence in the pedregal, known as Zacatepec. There his escort encountered a strong Mexican force, which exchanged shots and then fell back toward the western edge of the pedregal. The Americans pursued for a short distance and took five prisoners, but as they were unfamiliar with the trail through the lava, they soon abandoned the chase. Lee climbed to the top of Zacatepec and from that height was able to see that the enemy was in strength on the San Angel road and had thrown up a fortification on a hill near the village of Padierna. This settlement, which the Americans mistook for the village of Contreras, lay almost due west from the route Scott's troops were following. Lee's long-range examination convinced him that this position could be occupied without great loss.[22]

Unable to go farther that day Lee returned to San Augustin. The immediate conclusion to be drawn from his reconnaissance was plain: the Mexicans he had encountered manifestly had come from the San Angel road; if they could cross the western part of the pedregal Scott's men could too. When they reached the other

[22] Scott, in *Mexican Reports*, 304; Smith, *ibid.*, 349–50; Cadwalader, *Mexican Reports, Supplement*, 119; Graham, *ibid.*, 124; Hitchcock, 275; 2 Ripley, 211. Graham's report is the fullest.

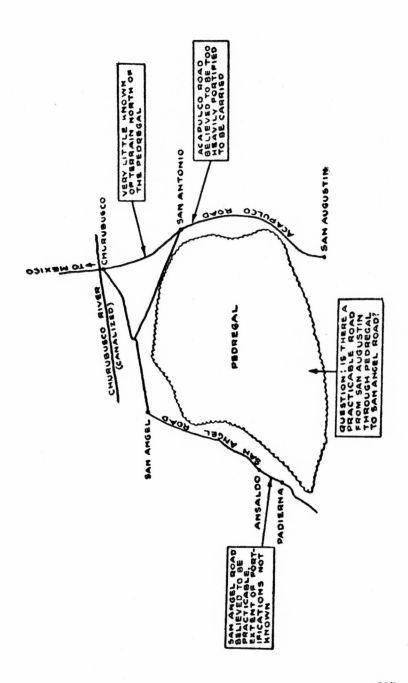

VERY LITTLE KNOWN OF TERRAIN NORTH OF THE PEDREGAL

ACAPULCO ROAD BELIEVED TO BE TOO HEAVILY FORTIFIED TO BE CARRIED

QUESTION: IS THERE A PRACTICABLE ROAD FROM SAN AUGUSTIN THROUGH PEDREGAL TO SAN ANGEL ROAD?

SAN ANGEL ROAD BELIEVED TO BE PRACTICABLE, EXTENT OR FORTIFICATIONS NOT KNOWN

TO MEXICO

CHURUBUSCO

CHURUBUSCO RIVER (CANALIZED)

SAN ANTONIO

ACAPULCO ROAD

SAN AUGUSTIN

PEDREGAL

SAN ANGEL

SAN ANGEL ROAD

ANSALDO

PADIERNA

257

side of the lava field, they would be on the San Angel road and could avoid San Antonio altogether. Lee's judgment that this was the best strategy was confirmed in his mind by the news that the reconnaissance up the Acapulco road had been halted by fire from the hacienda of San Antonio, where the Mexicans were on the alert and were as strongly fortified as had been reported.

That night Lee attended a council of war, summoned by the commanding general. Scott went over the reports one by one, beginning with the senior officer. Mason, who had reconnoitred on the Acapulco road, was all for assaulting San Antonio with the bayonet, and was convinced that infantry could take the place by a flank movement a short distance into the pedregal on the western side of the Acapulco road. Lee argued that the advance could be made with fewer casualties by moving through the pedregal and up the San Angel road. A silent auditor, Lieutenant Raphael Semmes, of the navy, was much impressed by both engineers. "The services of Captain Lee," he attested, "were invaluable to his chief. Endowed with a mind which has no superior in his corps, and possessing great energy of character, he examined, counselled, and advised with a judgment, tact, and discretion worthy of all praise. His talent for topography was peculiar, and he seemed to receive impressions intuitively, which it cost other men much labor to acquire. Mason, though a very young man, was scarcely, if at all, his inferior in this respect. . . ." [23]

General Scott gave no final orders before the council broke up, wisely waiting on developments, but he virtually decided to deliver his main attack by way of the San Angel road. [24] Lee was instructed to start early the next morning with the engineer company and 500 men from Pillow's division to put the track across the pedregal in condition for artillery. The rest of Pillow's troops and the whole of Twiggs's division were to protect the road builders. The other commands were to remain that day around San Augustin. Formal orders to this effect were issued before the night was over. [25]

Never, perhaps, in American history did a force of such limited

[23] *Semmes,* 379. Mason, an officer of great promise, died in 1853. *Cullum,* No. 629.
[24] Lee, in *Pillow Inquiry,* 78.
[25] G. O. 258, Aug. 19, 1847; *Pillow Inquiry,* 470–71.

numbers include so many men of future eminence as the column that filed westward from San Augustin on the morning of August 19. Twiggs and Pillow, the commanders, are now mere names, but some of their subordinates will long be remembered. Lee was in general charge of the reconnaissance; Lieutenant P. G. T. Beauregard was one of his assistants. Lieutenant G. B. McClellan of the engineer company was there with his captain, Gustavus W. Smith, who was subsequently a major general in the Confederate armies. Captain Joseph Hooker was assistant adjutant general to General Pillow. One of the two light batteries that accompanied the infantry was commanded by J. Bankhead Magruder, who, in the early spring of 1862, opposed McClellan on the peninsula of Virginia. Magruder's lieutenant was an awkward young man who had been transferred from the dismounted 1st Artillery, when Magruder had received his guns. That morning, perhaps for the first time, Lee saw this quiet "Mr. Jackson" who was to be his own most trusted lieutenant fifteen years thereafter, the "Stonewall" of the Army of Northern Virginia.

Under the direction of these men the troops slowly advanced, covering the working party engaged in the difficult work of turning a mule path into a road fit for artillery and wagons. By 1 P.M., on August 19, the road had been constructed to a point within range of the fortified position of Padierna, which was believed to be under command of General Valencia. The place was found to be armed with twenty-two guns, most of them heavy.

Lee saw that the road-making could go no farther till Valencia was driven off. He so reported to General Twiggs, returned the working parties to their regiments, and ordered the engineering tools repacked. General Twiggs thereupon directed Captain John McClellan[26] of the topographical engineers and Lieutenant George B. McClellan of the engineer company to go forward and find a location for the two American batteries. These officers, however, soon encountered a Mexican picket line and were forced to return. A regiment was then advanced, and the enemy was driven back. Lee accompanied these troops, who halted on the edge of a ravine, 30 yards from the Mexicans. Lee next selected a position for the batteries on the most favorable ground he could

[26] General Twiggs consistently spells John McClellan as John McLellan, but Cullum gave it as here printed.

find, sheltered somewhat from the enemy, with the wagons safe from the Mexican fire.[27] The batteries, brought up with much difficulty, began a cannonade with the enemy on most uneven terms. While Lee stood with the artillerists, a solid shot took off the leg of Preston Johnston, nephew of his friend Joseph E. Johnston. The boy dropped by the side of his gun and died that night.[28]

The ravine that lay between the American troops and the Mexican position was deep and rough and was coursed by a rapid stream that flowed northward. Swept by the Mexican fire, the declivity was considered impassable. Some expedient other than a frontal assault had to be found, and speedily. If this were not discovered, the American batteries would be destroyed and the opportunity lost, because Mexican reinforcements could already be seen advancing down the San Angel road in great numbers. The alternative quickly suggested itself. Almost at the same hour, several of the commanding officers near the front realized that the best movement was to attempt to turn the enemy's left, by advancing through the pedregal and westward across the San Angel road. Such a manœuvre, if successful, would force the enemy from his high ground and, at the same time, would cut him off from a retreat to Mexico City. General Pillow ordered Riley's brigade to start the operation, and close behind Riley he sent Cadwalader. A little later General Persifor F. Smith, of Twiggs's division, who had been on the left of Magruder's battery, filed away by the right flank, on his own initiative, and followed virtually the same route as Riley and Cadwalader.

All these troops, and a few others that General Scott sent on their heels, got safely across the pedregal and beyond the San Angel road. There they found themselves, some 3300 strong, in a situation full of advantage but, potentially, full of danger as well. They were in and around the little Indian village of San Geronimo,[29] on a high ridge that ran from southwest to northeast between two ravines. Half a mile south of them was the Mexican position

---

[27] Scott, *Mexican Reports*, 304; Twiggs, *ibid.*, 324; Smith, *ibid.*, 352; Lee, *Pillow Inquiry*, 79; 2 *Ripley*, 220; *English Soldier*, 251–52.

[28] Lee to Mrs. Totten, Aug. 22, 1847; *Pillow Inquiry*, 465.

[29] Names were much confused by the American commanders in this battle. Several of them in their reports mistook the village of San Geronimo for the ranch of Ansaldo, which lay just below it.

they had set out to turn. The approach to it was across a ravine and up a hill, through orchards, standing corn, and thick underbrush. North of the Americans and on the same side of the road with them another force of Mexicans was observed less than a mile away, mustered on elevated ground. This force consisted of all arms of the service and seemed to be preparing to advance. Estimates of its strength ran as high as 12,000. The Americans, in a word, were between two forces. If they could hold off the northern column they could keep it from reinforcing the Mexicans to the south of them, and then they might be able to deliver the intended attack on Padierna from the rear. But if the Mexicans discovered the real situation and were good enough soldiers to make a simultaneous attack from the north and from the south, the Americans might be wiped out. Roughly sketched, the situation was that shown on page 262.

General Persifor F. Smith, who believed himself the senior officer on the west side of the San Angel road, at once prepared to attack the large body of Mexican reinforcements to the north of his position, but before he could get his scattered troops deployed, night overtook him, and a heavy cold rain began to descend.[30] The troops had no shelter and little fire wood. Contact with the reserves on the eastern side of the road was uncertain; from Scott's headquarters the column was completely cut off by distance, darkness, and the nature of the ground.

Lee had come across the San Angel early in the evening, at the instance of General Scott, who was then at Zacatepec. Lee probably knew that the General believed it possible for the Americans west of the San Angel road to hold off the Mexican forces north of them while driving the other Mexican troops from the entrenched position at Padierna. Scott, indeed, had been much pleased with the prospect that the occupation of San Geronimo would prevent the reinforcement of Padierna. He had not been especially alarmed to find his advanced column between two Mexican forces. To strengthen the hold on San Geronimo he had sent Shields's brigade forward, unknown to Smith. But while Lee may have known this to be Scott's estimate of the situation, he brought no orders when he reported to General Smith.

[30] Santa Anna's report of Nov. 19, 1847, quoted in *Pillow Inquiry*, 537.

After sundown General Smith called Lee to confer with him and General Cadwalader. Two of the engineers had been up the ravine to the south of San Geronimo and had found it unguarded.

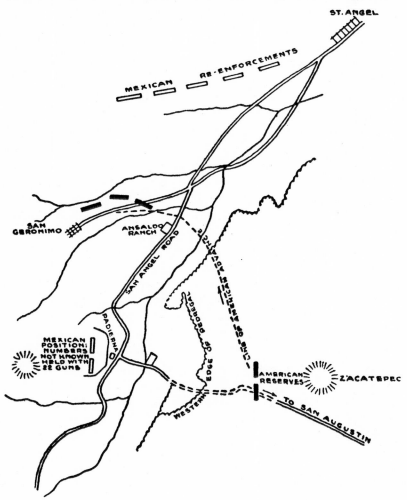

Position of American and Mexican forces adjacent to San Angel Road, at nightfall, August 19, 1847.

The occupants of the work at Padierna evidently were still of the belief that the Americans could and would attack only from the front. On the basis of this information a decision was reached to deliver an attack on Padierna from the rear, before daybreak, disregarding for the time the reinforcements to the north of San Geronimo. The opinion of the three officers, it would seem, was that the Mexicans were poor fighters and that, if the troops at Padierna were routed quickly, the others would not stand, much less attempt a counterstroke.

To cover the attack on Padierna, a strong demonstration by the troops in front of that place was desirable. But how was it to be assured? The forces west of the San Angel road were by this time wholly separated from those in the pedregal; the blackness of the night was unrelieved except by occasional flashes of lightning; a torrential rain was falling; the way across the pedregal was difficult and dangerous. But as soon as Smith stated that he would like to communicate his plan and position to Scott, Lee volunteered to carry the message to the commanding general, whom he believed to be still at Zacatepec. Smith accepted the offer. The understanding was, however, that Smith would deliver his attack, whether Lee returned from Scott or not.[31]

It was near eight o'clock when Lee left San Geronimo with a few men and started down the hill toward the pedregal. He had been over that part of the route only once, and it was too densely dark for him to observe any of the landmarks. There was nothing to guide him but his singularly developed sense of direction, and an occasional glimpse of the hill of Zacatepec when the lightning flashed. Groping his way along, step by step, he reached the road and crossed it in safety. Next, at some point in that black maze—he did not know exactly where—he must find the American outposts and risk being shot before he could give the counter-sign. Ere long, above the roar of rain, he heard the slow, uncertain tramp of a large body of men. From the direction of their advance they must be Americans, but what if they were not? Doubtless Lee stepped aside and waited until they were close enough for the next flash of lightning to show their uniforms. A

[31] Lee, in *Pillow Inquiry*, 75. There is a conflict of evidence here. Hunt (*Long*, 56–57) quoted an unnamed captain as saying that Lee stated he must return to Scott, as if he had orders to do so. The anonymous captain was not at the council of war. Smith was present, and he wrote in his narrative (*Mexican Reports*, 327) that Lee "offered to return to General Scott (a most difficult task) and inform him," etc. The text follows Smith. See also Smith in *Pillow Inquiry*, 100, and Cadwalader, *ibid.*, 84–85. There was no formal council of war in the church of San Geronimo. Hunt was misinformed on this point.

crash of thunder, a ghostly glare for an instant, and he recognized them. They were Shields's men, moving to join Smith.

Leaving one of his companions to guide these troops to San Geronimo, Lee plunged into the pedregal.[32] Around great blocks of lava he felt his way, and across crevasses he was forced to jump in the dark. When the lightning showed an abysm over which he could not spring, he had to skirt it, with every risk of losing his direction. There were fully three tortuous miles of this, in unrelieved night. At last, drenched and sore, Lee stumbled to Zacatepec, only to find that Scott had returned to San Augustin.

What should he do? Stay there till daylight and let Smith make his attack without the desired demonstration in his front? Not so long as the blood of "Light-Horse Harry" flowed in the veins of his son! Tired legs and bruised feet would have to carry him three miles more through the pedregal. So, on he went, gratified for every pick-stroke that had taken the edge from any of that accursed lava on the trail where the pioneers had labored to make a road. Three miles must have seemed thirty, and Lee's strong body was close to exhaustion when finally he saw dim lights in the houses at San Augustin. Still wet from the rain, every muscle numb and aching, Lee stepped into Scott's headquarters at 11 o'clock. He found the General calmly writing his report of the day's operations, confident of the outcome but naturally anxious for news from the other side of the pedregal. No information had come during the evening. Seven officers whom Scott had sent out in turn to carry messages to General Smith had all returned without reaching him.[33] The commander listened admiringly to Lee's report, cordially approved Smith's dispositions, and prepared immediately to order the desired demonstration against the front of the Mexican position at Padierna. He decided also to send part of Worth's division forward in case it should be needed.

Before the orders could be given two other callers were announced—General Twiggs and General Pillow. These division commanders had started from Zacatepec for San Geronimo during the evening, but had lost their way and had barely escaped falling into the hands of the enemy. Twiggs had injured his foot, and

---

[32] Lee, in *Pillow Inquiry*, 79.   [33] 2 *Scott*, 475.

the two had been forced to retrace their steps to Zacatepec, and thence, finding Scott gone, they had followed to San Augustin. Scott decided to keep Pillow with him for the night, but he sent Twiggs to collect troops for the demonstration.

As Twiggs was uncomfortable and in pain, and had already lost himself once in the pedregal, Lee accompanied him back toward Zacatepec. It was the third time he had made the journey that day, but there was nobody else at hand who knew enough about the road to guide Twiggs in his effort to locate those of his men who remained east of the San Angel road. This midnight mission doubtless was undertaken on horseback, and the darkness was not so Stygian, for the worst of the storm was over and through still-dripping clouds the moon now and again was visible to light the way. Slowly the General and Lee went forward until they reached Zacatepec, near which they found the headquarters of Brigadier General Franklin Pierce, senior officer in that part of the pedregal. They told him of Scott's orders to make a demonstration in front of the entrenched camp, but as Pierce had been hurt the previous day when his horse fell, he was unable to take charge of this operation. The command devolved on Colonel T. B. Ransom of the 9th Infantry.

It was now 1 o'clock. General Twiggs was worn out and returned to a battery position for rest, but Lee was so determined to see Scott's orders executed that he went on to Ransom's bivouac. There he explained what was required of Ransom and offered to guide the troops to what he considered the most advantageous position for a demonstration, namely, the ground occupied the previous day by the advanced American batteries. It took some time to get Pierce's wet and weary men in motion, and when they started they had to grope their way over the lava blocks. The rain had slackened, however, and ere long it ceased altogether. Day was dawning and Lee had been in the field nearly twenty-four hours when Ransom's men filed into the position where, on the 19th, Magruder, Collendar, and Jackson had fought.

The infantry were observed almost the moment they arrived, because the Mexicans were expecting a renewal of the attack from that quarter. Soon Lee found Ransom's men falling about him, as they answered the fire that was being poured into them. But the action did not last very long. Between 6 and 7 o'clock there was a nervous pause in the Mexican fire, visible confusion in the entrenched camp, and, in a few minutes, the roar of volleys from the crest of the hill above the Mexican guns. Then blue-coated men began to stream down the hillside through the growing light, and the Mexicans started to run. The attack that had been planned before Lee had left San Geronimo was being delivered from in rear of Padierna, and the Mexicans were being routed. Seventeen minutes after the first gun was fired, the whole earthwork was in the hands of the Americans, and those of the garrison who could escape were fleeing up the San Angel road. They were joined quickly by the thousands from the plateau above the American position, for these troops, who had been much mystified by the attack, quickly caught the panic and offered no resistance.[34]

Lee went over to the captured position and there found Joe Johnston, now acting lieutenant colonel of the Voltigeur regiment. Johnston had just heard of the death of his nephew late the previous evening and "his frame," in Lee's words, was "shrunk and shivered with agony." Lee held out his hand and burst into tears at the sight of his friend's grief.[35] As soon as he could compose himself, he rode back toward San Augustin to join Scott, whom he met on the way to the scene of action.[36]

The General realized that much depended now on the speed with which the enemy was followed up. He knew, as did the other commanders, that there was a crossroad north of the pedregal. At the village of Coyoacan, this crossroad divided. The upper, or northern fork, ran to the village of Churubusco. The lower fork led from the San Angel road to San Antonio, the advanced position of the enemy on the Mexico City-Acapulco highway. If, therefore, the United States troops could reach and

[34] Scott, *Mexican Reports*, 305 *ff.*; Twiggs, *ibid.*, 323; Smith, *ibid.*, 352; *Hitchcock*, 277; 2 *Ripley*, 235; P. F. Smith, *Mexican Reports*, 327 *ff.*; Pierce, *ibid.*, *Supplement*, 105; T. B. Ransom, *ibid.*, 113; I. I. Stevens, *Campaigns of the Rio Grande and of Mexico*, 66–67; Trist, in *Pillow Inquiry*, 123.

[35] Lee to Mrs. Totten, Aug. 22, 1847; *Pillow Inquiry*, 465; Johnston quoted in *Long*, 71; R. M. Hughes: *General J. E. Johnston*, 28–29; D. H. Maury (*op. cit.*, 40–41) mistakenly placed this incident at Chapultepec.

[36] It is impossible to say where Lee rejoined Scott, but it was before General Worth's column was turned back from the pedregal to the Acapulco road for a direct assault on San Antonio (*Pillow Inquiry*, 77).

hold the fork to San Antonio they would have a direct line of advance on that position from the flank and rear. General Scott had prudently anticipated this possibility and had left one brigade to mask San Antonio while ordering the rest of Worth's division to cross the pedregal and move up the San Angel road. As soon as he found that the enemy on the San Angel road had been routed, Scott directed Worth to hurry back to San Augustin, to advance up the Acapulco road, and to attack San Antonio from in front when Pillow and Twiggs approached it in rear, down the lower fork of the crossroad from Coyoacan. The situation around 7 A.M. was about that shown on page 268.

As he rode steadily toward Coyoacan on the crossroad leading from the San Angel road, Scott was in his glory, enjoying every moment of his triumph and giving his orders rapidly and with a quick understanding of each new development. He soon ordered Lee forward to reconnoitre the lower fork which Pillow's division was to follow, in the attack on the rear of San Antonio. Before this movement could be initiated, however, word came that the enemy had hurriedly evacuated San Antonio for fear of being enveloped, and was retreating up the road toward Mexico City.

Meantime, a hot fire was opened from the northeast through the standing corn beyond Coyoacan. The enemy evidently was making a stand somewhere along the upper fork of the crossroad on the way to Churubusco. A hasty examination was made of ground about which the engineers previously had been able to learn little. It was found the Churubusco ran due east through cultivated fields, more a mill stream or a canal than a river. Where it crossed the Mexico-Acapulco road, at the village of Churubusco, a heavy bridgehead had been thrown up, with a deep wet ditch. About 450 yards to the southwest of the *tête du pont* was the convent of San Mateo, which the Americans consistently misstyled San Pablo. This enclosure covered the flank approach to the bridgehead, by way of the northern fork of the crossroad, and had been converted into a temporary fort, with artillery and a strong garrison. To troops and officers just arriving the terrain was confusing. Some time elapsed before the United States forces understood the nature of the conventual buildings, hidden, as they were, by the head-high corn.

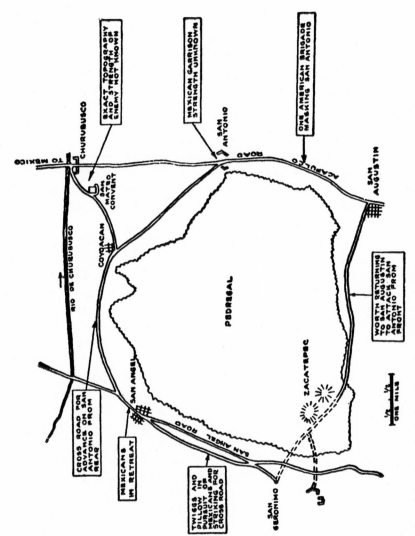

CHURUBUSCO

TO MEXICO

EXACT TOPOGRAPHY
AND STRENGTH OF
ENEMY NOT KNOWN

SAN
MATEO
CONVENT

COYOACAN

RIO DE CHURUBUSCO

SAN
ANTONIO

ACAPULCO ROAD

MEXICAN GARRISON
STRENGTH UNKNOWN

ONE AMERICAN BRIGADE
MASKING SAN ANTONIO

SAN
AUGUSTIN

PEDREGAL

WORTH RETURNING
TO SAN AUGUSTIN
TO ATTACK SAN
ANTONIO FROM
FRONT

ZACATEPEC

SAN ANGEL

SAN ANGEL ROAD

CROSS ROAD FOR
ADVANCE ON SAN
ANTONIO FROM
REAR

MEXICANS
IN RETREAT

TWIGGS AND
PILLOW IN
PURSUIT OF
MEXICANS AND
STRIKING FOR
CROSS ROAD

SAN
GERONIMO

½   ½
ONE MILE

General situation at beginning of American pursuit of Mexican army to Churubusco, about 7 A.M., August 20, 1847.

268

Worth advanced up the Acapulco road from San Antonio to Churubusco and deployed his troops against the bridgehead. Pillow joined him. The two divisions slowly but vigorously fought their way forward. Twiggs was ordered to take the convent. So confident was Scott of victory, despite the stubbornness of the Mexican resistance, that he decided to send Shields north of the river, with Pierce in support, to advance eastward to the Acapulco road, and to cut off the enemy's retreat to Mexico City from the bridgehead at the village of Churubusco. Lee was instructed to lead the troops across the Churubusco and to select a position for them. Lee himself is the best narrator of what followed: "Discovering a large mass of infantry on the Churubusco bridge, and apprehending a fire from batteries to defend the rear, I drew out towards the City of Mexico until I reached the large hamlet [in reality the ranch de los Partales] on the Mexican road about three fourths of a mile in the rear of the bridge of Churubusco. Throwing the left of his brigade upon this building which offered protection against the mass of cavalry stretching towards the gates of Mexico, and his right upon the building in the field in rear of which we had approached, General Shields formed his line obliquely to that of the enemy, who, not to be outflanked, had drawn out from his entrenchments and extended his line from the bridge to nearly opposite our left. General Pierce's brigade coming up just after General Shields' brigade had commenced the attack, took position to his right, enveloping the building in the field."

The general situation at this time is shown on page 270.

Lee's account continued: "Our troops being now hotly engaged and somewhat pressed, I urged forward the Howitzer battery under Lt. Reno, who very promptly brought the pieces to bear upon the head of their column with good effect. Perceiving that the enemy's cavalry were showing themselves on our left, and that our force was greatly outnumbered, I hastened back to the General-in-chief, who directed Major Sumner to take the Rifle regiment and a squadron to the support of that wing."[37] Even with this help the Mexicans could not be outflanked. The ground

[37] Lee, undated letter, probably to Mrs. Lee, H. A. White; *Robert E. Lee and the Southern Confederacy* (cited hereafter as *White*), 42. Lee represented Pierce's brigade as following Shields. The other accounts reverse the order.

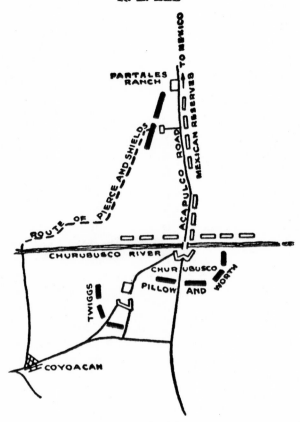

Disposition of American forces for final attack at Churubusco and Partales Ranch, August 20, 1847.

was too boggy and the enemy too strong. No offensive could be organized except a frontal attack on the road. Shields ordered this. Slowly the volunteers went forward in the face of a very heavy fire, and when they saw the Mexicans waver they charged. As they reached the road they met Worth's troops advancing up it, for the bridgehead had been taken, the convent of San Mateo had been stormed, and the victory was won.[38] Lee joined the infantry in pressing forward. Some of the cavalry pursued to the gates of Mexico.[39]

[38] Scott, *Mexican Reports*, 309–14; Shields, *ibid.*, 344; Smith, *ibid.*, 353.

[39] The American losses in the battles of Padierna (Contreras) and Churubusco were 1056; the Mexican casualties, never accurately reported, were estimated at about 6000, including 2637 prisoners (2 *Rives*, 487). After the battle the Americans learned that they

Lee doubtless sought repose as soon as he could get it after the close of the battle. He had been on his feet or in the saddle almost continuously for thirty-six hours, had thrice crossed the pedregal, and had been in all three of the actions, that of the 19th in the pedregal, that of Padierna, and that of Churubusco. But he had his reward. General Twiggs wrote of him in his report of the battles: "To Captain Lee, of the engineers, I have again the pleasure of tendering my thanks for the exceedingly valuable services rendered throughout the whole of these operations. . . ." [40]

More specifically, General P. F. Smith reported: "In adverting to the conduct of the staff, I wish to record particularly my admiration of the conduct of Captain Lee of the engineers. His reconnoissances, though pushed far beyond the bounds of prudence, were conducted with so much skill, that their fruits were of the utmost value—the soundness of his judgment and personal daring being equally conspicuous." [41]

Similarly, General Pillow mentioned him in this language: "I cannot in justice omit to notice the valuable services of Captain Lee of the engineer corps, whose distinguished merit and gallantry deserves the highest praise; and who, in the execution of his duties, was ably assisted by his assistants previously mentioned." [42]

In like strain, General Shields, remembering Lee's help in the marshy field above the Rio de Churubusco, said of him: "It affords me pleasure, and I but perform my duty, too, in acknowledging my great obligations to Captain R. E. Lee, engineers corps. . . ." And in the body of his report, describing the arrival of his forces on the field, he said: "I established the right upon a point recommended by Captain Lee, engineer officer, in whose skill and judgment I had the utmost confidence. . . ." [43]

Noting that General Twiggs had come to his camp during the night of August 19–20, General Pierce said that officer was "with

---

were right in supposing that the troops at Padierna were under General Valencia, who was at odds with General Santa Anna. The latter had commanded the troops north of San Geronimo on the San Angel road and later at Churubusco. Valencia had considered himself victor in the fighting of Aug. 19, and had refused to withdraw from Padierna on Santa Anna's orders. The total Mexican force engaged on Aug. 19–20 was around 17,000.

[40] *Mexican Reports*, 325. [41] *Ibid.*, 332.
[42] *Ibid.*, 337. [43] *Mexican Reports*, 344.

Captain Lee of the engineer corps, whose distinguished services on both days will not, I am sure, be overlooked. . . ." [44]

In short, every general under whom he served at Padierna (Contreras) and Churubusco had praise for Lee, precisely as they had at Cerro Gordo. General Scott added a final tribute when he named the officers of his staff who deserved commendation, among them "Captain R. E. Lee (as distinguished for felicitous execution as for science and daring)"—the only officer for whom he had such words.[45] Lee later received the brevet of lieutenant colonel, as of August 20,[46] and he gained much in professional prestige. When General Scott testified in the Pillow court of inquiry he said that Lee's two journeys across the pedregal on the night of August 19–20 constituted "the greatest feat of physical and moral courage performed by any individual, in my knowledge, pending the campaign." [47] Lee did not glorify his own exploits. On August 22, having no time to prepare a formal report to the bureau of engineers, he adopted an expedient common with the general staff and wrote an informal account of the recent battles, which he addressed to Mrs. Totten, wife of his commanding officer. In this there is no mention of any personal experience, except that of meeting Joe Johnston after the entrenched camp of Padierna had been captured.[48]

[44] *Mexican Reports*, Supplement, 105.   [45] *Mexican Reports*, 315.
[46] 1 *Cullum*, 420.   [47] *Pillow Inquiry*, 73.
[48] Lee to Mrs. Totten, Aug. 22, 1847; *Pillow Inquiry*, 461. *Cf. ibid.*, 301, 311.

CHAPTER XVII

Into the "Halls of the Montezumas"

The day after the battle of Churubusco the Mexicans sought an armistice. This was signed on August 24, 1847, ostensibly that negotiators might agree on a treaty of peace.[1] Scott observed both the spirit and the letter of the agreement, which forbade either side to construct or strengthen fortifications. He did not even reconnoitre the Mexican positions or work out a plan of operations to be followed in case the pourparlers failed. Lee remained during this period of rest chiefly at the pleasant village of Tacubaya, where numerous wealthy members of the English colony in Mexico City maintained summer homes. Above the village, General Scott had his headquarters in the bishop's palace.[2] The height of Chapultepec, the main defense of Mexico City, was only a mile to the northward.

On the evening of September 6, when it was manifest that no peace would be concluded and that hostilities would be resumed shortly, Scott called Lee and several other officers to his quarters and discussed the best method of attacking the city. No decision was reached other than that the American army would take the offensive within a few days unless the enemy did so meantime.[3] On the 7th the armistice was ended, and reconnaissance was at once undertaken. As Major Smith was sick and Lee was next in rank among the engineers,[4] the burden of directing the reconnaissance fell on the Virginian.

The military problem was an unusual one. The city of Mexico lies on slightly elevated ground, above fields in which scattered pools of water were always standing in the rainy, summer season.

---

[1] Scott, *Mexican Reports*, 314; text of the armistice, *ibid*, 356. For Hitchcock's claim that Scott had promised at Puebla to give the friends of peace an opportunity to act after the Mexican army had been defeated, see *Pillow Inquiry*, 524. The armistice in all its bearings is well explained in 2 *Rives*, 500 ff.
[2] *Semmes*, 427, 431.   [3] *Hitchcock*, 293.
[4] *Mexican Reports*, 355; *Pillow Inquiry*, 77, 313.

The only solid approach for an army was along one of the causeways that ran on straight lines toward the city gates. Three of
these causeways led up from the south and were commanded by
batteries at and near the gates, which were in themselves minia-
ture fortresses. The other two causeways ran from the west and
southwest and were open to fire from the city gates, and also from
Chapultepec, which was about a mile and a half from the nearest
of these gates. An approach from the south was difficult, but it
avoided the fire of Chapultepec. On the other hand, if Chapultepec could be stormed, an advance into the city from that direction would be less arduous than by an attack from the south. The
situation was this:

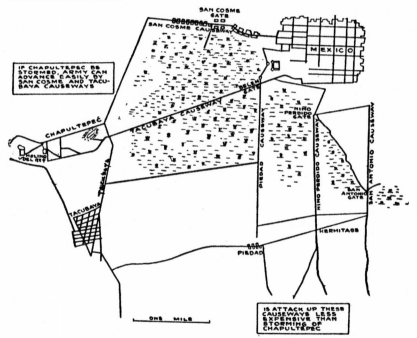

Alternative lines of American attack on Mexico City, as presented to General Scott,
September 7, 1847.

In gathering information from which Scott could make the best
decision, Lee was assisted by Lieutenants Beauregard and Tower.
They started with a study of the San Antonio and Nino Perdido

southern gates,[5] but they had not proceeded far with their work on September 7 when General Scott learned that Mexican troops in considerable numbers had been observed around Molino del Rey, which lay at the western foot of the height of Chapultepec. Two days previously the commanding general had been told that the Mexican authorities had collected many church-bells from the city and had sent them to Molino del Rey to be cast into cannon at a foundry alleged to be in operation there. Scott now connected the two reports and concluded that the troops had been sent to Molino del Rey to protect it while the ordnance was being made. He reasoned that the Mexicans greatly needed additional artillery, and that if it were fabricated he could not readily prevent its removal to the defenses of the city unless he stormed Chapultepec, which he was not prepared to do at the time. He hoped for the moment, in fact, that he might be able to avoid altogether a direct attack on that height.[6] Scott accordingly ordered General Worth, who was nearest the ground, to deliver a night attack on Molino del Rey, to destroy the foundry, to spike the cannon, and to return to his position by daylight. Later in the evening, on strong representation from Worth's staff, Scott consented that the attack might be deferred until daylight.[7]

Neither in the planning nor in the fighting of the battle of Molino del Rey on September 8 did Lee have any large part. The engineering work was done by Captain Mason and others. While the action was on, Lee acted as an aide to Scott in reporting the movements of the opposing forces.[8] By Worth's assault the enemy was driven from Molino del Rey and from the ground to the west, but Worth did not find any cannon foundry and did not think the position sufficiently important to hold it after he had sustained 787 casualties in taking it. The 5th Infantry, which attacked a powder magazine, known as Casa Mata, west of Molino del Rey, lost 38 per cent of its effective strength.[9] The fighting was the hottest of the entire campaign, considering the limited number of troops engaged. Scott's strategy in planning the battle and Worth's tactics in conducting it were both subjected to much criticism in the army. The chief gain to the Americans

---

[5] *Mexican Reports,* 355; *Pillow Inquiry,* 77.
[6] *Mexican Reports,* 355.　　　　　　　[7] *Semmes,* 433.
[8] *Mexican Reports,* 356, 426.　　　　　[9] 2 *Rives,* 536.

from the battle was a further demoralization of the Mexicans, among whom desertions increased greatly.

No sooner was the battle over than Lee resumed his reconnaissance to the south of the city, assisted still by Tower and Beauregard. They planned to work separately on each of the three southern causeways, but as they found the enemy in strength on the Nino Perdido and San Antonio roads, they were forced to reconnoitre jointly the Piedad road. They contrived to get to a ravine within a mile and a quarter of the city, and thence they could see the enemy busily at work strengthening the defenses of the San Antonio gate. The engineers discovered, also, that the enemy was running an entrenchment in a northwesterly direction from the gate of San Antonio toward the gate on the Nino Perdido road. The Mexicans manifestly were expecting an attack in that quarter and were preparing for it, though as yet they had mounted only five or six guns there.[10]

Lee's report of this situation was enough to induce General Scott the next morning, September 9, to make a personal examination in a wide sweep of the roads south of the city. The commander was depressed to find the enemy so actively at work, but he gave no orders for suspending the reconnaissance on that sector. On the contrary, while Lee was employed on September 10 in arranging for the defense of a new base at Miscoac, Beauregard, Tower, and I. I. Stevens tried to work their way farther around to the southeast of the city, with an eye to an attack on that sector.[11] Lee rejoined them on the morning of September 11, and with Lieutenant Tower conducted a further reconnaissance on the Nino Perdido road. Thus far he had not made up his mind whether the southern front offered a better line of attack than the western; but he now found a possible battery position, and he reasoned that if guns were planted there they could enfilade the San Antonio gate and part of the new entrenchments running thence to the Nino Perdido gate.[12] With this artillery aid he believed it would be possible for the army to storm Mexico City from the south. As for an attack on Chapultepec, he considered it practicable, but he began to doubt whether the American guns could do much damage to the lower part of the building,

[10] *Mexican Reports*, 426.   [11] *Mexican Reports*, 427.   [12] *Mexican Reports*, 427.

and he was satisfied that scaling ladders would be necessary in an infantry attack.[13]

That night Scott called a council of war in the church at Piedad. Lee and the other engineers were present with all the general officers except Worth and Smith, who were on special duty. Scott announced that he wanted the judgment of his subordinates regarding the best method of attacking the city. After the losses that had been sustained, he said, it was of vital importance to strike a decisive blow with minimum casualties. Personally, he explained, he favored an attack on Chapultepec and the western gates. He believed that one day's bombardment of Chapultepec would force its evacuation or make its capture easy, but he desired his officers to express their opinions freely. Lee and all the engineers except Beauregard announced themselves in opposition to Scott's plan and in favor of attacking the southern gates. The general officers, with Twiggs dissenting, also favored that course. Beauregard, however, made a detailed explanation of the comparative difficulties of the two operations and pronounced strongly in favor of assaulting Chapultepec. His argument convinced General Pierce, who went over to the side of Scott and Twiggs. With no further discussion, Scott decided that he would attack from the west, and thereupon adjourned the meeting.[14]

As the plan began to take form it called for a continuing feint against the southern defenses while preparations were made for the real attack from the west. Troops were marched to the southern approaches in daylight and then were moved westward during the night. Lee was instructed to start work immediately on the construction of four batteries that were to be used against Chapultepec.[15] The ordnance officers quickly selected sites, which Lee approved. Battery No. 1 was to be on the road leading from Tacubaya to the southeastern corner of Chapultepec. Battery No. 2, easily built by Benjamin Huger, was to be northeast of the bishop's palace above Tacubaya. Numbers 3 and 4 were to lie just south of Molino del Rey and were to play on the western

[13] *Hitchcock*, 301.
[14] The best account of this council is given in the excellent work of J. H. Smith, 2, 149. See also J. F. H. Claiborne: *Life and Correspondence of John A. Quitman* (cited hereafter as *Quitman*), 1, 353 *ff.*, and *Pillow Inquiry*, 143.
[15] Scott, *Mexican Reports*, 377; Quitman. *ibid.*, 410; Smith, *ibid.*, 428.

face of Chapultepec. Having laid off the site of Battery No. 1, Lee left the construction of it to Lieutenants Tower and Gustavus W. Smith, who worked so fast that by 7 o'clock on the morning of September 12 they were able to put into position the two 16-pounders and the 8-inch howitzer that were to constitute the armament. Theirs was a night-long task, with 1 o opportunity for sleep. When fire was opened that morning from Battery No. 1 it was speedily taken up by Battery No. 2, which contained one 24-pounder and one 8-inch howitzer.[16]

Preparation of Batteries 3 and 4 was more difficult, both because of the ground and also because of the distance the guns had to be brought. Lee had Lieutenant George B. McClellan as his assistant in this part of the task, and they worked together all night and on into the 12th. At Battery No. 4 a 10-inch mortar was brought into action during the day. At Battery No. 3 little could be done on the 12th until the fire of the other batteries caused that of the enemy to fall away. When this happened Lee prepared the ground and laid his platforms so that he could use the wall of the nearby aqueduct as a parapet. Ordnance officers by this time had an 8-inch howitzer and a 16-pounder at hand. These being duly mounted, Battery No. 3 joined the others in bombarding Chapultepec.[17]

When the effect of the fire began to show on Chapultepec, Lee went out with Lieutenant Tower to reconnoitre. Covered by guns in the batteries, they reached a point whence they could study in detail the approaches to Chapultepec and the building itself.[18] It was a position of great strength. A ridge some 600 yards in length ran almost east and west, rising to a height of about 190 feet. On the crest, which had been levelled off some sixty years before, a stout stone building had been constructed. This had been started as a palace, but had subsequently been turned into a military college. The Americans always called it a fortress, but it scarcely deserved the name, for most of its armament had been extemporized for the expected assault.

The chief reliance of the Mexicans was on the difficulties of the approach. The whole ridge was enclosed on the north, east,

---

[16] 2 *J. H. Smith*, 409.
[17] *Mexican Reports*, 377, 411, 423.   [18] Lee, in *Pillow Inquiry*, 143.

and south by a high brick wall. On the western side were the buildings of Molino del Rey. Inside the enclosure the ground rose so precipitously on the northern and eastern faces that the position was impregnable there. On the south was the regular approach, by a ramp cut into the rock, with a single sharp turn about half-way up. This, the engineers could see, had been strengthened with sandbags and was a formidable barrier. From the west the approach was easier. East of Molino del Rey, within the enclosure, was an open field, and then a marshy cypress grove that ran to the edge of the rocky ascent. Precisely what fortifications had been constructed along this ascent the American engineers probably could not discover, but they doubtless could see the parapet rising from the rocky ground to the terrace of the palace, and they suspected, if indeed they did not actually observe, that there was a deep ditch below the parapet wall.[19] A formidable position it was, weakened somewhat by the American guns, but by no means reduced!

Returning to the battery, Lee was soon visited by Beauregard, with a message that General Scott wished to see him. Lee had been up the whole of the previous night and had not had any sleep for more than thirty hours, but rest had to wait on orders from the commanding general. Off Lee went to Tacubaya, accompanied by Tower and Beauregard. He found the general not in his best humor. Why had not Lee reported to him sooner? It was important that he know what the effect of the American fire on Chapultepec had been, so that he could decide whether to attack that evening or on the morning of the 13th. Pillow, he explained, was to attack from the west and Quitman from the south. Their volunteer commands were to be strengthened by two storming parties of regulars, each 250 strong and supplied with scaling ladders. The troops would soon be ready for the assault. If they waited till the next day would the enemy be able during the night to repair the damage done by the bombardment? Lee answered that he feared the enemy would, and Tower was of the same mind. "Then we must attack this evening," said Scott, and turned away toward his quarters.

The three engineers hastily conferred and decided that there

19 2 *Rives*, 526–28, 544.

would hardly be time before nightfall to make the requisite preparations, to deliver the assault, and to follow it up. Lee, as the senior of the trio, thereupon approached Scott and told him that they believed it probably would be better to defer the attack until morning. Scott had cooled down somewhat, and, on second thought, he reasoned that if the Mexicans did reinforce Chapultepec that night the heavy batteries could drive them out the next morning. Moreover, he reflected, by attacking early in the day he would have a longer time in which to pursue whatever advantage he might gain. He accordingly acquiesced in the postponement, and had Lee and the other engineers explain to him where the opposing batteries were located, and what they had learned about the approaches to Chapultepec. Then he outlined fully his plan of operations, concluding with a request that Lee report to him that night.

Lee returned, as directed. Soon afterwards General Pillow rode up. At Scott's word, Lee then sketched the plan of attack that Scott had described to him that afternoon.[20] Even when this was done, and the conference had adjourned, Lee could not bring himself to take rest. He spent the rest of the night visiting the batteries, to be sure that instructions were understood and that all damage done by the Mexicans during the day was being repaired.

When dawn came on the 13th, Lee had been forty-eight hours without sleep and was close to collapse, but his orders took him very early in the morning to Pillow's division, which he was to guide in its advance.

Pillow's movement was part of an operation that can be followed in its several stages from the sketch shown opposite.

Worth's, Pillow's, and Quitman's divisions had been brought up under cover of darkness until all three of them were within striking distance of Chapultepec. Smith's brigade of Twiggs's division was marching to support Quitman. The storming party of 250 regulars from Worth's corps had reached Pillow, and a like force from Twiggs's had been sent Quitman. Twiggs's other brigade (Riley's) was to the east, in front of the San Antonio gate. The four heavy batteries were manned and ready for action. The

---

[20] Lee, in *Pillow Inquiry*, 143–44.

field artillery was divided among the infantry commands. Some of the cavalry were with Pillow; the rest were covering the advanced base and hospital at Miscoac.

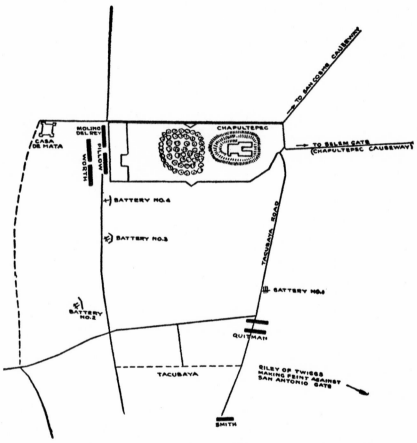

Position of American troops for attack on Chapultepec, September 13, 1847.

Scott's orders were for the heavy batteries to resume the bombardment on the morning of the 13th, while Riley made a demonstration in front of the San Antonio gate. At a given word from Scott the batteries were to suspend their fire. This was to be the signal for the assault. Pillow was to move from Molino del Rey eastward through the cypress grove within the enclosure of Chapultepec and was to storm the crest from the westward approach. Quitman simultaneously was to advance up the Tacubaya road, was to batter his way into the enclosure, and was to assault Chapultepec from the south, up the ramp cut in the face of the rock. Worth was to be held in reserve, to support Pillow and, if opportunity offered, to cut off the Mexican retreat. Nothing was known definitely concerning the strength of the Mexicans or the number of guns they had in the defenses of the city.

Every one realized that the action about to open would be the decisive engagement of the war. A thrill akin to that of the landing at Vera Cruz passed through the ranks as the men listened for the expected lull in the fire of the heavy batteries. Shortly after 8 o'clock in the morning Scott's messengers arrived at the headquarters of Pillow and of Quitman with word that he was about to give the signal for the opening of the battle. "Cease fire" was ordered. A moment's hush fell upon the army. The infantry were put in motion.

Lee set out immediately with Pillow from Molino del Rey and helped to guide the men of one storming party across the cultivated ground and into the cypress grove at the foot of the hill. They had not proceeded far when Pillow complained that he had been wounded. Lee saw the General safely placed out of the range of the fire,[21] and probably had some part in carrying out Pillow's order that Worth be asked to support him immediately with his entire division.

Pillow's men pushed forward, while Clarke's brigade came up from Worth, who held his other brigade for a turning movement north of Chapultepec. James Longstreet, Edward Johnson, George E. Pickett, and other young officers within the enclosure, urged their men on—past a temporary entrenchment the Mexicans had drawn up, over a mine field which the enemy had no time to explode, and on to a deep ditch directly under the ramparts of Chapultepec itself. Here there was a short pause while the scaling ladders were brought up. A little more, and the most daring were mounting the wall. They were thrown back, killed or wounded, but others quickly gained a foothold, and the whole storming column was streaming up the terraces. Regimental flags

---

[21] *Pillow Inquiry,* 529.

were soon flung out from the elevation, while cheers drowned the clash of arms.

Quitman, meantime, had been making his way toward the enclosure from the south, and part of his troops ere long mingled with the rejoicing regiments of Pillow. Soon Worth was thrown forward by Scott, on the northern side of the Chapultepec enclosure, to deal with a large force observed in that direction. A part of Pillow's command that had been unable to share in the assault was already there, and Lieutenant T. J. Jackson was serving a gun, almost single-handed, in an unequal duel with Mexican artillery.[22]

There is no record of Lee's movements from the time he saw Pillow carried to a place of safety until he reappears on the terrace of Chapultepec, when Scott and his staff rode up among the cheering troops, shortly after the palace had been stormed. Lee may have gone on with Pillow's men, but it is more probable that he returned to Scott, with a report of what had happened.[23] Now he hurried forward, under Scott's orders, to reconnoitre the approaches to the San Cosme gate, and to bring up the siege and engineering trains. For Scott sensed the demoralization of Santa Anna's troops and was determined to push Worth and Quitman on the heels of the enemy, into Mexico City itself.

By this time strain and sleeplessness had almost paralyzed Lee. It was with the greatest difficulty that he kept his saddle, but by a supreme effort of will he started on his mission. While he was discharging it he received a slight wound, which he did not even stop to have dressed. He examined the ground over which Worth had to advance before coming to the San Cosme gate at the northwestern side of the city. The wagons he got under way. Somehow he managed to return to Scott at Chapultepec, and he rode with the commanding general on the line of Worth's advance. Then he fainted—for the first and only time in his life.[24]

Before sunrise the next morning Lee was himself again and was soon despatched by Scott with orders for Quitman. He learned, before he set out, that after he had left the field the pre-

---

[22] *Mexican Reports*, 378–82, 400 *ff.*   [23] *Cf.* Smith in *Mexican Reports*, 428.
[24] *Mexican Reports*, 385, 428. Twenty-two years afterward, when a minister fainted in the pulpit at Lexington, Lee tactfully consoled him by relating this experience (*Jones*, 149).

vious evening Worth had fought his way to the San Cosme gate
and Quitman to the Belem gate. Darkness had found them both
practically within the city, their troops in good order and high
spirits, and ready to march to the plaza, even if the enemy fought
from house to house. Lee now heard even more pleasing news:
about 4 A.M. a delegation from the city council had arrived at
Scott's headquarters and had announced that Santa Anna had
evacuated the city.[25] All the Americans had to do was to march
in!

Lee carried the orders for Quitman to move cautiously to the
centre of the city. On his arrival he discovered that Quitman had
placed his entire command under arms soon after daylight and
had occupied the citadel. A little later, on report that a mob was
looting the public buildings, Quitman sent a column to the grand
plaza. Lee went with it and doubtless was in the square when
Captain Roberts of the rifle regiment, the officer designated for
that purpose by Quitman, raised the United States flag over the
palace amid the huzzas of the soldiers.[26] About 8 o'clock Scott
rode into the plaza from the Alameda, at the head of Worth's
division. He and his staff were in full dress, and he did not lose
a single thrill of the dramatic climax in which he was the central
figure. Napoleon himself would not have set the stage more
theatrically. The cavalcade and the mounted escort—

"filed to the right along the west side [of the plaza], and when
on a line with the front of the cathedral turned to the left; arms
were then presented, colors lowered, and drums beaten. General
Scott dismounted, uncovered his head, then passed through the
porte-cochère of the National Palace, followed by Generals Quitman and Smith and staff officers. In the *patio* he turned to them
and said: 'Gentlemen, we must not be too elated by our success';
then after a slight pause, 'let me present to you the civil and
military Governor of the City of Mexico, Maj.-Gen. John A.
Quitman. I appoint him at this instant. He has earned the distinction and shall have it.'

"The party then ascended a broad stairway, entered a handsomely furnished apartment facing the Grand Plaza, and General

---

[25] Scott, *Mexican Reports*, 383; Quitman, *ibid.*, 416–17.
[26] *Mexican Reports*, 417, 428.

Scott wrote [the order announcing the victory], which was read aloud to those about him." [27]

There followed twenty-four hours of scattered fighting in the streets with ruffians and with convicts that Santa Anna had released from prison before abandoning the city. These men fired from windows and roof-tops and had to be hunted down, a few at a time, with considerable losses. Scott did not hesitate to employ a strong hand in dealing with these miscreants. He could not afford to do otherwise, for after deducting the casualties of September 8 and 13, and the garrison left at Chapultepec, he had less than 6000 men with which to occupy and garrison Mexico City.[28]

In the bloody street encounters of the 14th and 15th, Lee did not share. Scott praised him for his conduct at Chapultepec,[29] and the Department of War later gave him the brevet of colonel,[30] but his fighting in Mexico was at an end. The artillery employed while the convicts were being driven out was the last Lee was to hear in action until 1861.

Labor did not end, however, with active hostilities. While the tired little army awaited reinforcements, Lee set himself and his brother engineers to making surveys and to preparing eight maps of Mexico City and the nearby defenses and battlefields. He personally undertook the topography of the general defenses of the city and adjacent fortified points.[31] Simultaneously, on orders from Colonel Totten, he began to collect material concerning the operation of the naval battery at Vera Cruz.

In December, 1847, reinforcements arrived and plans were made to occupy more of the cities of Central Mexico. Lee was designated to prepare routes to the various objectives. It probably was while Lee was making reconnaissances on one of these routes and was riding alone that he encountered a Mexican who fingered his lariat as if he were calculating whether he could get it swinging

[27] C. M. Wilcox: *History of the Mexican War*, 483, an eye-witness's account.
[28] Scott, *Mexican Reports*, 384.
[29] "Captain Lee, engineer, so constantly distinguished, also bore important orders from me (Sept. 13) until he fainted from a wound and the loss of two nights' sleep at the batteries" (*Mexican Reports*, 385). For Pillow's acknowledgment, see *ibid.*, 404.
[30] G. O. 47, *A. G. O.*, Aug. 24, 1848.
[31] Lee to Totten, *MS.*, Nov. 30, 1847; *Eng. MSS.*, 987; same to same, *MS.*, April 21, 1848, *ibid.*, 1018.

and throw it over the accursed Yankee before Lee could shoot him. Lee observed the man's motion, quietly took out his pistol from his holster and placed it in front of him. That was enough. The Mexican passed with polite salutation and went on his way. Lee always believed that if the Mexican had been given half a chance he would have used the rope.[32]

His study of the lines of advance completed, Lee returned to map making.[33] So intent was he on this that one night when Magruder of the artillery came to invite him to a dinner where his health had been proposed, Lee declined to go. Magruder insisted that the work was mere drudgery that another might perform; Lee answered that he was simply doing his duty—a remark that only his manifest sincerity saved from a note of self-righteousness.[34]

Not until April 21, 1848, were certain of the maps finished and forwarded to the engineers' bureau.[35] A little later Lee joined Beauregard and McClellan in reconnoitring Toluca, when ratification of the treaty of peace was still uncertain,[36] but apparently he made no further surveys. The maps he was unable to complete in Mexico he planned to deliver to the bureau after his return to the United States.[37] During almost the whole of this map work he had, in addition, the troublesome supervision of the engineering company, whose commanding officer, Lieutenant Gustavus W. Smith, reported to him as the senior officer of the corps in Mexico.[38] He was not wholly successful in procuring the information Colonel Totten desired on the siege of Vera Cruz.[39]

Thus engaged, Lee had little time and less inclination for the quarrels that broke out among some of the general officers of the army almost as soon as Mexico City was occupied. General Scott

---

[32] Packard, 158.

[33] Lee to Totten, MS., Jan. 1, 1848; Eng. MSS., 993; same to same, Feb. 1, 1848; Eng. MSS., 999.

[34] Jones, 133–34; Long, 64.

[35] Lee to Totten, MS., March 1, 1848; Eng. MSS., 1000; same to same, MS., April 1, 1848, ibid., 1012; same to same, MS., April 21, 1848; Eng. MSS., 1018.

[36] Lee to Totten, MS., May 1, 1848; Eng. MSS., 1016.

[37] Lee to Totten, MS., June 29, 1848; Eng. MSS., 1018; same to same, MS., Nov. 8, 1848; Eng. MSS., 1039.

[38] Lee to Totten, MS., Jan. 1, 1848; Eng. MSS., 993; same to same, MS., May 21, 1848, ibid., 1015.

[39] Lee to Totten, MS., Jan. 1, 1848; Eng. MSS., 993; same to same, MS., Feb. 1, 1848, ibid., 999.

considered that the successful plan of operations originated with him, and that he should have sole credit for it. General Pillow, on the other hand, had political ambitions as pronounced as those of Scott, and wished himself to appear a hero in the eyes of the American people. General Worth's aspirations were confined to his profession, but he felt that the decision to approach Mexico City by turning to the south of Lake Chalco was due to his activities, and he was anxious that the record show it. Each of the three generals had subordinates who were zealous partisans. If they did not disparage the achievements of others, they at least were quick to sound the praises of their chief.[40] On October 2, 1847, Scott opened a correspondence with General Pillow regarding that officer's claim in his reports to have initiated movements at Contreras and at Chapultepec. "General S. is sorry to perceive in General P's report of September 18," the commanding general wrote in summing up, "a seeming effort, no doubt unintentional, to leave General S. entirely out of the operations of September 13th."[41] A brisk, brief correspondence ended in dissatisfaction to both men.[42] Each thought the other wished to have all the glory.

Less than three weeks later the mails brought copies of New Orleans papers containing a communication signed "Leonidas," in which Pillow's part in the battle of Contreras-Churubusco was most inordinately and foolishly extolled.[43] The offended chief took no immediate action on this publication, perhaps because it made Pillow appear far more ridiculous than heroic. On November 10 came other newspapers, among them one including a letter that gave General Worth the credit for the turning movement below Lake Chalco.[44]

Scott read into all this a conspiracy to belittle him, and on November 12 he issued an ill-tempered order calling attention to the army regulation that forbade soldiers to write of military operations until after they had closed.[45] Worth at once wrote Scott to know if the order was aimed at him. Another warm

[40] 2 *Rives*, 621 *ff*.
[41] Scott to Pillow, Oct. 2, 1847; *Pillow Inquiry*, 629–30.
[42] *Pillow Inquiry*, 630–34.
[43] Pillow's memorandum, which he admitted to be the basis of this letter, appears in *Pillow Inquiry*, 389. The embroidered newspaper versions follow.
[44] 2 *Ripley*, 551.   [45] G. O. 349, *Pillow Inquiry*, 455.

exchange followed, at the close of which Worth preferred charges against Scott, who promptly put him under arrest for insubordination and proposed to court-martial him.[46] Colonel Duncan of Worth's division acknowledged himself as the author of the letter on the Chalco move, and was also detained for court-martial. And then, as if to make a clean sweep, Scott brought charges against Pillow and confined him to the City of Mexico.[47]

Needless to say, the suspension from command of two of the four major generals serving under Scott created a first-class sensation among the idle troops in the enemy's capital. It created more than a sensation when news of it reached Washington.

The administration had long been resentful of Scott's continual grumbling, and was glad of an opportunity to get rid of him. A court of inquiry was ordered on January 13, 1848, to hear Worth's charges against Scott, along with Scott's against Pillow. It was specifically set forth that Scott's complaints against Worth should not be brought to trial until the prior charges preferred against him by Worth had been considered. All three of the accused officers were ordered to be released from arrest. To crown it all, Scott was relieved of command, was directed to attend the court of inquiry, wherever held, and was told to report to the War Department when the court finished its hearings.[48]

Lee had not thought General Scott temperate in his dealings with Worth and Pillow. On his way back from his daily surveys of the western hills, while making his map, he often stopped at Tacubaya to chat with his young friend, Henry J. Hunt. That officer noted Lee's "desire to heal the differences between General Scott and some of his subordinate officers and the efforts he was making in that direction. . . . He was a peace-maker by nature."[49] But when Scott was relieved of command on February 18, Lee felt that the General had been mistreated, and his resentment rose high, though he was confident of Scott's vindication.[50] He told his chief what he knew of Pillow's movements on the morning of Chapultepec, when Pillow had been wounded, and he had frankly averred that Pillow could only have been hit by a bullet

---

[46] The correspondence is in *Semmes*, 360 ff.
[48] *Ex. Doc. 60, 1st sess., 30th Cong.,* 1040 ff.
[50] Lee to Mrs. Lee, March 15, 1848; *Fitz Lee,* 44.

[47] *Pillow Inquiry,* 373.
[49] Hunt, in *Long,* 70.

glancing from some object, perhaps a tree.[51] Now Lee spoke in plain terms to his brother:

"I think our country may well be proud of the conduct of both arms of the service. As to myself, your brotherly feelings have made you estimate too highly my small services, and though praise from one I love so dearly is sweet, truth compels me to disclaim it. I did nothing more than what others in my place would have done much better. The great cause of our success was in our leader. It was his stout heart that cast us on the shore of Vera Cruz; his bold self-reliance that forced us through the pass at Cerro Gordo; his indomitable courage that, amid all the doubts and difficulties that surrounded us at Puebla, pressed us forward to this capital, and finally brought us within its gates, while others, who croaked all the way from Brazos, and advised delay at Puebla, finding themselves at last, contrary to their expectations, comfortably quartered within its gates, find fault with the way they came there. With all their knowledge, I will defy them to have done better. I agree with you as to the dissensions in camp; they have clouded a bright campaign. It is a contest in which neither party has anything to gain and the Army much to lose, and ought to have been avoided. The whole matter will soon be before the court, and if it be seen that there has been harshness and intemperance of language on one side, it will be evident that there has been insubordination on the other.

"It is difficult for a general to maintain discipline in an army, composed as this is, in a foreign country, where temptations to disorders are so great, and the chance of detection so slight. He requires every support and confidence from his government at home. If he abused his trust or authority, it is then time to hold him to account. But to decide the matter upon an ex-parte statement of favorites; to suspend a successful general in command of an army in the heart of an enemy's country; to try the judge in place of the accused, is to upset all discipline; to jeopardize the safety of the army and the honor of the country, and to violate justice. I trust, however, that all will work well in the end."[52]

[51] Hitchcock, in *Pillow Inquiry*, 529. Pillow was reported to have said that his leg was "shattered," but the surgeons found no injury (*ibid.*).
[52] R. E. Lee to Smith Lee, March 4, 1848; Jones, *L. and L.*, 56–57.

A little later, he wrote:

"Mr. Gardener and Mr. Trist depart tomorrow. I had hoped that after the President had adopted Mr. Trist's treaty, and the Senate confirmed it, they would have paid him the poor compliment of allowing him to finish it, as some compensation for all the abuse they had heaped upon him; but I presume it is perfectly fair, having made use of his labors, and taken from him all that he had earned, that he should be kicked off as General Scott has been, whose skill and science, having crushed the enemy and conquered a peace, can now be dismissed, and turned out as an old horse to die." [53]

In still another letter to Smith, Lee noted the singular fact that when Santa Anna had been passing through Fredericktown, Md., in 1836, he chanced upon a court of inquiry sitting, at the instance of President Jackson, to investigate the conduct of General Scott. He added:

"Our present President thought perhaps he ought to afford the gratification to the same individual to see Scott before another court in presence of the troops he commanded. I hope, however, all will terminate in good. The discontent in the army at this state of things is great." [54]

Lee found himself, ere long, directly involved in the court of inquiry, which assembled in Mexico City on March 16, after meeting in Puebla. Part of Pillow's defense was that some of Scott's staff officers had violated the regulations by writing of military operations, and that they had not been punished in any way, though he had been put under arrest. Lee was one of those so accused, on the strength of the publication in *The Washington Union* of the letter he had written on August 22 to Mrs. Totten. She had duly received it, and had carried it to the engineers' headquarters, so that it might be read by the officers there. In the absence of Colonel Totten, his assistant, Captain Welcker, [55] gave a copy of the communication to the newspaper, not realizing that

[53] R. E. Lee to Smith Lee, undated; Jones, *L. and L.,* 54.
[54] R. E. Lee to Smith Lee, April 8, 1848; Jones, *L. and L.,* 57–58.
[55] The name is given as Welcher in the *Pillow Inquiry,* but the officer doubtless was Captain George L. Welcker.

he was violating any regulation. Pillow knew of the publication, if not of the circumstances attending it, and on March 28 he put Lee on the stand as a defense witness. Lee's examination was brief. He readily identified his letter and told how it came to be printed. The defense rested when it had brought out the fact that the letter was addressed to Mrs. Totten and not to the bureau. Scott at once offset this point by two questions:

"Had Major General Scott, at the time witness wrote the letter, any knowledge of the fact, or has the said Scott, as far as the witness knows, been since acquainted with the fact?"

Lee answered: "Not that I am aware of. He has never been informed by me, before or since."

"State the relationship of the engineer bureau to the Secretary of War, or is not that bureau part of the War Department?"—in other words, had not the letter been given out officially in Washington?

"The engineer bureau," said Lee, "is a part of the War Department. The chief engineer transacts business in the name or, certainly, under the authority of the Secretary of War." [56]

As the letter itself had been a plain narration of fact, exalting no commander, Lee's explanation and Scott's cross-examination effectually cleared the engineer of blame for any breach of the army law. Scott, however, kept the point in mind and when the hearing was resumed at Frederick, Md., after Scott's return to the United States, he put on witnesses to prove that what Lee had done was a common expedient among bureau officers who wished their chiefs to be informed when they were unable to prepare formal reports. [57]

Lee appeared before the court again in Mexico on March 31 and April 8, as a witness for the prosecution, but in both instances he testified only concerning actual troop movements and the orders given in front of Padierna and Chapultepec. [58] His evidence, though important for the facts it gave regarding the battles, had no decisive bearing on the case, which ended in the acquittal of Pillow. The charges against Scott and Worth were dropped. Lee's relations with the commanding general were

[56] *Pillow Inquiry*, 55.
[57] *Pillow Inquiry*, 301, 311.
[58] *Pillow Inquiry*, 75 *ff.*, 143 *ff.*

291

rendered warmer and more intimate by the stand the younger officer took in the controversy. He attended the dinner given to Scott by a wealthy Britisher the day after the General relinquished command,[59] and he was one of those among whom Scott directed that his wine be divided when he went home.[60]

While the court of inquiry had been sitting, peace negotiations had been in progress, and on February 2, 1848, a treaty had been signed at Guadalupe Hidalgo. The details of the subsequent discussion of the terms have no place here, but they were closely followed by Lee, who was anxious to go home, now that the fighting was over. He did not think much was to be gained by discussing the origins of the war. "That," he said, "ought to have been understood before we engaged in it. It may have been produced by the act of either party or the force of circumstances. Let the pedants in diplomacy determine." It was true, however, he said, "that we bullied [Mexico]. For that I am ashamed, for she was the weaker party, but we have since, by way of set-off, drubbed her handsomely and in a manner no man might be ashamed of." The United States could dictate a conqueror's peace, he said, but they should be just. "For myself," he wrote Mrs. Lee, "I would not exact now more than I would have taken before the commencement of hostilities, as I should wish for nothing but what was just, and that I would have sooner or later." Again, "we have the right, by the laws of war, of dictating the terms of peace and requiring indemnity for our losses and expenses. Rather than forego that right, except through a spirit of magnanimity to a crushed foe, I would fight them ten years, but I would be generous in exercising it."

When there was a prospect that Mexico might haggle over the revised treaty, as ratified by the United States Senate, Lee believed the country's representatives should submit it to Mexico and insist on its acceptance, or else "tear up the paper and make . . . arrangements to take the country up to the line from Tehuantepec to Osaqualco or whatever southern boundary they might think

[59] *Hitchcock,* 320.
[60] *Hitchcock,* 328. Some of this wine may have been purchased by Lee for Scott, or for the headquarters mess, before Lee left Vera Cruz (*cf.* R. E. Lee to Smith Lee, March 27, 1847; *Fitz Lee,* 37).

proper for the United States. I think we might reasonably expect that they would lose no time in ratifying the present treaty." He added grimly, "I might make a rough diplomatist, but a tolerably quick one." [61]

Hostilities had ended on March 6,[62] under the treaty, but the Mexican Congress was slow to act on the document. When word came at last that the peace had been ratified by the chamber of deputies, the favorable action of the senate being taken for granted, Lee rushed off the news to his brother Smith, happily jumbling politics and personal matters: "We all feel quite exhilàrated at the prospect of getting home, where I shall again see you and my dear Sis Nannie. Where will you be this summer? I have heard that the Commissioners start for Queretaro tomorrow. I know not whether it is true. General Smith will probably leave here for Vera Cruz on the 24th or 25th to make arrangements for the embarkation of troops. As soon as it is certain that we march out, and I make the necessary arrangements for the engineer transportation, etc., I shall endeavor to be off. I shall therefore leave everything till I see you. Several of your naval boys are here who will be obliged to 'cut out.' Love to Sis Nannie and the boys. Rhett Buchanan and all friends are well. Very truly and affectionately. . . ." [63]

Lee lost little time in realizing his hopes. On May 27, six days after he wrote Smith, he received orders to march the engineering company to Vera Cruz, and, as soon as he heard that ratifications of the treaty had been exchanged, to embark them for the United States. He reached Vera Cruz on June 6, sent off some of the officers and all of the men the next day, and sailed after them as soon as he could purchase a few gifts for his family and find a place aboard the steamer. McClellan went with the engineer company; Captain John G. Barnard and Lieutenant P. G. T. Beauregard travelled with Lee.[64] His own mount went on the

[61] Lee to Mrs. Lee, Feb. 8 and 13, 1848; *Fitz Lee,* 42–43; R. E. Lee to Smith Lee, March 4, 1848; Jones, *L. and L.,* 57; same to same, April 12, 1848, *ibid.,* 54–55.
[62] Lee to Totten, *MS.,* April 1, 1848; *Eng. MSS.,* 1012.
[63] R. E. Lee to Smith Lee, May 21, 1848; *Fitz Lee,* 45–46. The Mexican senate ratified the treaty on May 25. Ratifications were exchanged May 30, 1848 (2 *Rives,* 653, 655).
[64] Lee to Totten, *MS.,* June 7, 1848; *Eng. MSS.,* 1017.

same vessel with him. A white pony that he bought for his youngest boy was shipped on a later vessel, bound for Baltimore.

Twenty months of service in Mexico had been ended when Lee saw the castle and the towers of Vera Cruz fade from view, never again to be seen by him. They were probably the twenty most useful months of his training as a soldier. Their effect on him can be seen during nearly the whole of the War between the States. The lessons he learned on the road to Mexico City he applied in much of his strategy. Warnings he read in that campaign he never forgot.

He carried home with him the highest admiration of his former commander and the good opinion of his brother officers. As a result of their labors together, Scott had an "almost idolatrous fancy for Lee, whose military genius he estimated far above that of any other officer of the army," according to E. D. Keyes, who had abundant opportunity of knowing the mind of the General.[65] When there was talk of war between America and England, Scott is said to have declared that it would be cheap if the United States could absolutely insure the life of Robert E. Lee even at a cost of $5,000,000 a year.[66] In 1858 Scott referred to Lee in an official letter as "the very best soldier that I ever saw in the field." [67] Among other officers in Mexico, Lee gained a high professional reputation, though some of the late tributes to him may have been colored, in retrospect, by his subsequent campaigns in Virginia.[68] Yet Lee did not return from Mexico a national figure, in any sense. His skill in reconnaissance and his contribution to Scott's victories were known only to the army and to his intimates. This is humorously illustrated by the fact that when the commonwealth of Virginia began to vote awards to those who had distinguished themselves, the delegate from Alexandria decided to move that Lee share in them, but he had to write to Washington to get Lee's correct title and his record in Mexico.[69] At the same

[65] *Keyes,* 206–8.   [66] *Ibid.*

[67] *Jones,* 58. For other references to Lee's place in the esteem of Scott, see *Fitz Lee,* 42, and *Brock,* 166, quoting Reverdy Johnson.

[68] *Cf.* James May to C. F. Lee, April 22, 1861, quoting Major A. H. Bowman; *E. J. Lee,* 418.

[69] Francis L. Smith to J. S. Pendleton, MS., Dec. 19, 1848; *MS. A. G. O.* It is significant also that Lee is not mentioned in E. D. Mansfield's *Life and Services of General Winfield Scott* (1852).

time, if Lee was not a national figure when he returned to the United States in 1848, his reputation increased thereafter, as the part he played in the operations was seen in better perspective. Even more than that, the admiration expressed by Scott and by other friends during the decade after 1848 caused an appreciation of his soldierly qualities to spread gradually from the army to the general public.

Lee's Mexican experiences gave him, secondly, close observation of an army in nearly all the conditions, except those of retreat, that were apt to arise in the field. He had acquired his experience under an excellent, practical master, and in an army that, though small, was efficient and well-trained. All this helped him and made it easy for him in 1855 to transfer from the staff to the line. It so happened that while Lee was with Scott he had few dealings with the cavalry, which was little used during most of the battles in the valley of Mexico. This fact may account for the awkwardness that some critics have thought they observed in Lee's handling of that arm in 1862.

Even more valuable, in the third place, was Lee's training in strategy while in Mexico. As a member of Scott's "little cabinet," he sat in council when the most difficult of Scott's strategical problems were being considered by the General. His views, which were usually based on a better knowledge of the ground than his superiors possessed, were expressed fully and were received by Scott with real respect. More than once he had a part in planning operations that were executed where he could see the correctness or the errors of his reasoning—a very different matter from the blackboard studies of West Point.

Seven great lessons Lee learned from Cerro Gordo to Mexico City in strategy and in the handling of an army, seven lessons that were the basis of virtually all he attempted to do in Virginia fifteen years later:

1. Lee was inspired to audacity. This was, perhaps, his greatest strategical lesson in Mexico, for all the circumstances favored a daring course on the part of his teacher. The nucleus of Scott's army was professional; the forces that opposed them were ill-trained and poorly led. Scott could attempt and could achieve in Mexico what even he, bold as he was, would not have under-

taken against an army as well disciplined as his own. Some of his actions were little more than sham battles with ball cartridges, and were, in one sense, about as good schooling as could be devised for a beginner in the practice of strategy. When it is remembered that the son of "Light-Horse Harry" received his practical instruction, in that particular campaign, under as daring a soldier as Scott, and followed that by a study of Napoleon, it will not be surprising that audacity, even to the verge of seeming overconfidence, was the guiding principle of the strategy he employed as the leader of a desperate cause.

2. Lee concluded, from Scott's example, that the function of the commanding general is to plan the general operation, to acquaint his corps commanders with that plan, and to see that their troops are brought to the scene of action at the proper time; but that it is not the function of the commanding general to fight the battle in detail. Lee's later methods in this respect are simply those of Scott. Whether he was right in this conclusion is one of the moot questions of his career.

3. Working with a trained staff, Lee saw its value in the development of a strategical plan. Scott was very careful on this score. Although he could not keep the administration from naming politicians to command some of his divisions, he could surround himself with men who had been well grounded in discipline, promptness, and accurate observation. He did not exaggerate when he said publicly in Mexico City that he could not have succeeded in his campaign had it not been for West Point.[70] Scott relied on the young men who had been trained at the Military Academy, and they did not fail him. Lee kept this ideal of a trained staff and sought at a later time to build up such an organization; but he had become so accustomed to efficient staff work in the regular army that when he first took command in Virginia, in the great national tragedy, he did not realize how vast was the difference between trained and untrained staff officers.

4. The relation of careful reconnaissance to sound strategy was impressed on Lee by every one of the battles he saw in Mexico. Reconnaissance made possible the victories at Cerro Gordo and at

[70] *Hitchcock,* 310.

Padierna, and it simplified the storming of Chapultepec. Failure to reconnoitre adequately was in part responsible for the heavy losses at Molino del Rey. Lee had shown special aptitude for this work and he left Mexico convinced for all time that when battle is imminent a thorough study of the ground is the first duty of the commanding officer. Reconnaissance became second nature to him.

5. Lee saw in Mexico the strategic possibilities of flank movements. Cerro Gordo had been passed and San Antonio had been turned by flanking the enemy. At little cost of life, positions of much strength had been rendered untenable. These, too, were lessons that Lee never forgot. Second Manassas was Cerro Gordo on a larger terrain; the march across the pedregai to San Antonio and the San Angel road found a more famous counterpart in Jackson's movement to the rear of Hooker's army at Chancellorsville.

6. Lee acquired a confident view of the relation of communications to strategy. He saw Scott at Puebla boldly abandon his line of supply from the sea and live off the country. Within thirty-seven days Scott had battered his way into Mexico City. It is quite possible that this experience was one reason why Lee was emboldened to expose his communications in the Maryland campaign of 1862 and in the Pennsylvania campaign of 1863.[71]

7. Lee acquired in Mexico an appreciation of the value of fortification. The proper location of the batteries at Vera Cruz and at Chapultepec had contributed to the American victory. Lee had a hand in placing them and had every opportunity of observing the effect of their fire. At Cerro Gordo and at Padierna, he had examined fortifications that had been poorly defended but had been well laid out by Mexican engineers who were much more capable, as a rule, than the generals under whom they served. On both these fields and at Mexico City, immediately preceding the attack on Chapultepec, Lee may well have told himself that a competent defending force could have added much to Scott's difficulties by intelligent use of the light earthworks the Mexicans had constructed.

Along with these seven lessons in strategy, Lee had abundant

[71] *Cf.* Eben Swift: "The Military Education of Robert E. Lee," *Va. Mag. of History and Biography,* vol. 35, no. 2, April, 1927, p. 105.

opportunity during his months with General Scott to study human nature. The quarrels in the army, while distasteful and discreditable, were so much laboratory experience to Lee. He saw how dependent a commanding general was upon the good-will of his subordinates, and in Scott's failure to elicit that co-operation he read a warning that may have led him in the War between the States to go too far in the other direction. In addition, he had the most monitory of object lessons in the "political generals" whom Scott had to endure. Perhaps Scott's difficulties with Pillow gave Lee the clue to the handling of Wise and of Floyd in the campaign of 1861 in West Virginia, but his observation of Pillow's performances doubtless explains why Lee was so careful to keep politicians from holding important command in the Army of Northern Virginia. It is quite possible, indeed, that Pillow was in large measure responsible for the distrust of politicians that Lee exhibited later. From what he had seen of Pillow in Mexico and of Congress in Washington, he formed a poor opinion of the whole breed of politicians.

Lee's study of human nature in Mexico included men whom he was subsequently to meet as comrades or as enemies in the War between the States. Every one of the commanders of the future Army of the Potomac, except John Pope, served in Scott's expedition, though Meade did not get beyond Vera Cruz. Scores of the general officers of both the Confederate and Union armies were lieutenants or captains in the same campaign with Lee.[72] He doubtless met many of these young soldiers in the field, or in Mexico City after the fighting was over. Most of them belonged, as did he, to the "Aztec Club," formed in the Mexican capital during the tedious weeks of waiting for the treaty of peace to be agreed upon.[73] Grant was a member of this club. Lee did not meet him there, but he did see him one day when he went to visit Garland's brigade.[74] He kept, however, no remembrance of the circumstances or of the untidy young captain who was one day to dictate the terms of surrender Lee had to sign. It is probable, on the whole, that the extent of Lee's intimacy with his future antagonists has been exaggerated. The army was small, to be

[72] For lists of these officers, see 1 *Meade*, 196; *Fitz Lee*, 46–47.
[73] The original members' names will be found in Wilcox, *op. cit.*, 710–11.
[74] See *infra*, Volume IV. "The Ninth of April."

298

sure, but Lee was a busy staff officer during active operations and subsequently was engrossed in map work. He kept in touch with Joe Johnston and he saw Beauregard and Gustavus Smith daily and under conditions that gave him insight into the character and abilities of each of them. He may have been close enough to Captain Joseph Hooker of Pillow's staff to learn something of his qualities. George B. McClellan was the man of whom his knowledge was most detailed, and, in the event, most valuable. Lee encountered McClellan on reconnaissance work, labored with him in constructing batteries, observed him building roads and serving artillery, and, in so limited an engineering corps, could not fail to see both the strong qualities and the weakness of the officer he was to face at a time when his understanding of the man helped to compensate for many shortcomings of the Confederate staff. When these five are named—Joseph E. Johnston, P. G. T. Beauregard, Gustavus W. Smith, Joseph Hooker, and George B. McClellan—the list of those of whom Lee acquired useful "working knowledge" in Mexico is about complete. The general officers with whom he dealt most frequently and freely in 1847 had almost passed off the stage of action by the time Lee took command in Virginia. Patterson and Shields both fought south of the Potomac for a time, but neither of them faced Lee. This was the case, also, with Irvin McDowell, whom Lee met on the Rio Grande before he joined General Scott.

Between his return from Mexico and his participation in the War between the States Lee had no first-hand opportunity of observing large-scale field operations. His practical training in war prior to 1861 thus covered twenty months. McClellan was to see the Crimean campaign and was to learn something from it. Lee's only additional lessons were theoretical, acquired from his limited study at West Point in 1852–55. However, he was of a nature to apply readily what he had learned, and as there was comparatively little advance in military science between 1848 and 1861, except in the development of ordnance, his Mexican training, save in four respects, was not seriously deficient. Two of these have already been mentioned, viz., the fact that he did not encounter a first-class adversary, and, secondly, that he got little experience with cavalry. The third deficiency was, of course, that he belonged to an army of only 10,000 men at most, facing an enemy who did not have more than 17,000 men on any field and did not know how to employ even that number. It was one thing to bring Scott's small units together in the field and quite another to converge the columns of the Army of Northern Virginia in June, 1862, when one of the divisions was larger than Scott's whole army. Still, Lee's military training in this respect was progressive from 1861, and he was not called upon to lead 70,000 men until he had handled a small force in western Virginia and a somewhat larger army on the south Atlantic coast. Finally, it must be remembered that Lee had no experience with the transportation by railroad of an army in Mexico. All troop movements, except of cavalry, were on foot or by ship. Every ration and every round of ammunition had to go forward by wagon. He had to reckon new time schedules, both for his own army and for the enemy, when he dealt with railroads.

STRATFORD HALL, WESTMORELAND COUNTY, VIRGINIA, BIRTHPLACE OF ROBERT EDWARD LEE

From a photograph by Cook.

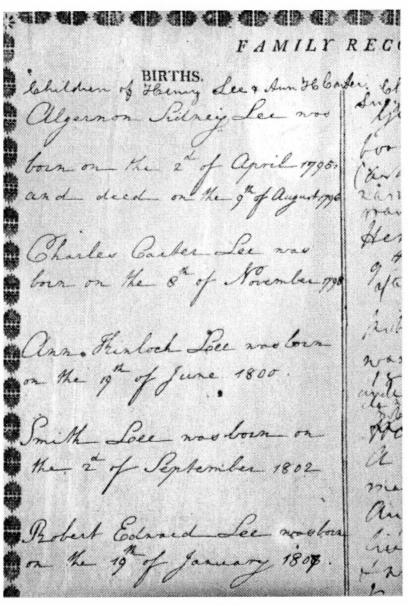

ENTRY OF THE BIRTH OF ROBERT EDWARD LEE, AUTOGRAPH OF ANN
HILL CARTER LEE, IN THE FAMILY BIBLE

Now in the possession of Robert R. Lee, son of R. E. Lee's oldest brother,
Charles Carter Lee.

MAJOR GENERAL HENRY ("LIGHT HORSE HARRY") LEE, FATHER OF GENERAL R. E. LEE

No well-authenticated portrait of the mother of Robert Edward Lee is known to be in existence, although what is believed by some to be a painting of her was found in Rome several years ago.

After a painting by Peale.

SYDNEY SMITH LEE, BROTHER OF ROBERT EDWARD LEE, IN THE DRESS
UNIFORM OF A JUNIOR OFFICER OF THE NAVY, FROM A PORTRAIT BY AN
UNKNOWN ARTIST

Smith Lee, who was four years older than Robert, was regarded by many as the
handsomer of the two.

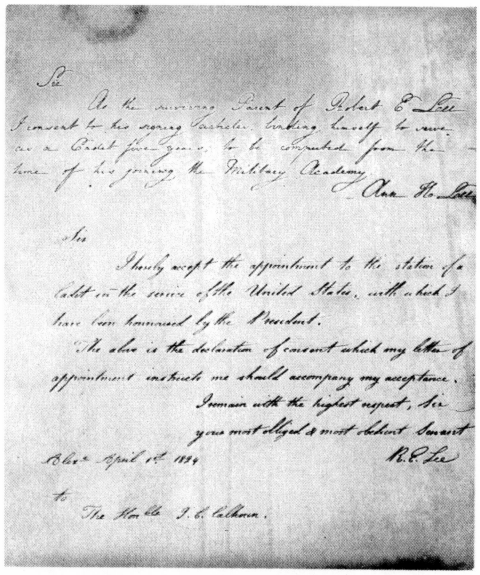

FACSIMILE OF LETTER OF ACCEPTANCE BY R. E. LEE OF APPOINTMENT TO THE
UNITED STATES MILITARY ACADEMY

This is the first signature of Lee now extant. Above his letter of acceptance in the formal assent of his
mother, in her handwriting, to his service for five years in the army of the United States.

Courtesy of the Adjutant General of the United States Army.

FACSIMILE OF THE FIRST ORDERS ISSUED LEE AFTER HE RETURNED HOME IN 1829
FROM THE UNITED STATES MILITARY ACADEMY

The first paragraph of the orders concerns Brevet Second Lieutenant Charles Mason, who graduated No. 1 at West Point when Lee was No. 2. Lee is instructed by Brigadier General Charles Gratiot, commander of the corps of engineers, to report "by the middle of November next . . . to Major Samuel Babcock . . . for duty at Cockspur Island in the Savannah River, Georgia."

ROBERT EDWARD LEE IN THE DRESS UNIFORM OF A LIEUTENANT
OF ENGINEERS
After a portrait painted in 1838 by William E. West

GEORGE WASHINGTON PARKE CUSTIS, FATHER-IN-LAW OF R. E. LEE

MARY CUSTIS, WIFE OF R. E. LEE
From a painting made by an unknown artist about the time of her marriage in 1831.

ARLINGTON, THE CUSTIS MANSION OVERLOOKING WASHINGTON, WHERE R. E. LEE WAS MARRIED AND WHERE HIS FAMILY RESIDED, WITH FEW LONG INTERMISSIONS, FROM 1834 TO APRIL, 1861

From a photograph by Cook.

"THE BEAUTIFUL TALCOTT," HARRIET RANDOLPH TALCOTT, NÉE HACK-
LEY, WIFE OF CAPTAIN ANDREW TALCOTT, LEE'S IMMEDIATE SUPERIOR
AT FORT MONROE

After a painting, made about 1832 by Thomas Sully, and now in
Virginia House, Richmond.

R. E. LEE IN THE DRESS UNIFORM OF A CAPTAIN OF ENGINEERS, UNITED
STATES ARMY, TAKEN ABOUT THE PERIOD OF THE MEXICAN WAR

After a photograph in the Confederate Museum, Richmond, from the
original daguerreotype.

FACSIMILE, FROM LEE'S LETTERBOOK AS SUPERINTENDENT OF THE UNITED STATES MILITARY ACADEMY, EXPLAINING WHY "CADET WHISTLER," LATER THE DISTINGUISHED ARTIST JAMES McNEILL WHISTLER, SHOULD NOT BE READMITTED TO WEST POINT. THE AUTOGRAPH IS THAT OF LEE'S CHIEF CLERK

Courtesy of the Librarian of the United States Military Academy.

FACSIMILE OF LEE'S FATEFUL RESIGNATION FROM THE ARMY OF THE UNITED STATES, WITH THE ENDORSEMENTS AND ACCEPTANCE OF THE RESIGNATION BY SIMON CAMERON, SECRETARY OF WAR

From the original in the War Department.

PHOTOGRAPH OF GENERAL LEE ISSUED IN BALTIMORE IN 1861 AND
REPRESENTING HIM WITH A HAT BEARING THE LETTERS "VA."

There is a possibility that this was retouched from a photograph taken prior to 1861,
as the uniform appears to be that of the United States army. If the photograph is
authentic, it is the only one posed, so far as is known, while Lee was in command of
the military and naval forces of Virginia.

LEFT TO RIGHT: BRIGADIER GENERALS JOHN B. FLOYD, HENRY A. WISE, AND W. W. LORING, WHOSE OPERATIONS IN WEST VIRGINIA IN AUGUST, 1861, GENERAL LEE WAS SENT TO CO-ORDINATE

From photographs in the Confederate Museum, Richmond.

CHAPTER XVIII

THE BUILDING OF FORT CARROLL

LANDING at New Orleans on his way home, Lee came up the Mississippi with his mare, Grace Darling,[1] and his orderly, Jim Connally. When his steamer reached Wheeling he left Jim to bring on the horse, and himself "took the cars" for Washington, which he reached on June 29, 1848, after having been absent a year and ten months, almost to the day. In some way he missed the carriage that had been sent to the city for him, but got a horse and rode over to Arlington. As he approached the house, members of the watching family did not recognize him at first, because they were looking for him in the vehicle, but his dog was not deceived. Spec's joyful barking quickly convinced the household that the soldier was back from the wars. A few moments more and he was embracing his loved ones in the hall.

"Where is my little boy?" he asked, after he had greeted the others. Answering his own question, he took up a youngster from the floor and kissed him joyfully. There was a shout of laughter from the other children and signs of acute distress from another little boy, who was proudly dressed for the occasion in a new dress. Truth was, Lee had picked up the wrong youngster! His smallest son and namesake had a guest, Armistead Lippitt, whom the father had mistaken for his own son.[2]

It was a happy time for the family. "Here I am once again, my dear Smith," he wrote his brother the next day, "perfectly surrounded by Mary and her precious children, who seem to devote themselves to staring at the furrows in my face and the white hairs in my head. It is not surprising that I am hardly recognizable to some of the young ones around me and perfectly unknown to the youngest. But some of the older ones gaze with

[1] This mare, which was regarded at Arlington as Lee's war horse, is difficult to identify. He mentions no Grace Darling in his published letters from Mexico.

[2] R. E. Lee, Jr., 4–6; R. E. Lee to Smith Lee, June 30, 1848; Jones, L. and L., 58–59; date from extract in R. E Lee, Jr., 4.

astonishment and wonder at me, and seem at a loss to reconcile what they see and what was pictured in their imaginations. I find them, too, much grown, and all well, and I have much cause of thankfulness and gratitude to the good God who has once more united us." [3] Needless to say, Mrs. Lee was no less grateful, for she had hung on every mail from Mexico, proud of the honors that had come to her husband, thankful for his safety, yet fearful that the next battle would claim him. [4]

He quickly distributed his gifts and arranged his luggage, including the unopened bottle of whiskey that a friend had forced on him before he had left for Mexico. [5] Not much time was lost in returning to the duties of peace. On the very day of his arrival he sent to the chief engineer another map of the Mexican defenses. [6] On July 3 he was assigned to "special duty" in Totten's office, an assignment which seemed less unattractive than in 1835, and gave him, besides, the boon of living at home. [7] On the 21st of the same month he was again named as a member of the board of engineers for the Atlantic coast defenses, from which board he had been dropped while on duty in Mexico. [8] With occasional brief absences—a visit to his sister in Baltimore and another to cousins near Middleburg—he passed the summer at Arlington and in Washington. He worked, during this time, on the last of the Mexican maps, performed miscellaneous office duty, [9] and had the pleasure of receiving his brevet commissions for Mexican service. They had been slow in passing through the bureaux, as had been those of all the officers whom the government rewarded in this way. He had not expected too much, nor had he been provoked at the delay. Before he had left Mexico he had discouraged any attempt to gain promotion for him by importuning the President: "I hope my friends will give themselves no annoyance

---

[3] R. E. Lee to Smith Lee, June 30, 1848, *loc. cit.*

[4] Mrs. Lee to Mrs. L. M. Stiles, Vienna, Austria, *MS.*, Nov. 1, 1847, copy of which Mrs. Frank Screven has generously given the writer.

[5] *Jones*, 169.   [6] Lee to Totten, *MS.*, June 29, 1848; *Eng. MSS.*, 1018.

[7] *Engineers' Orderly Book*, vol. 3, p. 514; also *MS. A. G. O.*; *cf.* R. E. Lee to Custis Lee, May 17, 1858: "[Bureau duty] is not altogether agreeable. But it makes you acquainted with the routine of duty. Brings you in contact with the high officials of the Government, and causes your deserts to be appreciated" (Jones, *L. and L.*, 93).

[8] *Ibid.*, 504; *MS. A. G. O.*, 238, with 60–L–61.

[9] R. E. *Lee, Jr.*, 5; *MS. Letters to Officers of Engineers*, Sept. 27, Nov. 8, Nov. 10, 1848, vol. 16, pp. 243, 292, 295; Lee to Totten, *MS.*, Oct. 1, Nov. 6, Nov. 7, 1848; *Eng. MSS.*, 1038–39, 1047.

on my account," he had written, "or any concern about the distribution of favors. I know how these things are awarded at Washington, and how the President will be besieged by clamorous claimants. I do not wish to be numbered among them. Such as he can conscientiously bestow, I shall gratefully receive, and have no doubt that those will exceed my deserts." [10] He could not have hoped for more than he received—brevet major for Cerro Gordo, brevet lieutenant colonel for Contreras-Churubusco, and brevet colonel for Chapultepec, the commission being issued in each instance as of the date of the battle. After the publication of general orders on August 24, 1848, he was "Colonel Lee," as army usage gave every man the title of his highest brevet.[11]

Now came a new assignment to duty. The port of Baltimore, Md., had been neglected by Congress in its appropriations for coast and harbor defenses. Between the city and bombardment, in case of hostile attack, stood only old Fort McHenry, famous as inspiring "The Star Spangled Banner," but even then too close to the city to afford it adequate defense. Army engineers had long recommended a new fort on Soliers' Point Flats, and the chief engineer had urged this in 1839, in 1842, and again in 1843. Following a new appeal by Baltimore in 1845 the United States acquired jurisdiction of the flats from the Maryland legislature. Major Cornelius A. Ogden of the corps of engineers laid off the site in 1847 and during the open season of 1848 began the preliminary work.[12]

To the construction of the fort Lee was assigned on September 13, 1848, and on November 15 he reported for duty in Baltimore, but he could do little more than officially take over the undertaking, as he had to leave almost immediately for Boston on duty with the board of engineers. He was in the latter city by November 18 and remained there until December 1. On his return to Baltimore the state of the work, the weather, and the scarcity of funds, led him to conclude that building operations should be suspended

---

[10] R. E. Lee to unnamed correspondent [probably Mrs. Lee], April 8, 1848; Jones, *L. and L.*, 57.

[11] *A. G. O.*, G. O. 47, Aug. 24, 1848; acknowledged in Lee to A. G., Nov. 4, 1848; MS. *A. G. O.*, 413–L–48.

[12] *Rept. Chief Eng. Army, Ex. Doc., 3d sess., 27th Cong.*, vol. 1, p. 243; *ibid., 1st sess., 28th Cong.*, vol. 1, pp. 102–3, *Senate Docs., 1st sess., 29th Cong.*, vol. 1, p. 251; *Ex. Docs., 1st sess., 30th Cong.*, vol. 1, p. 608; *cf.* 1 *Md. Hist. Mag.*, 32.

until the spring of 1849.[13] He accordingly stayed in Baltimore only a fortnight or so and then went to Washington, before Christmas, to procure maps for the use of the board of engineers.

General Totten—for he had been brevetted brigadier for his service at Vera Cruz—was careful, now as always, to keep his engineers occupied, so he set Lee to finishing the maps he had begun in Mexico City of the routes from that occupied capital to the places the American army had proposed to garrison in case the Mexicans had not accepted peace.[14]

Soon after these maps were done, Lee was sent off again with the board of engineers to make a study of the lands that should be held as public domain for the construction of fortifications in Florida. The bureau had previously reserved for this purpose all the islands on the coast, and it was now to decide whether any of these could be released. The engineers left Washington early in January, 1849, and by the middle of the month were in Mobile. Thence they made a circuit of the Florida coast from Pensacola all the way to Cumberland Island. It was not a hurried trip, and it must have interested Lee greatly, as it carried him to a country he had never before seen. Unfortunately, none of the letters that he wrote home while making this survey seems to have been preserved.[15]

While Lee was away his name was associated for the first time with one that was later to stand in dramatic contrast to it. Washington society, private and official, was preparing to give a "National Inaugural Ball" to Taylor and Fillmore. Lee was one of the 230 "managers" and was among the signers of the formal advertisement that announced on February 20, 1849, this "splendid compliment to the illustrious President and Vice-President elect from their fellow-citizens without distinction of party." The published card gave assurance that "the decorations will be in a style of elegance, and the supper in a tasteful profusion, hitherto unsurpassed." The interest of Lee's service on this committee,

---

[13] MS. A. G. O., Engr. order No. 22; Lee to Totten, MS., Dec. 1, Dec. 13, 1848; Eng. MSS., 1045; Totten to Lee, MS., Dec. 19, 1848; MS. Letters to Officers of Engineers, vol. 16, p. 349; same to same, MS., Dec. 23, 1848; loc. cit., vol. 16, p. 354; same to same, MS., Dec. 30, 1848; loc cit., vol. 16, p. 362.

[14] Lee to Totten, MS., Dec. 30, 1848; Eng. MSS., 1050.

[15] Lee to Totten, MS., Jan. 15, 1849; Eng. MSS., 1051; Totten to Lee, MS., Jan. 16, 1849; MS. Letters to Officers of Engineers, vol. 16, p. 383; same to same, MS., March 19, 1849; loc. cit., vol. 16, p. 476.

which probably never met, lies in the fact that among its congressional members was "Hon. A. Lincoln, Ill." [16]

The ball had been held nearly a month when, about April 1, Lee returned from Florida[17] and proceeded to Baltimore to resume work at Sollers' Flats. The family moved, also, at a later time, and took up its abode in a residence on Madison Avenue, now numbered 908. It is three storeys and of brick and was then almost new.[18] The house was quite pleasant, but the rooms were so small, in comparison with those of Arlington, that Lee averred his own chamber was "hardly big enough to swing a cat in." [19] To reach his station Lee had to take a bus daily to the wharf, where two oarsmen met him with a boat. He was rowed to Sollers' Point, and thence, after construction got under way, out to the flats. He had his dinner with a family living on the point.[20]

His task was in some respects an interesting one, certainly at the outset. The fort was to be built on a shoal about halfway from Baltimore to the mouth of the Patapsco River, and almost in midstream, between Sollers' Point and Hawkins' Point. Lee had to ascertain whether the foundation was solid, and if it was, he had to erect constructing wharves, drive piles, place the granite footings of the fort under water, and, when the surface of the river was reached, proceed in the regular way. He had acquired abundant experience in testing the character of river bottoms while on the Mississippi, and he was soon able to report that a stable, hard surface had been reached forty-five feet beneath the low-water level.[21] The work opened up quickly during 1849. He bestirred himself to procure piles for the foundation; abandoning the well started under Major Ogden at Sollers' Point, he dug another. Vigorously he pushed the completion of a scow, a pile driver, and a lighter, laid down the previous year. The building

---

[16] *Washington National Intelligencer*, Feb. 20, 1849, p. 4, col. 2.

[17] *Markie Letters*, 22–23; Lee to Totten, *MS.*, May 21, 1849; *Lee's MS. Letterbook of Sollers' Point*.

[18] *R. E. Lee, Jr.*, 11. The exact date of this move is not available. It may not have been until the autumn of 1849. For information as to Lee's residence the writer is indebted to Miss Mary N. Barton, reference assistant of the Enoch Pratt Library, Baltimore, Md.

[19] *Packard*, 158.   [20] *R. E. Lee, Jr.*, 10.

[21] Lee to Totten, *MS.*, May 21, 1849; *Eng. MSS.*, 1062; *Ex. Docs.*, *1st sess.*, *31st Cong.*, vol. 1, p. 227.

of a powerful crane was undertaken; he commenced the wharves from which the sea walls were to be reared; and he experimented in the laying of concrete under water with a tremie.[22]

All this required hourly supervision in a summer sun and on a site where it is safe to presume mosquitoes bred abundantly. Late in July Lee developed a fever that probably was malaria, and he wisely sought refuge at Ravensworth. Returning to Arlington, when he began to improve, he remained there by Totten's permission until the end of the first week in August. Then he went back to Baltimore.[23] On August 12 he placed his assistant, Captain J. G. Foster,[24] in charge at Sollers' Point and took train for Newport, R. I., where he joined his former West Point superintendent, Colonel Thayer, and the other members of the board of engineers in a study of the best location for new barracks, quarters, and a hospital at Fort Adams. Unluckily, Lee's sickness still dogged him. When Colonel Thayer designated him as one of two engineers to go from Newport to the Brooklyn Navy Yard to confer with a naval board on some problems connected with the drydock, Lee had to ask to be relieved. It was not until the end of August that he returned to Baltimore after the first and only illness prior to 1863 of which there is any record.[25] Work then settled into its usual channels at Sollers' Point. By the end of September, when the report-year closed, he was able to record the completion of nearly all the preliminary work and the erection of one hundred feet of the outer constructing wharf. Some $36,000 of the appropriation then remained unexpended, and, for the fiscal year of 1850–51, $50,000 was requested.[26]

The routine at Sollers' Point, the whole career of Lee indeed, was threatened about this time by a strange offer. The Cuban revolutionary junta in New York was preparing for a new descent

[22] Lee to Totten, MS., May 5, June 1, June 25, July 16, 1849; Eng. MSS., 1060, 1063, 1065, 1066; Totten to Lee, MS., June 22, 1849, containing instructions for the use of the tremie; MS. Letters to Officers of Engineers, vol. 17, p. 81.
[23] Lee to Totten, MS., July 26, July 31, Aug. 7, 1849; Eng. MSS., 1067, 1068, 1069.
[24] For Foster, see W. R. Livermore: John Gray Foster in Professional Memoirs, Corps of Engineers, vol. 11, pp. 249–52; New York Times, Sept. 3, 1874.
[25] Lee to Totten, MS., Aug. 10, Aug. 21, Aug. 28, 1849; Eng. MSS., 1070, 1073, 1074; Totten to Lee, MS., Aug. 11, Aug. 24, 1849; MS. Letters to Officers of Engineers, vol. 17, 173, 195. The report of the engineers on the Fort Adams project was forwarded Totten on Dec. 15, 1849 (cf. Totten to Lee, MS., Dec. 17, 1849; MS. Letters to Officers of Engineers, vol. 17, p. 329).
[26] Lee to Totten, MS., Sept. 1, 1849; Eng. MSS., 1075; Ex. Docs., 1st sess., 31st Cong., vol. 1, p. 217.

on the island. Some of the leaders had tendered command to General Worth and he had considered resigning his United States commission and organizing the expedition, but he had died before he had made a final decision.[27] Then the Cubans had turned to Jefferson Davis. He was senator at that time, chairman of the committee on military affairs and interested in Cuban affairs. He declined, but urged the committee to go to see Lee. They duly journeyed to Baltimore and asked Lee if he were willing to discuss the matter with them. Lee's martial impulses no doubt were fired by the thought of a campaign in which he would have full opportunity of planning and directing operations. All he had learned in Mexico could be applied. Southern sympathy would be with him, because filibustering against Spanish misrule was regarded as patriotic. Moreover, a strong element in Congress favored the seizure of Cuba. Success would mean ease and glory to the end of his days and perhaps a place as the Washington of Cuban liberty. But before Lee could consider either the comity or the feasibility of the expedition, he balked on a consideration of personal honor: he had been educated as a soldier at public expense; he held a commission in the army of the United States; was it right that he should entertain a proposal from another government while in the service of America? He debated the question and virtually reached his conclusion, but he determined to consult with Davis before deciding whether he would permit the proposal to be opened in detail to him by the junta. He accordingly went to Washington and confidentially discussed the matter. The Mississippi senator was disposed to canvass the chances of military success, but Lee explained that he wanted the judgment of Davis on the ethics of entertaining any offer from a foreign power. Davis's answer is not recorded, but Lee took the strictest view of his duty and declined to consider a proposal.[28] Suppose his decision had been to the contrary—what would have happened? The expedition came to disaster; would he have redeemed it, or would he in 1852 have ended his days in front of a

[27] A. J. Gonzales: *Manifesto on Cuban Affairs* (New Orleans, 1853), p. 6.

[28] W. F. Johnson, *History of Cuba*, vol. 3, pp. 38–39; Davis, *Lee Memorial Address*, Nov. 3, 1870; 7 *Rowland*, 283. The date of this episode cannot be fixed definitely, but it probably was late in 1849. The command was subsequently offered to General Quitman. See F. E. Chadwick: *The Relations of the United States and Spain*, 230.

Spanish firing squad? His judgment and his sense of duty made the question academic, but it may not be without some psychological significance that Colonel Lee, like his father before him, was attracted by a revolutionary struggle.

Two brief visits to Washington and Christmas at Arlington seem to have been Lee's only absence from Baltimore during the period from October 1, 1849, to the end of the report-year, twelve months thereafter.[29] When the results of the work for that time were assembled the showing was one of which no engineer need have been ashamed. The constructing wharves on two of the fronts of the projected fort had been completed, and a third of the wharf on the third front. All the piles for the wharf on the fourth front and the greater part for that on the fifth had been driven. Over 1200 feet of the wharves were ready. Piles under water for this part of the work numbered 822. The steam pile driver had been employed to start the foundation and the sheet piles for the sea wall on one front, and a machine had been devised for sawing off the foundation piles at a uniform depth under the water. To the other equipment had been added a dredge for levelling the surface of the shoal. This, like the saw, was built on the spot and was operated by the steam engine of the pile driver. A diving bell, too, had been constructed, not to mention a crane and a storehouse. It was anticipated by Lee that with the opening of the spring of 1851 masonry work could be commenced. The unexpended balance of $68,100 he planned to use by June 30, 1851. For the year 1851–52, $50,000 new money would be required.[30] As the work had reached a point where the completion of a fort might be expected, provided enough money was forthcoming, the War Department felt justified in giving a name to this creation of Lee's energy. On October 8, 1850, it ceased to be simply the "fort at Sollers' Point Flats" and became Fort Carroll,[31] in honor of Charles Carroll, last surviving signer

---

[29] Lee to Totten, *MSS.*, Nov. 3, Dec. 1, 1849, Jan. 9, Feb. 1, March 1, April 4, May 1, June 4, July 10, July 22, Aug. 23, Aug. 24, Sept. 1, and Oct. 3 (annual report), 1850; *Eng. MSS.*, 1077, 1079, 1081, 1084, 1085, 1086, 1087, 1088, 1089, 1090, 1093, 1094, 1095, 1096; Totten to Lee, *MS.*, Nov. 6, Dec. 24, 1849, Aug. 26, 1850; *MS. Letters to Officers of Engineers*, vol. 17, pp. 262, 334; vol. 18, p. 70.

[30] *Ex. Docs., 2d sess., 31st Cong.*, vol. 1, p. 355.

[31] Totten to Lee, *MS.*, Oct. 9, 1850; *MS. Letters to Officers of Engineers*, vol. 18, p. 121.

of the Declaration of Independence, who, at the age of ninety-five, had died in his native Maryland only eighteen years before.

With longer residence in Baltimore, the social life of the Lees became far more active. Colonel Lee's sister Ann (Mrs. William Louis Marshall) was still in the city and her husband had successfully made the change from the pulpit to the bar. Their only son, Louis Henry Marshall, had graduated at West Point in 1849, and in 1850 was on frontier-duty in New Mexico.[32] Through Mr. and Mrs. Marshall and through other connections of Lees and Custises, the family on Madison Avenue made many new friends Colonel and Mrs. Lee attended Mount Calvary Church,[33] and were active in the city's social life. When they went out to dinner the children were permitted to sit up and see them depart. Robert Lee the younger retained to the end of his days a lively memory of his father on such occasions—"always in full uniform, always ready and waiting for my mother, who was generally late. He would chide her gently, in a playful way and with a bright smile. He would then bid us good-bye, and I would go to sleep with this beautiful picture in my mind, the golden epaulets and all—chiefly the epaulets."[34]

The two older girls of the family lived in an ever-widening circle of young misses of their own age. Similarly, the boys were soon at ease in their new environment. The chief difference in the household was the absence of Custis. He was eighteen in 1850, and not unnaturally, in the afterglow of the Mexican War, decided to follow the profession of his father. Lee succeeded in procuring for him from the new Whig administration an appointment "at large" to the Military Academy. Under this appointment, in midsummer, 1850, Custis went to West Point. He had abundant ability, but at first he was somewhat indolent. Lee had to deal tactfully with him in order to arouse in him a determination to excel. That same firm purpose he sought to implant in the hearts of all his sons, and to cultivate it by frequent inquiry and encouragement. "He always insisted that I should get the

[32] *E. J. Lee*, 342. Mrs. Marshall's health was still poor (R. E. Lee to Smith Lee, June 30, 1848, *Fitz Lee*, 50).
[33] For this information the writer is indebted to Matthew Page Andrews of Baltimore.
[34] *R. E. Lee, Jr.*, 11. Some details of the social activities of the family are given in Mrs. R. E. Lee to Mrs. A. M. Fitzhugh, *MS.*, n. d. [1849?], March n. d., 1850, and Dec. 12, 1850; *Duke Univ. MSS.*

'maximum,' that he would never be perfectly satisfied with less"
—so wrote one of his sons.[35]

Through all its hopes and discouragements, Lee watched
Custis's career at West Point with continuing interest. When the
boy had been there ten months, Lee wrote him:

"Your letter . . . which I duly received, has given me more
pleasure than any that I now recollect having ever received. It
has assured me of the confidence you feel in my love and affection,
and with that frankness and candor you open to me all your
thoughts.

"So long as I meet with such return from my children, and see
them strive to respond to my wishes, and exertions, for their
good and happiness, I can meet with calmness and unconcern
all else the world may have in store for me. I cannot express my
pleasure at hearing you declare your determination to shake off
the listless fit that has seized you, and arouse all your faculties
into activity and exertion. . . . I do not think you lack either
energy or ambition. Hitherto you have not felt the incentive to
call them forth. . . . I am very much pleased at the interest taken
by the cadets in your success. . . . Prove yourself worthy of their
affection. . . . [Fitzhugh's] ambition is still to go to West Point,
and thinks there is no life like that of a dragoon. He thinks he
might get through the Academy, though he would not stand as
well as Boo [Custis]. I tell him he would get 200 demerits the
first year, and that would be an end to all his military resources." [36]

Steadily thereafter, Custis's academic standing rose, but late in
May, 1851, as he approached the end of his first year's work, a
vigilant inspector found liquor in the boy's room. Custis had not
brought it there; his roommates avowed they had not done so;
but all of them were forthwith put under arrest for violation of
paragraph 113 of the regulations. Colonel Lee was deeply hu-
miliated and more distressed, perhaps, than by anything that had
happened to him since the death of his mother. The loyal classmates of the Virginia cadet sought to save him from prospective

[35] *R. E. Lee, Jr.,* 14.
[36] R. E. Lee to G. W. C. Lee, May 4, 1851; J. G. de R. and Mary T. Hamilton:
Life of Robert E. Lee for Boys and Girls, 68.

dismissal. They offered, if Custis and his roommates were released, to take a pledge for the year not to violate the regulation the arrested youths were accused of breaking.[37] Custis refused to accept this favor at the hands of the cadets, and in so doing was upheld by his father. "I am fond of independence," the elder Lee wrote him. "It is that feeling that prompts me to come up strictly to the requirements of law and regulations. I wish neither to seek [n]or receive indulgence from anyone. I wish to feel under obligation to no one." [38] Fortunately, the superintendent of the academy took a just view of the conflicting testimony and, even before Colonel Lee wrote this letter, had approved a mild sentence of eight demerits against Custis.[39] The War Department subsequently confirmed this action.

Much relieved by this outcome of what might have been a blight upon the career of his able son, Colonel Lee wrote him this tactful letter:

"Baltimore 3 Aug 1851
"How is it with you, my dearest Mr. Boo? Times are pretty dull in B.—now for Speck, the Parrot & myself. No Mim, no children, no Mrs. Bonaparte, no baby! Still we get along, & at Sollers we hammer on, lustily. This past month, we have been laying stone by means of a Diving Bell. A troublesome operation with awkward, timid men. They are getting somewhat tutored now, & I hope this month to do better. Besides I have overcome many of the difficulties, by contrivances & arrangements to meet them. And you know all difficulties can be overcome by labour & perseverance. I was delighted at the contradiction in your last letter of that *slanderous* report against the room of those fine cadets Lee, Wood & Turnbull. I could not believe it before, to the extent of the report, & supposed it must have been greatly exaggerated. I am happy to have my impressions confirmed. I trust there will be no cause for even suspicions in future. I know there will be none as far as you are concerned. Your letter also did me good in other respects. It talked of being on the Colour Guard, of being relieved from Post, of taking your ease in your own tent. That sounded well. It assured me of your being released from

---

[37] For a description of this part of the West Point "code of honor," see *infra*, p. 333.
[38] R. E. Lee to G. W. C. Lee, *MS.* copy, June 22, 1851; *Lee MSS.*
[39] *MS. Records, U. S. Military Academy,* June 7, 1851, for which reference the writer is indebted to the kindness of Lieutenant C. E. Byers, acting adjutant.

arrest, of being on duty again, of coming right up to the mark, of no discouragement, no abatement in exertion, or relaxation in will. In a word, of standing up to the rack, fodder or no fodder. That was right. Keep up that spirit, and things will soon come right again. I was very sad before, when I thought of you confined to your room, trailing to meals after the guard, and deprived of the relaxation and enjoyment of your Comrades. It seemed unnatural. I could not realize that such a position was befitting my son. But now things look right again, I am cheered up. I am hopeful. . . . Think always of your devoted father."[40]

As the end of Custis's second year at the academy approached, Lee wrote him another and a more playful appeal.

"My dear Mr Boo: "Baltimore, February 1, 1852.
"This is not my day for writing to you. It is your mother's turn and she claims the privilege. But being not yet ready to take up the pen, I am merely getting it ready for her. I shall leave her to tell you of domestic events, and will at once jump to what is first in my mind, viz: that only four months have to *fly by*, you may say, before the June examinations and your furlough. Have you thought of that? Has it ever occurred to your mind that such an event is hastening on with irrepressible speed? Why, man, it will be upon you before you are aware. I must begin to prepare. I must get at my work and try and get through it before that time. . . . You must prepare too. You must press forward in your studies. You must 'crowd that boy Howard.'[41] You must be No. 1. It is a fine number. Easily found and remembered. Simple and unique. Jump to it fellow. . . ."[42]

Custis did. He "jumped to it" with so much ardor that he was soon one of the most promising cadets of the corps and was no longer an object of concern to his father. Colonel Lee, with hope for the future of his eldest son, could devote an untroubled mind

---

[40] Facsimile in *New York Times*, April 14, 1918, sec. VII., p. 5.
[41] The beloved O. O. Howard, later major general, U. S. V., whom Lee was subsequently to meet in battle.
[42] Reprinted in *Richmond Examiner*, May 10, 1864, p. 2, col. 5, after the text in "a New York Paper," which took it from the original found at Arlington by the Federals.

to his engineering duties and to the rearing of the younger children. Robert, the junior of the boys, long afterwards gave this picture of his father's efforts:

"He was always bright and gay with us little folk, romping, playing, and joking with us. With the older children, he was just as companionable, and I have seen him join my elder brothers and their friends when they would try their powers at a high jump put up in our yard [at Arlington]. The two younger children he petted a good deal, and our greatest treat was to get into his bed in the morning and lie close to him, listening while he talked to us in his bright, entertaining way. This custom we kept up until I was ten years old and over. Although he was so joyous and familiar with us, he was very firm on all proper occasions, never indulged us in anything that was not good for us, and exacted the most implicit obedience. I always knew that it was impossible to disobey my father. I felt it in me, I never thought why, but was perfectly sure when he gave us an order that it had to be obeyed. My mother I could sometimes circumvent, and at times took liberties with her orders, construing them to suit myself; but exact obedience to every mandate of my father was a part of my life and being at that time. He was very fond of having his hands tickled, and, what was still more curious, it pleased and delighted him to take off his slippers and place his feet in our laps in order to have them tickled. Often, as little things, after romping all day, the enforced sitting would be too much for us, and our drowsiness would soon show itself in continued nods. Then, to arouse us, he had a way of stirring us up with his foot—laughing heartily at and with us. He would often tell us the most delightful stories, and then there was no nodding. Sometimes, however, our interest in his wonderful tales became so engrossing that we would forget to do our duty—when he would declare, 'No tickling, no story!' When we were a little older, our elder sister told us one winter the ever-delightful 'Lady of the Lake.' Of course, she told it in prose and arranged it to suit our mental capacity. Our father was generally in his corner by the fire, most probably with a foot in either the lap of myself or youngest sister—the tickling going on briskly—and would come in at different points of the tale and repeat line after line of the poem—much to our disapproval—but to his great enjoyment."[43]

But life in Baltimore was not all enjoyment. Construction did not progress quite so satisfactorily at Fort Carroll in 1850–51 as during the previous report-year. Lee had some concern over the protection of the foundation piles from worms. The work of the board of engineers interfered with his work and necessitated two journeys—one to Boston in December, 1850, and one to New York in March, 1851. Worse still, the Thirty-first Congress adjourned on March 3, 1851, without making any appropriation for Fort Carroll, and construction had to be reduced, with every prospect that it would have to be halted altogether when the balances from previous appropriations were exhausted. There was a bit of annoyance, also, over the refusal of the government to allow double rations at Fort Carroll.[44] None the less, when Lee filed his annual report on October 15, 1851, he was able to record much progress. The constructing wharves were so far advanced that the remaining sections could be completed quickly whenever they were needed. An additional 194 lineal feet of the wharves had been made ready for use. Two hundred and twenty-six wharf piles had been driven, together with 324 sheet piles. For the foundations of the sea wall, 332 piles had been driven and had been cut off fifteen feet below the level of low water. Masonry had been begun, too. Three courses of it, 10 feet wide and 250 feet long, had been raised 6 feet above the foundations. Stone for seven additional courses was at hand. Workshops had been completed, and much machinery had been made ready. Nothing was needed, Totten commented, to insure rapid and very satisfactory progress on the fort—except regular appropriations. By economical management and slower operations, $40,600 remained available on

---

[43] *R. E. Lee, Jr.,* 9–10.
[44] Lee to Totten, *MSS.,* Nov. 4, Nov. 5, Nov. 28, Nov. 30, 1850, Jan. 6, Feb. 8, March 3, March 17, April 12, April 22, April 24, May 9, June 6, July 12, Aug. 6, Sept. 6, Oct. 2, 1851; *Eng. MSS.,* L. 1100, 1101, 1103, 1104, 1109, 1112, 1114, 1115, 1118, 1120, 1121, 1123, 1126, 1132, 1133, 1136, 1142, 1144; Totten to Lee, *MSS.,* Feb. 27, March 21, June 10, July 15, Aug. 8, 1851; *MS. Letters to Officers of Engineers,* vol. 18, pp. 291, 332, 455, 501, 554. The meeting of the board of engineers in Boston was to consider the defense of Portsmouth, N. H.

September 30, 1851, but this would all be used within twelve months, and nothing had been provided for work thereafter.[45]

Christmas, 1851, was spent at Arlington, whither, if practicable, the family always repaired at that season. Lee's own account of it was sent in a letter to Custis:

"We came home on Wednesday morning, [December 24]. It was a bitter cold day, and we were kept waiting an hour at Baltimore for the cars, which were detained by the snow and frost on the rails. We found your grandfather at the Washington depot, Daniel and the old carriage and horses. Your mother, grandfather, Mary Eliza, the little people and the baggage I thought load enough for the carriage, so Rooney and I took our feet in our hands and walked over. . . . The snow impeded the carriage as well as us, and we reached here shortly after it. The children were delighted at getting back, and passed the evening in devising pleasure for the morrow. They were in upon us before day on Christmas morning, to overhaul their stockings. Mildred thinks she drew a prize in the shape of a beautiful new doll; Angelina's infirmities were so great that she was left in Baltimore and this new treasure was entirely unexpected. The cakes, candies, books, etc., were overlooked in the caresses she bestowed upon her, and she was scarcely out of her arms all day. Rooney got among his gifts a nice pair of boots, which he particularly wanted, and the girls, I hope, were equally pleased with their presents, books and trinkets.

"Your mother, Mary, Rooney, and I went into church, and Rooney and the twins [who were visitors] skated back on the canal, Rooney having taken his skates along for the purpose. . . .

"I need not describe to you our amusements, you have witnessed them so often, nor the turkey, cold ham, plum puddings, mince pies, etc., at dinner. I hope you will enjoy them again, or some equally as good. . . .

"I had received no letter from you when I left Baltimore, nor shall I get any till I return, which will be, if nothing happens, tomorrow a week, 5th January, 1852. You will then be in the

<hr />

[45] *Ex. Docs., 1st sess., 32d Cong.,* vol. 1, p. 351. For the date of filing the annual report, see Totten to Lee, *MS.,* Oct. 21, 1851; *MS. Letters to Officers of Engineers,* vol. 19, p. 86.

midst of your examinations. I shall be very anxious about you. Give me the earliest intelligence of your standing, and stand up before them boldly, manfully; do your best, and I shall be satisfied." [46]

The driving of piles and the laying of stone continued, as the weather permitted, in the spring of 1852, with Lee more than ever confined to the fort because of a change of assistants late in March.[47] Some time had to be spent, also, in arranging for the care and preservation of old Fort Covington, the site of which had been declared a nuisance.[48]

Work was progressing regularly,[49] when on May 28, Lee received the following letter from Totten, dated at Washington on the 27th:

"You will prepare yourself to transfer the operations now under your charge temporarily to Lieut. [W. H. C.] Whiting, in order that you may proceed to West Point towards the close of the month of August and on the 1st of September next relieve Capt. [Henry] Brewerton of the Superintendency of the Military Academy, and of the command of the post of West Point, Capt. Brewerton to succeed to duty at Fort Carroll." [50]

This was a surprise, and not a pleasant one to Lee. Of course,

[46] R. E. Lee to G. W. C. Lee, Dec. 28, 1851; Jones, *L. and L.*, 76–77; an abbreviated text in Hamilton, *op. cit.*, 71.

[47] Lee to Totten, *MSS.*, Nov. 5, Dec. 4, 1851, Jan. 14, Feb. 2, March 1, April 6, 1852; *Eng. MSS.*, 1149, 1152, 1157, 1159, 1161, 1163. To this period belongs the famous "duty letter," in which General Lee is credited with saying to his son, "Duty is, then, the sublimest word in our language." The letter, which contains much advice to Custis, is supposed to have been written from Arlington, April 5, 1852. All the internal evidence and the little external evidence available leave no doubt that the letter is a forgery, probably concocted for his own amusement by some New England soldier who was stationed at Arlington during the war and chanced upon some of Lee's letters to his sons. There is a possibility, though more than a possibility, that the sentence on "duty" may have occurred in some letter of Lee's, but the chances are much stronger that the forger was echoing Kant's "Duty! thou sublime and mighty word." The whole case against the authenticity of the letter is set forth in two papers, "The Forged Letter of General Robert E. Lee," by Charles A. Graves, presented to the Virginia Bar Association at the annual meetings in 1914 and 1915. These papers appear in the annual *Reports* of the Association (vol. 27, pp. 176–215; vol. 28, pp. 299–315) and were separately reprinted. On Nov. 1, 1917, Professor Graves wrote a third article on the subject for *The New York Times*. This was republished in the *Report* of the bar association for 1917–18 (vol. 30, pp. 288–91) and was issued as a four-page reprint.

[48] Totten to Lee, *MSS.*, April 7, April 15, 1852; *MS. Letters to Officers of Engineers*, vol. 19, 207, 215; Lee to Totten, *MS.*, April 20, 1852; *Eng. MSS.*, 1166.

[49] Lee to Totten, *MS.*, May 5, 1852; *Eng. MSS.*, 1167.

[50] Totten to Lee, *MS.*, May 27, 1852; *MS. Letters to Officers of Engineers*, vol. 19, p. 259.

the superintendency of West Point was an honor, one of the few "plums" of the hard-worked engineer service. The superintendent was the titular head of a considerable command and the centre of a very pleasant society. He had a handsome house, and usually was left at the post for three or four years. In Lee's case the family would be able to see more of Custis, who was still a cadet at the academy. Service there would be heart-warming contrast to the mosquitoes and the discomfort of Sollers' Point. But Lee did not stop to weigh these advantages. He felt that he lacked experience for the position and he did not believe he could fulfill the expectations that Totten would have of him. Accordingly he wrote that same day an acknowledgment of the order:

"I learn with much regret the determination of the Secretary of War to assign me to that duty, and I fear I cannot realize his expectations in the management of an Institution requiring more skill and more experience than I command.

"Although fully appreciating the honor of the station, and extremely reluctant to oppose my wishes to the orders of the Department, yet if I be allowed any option in the matter, I would respectfully ask that some other successor than myself be appointed to the present able Superintendent." [51]

The bureau must have given consideration to Lee's request, for it was June 8 before an answer was sent to him. It was official and positive: his letter had been received and the chief engineer had to decline to change the assignment.[52] That was all, though doubtless Totten's reply had behind it a feeling that modesty alone had prompted Lee's application, which was not to be regarded too seriously. Lee apparently made no further reference to the new post until July 1. Then he wrote that he gathered from the letter of the 8th that he would not be relieved of the order assigning him to West Point, and if he were not, he requested that provision be made for the detail of the necessary officers for the ensuing academic year. Promptly enough came back the bureau's answer this time: "The department saw no

[51] Lee to Totten, May 28, 1852. The date of this letter is supplied from Totten to Lee, June 8, 1852, MS. *Letters to Officers of Engineers*, vol. 19, p. 263. The original of the letter has disappeared from the United States archives, and is not at West Point. The text is quoted from *White*, 47–48.
[52] Totten to Lee, June 8, 1852, *loc. cit.*

reason, and anticipated none for changing the order assigning him to West Point."[53]

That ended it. Lee began to prepare for the change, while keeping the work at the fort briskly under way. After a single trip to Washington at the end of July,[54] he completed his annual financial statement, and on August 21 announced to the department that he had turned over all balances to his assistant, Lieutenant W. H. C. Whiting, whom he was to meet again in very different circumstances. The final settlements were submitted at the same time, and on August 23, 1852, he set out for West Point. His concluding reports told of progress in the building of the sea walls and of a commencement in filling the coffer with concrete.[55]

Although he did not dream it at the time, this was the last engineering work Lee was ever to do for the United States. He had been at Sollers' Point three years and five months, and during that time he had carried the work through all its vexing stages, economically, expeditiously, and stably.[56] As Totten had written, all that was needed for its satisfactory completion was money. The work had not been especially interesting after the initial difficulties had been overcome. It gave Lee nothing that enlarged his knowledge of the art of war, unless it may have been that this experience with the slow and troublesome construction of stone forts of the old type unconsciously operated to make him still more an advocate of earthworks.

[53] Lee to Totten, MS., July 1, 1852; Eng. MSS., 1176; Totten to Lee, MS., July 3, 1852, MS. Letters to Officers of Engineers, vol. 19, p. 293.
[54] Lee to W. H. C. Whiting, MS., July 31, 1852; Lee's Sollers' Point Letter Book.
[55] Lee to Totten, MSS., July 10, July 31, Aug. 21 (2), 1852; Eng. MSS., 1177, 1183, 1184, 1185; Totten to Lee, MS., July 29, 1854; MS. Letters to Officers of Engineers, vol. 19, p. 319.
[56] For the state of work virtually as Lee left it, see Ex. Docs., 2d sess., 32d Cong., vol. 1, p. 152.

CHAPTER XIX

West Point Proves to Be No Sinecure

When Lee, on September 1, 1852, succeeded Captain Henry Brewerton and became ninth superintendent of the United States Military Academy,[1] he found a plant very different from the one he had known in the days of his cadetship. Scarcely any of the old buildings remained. The familiar north and south barracks were gone; the old mess hall was torn down the very year of Lee's return. A small hospital, inadequate by this time, had been reared in 1830. Band barracks had been erected in 1829. The hotel that was being built the year of Lee's graduation had a large new wing. There was a chapel dating from 1836, an academy constructed in 1838, ordnance and artillery laboratories finished in 1842, an observatory and library, the work of 1841, and—most impressive of all—the cadet barracks, just from the carpenters' hammer, a building 360 by 60 feet, with a wing 100 by 60 feet, the whole providing 172 rooms, 14 by 22 feet. A fine mess hall was nearing completion.[2] Of the old faculty only two remained, W. H. C. Bartlett and Albert E. Church. Both of them had been assistants when Lee had left the academy and both were now full professors, but they were paying for rising fame with multiplying gray hairs. The commandant of cadets was Captain Bradford R. Alden, but he left two months later. His successor was Major Robert S. Garnett, who was subsequently to fall in one of the first tragedies of the War between the States. Lee was soon on terms of close friendship with Garnett, who was of an old family from Tidewater Virginia. The instructor in artillery and cavalry was still

---

[1] 1 *Cullum*, 421; 1 *Cent. U. S. M. A.*, 236; *Ex. Docs.*, *2d sess.*, *32d Cong.*, vol. 2, p. 163; *MS. Letter Book of the Superintendent of West Point*, Sept. 1, 1852, p. 283. This last, which is the principal source on Lee's administration at West Point, is cited hereafter as *WPLB*, with the date and page.

[2] *Boynton*, 254 ff.; *Ex. Docs.*, *2d sess.*, *33d Cong.*, vol. 1, part 2, pp. 155–57. The old barracks had been condemned by the board of visitors in 1849 as "utterly unfit for occupation" (*Ex. Docs.*, *1st sess.*, *31st Cong.*, vol. 1, p. 142).

another Virginian, Major George H. Thomas, later to win fame on the battlefield. The adjutant of the academy, the officer with whom Lee had the most constant and intimate relationship, was young Seth Williams, of Maine, brevetted a captain for gallant conduct at Cerro Gordo and soon a staunch admirer of his new chief. When Williams was transferred, a year afterwards, Fitz John Porter took his place—the same Porter against whose corps Lee was to hurl his army at Mechanicsville and at Gaines's Mill.[3] The professor of drawing was Robert W. Weir, who was just then coming to distinction. Lee became very fond of him and later sat for a portrait which Weir painted with some understanding. This picture is one of the only two portraits made of Lee before the War between the States.

The work of the institution, Lee found, was on as high a general level as the official personnel. Brewerton had labored steadily during his term of service. Not long before he was relieved he had sought to improve the appearance of the corps on parade,[4] had extended instruction in fencing to the fourth class,[5] and had ordered the cataloguing of the library. Many of the major building enterprises had been initiated by him. No less an authority than Horace Mann had said in 1849, when serving on the board of visitors: "The committee [on instruction] would express the opinion that when they consider the length of the course and the severity of the studies pursued at the academy, they have rarely, if ever, seen anything that equalled either the excellence of the teaching or the proficiency of the taught." [6]

But Brewerton had some problems that Lee inherited. Many boys were being sent to the academy without proper preparation, and sometimes when they were dismissed for failure or for misconduct, discipline was impaired because the Secretary of War yielded to political considerations and ordered them restored to duty.[7] The curriculum was crowded, and some important subjects were being omitted; but neither Congress nor the War Department had acted on the recommendation of successive boards that the

---

[3] *Boynton*, 314 *ff.*; Lee to S. Cooper, *MS.*, Aug. 29, 1853; Lee to Totten, *MS.*, Sept. 1, 1853; *WPLB*, 47, 49.

[4] By barring the display of watch guards, chains, seals, etc. *2 Cent. U. S. M. A.*, 109.

[5] *2 Cent. U. S. M. A.*, 109.

[6] *Ex. Docs., 1st sess., 31st Cong.*, vol. 1, p. 250.   [7] *Ibid.*, 236, 240.

course of study be lengthened to five years.[8] The Secretary of War had declared against this change a month before Lee became superintendent.[9] Besides all this, the academy lacked a sufficient number of horses. Only forty animals had been available for the cavalry and artillery, and thirty of these had been condemned. Glanders appeared frequently.[10] There was great need of a riding school. The hall where the cadets were trained and the horses were given exercise was in dangerous dilapidation, and its abandonment had been urged by the board of visitors, but aside from the grant of an initial appropriation of $2000 nothing had been done to remove the risk to cadet and to mount.[11]

To supplying these and similar needs of the academy Lee had to devote himself from the outset of his administration. At the same time he discharged a daily routine that was usually tedious and sometimes exasperating. His correspondence was heavy and taxing. Records had to be kept and estimates made. The whole administration headed up to the superintendent, and his signature had to be attached even to letters requesting the chief engineer to permit cadets to receive a packet of socks from home.[12]

Dealings with the "academic board," as the faculty was still called in the regulations, demanded no little diplomacy and patience. Most of the chief instructors were civilians or soldiers who loved the easy, dignified life at West Point and had no desire to leave, but many of the assistants were restive young lieutenants or captains detailed from the staff and line. Lee approved the system that sent these junior officers back to the academy. He argued that it gave them an opportunity for carrying on advanced studies, and that it supplied the army with specialists.[13] But the arrangement involved difficulties. Duty at "The Point" was not uniformly desired. A captain might be requested for duty, but would bring influence to bear to avoid assignment.

[8] See board of visitors reports in *Ex. Docs., 2d sess., 31st Cong.,* vol. 1, p. 272; *ibid., 1st sess., 32d Cong.,* vol. 1, p. 367; *2d sess., 32d Cong.,* vol 2, p. 171.
[9] Report of Secretary C. M. Conrad, July 30, 1852, *Senate Doc., 98, 1st sess., 32d Cong.*
[10] *Ex. Docs., 1st sess., 31st Cong.,* vol. 1, p. 239; Lee to Totten, Sept. 15, 1853, *WPLB,* 51.
[11] *Ex. Docs., 1st sess., 31st Cong.,* vol. 1, p. 259; *ibid., 2d sess., 31st Cong.,* vol. 1, p. 273; *ibid., 1st sess., 32d Cong.,* vol. 2, part 1, pp. 368–69; *ibid., 2d sess., 32d Cong.,* vol. 2, p. 171.
[12] *E.g., WPLB,* 1852, p. 284 *ff.*
[13] Lee to Totten, *MS.,* Juiy 28, Dec. 9, 1854; *WPLB,* 125, 157.

Long correspondence might follow before another was selected.
The best that successive superintendents could do to moderate this
evil was to recommend two or three officers, in order of preference, hoping to get one or another of them by the time the next
session began.[14] Many of the instructors were chosen from the
artillery. The commander of one or another of these regiments
was apt to complain that he was furnishing more than his quota;
consequently, an effort had always to be made to equalize the
calls among the various units.[15] Care had to be taken, also, that
the ordnance bureau and the topographical engineers supplied
their quotas of instructors, so that the engineer corps would not
be crippled by inordinate details.[16] Occasionally, too, a number
of instructors were relieved at almost the same date, and the faculty had to be patched up in the middle of an academic session.[17]
Lee learned very early that it was his duty in circumstances of this
sort to play for time, but when he discovered that an officer wished
to leave, he let him go as soon as possible, affirming that he wanted
only willing instructors.[18] If members of the faculty found opportunity for advancement, Lee tried to assist them. When Captain
George W. Cullum, for example, was suggested as superintendent
of the assay office in New York, Lee arranged for Cullum to
discharge that service while retaining his position at the academy,
and he was disappointed when the Secretary of War withheld his
consent.[19] In cases where qualified instructors applied for places
elsewhere, Lee cheerfully wrote letters of recommendation.[20]

Lee assumed his routine in financial matters with confidence,
after so many years of dealing with the War Department. His
instinctive care in expending public funds had commended him
to his superior officers and had helped to advance him in the army.
The poverty of his youth had thus proved an advantage to him.
His thrifty impulses were never stronger than at West Point.
When an optimistic adventurer proposed to dig for buried treasure

[14] Cf. case of Captain E. K. Smith, Lee to Totten, MS., Sept. 8, Nov. 8, 1852; WPLB,
285, 298; cf., also, pp. 298, 300–301, 312.
[15] Lee to Totten, MS., Jan. 7, 1854; WPLB, 83.
[16] Same to same, MS., June 27, 1854; WPLB, 115.
[17] E.g., the proposed relief of Major G. H. Thomas and two other officers in April,
1854; Lee to Totten, MS., April 13, April 21, 1854; WPLB, 99, 101.
[18] Case of Lieutenant Chapman, Lee to Totten, MS., Jan. 9, 1854; WPLB, 85.
[19] Lee to Totten, MS., Oct. 28, 1853; Lee to Cullum, MS., Nov. 4, 1853; WPLB, 64,
66.
[20] Lee to Charles King, MS., Nov. 26, Dec. 13, 1853; WPLB, 72–73, 77.

at West Point, Lee wanted to stipulate that half the findings go to the post-fund of the academy.[21] In trying to replace the poor horses at the institution, Lee delayed buying in winter because of the shortage of stabling and the high cost of forage, and then he bargained for surplus animals left behind when the cavalry recruiting barracks were transferred from Carlisle, Pa., to Saint Louis, Mo.[22] He had to complain of certain unserviceable saddles the cadets were using, but, he said to the quartermaster-general, "I do not wish to expend a dollar more than necessary for the purpose, and if you think no other saddles can with propriety be furnished the cadets, they must do without them."[23] Even the expenses of the members of the board of visitors were subjected to close scrutiny. He was loath to pay the stated mileage allowance to a board member who was then in the East but claimed California as his home. When the board was overcharged for lodgings and food at West Point, Lee refused to pass the warrant approved by its secretary and referred the item to the War Department.[24]

While Lee was adjusting himself to his routine, his family was settling itself in the superintendent's house. Agnes and Annie remained in Virginia for at least a part of the winter, but the other children came with their mother to West Point.[25] The family horses were brought from Arlington, as was some of the furniture,[26] so that the household was quite comfortable. Living expenses were high, because the superintendent had to do much official entertaining, but fortunately, soon after he entered on his duties, Lee was assigned according to his brevet rank, with higher pay and allowances.[27] Every social pleasure was sharpened by the knowledge that Custis was nearby. The boy, who had shaken off his sloth and was rising rapidly in his class, usually came home on Saturday afternoon for a call, accompanied by one or more of the other cadets. "It is the only time we see him," Lee

[21] Lee to Totten, *MS.*, June 21, 1853; *WPLB*, 34.
[22] Lee to Totten, *MS.*, March 21, Sept. 27, Oct. 5, Oct. 8, 1853; *WPLB*, 11, 53, 57, 59.
[23] Lee to T. S. Jesup, Q. M. G., *MS.*, March 17, 1853; *WPLB*, 10–11.
[24] Lee to Totten, *MS.*, June *et seq.*, 1854; *WPLB*, 111, 115, 129.
[25] R. E. Lee to Annie Lee, Feb. 25, 1853; *R. E. Lee, Jr.*, 14–15.
[26] *Cf.* Lee to Mrs. Lee, Aug. 20, 1855; *E. J. Lee*, 434.
[27] *MS. A. G. O.*, vol. 8, Nov. 16, 1852; *S. O.*, 197. It was not until after the act of June 12, 1856, that the superintendent had the local rank of colonel, regardless of his regular rank (2 *Cent. U. S. M. A.*, 111). Captain Brewerton, in his time, had spent $6000 in addition to his pay in meeting the unescapable expenses of the superintendency.

explained to one of his absent daughters, "except when the Corps come under my view at some of their exercises, when my eye is sure to distinguish him among his comrades and follow him over the plain." [28]

During these early days of Lee's service, the life of the academy flowed on without incident. Early in October he made up his recommendations for new plant extensions. He asked $2000 for a new wharf, a small sum for additional conduits to bring water to the cadet barrack, and an appropriation for fencing and enclosing the grounds, always a matter of importance to one who, like himself, was a lover of order. Of major improvements he suggested a range of officers' quarters and stables for horses then without shelter. He also renewed the appeal for a riding hall. A little later he asked if the $3000 appropriated for study rooms for the professors might not be used to build small additions to the professors' houses, with the idea of adding a second story to these rooms when more funds were forthcoming. In this way the studies could be provided and the professors' small houses could ultimately be enlarged.[29] Before the end of the year Lee was able to forward plans for the new riding school, modelled after that at Saumur.[30]

The first serious breach of discipline that had to be reviewed by Lee occurred while these plans for the riding school were being prepared. A cadet reported sick one day in November, but was suspected of having subsequently slipped away and gone to New York. When inquiry was made by the commandant, the officer of the subdivision, a cadet lieutenant, refused to testify whether the suspect had been present when he inspected quarters. Lee was much disturbed by the discovery of such a state of affairs. The lieutenant's behavior, he said, was "highly reprehensible and destructive of the confidence reposed in cadet officers. If taught to practice such conduct here, they may learn to practice it in the army, which would put an end to its discipline and usefulness." He believed the lieutenant should be court-martialled, but, he added—in language he was to use many times in reporting the lapses of cadets—"should the department think [that] a milder

[28] R. E. Lee to Annie Lee, Feb. 25, 1853; *R. E. Lee, Jr.*, 15.
[29] Lee to Totten, *MS.*, Sept. 20, Oct. 9, Dec. 29, 1852; *WPLB*, 287, 293, 310–11.
[30] Lee to Totten, *MS.*, Dec. 31, 1852; *WPLB*, 311.

course would not correct this evil," he recommended the lieutenant's dismissal from the institution. The heaviest penalty that
could have been imposed by a court-martial would have been dismissal, and a lighter penalty was much more apt to be inflicted.
Consequently, the suggestion of outright dismissal without a court
was exceedingly serious for a lieutenant then in his last year. As
for the cadet who had been attracted by the lights of New York,
Lee wrote Totten that if the charges were true the boy had
"abused the indulgence of the Secretary of War, violated the
confidence of the surgeon, and outraged the discipline of the
Academy." He continued: "It is painful to be compelled to expose
such conduct, but I know of no other way of correcting it, or of
inculcating those principles of manliness and honour which are
the only safeguard of a soldier." He accordingly recommended a
searching inquiry to determine where the boy was on the day of
his alleged absence.[31]

All this was the course of a sympathetic soldier who understood boys, yet was determined to stiffen discipline he was surprised to find so lax. Happily for the cadet officer in question,
the issue did not have to be followed through. After a few days'
reflection, the lieutenant repented of his refusal to answer questions, and told what he knew of the affair. Thereupon Lee
promptly suggested that the boy be reprimanded in orders and deprived of his appointment, but that other proceedings against him
be dropped. Lee held to his opinion that, if guilty, the lad who had
slipped off should be given the fullest punishment, though he
reported that cadets were going to New York without permission
more frequently than had been supposed. Without further word
to the bureau of engineers, he set himself to breaking up this
practice. He must have been successful, for there is no reference,
in all his correspondence as superintendent, to another instance of
the same sort.[32]

While this case was being decided, Lee was engaged in a study
of the printed regulations of the school, preparatory to the publication of a new edition.[33] In this way he familiarized himself
with the modifications adopted during the twenty-three years he

[31] Lee to Totten, *MS.*, Nov. 30, 1852; *WPLB*, 301.
[32] Same to same, *MS.*, Dec. 9, 1852; *WPLB*, 303.
[33] Lee to Totten, *MS.*, Jan. 24, Feb. 14, March 4, 1853; *WPLB*, 317, 324–25, p. 5.

had been away from West Point. Without any overnight revolution or even a shakeup in personnel, he began to tighten up on discipline and on academic standards. His first step was to make the midyear examinations mean more to the cadets. Prior to 1849 the regulations had provided that only members of the fourth (freshman) class could be dismissed for failure to pass the January examinations. Cadets in the other classes were not dismissed or required to repeat the course if, in June, they made good their January deficiency. In 1849 the rule had been modified and the academic board had been given authority to dismiss at midterm any cadet who failed, regardless of the class to which he belonged. Until Lee's time, however, this new rule had never been applied to members of the first (senior) class. In the earliest examinations held after Lee became superintendent three cadets of the graduating class failed on engineering, and their case was brought before the academic board. Had their deficiency been in any other subject the board might have given them until June to regain their standing. But engineering had a certain sacrosanctity. First-classmen failing in it had been dismissed, as Lee subsequently explained, "on the very eve of graduation." The board deliberated and then voted to dismiss the three men who had fallen behind. One of them carried his case to Washington and precipitated a correspondence in which Lee vigorously defended the action of the board. Politics proved more potent than high scholarship. The young man was returned and, in the class of 1853, was duly graduated. He did not attain to distinction in the army.[84]

A case of this sort, where the board was overridden by the Secretary of War, was most destructive of discipline, as in 1849 the visitors had pointed out.[35] But Lee made no protest. After twenty-four years in the army, obedience to constituted authority had become so deeply implanted that it was almost a part of his religion. He found the secretary, C. M. Conrad, very much disposed to sacrifice morale to save a friend, and he was compelled to explain and to defend measures in which he should have had the

---

[84] Lee to Totten, *MS.*, Feb. 15, Feb. 21, 1853; *WPLB*, 325–26 and p. 1 (new volume).
[35] *Ex. Docs., 1st sess., 31st Cong.*, vol. 1, pp. 236, 240.

support of the secretary as a matter of course; but he met each inquiry with the same patience, the same tact.[86]

It must, none the less, have been with inward satisfaction that, on March 4, 1853, Lee saw Conrad retire, and a new secretary take the oath. The change marked the transfer of the government from Lee's own party to the Democrats, but it brought a personal friend to the head of the department, under a President who knew something of war at first hand. The new President was Franklin Pierce, whom Lee had often seen in Mexico, notably on that never-to-be-forgotten night in the pedregal in front of Padierna. The incoming secretary was Jefferson Davis. From the very hour that Davis assumed office, reversals of the superintendent of the military academy virtually ceased. Himself a West Pointer, the secretary understood that discipline at the academy could be no stronger than the faith of the War Department in the discretion of the superintendent. Lee's troubles were accordingly reduced. On the foundation of old friendship, new confidence and respect between himself and Davis were built up so stoutly in two years that all the strains of the War between the States could not overthrow them.

Very soon after Davis became his chief, Lee faced his first emergency as superintendent. One of the surgeons was absent and the other overworked himself in attending an unusual number of ill cadets. Lee suddenly found himself with a hospital full of sick boys, a disabled doctor—and nobody to administer treatment. He forthwith ordered Captain Gustavus W. Smith to New York with instructions to find a competent man and to send him to the Point on the next train. Smith met with no success. Conditions grew worse. Thereupon, Seth Williams was dispatched to the city, but even he failed to find a practitioner who would come to West Point and attend the sick cadets until the absent surgeon could return. Happily, Doctor Robert A. Murray of the army medical corps, then in New York, got another physician to look after his patients and hurried up to the academy. Lee learned his lesson, and thereafter if one of his surgeons was away he endeavored to get a substitute at once. It was sheer good fortune

[86] *Cf.* Lee to Conrad, *MS.*, Oct. 4, 1852, Feb. 10, 1853; *WPLB*, 289, 322–23.

that none of the boys died while the school was without doctors.[37]

If death spared West Point, it came that spring of 1853 to Arlington. Mrs. Custis's health had long been uncertain[38] and she had been very loath to be separated from her daughter and her grandchildren. Lee was distressed that she had to be denied the company of those she loved, and he urged Mrs. Lee to stay with her in the autumn of 1852, but later he thought it imperative that the children be under the discipline of their own parents.[39] Suddenly, in April, 1853, came word that Mrs. Custis was very ill. Mrs. Lee started for Arlington at once, only to find, on her arrival, that the gracious mistress of the estate was already dead. Somewhat contrary to every one's expectations, Mrs. Lee sustained the shock courageously, comforted no little by the fact that she had arrived in time to see her mother's remains and to make the funeral arrangements.[40] It was the first death in the family, barring that of "Black-Horse Harry," since the Lees had been married, and it grieved the son-in-law almost as deeply as it did the daughter. For years, Lee had called Mrs. Custis "Mother," and he gratefully owned, "She was to me all that a mother could be, and I yield to none in admiration for her character, love for her virtues, and veneration for her memory." To Mrs. Lee he wrote:

"May God give you strength to enable you to bear and say 'His will be done.' She has gone from all trouble, care and sorrow to a holy immortality, there to rejoice and praise forever the God and Saviour she so long and truly served. Let that be our comfort and that our consolation. May our death be like hers, and may we meet in happiness in Heaven." [41]

To Markie Williams he said: "The blow was so sudden and crushing, that I yet shudder at the shock and feel as if I had been

---

[37] Lee to G. W. Smith, *MS.*, March 12, 1853; *WPLB*, 9; Lee to Seth Williams, *MS.*, March 14, 1853; *ibid.*, 9; Lee to Totten, *MS.*, Oct. 17, 1853; *ibid.*, 62. For information concerning the presence in New York of Doctor Murray the writer is indebted to Colonel S. J. Morris, U. S. M. C., assistant to the surgeon general.

[38] Lee to Hill Carter, *MS.*, Jan. 25, 1840; *Shirley MSS; Markie Letters*, 29.

[39] R. E. Lee to Mrs. G. W. P. Custis, *MS.*, Dec. 20, 1852, Huntington Library; *Markie Letters*, 29.

[40] Mrs. Wm. Fitzhugh to Mrs. Abby Nelson, April, 1853; *Va. Mag. of History and Biography*, 35, 22–23. Mrs. Custis died April 23. She was then 65. *Cf.* William Burke to Mrs. Lee, *MS.*, May 8, 1853; *Duke Univ. MSS.*

[41] *Brock*, 162; *R. E. Lee, Jr.*, 18–19.

arrested in the course of life and had no power to resume my onward march." [42]

The first commencement of Lee's superintendency came not long after the death of Mrs. Custis. He had reorganized the battalion according to the height of the cadets,[43] and he had tried to provide a new dress cap, though in this he had not been successful.[44] No man could have been otherwise than proud of the four companies he presented the board of visitors when those funtionaries arrived on June 1.[45] The graduating class of fifty-three men contained many fine boys. At its head was John B. McPherson, doomed to fall in 1864 near Atlanta. The lad who graduated "No. 2" was William R. Boggs, subsequently a Confederate brigadier and chief of staff to E. Kirby Smith. Far down the list and inconspicuous in the class was a sharp-faced youngster known to his comrades as "Phil" Sheridan. And still nearer the bottom was a blond young giant of fine military mien but somewhat negligent in his studies, John B. Hood. Beginning on June 2, these youthful soldiers, along with the others, were examined before the board, and on June 16 they were formally graduated, with an address by Kenneth Rayner, a former Whig congressman from North Carolina.[46] The board concluded its deliberations soon thereafter and forwarded a report in which the academy and its administration were warmly praised. The extension of the course to five years was again approved.[47]

After commencement, summer leave—in the sequence that seemed more logical to third-classmen than any syllogism in the book! At Lee's coming there had been some question whether those cadets who entered in September were entitled to a leave of absence the second July following. Lee argued that they were, as otherwise they would get no leave during the whole of their cadetship. "I think [summer leave] a benefit," he said in words for which all West Pointers will thank him. "It is a great gratifi-

---

[42] June 23, 1853; *Markie Letters*, 31.   [43] *2 Cent. U. S. M. A.*, 109.

[44] Lee to Totten, *MS.*, March 15, 21, April 1, April 20, 1853; *WPLB*, 9–10, 13, 17, 22. Later in the year Lee proposed that a black welt instead of a black stripe be put on the "riding pantaloons" of the cadets, as the stripe was soon worn off by the sabre. Lee to Totten, *MS.*, Sept. 15, 1853; *WPLB*, 52.

[45] *Senate Docs.*, *1st sess.*, *33d Cong.*, vol. 2, p. 180.

[46] *Ibid.*, Lee to Daniel Goodenow, *MS.*, June 13, 1853; *WPLB*, 30–31; *2 Cent. U. S. M. A.*, 110.

[47] *Senate Docs.*, *1st sess.*, *33d Cong.*, vol. 2, pp. 180, 182.

cation. Its prospect holds out encouragement to better behavior;
and its enjoyment has a tendency to enlarge their ideas, ameliorate
many contracted notions, and renders them more happy and
contented during the rest of the course." [48] What Lee preached,
he practised. On July 5 he left West Point for a vacation in
Virginia. During his absence, the acting superintendent was Captain George W. Cullum, who held to Lee's policies rigidly and,
on his own account, opened war on trespassers. [49]

During this vacation occurred an important event in the life of
Lee. In early boyhood he had been drilled in his catechism by
Reverend Wiliam Meade. [50] From his youth he had been moral
and for years he had lived in the spiritual atmosphere Meade had
created in northern Virginia. Lee's correspondence does not contain the echo of a liaison, the shadow of an oath, or the stain of
a single obscene suggestion. He had always been religious in the
deeper sense of the word—as his mother's son he could hardly
have been otherwise—but he had not joined any church. He
attended service regularly, though even at West Point he frequently nodded during the sermon, much to the amazement of
his youngest son. [51] Prayer was a part of his life. As he grew
older all his religious impulses were deepened, and he felt an
increasing dependence on the mercy of a personal God. It is
probable that the Mexican War, the death of Mrs. Custis, and his
sense of responsibility for so many young men, brought the
great questions of faith closer to him. More particularly, as both
Mary and Annie were now of an age to be confirmed, Lee decided
that he ought also to submit himself formally to the Christian
faith. There is nothing to indicate any sudden spiritual upheaval.
Rather, his decision reflected a progression of religious experiences,
though it is plain from a later reference in a letter about Robert,
that he believed in conversion, in the nineteenth-century use of
the word. [52] On July 17, 1853, soon after he reached Arlington, he
and the two daughters, kneeling together, were confirmed at the

---

[48] Lee to Totten, *MS.*, March 25, April 1, 1853; *WPLB*, 14; Lee to G. Dean, May 24,
1853, *ibid.*, 28.

[49] Lee to Totten, *MS.*, July 5, 1853. For date of his return, see Lee to Stephen Lee,
Aug. 30, 1853, *ibid.*, 48.

[50] J. E. Cooke: *Life of General Robert E. Lee* (cited hereafter as *Cooke*), 18.

[51] *R. E. Lee, Jr.*, 12.   [52] See *infra*, p. 410, note 19.

chancel of Christ Church, Alexandria, by Right Reverend John Johns, Bishop of Virginia. Tradition has it that Bishop Johns said to him, "Colonel Lee, if you make as valiant a soldier for Christ as you have made for your country the Church will be as proud of you as your country now is." [53] His vows were not lightly taken. The religious note that was always strong in his private correspondence, after the outbreak of the Mexican War, became increasingly the dominant one of his life.

His vacation over on August 27, Lee had comparative quiet at the academy until almost the end of the year. To Lee's regret, Seth Williams was transferred in September;[54] and to his annoyance, glanders reappeared in the stables during the same month. The always troublesome estimates for the next fiscal year, together with his recommendations for improvements, had to be forwarded in October. Lee asked $5000 for betterments to the professors' houses, $20,000 for officers' quarters, $6500 for a second story to the overcrowded hospital, and $18,000 for the much-needed riding hall.[55]

With little besides these things to disturb him, and only a series of gunnery tests to stir his professional interest,[56] Lee had a bit more leisure time for his family life. In particular, he devoted himself to his youngest son, who had now reached the age where paternal influence was needed in his training. Lee began to consort more with the lad, and frequently took him with him when he went out for his daily exercise. He insisted that the boy learn to ride in the dragoon style with long stirrups and no posting, and he required him to keep his pony at a trot until he had become hardened to that gait. To encourage Robert in neatness, he purchased for him the bedding and room equipment of a cadet and regularly went through the ceremony of inspecting Robert's quarters. He was at equal pains to have the youngster taught to skate and to swim. His son's progress in study and in sport was a delight to the father.[57]

[53] Information courteously supplied from the records of Christ Church, Alexandria, Va., by the rector, Reverend William Jackson Morton, D.D. Cf. Packard, 155–56.
[54] Supra, p. 320.
[55] Lee to Totten, MS., Oct. 8, 1853; WPLB, 57. On Oct. 12, 1853, Lee forwarded Captain Cullum's estimate of the cost of a 300-foot pontoon bridge and train (Lee to Totten, MS., WPLB, 60).
[56] Lee to Totten, MS., Sept. 15, 1853, Jan. 20, Nov. 20, 1854; WPLB, 51, 86, 150.
[57] R. E. Lee, Jr., 11–13.

What Lee did with his own boy, for the development of discipline, he continued to do in different ways for other men's sons under his care. In July, at the instance of the academic board, the Secretary of War had approved a change in the regulations concerning demerit. Previously, a cadet could not be dismissed for "deficiency in conduct" until he had accumulated 200 demerits in twelve months. Now this extreme penalty could be imposed if 100 demerits remained against a cadet at the end of six months. Lee's idea was that many cadets allowed their demerits to pile up during the early months of a session, when the day of reckoning seemed far distant. Let the cadet know that he would have to face his record within six months, assured of dismissal for 100 demerits, and he would be more careful from the outset. So Lee reasoned and so the secretary ordered. Beneficial effects were soon apparent. The end of the first six months was to show only two fourth-class cadets liable to be sent home for having more than 100 demerits.[58]

All was proceeding peacefully when the commandant came to Lee and reported that on the night of December 16, 1853, a trio of third-class cadets had been absent from barracks from twelve o'clock until five, and that two fourth-class men had been away for an hour. The fourth-class men had liquor in their possession when they returned, and one of them, as well as one of the third-class men, was in citizen's clothes. It was a gross violation of the regulations. The men had been caught red-handed and had acknowledged their act. Bad as the infraction would have been in any case, it was rendered worse by the fact that among the offenders was Fitz Lee, the superintendent's nephew and son of his beloved brother Smith Lee. Fitz had entered the academy in 1852 and had not distinguished himself for scholarship or good conduct, but this was the first time he had been in serious trouble. Colonel Lee resolved his embarrassment by the simple expedient of declining to be embarrassed. He reported Fitz along with the rest and recommended the dismissal of all the culprits from the academy, or their trial before a court-martial.[59] The only points

[58] Lee to Totten, MS., June 22, Dec. 19, 1853, Jan. 9, 1854; WPLB, 35–36, 78–79, 84. For the rule, see Regulations for the Military Academy. . . . New York, 1853, § 72, p. 23.

[59] Lee to Totten, MS., Dec. 19, 1853; WPLB, 79.

in Fitz's favor were that he had been in uniform and had not had liquor on him. And neither point seemed likely to weigh against the uncontroverted fact that he had gone out of bounds at night.

But in his youth, as always, Fitz Lee had the ability to make friends who would stand by him in trouble. He had not won the plaudits of his professors, but he had the affection of his classmen. They were distressed at the prospect that he and his fellow-prowlers would be sent home. Bemoaning this, all the members of the third class revived that odd West Point custom that had been invoked in 1851 when Custis had been put under arrest. They offered, if the superintendent would relieve the trio of the charges against them, to pledge themselves for the remainder of the session not to commit the offense of which their comrades were accused. Lee forwarded the tender of this pledge to General Totten. Said he: "The subject being beyond my control, I have only to refer it to you, and although in a military point of view I consider this kind of convention between the authorities and the corps irregular, and that the oath which each member takes upon receiving his warrant a sufficient guarantee for his effort to perform his duty, yet I believe experience has shown the happiest results from these specific pledges and I therefore recommend it to your favorable consideration." [60] Jefferson Davis passed on the paper and declined to accept the pledge for the third-class men, inasmuch as the fourth class made no pledge for its members, who were equally culpable. The case went to court-martial, which put stiff punishment on Fitz Lee and two of his comrades. The two fourth-class men were allowed to resign. [61]

Light-hearted Fitz Lee did not regard his narrow escape very seriously. Because he then had 197 demerits he was required to remain at West Point during July and August, [62] while most of his classmates were on leave. Wearying of this dull life he slipped out of camp with another cadet about twelve o'clock one night and did not return until 2:30. He was caught and placed under arrest, with every prospect of ending speedily and ingloriously his career as a cadet. Colonel Lee could only forward the papers and

[60] Lee to Totten, *MS.*, Dec. 28, 1853; *WPLB*, 79.
[61] Lee to Totten, *MS.*, Jan. 7, 1854, Sept. 1, 1854; *WPLB*, 82, 125; S. O. 6, *A. G. O.*, Jan. 16, 1854.
[62] G. W. Cullum to Totten, *MS.*, July 18, 1854; *WPLB*, 122.

333

recommend a court-martial.[63] Again, and unanimously, all Fitz's classmates then at the academy offered to make a pledge not to commit his offense during the academic year. When the rest of the class returned the pledge was made unanimous, and in the third class all but two members proffered a like pledge for Fitz's companion in misadventure. The superintendent must have hesitated, but with the pledges in hand he finally wrote Totten: "Under all the circumstances of the case, I therefore recommend that the pledges be accepted, the charges be withdrawn, and that the cadets be released from arrest."[64] This time the secretary authorized acceptance of the pledges, and Fitz Lee was saved for the cavalry corps of the Army of Northern Virginia and for a long life of varied public service.

In the interval between Fitz Lee's escapades, his uncle was called upon to decide the case of another young cadet destined to even greater fame in another sphere. This young man was known to his comrades as "Curly" Whistler and he was registered at West Point as James A. Whistler, but in later years he styled himself James McNeill Whistler. The boy who entered West Point in July, 1851, was as erratic as the mature artist ever showed himself to be. Many and odd were the tales his classmates remembered of him—how he was witty but a dreadful horseman, and how he accepted proudly the West Point code of honor, but announced that he would not associate with men who talked of battles at dinner.[65]

Lee seems first to have come in official contact with this odd soldier when Whistler's mother, the fine Scotswoman whose later portrait was one of her son's greatest works, applied for a brief leave for "Curly" in order that he might come to New York and bid her farewell, as she was leaving for Europe. Lee granted permission, somewhat against his practice, though he was very explicit as to when Whistler had to report again for duty.[66]

The next spring Whistler developed rheumatism, with symptoms that suggested possible tuberculosis. He received the best attention the academy hospital offered, but he was in such poor

[63] Lee to Totten, *MS.*, July 24, 1854; *WPLB*, 122–23.
[64] Lee to Totten, *MS.*, July 28, Sept. 1, 1854; *WPLB*, 125, 132.
[65] E. R. and J. Pennell: *Life of James McNeill Whistler* (sixth edition), 22–23.
[66] Lee to Mrs. Anna M. Whistler, *MS.*, Sept. 28, 1852; *WPLB*, 288–89.

condition when Mrs. Whistler returned from Europe in May that Lee acquainted her with the facts on her arrival, apologizing for having to forward her such bad news.[67] The boy had to be given sick-leave soon thereafter, and could not attend the class examinations. During the summer he mended, and on August 28, 1853, he reported again and took the examinations. He was 37 in mathematics, 13 in French, significantly 1 in drawing, and in general standing 32. Lee hastened to notify Mrs. Whistler with the cheering announcement: "He will accordingly resume his position in his class, as if he had been present at the last examination, and prosecute the studies of its course."[68]

But "Curly" began to pile up demerits very fast and disdained uninteresting subjects of study. In June, 1853, he was quizzed on chemistry, of which he was a most indifferent student. Asked to discuss silicon, he started out boldly enough: "I am required to discuss the subject of silicon. Silicon is a gas——"

The examiner broke in: "That will do, Mr. Whistler."[69]

And it did. Very soon "Curly" was pronounced deficient in chemistry, and for that and other shortcomings was dismissed from West Point. He appealed from the decision of the academic board and asked for a re-examination in chemistry, instancing two fellow classmen who had even poorer records in chemistry than he, but had not been dismissed. To this Lee forwarded an answer that deserves to be quoted in full, both because it illustrates Lee's methods of dealing with the boys in his care, and also because it marked a turning-point in the career of Whistler. The letter was to General Totten and was dated July 8, 1854.[70]

"I have recd today the application of Cadet James A. Whistler for another examination in Chemistry, referred to me on the 6th Inst. It is true as stated by him, that his proficiency on first going over the course, entitled him to be transferred from the lowest to the next section, which was accordingly done on the commencement of the review of the course, viz.: on 25 March. It is also true that although his recitation marks on review were not as good as before, still his average mark for the whole time

[67] Lee to Mrs. A. M. Whistler, MS., May 26, 1853; WPLB, 29.
[68] Same to same, Aug. 31, 1853, MS.; WPLB, 49.
[69] Pennell: op. cit., 22.   [70] WPLB, 120–21.

was 2.2, and that for the whole time he received 130.6, a higher mark than any of those pronounced *deficient;* and higher than two of those pronounced *proficient,* viz: Cadets Hill and Pease, whose marks respectively were 129.8 and 125.4. During the review of the course however, Cadet Whistlers marks were 59.1, whereas Cadet Hills were 66.1 and Cadet Pease 58.1, showing that the two latter were improving, while the former was retrograding. It is also true as stated by Cadet W. I am sorry to say, that he passed a poor examination, and that by the Academic Board it was considered a complete failure, and that although his marks were better than those with whom he was classed, they could not in justice separate him from them and the vote for his deficiency was unanimous.—Cadets Hill and Pease on the contrary passed very satisfactory examinations. The subjects given him (Cadet W.) as to the others, though simple, were selected as involving the principles of Chemistry, separated in the course, with a view that he might shew his *proficiency,* of which there was doubt in the mind of his Instructor. I regret to say therefore that I know of no claim he has for a re-examination over any others that have come before the Board.

"In reference to his amount of demerit, I know of no grounds for his belief in the practicability of its reduction, except the indulgence that has hitherto been extended to him. From the period of his return from sick leave on the 28th Aug^t '53 to 31 Decr. the demerit recorded against him, amounted to 136, which under the present Reg^n. on the subject would have required his discharge, except that not having committed any grave offences, and on the recommendation of many of the reporting officers, and other considerations, I was enabled to remove 39, which reduced his amount below 100. Finding after Jany. that he was not more careful in his conduct, and fearing he might expect similar relief in June, I took occasion to caution him on the subject. On taking up the conduct Roll in June, I found he was again over the limit, and as I extended to some others in the same position, though not to the same extent, the priviledge of reconsidering their demerit, I again reconsidered his. After removing from the record book every report for which I could find any plea, and all that were favourably endorsed by the reporting officers, and reducing his demerit by 25, it was still 21 over the prescribed limit and now stands from the 1 Jan⁷. to 15th June 121. I can therefore do nothing more in his behalf, nor do I know of anything entitling him to further indulgence—I can only regret that one so capable of doing well should so have neglected himself, and must now suffer the penalty.

"The application of Cadet Whistler is herewith returned."

The War Department sustained Lee, and Whistler left the service, but in after years he had no grudge against West Point, and least of all against Lee. He always spoke with fiery admiration of his former superintendent.[71]

Still another youngster who later attained to a measure of fame gave Lee a bit of trouble during the months he was learning the strange and inscrutable ways of cadets. Large and splendid Archibald Gracie, Jr., a New York boy who held a cadetship from New Jersey, decided one day at review that it would be amusing to tread on the heels of the cadet in the file ahead of him. Around the field they tramped, Gracie indulging himself in this sport. When the cadet in front of him, fuming furiously, swore, *sotto voce,* that Gracie was going to get a drubbing, Gracie laughingly answered, "Not from you."

The offended cadet, Wharton Green, was as good as his word. After the review was over he started a fight on the very parade ground itself, and was giving Gracie the worst of it when the instructor in fencing came up and stopped the battle. Green stalked off at once; Gracie remained and, when questioned, gave his name and class. When asked who his antagonist was, Gracie answered, "You will have to ask him, for I'm no informer." He was of course placed under arrest, as fighting on the parade ground was a dire offense.

The next morning Lee was sitting in his office when Green entered. "Colonel Lee," he began, "Mr. Gracie was yesterday reported for fighting on the parade ground, and the 'other fellow' was not."

"Yes, sir, and I presume you are 'the other fellow.'"

"I am, sir, and I wish to submit the case in full for your consideration. Don't you think it very hard on him, Colonel, after

71 Pennell, *loc. cit.*

337

getting the worst of the fracas, to have to take all of the penalty incident?"

"Admitted," said Lee, "what then?"

"Simply this, sir. Whatever punishment is meted out to him, I insist on having the same given to me."

"The offense entails a heavy penalty," Lee reminded him.

"I am aware of the fact, Colonel, but Mr. Gracie is not entitled to a monopoly of it."

With a kindly smile Lee answered, "No, sir; you will get neither report nor penalty for this, and neither will Mr. Gracie get the latter. I will cancel the report. Don't you think, Mr. Green, that it is better for brothers to dwell together in peace and harmony?"

Young Green was equal to the occasion. "Yes, Colonel," he said squarely, "and if we were all like you, it would be an easy thing to do."

As soon as Gracie heard of Green's manful act, he wrung his hand in gratitude and from that day onward the two were warm friends.[72] Perhaps the memory of Lee's action may have been one reason why, some eleven years after, when Lee incautiously stepped upon the parapet of the Petersburg defenses, where he would have received a bullet on the instant, Gracie, then a gallant Confederate brigadier, quietly placed himself between Lee and the enemy.

[72] W. J. Green, *Recollections and Reflections*, 87–90.

CHAPTER XX

Lee Transfers from Staff to Line

As Lee dealt with his night-walking nephew, with the mischievous Gracie, and with that articulated frame of contradictions, "Curly" Whistler, so he dealt with all the cadets. He carried them on his heart, and spent many an anxious hour debating how best he could train them to be the servants of their country by making them masters of themselves. "When . . . I visited the academy," Jefferson Davis wrote years afterward, "and was surprised to see so many gray hairs on his head, he confessed that the cadets did exceedingly worry him, and then it was perceptible that his sympathy with young people was rather an impediment than a qualification for the superintendency." [1] Earnestly, however, Lee studied the boys. By the summer of 1854 he had come to know most of their frailties, their adolescent dodges, and all their good points, and he had made a consistent "administrative policy" out of the school's precedents and his own observations.

He believed that the best age for a boy to enter the academy was between seventeen and eighteen,[2] and he thought adequate preliminary training could be had at home.[3] From the hour they were admitted his attitude toward them he put into a single sentence: "These young gentlemen are not considered exactly in the light of enlisted men, and as much deference as possible is paid to their convenience and wishes in relation to personal matters." [4] Individual rights were not overridden and freedom of religious worship was always regarded.[5] In official dealings his funda-

[1] 150 *North American Review,* 57.
[2] Lee to N. Capen, *MS.,* Nov. 23, 1854; *WPLB,* 152.
[3] Lee to Mason Cleveland, *MS.,* March 31, 1853; *WPLB,* 16.
[4] Lee to Totten, *MS.,* March 4, 1854; *WPLB,* 95. The particular matter that elicited this observation was whether all cadets should be vaccinated.
[5] For instance, where he authorized cadets of particular creeds to attend outside religious worship, see Lee to Mrs. Adele Fowler, *MS.,* Nov. 9, 1853; *WPLB,* 68; Lee to Mrs. Agnel, *MS.,* April 21, 1853; *ibid.,* 23; Lee to B. O'Connor, *MS.,* Dec. 17, 1852; *ibid.,* 106; Lee to J. R. Torbert, *MS.,* Oct. 6, 1852; *ibid.,* 291.

mental was equal treatment for all,[6] though he felt that he had a special duty to the descendants of statesman and soldiers. When a grandson of Henry Clay was subject to dismissal because he had piled up a heavy demerit through inattention, Lee wrote: "I feel that regret that must be common to every American that the Grandson of Henry Clay, should be dismissed from the National Acady. of his country, and in consideration of the name of his Grandfather, and the devotion of the life of his father on the battlefield, respy. recommend that he be allowed to resign." [7]

If a cadet stood well in his classes and had little demerit, Lee was not apt to see much of him, except at examination or when he invited the lad to his house for supper Sunday evening.[8] But if the boy got into trouble of any sort, Lee was quick to know of it. If a cadet did not write home, Lee found out why.[9] In cases of serious illness he promptly notified the family, visited the boy, and gave him the best treatment possible in the academy hospital.[10] In the rare instances of death in the corps, his sympathy was personal and instant.[11] It was not always easy to be precise in writing of cadets' illnesses, because sometimes there was suspicion of malingering. "You must not suppose that any doubts are entertained as to the sincerity of his opinions as regards himself, or the treatment necessary for his recovery," he wrote one father who was anxious about his son. "But the medical officers have to be governed by their own judgment in his case and be guided by the same rules prescribed for all the cadets." [12]

Lee kept a close eye on the class reports, and when he perceived that a boy was in danger of failing he watched his standing week by week, consulted his instructors, and on occasion would call him in to discuss his case during his cadet office hour, which was between 7 and 8 A.M. Sometimes he wrote parents urging them to prod an indolent son or to encourage a disheartened student. If

[6] *Cf.* Lee to Sec. War, *MS.,* Dec. 29, 1852; *WPLB,* 309–10.
[7] Lee to Totten, *MS.,* Jan. 20, 1853; *WPLB,* 315; *cf.* Lee to Wm. Prather, *MS.,* Feb. 1, 1853; *ibid.,* 321; Lee to Totten, *MS.,* June 22, 1853; *Ibid.,* 35.
[8] *R. E. Lee, Jr.,* 17–18.
[9] *E.g.,* Lee to W. Palmer, *MS.,* Jan. 31, 1853; *WPLB,* 321.
[10] O. O. Howard: *Autobiography,* vol. 1, p. 54.
[11] Lee to Mrs. Adele Fowler, *MS.,* Feb. 2, 27, 1854; *WPLB,* 89, 94; Lee to Jacob Fort, *MS.,* March 29, 1853; *ibid.,* 15; Lee to Elijah Smead, *MS.,* May 18, 24, June 3, 1854; *WPLB,* 105, 108. For the death of a cadet, see Lee to Alpheus Frank, *MS.,* June 29, 1853; *WPLB,* 37.
[12] Lee to W. G. W., *MS.,* Feb. 9, 1854; *ibid.,* 89.

a prodigal returned to his books, he was more than apt to get commendation from the superintendent.[13] In those instances where a boy was in danger of dismissal for demerit, without having been guilty of any serious offense, Lee always took pains to explain that the cadet's character was not involved. Here is a typical letter:

"You must not however infer that his conduct has been in the least disgraceful or calculated to affect his moral character or standing. His amount of demerit has arisen from acts of carelessness, inattention to his duties, and to the regulations of police and discipline of the academy, which it is necessary for a good soldier to correct." [14]

When he could praise a boy's work, Lee did not stint his encomiums. In the case of a North Carolina cadet, who subsequently was killed in action while fighting at Frayser's Farm, in the Army of Northern Virginia, Lee wrote the father:

"It gives me great pleasure to assure you of the well-being of your son, and of the high estimation in which he is held at the Academy. There is none in his class more highly estimated for conduct, deportment and acquirement than himself, and he gives every promise of being an ornament to his family and an honour to the Institution. I congratulate you most sincerely on his high standing." [15]

Lee did his utmost to save the cadets from interruption of their studies by special leaves of absence. Much of his official correspondence had to do with applications for leaves he felt he could not grant. He uniformly declined to allow cadets to endanger their class standing by devoting time to weddings. "The cadets are placed here for a particular object," he said, "and if the indulgence in question is granted to one, it must be extended to all. You therefore see it would materially interfere with their course

13 *WPLB,* 171, 173, 176, 284; Lee to S. W. Downs, *MS.,* Nov. 1, 1853; *ibid.,* 65; Lee to S. Sanders, *MS.,* May 11, 1854; *ibid.,* 104; Lee to Geo. H. Devereux, *MS.,* Nov. 22, 1853; *ibid.,* 71; Lee to Wm. H. Terrill, *MS.,* April 19, 1853; *ibid.,* 20. For Lee's office hours, see *West Point Regulations,* 1853, § 356, p. 67.
14 Lee to J. B., *MS.,* Sept. 26, 1853; *WPLB,* 54.
15 R. E. Lee to Stephen Lee, *MS.,* Aug. 30, 1853; *WPLB,* 48. The cadet was Charles C. Lee, *Cullum,* No. 1714, who stood fourth in the class of 1856. *Cf.* Lee to Mrs. Burerev. *MS.,* Aug. 30, 1853; *WPLB,* 48.

of studies and instruction. Their presence at this time, to prepare for the approaching Jany. examination is particularly important to them, and it may be of more advantage to your son to maintain his present high standing in his class, than to enjoy the gaieties of the wedding. He will have other opportunities I hope to participate in these hereafter." [16] Leaves for Christmas, a perpetual cause of exchanges between home and academy, were granted by Lee only to those who had high standing in their classes, and, after 1853, only then to cadets who could go home and return within twenty-four hours.[17] Illness in the family, personal sickness, the departure of friends for the Far West, the presence in New York of intimates from a distance, even the arrival of the dead body of a parent—Lee accounted none of these a sufficient reason for absence from classes.[18] As for the endless applications to grant leave to cadets during the summers they were supposed to be in camp, Lee met all of them with resolute refusal and with the patient argument that such concessions would violate the principle of equal justice to all. "I think it would be unjust," he said in a typical letter, "to his class and the rest of his Corps, to grant him a leave of absence, equally desirable to them all, and retain them to perform his share of Camp duty." [19]

In case a cadet fell hopelessly behind in his work, or showed himself incompetent and certain to fail in his examination, Lee often urged parents to permit the boy to resign and thereby to save him the humiliation of dismissal. His letters to these disappointed fathers were the most difficult he had to write, but

---

[16] Lee to J. C. Van Camp, MS., Dec. 14, 1852; WPLB, 305. In this instance Lee was overruled by the War Department (Lee to Totten, MS., Dec. 17, 1852; ibid., 306). In the case of Cadet Archibald Gracie, Lee declined to allow the boy leave for a wedding but gave him permission to visit his sick mother (Lee to Archibald Gracie, MS., Oct. 6, 1852; ibid., 290–91). See also Lee to Totten, MS., Nov. 24, 1853; ibid., 72.

[17] WPLB, 80–81, 163, 164; Lee to Mrs. Ira M. Harrison, et al., MS., Dec. 22, 1852; ibid., 307; Lee to Mrs. Tennatt, MS., Dec. 7, 1854; ibid., 155; Lee to C. C. Paine, MS., Dec. 11, 1854; ibid., 158–59.

[18] Lee to Wm. Batcheler, MS., June 20, 1853; WPLB, 33 (illness in family); Lee to Totten, MS., Feb. 25, 1853; WPLB, 4 (personal sickness); Lee to Totten, MS., Jan. 20, 1853; WPLB, 315 (departure of friends for California and presence of friends in New York); Lee to Commodore J. T. Newton, MS., Sept. 26, 1853; WPLB, 55 (arrival of a corpse).

[19] Lee to Totten, MS., March 26, 1853; WPLB, 14–15; cf. same to same, MS., May 4, 10, 1853, May 31, June 21, 1854; ibid., 24, 25, ibid., 108, 111; Lee to James G. King, MS., April 6, 1853; ibid., 18; Lee to J. Watson Webb, MS., June 21, 1854; ibid., 112; Lee to Isaac E. Morse, MS., July 1, 1854; ibid., 116; Lee to G. R. Riddle, MS., July 7, 1854; ibid., 117; Lee to A. G. Brown, MS., July 7, 1854; ibid., 117; Lee to Henry Bennett, MS., Aug. 1, 1854; ibid., 128.

they were among the most tactful.[20] If anything could be said in extenuation of a boy's failure—youth, immaturity, or what not— Lee always mentioned it, and when a boy's conduct had been without serious demerit, Lee noted that, too. In advising a father to let his son resign before examination, Lee wrote: "He is a youth of such fine feelings and good character that I should not like to subject him to the mortification of failure, to which he might give more value than it deserves. For I consider the charac- ter of no man affected by a want of success, provided he has made an honest effort to succeed."[21] This last sentence might have been written on the eve of Appomattox.

Whenever he received the list of cadets deficient in conduct Lee went over it, as he did in Whistler's case, and reduced the demerit of those in whose behalf any valid excuse could be urged. If the number remaining was more than one hundred for six months, Lee held strictly to the rule that denied the privilege of resigna- tion to cadets who exceeded that figure. "If some inducement to good behavior," said he, "is not held out to those whose success at the examination may be doubtful, or failure certain, I fear it may have the effect of making them entirely reckless and in- different to order and discipline."[22] If cadets had to be dismissed, he regarded delay in action as injurious both to the boys and to the academy.[23] None the less, each such case was a personal distress to him. "I have just accomplished . . . the most un- pleasant office I am called on to perform," he wrote Markie Williams after the June examinations in 1854, "—the discharge of those cadets found deficient at the examination. There were fortunately only nine of them, but all very nice youths, some sons of officers of the Army, one of the Navy, who having neglected their studies, contrary to all advice and efforts to the contrary, must now suffer the penalty, which they acutely feel, but which they could not be made to realize. I have just closed their con-

[20] WPLB, Dec. 27, 1852, p. 307; Lee to J. Folsom, MS., Jan. 22, 1853; ibid., 316; Lee to Reuben Willets, MS., Jan. 29, 1853; ibid., 320 (advising against an attempt to have a boy reappointed to the academy); Lee to R. E. Campbell, MS., May 24, 1853; ibid., 27; Lee to Harmonys, Nephews & Co., MS., Oct. 21, 1853; ibid., 62–63; Lee to E. H. Her- bert, MS., Dec. 5, 1853; ibid., 74; Lee to Richard Berry, MS., Dec. 8, 1853; ibid., 75; Lee to C. F. M. Noland, MS., Nov. 15, 1854; ibid., 148; Lee to M. O. Wade, MS., Nov. 20, 1854, pp. 150–51; Lee to A. H. Moss, MS., Jan. 10, 1855; ibid., 172.
[21] Lee to R. E. Campbell, MS., May 24, 1853; WPLB, 27.
[22] Lee to Totten, MS., Jan. 17, 18, 1855; WPLB, 175–76, 177–78.
[23] Lee to Totten, MS., Feb. 23, 1854; WPLB, 92–93.

nection with the Academy, signed their last orders, taken leave of them, with sincere wishes for their happiness and prosperity. . . ." [24]

Lee wished no fuller record made of boys' dismissal than the rules required: "I think it unnecessary to multiply copies of what had better be forgotten than remembered," he told one mother who wanted a detailed report of her son's shortcomings.[25] To those who wrote him after their dismissal, he always sent friendly answers, not always devoid of the sort of preachments that crowded his letters to his sons.[26] At first he gave them general recommendations, if requested, but he found this a dangerous practice and toward the end of his superintendency he contented himself with reminding the ex-cadet that the certificate given him upon leaving West Point set forth his record.[27] As for outsiders, Lee was careful, then as always, whom he endorsed and he did not write many letters of this type. One of the few that put his name squarely behind the reputation of another man had been penned in 1851 when he had been asked to support the candidacy of an army officer for a professorship in Virginia. He responded cheerfully and never had reason to regret his action. For the applicant was Thomas Jonathan Jackson.[28]

Serious offenses at West Point often provoked Lee to urge that the cadet be brought before a court-martial, or be dismissed by the Secretary of War.[29] He placed under immediate arrest a dissatisfied cadet who raised a disturbance in a classroom.[30] When a cadet captain left the mess hall after having been assaulted by a cadet, Lee at once demoted the captain and asked for a court-martial of the assailant.[31] When dismissal occurred, Lee was opposed in every instance to re-examination or readmission.[32] It was painful to mete out punishment, especially to the young, he once wrote Totten, but "when it is necessary, true kindness re-

---

[24] *Markie Letters,* 49.

[25] Lee to Mrs. Margaret Hetzel, *MS.,* Jan. 31, 1855; *WPLB,* 181.

[26] *E.g.,* Lee to A. F. Devereux, *MS.,* Jan. 25, 1854; *WPLB,* 88.

[27] Lee to M. L. Montague, *MS.,* Feb. 15, 1853; *WPLB,* 326; Lee to W. H. Peck, *MS.,* Jan. 9, 1854; *WPLB,* 85; Lee to John P. Sherburne, *MS.,* Feb. 27, 1855; *ibid.,* 188.

[28] T. J. Arnold, *Early Life and Letters of Gen. Thomas J. (Stonewall) Jackson,* 216.

[29] Lee to Totten, *MS.,* Dec. 9, 1852, Feb. 23, 1854; *WPLB,* 303, 92–93.

[30] Lee to Totten, *MS.,* Jan. 31, 1854; *WPLB,* 89.

[31] Lee to Totten, *MS.,* Jan. 10, 1855; *WPLB,* 172–73.

[32] Lee to Totten, *MS.,* Jan. 7, 1853; *WPLB,* 313; Lee to P. C. Ricketts, *MS.,* Jan. 24, 1853; *ibid.,* 318; Lee to A. F. D., *MS.,* Jan. 25, 1854; *ibid.,* 88.

quires it should be applied with a firm hand, and not converted into a reward." [33] As long, however, as he could permit a boy to remain at West Point, Lee was usually willing to extend mercy on evidence of repentance, almost regardless of the gravity of the offense. It was so with boys who ran away from the academy and subsequently returned.[34] Each boy suspected of falsehoods received mercy. In one group of such cases Lee had to stretch logic about as far as it would go without breaking. It was painful to him, he wrote the chief engineer, to think that any member of the corps "could be guilty of the utterance or practice of a wilful falsehood, and if in your opinion the conduct of these young gentlemen, in this instance, does not admit of this severe imputation, I would ask that they be not brought to trial on a charge so injurious to their character and derogatory to that of the Corps of Cadets, but that the Dept. may place their conduct and its consequences in such a light that none may be at a loss to perceive how it is considered and the evil results of its being followed." By this involved language, he probably meant to suggest that the worse of the two offenders be dismissed from the academy. But a little later, when one of the boys repented, confessed his prevarication, and affirmed that it was common practice to dodge the officer of the day, Lee urged that some milder penalty than dismissal be imposed on him.[35]

Lee always accepted a cadet's confession and counted repentance as a point in any culprit's favor, but he thought the regulations should be very explicit in the matter of self-crimination.[36] He wanted no tattling, either. Once, when he was riding out with his youngest son, he came upon three cadets who were far out of bounds. The instant they saw Lee they jumped over the wall by the roadside and disappeared. "We rode on for a minute in silence," the junior Lee wrote, "then my father said: 'Did you know those young men? But no; if you did, don't say so. I wish boys would do what is right, it would be so much easier for all

---

[33] Lee to Totten, *MS.*, Jan. 7, 1853; *WPLB*, 313.
[34] Lee to Totten, *MS.*, Oct. 6, 7, 9, 11, Nov. 18, 1852; *WPLB*, 291, 292, 294, 299; Lee to R. M. P., *MS.*, Nov. 19, 1852; *ibid.*, 299. The boy involved in this case seems to have been dismissed by court-martial, despite Lee's willingness to accept his promise to mend his ways. For a similar case, see R. E. Lee to R. H. L., *MS.*, Sept. 6, 1852; *WPLB*, 284–85; Lee to Totten, *MS.*, Sept. 16, Oct. 15, 1852; *ibid.*, 286, 295.
[35] Lee to Totten, *MS.*, April 7, April 10, 1854; *WPLB*, 97, 98.
[36] Lee to Totten, *MS.*, March 4, 1853; *WPLB*, 5–6.

parties.'"[87] The cadets did not fail to appreciate the justice and the mercy of Lee's administration. Looking backward after four years of war and more than four decades of army service, General John M. Schofield wrote of Lee: "He was the personification of dignity, justice and kindness, and was respected and admired as the ideal of a commanding officer."[38]

Some of the young men who had tasted Lee's discipline were included among the forty-six who graduated in June, 1854, after a session that was wholly uneventful except for the incidents already noted. The class took for its ring emblem a mailed hand holding a sword with the motto, "When Our Country Calls." It was prophetic. For when war came, seven years later, thirty-seven of the forty-six entered the service—twenty-three as Federals and fourteen with the Confederacy.[39] At the head of the class, to Lee's gratification, stood his son Custis, who had maintained his improvement in his senior year and had qualified for the engineer corps. Archibald Gracie, Stephen D. Lee (who was not a kinsman of the superintendent), John Pegram, W. D. Pender, and J. B. Villepigue were also on the roll. The graduate whom Lee had come to know best, after his own son, was a stout gray-eyed lad of middle height and broad shoulders, with abundant hair and a dashing manner, a boy born to be a cavalryman and known already from his three initials as "Jeb" Stuart. He had visited the superintendent's home often[40] and had wholly won his heart. All seven of these graduates of 1854 became general officers in the Confederacy—Stephen Lee a lieutenant general, Pender and Stuart major generals, and the others brigadiers. Oddly enough, in this particular class the only Northerners who were to fight against Lee as general officers were Henry L. Abbot and O. O. Howard.

At this commencement of 1854 the board of visitors had nothing but compliments for the cadets themselves, for the academy, and for the superintendent. "The board cannot conclude this report," it said after summarizing conditions, "without bearing testimony to the eminent qualifications of the superin-

[87] *R. E. Lee, Jr.,* 12–13.
[38] J. M. Schofield: *Forty-six Years in the Army,* 15.
[39] B. J. Lossing: *Memoirs of Lieut.-Col. John T. Greble,* 24.
[40] *Cf.* O. O. Howard: *Autobiography,* vol. 1, p. 54.

tendent for the honorable and distinguished post assigned him by the government. Services conspicuous in the field, and when our country was engaged in a war with a foreign nation, have lost none of their luster in the exalted position he so worthily fills." [41]

The board had two definite suggestions, first, that Spanish be taught the cadets, and, secondly, that the course be made five years instead of four.[42] Instruction in Spanish had been previously proposed by the visitors of 1850[43] and the extension of the course had been favored by every board after 1850.[44] This time the board argued that a fifth year was necessary in order that the instruction might be given in important omitted subjects, and also in order to make good the poor preparation of many boys appointed to the academy. Secretary Davis saw the logic of this argument. He ordered instruction in Spanish begun with the next school year,[45] and on July 8 he opened, through General Totten, a lengthy correspondence with Lee on the scope of the projected five-year course and on the fairest way of separating the fourth class into two sections, to graduate a year apart. Lee referred the entire subject to the academic board and reported on September 8 that the board believed the fourth class should be divided according to the age of the cadets.[46] The board recommended, also, that the subjects most properly to be added to the course were constitutional and international law, elocution, history, composition, rhetoric, geography, and Spanish,[47] as already directed. Economics and physiology, two subjects advocated by some of the former visitors, were not included. No change was made in the military courses taught at the academy, except that Davis ordered separate

[41] *Ex. Docs., 2d sess., 33d Cong.,* vol. 1, part 2, p. 133. For Lee's amusing remarks on entertaining so many visitors at commencement, see *Markie Letters,* 48.
[42] *Ibid.,* 154, 130.
[43] *Ex. Docs., 2d sess., 31st Cong.,* vol. 1, p. 271.
[44] The instruction committee of the board of 1850 urged a five-year course, but the board did not endorse it that year (see *Ex. Docs., 2d sess., 31st Cong.,* vol. 1, p. 272). For the recommendation of the boards of 1851–53, see *Ex. Docs., 1st sess., 32d Cong.,* vol. 1, p. 367; *ibid., 2d sess., 32d Cong.,* vol. 2, p. 171; *Senate Docs., 1st sess., 33d Cong.,* vol. 2, p. 182.
[45] *2 Cent. U. S. M. A.,* 110. The professorship of Spanish was established by act of Congress, Feb. 16, 1857.
[46] Lee to Totten, *MSS.,* July 8, Aug. 22, Aug. 28, Sept. 8, 1854; *WPLB,* 120, 130, 131, 135.
[47] *Ex. Docs., 1st sess., 34th Cong.,* vol. 1, part 2, pp. 228, 243, 255. For the arrangement of the course by years, see *ibid.,* 248–49. Constitutional law had previously been taught with ethics, and Kent's *Commentaries* was the textbook during the whole of Lee's administration (see Lee to E. W. Morgan, *MS.,* Oct. 30, 1854; *WPLB,* 146).

instruction in cavalry and artillery.[48] The cadets who entered in June, 1854, were rearranged in two classes in September, not without some complaints,[49] but only a few of the new courses were undertaken for the session of 1854–55. Lee had no part in initiating this five-year system. It was not his proposal, though he has generally been given credit for it. After a few years' trial it was abandoned.

The decisions regarding the five-year course were made subsequent to Lee's return from a fortnight's vacation, July 9 to July 23, 1854.[50] After the fifth class was organized, the routine flowed on without sensation. Congress had appropriated $22,000 for the riding hall, $6500 for enlargements to the cadets' hospital, $8000 for cavalry stables, and $3000 for additions to the officers' quarters. The preliminary work for these improvements had begun, but the main construction was done in 1855.[51] A museum of artillery, which was recommended by the board of visitors in 1853, was started in 1854,[52] though no new structure was provided for it. Fresh needs appeared as old neglect was repaired. In his annual estimates Lee included $15,000 for a gas-house and the installation of gas in the cadet barracks, and $5000 for professors' houses. He renewed, also, his application for funds with which to build houses for the unmarried officers, who were occupying sixteen sets of quarters in the cadet barracks.[53] He had forwarded plans for such a building the previous January.[54]

While Lee was seeking these improvements at the academy, changes that were directly to affect him were being made in the army. Secretary Davis, in his report for 1853, had pointed out the numerical weakness of the regular armed forces of the United States and had asked that they be strengthened. Congress had not acted. On August 19, 1854, Lieutenant John L. Grattan, who had graduated under Lee the previous June at West Point, had been sent out with thirty men from Fort Laramie, Wyo., to make

---

[48] Lee to Totten, *MS.,* Dec. 19, 1854; *WPLB,* 162.
[49] *Cf.* Lee to George H. Crosman, *MS.,* Sept. 24, 1854; *WPLB,* 138–39.
[50] *WPLB,* 122, 123, 124. Lee arrived at West Point and resumed his duties on the morning of July 24. The vacation doubtless was spent in Virginia.
[51] *Ex. Docs., 1st sess., 34th Cong.,* vol. 1, part 2, 231, 241.
[52] *Boynton,* 297; *Senate Docs., 1st sess., 33d Cong.,* vol. 2, pp. 183, 197.
[53] Lee to Totten, *MS.,* Oct. 7, 1854; *WPLB,* 140; *Ex. Docs., 1st sess., 34th Cong.* vol. 1, part 2, p. 232.
[54] Lee to Totten, *MS.,* Jan. 5, 1854; *WPLB,* 82.

an arrest. The detachment had been attacked by Indians and every man in it save one had been killed. The survivor was badly wounded and subsequently died. This massacre created a sensation and sharpened Davis's argument when he appealed in December, 1854, for the enlistment of new regiments. Thirty million dollars, he pointed out, had been spent on Indian wars during the previous twenty-two years—enough to have paid troops who could have limited, or even prevented, the hostilities. With an army that had an authorized strength of 14,216, and seldom had more than 11,000 men under arms, Davis showed that the United States were guarding an Indian frontier of 8000 miles against 40,000 hostile Indian braves, to say nothing of the garrisons on the sea coasts and on the international borders.[55] This time Congress heeded the warning and by an act of March 3, 1855, authorized the establishment of two new regiments of infantry and of two of cavalry.[56]

Who would command the new troops? That was the question asked everywhere in the army. The matter was not long in the air. Almost as soon as the bill increasing the army had been signed by the President, Davis announced the appointments: As of March 3, 1855, Albert Sidney Johnston, hero of Davis's West Point days, was named colonel of the new 2d Cavalry and Lee was commissioned lieutenant colonel.[57] As he had in no sense been an applicant and had pulled no wires to win this post, Lee was surprised and not altogether pleased. The change from staff to line would bring no new compensation, for Lee was already drawing pay as colonel by brevet. Transfer meant farewell to the corps he loved and would certainly involve separation from his family. On the other hand, there was little prospect that he could rise to be chief engineer, for though Totten was now sixty-seven, he was still vigorous and not disposed to retire. Even if he should, two lieutenant colonels of engineers, four majors, and three captains were ahead of Lee.[58] In the army the outlook was different. All the general officers and most of the colonels were

---

[55] *Ex. Docs., 2d sess., 33d Cong.,* vol. 1, part 2, pp. 3–6.

[56] *Ex. Docs., 1st sess., 34th Cong.,* vol. 1, part 2, p. 3.

[57] It has been alleged, in the face of Mr. Davis's convincing denial, that the secretary gave the command of this regiment to Southern men in anticipation of an early war between North and South. *Cf.* Van Horne: *George H. Thomas,* 12.

[58] *Army Register of 1854,* p. 12; *Ex. Docs., 2d sess., 33d Cong.,* voi. 5 (Doc. 58).

old and there was talk of increasing the number of generals.[59]
Still again, service in the line meant a healthful, out-of-door life in
pleasant contrast to the confinement and office work of the superintendency. But none of these things weighed heavily with Lee.
He doubtless summed up his state of mind when he wrote Markie
Williams: "*Personal* consideration or convenience, would not induce me to sever my connexion with my Corps, or to separate
myself from my family. And the thought that my presence may
be important to the latter, or necessary to my children is
bitter in the extreme. Still in a military point of view I have no
other course, and when I am obliged to act differently, it will be
time for me to quit the service. My trust is in the mercy and
wisdom of a kind Providence, who ordereth all things for our
good. . . ." [60]

For these reasons Lee did not hesitate. "Promotion, if offered
an officer, ought in my opinion to be accepted, but it need not be
sought unless deserved," he afterwards said. On March 15 he
accepted,[61] and transmitted his letter to the adjutant general
through Totten, so that arrangements might be made to relieve
him as superintendent of the academy. He wrote his old chief:
"In thus severing my connection with the Corps of Engineers, I
cannot express the pain I feel in parting from its Officers, or my
grateful sense of your constant kindness and consideration. My
best exertions have been devoted to its service, and my warmest
feelings will be cherished for its memory." [62] On March 31, 1855,

[59] *Cf.* Scott's report, *ibid.*, 123: "Some forty or fifty officers, mostly in the higher
commissions, rendered non-effective by the infirmities of age, by wounds or chronic dis-
eases, now press down into lethargy, and then despair. . . ."

[60] March 14, 1855; *Markie Letters*, 52–53. Lee doubtless owed the tender of command to the good will and admiration of the Secretary of War, who virtually controlled
the new appointments. General Scott, of course, would have given Lee any command at
his disposal, but Scott was quarrelling with Davis, exchanging angry, written broadsides
with him, and could do Lee no good. "I tell you," he said emphatically to William
Preston, "that if I were on my death-bed tomorrow, and the President of the United
States should tell me that a great battle was to be fought for the liberty or slavery of the
country, and asked my judgment as to the ability of a commander, I would say with my
dying breath, let it be Robert E. Lee." (General William Preston, quoted in *Cooke*, 512.
Cf. ibid., 558.) Scott thought that Lee should have been made colonel and Johnston lieutenant colonel, but subsequently he said the appointments were satisfactory. Virginians
were gratified at the honor that had come to him and to other natives of the Old Dominion
elevated at the same time. (W. P. Johnston: *Life of Albert Sidney Johnston*, 185; *Richmond Dispatch*, March 8, 1855.)

[61] Lee to S. Cooper, *MS.*, March 15, 1855; *WPLB*, 191; the quotation is from R. E.
Lee to Custis Lee, Feb. 15, 1856; Jones, *L. and L.*, 89.

[62] Lee to Totten, *MS.*, March 15, 1855; *WPLB*, 192. Lee's surrender of his commission in the corps was announced in orders of July 19, 1855 (*A. G. O., MS., G. O.*, 19).

after disposing of the cases of some cadets involved in difficulty,[63] Lee turned over the command at West Point to Brevet Major Jonathan G. Barnard and went to Arlington.[64] Thence, almost daily, he rode over to Washington to complete the tedious labor of settling his accounts.[65]

He left the academy in good condition. Colonel C. C. Chesney of the British army said: "The writer visited West Point during the time of General Lee's charge and saw the institution very thoroughly, passing several days there. He is able, therefore, to testify to its completeness, and the efficiency of the course of study and discipline—never more remarkable, he believes, than at that period."[66] The school was the better for Lee's administration of its affairs, though he worked no revolution, in teaching or in discipline, and was no more, in the annals of the school, than an efficient, diligent superintendent. That he did not change the character of youth is shown by the fact that within a little more than three months after his departure the commandant had to call on the new cadets to use their bayonets on upper class men who interfered with them.[67]

As for the effect of the academy on Lee, it was immensely valuable in giving him added experience in dealing with one type of the young men he was to have under his command six years after he left West Point. He learned how to elicit the best endeavors of these men and how to cope with their weaknesses. Without dreaming that he was doing so, he likewise equipped himself to be a college president: when he went to Washington College he had to apply a different discipline, of course, but it was with a confident understanding of how the head of a school should deal with trustees, faculty, and students. It is hardly probable that he would have accepted the post at Lexington in 1865 if he had not been superintendent of the military academy.

His superintendency gave Lee useful understanding of a few of those who were to be his subordinates or adversaries in battle. He may have acquired no special knowledge of J. J. Reynolds,

---

[63] Lee to Totten, *MS.*, March 24, 1855; *WPLB*, 193.
[64] *Boynton*, 249; *A. G. O., MS.*, S. O., April 12, 1855.
[65] Lee to Totten, *MS.*, June 27, July 21, 1855; *Eng. MSS.*, 1405, 1419.
[66] C. C. Chesney: *Military View of the Recent Campaigns in Virginia*, vol. 1, p. 50, quoted in Bradford, *Lee the American* (cited hereafter as *Bradford*), 17.
[67] *2 Cent. U. S. M. A.*, 110.

assistant professor of philosophy, whom he subsequently encountered in West Virginia,[68] but he must have profited, at the outset of
the Seven Days' Campaign, by what he learned of Fitz John
Porter while that officer was his adjutant at West Point. He may
perhaps have seen enough of Phil Sheridan, in the last year of
that soldier's cadetship, to know what manner of man he was.
His memory of their behavior and standing at the academy was
valuable to Lee, also, in passing on the promotion of young West
Pointers who adhered to the South and served in the Army of
Northern Virginia. It was certainly so in one very important
instance—that of Jeb Stuart.

Beyond this it is not safe to go in assuming that Lee's three
sessions at West Point equipped him, as a Confederate leader, to
read the minds of his antagonists. Most of the cadets of his superintendency were not accounted old enough in 1862–65 to lead the
corps that confronted him. Only twenty-four Northern men who
had been at West Point under Lee became general officers in the
forces directly opposed to him while he was commander of the
Army of Northern Virginia. Most of these twenty-four were only
names to him. Just fourteen Southern cadets of his superintendency, in addition to his son Custis and his nephew Fitz, became
general officers in the army of Lee.[69]

The years as head of the academy added to Lee's professional
equipment, though to an undetermined extent. He had little
time for study because of his administrative duties. Had he sat
in the classes of D. H. Mahan while that professor was lecturing
on the art of war, he would have heard expounded again the
strategy taught in his cadet days, enriched by a better knowledge
of Napoleon and perhaps by some lessons drawn from the Mexican campaigns. There was, at that time, a "Napoleon Club"
among the officers at the academy, with Mahan as chairman and
critic. It held meetings several times a month and discussed papers
prepared by members of the academic board and staff. McClellan
and some others are known to have presented monographs to this
club, but unfortunately, as the records are said to have been

[68] *R. E. Lee, Jr.*, 40–41.
[69] This list was compiled by checking Cullum against Wright's *General Officers of the
Confederate Army* and the biographies in the *Confederate Military History*.

destroyed by fire, it is impossible to state how active a part Lee took in the discussions.[70]

The only present clue to his participation in the studies of the club is to be found in his reading, as attested by his borrowing from the library. During the two years and seven months of his superintendency he drew from the shelves six magazines and forty-eight books, some of the latter in several volumes, and some of them taken out more than once. He got three volumes of fiction, two of travel, and five of poetry, all of them probably for Mrs. Lee or his daughters, inasmuch as he had no taste for novels and scanty time for verse, though he knew more poetry than most soldiers.

On his own account, he got six works on geography (including maps), one on forestry, eight on architecture, five on military law, two on non-military biography, one on French and Spanish grammar, and fifteen on military biography, history, and the science of war. The books on architecture and on forestry doubt-less were to help him in his work of selecting new buildings and setting out trees at the academy. The studies in military law were for use in connection with courts-martial. Most of the others must have represented a review of military operations.

Of the fifteen books specifically related to war, seven concerned Napoleon. His principal study was of Gourgaud's and Montholon's *Mémoires pour servir à l'histoire de France sous Napoléon, écrits à Sainte-Hélène*, though he also used O'Meara and the *Memoirs* of the Duke of Rovigo. These are not now the most-esteemed books on Napoleon's campaigns, but they were, at the time, among the best that had been issued. The volumes Lee most frequently procured from the library dealt with Napoleon's Italian campaign of 1796 and with the Egyptian operations. There is every reason to assume that he read these volumes carefully and that he became reasonably conversant with Napoleon's military career through 1801. He seems also to have studied in detail the Russian campaign of the Corsican. In the editions he probably used, one of the volumes contained Napoleon's brief notes on

[70]Eben Swift: "The Military Education of Robert E. Lee," *loc. cit.*, 107–8. It is quite possible that some of the papers of the "Napoleon Club" may yet be unearthed in the records at West Point. Among them may be one by Lee.

353

Jomini's *Traité des Grands Opérations Militaires,* and Napoleon's lengthy notes on *Considérations sur l'Art de la Guerre,* originally printed in Paris in 1816. These latter notes are almost a volume in themselves, and though dictated by Napoleon on the work of an officer he did not admire, they include many of the Emperor's most discerning observations on defensive war.[71] Lee may have been particularly interested in this work because it was by an officer of engineers, and it is possible that one comment by Napoleon, in particular, may have found lodgement in his memory. This reads as follows:

"But must a capital be defended by covering it directly, or by the defending army's barring itself up in an intrenched camp in the rear of the invader? The first method is the safest: It allows of disputing the passage of rivers, and defiles, even of creating field positions; of receiving all the troops in the interior as reinforcements, whilst the enemy's forces would be insensibly decreasing. It would be a very bad measure to let oneself be shut up in an intrenched camp; running the risk of being forced, or at least blockaded, and of being reduced to cut one's way sword in hand to procure bread and forage. Four or five hundred wagons a day are required for supplying an army of 100,000 men with provisions. The invading army, being superior in infantry, cavalry, and artillery, by one-third, would prevent the convoys from arriving; and, without blockading them hermetically, as fortresses are blockaded, it would render all access to them so difficult, that there would be a famine in the camp.

"There remains a third way: to manœuvre incessantly, without submitting to be driven back on the capital which it is meant to defend or shut up in an intrenched camp in the rear. For this purpose it is necessary to have a good army, good generals, and a good commander-in-chief. In general, the idea of covering a capital, or any point whatever, by flank marches, carries with it

---

[71] It is not possible to say which edition of Gourgaud and Montholon was used by Lee, because four were listed in the catalogue of 1853. His withdrawals from the library, if correctly recorded, indicate that he may have used two editions. Other things being even, however, it is probably safe to assume that he used principally the English edition (Catalogue no. 4628), published by H. Colburn & Co., London, 1823-24. Major E. E. Farman, librarian of West Point, has very graciously checked these items for the writer.

the necessity of detaching troops, and the inconveniences attached to all division of force, in the face of a superior army." [72]

It is easy to trace the parallel between what Napoleon here advised and what Lee undertook in the campaign from the Rapidan to the James in 1864. Analogies between his operation and those of Napoleon in 1796 readily suggest themselves. The probability that Lee studied carefully the Egyptian campaign might be explained by a natural curiosity to see how the Emperor met a situation similar in some superficial respects, at least, to that which Scott faced landing in Mexico.

Lee probably gave some study, also, to Hannibal's campaign, through Rollin, and to Cæsar's battles as related in the pages of Jacob Abbott's biography, which was then a comparatively new book (1849). Lee's use of Russian and Turkish maps would indicate, further, that he followed at least some of the early movements of the Crimean War.

After his study of Napoleon, Lee's major military reading at West Point seems to have been of the American Revolution. He twice had from the library Sparks's life of Benedict Arnold, and he used, likewise, Sparks's sketches of John Stark, Charles B. Brown, Richard Montgomery, and Ethan Allen, which together form the first volume of the *Library of American Biography*. He probably was interested in the third volume of the *National Portrait Gallery* because it contained a sketch and an engraving of his father.[78] He twice drew from the library the second volume of the *Field of Mars,* a British encyclopædia of battles, naval and military, "particularly of Great Britain and her allies from the ninth century to the present period." The volume contained brief, alphabetical accounts, with dispatches and reports, of many of the most famous battles of history from the letter M to the end of the alphabet. Most of the battles of the southern campaign in which Lee's father had a part were treated in this volume. Yorktown was not included, as the book seems to have been printed

[72] *Memoirs of the History of France During the Reign of Napoleon,* vol. 4, pp. 304-5 (London edition, 1823).
[78] He declined, however, to be represented in a later volume of this work (Lee to John Livingston, *MS.,* Oct. 20, 1854; *WPLB,* 145).

in 1781 before the news of the final disaster of the Revolution reached Britain. *The Field of Mars* included, also, an essay on fortification, though this advanced no theories with which Lee was not already familiar.[74]

Thus it will be seen that Lee's studies were not profound, in any instance, but that his reading of Napoleon probably was critical and detailed. His use of Kausler's *Atlas* would indicate that he studied the terrain of Napoleon's great movements as closely as he could.[75]

The full list of Lee's withdrawals from the library at West Point during his superintendency, as given in the records, is as follows:

> *Field of Mars*, vol. 2.
> Kausler's *Atlas and Text*, 2 vols.
> Brown's *Domestic Architecture*.
> London's *Architecture*.
> Montholon's *Memoirs*, vols. 1 and 2.
> Gourgaud: *Mémoires de Napoléon*, vols. 1 and 2.
> *Mémoires du duc de Rovigo*, vols. 1 and 2.
> Montholon's *Memoirs*, vols. 3 and 4.
> Montholon's *Memoirs*, vols. 1 and 2.
> *Pickwick Papers*.
> Gourgaud: *Mémoires de Napoléon*, vol. 2.
> Hood's *Up the Rhine*, 2 vols.
> Hood's *Poems*.
> Ranlett's *Architecture*, vol. 2.
> *Putnam's Monthly* for February, April, and June, 1853.
> *Putnam's Monthly* for September, 1853.
> Hood's *Up the Rhine*, vol. 1.
> *Putnam's Monthly* for November, 1853.
> Hood's *Prose and Verse*.
> Holmes: *Poems*.
> Sobrino: *Grammaire Espagnole et Française*.
> Rollin's *Ancient History*, vol. 1.

[74] *The Field of Mars, Being an Alphabetical Digestion of the Principal Naval and Military Engagements, in Europe, Asia, Africa, and America, Particularly of Great Britain and Her Allies from the Ninth Century to the Present Period. . . . Embellished with Maps, Charts, Plans, and Views of Battles. . . .* London . . . MDCCLXXXI (vol. 2, M to Z).

[75] F. G. F. Kausler: *Atlas des plus mémorables batailles, combats et siéges des temps anciens, du moyen âge et de l'âge moderne en 200 feuilles* . . . (Carlsrouhe et Fribourg, 1831). This atlas contains no maps relating to America. For operations in the new world Lee probably used S. A. Mitchell: *A New Universal Atlas* . . . (Philadelphia, 1848).

Noble Deeds of American Women.
Lowell's *Poems,* 2 vols.
Atlas of New York.
Sparks's *American Biography,* vol. 3.
National Portrait Gallery, vol. 3.
Sparks's *American Biography,* vol. 1.
[A. W. Kinglake's] *Eothen.*
Irving's *Bracebridge Hall.*
Abbott's *History of Cæsar.*
Mitchell's *Atlas.*
Map of Orange County.
Kiebert's *Map of Turkey,* 4 sheets.
Cross's *Military Laws.*
Field of Mars, vol. 2.
Ranlett's *Cottage Architecture,* vol. 2.
Ranlett's *Cottage Architecture,* vol. 1.
Sparks's *American Biography,* vol. 3.
Carte de la Russie Européene, nos. 10 and 11.
Putnam's Monthly for August, 1854.
Downing's *Country Houses.*
Memoirs of the Duchesse d'Abrantes.
O'Meara's *Napoleon at St. Helena,* 2 vols.
[F. A. Michaux]: *North American Sylva,* vols. 1 to 3.
Cross's *Military Laws.*
Hood's *Prose and Verse.*
London's *Cottage Architecture.*
Gwitt's *Encyclopædia of Architecture.*
Kennedy on Courts Martial.
O'Brien's *Military Laws.*
DeHart on Courts Martial.[76]

In addition to reading from the shelves at West Point, Lee was building up a small military library of his own. It is not possible to say when he bought the various items of his collection, except as the time of publication sets the dates, but prior to the war he possessed, among others, these works:

Biot: *Traité Elémentaire d'Astronomie Physique* . . . 1841.
Carrion l'Cisas: *Essai sur l'Histoire Générale de l'Art Militaire,* . . . 2 vols., 1824.
Cormontaingne: *Mémorial pour la Défense des Places* . . . 1822.
Cormontaingne: *Mémorial pour l'Attaque des Places* . . . 1815.

[76] For this list the writer is indebted to Miss Margery Bedinger, former librarian of West Point. In addition to these books, Lee in 1855 read, for the second time at least, Suchet's *Mémoires* of the Peninsular War (*Markie Letters,* 51-52).

Emy: *Cours Elémentaire de Fortification* . . . 1834.

Fallot: *Cours d'art Militaire ou Leçons sur l'art Militaire et les Fortifications,* editions of 1839, 1841, 1844, and 1846.

Fonscolombe: *Résumé Historique des Progrès de l'Art Militaire* . . . 1854.

Jomini: *Précis de l'Art de la Guerre* . . . 1838.

Laisne: *Aide-Mémoire Portatif à l'Usage des Officiers du Génie* . . . 1840.

Merkes: *Résumé Générale concernant les Différentes Formes et les Diverses Applications des Redoubtes Casematées* . . . 1845.

Noizet-de-Saint-Paul: *Traité Complet de Fortification.*

Perrot: *Le Livre de Guerre* . . . 1, 1832.

de Pupdt: *Mémorial de l'Officier du Génie,* 7 vols.[77]

Most of these, it will be noted, are technical treatises for the engineer, and probably were acquired while Lee was serving with the board of engineers. None of them, however, contains any notes or marked passages in the handwriting of their owner.[78]

Men as well as books enlarged Lee's horizon while at West Point. The staff of the academy listed so many Southerners that some jealousies had been aroused, but it included men from most of the Northern states. Lee was a frequent guest in the home of Gouverneur Kemble, at Cold Springs, N. Y., and there he probably met ex-President Van Buren, his old commander General Scott, George Bancroft, and others of like distinction.[79] He did not need these contacts to give him an understanding of the Federal point of view. Having cut ditches in Georgia mud banks, run the Ohio-Michigan boundary, blasted rock from the bed of the Mississippi, repaired casemates in New York, served on Scott's staff in Mexico, and driven piles in Baltimore harbor, he already had an appreciation of the Union and of the elements that went into the making of it. Yet, while he was superintendent, he heard men of culture,

---

[77] These and other books formerly the property of General Lee are now in the Library of the Virginia Military Institute. The writer is indebted to Colonel William Couper of that school for a careful collation of them.

[78] Except on the title page of the volume of plates for O'Connor's *Art of War,* which was the copy he used at West Point. This note reads:
"Minute tactics learned from books which treat on the various arms
  General tactics, from duties of arms
  Strategy, from experience and criticisms on Campaigns and battles
  Staff duties arise from the march and operations of an army
  2. Kinds executive and administrative
  Military and civil duties of each."

[79] *Keyes,* 69; Marian Gouverneur: *As I Remember,* 126.

candor, and information discuss Napoleon's campaigns, the Crimean War, the sharpened sectional issues of slavery and states' rights, and a thousand other subjects that made for a national, indeed an international, mind. He had little to say on politics himself, but his justice toward the North long before this time had impressed Erasmus D. Keyes, a brilliant brother-officer: "Of all the hundreds of Southern men with whom I have been intimate," Keyes recorded, "[George H. Thomas] and Robert E. Lee were the fairest in their judgment of Northern men." [80] Keyes recorded further: "I will not deny that the presence of Lee, and the multiform graces that clustered around him, oftentimes oppressed me, though I never envied him, and I doubt if he ever excited envy in any man. All his accomplishments and alluring virtues appeared natural in him, and he was free from the anxiety, distrust and awkwardness that attend a sense of inferiority, unfriendly discipline and censure." [81]

[80] *Keyes,* 166.   [81] *Keyes,* 205.

CHAPTER XXI

EDUCATION BY COURT-MARTIAL

On April 12, 1855, Lee received orders to repair to Louisville, Ky., and to take command of the new 2d Cavalry, as its colonel was not ready to report for duty.[1] It was the first time since the Mexican War that he had left home without the assurance that the family would speedily join him at his new station. Except for the two years of the war with Mexico and the inspection tour in Florida he had not been separated from Mrs. Lee and the children for so much as three months continuously since 1840, when he had been relieved from work on the Mississippi. Now there was no hope of renewing the happy life of Arlington in some pleasant Eastern city. The 2d Cavalry had been established for frontier duty. The only question was where it would be placed. Whether to Texas, to the plains, or to California, Lee had to go with it. That was one heavy price he had to pay for his new commission as lieutenant colonel. So, without ado or long farewell, he left beloved Arlington, whither the family had returned from West Point.[2] Following the oft-travelled route he reached Louisville, and on April 20 assumed direct command of troops for the first time in his military career of twenty-six years.[3]

As the establishment of the two cavalry regiments had been at the instance of the military authorities, in the face of stiff opposition,[4] Secretary Davis had been put on his mettle to provide competent commanders and good recruits. Major E. V. Sumner, who well merited the honor, had been transferred from the 2d Dragoons and had been made colonel of the 1st Cavalry. Joseph E. Johnston had been named lieutenant colonel. In the 2d Cavalry, with Albert Sidney Johnston as colonel and Lee as second in command, W. J. Hardee and William H. Emory were com-

[1] *MS. A. G. O.*, vol. 11, S. O., 64.
[2] *Cf.* Lee to S. Cooper, *MS.*, April 2, 1855; *A. G. O.* For Lee's expressions of love for Arlington, see *Markie Letters*, 42, 45.
[3] *Fitz Lee*, 56.   [4] *Fitz Lee*, 52–53.

missioned major. Emory served only a short time, whereupon Davis offered the post to Braxton Bragg, and when he declined, the secretary named George H. Thomas, one of Lee's associates for a part of his superintendency at West Point. Among the captains were Earl van Dorn, E. Kirby Smith, and George Stoneman. Charles W. Field and John B. Hood were lieutenants. Altogether it was a roster of picked officers.[5] One troop of the regiment was recruited from each of eight states and one contained men from many states.[6]

Almost before Lee was able to form an estimate of his brother officers and his men, the 2d was ordered to Jefferson Barracks, Saint Louis, Mo. Thither Lee went, and soon found himself temporarily in command as ranking officer at the station.[7] He went to work vigorously to drill his troopers, not a little provoked when requisitioned clothing failed to arrive for two months. "Yesterday, at muster," he confided to Mrs. Lee, "I found one of the late arrivals in a dirty, tattered shirt and pants, with a white hat and shoes, with other garments to match. I asked him why he did not put on clean clothes. He said he had none. I asked him if he could not wash and mend those. He said he had nothing else to put on. I then told him immediately after muster to go down to the river, wash his clothes, and sit on the bank and watch the passing steam-boats till they dried, and then mend them. This morning at inspection he looked as proud as possible, stood in the position of a soldier with his little fingers on the seams of his pants, his beaver cocked back, and his toes sticking through his shoes, but his skin and solitary two garments clean. He grinned very happily at my compliments." [8]

Lee made the best of dull routine and separation from his family. He wrote often, cheerfully, and sometimes as though he were passing on to his children the philosophy with which he consoled himself. "We make a great deal of our own happiness and misery in this world," he told Agnes, "and we can do more for ourselves

[5] *Ibid.*, 53–54; *Long*, 74–75, 77. Fitz Lee later became a lieutenant in the regiment; (1 *S. H. S. P.*, 100.)

[6] In the reorganization of the army, when the dragoon and cavalry regiments were given one series of numbers, the 2d Cavalry became the 5th. (Voorhees Richeson: "History of the Fifth Cavalry," *U. S. Army Recruiting News*, Sept. 15, 1929, p. 8.)

[7] 1 *Cullum*, 421.

[8] Lee to Mrs. Lee, July 1, 1855; Jones, *L. and L.*, 70.

than others can for us. You must expect discomforts and annoyances all through life. No place or position is secure from them, and you must make up your mind to meet with them and bear them." [9]

He had need of these maxims very soon after he inscribed them. For he speedily got his first unpleasant dose of what was to become the irksome physic of his changed military life. This was court-martial service, which during the next five years was to compel him to ride hundreds of miles, and then to sit for tedious hours while witnesses testified and advocates argued. The War Department did not intend to waste talents: Both he and Albert Sidney Johnston were detailed to leave their regiment in the belief that its ranks would be slow in filling.[10] They were ordered across the state of Missouri to Fort Leavenworth, on the edge of Kansas, there to hear charges brought against several officers.[11]

The court convened on September 24, 1855, and when it was adjourned, Lee was sent to Fort Riley, farther westward in Kansas, to sit in judgment on a surgeon who was alleged to have abandoned his post of duty in the midst of an epidemic. It was a horrible affair, with a grisly record of fifty-nine deaths, seven of them in a single day, among a helpless garrison. Lee obligingly wrote out the more touching details for Mrs. Lee, including the demise of Mrs. Lewis Armistead, whose husband later fell in Pickett's charge at Gettysburg. "A soldier," Lee concluded, speaking in part for Armistead and in part, no doubt, for himself, "a soldier has a hard life and but little consideration." [12]

The courts-martial consumed so much time that the regiment, which now had 35 officers and 675 men, set out on October 27, without Lee or Major G. H. Thomas, to ride to Texas, there to relieve six companies of the 2d Dragoons who were ordered to the West.[13] When Lee at last was free at Fort Riley, he got still

[9] Lee to Agnes Lee, MS., Aug. 11, 1855. For the interesting letter of which this is an extract, the writer is indebted to John Stewart Bryan of Richmond.
[10] W. P. Johnston: *Life of Albert Sidney Johnston*, 186.
[11] *MS. A. G. O.*, vol. 11, S. O., 134, July 26, 1855.
[12] Lee to Mrs. Lee, Nov. 5, 1855, *Fitz Lee*, 57–58. *Cf.* Lee to Markie Williams, Sept. 16, 1853: ". . . I can advise no young man to enter the Army. The same application, the same self-denial, the same endurance, in any other profession, will advance him faster and farther" (*Markie Letters*, 37.)
[13] *Fitz Lee*, 58; *Ex. Docs., 1st sess., 34th Cong.* vol. 1, part 2, pp. 4, 131, 144.

another assignment to court-martial duty, but this time he was lucky: the court was held at Carlisle Barracks, Pennsylvania, early in January, so he had opportunity of coming East and of seeing his family again.[14] His stay was brief, and from Carlisle Barracks he was ordered to West Point for his fourth court-martial in as many months.[15] Hardly was he back home from West Point when orders arrived for him to join his regiment in Texas. Leaving on February 12, 1856, he went by steamer to Galveston, where he arrived on March 2. A long journey inland brought him on March 6 to San Antonio. In that familiar city, which had grown appreciably in the ten years since he had been there, he had to wait two weeks before he could set out for regimental head-quarters, which were located temporarily at Fort Mason, one hundred miles from San Antonio.[16] Five days' fast riding north-ward brought him to the fort, where Albert Sidney Johnston welcomed him.

On March 27, 1856, Johnston assigned Lee to command the two squadrons of the regiment then at Camp Cooper, 170 miles north of Fort Mason. At this outpost, which he was to call his "Texas home" for nineteen months, Lee arrived on April 9, relieving Major Hardee.[17] The camp was part of the Comanche reserve, on the clear fork of the Brazos River, 35 miles from the point of its junction with the main stream. Snakes were everywhere. Wolves prowled and howled at night. West of the camp a wild country stretched away to the "Staked Plains." The courses of some of the nearby rivers had not been mapped. Even to the eastward, on the road back to civilization, were large areas of country of which no one had full knowledge. North of the camp the Comanches roamed and hunted, always ready to send an arrow after the white man. Downstream from the camp were the lodges of a part of the tribe, under Chief Catumseh, whom the government was trying to "humanize," as Lee put it, with free

[14] MS. A. G. O., vol. 11, S. O., 235.
[15] MS. A. G O., vol. 12, S. O., 2. The West Point court-martial assembled on Jan. 12, 1856.
[16] Fort Mason, which does not appear on many maps, was north, 20 degrees west from San Antonio, between the Llano and the San Saba Rivers. The best map of the territory is that made in 1857 and published in the *Atlas of the Official Records*, Plate LIV. This map, however, does not show Camp Cooper.
[17] His movements are recorded in a meagre memorandum diary he kept while in the cavalry. Its principal entries are republished in *Mason*, 53–55. It is cited hereafter as *Diary*, with the page reference to *Mason*.

clothing and food. These Indians professed friendship, but they
were not trusted. Lee's impressions of them were anything
but favorable. Three days after he had reached Camp Cooper he
wrote Mrs. Lee: "Catumseh has been to see me, and we have had
a talk, very tedious on his part, and very sententious on mine. I
hailed him as a friend, as long as his conduct and that of his tribe
deserved it, but would meet him as an enemy the first moment
he failed to keep his word. . . . Yesterday I returned his visit,
and remained a short time at his Lodge. He informed me that he
had six wives. They are riding in and out of camp all day, their
paint and 'ornaments' rendering them more hideous than nature
made them, and the whole tribe is extremely uninteresting. . . ."[18]
He did not put himself out to conciliate them. When he was supposed to go through the ceremonial of disrobing, Lee contented
himself with taking off his necktie.[19] "These people give a world
of trouble to man and horse," he wrote not long afterwards, "and,
poor creatures, they are not worth it." [20]

Indians or no Indians, it was Lee's nature to make the best of his
surroundings. There were no buildings at Camp Cooper and no
lumber with which to construct any. He had to live in a tent and
to store all his belongings there. Like most good campaigners,
he had brought some chickens with him in a coop and he sought
to make them as comfortably productive as he could. In a letter
to his youngest daughter, he told her about them. "I have only
seven hens and some days I get seven eggs. Having no plank,
I have been obliged to make them a house of twigs. I planted
four posts in the ground and bored holes in each, three feet from
the ground, in which I inserted poles for the floor, and around
which were woven the branches that formed it. There are so
many reptiles in this country that you cannot keep fowls on the
ground. The sides and tops were formed in the same way, and
the whole is covered with branches with their leaves on, which
makes a shady house but furnishes little protection against rain.
Soldier hens, however, must learn not to mind rain. I converted
the coop they came in, into nests. They pick up so much corn
among the horses that I do not have to feed them, and they seem

---

[18] Lee to Mrs. Lee, April 12, 1856; *Mason*, 54.
[19] *Elliott MSS.*, May 24, 1856.
[20] Lee to Mrs. Lee, Aug. 25, 1856; Jones, *L. and L.*, 80.

quite domesticated. I have no cat, nor have I heard of one in this country. You will have to send me a kitten in your next letter. The Indians have none, as there are so many wolves prowling around that they frighten away all the mice. My rattlesnake, my only pet, is dead. He grew sick and would not eat his frogs, etc., and died one night." [21]

Lee's cheerfulness did not keep him from seeing the hardships and the futility of the life he was leading. The familiar sense of frustration, which had disappeared during the Mexican War and had not often reappeared at West Point, showed itself once again. He wrote an old friend: "Tell Robert I cannot advise him to enter the army. It is a hard life, and he can never rise to any military eminence by serving in the army." [22]

Only one professional interest was offered Lee at Camp Cooper: the War Department considered it desirable to locate a fort at some strategic point in that area and it designated Lee to suggest a site. For a time he made long rides almost daily to study the terrain and to find the most desirable location. Often he was attended by one of his lieutenants, John B. Hood, who had graduated from West Point during the first year of Lee's superintendency. Lee was fond of Hood, who was a most lovable young man, and he talked with him of many things besides fortification and drills. Perhaps he had an idea that Hood might be tempted to marry some girl of the frontier, simply as an escape from loneliness and he told him very earnestly, "Never marry unless you can do so into a family that will enable your children to feel proud of both sides of the house." [23]

The search for a good site for a fort did not require many days. Monotony of the darkest and dullest descended again, but, like most woes, it was relieved at length. Indians had been carrying on depredations on the edge of the Staked Plains and in the vicinity of Fort Chadbourne, presumably under the leadership of a chief named Sanaco. The department had determined to pursue them and, if possible, track them down. Lee was placed in charge of one expedition against them and was given four squadrons of

---

[21] Lee to Mildred Lee, *MS.,* April 23, 1856. For a copy of this unique letter, the writer is indebted to Mrs. C. W. Schaadt, of Richmond, Va.
[22] *Elliott MSS.,* May 24, 1856.
[23] J. B. Hood, *Advance and Retreat* (cited hereafter as *Hood*), 7–8.

cavalry that were to be collected, one from Camp Cooper, one from Fort Mason, and two from Fort Chadbourne. Leaving his own headquarters on June 13, 1856, Lee and his troopers spent four days marching to Fort Chadbourne, which was about ninety miles to the southwest. Finding that the troopers from Fort Mason had already arrived, Lee set out on June 18 with the four squadrons, the wagons, the guides, and the Indian interpreter, Jim Shaw. He rode northwestward, making for the headwaters of the nearer branches of the Colorado and the Brazos Rivers, in what is now Fisher County. Four days of slow marching with the wagons failed to uncover any signs of Indians. Smoke which had been supposed to come from Indian camps was found to be from a prairie fire. A sweep on an extended front was next made to the northeast and then toward Double Mountain, in the present Kent County. Indian trails were encountered, but all of them were pronounced by the guides to be old. "The water was salt," to quote the language of Lee's report, "the grass poor, and the country intersected by innumerable and almost impassable ravines." Lee accordingly determined to send back the wagons to the clear fork of the Brazos, and to make a farther scout westward. The men were to carry seven days' rations with them but no tents.

The first day the column was on the march it struck the trail of a small band of Indians, and that evening saw smoke rising to the westward, apparently some fifteen miles away. The next morning Lee divided his party and sent Major van Dorn ahead, with Captain O'Hara in support on van Dorn's right. With the second squadron Lee struck for the main course of the Brazos reasoning that if the Indians were retreating to the north they would make for that stream. Nothing was heard that day or the next either of the Indians or of the troopers from whom Lee's own little party was now separated. On the second day Lee came to the source of the north branch of the Brazos. "Halting the squadron," he stated in his report, "with a detachment of 10 men from each Comp^y under Capt. Smith, I crossed a wide high ridge 8 miles in extent, and reached the valley of a stream, the character of whose soil, growth and water differed entirely from any belonging to the Brazos. The stream appeared to take its rise among some high hills or mountains about 20 miles to the west, and wound through a wide valley running to the N.E. for about 25 miles, when it joined a larger valley from the west. At their junction was a high bluff or hill. The water of the stream was fresh, and I supposed it to be the Wichita."

No fresh trails of Indians were to be seen. The country along the upper Brazos was void of game and had very poor grass. "I saw nothing," Lee said, "to attract Indians to the country, or to induce them to remain." Lee consequently decided to turn back. On the second day he rejoined van Dorn and found that the major and his men had met a party of four Indians, had killed two of them and had captured a third, a woman. The fourth member of the party had escaped. This was the only reward for hard days in the hot sun—and Lee had missed even that brush!

The 4th of July, on the long journey back to camp, was spent in a thirty-mile ride, and ended on a branch of the Brazos, ended, as Lee wrote, "under my blanket, which was elevated on four sticks driven in the ground as a sunshade." He thought of Arlington and of the speech Mr. Custis always delivered on that day to celebrating friends. In Lee's bivouac, "the sun was fiery hot. The atmosphere like the blast from a hot-air furnace, the water salt; still my feelings for my country were as ardent, my faith in her future as true, and my hopes for her advancement as unabated, as if called forth under more propitious circumstances." [24]

Continuing the journey toward camp, Lee sent the four squadrons in a final sweep down the adjacent rivers, in separate columns, and on July 16 brought his men together again on the Concha River, at the crossing of the trail from Fort Chadbourne to Fort Mason. All the detachments had the same report: no Indians had been located, and no recent tracks had been observed. Two days later Lee broke up the expedition and sent each squadron back to its station. He reached Camp Cooper on July 23, after an absence of forty days. The distance covered by all the units had been 1600 miles, and the results had been negligible. He came back convinced that the Indians did not inhabit the country on the upper waters of the Colorado and Brazos, and simply passed

[24] Lee to Mrs. Lee, Aug. 4, 1856; *Mason*, 56.

through on their raids. No opportunity was given him for justifying or demonstrating this conclusion. His first long scout into
the Indian country proved to be his last.[25]

The dry hot weather continued after Lee's return to Camp
Cooper. The vegetable gardens dried up. The "clear fork" of the
Brazos ceased to deserve the name and became a chain of stag-
nant pools.[26] Lee tried to keep cheerful, but was depressed by
the heat and by the arrival of news that his sister Mildred, Mrs.
Edward Vernon Childe, who was only forty-five, had died in
Paris. He wrote of her: "The news came to me very unexpectedly,
and in the course of nature I might never have anticipated it, as
indeed I had never realized that she might precede me on the
unexplored journey upon which we are hastening. Though
parted from her for years, with little expectation but of a tran-
sient reunion in this life, this terrible and sudden separation has
not been the less distressing because it was distant and unlooked
for. It has put an end to all hope of our meeting in this world.
It has cut short my early wishes and daily yearnings, and so
vividly does she live in my imagination and affection that I
cannot realize she only exists in my memory. I pray that her life
has but just begun, and I trust that our merciful God only so
suddenly and early snatched her away because he saw that it was
the fittest moment to take her to himself. May a pure and eternal
life be hers, and may we all live so that when we die it may be
open to us." [27]

Soon after the tidings of Mrs. Childe's death, there came orders
for the detail that Lee must by this time have learned to expect
along with changing weather and hard fare: once again he was
summoned to court-martial duty—not at Fort Mason or Fort
Chadbourne, but 700 miles away, on the Rio Grande, at Ringgold Barracks. The assignment meant weary days of riding across
Texas, and the time was rather unfortunate, because there were
reports of the presence of Indians south of Camp Cooper, with the
possibility of an affray.[28] Lee made preparations to meet the
Indians, and then, on September 2, he had to leave Camp Cooper

[25] MS. A. G. O., Lee's report of July 24, 1856. There is a brief summary of the expedition in Lee to Mrs. Lee, July 28, 1856; Mason, 55–56.
[26] Lee to Mrs. Lee, Aug. 4, 1856; Mason, 56.
[27] Lee to Mrs. Lee, Aug. 11, 1856; Jones, L. and L., 80.
[28] Lee to Mrs. Lee, Aug. 25, 1856; Mason, 56–57.

in the expectation of being absent two and a half or three months. The journey turned out to be somewhat less unpleasant than Lee had anticipated. He was twenty-seven days on the road, which he estimated at 730 miles. One day he encountered high water and had all his effects thoroughly wetted, but he enjoyed the company of his friend Major George H. Thomas, who met him at Fort Mason, and for at least a part of the way he was not so completely in the wilderness as he was in the vicinity of his own station.

At Ringgold Barracks, where he arrived on September 28, 1856, he found a number of field officers and one of his classmates, Caleb Sibley. Another friend of the old days at West Point, Captain James A. J. Bradford, was on the court-martial.[29] The company was somewhat extensive and included a number of ladies. Work, however, was tedious, and the principal case before the court was protracted by the presence of two Texas lawyers, "accustomed," as Lee told Mrs. Lee, "to the tricks and stratagems of special pleadings, which, of no other avail, absorb time and stave off the question." Then, too, life was ruffled somewhat by the tone of at least one newspaper received at the barracks. A military writer had attacked Secretary Davis in *The New York Times,* and the same unknown author had criticised the new regiments, demanding that they be disbanded. Lee was resentful. He defended Davis and said on his own account, "They may suit themselves in everything relating to my services, and whenever they tell me they are no longer required they will not be obtruded on them." [30] In a somewhat different spirit, but with a certain resignation, he had answered Mrs. Lee the previous month when she had written him about the prospective appointment of a new brigadier general. A petition to the President, asking for Lee's promotion to that grade had been circulated the previous spring among Virginia public men and had been numerously signed. It had set out Lee's "life-long services in peace and war, his brilliant and pre-eminent distinctions won upon the field." [31] Perhaps it was to this that Mrs. Lee referred. Lee had answered:

"We are all in the hands of a kind God, who will do for us

[29] *Diary*, in *Mason*, 57; Lee to Mrs. Lee, Oct. 3, 1856; Jones, *L. and L.*, 81.
[30] Lee to Mrs. Lee, Oct. 24, 1856; *Fitz Lee*, 62.
[31] *MS. A. G. O.*, March 6, 1856; "Rec^d. (A. G. O.) Sept. 23, 1856."

what is best, and more than we deserve, and we have only to endeavor to deserve more, and to do our duty to him and ourselves. May we all deserve His mercy, His care, and protection. Do not give yourself any anxiety about the appointment of the brigadier. If it is on my account that you feel an interest in it, I beg you will discard it from your thoughts. You will be sure to be disappointed; nor is it right to indulge improper and useless hopes. It besides looks like presumption to expect it." [32]

On October 30, 1856,[33] the court adjourned to Fort Brown, on the site of the present Brownsville, near the mouth of the Rio Grande. Thither Lee went—by boat for part of the way—and there he landed on November 4.[34] He was now in closer touch with the outside world, and he had already made friends among the families of the other officers, who, like himself, had to travel about to form the courts-martial. His duties were not heavy. He had opportunity of visiting Matamoras, on the Mexican side of the river, and almost daily he walked along the banks of the Rio Grande, watching the birds and observing the rich flora.[35] Soon he recovered his old poise and wrote home in better spirits:

"The time is approaching when I trust many of you will be assembled around the family hearth at dear Arlington another Christmas. Though absent, my heart will be in the midst of you, and I shall enjoy in imagination and memory all that is going on. May nothing occur to mar or cloud the family fireside, and may each be able to look back with pride and pleasure at his deeds of the past year, and with confidence and hope to that in prospect. I can do nothing but hope and pray for you all. . . . Things seem to be going as usual in the states. Mr. Buchanan, it appears, is to be our next President. I hope he will be able to extinguish fanaticism North and South, cultivate love for the country and Union, and restore harmony between the different sections." [36]

During the week before Christmas he scoured the poor shops

---

[32] Lee to Mrs. Lee, Sept. 1, 1856; Jones, *L. and L.*, 81.

[33] The diary (*Mason*, 57) gave the date as Sept. 30, but as there exist letters from Ringgold Barracks dated as late as Oct. 24 (*Fitz Lee*, 62), the correct date doubtless was Oct. 30.

[34] *Mason*, 57.　　　　　　　　　　　　[35] *Jones*, 164–65.

[36] Lee to Mrs. Lee, undated, December, 1856; part in Jones, *L. and L.*, 81–82, and part in *Mason*, 58.

of Fort Brown for presents, and on Christmas morning he had something for every officer's child in the garrison, though he had known them only a few weeks and expected to leave them soon. He went to church and then to dinner with Major and Mrs. George H. Thomas. "I thought of you all and wished to be with you," he wrote home. "[My day] was gratefully but silently passed." [37]

His own best Christmas gift was a full file of his Alexandria newspaper, the most recent issue only three weeks old. This reached him by a steamer that docked during the holidays. In writing to his wife of this happy arrival, Lee set down for the first time, as far as is known, his reflections on the slavery question that was then inflaming sectional hate. He had participated in the discussions among the officers at West Point during his superintendency; while he was on court-martial duty at Fort Leavenworth he may have seen at first hand some of the passions aroused in "bleeding Kansas"; he had been in contact with slavery all his life, though he had never owned more than some half-dozen slaves,[38] and they had probably been inherited or given him by Mr. Custis. He had believed steadfastly in gradual emancipation,[39] and had sent to Liberia such of his servants as wished to go.[40] But of all he thought and said on a subject that puzzled open-minded Southerners, nothing of any consequence remains prior to this letter, written about seven weeks after the first national election in which the Republican party had presented a candidate:

"The steamer also brought the President's message to Cong; & the reports of the various heads of Depts; the proceedings of Cong: &c &c. So that we are now assured, that the Govt: is in operation, & the Union in existence, not that we had any fears to

[37] Lee to Mrs. Lee, Dec. 27, 1856; Jones, *L. and L.,* 83.

[38] There are no references in any of Lee's letters to slaves of his own and until the rediscovery of his will in the records of Rockbridge County, Virginia, it was not positively known that he ever held any servants in his own name. That document, written in 1846, showed that he then owned a Negro woman Nancy and her children, who were at the White House plantation. He directed that after his death they be "liberated as soon as it can be done to their advantage and that of others" (*Rockbridge County Will Books,* 1870).

[39] So Rooney Lee told Reverend David Macrae; *cf.* his *Americans at Home* (cited hereafter as *Macrae*), I, 163.

[40] Lee's interview with Reverend John Leyburn, 30 *Century Magazine,* 167. See *infra,* Volume IV. *Cf.* the "Saunders interview" in *R. E. Lee, Jr.,* 231.

the Contrary, but it is Satisfactory always to have facts to go on. They restrain Supposition & Conjecture, Confirm faith, & bring Contentment: I was much pleased with the President's message & the report of the Sec^y of War, the only two documents that have reached us entire. Of the others synopsis [sic] have only arrived. The views of the Pres: of the Systematic & progressive efforts of certain people of the North, to interfere with & change the domestic institutions of the South, are truthfully & faithfully expressed.[41] The Consequences of their plans & purposes are also clearly set forth, & they must also be aware, that their object is both unlawful & entirely foreign to them & their duty; for which they are irresponsible & unaccountable; & Can only be accomplished by *them* through the agency of a Civil & Servile war. In this enlightened age, there are few I believe, but what will acknowledge, that slavery as an institution, is a moral & political evil in any Country. It is useless to expatiate on its disadvantages. I think it however a greater evil to the white than to the black race, & while my feelings are strongly enlisted in behalf of the latter, my sympathies are more strong for the former. The blacks are immeasurably better off here than in Africa, morally, socially & physically. The painful discipline they are undergoing, is necessary for their instruction as a race, & I hope will prepare & lead them to better things. How long their subjugation may be necessary is known & ordered by a wise Merciful Providence. Their emancipation will sooner result from the mild & melting influence of Christianity, than the storms & tempests of fiery Controversy. This influence though slow, is sure. The doctrines & miracles of our Saviour have required nearly two thousand years, to Convert but a small part of the human race, & even among Christian nations, what gross errors still exist! While we see the Course of the final abolition of human Slavery is onward, & we give it the aid of our prayers & all justifiable means in our power, we must leave the progress as well as the result in his hands who sees the end; who Chooses to work by slow influences; & with whom two thousand years are but as a Single day. Although the Abolitionist must know this, & must See that he has neither the right or power of operating except by moral means & suasion, &

---

[41] President Pierce defended the repeal of the Missouri Compromise and devoted the greater part of his message of Dec. 2, 1856, to an argument against Northern interference with slavery in the South. Richardson: *Messages and Papers of the Presidents.* 5, 397 ff.

if he means well to the slave, he must not Create angry feelings in the Master; that although he may not approve the mode by which it pleases Providence to accomplish its purposes, the result will nevertheless be the same; that the reasons he gives for interference in what he has no Concern, holds good for every kind of interference with our neighbours when we disapprove their Conduct; Still I fear he will persevere in his evil Course. Is it not strange that the descendants of those pilgrim fathers who Crossed the Atlantic to preserve their own freedom of opinion, have always proved themselves intolerant of the Spiritual liberty of others?" [42]

This was the prevailing view among most religious people of Lee's class in the border states. They believed that slavery existed because God willed it and they thought it would end when God so ruled. The time and the means were not theirs to decide, conscious though they were of the ill-effects of Negro slavery on both races. Lee shared these convictions of his neighbors without having come in contact with the worst evils of African bondage. He spent no considerable time in any state south of Virginia from the day he left Fort Pulaski in 1831 until he went to Texas in 1856. All his reflective years had been passed in the North or in the border states. He had never been among the blacks on a cotton or rice plantation. At Arlington the servants had been notoriously indolent, their master's master. Lee, in short, was only acquainted with slavery at its best and he judged it accordingly. At the same time, he was under no illusion regarding the aims of the Abolitionists or the effect of their agitation.

When writing in this wise on the slavery question, Lee had been in Texas nearly ten months. Although oppressed often by the thought of his separation from his family, and by the news that Mrs. Lee was ill again,[43] he was becoming inured to the life of camps and courts-martial. After that Christmas at Fort Brown he had little to say in his letters home about the hardships of a soldier's life.[44] Those hardships continued, however. He passed

[42] Lee to Mrs. Lee, Dec. 27, 1856; *Lee MSS.*, Library of Congress. A very defective version, from which are omitted Lee's most severe references to Northern abolitionists, appeared in Jones, *L. and L.*, 82–83.

[43] Lee to Mrs. Lee, Jan. 7, 1857; Jones, *L. and L.*, 84.

[44] Lee to Mrs. Lee, *MS.*, Jan. 17, Jan. 24, 1857; Lee to Mrs. A. M. Fitzhugh, *MS.*, Sept. 8, 1857; *Duke Univ. MSS.*

his fiftieth birthday at Fort Brown, and from there he went to San Antonio on February 6, only to be ordered to a new court at Indianola.[45] Before the time arrived for that tribunal to sit he was ordered back to Fort Brown once more.[46] Thence he went overland to Indianola, arriving by March 20. En route he stopped at Sarassa and had the pleasure of seeing M. and Mme. Monod, with whom he had stopped for the night, eleven years before, on his way to report to General Wool at San Antonio. Madame made an impressive entrance: it was "foreshadowed," in Lee's words, "by the coming-in of her stately cats, with visages grave and tails erect, who preceded, surrounded and followed her. Her present favorite, Sodoiska, a large mottled gray, was a magnificent creature, and in her train she pointed out Aglai, her favorite eleven years ago when I first visited her. They are of French breed and education, and when the claret and water was poured out for my refreshment they jumped on the table for a sit-to." [47] These felines interested Lee the more because he was in search of a cat to preside over his tent at Camp Cooper[48]—partly for mousing and partly for company.

The court at Indianola adjourned within ten days, and Lee started back to Camp Cooper by way of San Antonio and Fort Mason. He reached Fort Mason on April 11, while a heavy cold norther was blowing. Picketing his horses under the shelter of a thicket to protect them from the wind, he betook himself to a tent, but he could not forget his animals and he went out during the night in a futile attempt to relieve their distress. The next day was Easter Sunday. "My [services]," he wrote home, "have been performed alone in my tent, I hope with a humble, grateful and penitent heart, and will be acceptable to our Heavenly Father. May He continue His mercies to us both and all our children, relatives and friends, and in His own good time unite us in His worship, if not on earth, forever in heaven." [49]

Six days later, April 18, 1857, Lee was back at Camp Cooper,

[45] Diary in Mason, 62; MS. A. G. O., vol. 13, S. O., 17, Feb. 12, 1857.
[46] A letter in Fitz Lee, 66, Feb. 16, 1857, is dated at Fort Brown.
[47] Lee to Annie Lee, March 27, 1857; Fitz Lee, 67.
[48] Ibid., and Lee to Mrs. Lee, Feb. 16, 1857; Fitz Lee, 66.
[49] Lee to Mrs. Lee, April 12, 1857. This letter is wrongly dated April 4, in Jones, L. and L., 84–85. The correct date is established by Lee's mention of Easter Sunday, which fell on April 12 in 1857.

after some empty alarums of Indians by the way. He found his tent still standing, though it had been blown down often in the seven months of his absence,[50] and he got, no doubt, from his captains and lieutenants fuller details of their brushes with the Indians than they had been able to write him during the winter. There had been four clashes, in which two cavalrymen and more than a dozen redskins had been killed. Lee's opinion of these casualties had been expressed in January to Mrs. Lee: "It is a distressing state of affairs that requires the application of such treatment; but it is the only corrective they understand, the only way in which they can be brought to keep within their own limits." [51]

A return to Camp Cooper did not bring immunity from the perennial nuisance of court-martial duty. If Lee was not to go to a court, a court would be brought to him. A week after he pulled up the flap of his old tent he was entertaining a court-martial, was its president, in fact, and was embarrassed, besides, to provide decent food for Mrs. George H. Thomas, who accompanied her husband on his journey thither. Said Lee: "The major can fare as I do, but I fear she will fare badly, for my man Kumer is both awkward and unskilled. I can, however, give them plenty of bread and beef, but with the exception of preserved vegetables, fruits, etc., I can give them very little else. I sent yesterday to the settlements below and got a few eggs, some butter, and one old hen. I shall not reflect upon her. . . ." [52]

The court adjourned, leaving no comment on the diet Camp Cooper provided. Summer came, with heat and sickness. A soldier's child died, and Lee for the first time had to officiate in reading the Episcopal burial service.[53] The thermometer went above 100, and there was another death among the children of the camp:

"He was as handsome a little boy as I ever saw—the son of one of the sergeants, about a year old; I was admiring his appearance

---

[50] Lee to Mrs. Lee, April 19, 1857; Jones, *L. and L.,* 85; *Mason,* 62.
[51] Lee to Mrs. Lee, undated, January, 1857; *Mason,* 61–62.
[52] Lee to Mrs. Lee, April 26, 1857; Jones, *L. and L.,* 86.
[53] Lee to unnamed correspondent (probably Mrs. Lee), June 9, 1857; Jones, *L. and L.,* 86.

the day before he was taken ill. Last Thursday his little waxen form was committed to the earth. His father came to me, the tears flowing down his cheeks, and asked me to read the funeral service over his body, which I did at the grave for the second time in my life. I hope I shall not be called on again, for, though I believe that it is far' better for the child to be called by its heavenly Creator into his presence in its purity and innocence, unpolluted by sin, and uncontaminated by the vices of the world, still it wrings a parent's heart with anguish that is painful to see. Yet I know it was done in mercy to both—mercy to the child, mercy to the parents. The former has been saved from sin and misery here, and the latter have been given a touching appeal and power-ful inducement to prepare for hereafter. May it prove effectual, and may they require no further severe admonition." [54]

It was quite indicative of Lee's relations with his men that one of them should have asked him to read the burial service. There was already between him and them the fullest understanding. They knew him to be a capable soldier; he saw to it that their rights were fully respected and that justice was done them. In fact, that very reputation for fair dealing sometimes made the men a bit concerned when they were called before him. Once, when a soldier was under examination for some offense, Lee assured him quietly, "You shall have justice." Thereupon the soldier forthrightly answered, "That is what I am afraid of, sir." [55]

Living among these men and directing their drill, in the midst of the hot weather of the summer of 1857, with the thermometer registering 112 degrees in the coolest tent, Lee received a wild rumor that the Comanches were about to descend on the camp and on the nearby reservation, where their quieter brethren re-sided. The Indians saddled their ponies and prepared for fight or flight, but Lee refused to believe an attack would materialize, and he was right. [56] The camp settled back to more heat and more tedium, but Lee had to set off for the usual court-martial—this time no farther away than Fort Mason.

Although he had no idea that such fortune awaited him when

---

[54] Lee to unnamed correspondent (probably Mrs. Lee), June 22, 1857; *Jones*, 375.
[55] *Packard*, 157.   [56] Lee to Mrs. Lee, June 29, 1857; *Mason*, 63.

he rode away, Lee was never to see Camp Cooper again. Arriving at Fort Mason in time for the assembly of the court on July 15,[57] he had been there only eight days when an express arrived with orders to proceed at once to San Antonio and to take command of the regiment, as Colonel Albert Sidney Johnston had been called to Washington by the War Department.[58] Lee left as soon as practicable, reached San Antonio on the 28th, and assumed command the next day. Life was now much more pleasant. San Antonio was not a Washington or a New York, but it was immeasurably a more acceptable post than poor Camp Cooper. Instead of a tent there were quarters, a whole house, indeed, which Lee occupied on August 1, 1857.[59] He found friends there, too, among them the family of Major R. H. Chilton, paymaster, who was to serve later as his chief of staff. The pleasure he had in Major Chilton's two little daughters, Laura and Emmie, was to be, in retrospect, "the purest if not the greatest," Lee had in Texas.[60]

Life flowed quietly on at San Antonio, with daily duties none too exacting and with pleasures moderate enough. Although Lee had now been in Texas a year and seven months, there seemed to be no prospect of an early summons home. The months stretched out ahead, with no promotion and little opportunity—the familiar story of most of Lee's military career, differing only in setting. Then, on October 21, with no warning, there came news that on October 10 Lee's father-in-law, G. W. P. Custis, had died at Arlington.[61] This meant grief to Mrs. Lee and heavy responsibility besides, for there was no adult male member of the Lee family at Arlington to direct affairs. Custis Lee was on duty in the West. Rooney, who was only twenty, had entered Harvard in 1854 but had left to accept a commission as lieutenant of infantry and was already on the way to Texas.[62] Mrs. Lee was alone and sick. There was nothing for Lee to do except to procure immediate leave and to start at once for Virginia. His superiors gave him all possible assistance. His orders to attend a court of inquiry on November 11 were

[57] *MS. A. G. O.*, vol. 6, S. O. 89, June 18, 1857. [58] *Diary* in *Mason*, 63.
[59] *Ibid.*, 64. A misprint in this entry made the date on which Lee took command of the regiment appear as Oct. 28. It should be July 28.
[60] Lee to Laura Chilton, *MS.*, Nov. 22, 1869; *Chilton Papers*, Confederate Museum.
[61] *Diary* in *Mason*, 63; *Brock*, 162. [62] *E. J. Lee*, 499.

cancelled,[63] he was granted a two months' leave of absence, and on October 24, 1857, he left San Antonio for home.[64]

"In Texas," an anonymous brother officer testified of Lee, ". . . he examined everything thoroughly and continuously, until master of every detail, ever too conscientious to act under imperfect knowledge of any subject submitted to him. And with all his stern sense of duty, he attracted the love, admiration, and confidence of all. The little children always hailed his approach with glee—his sincerity, kindliness of nature, and cordial manners attracting their unreserved confidence." [65]

He had gained some new experience, of course, during the nineteen months he had been on duty in Texas. He had adjusted himself to camp life, to hard riding, and to rough fare. Physically, he had unconsciously been in training for the desperate years that lay ahead. His leading of troops taught him little, but his acquaintance with the private soldier's state of mind was invaluable. Then, again, tedious as was his endless court-martial duty, it was instructive. For as he listened to case after case, he understood better than ever before how weak, jealous, indolent, and sensitive men reacted to army life. He saw why they lapsed in their duty, and what were the temptations before which they most often fell. At West Point, during his superintendency, he had seen the current raw material of command; in Texas he had dealt with the worn as well as with the recently finished product.

[63] MS. A. G. O., vol. 13, S. O. 141, Oct. 1, 1857; ibid., vol. 13, S. O. 146, Oct. 12, 1857.
[64] Diary in Mason, 63; Lee to S. Cooper, MS., Nov. 24, 1857; MS. A. G. O.
[65] Mason, 64.

CHAPTER XXII

The Lees Become Land-Poor

On November 11, 1857, Robert E. Lee reached Arlington on the saddest of all his ante-bellum home-comings. The shadow of Mr. Custis's death still hung over the plantation. The old gentleman had been ill only four days from pneumonia when he had realized that his end was near at hand. On the morning of October 10, after having been unconscious most of the night, Mr. Custis had roused himself, had embraced Mrs. Lee and the children, and had directed that his rector be summoned. After the clergyman had arrived, Mr. Custis had asked that the prayer for the dying be said, and while it was being repeated, he passed away. He was then in his seventy-seventh year.[1]

The absence of his father-in-law, however, was less of a shock to Lee than the plight of his wife. When he had left home in 1856 she had been in her usual health, which had been fair after she had recovered from the pelvic infection which, in 1836, had caused her so much suffering. Lee had heard in January, 1857, that she was ill, and he had yielded at that time to his impulse to give advice,[2] but he does not seem to have realized the seriousness of her condition. Perhaps she kept it from him, lest it add unhappiness to the hardships he had to sustain in Texas. "I almost dread him seeing my crippled state," she had written in February, 1857, to a kinswoman. Arthritis had assailed her right hand and arm at that time and probably was slowly spreading. Often she was kept awake at night by the pain.[3] Lee now found her scarcely able to move about the house, and, though she was only forty-nine, aging very rapidly. Overnight, and without warning, he had to face the fact that his wife had become an invalid. That was enough to add the deepest gloom to his return.

[1] Decker and McSween: *Historic Arlington*, 45. He had been born at Mount Airy, April 30, 1781 (*Brock*, 162).
[2] Lee to Mrs. Lee, Jan. 7, 1857; Jones, *L. and L.*, 84.
[3] Mrs. R. E. Lee to Mrs. Hackley, *MS.*, Feb. 19, 1857; *Talcott MSS.* (*VHS*).

Lee soon found that Mr. Custis's will had put a heavy burden on him. He had been named one of the four executors, and as the others failed to qualify, he had to discharge all the duties of settling a troublesome estate under a complicated testament.[4] Mr. Custis had drawn up the paper in 1855, apparently without consulting counsel. He left Mrs. Lee a life interest in Arlington and its contents and in adjacent properties. On her demise all this property except the minor plate was to pass in fee to Custis Lee, "he my eldest grandson taking my name and arms." His "White House" plantation of 4000 acres in New Kent County, Mr. Custis left to Rooney Lee, and the "Romancock"[5] property of like acreage he bequeathed to his youngest grandson, Robert E. Lee, Jr. To Colonel Lee he left a lot in "Square 21" of Washington City. Each of Mr. Custis's granddaughters was to receive $10,000. One paragraph of the will provided that Smith's Island, off North-ampton County, and sundry lands in Stafford, Richmond, and Westmoreland Counties, should be sold to provide these legacies. Another section said that these properties and "my estates of the White-House in the County of New Kent and Romancock in the County of King William" were to be "charged with the payment of the legacies to my granddaughters." The will then read: "Smith's Island and the aforesaid lands in Stafford, Richmond and Westmoreland only are to be sold, the lands of the White House and Romancock to be worked to raise the aforesaid legacies to my four granddaughters." This was confusing and contra-dictory enough, but a final tangle was added by a provision that when the legacies should have been paid, and the properties had been cleared of debt, all the Custis slaves were to be emancipated, "the said emancipation to be accomplished in not exceeding five years from the time of my decease."[6]

The courts manifestly would be required to construe this docu-ment and to determine the nature and extent of the liens on White House and Romancock. The beneficiaries under the will were of the same family. If, therefore, all went well and the

[4] They were Robert Lee Randolph of Eastern View, Right Reverend William Meade, and George Washington Peter.
[5] This harsh name, which is spelled throughout the will as it is here given, was subse-quently softened to "Romancoke."
[6] Will of G. W. P. Custis, MS. Records Alexandria County, Virginia. This docu-ment was probated Dec. 7, 1857.

miscellaneous landed properties yielded enough to pay the greater part of the legacies without draining the White House and Romancock for too long a time, a settlement would be a matter of no great difficulty. The immediate trouble was that Mr. Custis left more than $10,000 of debts[7] and virtually no money with which to operate the estate. He had wide-spreading acres and 196 slaves,[8] but he had always been a negligent farmer and an easy-going master, and he had become more careless as he had grown older. For some time after 1851 he had devoted himself chiefly to the painting of feeble pictures of Washington's battles.[9] His Arlington tract of 1100 acres, in the Virginia phrase, was sadly "run down." His fences had fallen, his roof leaked, his very lawn was being invaded by bushes and weeds. Arlington would not have sustained the family during the life of Mr. Custis had he not received a fair income from some of his other farms that were rented out to capable planters. His servants, who for years had done little but tend their own gardens, were not disposed to turn to hard work. Instead of inheriting easy luxury, the Lees found themselves "land-poor."

As executor, Lee saw that if his daughters' legacies were to be paid, Arlington must be made self-supporting. If the house was to be saved from ruin, it had to be repaired. To do all this called for the expenditure of at least a part of his salary, and also for his presence on the ground. He could not hope to effect the necessary revolution through some one else while he was absent in Texas. Embarrassing as was the application, and serious as might be the effect on his career of protracted separation from his regiment, he had no choice except to ask for a lengthy leave of absence. He applied for two months' leave soon after he reached home,[10] and before that expired he got an extension to December 1, 1858, by which time he hoped to be able to rejoin his regiment.[11] In all this, of course, he had the support of his "true and warm

---

[7] R. E. Lee to Custis Lee, MS., March 17, 1858; *Duke Univ. MSS.*

[8] Inventory of the estate of G. W. P. Custis, Jan. 1, 1858; *MS. Records, Alexandria County, Virginia;* R. E. Lee to Mrs. A. M. Fitzhugh, MS., Nov. 22, 1857; *Duke Univ. MSS.*

[9] B. J. Lossing: "Arlington House," *Harper's Magazine,* September, 1853, pp. 435, 445 *ff.*

[10] *MS. A. G. O.,* vol. 13, S. O. 154, Nov. 27, 1857.

[11] *MS. A. G. O.,* vol. 14, S. O. 7, Jan. 21, 1858.

friend," as he styled General Scott.[12] It had been only in the previous spring that his old chief had advocated a commission for Rooney Lee "mainly," as Scott had said, "on the extraordinary merits of the father, the very best soldier I ever saw in the field." [13] As commanding general of the army, Scott would grant whatever leave the circumstances of Colonel Lee required—and would be ready to argue that it was far less than the country owed Lee.

So Lee settled down in the winter of 1857–58 to become temporarily a farmer—with scant equipment, little money, many debts, and indifferent help. He had often longed to lead the life of a planter, but now that he had to do so, with a neglected estate, deeply involved, he entered upon one of the darkest, most unhappy periods of his life. He wished, of course, for Mrs. Lee and the children to be comfortable, and he wanted the property to be in good order when it passed to his son. But he could do little, at that season, for the repair of the house or for the cultivation of the farm. He soon became restless and unsettled regarding his future. He felt that he was at the crossroads. Should he stay in the army, or was it his duty to resign and devote himself to Arlington, on which $10,000, exclusive of the payment of the debts, would have to be spent?[14] He decided that his course of action should depend chiefly on what his sons had in contemplation. Custis was still in the West, and not particularly pleased with his post. Rooney wanted to marry his cousin, Charlotte Wickham, of Shirley, and start housekeeping at White House, but he had just been ordered to join the expedition sent against the Mormons and he could not afford to resign at such a time. Lee explained all this in a letter to Custis and continued:

"As to myself and future plans, I shall defer my determination until the fall, as it will not be necessary to determine till then. In the meantime, you must think over the matter and decide what you would prefer doing. If you wished to resign and take this place, and Rooney to get married and settle down at the White

[12] R. E. Lee to Custis Lee, Feb. 15, 1858; Jones, *L. and L.,* 89–90.
[13] See *supra,* p. 294; Winfield Scott to J. B. Floyd, May 8, 1857; Jones, *L. and L.,* 127–28.
[14] R. E. Lee to Custis Lee, *MSS.,* Jan. 17, Feb. 15, 1858, *Duke Univ. MSS.* The original of the second of these letters contains much matter, omitted without any indication of that fact, from Jones's version, quoted *supra.*

House, there would be no necessity for my leaving the Army. I had thought myself of applying for your appointment in any new regiment that might be raised this winter, if I saw any chance of success, and am glad you have mentioned the subject. I am doubtful whether you would be benefited or not. That also depends upon your taste and feelings. The service in the Engineer Corps is preferable to that in the regiment. No place is without its drawbacks and you must not expect unalloyed pleasure anywhere. Promotion, if offered an officer, ought in my opinion to be accepted. But it need not be sought unless deserved. A captaincy in the engineers in time of peace, in responsibility, dignity, and usefulness, would rank with a field officer of the line. In time of war, it might be different. . . ."[15]

There was, in this letter, a suggestion of his strong wish to remain in the army,[16] and perhaps an indirect confession that his former service with the engineers was preferable to his new cavalry command, but desire and ambition alike were subordinated to the need of the family. He was not alone in this. If he was willing to abandon his profession in order to improve Arlington for his son, Custis was equally anxious to increase his father's happiness and at his own expense. On March 17, 1858, Lee received a letter from Custis, written February 18, in which the boy sent his father a deed to Arlington and all the other property inherited under his grandfather's will. The transfer had already been suggested by Custis, so it was no surprise to the senior Lee. He sat down at once and thanked his son but of course declined the gift. He said:

"I am deeply impressed by your filial feeling of love and consideration, as well as your tender solicitude for me, of which, however, I required no proof, and am equally touched by your generosity and disinterestedness. But from what I said in a previous letter you will not be surprised at my repeating that I cannot accept your offer. It is not from an unwillingness to re-

---

[15] R. E. Lee to Custis Lee, Feb. 15, 1858; Jones, *L. and L.*, 89.

[16] *Cf.* Lee to unnamed correspondent, n. d., 1859: "You have heard me say that the cordiality and friendship in the army was the great attraction of the service. It is that, I believe, which has kept me in it so long, and it is that which now makes me fear to leave it. I do not know where I should meet with so much friendship out of it" (P. A. Bruce: *Robert E. Lee*, 93).

ceive from you a gift you may think proper to bestow, or to be
indebted to you for any benefit great or small. But simply
because it would not be right for me to do so. Your dear grandfather distributed his property as he thought best, and it is proper
that it should remain as he bestowed it. It will not prevent me
from improving it to the best of my ability, or of making it as
comfortable a home for your mother, sisters, and yourself as I
can. I only wish I could do more than I shall have it in my
power to do. I wish you had received my previous letter on this
subject in time to have saved you the trouble of executing the deed
you transmitted me."

Here Lee's amusing propensity for giving advice to his children
asserted itself even more strongly—and certainly with less of tact
—than usually. He added:

"And indeed I also regret the expense you incurred, which I
fear in that country is considerable, as I wish you to *save all* your
money, and invest it in some safe and lucrative way, that you
may have the means to build up old Arlington, and make it all
we would wish to see it. The necessity I daily have for money
has, I fear, made me parsimonious. In order that you may know
the full extent of your grandfather's will, I enclose you a copy." [17]

Custis probably was actuated by a desire to have his father own
a property on which he, and not the son, would have to spend
money. Lee must have felt that his boy's generous letter, which
unfortunately has been lost, was full compensation for all the
labor he put on Arlington. His own affairs, however, were not so
embarrassed as Custis may have thought. The Custis property
was in distress, but Lee himself had always lived within his income and had been able to save a part of his salary.

On April 26, Lee had to leave for Newport Barracks, Kentucky,
by way of Cincinnati to serve on a court-martial,[18] convened to
try Brigadier General Twiggs, but he was not long detained and
was back in Washington on May 5, with a day in Baltimore on
his return journey. He found his sister, Mrs. Marshall, in poor

[17] R. E. Lee to Custis Lee, March 17, 1858; Jones, *L. and L.*, 90–91. In printing this
letter, Doctor Jones omitted the important statement, the crux to Lee's whole problem at
Arlington, that the Custis estate was $10,000 in debt. *Cf.* the original, *Duke Univ. MSS.*
[18] *MS. A. G. O.*, vol. 14, S. O. 42, March 19, 1858.

health, but he had the pleasure of seeing numerous kinspeople and old friends.[19] He was at work again in time to put in a good crop of corn, his first large venture as a planter.

His labor was aggravating and the results doubtful. Arlington was far more difficult to administer than West Point or a fort under construction. The rain interfered, and agrarian discontent, which was as general then as thereafter, overtook him in mid-summer. "I am getting along as usual," he wrote Rooney in August, "trying to get a little work done and to mend up some things. I succeed very badly." [20] The affairs of his family claimed much time. Rooney had gone off to his command in the West, with his father's benediction and a letter of parental advice, "which," Lee somewhat apologetically explained, "proceeds from my great love and burning anxiety for your welfare and happiness." [21] The young man was anxious to marry without further delay and had to be tactfully discouraged for the time, acceptable though his fiancée was in every way.[22] While urging Rooney to stay in the West until he had established a name for himself in the army, Lee was working to get Custis an assignment in the engineer bureau in Washington, in order that the young man might "see how [he] would like to become a farmer." [23]

Mrs. Lee and his daughters were at the time even more of a concern than were the boys. The condition of Mrs. Lee was somewhat better, but she had to be taken to the Hot Springs during August, while the younger children were left with the ever-generous Mrs. Fitzhugh at Ravenswood.[24] Later in the year, two of his daughters were ailing.[25] He had to play the nurse, while attending to the farm, but he contrived to do both and still kept in contact with the army. Unknown to him, James M. Porter of Pennsylvania, founder of Lafayette College, and former nominee for Secretary of War, had been urging Lee's promotion as

[19] Lee to Mrs. A. M. Fitzhugh, MS., May 5, 1858; Duke Univ. MSS.; R. E. Lee to Custis Lee, May 17, 1858; Jones, L. and L., 91–93. For the erroneous transcription of Twiggs's name as Scruggs, see infra, 414, n. 34.
[20] R. E. Lee to W. H. F. Lee, Aug. 7, 1858; Jones, L. and L., 95.
[21] R. E. Lee to W. H. F. Lee, May 30, 1858; Jones, 376.
[22] R. E. Lee to W. H. F. Lee, Aug. 7, 1858; Jones, L. and L., 94–95.
[23] R. E. Lee to Custis Lee, May 17, 1858, Aug. 19, 1859; Jones, L. and L., 92, 103.
[24] R. E. Lee to Mrs. A. M. Fitzhugh, MS., Aug. 12, Sept. 6, 1858; Duke Univ. MSS.
[25] R. E. Lee to Custis Lee, May 30, 1859; Jones, L. and L., 100.

brigadier general to succeed Persifor F. Smith, who had recently died. Porter had said:

"Col. Lee is one of the most accomplished and best educated officers in the Army. . . . He is a highly finished gentleman in his manners and deportment and one of the best educated men, both in a military point of view and as a general scholar, that we have in this country. I have always considered him a model officer; the pattern of a soldier and a gentleman. He is in the prime and vigor of life, and admirably adapted for the command of our forces." [26]

The recommendation came to naught, but it shows that Lee's professional reputation, which was limited to army circles at the close of the Mexican War, was gradually spreading. When Scott was ill about this time there was some talk in the army of Lee as his successor.[27] Lee had no repinings that he was not named in Smith's stead, nor did he complain because he was not given a place in the Utah expedition, but he did think a mistake was made in placing two sick men in charge of the later stage of the campaign—General W. S. Harney and Lee's old colonel, Albert Sidney Johnston, now a brevet brigadier general. "I do not think it right," he said, "to commit the honor of the country and the lives of the soldiers to persons so prostrated." [28]

There was already beginning to creep into his correspondence some of the misgiving of a man long separated from his profession. His leave was to expire on December 1, 1858, but as that date approached, Lee realized that he could not quit Arlington with his work as executor half-done. The farm was by no means in the order he desired. Moreover, the court had not yet construed those parts of Mr. Custis's will in which provision had been made both for the emancipation and for the employment of the slaves on the farms, as well as for the sale of certain properties, to provide the specified bequests for the daughters. Lee set forth his situation very fully in a letter of October 22, 1858, addressed to General Scott's assistant adjutant general. This read as follows:

"I have been occupied ever since my arrival from Texas, in

[26] J. M. Porter to James Buchanan, May 25, 1858; MS. A. G. O., L., 48.
[27] Long, 37.   [28] R. E. Lee to Custis Lee, May 17, 1858; Jones, L. and L., 92.

settling the estate of the late G. W. P. Custis, and have earnestly endeavored so to arrange it, so as to enable me to return to my Regt this Fall. I find it however impossible to do so, and without going into a narration of matters still unfinished and requiring my personal attention, I will only state that the terms of Mr. Custis' will are found to be so indefinite and admit of so many different versions, that I have been compelled to apply to the Circuit Court of Virg^a for their true and legal construction, and specific rules for my government as Executor.

"These I had hoped to receive before this time, but the earliest period I can now obtain them, is at the next November term of said Court; which if received will not enable me to put in train of execution, before the expiration of my present leave of absence, 1st Dec^r.

"The most important point to be determined by the Court is the period of the emancipation of the slaves, which is dependent upon the conditions of the will. Justice to them requires their earliest fulfilment. I therefore feel compelled to ask an extension of my present leave of absence till 1st May next.

"The leave of absence granted by the Commd Genl of the Dept of Texas, authorized me to ask for such an extension as was necessary for the arrangement of my business.

"Should however the Commd Genl of the Army consider my presence with my Regt this winter necessary, I will cheerfully join it at any time he may designate." [29]

Scott "heartily approved" this application,[30] which was accordingly granted.[31] Not all this additional leave, however, was spent at home. On December 15, Lee was at West Point, sitting on an irksome court of inquiry assembled to hear some foolish charges against Professor Mahan. This held him until after Christmas, and forced him to hurry back home for the necessary but unpleasant task of hiring out some of the idle Arlington Negroes.[32] The only pleasure Lee had on this journey was a report of

[29] Lee to Irvin McDowell, A. A. G., Oct. 22, 1858; *MS. A. G. O.*
[30] Endorsement on *Idem.*
[31] *MS. A. G. O.*, vol. 6, S. O. 153, Oct. 29, 1858.
[32] *Ibid.*, vol. 6, S. O. 167, Dec. 1, 1858; Lee to Andrew Talcott, *MS.*, Dec. 21, 1858; *Talcott MSS. (VHS)*; R. E. Lee to Custis Lee, Jan. 2, 1859; Jones, *L. and L.*, 97. Lee reached home on Dec. 29, 1858.

Rooney's soldierly bearing and good conduct, given him in New York by Rooney's colonel, Charles A. May.[33]

The winter of 1858–59 and the spring of 1859, were in many ways the gloomiest Lee had experienced. The circuit court adjourned in November, 1858, without construing the Custis will,[34] and the pressure on Lee's finances, for the improvement of the property, was so manifest that the always thoughtful Mrs. Fitzhugh was constrained to send him $1000 to be used as he saw fit. Lee had determined to keep the expenditures at Arlington within his means and he could not accept the check, which he acknowledged with warmest gratitude.[35] Remaining continuously at home, except for about seven weeks' service on a board convened in Washington, to consider the equipment of the cavalry,[36] he worked hard, but, as he thought, to very little purpose. He got the house and the stable safe from leaks and, as he said, "ameliorated some things," but the embarrassment of limited means could not be overcome. The improvements, he wrote Custis, were "very meagre. . . . I have been able to do nothing to the grounds around the house, except to clean up on the hill, and have been obliged to limit myself to what is most essential, and promises something for man and beast to eat, and to furnish shelter and protection. You will find things, therefore, I fear rough and unsightly, as much as I desire to polish up your mother's habitation, and to prepare for you an acceptable home." [37]

His other worries continued. Mrs. Lee's health at the end of the spring of 1859 was as bad as it had been when Lee returned from Texas. By July, Lee had begun to despair of her recovery. His ailing daughters, except Mildred, got no better. "I have no enjoyment in life now," he wrote in distress, "but what I derive from my children." [38] He did not spare himself to make those

[33] R. E. Lee to W. H. F. Lee, Jan. 1, 1859; Jones, *L. and L.*, 96.
[34] R. E. Lee to Mrs. A. M. Fitzhugh, *MS.*, Nov. 20, 1858; *Duke Univ. MSS.*
[35] R. E. Lee to Mrs. A. M. Fitzhugh, *MS.*, Nov. 20, Dec. 13, 1858; *Duke Univ. MSS.*
[36] R. E. Lee to Mrs. A. M. Fitzhugh, *MS.*, Jan. 30, Feb. 17, 1859; *Duke Univ. MSS.*; *MS. A. G. O.*, vol. 6, S. O. 13, Jan. 20, 1859; undated *MS.* memorandum, *A. G. O.*, of Lee's assignments, 1858–59. He served on the equipment board, Jan. 25–March 1, and March 2–12, 1859. D. H. Maury, who was also a member of this board, has left a brief account of its work (*op. cit.*, 107).
[37] R. E. Lee to Custis Lee, Jan. 2, May 30, July 2, 1859; Jones, *L. and L.*, 97–98, 99, 102.
[38] R. E. Lee to Custis Lee, May 30, July 2, 1859; Jones, *L. and L.*, 100, 101.

young Lees happy. Whatever the load he carried, he had a cheerful mien in their presence. Once, in the autumn of 1858, he came upon Annie and Katherine Stiles, a friend from Georgia, weeping together as Katherine made ready to leave after a visit. "No tears at Arlington," he gaily told them, "no tears!" [39] The time was not far distant when there would be nothing but tears at Arlington!

Lee's only relief from nursing his family and managing the farm in 1859 was in a number of brief visits. In March he travelled to Richmond and thence to Shirley, the beloved old home of his mother, where, on the 23d, Rooney was married to his distant cousin, Charlotte Wickham. The wedding was of the generous, old-fashioned sort, where the guests lingered long. Lee was one of the trustees under the generous marriage settlement of Charlotte, and on April 1 he was in Richmond, probably in connection with the recordation of the deed of trust.[40] The next month Lee made a brief trip to Goodwood, his first vacation since his return to Virginia. He went, also, to the White House at the end of May, to prepare it for Rooney and Charlotte, who were soon to move there; and he journeyed to Baltimore in July to see Mrs. Marshall, whose eyesight was endangered.[41] But even changes of scene, which he regarded as the best physic,[42] did not raise his depressed spirits. Absence from his command troubled him deeply, the more so as circumstances had protracted it. He had hoped to return to his regiment on May 1, for the summer at least, but he had to ask once again that his leave be prolonged, and on June 14 had it extended four months more.[43] He explained this to Custis: "It was this desire [to have Robert with me], the unsettled business of your grandpa's estate, your mama's condition,

---

[39] Miss Stiles in *Richmond Times-Dispatch*, Jan. 20, 1907.

[40] Information supplied by Honorable Henry T. Wickham; Records Chancery Court of Richmond, Va., MS. *Deed Book* 73-A, p. 553. Charlotte Wickham, christened Georgiana, was the posthumous child of George Wickham, U. S. N., and of Charlotte Carter, daughter of Williams Carter of Shirley. Her mother dying while she was a baby, Charlotte was reared by her maternal grandfather at Shirley. George Wickham, her father, was the son of John Wickham and his wife, Elizabeth Selden McClurg of Richmond, Va.

[41] Jones, *L. and L.*, 98, 100, 101; R. E. Lee to Custis Lee, MS., May 30, 1859; *Duke Univ. MSS.*

[42] Cf. "[An excursion] to some healthy and interesting region will do more to renovate and invigorate the system, and enable it to throw off any general or even local disease, than anything else in the world" (Lee to Talcott, MS., Aug. 7, 1838; *Talcott MSS. (VHS)*).

[43] MS. *A. G. O.*, vol. 6, S. O. 104, June 14, 1859.

and the hope I at one time entertained of seeing you, my dear son, that induced me to forego my purpose of returning to Texas this summer, and to remain till the fall. God knows whether I have done right, or whether my stay will be an advantage. I am very doubtful on the subject and feel that I ought to be with my regiment, and this feeling deprives me of half the pleasure I should derive from being here under other circumstances." [44]

The handling of the slaves, always a difficult matter to a conscientious man, added to Lee's distress. The Negroes at Arlington numbered sixty-three, and the majority of them belonged to a few large families. They were more than Lee could work advantageously with his available capital and land, consequently he had to hire out a few of them by the year in order to supplement the income from the property. The demand for servants was so limited in northern Virginia, and the return was so small that he was compelled to send some of the Arlington Negroes to work in eastern Virginia. This may have caused something of a rebellion among them, for two of them, a man and a young woman, ran away in the hope of reaching Pennsylvania. They were captured in Maryland and were returned to Arlington. Thereupon Lee sent them to labor in lower Virginia, where there would be less danger of their absconding.[45] That probably was the extent of the punishment imposed on them. There is no evidence, direct or indirect, that Lee ever had them or any other Negroes flogged. The usage at Arlington and elsewhere in Virginia among people of Lee's station forbade such a thing. But false stories were spread, and on June 24, 1859, *The New York Tribune* printed two communications on the affair. One of them read as follows:

SOME FACTS THAT SHOULD COME TO LIGHT

To the Editor of the N. Y. Tribune.

Sir: It is known that the venerable George Washington Parke Custis died some two years ago; and the same papers that announced his death announced also the fact that on his deathbed he liberated his slaves. The will, for some reason, was never

[44] R. E. Lee to Custis Lee, July 2, 1859; Jones, *L. and L.*, 101–2.   [45] *Ibid.*

allowed any publicity, and the slaves themselves were cajoled along with the idea that some slight necessary arrangements were to be made, when they would all have their free papers. Finally they were told *five years* must elapse before they could go. Meantime they have been deprived of all means of making a little now and then for themselves, as they were allowed to do during Mr. Custis's life, have been kept harder at work than ever, and part of the time have been cut down to half a peck of unsifted meal a week for each person, without even their fish allowance. Three old women, who have seen nearly their century each, are kept sewing, making clothes for the field hands, from daylight till dark, with nothing but the half-peck of meal to eat; no tea or coffee—nothing that old people crave—and no time given them to earn these little rarities, as formerly. One old man, eighty years old, bent with age, and whom Mr. Custis had long since told "had *done enough,*" and might go home and "smoke his pipe in peace," is now turned out as a regular field hand. A year ago, for some trifling offense, three were sent to jail, and a few months later three more, for simply going down to the river to get themselves some fish, when they were literally starved.

Some three or four weeks ago, three, more courageous than the rest, thinking their five years would never come to an end, came to the conclusion to leave for the North. They were most valuable servants, but they were never advertised, and there was no effort made to regain them which looks exceedingly as though Mr. Lee, the present proprietor, knew he had no lawful claim to them. They had not proceeded far before their progress was intercepted by some brute in human form, who suspected them to be fugitives, and probably wished a reward. They were lodged in jail, and frightened into telling where they started from. Mr. Lee was forthwith acquainted with their whereabouts, when they were transported back, taken into a barn, stripped, and the men received thirty and nine lashes each, from the hands of the slave-whipper, when he refused to whip the girl, and Mr. Lee himself administered the thirty and nine lashes to her. They were then sent to Richmond jail, where they are now lodged.

Next to Mount Vernon, we associate the Custis place with the "Father of this free country." Shall "Washington's body guard" be

391

thus tampered with, and never a voice raised for such utter helplessness?

A.

Washington, June 21, 1859.

The other letter was briefer but equally exaggerated:

To the Editor of The N. Y. Tribune.

Sir: I live one mile from the plantation of George Washington P. Custis, now Col. Lee's, as Custis willed it to Lee. All the slaves on this estate, as I understand, were set free at the death of Custis, but are now held in bondage by Lee. I have inquired concerning the will, but can get no satisfaction. Custis had fifteen children by his slave women. I see his grandchildren every day; they are of a dark yellow. Last week three of the slaves ran away; an officer was sent after them, overtook them nine miles this side of Pennsylvania, and brought them back. Col. Lee ordered them whipped. They were two men and one woman. The officer whipped the two men, and said he would not whip the woman, and Col. Lee stripped her and whipped her himself. These are facts as I learn from near relatives of the men whipped. After being whipped, he sent them to Richmond and hired them out as good farm hands.

Yours,

A CITIZEN.

Washington, June 19, 1859.

This was Lee's first experience with the extravagance of irresponsible antislavery agitators. The libel, which was to be reprinted many times in later years with new embellishments, made him unhappy, but it did not lead him to any violent retort. All he had to say to Custis about the criticism was: "*The N. Y. Tribune* has attacked me for my treatment of your grandfather's slaves, but I shall not reply. He has left me an unpleasant legacy." [46]

The summer dragged itself out. A visit to Capon Springs, for the health of Mrs. Lee and of Agnes, was interrupted by a hurried call from Lee's niece, Mary Childe, who begged Lee to join her at Saratoga Springs, N. Y., where her father was very ill. Lee dutifully started from the Capon spa, but fortunately got a letter,

---

[46] R. E. Lee to Custis Lee, July 2, 1859; Jones, *L. and L.,* 102.

as he was passing through Alexandria, stating that Childe was better and that Lee need not come. He accordingly went out to Arlington, where he found that he had missed a visit from Lieutenant "Jeb" Stuart,[47] who was then on leave, visiting friends and relatives in Virginia.

On October 6, Lee was at Fort Columbus, New York harbor, for a brief court-martial.[48] Then, or about that time, General Scott offered him the position of military secretary, with the same rank as Lee then held, that of lieutenant colonel.[49] But Lee had made the change from the staff to the line, and though he was devoted to the old General, and would have done anything in his power to serve him, he did not wish to return to staff duty, where experience had shown him promotion was slow. Scott expected he would decline and was not piqued when he did so.

[47] R. E. Lee to Custis Lee, *MS.*, Aug. 17, 1859; *Duke Univ. MSS.;* same to same, Aug. 19, 1859; Jones, *L. and L.*, 104.
[48] *MS. A. G. O.*, vol. 6, S. O. 179, Oct. 3, 1859.   [49] *Keyes,* 317.

CHAPTER XXIII

An Introduction to Militant Abolitionism

Lee returned home from the court-martial in New York and put all his energy behind the autumn work at Arlington in the belief that he could soon complete the last of the necessary repairs and rejoin his regiment. He was busy at this on the morning of October 17, 1859, when Lieutenant "Jeb" Stuart arrived with a sealed note from Colonel Drinkard, chief clerk of the War Department. The message was a brief order for Lee to report to the Secretary of War immediately.[1]

Setting out at once, in civilian clothes, Lee soon learned that the government had received from John W. Garrett, president of the Baltimore and Ohio Railroad, news of a mysterious insurrection at Harpers Ferry, Va. Trains had been stopped; firing had been heard; rumor had it that strangers had entered the town in large numbers and were inciting the slaves to a rising. What that might imply, nobody had to tell Lee, for he had been at Fort Monroe when the Nat Turner insurrection had occurred, that bloody massacre which the South for almost twenty years had been fearing the Negroes would repeat. The place of the insurrection seemed chosen with a design that made it potentially the more serious, for in Harpers Ferry, at the junction of the Shenandoah and the Potomac Rivers, the United States maintained an armory and arsenal, where rifles were made and stored.[2]

It might be a serious affair, calling for instant action. Troops had been ordered from Fort Monroe during the morning; the service of Maryland militiamen had been accepted; a detachment of marines from the Washington navy yard had been ordered to the scene; Lee was to take command of all the forces, acting

---

[1] J. B. Floyd, Secretary of War, to Colonel Drinkard, *MSS.*, Oct. 17, 1859 (two letters), *A. G. O.*

[2] O. W. Villard: *John Brown. A Biography After Fifty Years* (cited hereafter as *Villard*), 433.

with his brevet rank of colonel. Orders were quickly issued,[3] and Lee went with the secretary to the White House, accompanied by Lieutenant Stuart, who had been at the War Department negotiating for the use of his patent on a sword-attachment when he had been requested to carry the message to Arlington. Sensing trouble, Stuart had immediately asked the privilege of going with Lee.[4]

Not knowing the magnitude of the rising, the President and his military adviser prepared for the worst, and drew up a proclamation, which Lee was authorized to issue if conditions justified. Armed with this document, and without waiting to put on a uniform, Lee hurried with Stuart by train to the Relay House, eight miles from Baltimore, whither the marines had gone from Washington at 3:30 P.M. to take the train for Harpers Ferry.[5] The two officers arrived after the cars for Harpers Ferry had left, but Lee was told that a locomotive would soon be brought up to carry him to his destination. He accordingly telegraphed orders to the marines on the train ahead of him to stop at Sandy Hook, slightly more than a mile from Harpers Ferry, and to await his arrival. The senior line officer with the marines was a lieutenant, Israel Green. They were accompanied by Major W. W. Russell, but he was a paymaster and could not take command. By this time alarm was general. Rumor had swollen the number of insurgents to 500. Lee so notified the secretary at 7:45 P.M.[6]

Aboard a roaring locomotive, Lee reached Sandy Hook at 10 o'clock and found the marines waiting for him there, along with four companies of Maryland militia, under a brigadier general of that state. Lee learned quickly that the bridge to Harpers Ferry was open, that the number of the insurgents had been greatly exaggerated, and that those who had survived a day of desultory fighting with the militia had taken refuge in the fire-engine house, within the armory enclosure. They had carried with them a number of hostages whom they had captured during the night of October 16–17, when they had first descended on Harpers Ferry. Firing, slow and half-hearted, was still in progress. The leader

[3] MS. A. G. O., vol. 6, S. O. 194, Oct. 17, 1859.

[4] H. B. McClellan: *The Life and Campaigns of . . . J. E. B. Stuart* (cited hereafter as *H. B. McClellan*), 28; *Villard*, 449.

[5] The B. & O. at that time had no direct line between Washington and Harpers Ferry.

[6] Lee to Secretary of War, MS., Oct. 17, 1859, 7:45 P.M.; A. G. O.

of the band, Lee heard, was a man styling himself Smith, who had been seen at Harpers Ferry and in Maryland before the attack. Lee ascertained, too, that Harpers Ferry was already swarming with Virginia militia and armed citizens, and that the engine house could be surrounded with little difficulty. There were troops enough, and to spare, for the only work ahead—that of storming the place. For this reason Lee telegraphed instructions to Baltimore that the troops dispatched from Fort Monroe should not be sent on. The message was duly received by the commanding officer, Captain E. O. C. Ord, whose name Lee was to hear more than once in the years that lay ahead.[7] Lee decided, also, to refrain from issuing the President's proclamation, because he did not deem the rising of such moment as to justify the document.[8] At 11 o'clock P.M. that night (October 17), he crossed the river and placed the militia in the armory enclosure with marines. His inclination was to attack at once, but he feared that if he entered the engine house in the darkness the hostages, who included some of the most prominent men of the neighborhood, might be slain in the mêlée.[9] He determined to survey the ground, to make ready for an assault on the engine house at daylight, and, meantime, to drew up a summons to the insurgents, in case they might be induced to yield and to give up their prisoners. This was the letter he addressed to the men in the armory, of whose identity he was not yet certain, though it was reported, about this hour of the night, that the leader of the gang was one John Brown, a notorious antislavery partisan from Kansas:[10]

[7] Lee to the Adjutant General, U. S. A., MS., Oct. 18, 1859; A. G. O. Cf. Correspondence Relating to the Insurrection at Harper's Ferry, 17th October, 1859 (Maryland Senate Document Y, March 2, 1860, p. 19; cited hereafter as Md. Doc. Y).

[8] The only mention of this proclamation is in Lee's MS. report of Oct. 19, 1859, A. G. O. Along the side of the paragraph referring to the proclamation is the contemporary pencilled word "omit." Nothing in the published document, the "Mason Report," indicates this omission. That is why the incident escaped the biographers of Brown. The content of the proclamation is not known. It probably established temporary martial law. The "Mason Report" is the Report of the Select Committee of the Senate appointed to inquire into the late Invasion and Seizure of the Public Property at Harper's Ferry (Senate Com. Report No. 278, 1st sess., 36th Cong., Washington, 1860; the "testimony" in this report has separate pagination).

[9] Governor Henry A. Wise of Virginia telegraphed Lee to "make no terms with the insurgents before I reach you" (Md. Doc. Y, p. 20), and subsequently believed that Lee had acted on his suggestion, but "Jeb" Stuart thought it doubtful whether Lee ever received Wise's message and was sure Lee acted on his own initiative. See Stuart's statement in Jones, L. and L., 106–7.

[10] Cf. report of Associated Press Correspondent Fulton, dated midnight, Oct. 17–18 1859; Md. Doc. Y, p. 19.

Headquarters Harper's Ferry,
October 18, 1859.

Colonel Lee, United States Army, commanding the troops sent by the President of the United States to suppress the insurrection at this place, demands the surrender of the persons in the armory buildings.

If they will peaceably surrender themselves and restore the pillaged property, they shall be kept in safety to await the orders of the President. Colonel Lee represents to them, in all frankness, that it is impossible for them to escape; that the armory is surrounded on all sides by troops; and that if he is compelled to take them by force he cannot answer for their safety.

R. E. LEE
Colonel Commanding United States Troops.[11]

Lee gave this message to Stuart about 2 A.M. and told him to deliver it, under a white flag, at the door of the engine house when directed to do so by a subsequent order. Lee intended to have the militia paraded and drawn up around the armory by the time he gave that order so that the insurgents would see he was not bluffing when he said the place was surrounded. Stuart was then to read the message to the insurgents, and was to tell them that if they accepted the terms they were to surrender their arms at once and give up their hostages. Lee did not believe the insurgents would do this, and he had to figure on the possibility that after they had refused his terms, they would threaten to kill, or might actually slay their captives, unless allowed safe conduct from the place. How would Lee guard against this? He decided that if he stormed the engine house the instant the insurgent leader declined to surrender he could probably save the hostages. Accordingly he told Stuart not to entertain any counter-proposal, but to give a signal the very moment the insurgents rejected his demand. On that signal, a storming party was to batter in the door and attack the insurgents with the bayonet. No shots were to be fired, lest some of the hostages be hit.[12]

Who were to form the storming party? Lee felt that as the insurrection was apparently directed against state authority, the

---

[11] *Mason Report*, 43–44.   [12] Lee in *Mason Report*, 41–42.

militia, if they desired to do so, should have the honor of capturing the invaders. About 6:30, therefore, he asked Colonel
Shriver, head of the Maryland volunteers in Harpers Ferry,
whether his men wanted to deliver the assaults. Shriver immediately declined. His soldiers, he said, had only come to help the
people of Harpers Ferry. "These men of mine," he went on,
"have wives and children at home. I will not expose them to such
risks. You are paid for doing this kind of work." Lee then
inquired of Colonel Robert W. Baylor, senior officer of the
Virginia militia companies, whether he wished to organize the
forlorn hope. Baylor also declined. Lee thereupon turned to
Lieutenant Green of the marines, to know if he wished the honor
of "taking those men out." Green doffed his hat and warmly
thanked Lee, who thereupon told him to pick twelve men from
his detachment as a storming party. Green immediately did so
and selected a dozen others as a reserve. Three were told off
to break in the doors of the engine house with hammers, and all of
them were instructed personally by Lee to employ only the bayonet. He explained to them, also, how to distinguish the captured
civilians, and he ordered them not to injure the slaves in the
building, unless the Negroes offered resistance. This last order
was prompted by lack of knowledge whether the Negroes were
in the conspiracy.

It was 7 o'clock on the morning of October 18 when arrangements were complete, and the light was sufficient for the assault
to be made. In civilian clothes still, and unarmed, Lee took his
stand on a slight elevation, about forty feet from the doors of the
engine house. Stuart was ready with his flag of truce. He and
Green had agreed that a wave of Stuart's hat was to be the signal
that the insurrectionists rejected the terms. Green and his selected
twenty-four men were close by but out of the line of fire, which
had virtually ceased during the night. The militia were in position, surrounding the building at a little distance. The whole
population of the town and most of the countryside had gathered
to witness the assault. Fully 2000 people were looking on when
Stuart advanced with his flag to the entrance of the engine house.
In answer to his summons, a gaunt, begrimed old man opened
one of the doors about four inches and thrust out a carbine.

Stuart, who had been on duty in Kansas, immediately confirmed the identification of this man. He was none other than "Ossawatomie" John Brown. Stuart read Lee's terms, which Brown at once began to argue. He wanted assurance that he would be permitted to leave the town with his prisoners and his wagon. He must be free to cross the bridge into Maryland, and to go along the road by the canal to a certain point. Then he would liberate his captives. Almost before Stuart could announce that Lee would entertain no counter-proposal, Brown was advancing another compromise. The hostages in the engine house overheard all this, of course, and some of them began to importune Stuart to call to Colonel Lee and see if he would not modify the terms set forth in the note. One voice from within cried out in a very different tone, "Never mind us, fire!" The speaker was Lewis W. Washington, grandnephew of the general. Lee, who knew him well, recognized his inflections and remarked quietly, "The old revolutionary blood does tell!"[18]

Stuart continued trying to explain that Lee would not consider any other terms. Brown babbled on; the hostages kept up their appeal. It was a long parley. Finally Stuart broke away, stepped from in front of the house, and waved his hat. On the second three of Green's marines advanced with their sledgehammers and tried to batter down the doors with them. The defenders opened fire almost as soon. In a moment it became evident that the doors were secured in such a way that they would spring inward under every blow. Green ordered the men to drop the hammers and move away. Looking about him, he saw a long ladder lying on the ground nearby, and he told some of his men to pick this up and use it instead of the sledges. Major Russell, with nothing in his hand but a rattan switch, advanced with these marines to the doors. One thrust of the improvised battering-ram was futile. At the next a ragged hole was splintered in one door. Lieutenant Green came from the abutment, where he had been directing the attack, and crept through the hole, armed only with his light dress sword. Russell followed him. The next man, a marine private, was shot down, mortally wounded. The fourth was struck in the face by a bullet. A few seconds more and the de-

[18] *Mason Report*, 67.

tachment was all inside. Three minutes after Stuart had given his signal, the affair was over. There were four dead men on the floor, two of whom had been killed prior to the assault that morning. One man was dying from an earlier bullet. Brown himself was bleeding from wounds inflicted by Lieutenant Green's sword and was thought to be mortally wounded. Two others were uninjured. The hostages, thirteen in number, were dirty and half-famished, but all of them had escaped bullets and bayonets. Colonel Lewis Washington refused to come out until a pair of gloves were brought, so that his neighbors might not see his soiled hands.[14]

The dead and the wounded were carried from the building and were laid on the grass. John Brown was soon removed to the paymaster's adjacent office. The day before there had been talk of violence on the part of half-drunken rowdies, but there was nothing of the sort now. Lee's authority was fully respected, and he was left to handle the situation as he saw fit. He had not regarded the affair at any time after his arrival as of great consequence,[15] and he now considered the "invasion" at an end. In a brief report filed about this hour for the Secretary of War, he no longer dignified John Brown's men as insurrectionists, but dismissed them as "rioters."[16] A little later in the day, however, he took care to send two parties across the Potomac into Maryland to search for missing men and to seize Brown's depot of arms.[17]

About 1 o'clock that afternoon arrived Governor Henry A. Wise of Virginia, Senator James M. Mason, and other dignitaries. All of them wanted to see and question Brown, whose injuries had been found by a surgeon to be superficial. Lee had Brown's wounded lieutenant, Aaron Stevens, brought over from the hotel and laid beside his chief, but before permitting Brown to be quizzed he told him that he would exclude all the visitors if they annoyed him or caused him pain.[18] Brown was willing, indeed anxious, to talk, and for three hours answered his questioners and argued with them on slavery. Lee's part in the interview was

---

[14] The best general narrative of the storming of the engine-house is in *Villard*, 451–55; for Lee's official account, see *Mason Report*, 40–43. Stuart's letter describing the affair is in *H. B. McClellan*, 29–30; Green, years afterwards, wrote his version in *North American Review*, December, 1885.

[15] Green, *loc. cit.*, 568.

[16] Lee to Secretary of War, MS., Oct. 18, 1859 [received 10:30 A.M.]; *A. G. O.*

[17] Lee's report, *loc. cit.*, 42.   [18] *Villard*, 456.

confined to noting the names of those whom Brown mentioned as members of his party. After he left Brown, Lee took the names Brown had given him and checked them, with Stuart's assistance, by the known dead and captured, and by a roll of the band that had been found at Brown's Maryland headquarters.[19] Some papers that seemed to throw light on the real purpose of the foolish attempt, Lee forwarded to the War Department by Major Russell, who was ready to return to Washington. In successive brief reports during the day he kept the secretary apprised of events.

As for the troops, Lee thought the militia might readily be dismissed but he deemed it necessary to keep the marines on the ground temporarily. His one concern was over the disposition of Brown and the other prisoners, and on this point he asked the instructions of the Secretary of War.[20] No decision having been reached at that time determining how the prisoners were to be tried, the War Department instructed Lee to place Brown and the other survivors in the joint custody of the United States marshal and of the sheriff of the county (Jefferson) where the insurrection had been attempted.[21] Lee made a final check of the conspirators on the morning of October 19 with Andrew Hunter, whom Governor Wise had designated as prosecutor;[22] then Lee had the prisoners removed by train to Charlestown, the county seat, under Lieutenant Green and an escort of marines.

As this seemed to him the last scene in his part of the drama, he began to draft his final report and to prepare the marines for their return to Washington. That night, about 9 o'clock, a wild tale came to Harpers Ferry that an attack had been made by insurrectionists on the village of Pleasant Valley, Md., some five miles away. Lee thought the story improbable but proceeded there in person with Stuart, Green, and twenty-five marines, only to find the village quiet and the report entirely false.[23] He returned to Harpers Ferry, brought his report down to that hour, took his command back to Washington on the train leaving at 1:15 A.M., and the next morning, October 20, completed the report and

[19] Lee in *Mason Report*, Testimony, 46.
[20] Lee to Secretary of War, Oct. 18, two MS. reports and one telegram; *A. G. O.*
[21] *Villard*, 470.
[22] Lee in *Mason Report*, Testimony, 46.   [23] Lee's report, *ibid.*, 43; *Villard*, 470–71.

presented himself at the War Department.[24] The Virginia state authorities had not complained at the withdrawal of the marines and had, if anything, been disposed to take the whole case in their hands; but shortly after Lee's departure Governor Wise entered a protest at the withdrawal of the Federal force and pointed out the unprotected condition of Harpers Ferry.[25]

After a few days at home, and about a fortnight's service on a board of officers considering the form of ceremonials and parades,[26] Lee was ordered back to Harpers Ferry. The radical abolitionist element in the North had been aroused to a frenzy by the assumed "martyrdom" of Brown. Irresponsible men were filling the mails with threats to rescue him and to harry Virginia in revenge for the impending execution of the man. Governor Wise had become deeply alarmed lest these threats be carried out, and while ordering Virginia militia and cadets to Charlestown he had asked President Buchanan to send Lee to Harpers Ferry again with sufficient troops to repel any attempt to seize the arsenal. The President had regarded the reports Wise forwarded him as "almost incredible," [27] but on November 29, he had the Secretary of War issue the necessary orders to Lee.[28] Lee first went to Baltimore to make arrangements for transferring the four companies of troops that were being sent him by steamship from Fort Monroe. Then he proceeded with them to Harpers Ferry, where he arrived about noon on November 30 and posted guard.[29] The next day he met Mrs. John Brown. She had come to ask permission to say farewell to her husband, who had been convicted and was to be hanged at Charlestown on December 2. Lee had no control over the prisoner or the execution and could only refer the sad woman to General William B. Taliaferro, commander of the Virginia troops.[30]

The day of Brown's execution passed without the appearance

[24] Lee in *Mason Report*, Testimony, 46. *Cf.* Lee's brief diary entries for this period in R. W. Winston: *Robert E. Lee* (cited hereafter as *Winston*), 71–72.

[25] Henry A. Wise to President Buchanan, MS., Oct. 24, 1859; MS. *A. G. O.; Calendar Va. State Papers*, vol. 11, 81–82.

[26] MS. *A. G. O.*, Nov. 2, 22, 1859; vol. 6, S. O., 214, 229. He served with this board Nov. 10–22, 1859.

[27] *Villard*, 524.

[28] MS. order of Nov. 29, 1859, in Lee's autograph, signed by the Secretary of War, *A. G. O.*

[29] MS. *A. G. O.*, Lee to A. G., Nov. 30, 1859.

[30] Lee to Mrs. Lee, Dec. 1, 1859; *R. E. Lee, Jr.*, 22–23.

of any of the desperadoes who were supposed to be massing. At Harpers Ferry nothing more exciting happened than the arrival of Brown's body and its transshipment to Philadelphia. Although Lee improved the idle time of the troops by drilling them in target practice, he and the men alike were glad when orders came on December 9 for a return on December 12 to their station.[31] The country continued to debate bitterly the rights and the wrongs of Brown's attempt, but the affair seems to have affected Lee very little. It influenced his views of pending political questions not at all, for he had very quickly made up his mind regarding Brown. "The result," he said in his report of October 19, written within thirty hours after the capture of the engine house, "proves that the plan was the attempt of a fanatic or madman. . . ."[32] He did not believe that the Negroes would respond to such appeals as Brown had made, and he troubled himself no more about it. From the time of his return home after his second journey to Harpers Ferry there is only a casual reference or two to John Brown in the whole of his correspondence during the rest of his life. If he felt depression at the display of hysterical sympathy with Brown, and at the appearance of bitter anti-Southern spirit in the North, he doubtless reflected that there were also extremists in his own section.

Lee had expected that the work at Arlington would have progressed far enough by the end of October to make it possible for him to leave at that time for Texas,[33] and he had procured an assignment of duty in Washington for Custis, so that the prospective master of Arlington might supervise the estate.[34] Orders had been issued prior to December 14 for him to join his regiment, but these had been suspended, at Senator Mason's request and without Lee's knowledge, in order that he might be a witness in the Harpers Ferry investigation.[35] He was called on January 10, 1860, but was asked only a few unimportant questions—chiefly to explain how he had prepared his list of the raiders and what he had found about the guarding of the armory in normal times.[36]

[31] MS. A. G. O., Lee to A. G., Dec. 10, 1859. [32] Mason Report, 42.
[33] MS. A. G. O., Lee to A. G., Oct. 1, 1859. [34] Jones, L. and L., 109.
[35] J. M. Mason to Secretary of War, MS., Dec. 13, 1859; Secretary of War to J. M. Mason, MS., Dec. 14, 1859; MS. A. G. O.
[36] Mason Report, Testimony, 46–47. For Lee's report on a controversy with the Maryland volunteers, regarding captured arms, see Lee to A. G., MS., Dec. 24, 1859; A. G. O.

This duty discharged, Lee was assigned on February 6, 1860, to temporary command of the Department of Texas, according to his brevet rank, with headquarters in San Antonio. It was a distinction, of course, to have departmental command, but as it was an accidental appointment, due to the fact that no colonel of the army was in Texas, Lee attached no importance to it.[37]

After he waved good-bye to his family and set out for Texas on February 10, 1860,[38] Lee was to spend less than three months of the remaining ten years of his life under the friendly old roof of Arlington. Like the fated victim in a Greek tragedy, he was coming under the influences of forces he could not control, forces against which it was futile for him even to struggle. Those last months of homely hard work at Arlington had merely rendered his destiny more certain. Some other Southern-born officers, sent for long tours of duty on distant stations, had lost contact with their states and with the social implications of the doctrine of states' rights. The development of the concept of a nation had eclipsed in their minds the older principle that a man's first duty was to his state. It had never been so with Lee. Often his post of duty had been close to Virginia. Always he had come back to Arlington as frequently as he could, no matter where he had been assigned. The spirit of Virginia had been alive in his heart every hour of his life. It had become more potent than ever during 1857–59, when he had sensed her feeling, had seen her reaction to the hostility of abolitionists, and had mingled much with his countless cousins, whose faith in Virginia's political rightness was as unquestioning as their belief in God. While in Texas, during the next fourteen months, he was to read of the coming crisis in a full understanding of how Virginia interpreted it. Having ploughed her fields, he had a new sense of oneness with her. He was a United States officer who loved the army and had pride in the Union, but something very deep in his heart kept him mindful that he had been a Virginian before he had been a soldier.

[37] *Cf.* Lee to unnamed correspondent, 1860: "My present position being but accidental . . ." (*Mason,* 70).
[38] R. E. Lee to Mrs. A. M. Fitzhugh, *MS.,* Feb. 9, 1860; *Duke Univ. MSS.*

CHAPTER XXIV

Colonel Lee Declares the Faith That Is in Him

Pitying his tired fellow-travellers more than himself, Lee reached New Orleans on the afternoon of February 13, 1860, and humorously admitted the next day, in a letter to Custis, that he had failed to bring some rather personal belongings with him: ". . . imagine my horror this morning when I found I had left my shaving-brush and pants behind. The first I constantly leave, but my pants, my *new pants,* I cannot account for. . . . I could hardly believe my own eyes when I found them out of their accustomed place. Take care of them, or use them as may be most convenient." [1]

From New Orleans on February 15, Lee sailed by steamer for Indianola, and thence he went to San Antonio, arriving on February 19. As he expected to direct the department for a short time only, he did not open elaborate private quarters, but thriftily boarded on the plaza. The next day he assumed command. [2] He found part of the forces disorganized by a series of plundering raids, made by Indians in northern Texas. On February 3, the animals of residents in the vicinity of Camp Colorado had been driven off. On February 17 many mules were stolen from Camp Cooper, perhaps by collusion. The garrison had been so reduced at the time, because of numerous detachments for scouting expeditions, that the band men had to be sent in pursuit of the thieves. Twenty-three mules were recovered, but forty others and three horses were lost. The very next day all the animals from the Indian agency near Camp Cooper were whipped into the

---

[1] R. E. Lee to Custis Lee, Feb. 14, 1860; Jones. *L. and L.,* 109.
[2] *Diary* in *Mason,* 68.

wilds by marauders, and a citizen was shot within two or three miles of a fort by three Indians on foot. Lee attributed these outrages to the lack of adequate troops in Texas, and also to the fact that the horses of the troopers were so worn down by hard riding that they could not overtake fleeing robbers.[3] The War Department promptly took cognizance of these and of other depredations by the Comanches and Kiowas, and authorized a large expedition sent out against the Indians as soon as the grass on the prairies would suffice for the horses.[4] Until this could be done, Lee worked as best he might to restore order.

The situation in the North had improved to such an extent by March 15 that Lee left San Antonio on that date for the Rio Grande to deal with Juan Cortinas. This man had been a bandit and desperado for ten years and in various ways had defied the Texas authorities. With something more than fifty men, on September 28, 1859, he had seized the town of Brownsville, where there were no United States troops and only a few American citizens. Cortinas had a free hand to murder and to rob, and then, for a time, he played hide and seek on both sides of the Rio Grande. On October 22 he worsted an irregular force sent out against him, and captured two light field-pieces from it. This success greatly emboldened him and gave to his activities almost the appearance of an insurrection. On the night of December 5, however, Lee's old West Point acquaintance, Major S. P. Heintzelman, arrived at Brownsville with 117 men, took over the demoralized Texas Rangers, and on December 27, near Rio Grande City, attacked and routed Cortinas's bandits. Thereafter the thieving band disintegrated rapidly.[5] With the leader on the run and his followers dispersed, Lee anticipated no trouble, "but," he wrote Custis, "there are so many contradictory reports that I think it better to see for myself, that I may if possible give quiet there and rest to the authorities at Washington."[6]

[3] W. W. Lowe to G. H. Thomas, *MS.*, Feb. 21, 1860; G. H. Thomas to Dept. Texas, *MS.*, Feb. 22, 1860; Lee to A. G., *MS.*, Feb. 20, 1860; Lee to Hdqrs. Army, *MS.*, March 6, 1860; *A. G. O.*

[4] H. L. Scott to A. G., *MS.*, March 10, 1860; *A. G. O.*

[5] Heintzelman's full report of March 1, 1860. *House Ex. Doc. 81, 1st sess., 36th Cong.*, p. 2; conveniently reprinted in *House Report No. 701, 2d sess., 45th Cong.*, Appendix, p. 75 *ff.*

[6] R. E. Lee to Custis Lee, March 13, 1860; Jones, *L. and L.*, 110.

Accompanied by a single company of cavalry, Lee pushed on toward Ringgold Barracks, but turned to the southwest and made for the Rio Grande in the vicinity of Eagle Pass, when he heard a rumor that Cortinas was in that quarter. From Eagle Pass, Lee and his men rode down the river to the barracks, where they arrived on March 31.[7] Once on the Rio Grande, Lee saw it would be impossible to catch Cortinas, or to prevent his return, unless the Mexican Government also took action against the bandit. Lee had been authorized to demand co-operation and to enter Mexico, if need be, in pursuit of Cortinas, so he called the Mexicans to their duty in this letter, written in a style he probably had acquired thirteen years before from General Scott:

> Hd. Qrs. Ringgold Barracks, 2d April, 1860.
> His Excy. Andres Trevino,
>   Govr. of State of Tamulipas, etc.,
>   Victoria, Mexico.
> Sir: In consequence of the recent outrages of Cortinas and his followers upon the persons and property of American citizens, I have been instructed by the Sec'y of War of the U. S. to notify the authorities of Mexico on the Rio Grande frontier, that they must break up and disperse the bands of banditti which have been concerned in these depredations and have sought protection in Mexican territory. Further, that they will be held responsible for the faithful performance of this plain duty on their part. I have, therefore, the honor to request that your Excellency will cause to be dispersed any bands within the States under your jurisdiction, having for their object depredations upon American soil.[8]

From Ringgold Barracks, on April 3, Lee conducted a careful inspection of the lower Rio Grande valley and not until April 11 did he reach Fort Brown.[9] On the way he had some correspondence with the authorities at Reynosa,[10] and later he received a protest from General G. Garcia of the Mexican army, over the action of some of the Texas Rangers, who had gone across the river

---

[7] *Diary* in *Mason*, 68.
[8] *Ex. Doc. 81, 1st sess., 36th Cong.*, p. 84; Jones, *L. and L.*, 111.
[9] *Diary* in *Mason*, 68–69.
[10] *House Report, No. 701, 2d sess., 45th Cong.*, Appendix, p. 84.

into Mexican territory at that point, forty miles west of Matamoras, in quest of Cortinas. Lee answered with some sharpness:

Hd. Qrs. Fort Brown, Texas, 12th April, 1860.
Gen'l G. Garcia,
    Commr. in Chief of the line of the Bravo,
        Matamoras, Mexico.

Gen'l: I had the honor to receive your letter of the 6th inst. on my way to this place, and postponed replying till my arrival. I regret that you consider the visit of Captain Ford of the Texas Rangers to the town of Reynosa, a cause for complaint, as that officer in his official report of the occurrence supposed he was acting in accordance with your sanction and the general understanding between yourself and Major Heintzelman, commanding the U. S. troops on the Rio Grande, viz., that the outlaw Cortinas and his band should be pursued and arrested wherever found.

I was gratified to learn from the authorities of the city of Reynosa and am pleased to have it repeated in your letter of the 6th that the authorities and public force of Mexico, under the orders of the superior authorities, will pursue and punish Cortinas and his followers; as the vindication of the violated laws of the United States will conduce to the restoration of quiet on our frontiers, and of amicable feelings between the two countries. For the attainment of this object I shall employ, if necessary, all the force in this Department, and I beg leave to inform you that I have been directed by the Honble Sec'y of War of the U. S., to notify the Mexican authorities on the Rio Grande, that they must break up and disperse the bands of banditti concerned in the outrages against the persons and property of American citizens. I shall therefore consider it my duty to hold them responsible for its faithful performance. As this agrees with the orders of the superior authorities of your own Govt. and I am sure is in accordance with your own sentiments, I feel confident of your cordial cooperation in the only means of preserving peace between the two countries. I have been informed that there are now in Matamoras persons that were engaged with Cortinas in his depredations upon American soil, ready, if opportunity favors, to renew these aggressions. If this is the case, I shall expect as an evidence of the friendly relations between the Govts. of the U. S. and Mexico, that they be apprehended and punished agreeably to the orders of the superior authorities of Mexico.[11]

Lee did not think the Mexicans would act against Cortinas, and though the bandit was reported to be 135 miles away, moving into the interior, Lee would have crossed the river and would have started in pursuit if he had believed his feeble horses could have found food in the country they would have had to cover.[12] As time passed and Lee heard nothing more of the bandit, he decided that Cortinas had left the Rio Grande, and he accordingly planned to return to San Antonio. The day before he had arranged to start, however, he got a report that Cortinas was back on the Rio Grande. To trap him, Lee sent two companies across the river, only to find, once again, that rumor outrode the bandit. More correspondence with the Mexican authorities followed. Finally they promised to arrest Cortinas, and Lee set out for San Antonio. He covered the 264 miles between May 8 and 17[13] Two months later Lee was able to report that even rumors of Cortinas's presence on the north bank of the Rio Grande had ceased and that he proposed to withdraw some of the troops from unhealthy districts on the river.[14]

From the time of his arrival at San Antonio until late in the autumn Lee had only his routine duties to occupy him. He drew up a plan for the establishment of a military post at the head-waters of the Concha, but could do nothing to carry out the idea, as the Secretary of War had no funds available for it.[15] He had a few things to cheer him, such as the arrival of his first grand-child, whom Rooney and Charlotte insisted on naming after him. "I wish," he said, "I could offer him a more worthy name and a better example. He must elevate the first, and make use of the latter to avoid the errors I have committed. I also expressed the thought [in a separate letter to Charlotte] that under the circumstances you might like to name him after his great-grand-father, and wish you both, 'upon mature consideration,' to follow

---

[11] *House Report, No. 701, loc. cit.*, 84; Jones, *L. and L.*, 112.
[12] R. E. Lee to Custis Lee. April 16, 1860; Jones, *L. and L.*, 113–14.
[13] *Diary* and fragment of a letter to Mrs. Lee, May 2, 1860; *Mason*, 69.
[14] Lee to A. G., *MS.*, July 19, 1860; *A. G. O.*
[15] Lee to Hdqrs. Army, *MS.*, Aug. 13, 1860; *A. G. O.*

your inclinations and judgment. I should love him all the same, and nothing could make me love you two more than I do." [16]

A certain amusement Lee found in the observance of Saint John's Day, when every Mexican in San Antonio rode wildly up and down the streets. "I did not know before," he said, "that Saint John set so high a value upon equitation." [17] He interested himself in the building of an Episcopal church at San Antonio, [18] and he was rejoiced that his youngest son, Robert, was preparing for confirmation. [19] Despite his separation from his family, he tried to be philosophical. ". . . We want but little," he wrote Rooney. "Our happiness depends upon our independence, the success of our operations, prosperity of our plans, health, contentment, and the esteem of our friends." [20] But under the surface of cheerfulness, this was a time of deep depression with Lee. He only hinted at it vaguely in one of his letters:

"At this distance from those you love and care for, with the knowledge of the vicissitudes and necessities of life, one is rent by a thousand anxieties, and the mind as well as body is worn and racked to pieces. But I will not, dear Cousin Anna, impose my sad thoughts upon you, for a man may manifest and communicate his joy, but he should conceal and smother his grief as much as possible. Touching your kind wishes for my speedy return, you know the embarrassment that attends it. A divided heart I have too long had, and a divided life too long led. That may be one cause of the small progress I have made on either hand, my professional and civil career. Success is not always attained by a single undivided effort, it rarely follows a halting vacillating course. My military duties require me here, whereas my affections and urgent domestic claims call me away. And thus

---

16 R. E. Lee to W. H. F. Lee, June 2, 1860; *Jones,* 381. *Cf.* same to same, April 2, 1860, Jan. 29, 1861; Jones, *L. and L.,* 112–13, 121–22. An account of the christening appears in Lee to Mrs. Lee, *MS.,* Jan. 23, 1861; *Lee Papers.*
17 Lee to Mrs. Lee, June 24, 1860; Jones, *L. and L.,* 115.
18 *R. E. Lee, Jr.,* 33.
19 Lee to Mrs. Anna Fitzhugh, *MS.,* June 6, 1860; Confederate Museum. Lee's reference, which evidences his belief in the doctrine of religious conversion, is as follows: "I know you will sympathize in the joy I feel at the impression made by a merciful God upon the youthful heart of dear little Rob. May He that has opened his eyes to the blessing of Salvation, taught him the way, and put in his heart the good resolution he has formed, enable him to do all things to secure and accomplish it. . . ."
20 R. E. Lee to W. H. F. Lee, Aug. 22, 1860: *Jones,* 381.

I live and am unable to advance either. But while I live I must toil and trust." [21]

Slow promotion, as well as homesickness, had something to do with this mild but melancholy expression of the old sense of frustration. He was now fifty-three, and had been twenty-two years in advancing from the grade of captain to that of lieutenant colonel. Between him and the rank of general officer stood nineteen colonels and three lieutenant colonels, while four other lieutenant colonels had been commissioned the same day that he had been. Twenty-two men at least between him and titular brigade command! After holding a commission for thirty-one years his pay was only $1205 per annum, and his gross return from the government—pay, rations, quarters, travel, and everything— only $4060.[22] This was very discouraging to the father of four unmarried daughters, and the husband of an invalid wife. What made it worse was the belief that he did not know how to advance his interests in the army. There was Joe Johnston, for instance. Johnston had belonged to the topographical engineers, but he had early undertaken special duties in order to win promotion. Lee had realized what Johnston was after, had seen how he was proceeding to get what he wanted, and yet Lee had felt himself wholly incapable, somehow, of doing the same thing.[23] Johnston, who was a cousin of the Secretary of War, had been on detached duty in Washington and had been assigned important duties. Lee was glad to see his friend advanced and cheerfully admitted that Johnston was worthy of the honor, but he was stung by what he considered the injustice of Floyd's preferment of Johnston. "I think it must be evident to him," Lee confided to Custis, "that it never was the intention of Congress to advance him to the position assigned him by the Sec'y. It was not so recognized before, and in proportion to his services he has been advanced beyond anyone in the army and has thrown more discredit than ever on the system of favoritism and making brevets." [24]

---

[21] R. E. Lee to Mrs. Anna Fitzhugh, *MS.*, June 6, 1860; *loc. cit.*
[22] Army Register, 1860; *Ex. Doc. 54, H. of R., 2d sess., 36th Cong.*
[23] *Cf.* "Joe Johnston is playing Adjt. Gen'l. in Florida to his heart's content. His plan is good, he is working for promotion. I hope he will succeed" (Lee to John Mackay, *MS.*, Feb. 3, 1846; *Elliott MSS.*).
[24] R. E. Lee to Custis Lee, April 16, 1860; Jones, *L. and L.*, 113.

While Johnston was in Washington, death made vacant the office of quartermaster general, long held by Thomas S. Jesup. The office carried with it the rank of brigadier general and, of course, was much sought after. Scott is reported to have been asked to suggest a successor to Jesup and is said to have declined to do so, preferring instead to name four men, any one of whom he considered qualified. The four were Joseph E. Johnston, Robert E. Lee, Albert Sidney Johnston, and Charles F. Smith.[25] As among these possible appointees, Floyd chose Joseph E. Johnston.[26] Lee cheerfully wrote his congratulations to the fortunate brigadier:

San Antonio, Texas, July 30, 1860.

My dear General: I am delighted at accosting you by your present title, and I feel my heart exult within me at your high position. I hope the old State may always be able to furnish worthy successors to the first chief of your new department; and that in your administration the country and army will have cause to rejoice that it has fallen upon you. Please present my cordial congratulations to Mrs. J., and say that I fear, now that she will have you constantly with her, she will never want to see me again. May happiness and prosperity always attend you is the sincere wish of

Very truly yours,

R. E. Lee[27]

His old classmate's attainment to the rank of the general officer made Lee look on himself, more than ever, as a failure, a man whose errors of judgment and slowness in promoting his own interests had left him far down the ladder.[28]

In this depression of mind, as the autumn of 1860 opened, Lee found himself involved in the darkest of American tragedies. He had bantered Cassius Lee years before about the superiority of the Whigs, and he had watched the outcome of the successive presidential elections with more than the average man's interest, but this had primarily been because of the effect that changes of

25 Robert M. Hughes: *General Johnston*, 33.
26 Named as of June 28, 1860.   27 Robert M. Hughes, *op. cit.*, 34.
28 His letters of 1860–61 contain several references to his "errors." *E.g.*, R. E. Lee to W. H. F. Lee, June 2, 1860, Jan. 29, 1861; Jones, *L. and L.*, 113–22.

administration had on the War Department and on the army. Of Congress he had seen enough to view it without illusion, but he had served in no Southern state except Texas in nearly thirty years, and he had not had close contact with the passions the slavery question had aroused there. It was his nature, moreover, to leave politics to the politicians.

It could no longer be so. The wrath aroused by the John Brown raid had not cooled. Politics had become the affair of every man and the concern of every soldier, for the old amity among the states was gone. Men all around Lee were talking of secession if the "Black Republicans" carried the presidential election. The Republican ticket, Lincoln and Hamlin, had no support in Texas. Douglas and Johnson, the nominees of the Northern element of the disrupted Democratic party, had only a scant following. Lee himself had believed in July that Judge Douglas should withdraw "and join himself and party to aid in the election of Breckinridge" and the defeat of Lincoln, but he had added regretfully, "Politicians I fear are too selfish to become martyrs." [29] The real contest in the Lone Star State was between Bell and Everett, the Whig candidates, and Breckinridge and Lane, chosen by the Southern Democrats who had left the Charleston convention because of disagreement over the party's declaration on slavery in the territories. When the state elections of October 9 in Pennsylvania and Indiana were carried by the Republicans,[30] the Southern Democrats in Texas argued that the only possible way to defeat Lincoln was to throw the whole strength of the South to Breckinridge.[31] This view prevailed. In the fateful election of November 6, 1860, Texas's vote was Breckinridge, 47,548, Bell, 15,463. Lee's own state went for Bell by a plurality of 358 over Breckinridge. But Lincoln was elected. In four days the South Carolina legislature issued a call for a convention to withdraw the state from the Union; sentiment for secession grew stronger over night; and everywhere in Texas the people were flying the "Lone Star" flag. Governor Sam Houston was opposed to secession, and as his opponents were sure he would not call an extra

[29] Lee to Major Earl Van Dorn, *MS.*, July 3, 1860; Library of Congress.
[30] J. F. Rhodes: *History of the United States from the Compromise of 1850* (cited hereafter as *Rhodes*), vol. 3, p. 114.
[31] D. G. Wooten: *Comprehensive History of Texas* (cited hereafter as *Wooten*), vol. 2, p. 83.

session of the legislature, they began to agitate for a "popular convention" chosen without a formal legislative call.[32] Much influence in behalf of secession was exerted by the Knights of the Golden Circle, a secret organization somewhat similar to the post-bellum Ku Klux Klan. The K. G. C. had "castles" all over the state. It was believed they could on four days' notice put 8000 fully equipped men in the field.[33]

From Lee's own state such newspapers as he received during the first weeks after the election told of much dissatisfaction and of many appeals for secession, but of no action to that end. Lee was profoundly concerned but not despairing. "The Southern states," he wrote Custis, "seem to be in a convulsion . . . It is difficult to see what will be the result, but I hope all will end well." He was expecting at the time to be relieved of command of the Department of Texas by the return of General D. E. Twiggs,[34] and he thought that after the General's arrival he would be sent on an expedition into the Comanche country. In the letter just quoted he told his son of this: "But I shall not mind that, nor regret my departure from San Antonio, except so far as it will take me farther from you all, and render my communication with you more distant and precarious. But God's will be done! It will only prepare us for a longer separation soon to come. My little personal troubles sink into insignificance when I contemplate the condition of the country, and I feel as if I could easily lay down my life for its safety. But I also feel that would bring but little good." [35]

His distress over the threat to the Union, and his lack of sympathy with the extreme policies proposed by many of those about him, caused Lee to withdraw into himself and to guard his tongue. From this period date the first of the references to the reserve he showed so strongly in later years that it has been

---

[32] 2 *Wooten*, 85–86.

[33] Charles Anderson: *Texas Before and on the Eve of the Rebellion.* . . . (Cincinnati, 1884) (cited hereafter as *C. Anderson*), pp. 8, 17–18.

[34] Jones (*L. and L.,* 115–16, and elsewhere) consistently misread "Twiggs" in the *Lee MSS.* for "Scruggs." There was no "Scruggs" among the general officers of the army. If Twiggs had not returned, Lee would have been superseded on the arrival in Texas of Colonel C. A. Waite of the 1st Infantry, whose commission antedated Lee's (L. Thomas to A. G., *MS.,* Oct. 24, 1860; *A. G. O.*).

[35] R. E. Lee to Custis Lee, Nov. 24, 1860; Jones, *L. and L.,* 115–17.

mistakenly assumed to be a part of his personality from youth. "I knew him well," wrote a Kentuckian, who was thrown with him often in the fall of 1860, "perhaps I might say, intimately, though his grave, cold dignity of bearing and the prudential reserve of his manners rather chilled over-early, or over-much intimacy."[36] There is no earlier comment on Lee's "coldness." On the other hand, his exuberance of spirit was often noted, especially in his youth.

As the exciting days passed it looked for a time as if secession might be accomplished peaceably and by consent. General Scott believed the Southern states should not be forced to remain in the Union or punished for leaving it, though he had no sympathy with secession. Horace Greeley said in the *Tribune:* "We hope never to live in a republic whereof one section is pinned to the residue by bayonets." [37] This "Greeley policy" was strengthened by a reaction on the part of some who had voted for Lincoln without realizing what the consequences might be.[38] Lee sensed this movement, and momentarily he, too, reasoned that the Union might simply be dissolved. In such a case his command would, of course, be withdrawn from Texas and might be disbanded. If, on the other hand, the Union were preserved, he was still ambitious to win advancement. In a letter to Custis, he stated the alternatives half-awkwardly and half-seriously: "If the Union is dissolved, which God in his mercy forbid, I shall return to you. If not, tell my friends to give me all the promotion they can." [39] That, surely, was not the language of one who believed war was inevitable. Neither was it the language of a man who knew the adroit, secret methods of getting the promotion he naturally desired.

Passion continued high while Lee still hoped. Events rushed on. A committee of Texans on December 3 joined in a call to the

---

[36] *C. Anderson,* 24. The rest of the passage is worth quoting as the estimate of a man who was strongly Unionist in sympathy, a brother of Major Robert Anderson's, of Fort Sumter: "And of all the officers or men whom I ever knew he came (save one other alone) the nearest in likeness to that classical ideal Chevalier Bayard. . . . And if these, our modern, commercial, mechanical, utilitarian ages, ever did develop a few of these types of male chivalric virtues, which we attribute solely to those 'ages of faith,' Robert E. Lee was one of the highest and finest models."

[37] 3 *Rhodes,* 141 *ff.*   [38] 3 *Rhodes,* 144.

[39] R. E. Lee to Custis Lee, Dec. 5, 1860; Jones, *L. and L.,* 118.

people to elect a convention to decide whether the state should secede. The next day President Buchanan in his annual message to Congress declared that secession was "neither more nor less than revolution," a sentence that stuck in Lee's mind. On December 6 the people of South Carolina elected a convention, every member of which was a secessionist. Then, on the 7th, seeing that a convention might be called in spite of him, Governor Houston summoned the Texas legislature to meet on January 21, 1861, in extra session. The air was full of boasts and threats; the advocates of immediate secession were asserting that they spoke for the entire South, and some were hinting that disaster would overtake the border slave states unless they joined the secession movement.

Lee's wrath slowly rose as this attitude showed itself among "Cotton-state" extremists with whom he had little in common. He did not admit the unity of Southern interests. Save as he felt that the citizens of every state had equal rights in the territories, he had no regard at the time for the South as a section, much less as a confederation. His mind was for the Union; his instinct was for his state, Virginia. He felt powerless to help in preserving the Union, but with the religious faith that had been growing steadily since the Mexican War, he could not believe a beneficent Providence would permit its destruction. As for his state, he looked on Virginia much as he did on his family. He did not then or thereafter stop to reason out the nature of this feeling, which was instinctive.

He set forth these views in a letter he wrote Custis on December 14. He told first of the arrival of General Twiggs and of his own prospective departure for the headquarters of his regiment at Fort Mason:

"He [General Twiggs] thinks the Union will be dissolved in six weeks, and that he will then return to N[ew] O[rleans]. If I thought so, I would not take the trouble to go to Mason, but [would] return to you now. I hope, however, the wisdom and patriotism of the country will devise some way of saving it, and that a kind Providence has not yet turned the current of His blessings from us. The three propositions of the President are eminently just, are in accordance with the constitution and ought to be cheerfully assented to by all the States.[40] But I do not think the Northern and Western States will agree to them."

Then he went on:

"It is, however, my only hope for the preservation of the Union, and I will cling to it to the last. Feeling the aggressions of the North, resenting their denial of the equal rights of our citizens to the common territory of the commonwealth, etc., I am not pleased with the course of the 'Cotton States,' as they term themselves. In addition to their selfish, dictatorial bearing, the threats they throw out against the 'Border States,' as they call them, if they will not join them, argue [sic] little for the benefit While I wish to do what is right, I am unwilling to do what is wrong, either at the bidding of the South or the North. One of their plans seems to be the renewal of the slave trade. That I am opposed to on every ground. . . ."[41]

He added the practical counsel that Custis should pay all debts as soon as possible and should "hold on to specie."[42] Almost before this letter had left San Antonio, Lee declared himself even more fully when Charles Anderson came to him with a copy of a confidential pamphlet General Scott had sent him. Anderson explained that Scott had asked him to show this document to General Twiggs, to Lee, and to such other officers as Anderson thought proper. Anderson had already lent it to General Twiggs, who had grumbled over it, and had remarked, on Anderson's statement that he intended to pass it on to Lee, "Ah! I know General Scott fully believes that God Almighty had to spit on his hands to make Bob Lee and Bob Anderson."

After Anderson left, Lee read the paper, which proved to be an

---

[40] Buchanan urged an "explanatory amendment" on slavery containing (1) a recognition of "the right of property in slaves in the states where it now exists or may hereafter exist"; (2) the duty of protecting this right in the territories, "throughout their territorial existence, and until they shall be admitted as states into the Union, with or without slavery, as their constitutions may prescribe," and (3) enforcement of the fugitive-slave laws, with a declaration of the unconstitutionality of state laws modifying them (5 Richardson: *Messages and Papers of the Presidents*, 5, 638).

[41] R. E. Lee to Custis Lee, Dec. 14, 1860; Jones, *L. and L.*, 118–19.

[42] This does not appear in Jones's version but is in the original which is among the *Duke Univ. MSS.*

exposition of General Scott's views on the steps that might be taken to prevent war, and on the strategy that should be followed in case hostilities should be opened.[43] Lee doubtless reflected that the publication of Scott's plan would be accepted in Texas as proof of the overt intentions of the Federal Government and might thereby aggravate the probability of war that Scott, Anderson, and he alike were anxious to avert.

He accordingly sent for Anderson, who called in company with Doctor Willis G. Edwards. Lee returned him the pamphlet. "My friend," said he, "I must make one request of you, and that is, that you will not suffer these *Views* to get into the newspapers." Anderson promised, though he did not understand why Lee was so solicitous on this point. The conversation then shifted, inevitably, to the crisis. Anderson spoke out vigorously. Lee remarked, "Somebody surely is grievously at fault, probably both factions." Anderson, strongly Federalist in his views, answered that he had previously thought both sides were to blame, but that he had concluded there was a definite conspiracy against the Union, by men who were only alleging abolition as an excuse. Lee made no answer. Then Doctor Edwards raised the question whether a man's first allegiance was due his state or the nation. Lee's courteous reticence vanished. Instantly he spoke out, and unequivocally. He had been taught to believe, he said, and he did believe that his first obligations were due Virginia.[44]

His own position plain to all his intimates, Lee left San Antonio on December 19 for the comparative isolation of Fort Mason, the headquarters of the 2d Cavalry.[45] He had not been with his regiment for two years and two months; in fact, from the time he had taken command at Louisville, in 1856, until he left Texas for the last time in February, 1861, he was with his own soldiers only fourteen months and with other troops a little more than two months. That constituted his experience as a line officer prior to the time he resigned from the United States army.[46] In Mexico,

[43] It was entitled: *"Views Suggested by the Imminent Danger, Oct. 29, 1860, of a Disruption of the Union by the Secession of One or More of the Southern States."*

[44] *C. Anderson,* 29–31. Anderson fixed the date of this conversation as Dec. 15, 1860, or about that time. The *Views* were republished in *The Washington National Intelligencer,* Jan. 18, 1861.

[45] He arrived on Dec. 22; *Diary* in *Mason,* 70.

[46] The total strength of the Second Cavalry, as of Feb. 26, 1861, was 739 officers and men.

of course, during 1847, he had enjoyed larger opportunities, but always as a staff officer, even though a most favored one.

Neither Lee nor his men were in a mood to improve their renewed acquaintance by hard drilling or field manœuvres after the lieutenant colonel came back to headquarters. They discharged their routine duties, of course, but in bewilderment of mind they saw their world being dissolved about them. Every mail brought reports of some new tragedy. While Lee had been riding toward Fort Mason, South Carolina's convention had voted unanimously for secession, and hotheads had rejoiced as though the division of the Union were as great an act as its creation. In Congress the Crittenden compromise was voted down almost in the hour of South Carolina's secession. On December 26, Colonel Robert Anderson, commanding the United States coast defenses at Charleston, S. C., moved his troops from an exposed position at Fort Moultrie to the security of Fort Sumter, in the harbor. Men held their breath, not knowing whether the next day would see madness sweeping the country into the agonies of war, or whether sanity would assert itself in a new compromise that all would accept as a better alternative than bloodshed among brothers.

The new year came, the blackest in American history. On January 9, the steamer *Star of the West* was fired on by South Carolinians as she attempted to enter Charleston harbor, with reinforcements for the garrison of Fort Sumter. On the same day Mississippi seceded. Florida followed on the 10th, Alabama on the 11th, and Georgia on the 18th. Every hour the prospect seemed darker, but earnest men, in and out of Congress, were still at work and had not despaired of effecting a settlement.

At Fort Mason, Lee watched events and spent some of those dismal January days in reading Everett's *Life of Washington*, which had been prepared for the *Encyclopædia Britannica* and had been separately republished. It was a hasty work of no originality, and it traced the career of Lee's hero with scant interpretative comment. One passage, however, suggested a parallel that probably did not escape Lee's eye. It was this:

"Washington, by nature the most loyal of men to order and law, whose rule of social life was obedience to rightful authority, was from the first firmly on the American side; not courting, not contemplating, even, till the eve of the explosion, a forcible resistance to the mother country, but not recoiling from it when forced upon the colonies as the inevitable result of their principles." [47]

That was almost precisely the state of mind in which, on January 23, 1861, Lee wrote in a letter home his fullest and most important statement of his conception of his duty in the crisis. He said:

". . . I received from Major Nicholls Everett's life of Washington, you sent me and enjoyed its perusal very much. How his spirit would be grieved could he see the wreck of his mighty labors! I will not, however, permit myself to believe till all ground of hope is gone that the work of his noble deeds will be destroyed, and that his precious advice and virtuous example will so soon be forgotten by his countrymen. As far as I can judge by the papers, we are between a state of anarchy and civil war. May God avert from us both. It has been evident for years that the country was doomed to run the full length of democracy. To what a fearful pass it has brought us. I fear that mankind will not for years be sufficiently Christianized to bear the absence of restraint and force. I see that four states have declared themselves out of the Union; four more will apparently follow their example. Then, if the Border States are brought into the gulf of revolution, one-half of the country will be arrayed against the other. I must try and be patient and await the end, for I can do nothing to hasten or retard it." [48]

In another letter of the same date, written probably to Custis, he said:

"The South, in my opinion, has been aggrieved by the acts of the North, as you say. I feel the aggression, and am willing to take every proper step for redress. It is the principle I contend for, not individual or private gain. As an American citizen, I take great pride in my country, her prosperity and institutions, and would defend any State if her rights were invaded. But I can anticipate

[47] Edward Everett, *Life of George Washington*, 94.
[48] *MS. Lee Papers*, copy of which was graciously supplied the writer by Mrs. Mary Custis Lee De Butts. Jones (*op. cit.*, 137) gave a very incorrect version of this letter.

no greater calamity for the country than a dissolution of the Union. It would be an accumulation of all the evils we complain of, and I am willing to sacrifice everything but honor for its preservation. I hope, therefore, that all constitutional means will be exhausted before there is a recourse to force. Secession is nothing but revolution. The framers of our Constitution never exhausted so much labor, wisdom and forbearance in its formation, and surrounded it with so many guards and securities, if it was intended to be broken by every member of the Confederacy at will. It was intended for 'perpetual union' so expressed in the preamble,[49] and for the establishment of a government, not a compact, which can only be dissolved by revolution, or the consent of all the people in convention assembled. It is idle to talk of secession. Anarchy would have been established, and not a government by Washington, Hamilton, Jefferson, Madison, and the other patriots of the Revolution. . . . Still, a Union that can only be maintained by swords and bayonets, and in which strife and civil war are to take the place of brotherly love and kindness,[50] has no charm for me. I shall mourn for my country and for the welfare and progress of mankind. If the Union is dissolved, and the Government disrupted, I shall return to my native State and share the miseries of my people, and save in defence will draw my sword on none." [51]

In a similar spirit, he wrote Markie Williams:

"God alone can save us from our folly, selfishness and short sightedness. The last accounts seem to shew that we have barely escaped anarchy to be plunged into civil war. What will be the result I cannot conjecture. I only see that a fearful calamity is upon us, and fear that the country will have to pass through for its sins a fiery ordeal. I am unable to realize that our people will destroy a government inaugurated by the blood and wisdom of our patriot fathers, that has given us peace and prosperity at home,

[49] Here, of course, as illustrating his lack of familiarity with constitutional law, Lee confused the preamble of the Articles of Confederation with that of the Constitution of 1787, which proposed a "more perfect union."
[50] This, it will be observed, was an echo of the *Tribune* editorial (*supra*, p. 415) that was the basis of the "Greeley policy."
[51] Jones, *L. and L.*, 120–21. In a letter to A. C. Brackett (n. d., n. p.), he is quoted as saying: "I fear the liberties of our country will be buried in the tomb of a great nation" (*Battles and Leaders of the Civil War*, cited hereafter as *B. and L.*), I, 36 n.

power and security abroad, and under which we have acquired a colossal strength unequalled in the history of mankind. I wish to live under no other government, and there is no sacrifice I am not ready to make for the preservation of the Union save that of honour. If a disruption takes place, I shall go back in sorrow to my people and share the misery of my native state, and save in her defence there will be one soldier less in the world than now. I wish for no other flag than the 'Star spangled banner' and no other air than 'Hail Columbia.' I still hope that the wisdom and patriotism of the nation will yet save it.

"I am so remote from the scene of events and receive such excited and exaggerated accounts of the opinions and acts of our statesmen, that I am at a loss what to think. I believe that the South justly complains of the aggressions of the North, and I believed that the North would cheerfully redress the grievances complained of. I see no cause of disunion, strife and civil war and pray it may be averted.

"My own troubles, anxieties and sorrows sink into insignificance when I contemplate the sufferings past and prospective of the nation. Yet I am very desirous to be near those who claim my protection, and who may need my assistance. Nothing prevents my endeavouring to do so but the necessity of my presence with the Regiment. There is no other field officer with it." [52]

On the convictions expressed in his talk with Anderson, and on those set forth in these letters, which were written nearly three months before he resigned from the army, the whole of Lee's subsequent course was based. He refused to despair until the very last hour, but he believed that the country stood between anarchy, through the dissolution of the Union, and war, through secession. Like Buchanan, he regarded secession as nothing but revolution. Prior to the war, he never believed in secession as a right. In January, 1861, it was not justified in his opinion, even as revolution, but if it came, he would not serve a Union that had to be maintained by force.

The plain inference from the concluding sentence of the second letter quoted above is that if secession destroyed the Union, Lee

[52] Jan. 22, 1861; *Markie Letters*, 58–59.

intended to resign from the army and to fight neither for the South nor for the North, unless he had to act one way or the other in defense of Virginia. In this, he showed that he was no constitutional lawyer. Apparently he did not stop to reason that Virginia could not be neutral in a war between the states, but must either fight with the North against the South or with the South against the North. Perhaps his optimism and his devotion to the Union led him to close his mind to this hard logic of action. But Mrs. Lee correctly stated his position when she said, "From the first commencement of our troubles he had decided that in the event of Virginia's secession, duty . . . would compel him to follow."[53] In the light of his own words and hers, it is hard to understand why it has been so widely believed that he waited until the secession of Virginia to determine what he would do.[54] There is not the slightest doubt that before he left Texas he had decided, without any mental struggle, or thought of personal gain or loss, to stand with Virginia, though he hoped with all his heart that the Union would be preserved.

Time and circumstance were not to shake him from this position. His political philosophy was born in him, a part of his very ego. Reaction to particular events was merely the steadfast response of a determined soul to developments he deplored but could not deflect. His one hope was inspired by a religion as simple as his instinctive allegiance to Virginia. After Louisiana seceded, on January 26, and the Texas convention met in bel-

[53] Quoted (second-hand, unfortunately) in *Long*, 91.
[54] *Cf.* Taylor's *General Lee*, 20: ". . . those who knew him best understood that there was no struggle of this kind, although it was a serious trial to him to separate himself from a service to which he had devoted the best years of his life and all the ability he possessed." This view of Taylor's, based on an intimate knowledge of Lee, is confirmed by a score of circumstances, among them those attending an interview Lee had in November, 1865, with a British visitor, Herbert C. Saunders. When Saunders, in July, 1866, sent him the manuscript of an article he proposed to publish, Lee declined to be quoted but, as explained in Volume IV of this work, he revised Saunders's manuscript. Saunders had written: "This right [of secession] he [*i.e.*, Lee] told me he always held as a constitutional maxim. . . . As to the policy of secession on the part of the South he was at first distinctly opposed to it, and it was not until Lincoln issued a proclamation for 75,000 men to invade the South which he deemed clearly unconstitutional that he had then no longer any doubt what course his loyalty to the Constitution and to his State required him to take" (*MS.*, July 31, 1866; Washington and Lee University, first cited and reproduced in *Winston*, 391 *ff.*). Lee made various changes in this statement, and struck out altogether the reference to the "doubt" in his mind. The last sentence, as finally revised by Lee read thus: "As to its exercise [*i.e.*, of the right of secession] at the time on the part of the South, he was distinctly opposed, and it was not until Lincoln issued a proclamation for 75,000 men to invade the South which was deemed clearly unconstitutional that Virginia withdrew from the U. States."

ligerent temper on the 28th, he wrote in deepest distress: "The country seems to be in a lamentable condition and may have been plunged into civil war. May God rescue us from the folly of our own acts, save us from selfishness and teach us to love our neighbors as ourselves." [55]

Demoralization had now come over the army commanders in Texas. General Twiggs believed that he would soon be compelled to surrender his forces. Pay had stopped and all allowances were reduced. Every one was waiting for a turn of events that each one shaped according to his own hopes or fears. Lee hoped that if Texas seceded the United States troops would be ordered away. "I certainly shall not want to stay," he told Mrs. Lee.[56] An Indian raid in the country below Fort Mason called forth the usual pursuit, but the interest in it was dwarfed by greater events.[57]

On February 1 the Texas convention, which the legislature had voted to recognize, passed an ordinance of secession by a vote of 166 to 7.[58] This ordinance provided for a referendum, but the convention proceeded to act as if ratification by the people were certain, as indeed it was. Secession was now a reality in seven states, and plans for the establishment of a separate Southern government were under way. Offsetting, to some extent, these grim omens of internecine strife, was the news that a peace conference, called at the instance of Virginia, had met in earnest mood on February 4 in Washington. On the same day the people of Lee's mother state elected a convention but chose to it a two-to-one majority of delegates opposed to secession. Virginia voters overwhelmingly decided, further, that no ordinance of secession should be valid unless and until it was approved by the voters at the polls.[59]

For these reasons, hope was not dead when Lee received a

---

[55] R. E. Lee to Custis Lee, Jan. 30, 1861; Jones, *L. and L.*, 122. Jones's transcription of this letter makes a new sentence begin with the word "*Save*." Although Lee never hesitated as to his own duty, he was anxious that his children's interests should not suffer. In this letter to Custis, he spoke of the money that was being accumulated to pay off the legacies provided in the will of his father-in-law. He had intended, he said, to buy Virginia bonds, but Virginia might secede, in which case the investment might be lost. Custis, however, was to act as the other executors advised (*Duke Univ. MSS.*).

[56] Lee to Mrs. Lee, Jan. 23, 1861; MS., Lee Papers.

[57] R. E. Lee to Custis Lee, Jan. 30, 1861; Jones, *L. and L.*, 122.

[58] 2 *Wooten*, 104.

[59] Provision for the election of a convention had been made on Jan. 12, 1861, at a special session of the general assembly of Virginia.

wholly unexpected message from Twiggs's headquarters in San Antonio, under date of February 4: by direct order of the War Department Lieutenant Colonel Lee was relieved of duty with his regiment and was directed to report in person to the general in chief in Washington by April 1.[60]

What did this mean? Was it the preliminary of promotion? Was it simply a new assignment to duty? If so, why the reference to reporting to the general in chief? Why not simply to the War Department? Did General Scott want Lee close to him in a crisis, a crisis that might involve Virginia? Lee did not know, but he feared Scott wished to consult him regarding plans for hostilities. He suspected, moreover, that he was being transferred permanently from Texas and he accordingly prepared to move all his belongings, which were bulky and somewhat valuable. On February 13, relinquishing command of his regiment, he climbed into an ambulance at Fort Mason for the journey to San Antonio, whence he was to proceed to the coast.[61]

As the vehicle was about to start, one of Lee's young officers asked: "Colonel, do you intend to go South or remain North? I am very anxious to know what you propose doing."

"I shall never bear arms against the Union," Lee answered simply, "but it may be necessary for me to carry a musket in defense of my native state, Virginia, in which case I shall not prove recreant to my duty."

The driver cracked the whip, the ambulance started, and Lee called back, "Good-bye; God bless you!" [62] It was the last time Lee ever saw any of his troopers except as prisoners of war or as visitors after Appomattox.

On the long road to San Antonio,[63] Lee stopped at a familiar spring for lunch, and found one of his officers, Captain George B. Cosby, already there. As they ate together and chatted, Cosby expressed the opinion that Lee was being called to Washing-

---

[60] For the date and channel of delivery of these orders, see Lee to L. Thomas, A. A. G., *MS.*, April 1, 1861; *A. G. O.*

[61] *Diary* in *Mason*, 71.

[62] R. W. Johnson: *A Soldier's Recollections in Peace and War*, 132–33.

[63] Lee sometimes spent the night, while on his travels around Fort Mason, at the little hotel in Fredericksburg, operated by a German named Nimitz. The proprietor always assigned Lee to the same quarters, which he later preserved and exhibited as "General Lee's room" (36 *Confederate Veteran*, 51; Decca Lamar West in *Texas Monthly*, April, 1930, p. 323).

ton to confer on a campaign against the South in case of war. Lee replied that he feared Cosby's surmise was correct, and if it were, he would resign. Cosby subsequently wrote of Lee: "He further said that he had confidence that Virginia would not act on impulse, but would act as she had in the past, and would exhaust every means consistent with honor to avert civil war. That, if she failed and determined to secede, he would offer her his services. That he had ever been taught that his first allegiance was due his mother State; that he fervently hoped that some agreement would be reached to avert such a terrible war; and there was no personal sacrifice he would not make to save his beloved country from such a dreadful calamity; but under no circumstance could he ever bare his sword against Virginia's sons. As he spoke his emotion brought tears to his eyes, and he turned away to avoid showing this emotion which was greater than he afterwards showed when he lost or won some great battle." [64]

Sick and sad at heart, Lee continued on his journey, pondering many things, and not least the new developments in Texas, especially as they concerned General Twiggs. That veteran officer, who had taken over from Lee the command of the department on December 13, 1860,[65] was a native Georgian, seventy years old, and a strong "states' rights man." He had been slow to resume his duties in Texas after the election of Lincoln because he believed the Union was certain to be dissolved, and he had been frank to say in his official correspondence that he would not fire on American citizens.[66] Repeatedly he asked Washington for instructions, stating that he did not assume the government desired him to carry on civil war in Texas and that he consequently would turn over the army property in his department to the government of the state after Texas seceded.[67] He had asked on January 13 that he be relieved of command, but orders had not been issued until January 28, and then the necessary papers had been

---

[64] Geo. B. Cosby in 13 *Confederate Veteran*, 167–68.

[65] R. E. Lee to Custis Lee, Dec. 14, 1860; Jones, *L. and L.*, 119.

[66] D. E. Twiggs to A. G., Jan. 18, 1861; *Official Records of the Union and Confederate Armies*, series I, vol. 1, p. 581. This work will be cited hereafter as *O. R.* and all citations, unless preceded by Roman numerals, will be to Series I. Numerals immediately following "O. R." refer throughout to volume numbers.

[67] *O. R.*, 1, 582.

sent by mail.[68] While the orders were on their way, with Twiggs wholly in the dark concerning the policy of the Government, Texas had seceded and her representatives had opened negotiations with General Twiggs for the transfer of army property in Texas. Twiggs followed the course he had notified the government he would pursue. On the days Lee was being driven from Fort Mason to San Antonio, General Twiggs's commissioners were arguing with the Texas committee of safety in regard to what the United States troops should carry with them as they marched out of Texas. The question was close to settlement when, on February 15, the order of January 28, relieving Twiggs of command, was received by him. Colonel C. A. Waite, of the 1st Infantry, next senior officer in the department, was named his successor.[69] Waite was from New York and was a strong Unionist. The Texans reasoned that he would not surrender the Federal property, so before daylight on February 16 they abandoned diplomacy for force, marched into San Antonio and seized the government stores.[70]

The first intimation that Lee had of any of this was when his ambulance drew up in front of the Read House in San Antonio about 2 o'clock that afternoon. Immediately the vehicle was surrounded by a crowd of curious men, on whose coats or shirts Lee observed crude red insignia. Soon he saw Mrs. Caroline Darrow, the wife of a friend, coming across the square to meet him.

"Who are these men?" he asked as soon as he had greeted her.

"They are McCulloch's," she answered. "General Twiggs surrendered everything to the state this morning, and we are all prisoners of war."

The shock of her announcement upset Lee's poise for a moment. Tears came into his eyes. His lips trembled in spite of him. "Has it come so soon as this?" he said.[71]

Prisoners of war! Was he one of them? Had he driven into a trap? Was he included in a formal surrender? He must have asked himself these questions as he walked over to the hotel and registered. What should he do? Technically, he was no longer

---

[68] O. R., 1, 581, 584.   [69] O. R., 1, 590.
[70] Twiggs's report, O. R., 1, 503.
[71] Mrs. Caroline B. Darrow in 1 B. and L., 33.

an officer on duty in the Department of Texas. If he insisted on
that fact, he might be able to leave the state and report to the
War Department, according to orders. To determine the precise
state of affairs, he took off his uniform, put on civilian clothes,
and went across to headquarters.[72] There he found the secessionists in complete control. The authority of the United States was
at an end.

Either then or a day or two later, while he was trying to make
arrangements to travel to the coast, the Texas commissioners
bluntly told Lee that if he would forthwith resign his commission
and join the Confederacy, he should have every facility, but that
if he refused he would not be allowed transportation for his
effects. Holding that his allegiance was to Virginia and to the
Union, not to any revolutionary government in Texas, Lee was
indignant at such a proposal.

He left the commissioners and sought out his friend Charles
Anderson, to whom he told the story of the Texans' offer with a
wrath that Anderson was surprised to see him exhibit. Nothing
had been said by the commissioners, apparently, about detaining
Lee personally; consequently he determined to entrust his belongings to Anderson, there in San Antonio, and, regardless of
threats, to set out for home by way of Indianola. It was better,
far, to risk his property than his honor. Would Anderson care
for his boxes and his equipment until they could be forwarded?
His friend promised quickly enough, and started with him to the
storage merchant's.

On their way thither, or as they prepared to separate, Lee
thought he should make his position still plainer to the man who
was helping him. He asked if Anderson remembered their conversation in the presence of Doctor Edwards some time previously? Anderson recalled it distinctly. Lee then said: "I think
it but due to myself to say that I cannot be moved by the conduct
of those people from my sense of duty. I still think, as I then
told you and Doctor Edwards, that my loyalty to Virginia ought
to take precedence over that which is due the Federal Government. And I shall so report myself at Washington. If Virginia
stands by the old Union, so will I. But if she secedes (though I

---

[72] *Ibid.*

do not believe in secession as a constitutional right, nor that there is sufficient cause for revolution), then I will still follow my native state with my sword, and if need be with my life. I know you think and feel very differently, but I can't help it. These are my principles, and I must follow them." [73]

In sad reflection on the political tragedy he was witnessing, Lee slept little that first night in San Antonio, and it must have been with some difficulty that he met curious inquiries with the statement that he was neutral in the controversy between Texas and the Union.[74] By discretion and silence he avoided a commitment that might have had a momentous effect on his own career and on the whole course of the war. For what might not have happened if he had been in command of the department instead of Twiggs when the Texans demanded surrender? His own state had not seceded; he would have had no hesitancy in obeying the orders of the War Department; he certainly would have refused to surrender government property. Would he then have clashed with the Texans? Would he have been the first to face secession fire? The experience of Colonel Waite indicates that it might have been so. Waite was soon at odds with the Texans. They refused him transportation, and, on April 23, arrested him and several of his officers as prisoners of war,[75] though they promptly paroled them.[76]

As speedily as he could, Lee prepared to leave San Antonio. When friends came to say good-bye, his views were freely expressed and fully understood. To one officer he said simply and in the deepest distress: "When I get to Virginia I think the world will have one soldier less. I shall resign and go to planting corn." [77]

Hurrying away from San Antonio, Lee went to Indianola, where he arrived on February 22. By steamer he reached New Orleans on February 25 and made his way homeward through a troubled

[73] C. Anderson, *op. cit.*, 32. An earlier, incomplete version of this episode will be found in 11 *SHSP*, 443 ff. Anderson's article was written in 1884, twenty-three years after the incidents he described, but his statements fit in so perfectly with Lee's private letters, which Anderson probably had not read, that Anderson's testimony commends itself as valid. His credibility is increased by the fact that he was vehemently anti-Confederate.
[74] Mrs. Darrow, *loc. cit.*   [75] *O. R.*, 1, 576.
[76] II *O. R.*, 1, 86. The Roman numerals refer to the Second Series of the *Official Records*.
[77] R. M. Potter, quoted in 1 *B. and L.*, 36 n.

country.[78] A separate government, the Confederate States of America, had been set up at Montgomery, Ala., and Lee's friend, Jefferson Davis, had been chosen its President before Lee had reached the Texas coast. The mails, however, were still passing freely between the North and the South, commercial intercourse was as yet unhindered, the free navigation of the Mississippi had been pledged by the Confederate Congress,[79] and, what was infinitely more important, not a blow had been struck. The Federal administration was perplexed about Fort Sumter, but was generally expected to withdraw its garrison and thereby to avert a clash. General Scott, though strongly for the maintenance of Federal authority, advised this course.[80] Tense as was the situation, there was nothing to compromise Lee's status as an officer of the United States army when he reached Alexandria on March 1, took carriage, and soon joined his loved ones at Arlington.[81]

[78] *Diary* in *Mason*, 71. Lee, it would seem, never recovered his baggage. It was shipped to Virginia by way of New York, where it was seized (*Baltimore American*, May 23, 1861, p. 1, col. 1).

[79] 3 *Rhodes*, 296.　　　　　　　　　　　　[80] 3 *Rhodes*, 332–33.

[81] *Diary* in *Mason*, 71. A few days before his arrival his family had received a visit from two very interesting young men, Charles Francis Adams and Henry Adams (*Autobiography of Charles Francis Adams*, 90–91).

CHAPTER XXV

The Answer He Was Born to Make

"Our country," Lee had written one of his sons before he left Texas, "requires now everyone to put forth all his ability, regardless of self." [1] That maxim he applied in the bewildering situation he faced when he reached home. On the Virginia side of the Potomac opinion was divided concerning the occasion for secession, but there was almost complete agreement touching the right. North of the river, just half-an-hour's ride from Arlington, cross-currents of sentiment were sweeping. In Congress and at the White House efforts were still being made to avert war; in the departments preparations were under way to face any emergency. President Buchanan was fighting to save states for the Union; General Scott and the politicians interested in the army were angling for individual soldiers whose knowledge would be useful should the conflict come. The atmosphere in which many officers were received by their superiors had suddenly changed. There was unconcealed interest in the probable course that would be followed by captains and colonels the prospect of whose resignation, in ordinary times, would have been heard with rejoicing because promotion would be opened to other men.

Lee was not aware of this change when he called at General Scott's office soon after he reached home. In the outer room he met his friend Lieutenant Colonel Erasmus D. Keyes, associate of his West Point superintendency, and the man whom Scott had named as his military secretary when Lee had declined that post.

The two shook hands. "Lee," said Keyes, "it is reported that you concurred in Twiggs's surrender in Texas. How's that?"

Lee became serious on the instant, but without showing any resentment of the suggestion of disloyalty, he said calmly: "I am here to pay my respects to General Scott; will you be kind enough, Colonel, to show me to his office?"

[1] Letter of Feb. 16, 1861; *Jones*, 387–88.

Keyes said no more, but ushered Lee into Scott's room.[2] The door was shut, and for three hours the old General and his favorite lieutenant talked together. What they said to each other, in the confidence of long and trustful association, neither ever afterwards revealed. All the evidence regarding their conversation is negative in character or is reported at second-hand. But Scott's known opinion of secession, his admiration for Lee, and his desire to assure good leadership for the army make it possible to reconstruct the substance of at least a part of what was said. Scott told Lee that he was soon to be made a colonel, and then, probably, he hinted that if he found himself too feeble to take the field he would recommend Lee as his second in command. There can be little doubt that Scott deliberately sought to appeal to Lee's ambitions, but that, knowing Lee as he did, Scott did not try to buy his allegiance with promises, which, indeed, Scott was not authorized to make.[3] If Lee replied to Scott's overtures it was to repeat what he had said to Charles Anderson in Texas—that if Virginia seceded, he would follow her because he considered that his first obligation was to her.[4] Scott, of course, was of a temper to argue this and probably ended a lengthy oration with the request that Lee go home, think the subject over, and await further developments.[5] When Lee left, Scott's manner was "painfully silent." [6]

[2] *Keyes*, 205–6. Keyes gave no date for this interview, but the circumstances indicate it occurred soon after Lee's return.

[3] The papers (Library of Congress) of Joseph Holt, Secretary of War under Buchanan in 1861, show no correspondence between him and Scott regarding Lee.

[4] The evidence on which these conclusions are based is as follows: 1. After the war, Lee wrote Reverdy Johnson (*R. E. Lee, Jr.*, 27): "I never intimated to any one that I desired the command of the United States Army; nor did I ever have a conversation with but one gentleman, Mr. Francis Preston Blair, on the subject, which was at his invitation." If the only conversation was with Blair, then, obviously, to the best of Lee's recollection, there had been no discussion of the subject with Scott. 2. An unnamed kinswoman of Mrs. Lee is quoted by Long (*op. cit.*, 92) as stating: "[Mrs. Lee] mentioned that General Scott, in one of their interviews, said that in the event of his resignation, which from his advanced age must soon become a necessity, if Robert had remained with the North he (General Scott) believed he would be given the command of the Union army." 3. Charles Anderson, Lee's friend in Texas, said (*op. cit.*, 33) that Scott subsequently told of an interview with Lee after that officer's return. According to Anderson, Scott said he informed Lee that, in addition to his speedy promotion to the rank of colonel, he, Scott, was authorized to offer Lee the command of the armies, second only to Scott himself. Anderson stated that Lee thanked Scott and then told him precisely what Lee had stated to Anderson as they had walked together to the storage merchant's in San Antonio.

[5] Lee's orders were that he should report April 1. On that date (Lee to A. G., *MS.*, April 1, 1861, *MSS. A. G. O.*), Lee duly informed the War Department that he had reported to Scott and was then at Arlington.

[6] *Keyes*, 206.

Lee went home and in agony of spirit watched the course of events. At the time of his interview with Scott, the peace conference had risen and had suggested a constitutional amendment that Congress was in no mood to pass, but a different amendment, preserving slavery in the states that had it, had been approved by the House on February 28, and received a two-thirds vote in the Senate the day after Lee reached home.[7] In Virginia, volunteers were drilling and the fire-eaters were predicting early secession, but the state convention was safely under the control of a conservative majority that was as anxious as Lee himself to preserve the Union. Virtually the only point of agreement between the radical secessionists and the Southern Whigs in the convention was that all of them were determined that Virginia would not be party to the "coercion" of any Southern state for its withdrawal from the Union. The situation in the Old Dominion seemed further stabilized by the fact that no matter what the convention did, the people of the state would be the final judges of secession. Every Virginian, however, held his breath on March 4, when Lincoln delivered his inaugural. His views on many aspects of the crisis were those of Lee. The new President was cautious in the utterances, but his announcement of his purpose to hold government property in the South and to collect taxes there was accepted by Virginians as a threat of force.[8]

All the while Scott probably was quietly at work, seeing if he might not hold Lee to the Union. Keyes thought that Scott did not expect Lee to fight against the South, but that the General believed it possible to put Lee at the head of an army so powerful that war could be prevented.[9] General Twiggs was dismissed from the army on March 1 for his surrender of Texas.[10] Colonel E. V. Sumner of the 1st Cavalry was named brigadier general to succeed him on March 16. Lee was at once made colonel and was given Sumner's regiment.[11] This commission, which was signed by Abraham Lincoln, Lee did not hesitate to accept when, on March 28, it was forwarded to him.[12]

Between the date he was promoted and the time he received

---

[7] 3 *Rhodes*, 306–13.
[8] 3 *Rhodes*, 318 n.
[9] *Keyes*, 206.
[10] *O. R.*, 1, 597; G. O. 5.
[11] *MS. A. G. O.*, G. O. 7, March 20, 1861.
[12] Lee to A. G., *MS.*, March 30, 1861; *A. G. O.*, 1861.

his commission, Lee probably got a letter written him on March 15 by L. P. Walker, Confederate Secretary of War. This was a direct offer of a commission as brigadier general, the highest rank then authorized, in the army the South was raising. "You are requested," the letter read, "to signify your acceptance or nonacceptance of said appointment, and should you accept you will sign before a magistrate the oath of office herewith and forward the same, with your letter of acceptance to this office."[13] After the long years of slow promotion the honors were coming fast— a colonelcy in one army and a like offer of a generalship in the rival service, all in a breath! There is no record of any reply by Lee to this tender from the new Confederacy. It is probable that he ignored the offer, and it is certain that he was not lured by the promise of high position. He owned allegiance to only two governments, that of Virginia and that of the Union, and there could be no thought of a third so long as these two did not conflict and Virginia did not throw in her destiny with the Confederate States.

For a few days it seemed as if the conflict of allegiance might be avoided. As late as April 3 the expectation was general that Fort Sumter would be evacuated and a clash avoided.[14] On April 4 a test vote in the Virginia convention showed a majority of two-to-one against secession.[15] Lee would not despair of the Union. He was for forbearance to the last, recognizing no necessity for recourse to arms.[16] The maintenance of slavery meant nothing to him. He felt that if he owned all the slaves in the South he would cheerfully give them up to preserve the Union.[17] He would hold to the army and to the flag as long as he could in honor do so.[18] But during those days of suspense, Lee was confirmed in his point of view. He had been determined from the outset that he would adhere to Virginia and defend her from any foe. Now, fully, he realized that though he considered secession neither more nor less than revolution, he could not bring himself to fight against the states that regarded secession as

---

[13] IV O. R., 1, 165–66. [14] 3 Rhodes, 337.

[15] Journal of the Committee of the Whole, Virginia Convention, 1861, pp. 31–33.

[16] Lee to Mrs. Marshall, April 20, 1861; R. E. Lee, Jr., 25, 26.

[17] Long, 92–93, quoting one version, probably rhetorical and overdrawn, of the interview with Francis P. Blair.

[18] Long, 91, quoting Mrs. Lee.

a right. He could not think of himself as fighting with the South against the Union, unless Virginia's defense were involved, but neither, as the possibility seemed to be brought nearer, could he reconcile himself to fighting with the Union against the South. "That beautiful feature of our landscape," he said sadly one day, as he pointed to the capitol across the Potomac, "has ceased to charm me as much as formerly. I fear the mischief that is brewing there." [19]

This was Lee's state of mind when, on April 7, his old comrade of Mexican days, P. G. T. Beauregard, took a decisive step at Charleston, S. C., where he was then in command of the Confederate forces. Believing that Fort Sumter was about to be reinforced, Beauregard ordered supplies of fresh food cut off from the Federal garrison. The next day, April 8, a confidential messenger from President Lincoln announced to Governor Pickens of the Palmetto State that Sumter would be revictualed by United States ships. On the instant all the passions that had been rising since 1830 in South Carolina suddenly overflowed, and at daylight on April 12 the bombardment of Fort Sumter began. On the 14th Sumter surrendered without the loss of a single life on either side. The next day, to a nation that had gone mad, Lincoln issued his proclamation calling for 75,000 soldiers "to suppress combinations" and "to cause the laws to be duly executed." [20]

The North and the South were arrayed, and blows had passed, though no blood had yet been shed—what would the border states do? What would be the action of Virginia? For the answer, Lee turned his eyes from Sumter to Richmond, where the convention was still in session. He was at a distance and knew little of the inner workings of that body. All his information was derived from the newspapers, which were too excited to be explicit.

Late on April 16, or on the 17th, he heard that the Virginia convention had gone into secret session. That was the only news from Richmond; but from Washington, on the 17th, there arrived a letter and a message. The letter bore Scott's signature and requested Lee to call at his office on the 18th. The message

[19] Thomas B. Bryan, to whom he addressed this remark, in *Military Essays and Recollections*, 3, 14.
[20] III *O. R.*, 1, 67–68.

was conveyed in a note from a Washington cousin, John Lee. It was that Francis P. Blair, Sr., a publicist of Lee's acquaintance, formerly editor of *The Congressional Globe,* desired Lee to meet him the next morning at his house in Washington.

What was afoot now? Were the two calls related? The answer, in its entirety, Lee did not learn during his lifetime. He never realized how anxious some men high in office and influence had been to save his services to the United States army. In addition to what General Scott had done, Francis P. Blair, Sr., father of Colonel Lee's Missouri friend, Montgomery Blair, had been at work. He had been to President Lincoln, who had authorized him to "ascertain Lee's intentions and feelings." [21] Blair had also discussed the subject with Secretary Cameron and had been directed by him to make a proposition to Lee. It was to explain this that Blair had sent the message to Arlington.[22]

Duly on the morning of April 18 Lee rode over the bridge and up to the younger Blair's house on Pennsylvania Avenue, directly opposite the State, War and Navy Building,[23] where he found the old publicist awaiting him. They sat down behind closed doors. Blair promptly and plainly explained his reason for asking Lee to call. A large army, he said, was soon to be called into the field to enforce the Federal law; the President had authorized him to ask Lee if he would accept the command.

Command of an army of 75,000, perhaps 100,000 men; opportunity to apply all he had learned in Mexico; the supreme ambition of a soldier realized; the full support of the government; many of his ablest comrades working with him; rank as a major general—all this may have surged through Lee's mind for an instant, but if so, it was only for an instant. Then his Virginia background and the mental discipline of years asserted themselves. He had said: "If the Union is dissolved and the government disrupted, I shall return to my native state and share the miseries of my people and save in defence will draw my sword on none." There he stood, and in that spirit, after listening to all Blair had to say, he made the fateful reply that is best given in his own

[21] 4 Nicolay and Hay: *Abraham Lincoln,* 98.

[22] Simon Cameron gave two somewhat contradictory versions of the offer to Lee, but there seems no valid reason to criticise the essential accuracy of the statement of 1887, quoted in Jones, *L. and L.,* 130.

[23] No. 1651 Pennsylvania Avenue.

436

simple account of the interview: "I declined the offer he made me to take command of the army that was to be brought into the field, stating as candidly and as courteously as I could, that though opposed to secession and deprecating war, I could take no part in an invasion of the Southern States." [24] That was all, as far as Lee was concerned. He had long before decided, instinctively, what his duty required of him, and the allurement of supreme command, with all that a soldier craved, did not tempt him to equivocate for an instant or to see if there were not some way he could keep his own honor and still have the honor he understood the Presi-dent had offered him. Blair talked on in a futile hope of con-verting Lee, but it was to no purpose. [25]

Bidding farewell to Blair, Lee went directly to Scott's office. He sensed Scott's deep interest in his action, and as soon as he arrived he told him what Blair had offered and what he had answered. [26] "Lee," said Scott, deeply moved, "you have made the greatest mistake of your life; but I feared it would be so." [27]

Deep as was the difference between the two men on a public question that made personal enemies of many lifelong friends, Scott did not stop with this sad observation, but expressed the belief that if Lee were going to resign he ought not to delay. "There are times," Scott is reported to have said, "when every officer in the United States service should fully determine what course he will pursue and frankly declare it. No one should continue in government employ without being actively em-ployed." And again, "I suppose you will go with the rest. If you purpose to resign, it is proper that you should do so at once; your present attitude is equivocal." [28]

[24] Lee to Reverdy Johnson, Feb. 25, 1868; *R. E. Lee, Jr.*, 27–28.
[25] For the conflict of testimony on this point, see Appendix I–1.
[26] Lee to Reverdy Johnson, *loc. cit.*
[27] *Mason*, 73, doubtless on the authority of Mrs. Lee.
[28] E. D. Townsend: *Anecdotes of the Civil War*, 29. The writer has hesitated to cite Townsend as a witness, because all the internal evidence is against his account of the in-terview of April 18. He erred in the following particulars: (1) He stated Lee was on leave; (2) he assumed that Scott knew little or nothing of Lee's movements, though Keyes testified that Lee had previously been to Scott's office and Mrs. Lee stated, though indirectly, that there were several meetings between them; (3) he gave the wrong date for the interview; (4) he failed to mention what it is hard to see how, if he heard the whole conversation, he could have forgotten, namely, that Lee told Scott he had been offered command of the Federal army and had declined the post. Moreover, after his frank statements of his intentions, Lee would hardly have said at the end of the inter-view, as Townsend alleged: "The property belonging to my children, all they possess, lies in Virginia. *They will be ruined if I do not go with their state.* I cannot raise my

This added a complication that Lee pondered as he left his old commander for the last time. He loved the army and the Union too well to leave either until he was in honor compelled to do so. Though willing to resign rather than to fight against the South, he had clung to the hope that he would not have to act unless Virginia seceded and the people voted affirmatively on an ordinance of secession. But Scott had now said that he should not remain in the army if he was unwilling to perform active duty. Those 75,000 soldiers, of whom Blair had talked, would not have been asked of the states if they had not been intended for early service in the field. And if they were so intended, Lee, as an officer of the army, might be called upon immediately for duty he could not conscientiously perform. Then he would have to resign under orders.[29] That was a disgrace to any soldier.

As his brother Smith was on duty in Washington, Lee stopped to discuss this new question with him. They could come to no immediate conclusion on it and parted in the expectation of meeting again before either of them took any action. At length, over the route he had so often travelled, Lee rode out of Washington, across the bridge and up the quiet hills to the home whose white columns he could see for most of the way. He was never again to make that journey in that same fashion. The next time he was to cross the Potomac, it was to be upstream, from the South, with bands playing and a victorious, a cheering army around him.

But he did not leave his problem behind him as he turned his back on his country's capital. He carried it with him; he wrestled with it. *Was* his position equivocal? Ought he to resign at once, regardless of what Virginia did? He felt that Scott was right, but his own mind was so opposed to secession, and his devotion to the Union and to the army proved so strong, now it was put to the

hand against my children." The italicized sentence does not sound like Lee, though the rest may well have come from his lips. At the same time, what Townsend quoted Scott as saying to Lee is what might have been expected from an old officer to a younger friend. Probability is lent to the substantial accuracy of this part of Townsend's otherwise doubtful account, by the fact that Lee in his letter of April 20 to Scott, said: "Since my interview with you on the 18th inst., I have felt that I ought no longer to retain my commission. . . ." In order that the reader may judge for himself whether it is permissible to accept as authentic these sentences from a document that otherwise is suspect, the full quotation from Townsend is printed in Appendix I–2.

[29] R. E. Lee to Smith Lee, April 20, 1861; Jones, *L. and L.*, 134.

test, that he delayed the actual writing of his resignation, hoping against hope.

All this time he had not known what had happened after the Virginia convention had gone into secret session on the 16th. *The Washington Star* of April 18 contained an unverified report that the Virginia convention had passed an ordinance of secession and had caused three ships to be sunk at the mouth of the Elizabeth River, but *The Alexandria Gazette* of the same day contained a dispatch from Richmond, dated April 17, 5 P.M., affirming that the convention was still in secret session and that no ordinance withdrawing the state from the Union had been passed.

The next morning, April 19, Lee went into Alexandria on business and there he read the news he had hoped he would never see: Virginia had seceded! [30] To his mind that meant the wreck of the nation, "the beginning of sorrows," the opening of a war that was certain to be long and full of horrors. But of all that he thought and felt in the first realization that his mother state had left the Union, his only recorded observation is one he made to a druggist when he went into a shop to pay a bill. "I must say," he remarked sadly, "that I am one of those dull creatures that cannot see the good of secession." [31]

If Lee had any doubt of the truth of the report in the Alexandria paper that morning, it was soon removed. That afternoon, *The Washington Star* took the news for granted.[32] By nightfall on the 19th, Lee had no alternative to believing it. When other hopes had failed him before this time, Lee had told himself that secession could not become an accomplished fact until the voters of Virginia had passed on the ordinance of secession, as they had specifically reserved the right to do, but now Lee's judgment told him that war would not wait on a referendum. Virginia would certainly consider that her safety required the seizure of Federal depots within her borders. Had not Texas similarly provided for

[30] The ordinance had been passed on the afternoon of April 17 in secret session, but had not been announced until shortly before noon the next day (*Journal of the Virginia Convention of 1861*, p. 164). Every effort was made to keep the state's action from becoming known until troops could seize the Federal navy-yard at Gosport and the arsenal at Harpers Ferry.

[31] John S. Mosby: *Memoirs*, 379. The druggist took pains to write down Lee's words on his journal opposite the entry of the payment.

[32] Joseph E. Johnston, in his *Narrative of Military Operations* (cited hereafter as *Johnston's Narrative*), 10, stated that April 19 was the earliest date on which the secession of Virginia was known in Washington.

439

a referendum on secession, and had not he, with his own eyes, seen how the Texas committee of safety had committed an act of war by seizing United States property without waiting for the people to confirm or disavow the ordinance of the convention? The Federal Government, for its part, would certainly take prompt action since the state just across the river from its capital had left the Union. As one of the senior field officers in Washington, he might be summoned at any hour to defend Washington by invading Virginia—which he could not do. Duty was plain. There could be no holding back. The time had come. All the Lees had been Americans, but they had been Virginians first. From Richard the emigrant onward, the older allegiance had been paramount with each of them until the Revolution came. Had not his own father called Virginia "my native country"? In a crisis that seemed in his day to threaten the Union, had not "Light-Horse Harry" said: "Should my efforts . . . be unavailing, I shall lament my country's fate and acquiesce in my country's will . . ."?[33] Now revolution and the older allegiance were the same. The son must be as the sire. Washington, his great model, had embraced a revolutionary cause. Dearly as Lee loved the Union, anxious as he was to see it preserved, he could not bear arms against the South. Virginia had seceded and doubtless would join the South; her action controlled his; he could not wait for the uncertain vote of the people when war was upon him. So after midnight on the 19th he sat down and wrote this letter, not more than fifteen hours after he had received positive information that Virginia had seceded:

Arlington, Virginia (Washington City P.O.)
20 April 1861.

Hon. Simon Cameron
    Secty of War
Sir:
    I have the honor to tender the resignation of my commission as Colonel of the 1st Regt. of Cavalry.
Very resp'y Your Obedient Servant.
R. E. LEE
Col 1st Cav'y.[34]

[33] See *supra*, p. 169.   [34] *MS. A. G. O.*, 69, L., 61.

His resignation was not prompted by passion, nor did it carry with it resentment against the Union he left. On the contrary, if there was any resentment, it was against the authors, Northern and Southern, of the consummate wickedness of bringing about division within the Union. There was a pang and a heartache at the separation from brother officers whose patriotism he had seen vindicated in the hardships of campaigning and in the dangers of battle. He was willing to defend Virginia, whatever her allegiance, but he did not desire to fight against the flag under which he had served. If he must see the Union wrecked by men who would not forbear and plead for justice through constitutional means, if he must tear himself from the service of a nation of which he had been proud, then the hope of his heart was that he might never again be called to draw a sword which only Virginia could command. It was in this spirit that he wrote farewell to General Scott, that loyal old friend, who had admired him, taught him, and advanced him. He penned this letter:

General: Arlington, Va., April 20, 1861.

Since my interview with you on the 18th inst. I have felt that I ought no longer to retain my commission in the Army. I therefore tender my resignation, which I request you will recommend for acceptance. I would have presented it at once, but for the struggle it has cost me to separate myself from a service to which I have devoted all the best years of my life and all the ability I possessed.

During the whole of that time—more than a quarter of a century—I have experienced nothing but kindness from my superiors and a most cordial friendship from my comrades. To no one, General, have I been as much indebted as to yourself for uniform kindness and consideration, and it has always been my ardent desire to meet your approbation. I shall carry to the grave the most grateful recollections of your kind consideration, and your name and fame will always be dear to me.

Save in defence of my native State, I never desire again to draw my sword.

Be pleased to accept my most earnest wishes for the continuance of your happiness and prosperity, and believe me, most truly yours,

R. E. Lee.[35]

He came downstairs when he had finished the letters. Mrs. Lee was waiting for him. She had heard him pacing in the room above her and had thought she had heard him fall on his knees in prayer. "Well, Mary," he said calmly, "the question is settled. Here is my letter of resignation and a letter I have written General Scott." [36]

She understood. Months later she wrote a friend, "My husband has wept tears of blood over this terrible war, but as a man of honor and a Virginian, he must follow the destiny of his state." [37] The other members of the family understood, also. Arlington became as still and gloomy as if a death had occurred, because as one of his daughters confided to a kinswoman the following Sunday, "the army was to him home and country." Rooney, who hastened to consult his father as soon as the state seceded, was in deep depression as he saw how jubilant the people were. They had lost their senses, he held, and had no conception of what a terrible mistake they were making. Custis was no believer in secession. Had he been able to dictate policy, he said, he would have called the movement revolution and would forthwith have seized and fortified Arlington Heights.[38]

Lee dispatched his resignation to General Scott that morning, probably by special messenger, and before night it had been forwarded to the Secretary of War.[39]

---

[35] *R. E. Lee, Jr.*, 24–25. This is a text slightly different from and seemingly superior to that in *Jones*, 132–33. In the version printed by E. G. Booth (*In War Time*, 59) there is a final "(all with highest manifestations)."

[36] Jones, *L. and L.*, 133, quoting Mrs. Lee's own account of the incident. There is no foundation for the story (18 *S. H. S. P.*, 143) that he was prompted to his decision by the statement of "an old lady" that "the path of duty is the path of sacrifice."

[37] December, n. d., 1861; quoted in 1 *Macrae*, 225.

[38] "War Time in Alexandria," *South Atlantic Quarterly*, July, 1905, vol. 4, no. 3, p. 235.

[39] Endorsements on Lee to Cameron, *MS.*, April 20, 1861 (*MS. A. G. O.*, 69L61). The bureau chiefs endorsed that all Lee's accounts were clear. The second auditor stated that Lee settled monthly (*ibid.*). Formal announcement of the resignation was made in S. O. 119, April 27, and the resignation was there stated to have been accepted to take effect as of April 25. This was probably the date when the resignation was reached after it had gone the rounds of the bureaus and had been returned to the office of the adjutant general. Lee was surprised when he learned that acceptance of his resignation was dated April 25, and he explicitly directed that no pay or allowance be accepted for any time after April 20 (Lee to Mrs. Lee, May 2, 1861, *R. E. Lee, Jr.*, 30).

THE ANSWER HE WAS BORN TO MAKE

After he had sent off the paper, he sat down to explain his act to his sister, Mrs. Marshall, and to his brother Smith. Mrs. Marshall's husband was Unionist in his sympathies. Her son Louis was now a captain in the United States army. She herself sided with her husband and son, though she could not quite forget her Virginia uprearing. Lee took her situation into account and wrote her as tactfully as he could:

Arlington, Virginia, April 20, 1861.

My Dear Sister:

I am grieved at my inability to see you. . . . I have been wait-'ng for a "more convenient season," which has brought to many before me deep and lasting regret. Now we are in a state of war which will yield to nothing. The whole south is in a state of revolution, into which Virginia, after a long struggle, has been drawn; and, though I recognize no necessity for this state of things, and would have forborne and pleaded to the end for a redress of grievances, real or supposed, yet in my own person I had to meet the question whether I should take part against my native state.

With all my devotion to the Union and the feeling of loyalty and duty of an American citizen, I have not been able to make up my mind to raise my hand against my relatives, my children, my home. I have therefore resigned my commission in the Army, and save in defence of my native state, with the sincere hope that my poor services may never be needed, I hope I may never be called on to draw my sword. I know you will blame me; but you must think as kindly of me as you can, and believe that I have endeavored to do what I thought right.

To show you the feeling and struggle it has cost me, I send you a copy of my letter of resignation. I have no time for more. May God guard and protect you and yours and shower upon you everlasting blessings, is the prayer of your devoted brother,

R. E. LEE.[40]

He had left Smith Lee on the 18th with the understanding that they would confer again regarding their course of action. He

[40] *R. E. Lee, Jr.,* 25–26.

therefore wrote to explain why he had resigned before consulting with him further:

Arlington, Virginia, April 20, 1861.

My Dear Brother Smith: The question which was the subject of my earnest consultation with you on the 18th inst., has in my own mind been decided. After the most anxious inquiry as to the correct course for me to pursue, I concluded to resign, and sent in my resignation this morning. I wished to wait till the Ordinance of Secession should be acted on by the people of Virginia; but war seems to have commenced, and I am liable at any time to be ordered on duty, which I could not conscientiously perform. To save me from such a position and to prevent the necessity of resigning under orders, I had to act at once, and before I could see you again on the subject, as I had wished. I am now a private citizen, and have no other ambition than to remain at home. Save in defence of my native state, I have no desire ever again to draw my sword. I send you my warmest love.

Your affectionate brother,
R. E. Lee.[41]

Lee gave no advice to Smith regarding his own course, nor did he counsel Custis, who was as loath as he to quit the service of the United States. "Tell Custis," he subsequently wrote, "he must consult his own judgment, reason and conscience as to the course he may take. I do not wish him to be guided by my wishes or example. If I have done wrong, let him do better. The present is a momentous question which every man must settle for himself and upon principle." [42]

When he took up his daily paper, *The Alexandria Gazette,* it was to discover that others beside himself were interested in the action he had taken. For an editorial article read as follows:

"It is probable that the secession of Virginia will cause an im-

41 *R. E. Lee, Jr.,* 26–27.

42 Lee to Mrs. Lee, May 15, 1861; *Fitz Lee,* 94. In the summer of 1868, *Harper's Weekly* charged that Lee had remained on General Scott's "staff" to the last minute in order to learn that officer's plan of operations. Major Sidney Herbert, editor of *The Troy Messenger and Advertiser,* denied this libel and wrote Lee on the subject. Lee, of course, confirmed the denial and pointed out that except when with the general staff in Mexico he had never been a member of General Scott's military family. See *Columbus* (Ga.) *Inquirer,* quoting Lee to Herbert, June 29, 1870; reprinted in *The Alexandria Gazette,* July 14, 1870.

mediate resignation of many officers of the Army and Navy from this State. We do not know, and have no right to speak for or anticipate the course of Colonel Robert E. Lee. Whatever he may do, will be conscientious and honorable. But if he should resign his present position in the Army of the United States, we call the immediate attention of our State to him, as an able, brave, experienced officer—no man his superior in all that constitutes the soldier and the gentleman—no man more worthy to head our forces and lead our army. There is no man who would command more of the confidence of the people of Virginia, than this distinguished officer; and no one under whom the volunteers and militia would more gladly rally. His reputation, his acknowledged ability, his chivalric character, his probity, honor, and—may we add, to his eternal praise—his Christian life and conduct —make his very name a 'tower of strength.' It is a name surrounded by revolutionary and patriotic associations and reminiscences." [43]

It was not a pleasant article for a modest man to read, and it was disquieting, besides, with its assurance that some, at least, were looking to him to lead the army of Virginia, against the Union and the old flag, if war came. . . He could only pray it would not.

During the day Lee saw his neighbor and friend, John B. Daingerfield, and showed him a copy of his letter of resignation. The rest of that fateful 20th of April was doubtless spent at Arlington. Nothing of consequence occurred except the receipt, late in the evening, of a letter from Judge John Robertson, of Richmond. The judge was then in Alexandria and asked for an interview the next day. Lee set 1 o'clock as the hour and offered to meet him in town. [44] Meantime, Lee waited and pondered. Surrounded by objects familiar through thirty years of tender association, and with his invalid wife in her chair, he must have realized that if hostilities came, war and invasion would soon bring Arlington within the lines of the Union army. The Federals

[43] *The Alexandria Gazette*, April 20, 1861.
[44] John Robertson to Governor John Letcher, *MS.*, April 23, 1861; *MSS. Va. State Library*, for an abstract of which document, now missing from its place in the archives, the writer is indebted to Professor Charles W. Ramsdell of the University of Texas.

could not long permit so commanding a position, so close to the capital, to remain unguarded. But in none of his letters prior to his resignation and in none of his reported conversation is there even a hint that he had any selfish regard for the fate of Arlington, either in delaying his resignation until Virginia's secession, or in deciding to leave the army when he did.

Sunday morning, April 21, dressed in civilian clothes, Lee went into Alexandria with one of his daughters to attend service at Christ Church. The town was wild. Overwhelmingly Southern in their sentiment, the people rejoiced at the secession of Virginia as if it meant deliverance from bondage. In their enthusiasm they fancied they were repeating the drama of 1776 and that the spirit of a Washington gave its benediction to a new revolution.

In all this rejoicing Lee took no part. His resignation was not generally known as yet, though his neighbors and friends had been waiting to see what he would do.[45] His sorrow, his sense of the fitness of things, and his knowledge that war would be long and terrible kept him from any statement of his action. In the church, as he prayed, it must have been for his divided country. When the Psalter for the morning of the 21st day was read, he doubtless felt there was more than coincidence in these verses and the responses:

"13 What time as they went from one nation to another: from
    one kingdom to another people;
"14 He suffered no man to do them wrong; but reproved even
    kings for their sakes. . . ."[46]

At length the service was over. The congregation stopped to talk of the inevitable theme, and then straggled slowly into the churchyard. When Lee reached the open air he became engaged in serious conversation with three men, who were unknown to the congregation and whose identity has never been established. His neighbors and friends thought the strangers were commissioners from the governor of Virginia,[47] but it seems more probable that

---

[45] Mrs. Burton Harrison: *Recollections Grave and Gay* (cited hereafter as *Mrs. Burton Harrison*), 24–25.

[46] Psalm 105.

[47] Robertson to Letcher, *MS.*, April 23, 1861, *loc. cit.*; "War Time in Alexandria," in *South Atlantic Quarterly*, July, 1905, 235; *Mrs. Powell*, 249. It was assumed, subsequently, by all Lee's Alexandria neighbors that the visitors, in Letcher's name, formally

they were companions of Judge Robertson, who explained that the judge had gone to Washington and had been detained there but would soon arrive to keep his appointment. Lee had not been in communication with the state convention or with the governor. He had no information as to the military plans. Perhaps the visitors acquainted him with what had happened and intimated that his service was desired by his mother state, but in Judge Robertson's absence there could have been nothing official. Lee waited and chatted several hours and then, concluding that Robertson would not return, rode back to Arlington.

That evening a messenger arrived at the mansion with a letter from Robertson. He apologized for his delay and—this was the important item—invited Lee, in the name of the governor, to repair to Richmond for conference with the chief executive.[48] Lee realized, of course, that this meant participation in the defense of Virginia, but he did not hesitate an hour. The very reason that had impelled him to resign from the United States army, his allegiance to Virginia, prompted him to sit down at once and to write an answer to Robertson. Virginia's action in withdrawing from the Union carried him with her, and if she called him now it was his duty to obey. In a few words he notified the governor's representative that he would join him in Alexandria the next day in time to take the train for Richmond.[49] There was no questioning, no holding back, no delay. The road from Arlington, though lit with glory, led straight to Appomattox. But Lee never regretted his action, never even admitted that he had made a choice. With the war behind him, with the South desolate and disfranchised, and with her sons dead on a hundred battlefields, he was to look back with soul unshaken and was to say: "I did only what my duty demanded. I could have taken no other course without dishonor. And if it all were to be done over again, I should act in precisely the same manner."[50]

offered Lee the command of the Virginia forces. The chronology of events, however, disproves this. For sundry other details, probably in part apocryphal, of Lee's movements after church, see Wedderburn, *op. cit.*

[48] Robertson to Letcher, *MS.*, April 23, 1861, *loc. cit.*

[49] Robertson to Letcher, *MS.*, April 23, 1861, *loc. cit.* For the circumstances of the summons of Lee to Richmond, see Appendix I–3.

[50] To Wade Hampton, June, 1868; *Jones*, 142.

CHAPTER XXVI

On a Train en Route to Richmond

DRESSED in civilian clothes and silk hat,[1] Lee departed from Arlington on the morning of April 22, never to enter its friendly portals again. Driving to Alexandria, he joined Judge Robertson, checked his trunk, and, with sombre face, climbed aboard the train of the Orange and Alexandria Railroad, bound for Gordonsville, whence he was to travel via the Virginia Central to Richmond.

The first stage of his journey took him through a rolling countryside. Soon the Blue Ridge Mountains were faintly visible to the west, guarding the Shenandoah Valley. Every few miles the train would stop at some station, where an anxious crowd waited for the newspapers and inquired whether Virginia had yet been invaded. Well it was for him, as he gazed out of the window, that he did not know what the names of these simple places were soon to signify to him, or how many of those who looked up at him from the platforms were to die at his word. Else even his resolute heart might have grown faint. Here was Manassas Junction, where passengers who had come down the Manassas Gap Railroad took the train. Three months to the very day was to see the station and the road filled with bleeding men, and all the quiet fields covered with the victims and the debris of a great battle. Seventeen months and a little more were to find him close by, after one of the greatest of his victories. Did any of his fellow-passengers talk of crossing Thoroughfare Gap, of visiting Centreville, of passing Groveton Heights? The words were well-nigh meaningless to him, if they were uttered, but ere long they were to be forever associated with his name. Soon he was at Bristoe Station, in the very railway cut from which two of his brigades were to be repulsed bloodily one autumn day in 1863.

[1] W. W. Scott, who saw him that day at Orange, in *William and Mary Quarterly,* 2d Series, 6, 279.

448

Catlett's Station, the conductor called, Catlett's Station, where "Jeb" Stuart was to capture the enemy's headquarters in a midnight hour of groping; Warrenton Junction next—how many times he was to look at its name on his map! Rappahannock bridge that was to be the scene of a dark tragedy for some of his soldiers; Fleetwood Hill and Brandy Station, at the mention of which every reader of history was to hear a bugle call; Culpeper, future objective of many of his marches—all these he passed. Clark's Mountain rose in the distance, and he crossed the Rapidan River, down which were Raccoon Ford, Germanna, Ely's Ford. Presently he was at Orange Courthouse, whence two roads lead eastward into the tangled country that the natives rightly had styled the Wilderness. He changed cars at Gordonsville, for the protection of which so many of his plans were later to be shaped; then he came down the Virginia Central Railroad, that was for many months to hold his army together. Trevilian's Station, Louisa, Frederick's Hall, Beaver Dam—all of them were to become a part of his biography. With much blowing of the whistle and grinding of the brakes, he reached Hanover Junction, where the Virginia Central crossed the Richmond, Fredericksburg and Potomac Railroad. The village had been unknown to fame, but it was to become, after Richmond, the chief object of his care for many anxious seasons.

At Orange and at Louisa he had to go to the rear of the car and bow to the crowds that insistently called for him.[2] For the rest of the long journey he observed and pondered. Was he prepared for what lay ahead in that country that the fates seemed to spread out before him, as if to show him its simple beauty in peace, ere he saw it ruined by war? No, he was not prepared: no man could be. But did he possess the qualities that would make it possible for him to equip himself for leadership?

He was then fifty-four years of age and stood five feet eleven inches in height, weighing slightly less than 170 pounds. In physique he was sound, without a blemish on his body.[3] In the

---

[2] W. W. Scott, *loc. cit.*, and Jones, *L. and L.,* 137.
[3] The undertaker who prepared his body for burial in 1870 attested that even then there was no blemish. (Information supplied by Gutzon Borglum.) His height, etc., are given with accuracy by E. C. Gordon, in Riley, *General Robert E. Lee after Appomattox,* 78 (cited hereafter as *Riley*).

whole of his previous life he had suffered only one recorded illness and that had not been severe.[4] Without having the bulging muscles of bovine strength, he was possessed of great powers of endurance, as he had demonstrated that night on the pedregal in front of Padierna. Only at the end of the long-continued strain of the days preceding the attack on Chapultepec had his body failed him, and then only for a few hours.[5] When he was past forty he had competed with his sons in high jumps at Arlington.[6] He had skated and danced and had been an excellent swimmer. His vision and teeth were fine, his hearing was unimpaired, and his voice, which was of the lower middle register, was rich and resonant. Few men were the inheritors of a stronger nervous system. From the most strenuous efforts he could relax almost instantly, and if he sat down unoccupied, even in a church, he had to be on his guard lest he dropped quickly asleep.[7]

In appearance one fellow-traveller, who saw him that April day, considered Lee "the noblest-looking man I had ever gazed upon . . . handsome beyond all men I had ever seen."[8] His fine large head, which had a circumference of twenty-three and one-half inches,[9] was broadly rounded, with prominent brows and wide temples, and was set on a short, strong neck. His hair was black, with a sprinkle of gray; his short mustache was wholly black. Brown eyes that seemed black in dim light and a slightly florid complexion gave warmth and color to his grave face. His mouth was wide and well-arched. His lips were thin.[10] A massive torso rose above narrow hips, and his large hands were in contrast to very small feet.[11] Sitting behind a desk, or on a horse, his shoulders, neck, and hands made him appear a larger man than he actually was.[12] His finest appearance was when mounted, for he was an admirable rider, with the flat legs of the ideal cavalryman, and he always used the dragoon seat, with long stirrups.

---

[4] *Supra*, p. 306.
[5] See *supra*, p. 313.
[6] *R. E. Lee, Jr.,* 9.
[7] *R. E Lee, Jr.,* 12.
[8] T. S. Garnett, *loc. cit.*
[9] Lee to Talcott, May 23, 1834, with reference to the purchase of a hat, *Talcott MSS.* (*VHS*).
[10] E. V. Valentine, the sculptor who made measurements of Lee's head for a bust, was insistent that the portrait of Lee painted in 1831 and reproduced in this volume shows Lee with much thicker lips than he had.
[11] A pair of dress boots given by him to E. V. Valentine were No. 4½ C (*Riley,* 152), but probably were too small for him.
[12] Gordon in *Riley,* 78.

His manners accorded with his person. In 1861, as always, he was the same in his bearing to men of every station, courteous, simple, and without pretense. Of objective mind, free of any suggestion of self-consciousness, he was considerate in his dealings with others, and of never-failing tact. He made friends readily and held them steadfastly.

Close relations never lowered him in the esteem of his associates. He was clean-minded and frank with his friends, and confided in them more freely than has been supposed. Always he was unselfish, talked little of himself, and was in no sense egotistical. Although he was slow to take offense and was not quick to wrath, his temper was strong. Except when he was sick, he rarely broke the bounds of self-mastery for more than a moment. Then he was best left alone. In all that has been recorded of him prior to 1861, the only instance in which he is reported to have let his indignation overcome his self-control was when he told Charles Anderson of the threat of the Texas commissioners to refuse him transportation to the coast unless he resigned from the United States army and accepted a Confederate commission.

The company of women, especially of pretty women, he preferred to that of men. In the presence of the other sex, he displayed a gracious, and sometimes a breezy gallantry; but no suggestion of a scandal, no hint of over-intimacy, was ever linked with his name. His conversation with his younger female friends was lively, with many touches of teasing and with an occasional mild pun, but it was not witty. He had a good sense of humor, which his dignity rarely permitted him to exhibit in laughter. Those who observed him closely, in the midst of comical incidents, believed that he "laughed inwardly." The bitter strife that lay ahead was to check even these occasional evidences of mirth, as if the memory of the dead came to him just at the instant he had been tempted to smile at the narration of some hilarious story. In dealing with children his manners were at their finest. For them he always had a smile, no matter where he met them, and without indulging in foolish talk or grimaces, he won their confidence almost invariably. There is only one case of record—and that after the war—when a child would not talk confidently with him on first acquaintance. The farther he was from his own offspring, and the longer the separation, the more he craved the company of other children.

His manners reflected his spiritual life. It has been in vain that some of his biographers have asked if his calm dignity did not cover some deep spiritual conflict. It was not so. His was a simple soul, humble, transparent, and believing. Increasingly through the years prior to that historic railway journey to Richmond, religion had become a part of his very being. So far as may be judged from his letters, he had not passed through a single period of doubt as to the existence of a personal God. The religious controversies of his mature years never touched him. Creeds meant little to him. Reading daily his Bible and his prayer book, spending much time on his knees, he believed in a God who, in His wisdom, sent blessings beyond man's deserts, and visited him, on occasion, with hardships and disaster for the chastening of the rebellious heart of the ungrateful and the forgetful. As Robert E. Lee viewed it, on the eve of his plunge into the bloody tragedy of a war among brothers, life was only a preparation for eternity. Whatever befell the faithful was the will of God, and whatever God willed was best. In every disaster, he was to stand firm in the faith that it was sent by God for reasons that man could not see.

The application of this faith was as simple as its content. Self-denial and self-control were the supreme rule of life. It was the basis of his code of conduct. He loved good food—fried chicken, game, barbecued shoat, roast beef[13]—but he was ready to eat thankfully the hardest fare of the field. In the confused councils he was doomed to share, he bore the contention of braggarts and swaggerers with self-control because it was his duty as a soldier to be patient and his obligation as a Christian to be humble. In dealing with alcoholic beverages, his habits were abstemious lest he endanger his self-mastery. He had built up, in this way, a dislike for tobacco, which he never used, and a hatred for whiskey. "I think it better to avoid it altogether, as you do," he had written one of his sons, with reference to strong drink, "as its temperate use is so difficult." [14] Even wine he drank rarely and in small quantities.

[13] *Cf.* Mrs. James Chesnut: *A Diary from Dixie,* 93 (cited hereafter as *Mrs. Chesnut*).
[14] R. E. Lee to W. H. F. Lee, May 30, 1858; Jones, *L. and L.,* 94.

His ideals had their embodiment, for unconsciously he was a hero-worshipper. He viewed his father not as "Light-Horse Harry" was in the tragic years of his speculation, but as he might have been if the promise of his Revolutionary record had been fulfilled. Above his father and every other man he had always placed Washington. The Father of his Country was no mere historical figure to him, great but impersonal and indistinct. Through Lee's long years of association with Mr. Custis, who knew Washington better than did any man alive in 1850, Washington was as real to him as if the majestic Virginian had stepped down nightly from the canvas at Arlington and had talked reminiscently with the family about the birth of an earlier revolution. Daily, for almost thirty years, whenever Lee had been at home, his environment had been a constant suggestion of the same ideal. He had come to view duty as Washington did, to act as he thought Washington would, and even, perhaps, to emulate the grave, self-contained courtesy of the great American rebel. The modesty of his nature doubtless kept Lee now from drawing the very obvious analogy between his situation and that of Washington in 1775, but the influence and the ideal were deep in his soul. He would not have shaped such a question, even in his own mind, but those who knew him as the inheritor of the Mount Vernon tradition must have asked if he was destined to be the Washington of the South's war for independence.

In intellect he was of an even higher order than had been demonstrated in his record of thirty-two years of army service without a single failure to his discredit. His mind was mathematical and his imagination that—and only that—of an engineer. The best of his results always were attained when originality and initiative could be employed. Routine office duties bored him. Although a specialist in his work and in his reading, his culture was wider than that of most soldiers. Well-grounded in Greek and in Latin, he kept some of the spirit of the classics when he had forgotten the texts. French, which he had mastered when he was in his first full vigor of mind, remained longer with him than the language of the antique world. For Spanish he had an enthusiasm born of a belief in its utility. Of some phases of American history, and particularly of those in which his family had figured, he had

453

a measure of precise knowledge. Fiction he avoided as an intellectual narcotic, but poetry he enjoyed and tenaciously remembered. His principal reading, never wide, was chiefly of the newspapers, to which he looked for that part of his information on public affairs not supplied by his conversation. There was music in his family, and a real if undiscriminating love of art. Essentially an out-of-doors man, the pictures he enjoyed most were those of Nature's own painting, and his most understanding affection was for her creatures, horses, dogs, cats even. As other men might admire a great portrait, he delighted to look at a sunset or at a garden. Birds were a particular care to him. His own contribution to physical beauty was through the promotion of orderliness and in the planting of trees.

Prolonged travel had been his lot as an army officer, in New England, along the whole of the South Atlantic seaboard, and on the frontier, but he had been in no foreign land except Mexico. In his journeyings he was extremely sensitive to the natural charm of a picturesque country, and interested in the fertility of farm lands, but he never lingered to admire them, if delay would interfere with the precision of his schedule.

Outside his profession his chief interests were not cultural but agricultural and social. The ideal life, had he been able to fashion it, would have been to entertain or to visit pleasant people and friendly kinfolk, while riding daily over a small plantation that was tilled by white men and was improving in value and in appearance. As for society, he learned more from men than from books. His dignity cloaked no diffidence. The company of humans he sought and loved, unwearied by small talk and unvaryingly patient with dull minds. All manner of acquaintances were his—generals, professors, planters, politicians, engineers, laborers—for his life in isolated forts and at frontier stations had been relieved by assignments to the centres of thought and of political action. In meeting and remembering new acquaintances he had a singularly developed and highly useful memory for names.

Men had been the raw material of his work as an engineer and as an administrator. Alike to giving and to taking orders he had long been disciplined. His superiors, as a rule, had been trained; his laborers had often been inexperienced and awkward. He had always been able to satisfy, and more than satisfy, the officers to whom he was responsible, while getting much toil from those in his charge. His methods were systematic. Essentially of a scientific mind, he would first study his problem exhaustively. Once he had found what he deemed the best solution within the money and resources at his disposal, he would start at the rough beginnings, with the simple tools at his command. The prospect of organizing a long and difficult project had no terrors for a man who had worked at Cockspur Island, at the Des Moines Rapids, and at Sollers' Point. Rapid in his work, and happily free of any trace of laziness, he was as mindful of detail[15] as he was resourceful in design. Inborn thrift, his mother's thrift, strengthened by the discipline of his youth, made him economical in the public service, accurate in accounting, and prompt in report. Rarely had he enjoyed the luxury of more than one assistant; so frequently had he carried the whole burden on his own shoulders that it was second nature to make his decisions alone, and alone to direct the execution of his plans. With pride in his profession, he had all the engineer's zest for action and a profound aversion to delay. His delight was in getting results—and results were Virginia's instant need with the clouds of war blowing fast toward the capital whither Lee's train was carrying him.

After the first duty of helping to organize an army—in what capacity he did not yet know—Lee had to anticipate a bloody and a bitter war. What did he know of the grisly art he would have to apply?

In those two unchanging fundamentals of military service, discipline and co-operation, Robert E. Lee had received the precise training of a professional soldier. Obedience to orders was part of his religion. Adverse decisions on his acts he had schooled himself to accept in precisely the same spirit as approval. He could elicit the support of his superiors without flattery, and in the few instances where he had ever had subordinates, he had

---

[15] In the autumn of 1860 some one from Arlington ordered a coulter of special design from a foundry in Washington. It had not been paid for when Lee joined the Confederacy. Learning subsequently of the debt, he arranged through secret channels to pay the maker two dollars in gold, late in 1861, and, busy as he was, he wrote a personal note of apology for the delayed settlement. This incident has often been cited as an illustration not only of his sense of honor but also of his attention to details (*Jones*, 286; *Long*, 39).

won their allegiance without threats. He was a diplomat among engineers. Fully qualified to deal with the politician in executive office, he was suspicious of him in the field or in the forum, and none too confident of his sagacity in legislation, though he was as meticulous as his great model, Washington, in subordinating himself, at all times and in all things, to civil authority. His dealings with his brother officers had never been darkened by scheming or marred by jealousy. Of much that West Point taught and of all that it failed to inculcate, his observation had been close and personal. A knowledge of the capacity of some of his prospective opponents had been gained by his service at the academy, in Mexico, and in Texas. His tedious attendance upon dull courts-martial had not been time wasted, for there he had seen the rivalries, the animosities, and the occasional demoralization of camp life uncovered. Even the Pillow court of inquiry had been a useful part of his military education, for it had shown him how selfish political ambitions could rive an army in the field.

Familiarity with the history of war, another fundamental of the training of a leader, was his in limited measure. The American Revolutionary campaigns he had surveyed carefully. His reading of "Light-Horse Harry's" *Memoirs* had been emulous and detailed. Napoleon was the great captain whose battles he had most carefully followed from Jomini, and from such other books as were available. The operations in Italy, the descent on Egypt, and the Russian campaign he must have known with thoroughness. To the Crimean War he had devoted at least casual study. With Hannibal and with Julius Cæsar he was not wholly unacquainted.

From these masters of war, and most of all from General Winfield Scott, he had learned the theory of strategy, and had learned it well. He had participated, too, in nearly all the strategical preparation of the most successful series of battles ever fought prior to 1861 by an American army. The strategy he had seen Scott apply had primarily been that of flank attack, based on careful reconnaissance and, where possible, on surprise. Cerro Gordo and Padierna, the two battles which were fought on the basis of Lee's own study of the ground, seem to have meant more in shaping his views of strategy than all his reading. Chapultepec, also, had made a deep impression on him and perhaps suggested the final assault at Gettysburg. The strategical function of the high command he had learned from those same battles in Mexico. That function, as he saw it, was to develop the lines of communication, to direct the reconnaissance, to ascertain the precise position of the enemy, and then to bring all the combatant units into position at the proper time and to the best advantage. In Mexico Scott had never tried to handle his troops in action. He had left that to the divisional commanders; Lee's instinct was to do the same thing.

But if Lee was, in the spring of 1861, a well-schooled theoretical strategist, whose interest lay in that field of war, Scott's methods and his own lack of opportunity had given him a very limited knowledge of tactics. He was adept enough, of course, in the drill and manœuvres of the cadet battalion at West Point, but of larger tactical experience he had little. Twenty-six of his thirty-two years in the army had been spent on the staff, and only six in the line. Of these six years something less than three had been passed with troops. At no time had he commanded more than 300 men in the field, and even that number simply for one brief uneventful scout through a desert. Since he had left West Point he had never served with infantry or with artillery, except in the battery at Vera Cruz.

Thanks, however, to the advantages that Scott had afforded him during the campaign from Vera Cruz to Mexico City, he had far more than the staff officer's approach to the duties that awaited him in excited Richmond. In reconnaissance his experience had been sufficient to develop great aptitude. One of the most compelling commandments of his military decalogue was to examine in person, fully and carefully, the ground of advance and anticipated action. He was an excellent topographer and not without training as an intelligence officer. Those anxious summer days spent at Puebla in 1847, when he had questioned travellers regarding the approaches to Santa Anna's capital, were to yield him many a dividend of advantage in the Virginia campaigns. He had seen something of what sea power meant, and he had watched observantly as Scott had made the hard calculation of the chances the army must take when it prepared to abandon its line of communications and to subsist on the country through which it was to advance. Fortification, as an engineer, he knew thoroughly. Nearly every contemporary form of coast defense he had studied, and in the location and design of some types he was as well trained as any American soldier. The nascent art of field fortification he had examined in Mexico, but always from the standpoint of the attack.

Such was the positive equipment of Robert E. Lee at the beginning of the War between the States. It was, on the whole, the best equipment with which any soldier entered the struggle, for the capable leaders of Scott's divisions of 1847 were then either dead or too infirm for action, and few of the brigadiers of the Mexican campaigns had displayed special ability. The absence of any retirement law for their seniors had kept most of the colonels of 1846–48 from becoming general officers before they had passed the age when they could adapt themselves to the intricate problems of a war in the United States.

Admirable as was the training of Lee it was not complete. He had scant knowledge of militia and little experience with hastily trained volunteers, wide as was his acquaintance with inexpert civilian labor. Only the regular soldier did he know well. Again, from the narrowness of his subordinate command, there was danger that his view would be microscopic. In the third place, all his battle experience had been on the offensive, though the situation and comparative weakness of the South were to compel it to hold to a defensive in the larger sense of the word. Furthermore, having labored so long on detached projects, he was disposed to do work that could have been passed on to others. Most of all was he lacking in any detailed knowledge of the service of supply. Belonging to the élite corps of the army, he had never performed lengthy duty as quartermaster or as commissary, and he had not sought any such detail for the sake of promotion, as his friend Joe Johnston had. Nor had he and most of the other Confederate leaders been reared in a society that gave them a background for this homely but essential part of the work of a successful commanding general. Industry, with a few exceptions, had not attracted the best brains of the South. In plantation life, while provision had to be made for clothing and feeding hundreds, this had been the task of the overseers—and overseers were not apt to be chosen to lead armies.

With Lee's excellent training in some directions set down in one column and his lack of equipment in some particulars placed opposite it, any person who knew him intimately would have said that the man who was now approaching Richmond would show himself a fine strategist, though he might perhaps be a bit theoretical, a popular leader though not a facile tactician—in short, an excellent man to organize an army, to make reconnaissance and to plan battles, but an unknown quantity in handling troops in action. What surprises one who studies the military education of Lee is the entire absence of anything to forecast his great skill in troop movements. His experience in logistics had been confined to what he had observed in Mexico, where no railroad existed, coupled with the little he had learned during the Harpers Ferry insurrection. Yet from the hour he had responsibility for using the railroads to effect rapid concentration, he employed them as if he had spent his life in practising how to bring great bodies of men to a desired point at a predetermined moment.

All these were the abstract considerations that might have been argued in the case of any soldier whose background was known. There remained the basic, if less tangible, factor of temperament. He was a gentleman in every impulse: was he too much a gentleman for the dirty business of war? Was there enough of steel in his soul? That respect for civil authority—would it tie his hands in a revolution? Feeling that his duty was performed when he had obeyed his orders and had done his utmost, would he fight for his opinions? Would he escape the "subordinate complex" which is all too familiar in war? If the Southern cause ever depended on him and on him alone, was there in him the stuff of which military dictators are made?

If he thought at all of these things, as his train rolled down to the valley of the Chickahominy, it must have been in the humble conviction that he was not equal to the task that lay ahead, a task of which he was one of few Southern men to realize the full magnitude. Far better than the throngs that cheered the new Palmetto flag, he knew the might and the prestige of the old standard that had been hauled down. The crowds that filled the stations along his route may have been talking of easy victories and early independence, but he had measured the strength and determination of the North, and he foresaw a bloody test, a long war, a doubtful issue.

The passengers on the train began to stir. Peake's Turnout was passed, Atlee's was reached. To the southeast was a little village bearing the unpretending name of Mechanicsville, and beyond that a sleepy crossroads called Cold Harbor. Richmond was close now, Richmond that was soon to be "a torch and a trumpet." It had been a quiet city of 37,000 people when madness had seized the country, a place of peace and pleasantness. John Smith had come there at Whitsuntide in the year when Jamestown had been settled; a fort had been erected at the "falls of the James" before the massacre of 1622; slowly through the eighteenth century it had been built up until, in 1779, it had become the capital of the commonwealth, in succession to Williamsburg. On picturesque hills, that followed a wide bend in the river, successful merchants had reared ample homes. Flour that was sent "across the line" to South America had early been stencilled with the city's name; a capitol that Jefferson himself had modelled after an old Roman temple at Nîmes had been erected on the finest eminence. A generation later a canal had been started that was to link Richmond with the headwaters of the Ohio and rescue for Virginia the trade of the old Northwest that New York was diverting through the Erie. John Marshall had lived in Richmond and had been buried there; Edgar Allan Poe had called it home. To its large hotels the wealthy planters had come; from its platforms Clay, Webster, Thackeray, and Dickens had spoken. Wealthy for the time, with strong banks, varied manufactories, profitable shipping, and ample railroad connections with almost every part of the state, boasting a state arsenal and a large rolling mill, Richmond was the heart of Virginia, financially and economically. Most of all was she rich in her people. None of them had a mighty fortune; few of them were very poor, but nearly all of them had lived long in the town and had the homogeneity not less of understanding than of blood. Together they rejoiced; as one they labored. *Noblesse oblige* was written larger in the civic code than any ordinance the common hall ever drafted. As Whigs and as Democrats, as "Union men" and secessionists, the voters had divided often and violently; but always for their city's honor they had been a unit. Fire and pestilence and the gray adversity that had followed "flush times" had left them like-minded. Save for long-forgotten Indian fights and a brush with the British, when Arnold had occupied the place in 1781, Richmond had never heard the clash of combat, but now that the evil day was come she had cast her lot whole-heartedly with the South. All that she had symbolized in peace was to be forgotten in the battles that were to be waged for her. Alarms were to bewilder her; the first slaughter was to stun her; but soon she was to show the staunch-ness of her soul. She had meant little in the life of the gentleman who sat erect in his silk hat as the train pulled into the station, but from the moment the conductor cried, "All out for Richmond," the safety of that city was to be the supreme care of the military life of Robert E. Lee.

CHAPTER XXVII

Virginia Looks to Lee

FROM the train-shed at 17th and Broad Streets, on the afternoon of April 22, 1861, Colonel Lee made his way to a carriage and rode through Richmond streets to the Spotswood Hotel at the southeast corner of 8th and Main Streets, where he took a room.[1] The conversation he overheard, as he walked through the lobby and as he ate his supper, was all of defense against invasion, of preparation, and of speedy alliance with the Southern Confederacy. The day before, while the ministers had been dismissing their anxious, prayerful congregations, the tocsin had been sounded from the guard house in the Capitol Square, and word had quickly spread that the *Pawnee,* a Federal warship, was steaming up James River to bombard the unprotected city. The volunteer companies had rushed to arms, the Fayette artillery had galloped with its field guns to an eminence overlooking the stream, the governor himself had gone to the waterfront, the soldiery had lined the riverbank, old men had taken down their fowling pieces, and curious, unarmed thousands had hurried to the hill-tops to watch for the coming of the sloop. She had not appeared, though the martial waiting had been continued until nightfall. Then Richmond had been told that the rumor had originated in a misreading of telegrams.[2] The excitement of this first of Richmond's many war "scares" had not died away when Lee arrived.

The town was buzzing, also, over the arrival of Alexander H. Stephens, Vice-President, as special commissioner from the Confederate States of America to the commonwealth of Virginia, with letters of credence, authorizing him to "negotiate of and

---

[1] *Cf.* Lee to Mrs. Lee, May 16, 1861; *R. E. Lee, Jr.,* 31.
[2] Sally Brock: *Richmond during the War* (cited hereafter as *Miss Brock*), 24; T. C. De Leon: *Four Years in Rebel Capitals* (cited hereafter as *De Leon*), 104; George Cary Eggleston: *A Rebel's Recollections* (cited hereafter as *Eggleston*), 24; 42 *S. H. S. P.,* 121; *O. R.,* 51, part 2, p. 24.

concerning all matters and subjects interesting to both Republics." [3] All secessionists welcomed Mr. Stephens and advocated a speedy union of Virginia with the other Southern States. Most Whigs, now that war was upon them, favored the same course. Virginia, as they saw it, could not remain neutral. Would the convention, which had been sitting in secret session, display the same spirit and vote Virginia into the Confederacy, pending final action by the people on the ordinance of secession? In the hotels and in the streets every man was a constitutional lawyer, as he debated this question and discussed Stephens's mission.

Lee's military instinct told him that the crowd was right: Virginia alone could not resist. If there must be war there must be alliance with the South. He did not mingle with the noisy debaters, however. Instead, he hastened to the capitol, where he met Virginia's governor. John Letcher was then fifty-eight, a bald-headed, florid, bottle-nosed lawyer from Rockbridge County, in the Shenandoah Valley. Not a brilliant man, he was a level-headed conservative Democrat, and he had refused to endorse secession until Lincoln had called for troops. Lee was to see much of Letcher during the next few months and he was to profit by Letcher's integrity, his determination, his common sense, and his familiarity with the mind of the Virginia people. Letcher did not flatter himself that every politician was a soldier. During that tempestuous April week he was one of the few public men who did not have on his tongue the very plan by which victory could be achieved, quickly and surely.

The governor had an explanation to make; an explanation to make and a question to ask. The state convention, he said, had provided by an ordinance of April 19 for the appointment of a "commander of the military and naval forces of Virginia," with the rank of major general, and with authority to direct the organization and operations of the troops, under the governor's constitutional control.[4] The advisory council had recommended Lee for this post.[5] Letcher had formally tendered it to him on April 21 and had sent a messenger,[6] whom Lee had probably passed on

---

[3] O. R., 51, part 2, pp. 18, 24; IV O. R., 1, 242.
[4] *Ordinances Adopted by the Convention of Virginia in Secret Session in April and May, 1861*, p. 9.
[5] O. R., 51, part 2, p. 21.   [6] *MS. Executive Journal of Virginia*, April 21, 1861.

the road. Would Lee accept the office created by the convention?

That was the question Letcher put, so directly and with so little dramatic touch, that neither the language of his tender nor of Lee's reply has been preserved.

Lee's answer had been shaped by the very reasons that had led him to resign from the army. He felt that his first allegiance was to Virginia. When he had said he would unsheathe his sword only in her defense, that was equivalent to saying that when she called, he would respond. There was, consequently, no hesitation now; in a few brief words he accepted the task of defending his native state. Doubtless he told the governor that he had not resigned in the expectation or in the desire of further military service, and he probably added that he wished an abler man had been found for the task Virginia assigned.

That was all. Before the convention adjourned its night session Lee's name was sent in by Governor Letcher for confirmation, with a simple note that Lee had determined to resign from the United States army before the convention had created the office to which Lee was nominated.[7] The convention at once and unanimously approved the choice;[8] word that Lee would take command was telegraphed to Norfolk, then considered the most threatened point in the state,[9] and the weary new general retired to his bed in the Spotswood Hotel with a greater burden than he had ever borne.

The next morning, April 23, Lee opened a temporary office either in the Richmond Post-office or in the old state General Court building.[10] Without an adjutant, or even a clerk, he drafted his General Order No. 1, announcing that he had assumed command, and Governor Letcher made a statement to the same effect.[11] Before Lee was able to do much more, a committee from the convention waited on him to escort him to the capitol, where he was to receive formal notice of his appointment. Accompanied by four members of the convention, Marmaduke Johnson of Richmond, P. C. Johnston, representing Lee and Scott Counties, W. T. Sutherlin of Danville, and John Critcher of his own native

[7] *Journal of the Virginia Convention of 1861*, pp. 184–85.
[8] *Journal of the Virginia Convention of 1861*, pp. 184–85.
[9] O. R., 2, 774.
[10] Cooke, *op. cit.*, 40, named the post-office. Earle Lutz's researches indicate the court building.
[11] O. R., 2, 775–76.

Saturday Apl 20 1861

Govr Tendered to Col Robert E. Lee the office of Commander in Chief of Military forces of Va Special Messenger sent to communicate with him in event of his acceptance;

Tuesday Apl. 23 1861

Govr nomd to Convn Genl Robert E. Lee to be commander of Military & naval forces of Va with rank of Major Genl confirmed by Convn & comny. sened

Facsimile of entry in the Executive Minute Book of Governor John Letcher, of Virginia, covering the nomination and confirmation of General Robert E. Lee "as commander of the military and naval forces of Virginia."

From the original in the Virginia State Library.

county of Westmoreland, Lee climbed the hill shortly before noon and entered the capitol, where the convention was sitting behind closed doors.

When he arrived some necessary motions were under discussion on the floor, and there was a brief delay in the rotunda. Lee's mind was running ahead to the exactions of the hour and to the necessities of united action by all the Southern states. Virginia came first in his devotion, but he saw plainly that neither her defense nor the triumph of her cause could be assured unless the South halted all centrifugal tendencies and remained one republic. In this thought, as he waited, Lee looked up at the ivory-tinted statue of his great hero, Washington, a marble that exhibits the perfect poise and all the high determination of an earlier revolutionary—and he said aloud: "I hope we have seen the last of secession." Some, at least, of those who stood around him did not understand what he meant.[12]

The doors were opened. Lee entered on the arm of Marmaduke Johnson. A crowded room greeted his eye, the same room in which his father, pleading vainly against the Virginia resolutions of 1798, had affirmed that he would share the calamities he could not prevent. The convention rose to receive him. On the speaker's platform stood the president of the convention, John Janney. To his right was the emaciated, unhealthy figure of Vice-President Stephens, his eyes shining, his thin lips taut. Beyond him was Governor Letcher. On the left of Janney was Judge John J. Allen, president both of the court of appeals and of the governor's advisory council. By his side were the other two members of the council, Colonel Francis H. Smith, superintendent of the Virginia Military Institute, and a keen-eyed man with a great dome of a head and pleasant composure of countenance, Matthew Fontaine Maury, the oceanographer who had resigned his post at the Naval Observatory in Washington to share in the defense of his native Virginia.[13]

This much Lee observed at first glance. Then, when they were

---

[12] John Critcher, 5 *Va. His. Mag.*, 221; *Memoirs J. S. Mosby*, 379.

[13] *Southern Generals, Who They Are and What They Have Done* [Anonymous] (cited hereafter as *Southern Generals*), 42; *The Early Life, Campaigns and Public Service of Robert E. Lee* [and] . . . *His Companions in Arms*, by a Distinguished Southern Journalist, 54.

three short paces within the entrance,[14] Johnson announced: "Mr. President, I have the honor to present to you, and to the convention, Major General Lee."

Lee halted. The members of the convention took their seats again. President Janney remained standing and, a moment later, addressed Lee in full and rounded periods. "Major General Lee," he said solemnly, "in the name of the people of your native state, here represented, I bid you a cordial and heartfelt welcome to this Hall, in which we may almost yet hear the echo of the voices of the statesmen, the soldiers and sages of by-gone days, who have borne your name, and whose blood now flows in your veins.

"We met in the month of February last, charged with the solemn duty of protecting the rights, the honor and the interests of the people of this Commonwealth. We differed for a time as to the best means of accomplishing that object; but there never was, at any moment, a shade of difference amongst us as to the great object itself; and now, Virginia having taken her position, as far as the power of this Convention extends, we stand animated by one impulse, governed by one desire and one determination, and that is that *she shall be defended;* and that no spot of her soil shall be polluted by the foot of an invader.

"When the necessity became apparent of having a leader for our forces, all hearts and all eyes, by the impulse of an instinct which is a surer guide than reason itself, turned to the old county of Westmoreland. We knew how prolific she had been in other days of heroes and statesmen. We knew she had given birth to the Father of his Country; to Richard Henry Lee, to Monroe, and last, though not least, to your own gallant father,[15] and knew well, by your own deeds, that her productive power was not yet exhausted.

"Sir, we watched with the most profound and intense interest the triumphal march of the army led by General Scott, to which you were attached, from Vera Cruz to the capital of Mexico; we read of the sanguinary conflicts and the blood-stained fields, in all of which victory perched upon our own banners; we knew of

14 So affirmed Colonel John Bell Bigger, long-time clerk of the house of delegates of Virginia, who got his information from John L. Eubank, secretary of the convention. Contemporary accounts state that Lee halted about midway of the short, central aisle.

15 The services of "Light-Horse Harry" Lee had been described to the general assem-

the unfading lustre that was shed upon the American arms by that campaign; and we know, also, what your modesty has always disclaimed, that no small share of the glory of those achievements was due to your valor and your military genius.

"Sir, one of the proudest recollections of my life will be the honor that I yesterday had of submitting to this body the confirmation of the nomination made by the governor of this state, of you as Commander in Chief of the military and naval forces of this Commonwealth. I rose to put the question, and when I asked if this body would advise and consent to that appointment, there rushed from the hearts to the tongues of all the members, an affirmative response, that told with an emphasis that could leave no doubt of the feeling whence it emanated. I put the negative of the question for form's sake, but there was an unbroken silence.

"Sir, we have, by this unanimous vote, expressed our conviction that you are at this day, among the living citizens of Virginia, 'first in war.' We pray God most fervently that you may so conduct the operations committed to your charge, that it will soon be said of you, that you are 'first in peace,' and when that time comes you will have earned the still prouder distinction of being 'first in the hearts of your countrymen.'

"I will close with one more remark.

"When the Father of his Country made his last will and testament, he gave his swords to his nephews with an injunction that they should never be drawn from their scabbards, except in self-defense, or in defense of the rights and liberties of their country, and that, if drawn for the latter purpose, they should fall with them in their hands, rather than relinquish them.

"Yesterday, your mother, Virginia, placed her sword in your hand upon the implied condition that we know you will keep to the letter and in spirit, that you will draw it only in her defense, and that you will fall with it in your hand rather than that the object for which it was placed there shall fail." [16]

bly of Virginia by admirers only a few weeks before, and an appropriation had been made on March 28 to remove his body from Cumberland Island to the grounds of the Virginia Military Institute (*Acts of the General Assembly of Virginia*, 1861, p. 58).

[16] *Journal of the Virginia Convention of 1861*, pp. 186–88. The text of this address, with that of Lee's reply, is very inaccurately printed in *Long*. Most of the biographers have followed Long, whose errors, of course, are attributable to and excused by his blindness.

Lee had anticipated no such welcome as this and must have been embarrassed by Janney's praise. He had never made a speech in his life, but he saw that he was expected to reply and he answered, slowly and distinctly: "Mr. President and Gentlemen of the Convention,—Profoundly impressed with the solemnity of the occasion, for which I must say I was not prepared, I accept the position assigned me by your partiality. I would have much preferred had your choice fallen on an abler man. Trusting in Almighty God, an approving conscience, and the aid of my fellow-citizens, I devote myself to the service of my native State, in whose behalf alone will I ever again draw my sword." [17]

The chair was thereupon vacated, and the members gathered about him,[18] to congratulate him and to voice their confidence in him. His previous reputation and his fine appearance made a most favorable impression upon them. Said Stephens: "All the force which personal appearance could add to the power and impressiveness of words . . . was imparted by his manly form and the great dignity as well as grace in his every action and movement. All these, combined, sent home to the breast of every one the conviction that he was thoroughly impressed himself with the full consciousness of the immense responsibility he had assumed." [19] Wrote Jubal A. Early, member from Franklin and later one of Lee's corps commanders: "Those who witnessed his appearance before the convention, saw his manly bearing, and heard the few grave, dignified and impressive words with which he consecrated himself and his sword to the cause of his native state, can never forget that scene. All felt at once that we had a leader worthy of the State and the cause." [20]

As soon as the news of Lee's appointment and acceptance reached the larger public, it aroused high enthusiasm and evoked much praise. *The Richmond Enquirer* quoted with satisfaction a report that General Winfield Scott had said he had rather have

[17] *Journal of the Virginia Convention of 1861*, p. 188. It is probable that Lee had been told that a response was in order, for his words were too well chosen to have been fashioned without deliberation. It is hardly necessary to point out how they echo the language of his letters of April 20 to his kinspeople and to General Scott. Perhaps, also, he unconsciously adopted the style of Washington's farewell to Congress, Dec. 23, 1783, which he had read in Texas, from Everett's *Life of Washington*, 150–53.
[18] *Southern Generals*, 42.
[19] A. H. Stephens: *A Constitutional View of the War Between the States* (cited hereafter as *Stephens*), 2, 384.
[20] Quoted in *Jones*, 2.

received the resignation of every general than that of Lee.[21] "A more heroic Christian, noble soldier and gentleman," said *The Richmond Dispatch*, "could not be found."[22] And again, "Of him it was said before his appointment, and of him it may be well said, no man is superior in all that constitutes the soldier and the gentleman—no man more worthy to head our forces and lead our army. There is no one who would command more of the confidence of the people of Virginia than this distinguished officer, and no one under whom the volunteers and militia would more gladly rally. His reputation, his acknowledged ability, his chivalric character, his probity, honor, and—may we add to his eternal praise—his Christian life and conduct make his very name a 'tower of strength.' . . ."[23] *The Lynchburg Virginian* was no less laudatory: "We rejoice that this distinguished officer and worthy son of Virginia has withdrawn from Lincoln's army and thrown himself upon the bosom of his native State. It was what we expected of the man. Captain Maury has done likewise; and thus, these two noble men, the very flower of the Army and Navy of the late United States, respond to the call of their glorious old Mother. . . ."[24] In different strain, the wife of ex-President Tyler wrote: "Col. Lee, a splendid man every inch of him, is in command of the Virginia forces. . . . He can only lead to victory, if this shocking war continues."[25] J. M. Broadus, addressing his brother, John A. Broadus, a minister of high prestige, expressed faith in Lee as "a prudent and skillful warrior. I hope he may not precipitate hostilities. Virginia is not ready for a conflict, but she is making herself so as rapidly as possible."[26] In the North, issues overshadowed men. Lee's resignation and his acceptance of the Virginia command attracted little attention for a few weeks. Then denunciation of the "traitor" became general, and Lee's personal honor and private conduct were assailed in libellous *crescendo*. James G. Blaine, looking back upon it, expressed the belief that Lee's assumption of command "was a powerful incentive with many to vote against the Union."[27]

[21] *Richmond Enquirer*, April 27, 1861, p. 2, col. 1.
[22] *Richmond Dispatch*, April 26, 1861, p. 3, col. 2.
[23] *Richmond Dispatch*, May 1, 1861, p. 2, col. 4.
[24] Quoted in *Richmond Enquirer*, April 25, 1861, p. 2, col. 6.
[25] *Letters and Times of the Tylers*, 2, 648.
[26] A. T. Robertson: *Life and Letters of John A. Broadus*, 183–84.
[27] I. G. Blaine: *Twenty Years of Congress*, 1, 302–3.

Some of the very qualities that Lee's admirers saw in him were put to the test within a few hours after he left the convention hall and went to his office to begin work. A message came that Vice-President Stephens wished to see him that evening at the Ballard House. Lee called. He found the Confederate emissary perplexed but candid. The Confederacy, Stephens explained, of course desired an immediate military alliance with Virginia, and hoped that the Old Dominion would join the other Southern states as soon as the voters ratified the ordinance of secession. This would involve the control of military operations in Virginia by the Confederate authorities—a manifest necessity of war. The Confederacy had no military rank at the time higher than that of brigadier general; Lee, a Virginia major general, might find himself under orders of a titular subordinate. The Virginia convention, Stephens went on, would certainly see that this contingency might arise and, if Lee raised any question of rank, the convention might refuse to enter into a military agreement.

What did Lee propose to do? "He understood the situation fully," to use Stephens's own language. "With a clear understanding of its bearing upon himself personally, he expressed himself as perfectly satisfied, and as being very desirous to have the alliance formed. He stated, in words which produced thorough conviction in my mind of their perfect sincerity, that he did not wish anything connected with himself individually, or his official rank or *personal* position, to interfere in the slightest degree with the immediate consummation of that measure which he regarded as one of the utmost importance in every possible view of public considerations." [28]

With this assurance, Lee bade good-evening to Stephens, who prepared to press with renewed confidence for an early alliance. Lee started for the Spotswood Hotel fully committed to the Confederate cause. His first thought had been of Virginia. He had even resented the belligerent attitude of some of the leaders in the cotton states during the preliminaries of secession. These men, he had believed, were trying to involve the other border states in their quarrel. Now it was different. It was increasingly plain that Virginia would be assailed; in her exposed position she would

[28] 2 *Stephens,* 385.

need the assistance of the South. Virginia's welfare—the very factor that had made him almost hostile to the cotton states— now put him on the side of alliance and common effort.

As he tramped back from the Ballard House, through the shadows of the spring night, did he reflect how fast and how far the Southern revolution had carried him? On Saturday morning he had written to General Scott, to Smith Lee, and to Mrs. Marshall. He had hoped then that he would have to take no part in the quarrel that had forced his resignation. Now it was Wednesday evening and he was a major general in arms against the United States, urging the affiliation of the commonwealth with the militant new Confederacy. The rapid approach of war had quickly and inexorably revealed which were the deepest loyalties of his soul.

CHAPTER XXVIII

CAN VIRGINIA BE DEFENDED?

THE seven weeks that followed the appointment of Lee to the command of the Virginia forces are the least known of his military career, but certainly among the most interesting. They are little known because the confused events of the period were eclipsed by his conduct of field operations the next year. They are interesting because they disclosed Lee's powers as an organizer, and also because they represent the solution adopted by a trained military mind for problems that recur in every democratic society that is forced to raise an army from untrained citizens on the outbreak of a war for which there has been no adequate defensive preparation. A close study of what Lee did in Virginia in April-June, 1861, would have prevented some of the blunders of the Spanish War in 1898 and might have simplified the far vaster mobilization of 1917.

Lee found himself the military and naval commander, under the governor and convention, of a state of 1,596,652 people, of whom only 1,047,579 were whites.[1] Virginia was the most populous state of the South and the fifth in the Union. Her territory extended from the Atlantic Ocean to the Big Sandy River, within 115 miles of Cincinnati. On the longest axis in the general direction of east and west, Virginia was then 425 miles in width. From the farthest point north, in the "Panhandle counties" opposite Pittsburgh, the distance directly south to the North Carolina boundary was 300 miles. The gross area was 67,230 square miles, or roughly that of New England. Strategically, Virginia occupied the line of the Potomac and of the Ohio. She had strong, defensive rivers and mountains, but she was exceedingly vulnerable to attack by a power commanding the sea. The highways of the state were numerous and of every degree of excellence and bad-

[1] Doc. XIV. *Journal of the Va. Convention of 1861.*

ness. The railroads, which had a gross mileage of about 1150 miles, included continuous trackage from Norfolk to Bristol, from Richmond to the Alleghany Mountains, from Alexandria to Lynchburg, from the Potomac River into North Carolina, and a number of shorter lines.

That this large state would have to be prepared immediately for defense was apparent to all. She had already committed acts of war, though for self-preservation, and she must accept the consequences. The Federal authority had been overthrown everywhere in Virginia except at Lee's old post, Fort Monroe, which had been too powerful for the state's volunteers to assault. Harpers Ferry, familiar to the whole country because of the John Brown raid, had been mistakenly believed by the Virginians to have in its Federal arsenal not less than 16,000 modern small arms, badly needed for the defense of the state, together with immensely valuable machinery for the manufacture of muskets and rifles. As soon as the secessionist leaders had been convinced that the convention would withdraw Virginia from the Union, they had determined to capture the Harpers Ferry arsenal, which was held by a small detachment of United States troops. On the night of April 18 Virginia volunteers had descended on the place, only to find that the commander of the guard had received information of their approach and had set fire to the buildings before withdrawing into Maryland.[2] The machinery had escaped the flames, but most of the small arms had been destroyed. The site being as vulnerable as it was important, the Virginia volunteers who occupied Harpers Ferry were more or less in the attitude of holding a wolf by the ears.

In another corner of the state, at Norfolk, the United States had maintained a large navy yard, where the coming of secession had found ten warships of various classes anchored or undergoing repairs, close to warehouses that contained large stores and much equipment. Norfolk volunteers had promptly sunk some hulks at the mouth of the Elizabeth River in an effort to prevent the escape of the naval vessels. The troops had believed themselves successful in blocking the river, and they had been mustering for the difficult task of storming the navy yard and of boarding the

[2] 11 *Calendar Virginia State Papers*, 174–76; *O. R.*, 2, 4; General John B. Imboden in 1 *B. and L.*, 111 ff.

warships, when the sloop *Pawnee*—the same craft that alarmed Richmond the next day—had steamed through the obstructions on the night of April 20, and had landed a contingent of about 500 men at the navy yard. They had proceeded to set fire to the buildings and vessels and, about midnight, had left aboard their ship, with the *Cumberland* in tow. The next day the Virginians had occupied the navy yard, and had thrown up works to prevent a return of the Federals. On the 22d General Walter Gwynn had taken command at Norfolk, on orders from Governor Letcher.[3] Virtually all that was known of the situation, when Lee set to work, was that the fire had burned most of the warships to the water's edge, that the new frigate *Merrimac* and perhaps one or two others could be raised, that damage to the stores had been slight, and that a great number of unmounted naval guns and some 2800 barrels of powder had fallen into the hands of the Virginians.[4]

These overt acts would certainly be answered, and speedily, by the Federal Government. It could not permit its power to be flouted at Harpers Ferry and at Norfolk. President Lincoln, in his proclamation of April 15, had given the Southern forces twenty days in which "to disperse and return peaceably to their respective abodes." [5] This was generally interpreted to mean that the President would wait until May 5 and then would begin the invasion of the South. He might not delay even that long in employing the navy, which was ready for action.

Twelve days, then, Lee had—from April 23 to May 5—in which to prepare Virginia for the first shock of the invasion that was certain to be visited on the Old Dominion sooner than on any other state, because she was on the frontier. What resources could he command for so huge an undertaking? Enthusiasm, yes, for many of the volunteer companies had assembled, in addition to those that had marched on Norfolk and on Harpers Ferry, and they were clamoring to be mustered into service. Some arms

---

[3] Gwynn on April 26, 1861, was nominated to the Virginia convention as a brigadier general of volunteers, 11 *Calendar Virginia State Papers*, 121.
[4] *Official Records of the Union and Confederate Navies*, series IV, vol. 4, 306 ff. (cited hereafter as *N. O. R.*, with Series I implied except where Roman numerals preceding the letters indicate the second, third, or fourth series); *O. R.*, 2, 771; 1 *B. and L.*, 693.
[5] III *O. R.*, 1, 68.

Virginia had and facilities of a sort for equipping and uniforming a number of troops. The militia had a paper organization; the commonwealth had decent local credit. A measure of help could be expected from the Confederacy, for it had been making ready since February. But of organization there was little and of naval vessels there were almost none.

How did Lee view this prospect? He was convinced that war would come;[6] that it would be prolonged, he feared for reasons all too valid. "The war may last ten years," he wrote Mrs. Lee, when he had been in Richmond only eight days.[7] "He warned those around him," one member of the military committee of the convention attested, "that they were just on the threshold of a long and bloody war, and advised them if they had any idea that the contest in which they were about to engage was to be a slight one, to dismiss all such thoughts from their minds, saying that he knew the Northern people well, and knew that they would never yield in that contest except at the conclusion of a long and desperate struggle."[8] The fullest expression of Lee's mind at this time, oddly enough, is to be found in a letter of May 5 to a little girl in the North, the daughter, no doubt, of friends of happier days. She had asked for his photograph, which he sent her with a letter that concluded: "It is painful to think how many friends will be separated and estranged by our unhappy disunion. May God reunite our severed bonds of friendship, and turn our hearts to peace! I can say in sincerity that I bear animosity against no one. Wherever the blame may be, the fact is that we are in the midst of a fratricidal war. I must side either with or against my section of country.[9] I cannot raise my hand against my birthplace, my home, my children. I should like, above all things, that our difficulties might be peaceably arranged,

[6] Cf. R. E. Lee to C. F. Lee, April 25, 1861: ". . . I fear it is now out of the power of man [to restore peace to the country]." E. J. Lee, 419–20; Lee to Mrs. Lee, April 26, 1861; "War is inevitable." R. E. Lee, Jr., 29; Lee to Mrs. Lee, May 13, 1861: "Do not put faith in rumors of adjustment. I see no prospect for it." Jones, L. and L., 140.

[7] Lee to Mrs. Lee, April 30, 1861; Fitz Lee, 93.

[8] John Echols in 11 S. H. S. P., 452. For a prediction that the war would last four years, see an anonymous and perhaps in part apocryphal account of an interview with some would-be mediators, quoted in Jones, 483.

[9] This reference to "my section of country" is highly important evidence of the promptness with which Lee's allegiance to Virginia became blended with allegiance to the South. It is probably the first reference of its kind in Lee's correspondence.

and still trust that a merciful God, whom I know will not unnecessarily afflict us, may yet allay the fury for war. Whatever may be the result of the contest, I foresee that the country will have to pass through a terrible ordeal, a necessary expiation, perhaps, of our national sins. May God direct all for our good, and shield and preserve you and yours."[10] To another and older friend, Reverend Cornelius Walker, he wrote: "I shall need all your good wishes and all your prayers for strength and guidance in the struggle in which we are engaged and earnestly and humbly look for help to Him alone who can save us, and who has permitted the dire calamity of this fratricidal war to impend over us. If we are not worthy that it should pass from us, may He in His great mercy shield us from its dire effects and save us from the calamity our sins have produced. Conscious of my imperfections and the little claim I have to be classed among Christians, I know the temptations and trials I shall have to pass through. May God enable me to perform my duty and not suffer me to be tempted beyond my strength."[11]

Lee could not proceed according to any formally drafted plan, matured at leisure or taken from a vault where it had been placed in advance by a general staff that had foreseen all the contingencies and had drafted all the orders. His plan, on the contrary, had to be shaped virtually as it was being executed, in an atmosphere of excited haste and with scant trained assistance. Yet as Lee's successive steps are retraced from his dispatches, their logic appears, and it is possible to see why he acted when he did. Emergencies forced him to extemporize. Limitation of men and of materials restricted him. He was compelled, on occasion, to attempt simultaneously many preparations he would have preferred to undertake successively. He held fast, however, to the essentials of a systematized if hurried programme.

He postulated everything on the maintenance of a strict defensive as long as possible. That was put above everything else. He saw Virginia could not undertake an offensive or even an

[10] Lee to "My dear Little H——," May 5, 1861; *New York Times*, Aug. 6, 1861, p. 3, col. 4.
[11] May 8, 1861; *Virginia Historical Society MSS.*, presented by Miss Mary Cushing Dame; printed in *Richmond News Leader*, June 23, 1932. Significantly enough, Lee wrote "the dire calamity of this Civil War," but scratched out "Civil" and wrote "fratricidal."

476

offensive-defensive, and he reasoned that if limited operations were temporarily successful, they would quickly bring upon Virginia attacks that would complicate if they did not defeat his preparation.

He enunciated this defensive policy as soon as he entered upon his duties. "You will act on the defensive," he wrote on April 24 to the officer whom Letcher had placed in charge on the Rappahannock River.[12] He put his instant disapproval on a wild plan to attempt to throw Virginia troops into Baltimore.[13] "It is important," he said, "that conflict be not provoked before we are ready."[14] Lest seizure lead to reprisals, he earnestly urged that ships should not be detained in Virginia waters unless they were necessary for the defense of the state.[15] The most that he would countenance on any of the fronts was the removal of the buoys and the destruction of the lightships in the Potomac River off Alexandria.[16]

In holding to this basic strategy, while organizing the Virginia forces, Lee had to restrain the ardor of men who believed that an early offensive meant an easy victory over an effete foe. Soon after the secession of Virginia, L. Pope Walker, the Confederate Secretary of War, sent to Richmond a friend who might be termed an "unofficial observer." This gentleman, D. G. Duncan, was very critical of Lee's caution. In daily telegrams to Walker, Duncan lamented the manner in which the Virginia commander sought, as he averred, to repress the enthusiasm of the people.[17] Duncan went so far as to hint that there was treachery in Virginia,[18] though ultimately he was convinced that Lee was acting with vigor.[19] So far as is known, Lee paid no heed to Duncan, but he could not wholly ignore the boasts of the uninformed or the invective of the bitter, for he regarded every overconfident expression as dan-

---

[12] Lee to Daniel Ruggles, *O. R.*, 2, 778.   [13] 29 *S. H. S. P.*, 165-66.

[14] Lee to P. St. George Cocke, 11 *Calendar Virginia State Papers*, 112. *Cf.* Duncan to Walker, April 26, 1861, *O. R.*, 51, 2, p. 39.

[15] *Cf. O. R.*, 51, part 2, pp. 28, 30.

[16] *MS. Exec. Papers of Va.*, April 24, 1861; *O. R.*, 2, 778; Lee to Philip St. George Cocke, April 24, 1861; *Cocke MSS.*

[17] *E.g.*, *O. R.*, 51, part 2, p. 39.

[18] *O. R.*, 51, part 2, p. 71. He was not alone in thinking Lee was unsympathetic with the Southern cause. Under date of June 12, 1861, Mrs. Chesnut quoted "Jim Velipegue" [John Villepigue?] as saying: "At heart Robert E. Lee is against us; that I know" (*Mrs. Chesnut*, 63).

[19] *O. R.*, 51, part 2, p. 71

gerous, and every disposition to minimize the fighting qualities of the North as an obstacle to adequate preparation in the South. Braggadocio was worse than that. He wrote Mrs. Lee when he had been in Richmond three weeks: "I agree with you in thinking that the inflammatory articles in the papers do us much harm. I object particularly to those in the Southern papers, as I wish them to take a firm, dignified course, free from bravado and boasting." [20] Later on, when all serious men should have seen that the calamity of a long and bitter war had fallen on America, an indulgent father brought a young hopeful of five years to Lee's office to present a Bible to the General. An aide pleaded Lee's preoccupation, but the General heard the conversation and insisted that the visitors be admitted. Having made the gift, the little boy was sitting on Lee's knee when the father demanded of him: "What is General Lee going to do with General Scott?" The lad, having been coached in advance, replied promptly: "He is going to whip him out of his breeches." Lee's manner changed instantly. He stood the youngster on his feet, looked at him intently, and spoke to the father over the tiny fellow's shoulders. "My dear little boy," he said very earnestly, "you should not use such expressions. War is a serious matter, and General Scott is a great and good soldier. None of us can tell what the result of the contest will be." [21]

In this spirit, having determined on a defensive policy, Lee had to ask himself seven questions:

1. How could he offset the sea power of the North, with its immediate, constant threat to Virginia, open as the very heart of the state was to invasion up her long tidal rivers?

2. Should he attempt to hold Harpers Ferry, and could he retain Norfolk, with its dry dock, its machinery, and its proximity to the sea?

3. How were competent officers to be procured in sufficient numbers for the troops that were to be called into the field?

4. On what basis and with what personnel was the general staff to be organized?

---

[20] May 13, 1861; Jones, *L. and L.*, 140.
[21] Jones, 409–10; 11 *S. H. S. P.*, 423. Lee was careful to make compensation to the lad. He rode him on his horse subsequently and gave him a copy of G. W. P. Custis's *Recollections of General Washington*, which Mrs. Lee had republished.

5. Prompt mobilization and early training were necessary: how were they to be effected?

6. In what way were the necessary arms and equipment to be provided and distributed?

7. When mobilized, armed, trained, where could the Virginia forces be disposed to meet effectively the advance of a superior enemy, that not only controlled Chesapeake Bay, but was able to move into Virginia simultaneously from the north, the east, and the west?

His answer to the first of these questions was a vindication of all that Mahan was later to argue regarding sea power. The readiness of the Federal navy was more to be regarded at this time than the mobilization of a great Federal army. Virginia must be saved from the possibility of a fleet movement up the Rappahannock, the York, or the James, all of which were navigable to points within striking distance of Richmond. Governor Letcher had been quick to sense this danger. Embarrassed as he had been by the lack of military experience and of trained advisers,[22] he had taken the first defensive steps immediately after the ordinance of secession had been passed. On April 20 the convention had created the advisory commission of three that Lee had seen in the hall of the convention, Judge Allen, Colonel Smith, and Captain Maury.[23] With the help of these men the governor had proceeded to organize for the defense of the rivers. Powder had been hurried from Norfolk. Subsistence and quartermaster services had been set up,[24] commanders had been named on the Potomac and on the Rappahannock,[25] a veteran naval officer had been named to conduct the Norfolk navy yard,[26] heavy ordnance had been transported from that city, though there were no carriages for it;[27] some light artillery had been sent to the Potomac,[28] and the state's engineer had been dispatched to

[22] 11 *Calendar Virginia State Papers,* 160–61.

[23] See *supra,* p. 465; F. H. Smith, *Virginia Military Institute,* 178; *Ordinances Adopted in Secret Session,* p. 6. On April 29, *ibid.,* p. 6, the convention increased the membership to five by the addition of General Thomas S. Haymond and Robert L. Montague, vice-president of the convention (F. H. Smith, *op. cit.,* 178). The commission served until June 19, 1861, when it was abolished (*Ordinances Adopted at the Adjourned Session,* 51; IV, *O. R.,* 1, 396).

[24] *O. R.,* 51, part 2, p. 21.

[25] *O. R.,* 2, 775; *O. R.,* 51, part 2, p. 21.

[26] *O. R.,* 2, 771.

[27] *O. R..* 2, 783, 778.

[28] *O. R.,* 2, 777.

Gloucester Point and to Yorktown, at the mouth of the York River, to lay out batteries there.[29] Lee pushed this work with the most insistent vigor. The state engineer proved to be none other than Lee's chief of happier days, Colonel Andrew Talcott.[30] Lee was happy to renew association with this able officer, though, he wrote Talcott, "I sincerely lament the calamitous times in which we have fallen." [31] From the York, Talcott proceeded to Norfolk, where he found the utmost confusion prevailing, and thence, by Lee's orders, he went up the James River to select the most suitable sites for batteries.[32]

Lee left the location of these works entirely to the discretion of the energetic old colonel, in whose judgment he had full confidence. But when the batteries had been designed and staked off, who was to construct and to arm them? Perhaps, for answer, Lee went back in memory to the siege of Vera Cruz when he had seen sailors quickly mount long guns. Perhaps his choice was that of necessity. Whatever the prompting, he turned over this part of the task to the naval personnel of Virginia, which had been quickly and efficiently organized from resigning United States officers.[33] An admirable job the navy made of it. Steadily through the days when it seemed impossible to procure transportation with which to move from Norfolk the cumbersome guns that often weighed more than three tons, the officers worked fast and successfully. There were, however, one or two close races between the Virginia navy on land and the Federal navy in the Chesapeake. At Gloucester Point things came to such a pass that six-pounder field artillery was employed by the local commander against a Federal warship that seemed to be threatening to enter the river, but within three days thereafter nine-inch columbiads had been planted, and the battery was prepared to execute Lee's orders to challenge all passing ships and to fire on those that refused to stop.[34] Thenceforward the fortification of Gloucester Point went on, with nothing more serious to interrupt it than some friction between the civilian engineer and the military.[35]

29 *O. R.*, 2, 781–83.   30 *Talcott MSS.* (F); *IV O. R.*, 1, 389.
31 Lee to Talcott, April 30, 1861, *Talcott MSS.* (VHS).
32 *O. R.*, 2, 781–83, 788–89; *Talcott MSS., loc. cit.*
33 Lee's report, *O. R.*, 2, 927.
34 *N. O. R.*, 4, 381; *O. R.*, 2, 812, 815–16, 821; *O. R.*, 51, part 2, p. 80.
35 For the progress of the work at Gloucester Point, see *O. R.*, 2, 829–30, 843–44, 859, 949, 967–68, 970; *O. R.*, 51, part 2, pp. 120, 137.

Across the river from Gloucester Point, at the ancient settlement of Yorktown, a battery was also constructed, and forces were slowly accumulated nearby. Once the channel of the York was commanded, the situation around Yorktown was not regarded as immediately threatening, because the land approaches were protected against a surprise attack by an informal armistice between the Virginians and the Federal forces at Fort Monroe.[36]

On the James, Talcott recommended, at the outset, only the fortification of Jamestown Island. A heavy battery was accordingly built there, almost under the eaves of the crumbling church near the site where the first law-making body in Anglo-Saxon America had met in 1619.[37] Along the Rappahannock the people were very apprehensive of an early Federal attack. Lee did not believe this would materialize speedily, but as volunteers had been called out at Fredericksburg, he felt they should be retained in that vicinity. Directing that a small battery be erected below Tappahannock, he had to concern himself more with allaying the fears of the populace than with guarding against an ascent of the river.[38] As for the Potomac, little could be done for the defense of Alexandria—nothing, in fact, that would have any other effect than to risk the destruction of the city in case of a Federal offensive. Along the lower tidal estuaries of that river there was likelihood of a naval attack and a possible landing, especially on Aquia Creek, which was the northern terminus of the direct railroad to Richmond. Batteries were accordingly placed around the Aquia. Much correspondence and many divergencies of opinion were developed over the fortification of Mathias Point on the Potomac.[39]

Considered as a whole, the fortification of the rivers progressed satisfactorily from the beginning and occupied so little of Lee's time that he was able at an early date to turn to the defense of Norfolk and of Harpers Ferry, which jointly constituted the second aspect of his military problem.

The property seized by Virginia at the Norfolk shipyard was

[36] *O. R.,* 51, part 2, pp. 90–91; *O. R.,* 2, 839, 854, 862, 865.

[37] *N. O. R.,* 6, 700 *ff.*; *O. R.,* 51, part 2, pp. 70, 119.

[38] 11 *Calendar Virginia State Papers,* 107; *O. R.,* 2, 776, 807, 907, 920–22; *O. R.,* 51, part 2, p. 107.

[39] *O. R.,* 2, 815, 843, 845, 874, 878, 917, 959, 961, 963–64, 973, 974, 976; *O. R.,* 51, part 2, pp. 141–42. For details of the subsequent attacks on Mathias Point see *O. R.,* 2, 55 and 135 *ff., N. O. R.,* 4, 542 *ff.*

found to include 1198 guns,[40] and was worth some $7,307,000, according to the state's appraisal,[41] but the value to the new government of such a plant and dry dock, with much of the machinery intact,[42] could not be computed in terms of money. If Norfolk could be held, at least one and perhaps three of the scuttled warships could be raised and refitted, and the South would have the means of building other naval vessels until perhaps a formidable fleet might be gathered to dispute with the North the control of Hampton Roads. With Norfolk lost, the South would have no shipyard comparably so well suited for the construction of war vessels. Norfolk, moreover, was strategically located in relation to North Carolina. A railroad ran from Norfolk to Weldon. From Norfolk, also, the Elizabeth River and the Dismal Swamp Canal afforded access for light ships to a point within fifteen miles of Elizabeth City, N. C. To possess Norfolk was, therefore, to hold the key to eastern Carolina.

Unfortunately, the defense of Norfolk was difficult for a government that did not control Hampton Roads. In relation to the rest of the commonwealth, the city was at the end of the Petersburg and Norfolk Railroad. This railway ran through Suffolk near the head of the Nansemond River, which empties into Hampton Roads almost opposite Newport News. From the mouth of the Nansemond, at Pig Point, the distance to Suffolk is only about eighteen miles, most of it navigable for light transports. By dispatching small ships up the Nansemond, the Federals might easily cut off Norfolk from Richmond and might then send a land force against the navy yard itself, which could readily be turned from the west.

Cognizant of all this, Lee nevertheless prepared to fight for so valuable a prize. When he entered on his duties he found that the governor had authorized the commanding officer at Norfolk to accept additional volunteers as soon as he could use them.[43] Work was being started on four batteries laid out by Colonel Talcott—one of fourteen guns at the Naval Hospital, one of

---

[40] Doc. XL, *Journal of the Virginia Convention of 1861*, p. 32.
[41] *Ibid.*, Doc. XL, p. 128.
[42] For a statement of what was destroyed by the Federals, see II *N. O. R.*, 2, 109.
[43] For a very interesting picture of the condition and activities of the volunteers, see W. H. Taylor: *General Lee, 1861–65* (cited hereafter as *Taylor's General Lee*), 15–16. Taylor was one of the early volunteers.

fifteen guns at Fort Norfolk, one of twelve guns at Pinner Point, and one of twenty guns at Craney Island.[44] Lee directed that the construction of these batteries be pushed and that they be supplemented by works at the mouth of the Nansemond to keep the Federals from ascending that stream. During the weeks that followed he was painfully alert to the possibilities of an attack in that quarter.[45] On May 1 there came news that the Federal ships were sounding up the Elizabeth River as if preparing for an attempt to recapture the navy yard.[46] This created a near panic in Norfolk[47] and forced Lee to take additional precautions quickly. He ordered all the valuable metals away from the town,[48] together with the surplus powder;[49] he hurried cartridges to the soldiers there, and he directed the commanding officer to make them on his own account.[50] To Norfolk, also, he forwarded the first troops that came to Virginia from Georgia and Alabama.[51] The result he had to leave to the fortunes of war.

The machinery at Harpers Ferry was scarcely less important to the Confederate army than the Norfolk dry dock and shops were to the sea forces. There had been reports that 4000 to 5000 small arms had been salvaged at Harpers Ferry out of 16,000 reputed to have been in the arsenal when it had been set afire.[52] Actually, only 4287 finished small arms had been in storage at Harpers Ferry at the time the Virginians descended upon the place.[53] Few had been secured, and most of them had been carried off by individuals. A considerable number of arms, however, had been in the course of manufacture in the shops, which were virtually intact, with all their machinery, thanks to the vigilance of a Southern sympathizer, Master-Armorer Armistead Ball.[54] Manifestly, if Virginia could retain Harpers Ferry, the manufacture of small arms would go on more rapidly than if the shops were moved. Much time would inevitably be lost if the machinery had to be taken down, shipped to some distant city and set up

[44] *O. R.*, 2, 781–83.
[45] *O. R.*, 2, 791, 882–83, 884; *O. R.*, 51, part 2, pp. 61–62.
[46] *O. R.*, 51, part 2, pp. 61–62.   [47] *Cf. O. R.*, 51, part 2, p. 69.
[48] *O. R.*, 2, 795.   [49] *O. R.*, 2, 800–801.
[50] *O. R.*, 2, 803–4.   [51] *O. R.*, 2, 800–801, 803–4.
[52] *O. R.*, 51, part 2, p. 24.   [53] *O. R.*, 2, 6.
[54] Jefferson Davis: *The Rise and Fall of the Confederate Government* (cited hereafter as *Davis*), 1, 317–18.

again.[55] But there was one great difficulty about retaining the shops at Harpers Ferry: a strong expedition sent out from Washington along the line of the Manassas Gap Railroad could cut off communication from the south. A superior force could easily be collected in Pennsylvania and brought by rail to Hagerstown, within seven miles of Williamsport. Thence it might get in rear of Harpers Ferry. The same thing could be done from the west, via Martinsburg. The town itself was badly placed to stand a siege by an army advancing on any of these routes, because it was in a flat dominated on three sides by very high ground. On the north the "Maryland Heights" were across the Potomac, the new "international frontier." To occupy Maryland Heights was to take the offensive and perhaps to affront the state of Maryland, which was then hesitating, as most Virginians believed, between secession and allegiance to the Union.[56]

Resolving this dilemma, Lee decided to continue the removal of surplus machinery from Harpers Ferry, which he found in progress,[57] and to haul all the machines to Richmond as speedily as possible, but, meantime, to operate the shops as long as any part of the equipment remained.[58] While he was planning this there came into his office a tall, sober-faced young professor, in the uniform of the Virginia Military Institute, to consult with him regarding the use of the cadets of that school, who had been brought to Richmond as drillmasters. Lee had not seen him, so far as is known, since they had left Mexico in 1848, but he had recommended him for his post at the institute and of course recognized him as Major Thomas J. Jackson. Governor Letcher had known Jackson in Lexington, where the institute was located, and he nominated him to the convention for commission as colonel of infantry. Simultaneously, he directed Lee to put Jackson in command at Harpers Ferry as soon as he was confirmed.[59] The convention accepted the appointment, though the nominee

[55] The shipment in itself would be a tremendous task, for the only railroad from Harpers Ferry that was not in the hands of the enemy was the feeble line to Winchester, thirty miles to the south. At Winchester the machinery would have to be unloaded, put aboard wagons, and hauled eighteen miles to Strasburg, whence it could be handled by rail to Manassas Junction and thence via Gordonsville to Richmond.

[56] On this important phase of the situation on "the frontier," see *Johnston's Narrative*, 17–18. For various plans to assist secessionists in Maryland and for Virginia's dealings with that state, see *O. R.*, 2, 773; 779, 794, 824, 825; *O. R.*, 51, part 2, pp. 24, 34–35, 56; 11 *Calendar Virginia State Papers*, 112.

[57] *O. R.*, 2, 772.   [58] Cf. *O. R.*, 2, 781.   [59] *O. R.*, 2, 784.

was so little known that some of the members asked, "Who is this Major Jackson?"[60] Promptly and cheerfully enough, Lee ordered Jackson to his post,[61] doubtless without imagining that circumstance and Governor Letcher had combined to bring under his command the one Southern soldier, above all others, who was to show himself the ideal lieutenant. The only thing to suggest during the next few months that Lee had any consciousness of a special relationship between himself and Jackson is the fact that, from the outset, his orders to Jackson were direct and downright, as if he knew he was dealing with a man who would understand and obey, without the stimulus of euphemism or diplomatic flourishes.

When Jackson arrived at Harpers Ferry he found something more than 2000 volunteers and militia there. Increasing hourly, they had little equipment and even less powder and shot. There were too many general officers and too few drillmasters. However, Major General Kenton Harper, the senior militia officer on the ground, had acted with promptness and good judgment. On his own initiative he had negotiated with the Maryland local authorities to give him notice of the approach of the enemy, and he had gained their unofficial consent to occupy Maryland Heights, in case of necessity. Jackson acted with the greatest energy. The machinery immediately required in Richmond was moved rapidly; more volunteers were brought up, were organized and were drilled; arms taken from the arsenal at the time of the fire were traced;[62] outposts were established; and, though reports reached Virginia that 5000 men were mustered at Chambersburg, Pa., within easy reach of Harpers Ferry,[63] a spirit of confidence was gradually created.

Lee was much gratified at Jackson's accomplishments. He prepared to send new troops to him and, in order to keep Harpers Ferry from being turned by way of the Manassas Gap Railroad, he decided to increase the force that Governor Letcher had already sent to Manassas Junction. He had to gamble, of course, whether he would be able to hold Harpers Ferry, but he felt that the machinery in the shops and the strategic value of the position justified the risks.

[60] F. H. Smith: *Virginia Military Institute*, 136.
[61] *O. R.*, 2, 784-85.   [62] *O. R.*, 2, 786.   [63] *O. R.*, 51, part 2, p. 58.

The construction of river batteries and the defense of Norfolk and of Harpers Ferry were tasks that would not wait on organization. Lee had to use the men and materials at hand. As soon as these first defensive measures had been taken he turned to the third aspect of his problem, which was the selection of officers and the creation of a staff. Until this was done, it went without saying that nothing that had been gained was secure, and that a general call for troops, which was next in order, could not be sent out.

The militia law of Virginia had provided an elaborate organization of staff and line, with four divisions, each of them commanded by a major general. The officers of high rank in the militia were, in the main, "prominent citizens" or elderly men of political influence. The staff of the militia had never functioned and was incomplete in 1861. The volunteers, though numerous, had never been regimented and had no officers above the rank of captain. For the first operations, Governor Letcher, of necessity, had chosen the most available men, chiefly of the militia. He had utilized the company officers of the units that had been ordered on duty, whether of militia or of volunteers. As respected field officers, this arrangement was manifestly so unsatisfactory and so little suited to a real emergency that it had to be changed as speedily as possible. The convention had provided that company officers should be elected by the men, but that the field officers should be appointed by the governor.[64] The convention also invited all "efficient and worthy Virginians . . . in the Army and Navy of the United States to retire therefrom and to enter the service of Virginia." The governor had been directed to assign these officers "such rank as will not reverse the relative rank held by them in the United States service and will at least be equivalent thereto." [65] Although some of these officers were at distant posts and would be slow in arriving, the invitation extended by the convention assured ultimately a limited supply of trained soldiers, for nearly all the Virginians of distinction in the Federal army had resigned, except General Scott and Major George H. Thomas. A commission was set up by the governor, at the instance of the

[64] Cf. Lee to P. St. George Cocke, April 24, 1861; O. R., 2, 777.
[65] O. R., 51, part 2, p. 22.

advisory council, to correspond with available men[66] as the convention had directed. Caution was shown from the outset in giving high commissions to politicians—even to so influential a person as ex-Governor Henry A. Wise.[67] To make it certain that professional soldiers were given first consideration, the convention went still further and provided that all names should be submitted to it for confirmation. As Lee himself recommended only experienced men for field command, this requirement imposed no handicap. By May 1 Lee was sending out commissions in the army of Virginia to a number of men who later attained distinction. Besides Jackson, Virginia called on Joseph E. Johnston, John Bankhead Magruder, Richard S. Ewell, Harry Heth, Samuel Jones, J. C. Pemberton, William Mahone, L. L. Lomax, John McCausland,[68] and others. As officers of experience reported, they were welcomed and immediately assigned to duty. "I am glad to see you. I want you to help me," Lee told Lieutenant John B. Hood, as he shook that officer's hand on arrival; and before two hours had elapsed Hood was on his way to his post.[69] In a few instances Letcher made nominations without consulting either Lee or the advisory council, and the senior naval officers apparently did the same thing, but friction was slight at the outset.[70] Lee had reasonable prospect of procuring competent brigade officers and a fair number of good colonels and lieutenant colonels by the time he was ready to bring the full force of volunteers into the field. His task was somewhat complicated, however, because neither he nor any one else knew precisely how desirable a commission in the army of the commonwealth might be. On April 25 the state convention had ratified a pact for temporary union with the Confederacy, and had accepted the Southern Constitution, subject to revocation in case the people of Virginia declined to approve the ordinance of secession at the polls on May 23. The treaty provided that military operations should be under "the chief control and direction of the President of [the] Confederate

[66] O. R., 51, part 2, pp. 36, 37.   [67] O. R., 51, part 2, p. 30.
[68] O. R., 51, part 2, pp. 36, 40, 50, and 52; MS. Virginia Executive Papers, April 26, 1861; Richmond Dispatch, May 3, 1861, p. 1, col. 6; R. S. Garnett to P. St. G. Cocke, May 1, 1861; Cocke MSS.
[69] Hood, 16.
[70] See the case of T. T. Fauntleroy, Doc. XXII, Virginia Convention of 1861; See also the case of William Smith, former governor, 10 S. H. S. P., 433–44.

States, upon the same principles, basis and footing" as if the Old Dominion were a member of the Confederacy.[71] This might well mean that every Virginia commission would be vacated. It is to be written down to their love of their native state that few Virginians hesitated on this account.

The organization of the general staff proceeded simultaneously, if less satisfactorily, under an ordinance adopted by the convention on April 21 and amended three days later. The adjutant general's, quartermaster's, subsistence, medical, and pay departments and an engineers corps were set up. Their respective heads were to be named by the governor and were to be confirmed by the advisory council. The adjutant general's department was to be distinct from the office of the state adjutant general, whose functions were limited to the militia.[72] As the general staff of the militia proved to be useless, some commanders having been compelled to take the field without a single staff officer,[73] it was scrapped in its entirety. Desirable men were not easy to find for the new posts, because most Virginians of military age wished to serve with the combatant units. Engineers were particularly hard to procure.[74] By a series of brief general orders Lee sought to establish system as rapidly as practicable within the departments,[75] and as a short cut he adopted the old regulations of the United States army wherever applicable.[76] If the staff was not so efficient as Lee had hoped, it was chiefly because the men appointed to the Virginia staff realized that the Confederate States would soon assume charge of the departments and might supersede them.

Virtually no attempt was made to set up an intelligence service as a part of the general staff. Reports of the plans and movements of the Federal forces were gleaned from Northern newspapers, or were gathered slowly from travellers and from private letters.

[71] *Ordinances Adopted in Secret Session*, 3, 5, 6; IV *O. R.*, 1, 242, 243. Congress voted and President Davis approved the admission of Virginia to the Confederacy on May 7 (IV *O. R.*, 1, 294).
[72] *Ordinances Adopted in Secret Session*, 13.
[73] General P. St. George Cocke, for example; *O. R.*, 2, 818.
[74] For the organization and operations of the general staff, see *O. R.*, 2, 786–87, 822, 857, 866, 876, 877; *O. R.*, 51, part 2, p. 36.
[75] *Ordinances Adopted in Secret Session*, 26; *O. R.*, 51, part 2, pp. 51, 53, 68, 88; *Richmond Enquirer*, May 7, 1861, p. 3, col. 6; *ibid.*, May 14, 1861, p. 3, col. 6; *Richmond Whig*, May 18, 1861, p. 3, col. 3.
[76] R. S. Garnett to P. St. George Cocke, April 28, 1861; Lee to Cocke, May 16, 1861; *Cocke MSS.*

Some of the most important movements were wrongly reported or were not discovered at all.[77] The Virginia press, in its zeal to inform its readers, informed the enemy as well, and helped to create in Lee a dislike for newspaper methods that he held to the end of his days.[78]

The personal staff of the commanding general, like the general staff, had to be built up in an atmosphere of impermanence. Although he had started without a single assistant, Lee was determined to employ only trained men, so far as they were procurable. "It is necessary," he wrote in an early veto on nepotism, "that persons on my staff should have a knowledge of their duties and an experience of the wants of the service to enable me to attend to other matters." [79] It was an ideal he never fully realized.

Fortunately, R. S. Garnett, who had been Lee's adjutant at West Point, joined Virginia early, and accepted the new post of adjutant general. After April 26, Colonel Garnett was with Lee and relieved him of much of the correspondence and of virtually all the drafting of orders. With Garnett in charge of the office, Lee soon moved his headquarters to the top floor of the Mechanics Institute,[80] where he collected a few clerks and, ere long, the staff of two aides and a military secretary allowed him under ordinance of the convention.[81] Lieutenant Walter H. Taylor reported soon thereafter and soon made himself indispensable at Lee's headquarters. Other officers assisted him during the summer,[82] notably Lieutenant Colonel George Deas and Lieutenant Colonel John A. Washington, the latter a long-time friend in northern Virginia, a gentleman of the highest type and a true aristocrat. Promptness and system were not attained without an effort, and for the first weeks orders were sometimes slow in reaching officers.[83]

[77] Instances of the crude intelligence service of early weeks will be found in O. R., 2, 838–39, 853, 864, 865, 876, 895, 899, 935, 967.

[78] Cf. O. R., 51, part 2, p. 115.

[79] R. E. Lee to C. F. Lee, April 25, 1861; Long, 102.

[80] Hood, 17.   [81] Ordinances Adopted in Secret Session, 10.

[82] W. H. Taylor: Four Years with General Lee (cited hereafter as Taylor's Four Years), 11; Taylor's General Lee, 21; John M. Brooke and Thos. J. Page of the Virginia Navy served temporarily as aides; O. R., 2, 800–801; Colonel Deas also acted as inspector general, O. R., 51, part 2, pp. 77, 140; Cocke MSS., S. O. 68, May 15, 1861; Colonel Washington became aide-de-camp on May 13, 1861, O. R., 51, part 2, p. 88; Captain F. H. Smith was named military secretary on May 27, 1861; O. R., 51, part 2, p. 114. Richmond Enquirer, May 31, 1861, p. 3, col. 5. For the staff of Lee as it was subsequently developed see Appendix I–4.

[83] Cf. W. B. Taliaferro to Lee, May 11, 1861; O. R., 2, 835.

All work had to be done at a furious rate, amid countless inter-ruptions, ceaseless alarms, and the wildest public confusion. Every one wanted to fight; few were willing to recognize that war calls, first of all, for ordered preparation. The public seemed to think that arms and ammunition and all the equipment of an army could be provided instantly and by magic, and that all that was needed was the word to go forward and overwhelm the enemy. Lee had to do a prodigious volume of work, but he kept his head, and by May 1, or about that time, having been in command only one week, he had taken the first necessary steps to fortify the rivers, to hold and to strengthen Norfolk and Harpers Ferry, and to select field and staff officers. This initial stage of his labors brought Lee close to May 5, the date of the expiration of the period that Lincoln had allowed for the dispersion of the seces-sionists. As evidence began to accumulate that Federal forces were mobilizing in strength and might start an offensive at any time, Lee became more apprehensive for the safety of Harpers Ferry and of Norfolk, and decided to issue the call for a general mobilization of volunteers. That opened a new and a still more difficult period in Virginia's preparations for war.

CHAPTER XXIX

THE VOLUNTEERS ARE CALLED OUT

IMMEDIATELY following secession the governor and the advisory council had seen the folly of calling out more troops than Virginia needed at Harpers Ferry, at Norfolk, and at other exposed points. Student companies that had hurried to Richmond from the University of Virginia without orders had been sent back to school. The Confederate Government had been requested not to forward thirteen proffered regiments until Lee had been consulted.[1] But the uninformed public had been insistent and the waiting volunteers had become restive. Despite strong pressure, Lee had postponed a general mobilization of volunteers in the knowledge that arms were limited, that field officers were lacking, and that the general staff had not been organized to transport, to quarter, and to feed the thousands who were anxious to defend their state. Now that the prospect of invasion was imminent he had to bring the waiting volunteers into the field. Delay after May 5 might be as dangerous as haste before that time would have been confusing.

Estimates prior to the dissolution of the Union were to the effect that the state would require about 15,000 soldiers.[2] Lee listed the places that had to be defended, reversed the figures and promptly raised the total to 51,000.[3] To supply this number of men Virginia had a partly organized militia of about 131,000, exclusive of the armed volunteers, who were supposed to number 12,000.[4] In addition, the convention had authorized the establishment of a "provisional army," which was really to be a regular army of some 8000 men, enlisted for three years.[5] A navy of

---

[1] O. R., 51, part 2, pp. 24, 37; IV O. R., 1, 231, 272.
[2] 11 Calendar Virginia State Papers, 164.   [3] O. R., 2, 927.
[4] Report of the adjutant general, IV O. R., 1, 382 ff.; O. R., 2, 940. The figures 143,-000, in the adjutant general's report, include 12,000 volunteers.
[5] Ordinances Adopted in Secret Session, pp. 7-8, 9-11.

2000 men had likewise been sanctioned.[6] Recruiting for the provisional army and for the navy was to be undertaken simultaneously with the enlistment of volunteers. This double appeal for men presented a difficulty. Another difficulty was the sharp division of opinion as to the term of enlistment of the troops who were to be accepted. Some bombastic orators whose overconfidence angered Lee were affirming that an early victory made long enlistments unnecessary. Lee thought that all soldiers should be sworn in for the duration of the war. The convention, after debate, decided to fix the term at one year—a course that was to plague the Confederacy in the spring of 1862.[7]

Making the best of what he could not change, Lee devised this method of mobilization: He directed the commanding officers at Harpers Ferry, at Norfolk, at Fredericksburg, at Richmond, and at Culpeper Courthouse to accept companies of volunteers from designated nearby counties, in numbers not to exceed specified totals of each of the three arms of the service. By fixing the company as the unit, he passed the task of individual recruiting to the localities where men of station were willing to collect enough men to form a company, either as a patriotic service or as a means of procuring commissions, through company elections, as captains or lieutenants. At other centres of population where good railroad connections were available, he named special recruiting officers who were to issue calls to the counties, accept companies, arm them, and either begin their training there or else send them to places where they were needed and could be drilled. No time schedule for a general concentration was attempted. From some of the mobilization centres the commanding officers were directed to forward the troops by companies as rapidly as they were organized and armed.[8]

The first call, which covered only one section of the state, was

[6] *Ordinances Adopted in Secret Session*, pp. 11–12.

[7] *Ordinances Adopted in Secret Session*, 19; *Taylor's Four Years*, 11; *Taylor's General Lee*, 22–23; *Richmond Enquirer*, May 10, 1861, p. 3, col. 7; *O. R.*, 2, 797. On June 29, 1861, after the Virginia troops had been incorporated in the Confederate States army, the War Department refused to accept any more men unless for three years or the war, IV *O. R.*, 1, 411–12, but in the crisis just before the first battle of Manassas, President Davis set this ruling aside (*O. R.*, 51, part 2, p. 177).

[8] *Richmond Enquirer*, May 10, 1861, p. 3, col. 7; *O. R.*, 2, 797, 798–99, 801, 802, 803, 806, 807, 808, 813, and 823. Besides the towns mentioned, Lynchburg, Staunton, and Abingdon were named as mobilization centres. For the Eastern Shore, see *O. R.*, 51 part 2, pp. 117, 162. For western Virginia, see *infra*, pp. 502–3.

sent out on May 3, the very day that Lincoln signed his second proclamation for 42,000 additional volunteers, ten regiments of regulars, and 18,000 seamen.[9] Other calls for different parts of the commonwealth Lee issued on May 6, May 7, and May 9. He watched the response closely.[10] In most counties the enlistment was general and hearty. From western Virginia there came varying stories of support and of disaffection, and on the lower Peninsula, for some reason, volunteers came in slowly.[11] The stern eye of Colonel Thomas J. Jackson found encouragement in the quality of the men, untrained though they were.[12] "The whole state is clad in steel," ex-President Tyler wrote.[13] Anxious as Lee was to bring Virginia's man-power quickly into the field, he declined to accept volunteers under the age of eighteen. "Those are beautiful boys, sir," he said of some lads he sent back home, "and I very much disliked to refuse them; but it will not do to let boys enlist now. I fear we shall need them all before this war closes." [14] Ere long it became apparent that the provisional army could not be recruited for three years in competition with one-year volunteers.[15] The provisional army had accordingly to be abandoned.[16] It served one useful purpose, however, if only one, in that it gave the governor and the commanding general an organization in which to commission quickly a number of desirable officers for whom volunteer regiments or companies were not available. This experience with the provisional force showed that the war was not to be fought either with regulars or with militia, but with volunteers.[17]

Mobilization meant training, and that was the fifth aspect of Lee's labor of preparation. In addition to the simple drilling provided at the mobilization centres, a camp of instruction named

[9] III O. R., 1, 146.   [10] Cf. Lee to P. St. George Cocke; O. R., 2, 813.

[11] O. R., 51, part 2, pp. 88–89. For a good case of ingenious recruiting, see Angus W. McDonald to L. P. Walker, O. R., 2, 952–53.

[12] O. R., 2, 810.

[13] John Tyler to Mrs. Gardiner, 2 Letters and Times of the Tylers, 644.

[14] Jones, 484.   [15] 11 Calendar Virginia State Papers, 159.

[16] Its remaining officers were discharged as of Sept. 1, 1861; Richmond Examiner, Aug. 31, 1861; p. 2, col. 5.

[17] Virginia provided that where volunteers did not equal 10 per cent of the total population of a county, the residue had to be supplied by the militia; O. R., 5, 817, 888. In several emergencies later in the year when sufficient volunteers were not at hand, the militia were called out en masse, though in at least one instance this aroused some local resentment (O. R., 2, 859; O. R., 51, part 2, 145, 158–59, 172, 180).

after Lee was established at Richmond. The cadets of the Virginia Military Institute who had been brought to the city as drillmasters were speedily put to work and some of them were subsequently sent to Harpers Ferry for similar service. They were invaluable. In fact, although the Institute supplied many competent officers during the war, it probably did nothing that helped more materially than furnishing these well-equipped young cadets of soldierly bearing and high morale at this stage of the mobilization. In addition to Camp Lee, an artillery school of instruction was established nearby, at Richmond College,[18] with V. M. I. cadets again in charge of the raw gunners. The training and review of these men, which Lee occasionally found time to observe in person, gave Richmond its first glimpse of the picturesque side of a war whose horrors the city was soon to witness.[19] New color, thrills, and romance were added, a little later, when the first troops from other Southern states began to arrive at Camp Lee, the South Carolinians with their palmettos, and the picturesque Louisiana Tigers.[20]

Not all the phases of mobilization went as smoothly as the reviews at Camp Lee. Some blunders were made, particularly at Lynchburg. The call sent out from that city did not specify the number of troops that were to be received. The men from so many counties were directed to report there that some of them had to be sent elsewhere.[21] It was at Lynchburg, also, that the first friction between the state and the Confederate authority occurred.[22] With these and some other minor exceptions, however, mobilization and training proceeded better than might have been anticipated. The end of May was to find numerous large camps established in various sections and crowded with youthful volunteers.[23] Within four weeks after the men had been called to the colors seventeen regiments were formed and nineteen

[18] O. R., 51, part 2, pp. 21–22; F. H. Smith: *Virginia Military Institute*, 179, 181. For the later history of Camp Lee, located at the fair grounds on the present site of the Broad Street Terminal, see 26 S. H. S. P., 241–45. By June 2 every disposable drillmaster in the state was on duty (Garnett to Cocke, June 2, 1861; *Cocke MSS.*). For the artillery camp at Richmond College, see F. S. Daniel: *Richmond Howitzers in the War*, 12–14.
[19] For descriptions of Lee's appearance at Camp Lee, see *Miss Brock*, 50; *Mrs. Chesnut*, 72.
[20] *Miss Brock*, 29, 33, 35, 36.
[21] O. R., 2, 781, 829, 851–52.
[22] O. R., 51, part 2, p. 56. See infra, p. 501.
[23] O. R., 2, 895, infra, p. 521.

others were being organized from companies that had been brought together and had been given some training.[24] Rail transportation in sufficient quantity for moving all these troops was made available. Lee left this part of the mobilization largely to the railroad authorities. He contented himself with seeing to it that physical connection was established at strategic points, and that military commanders should not use rolling stock without authority.[25] On occasion it became necessary to suspend passenger traffic in order to move troops.[26]

Beyond a certain stage, mobilization was futile and training was impossible without arms and equipment. Providing these was the sixth aspect of Lee's problem, and during the first period of the war it remained a more difficult matter, by far, than finding troops.[27] Virginia had collected a certain volume of munitions. During the early months of 1861 she had established a department of ordnance, had appropriated $800,000 for the purchase of arms and ammunition, and had authorized the counties and cities to borrow money for equipping the militia.[28] The war had come, however, before this legislation of 1861 had yielded results.

The sources of supply from which Virginia hoped to draw were as follows:

1. When received into the service of the state, some 5000 volunteers—and not 12,000 as had been estimated by the adjutant general —carried arms that had been issued by the commonwealth or separately bought.[29]

2. Virginia had in storage at Richmond and at Lexington something over 60,000 small arms, though 54,000 of these were old flintlock muskets, wholly inferior to the percussion muskets

---

24 *O. R.*, 51, part 2, p. 123.

25 IV *O. R.*, 1, 240–41, 405–6; *O. R.*, 51, part 2, pp. 37, 163; *Richmond Enquirer*, May 3, 1861, p. 3, col. 7; May 7, p. 3, col. 6, May 14, p. 3, col. 6; MS. *Executive Papers of Va.*, E. C. Marshall to John Letcher, May 8, 1861; *O. R.*, 2, 831, 858, 866, 937; Doc. XXVI, *Va. Convention of 1861*, p. 7; *Ordinances Adopted in Secret Session*, 53–54, 55–56.

26 D. H. Wood to Colonel Dodamead, July 8, 1861; MS. *Ga-ga-1-37*, Confederate Museum, Richmond, Va.

27 Lee's Report, *O. R.*, 2, 928.

28 *Acts of the General Assembly of Virginia*, 1861, pp. 27, 28, 35.

29 *O. R.*, 2, 928. For the adjutant general's figures, see *ibid.*, 940. The adjutant general must have counted volunteer companies that did not enlist or were disbanded, together with all arms in the hands of western Virginia companies who refused to acquiesce in secession.

with which the Federals were certain to be armed from the outset.[30]

3. The state hoped that a considerable number of the arms damaged in the evacuation of the Harpers Ferry arsenal by the United States troops, or in process of manufacture,[31] could be restored or completed and issued.

4. There was a possibility that arms might be imported and that a limited supply might be had, by loan or purchase, from some of the Southern states if any of them had a surplus.

These were the only sources, and Harpers Ferry was to yield little.

In order that the best use might be made of the arms that were available the convention authorized Lee to distribute them to Virginia troops and, inferentially, to the secessionists of Maryland.[32] It was a burdensome assignment. The demands from the outset were insistent. Sometimes after volunteers had been received, and occasionally when they were in the face of the enemy, their armament was tragically inadequate. Upon General Cocke's arrival on the Alexandria line, for instance, he found that by no means all his pitiful little force of 300 or 400 men were armed, and those who carried any weapons had only flintlocks of the model of 1818.[33] Again, 800 volunteers reported for muster at Williamsburg; just 300 of these had arms, and half of these were antiquated.[34] Among 300 men from the western counties there were only 55 muskets of the same outmoded type, in bad order.[35] Some commanders, even Colonel T. J. Jackson, demanded more muskets than they had prospects of issuing promptly, and had to be denied.[36] In Lynchburg there was a near-mutiny because men who had volunteered as riflemen had flintlocks issued to them.[37] At a very critical stage of operations in western Virginia, when every volunteer counted in determining whether that section would side with the commonwealth or turn against her, one

---

[30] Adjutant general's report, IV *O. R.*, 1, 382 *ff*. It is impossible to be precise as to the number of small arms. There were 62,190 as of Oct. 1, 1860, to which number 5000 were subsequently added by purchase, but some of these 67,190 were doubtless issued early in 1861 to certain of the 5000 volunteers who had arms when mustered in.

[31] 11 *Calendar Virginia State Papers*, 182–83.

[32] *Ordinances Adopted in Secret Session*, 27.

[33] *Cocke MSS.; O. R.*, 2, 26–27.

[34] *O. R.*, 2, 854.

[35] *O. R.*, 2, 847.

[36] *O. R.*, 2, 832–33, 836.

[37] *O. R.*, 51, part 2, p. 111.

company reported with no arms whatsoever, and two others had to be sent home, as there were no muskets for them.[38] General Joseph E. Johnston, on taking charge at Harpers Ferry, stated flatly that the dispatch of troops without arms simply made his command "more helpless."[39]

These were typical illustrations of a situation that Lee met as best he could. He had to dole out arms very cautiously in advance of actual enlistment,[40] and he used his scant supply of percussion and "altered" muskets where he expected the troops to be called speedily to the field.[41] "Sir," he said to one man who protested against the inferiority of his company's armament, "your people had better write Mr. Lincoln and ask him to postpone this thing for a few months until you can get ready for him."[42] A thousand muskets were procured from North Carolina and were sent to Jackson.[43] New efforts were made to recover arms seized by individuals at Harpers Ferry, and the shops there were operated, in accordance with Lee's plan, as long as he believed it could be done without subjecting the machinery to the risk of capture.[44] Georgia was urged to lend Virginia any surplus arms she possessed, and was diplomatically asked not to look to the hard-pressed Old Dominion to furnish muskets to the Georgia troops sent to Virginia.[45] The Confederate States Government received similar notice.[46] The store of percussion muskets was exhausted by the end of May,[47] but through economy, patience, and care in not issuing more than were immediately required by the men at any one mobilization centre, the supply of flintlocks held out. Every requisition from Virginia troops was met, and probably more than 10,000 muskets were issued to troops from other states. When the Virginia forces were to be taken over by the Confederate States, Lee's report was to show some 46,000 guns in the hands of the mustered volunteers.[48] It is enough to note, for

[38] O. R., 2, 52.   [39] O. R., 2, 922.   [40] E.g., O. R., 2, 788, 794.
[41] O. R., 2, 835, 858. "Altered" muskets were flint-lock weapons changed to use percussion caps.
[42] J. Ryland in Alfred Bagby: King and Queen County, Virginia, 225.
[43] O. R., 2, 822.   [44] O. R., 2, 806, 814–15, 825.
[45] IV O. R., 1, 356; Candler: Confederate Records of Georgia, 3, 89–90.
[46] O. R., 2, 877.
[47] Endorsement of R. S. Garnett on requisition of P. St. George Cocke, May 31, 1861; Cocke MSS.
[48] O. R., 2, 928; 11 Calendar Virginia State Papers, 164–65; cf. IV O. R., 1, 354.

comparison, that during 1861 the North was able to issue to its soldiers 1,276,686 firearms.[49]

As it was with infantry small arms, so it was with arms and equipment for cavalry. The militia included five regiments of cavalry, which had never been armed, and the volunteers on December 15, 1860, had numbered 50 troops, 24 of which had sabres and pistols, while 24 had only pistols.[50] The state had such scant cavalry stores that all had been issued by May 12.[51] Attempts to procure additional arms from Georgia failed, and Lee could only advise that the men take their double-barrel shotguns with them, or privately purchase such weapons where available.[52]

The same story seemed in a fair way of being repeated with percussion caps and small-arms ammunition. The supply of caps was very limited. An agent sent North to purchase a cap machine prior to secession was barely able to return home, empty-handed and in disguise.[53] Early attempts to procure caps in Kentucky and the West yielded little; schemes to construct machines for their manufacture could not be executed quickly; some were found in Norfolk and some were forwarded from Tennessee; but by the end of May all that could be scraped together had been issued to troops and none remained in storage.[54] A later windfall of 1,000,000 from some undisclosed source of supply saved the day.[55]

As for powder, the state had only 50,000 pounds and some 226,000 ball cartridges on December 15, 1860.[56] The increase of this scant stock was very much in mind when the capture of the Norfolk navy yard was undertaken.[57] The seizure of 300,000 pounds in that city met immediate needs, though so little rifle powder was taken that cartridges had to be loaded with coarse cannon powder. Lee urged close economy in the use of ammuni-

---

[49] R. M. Johnston: *Bull Run, Its Strategy and Tactics* (cited hereafter as *Johnston's Bull Run*), 7.

[50] Adjutant general's report, IV *O. R.*, 1, 382 ff.

[51] Lee to J. A. Early, *O. R.*, 2, 835. *Cf.* Lee to T. J. Jackson, *ibid.*, 836.

[52] *O. R.*, 2, 851–52, 905; IV *O. R.*, 1, 356. For examples of the manner in which cavalry equipment was improvised, see Early in *O. R.*, 2, 912, and *O. R.*, 51, part 2, p. 111.

[53] 11 *Calendar Virginia State Papers*, 164.

[54] *O. R.*, 51, part 2, pp. 41, 48, 53; *O. R.*, 2, 809, 894; 11 *Calendar Virginia State Papers*, 128.

[55] 11 *Calendar Virginia State Papers*, 165.

[56] Adjutant general's report, IV *O. R.*, 1, 382 ff.　　　[57] *O. R.*, 51, part 2, p. 19.

tion, and called on the post commandants to take the powder he forwarded to them, and to prepare their own cartridges.[58]

Of field artillery the twelve volunteer companies in Virginia had thirty pieces in December, 1860, including about a dozen new Parrott guns.[59] The state had some 300 old light cannon in addition,[60] but most of these were unmounted and lacked harness and equipment. The principal task of the ordnance bureau, therefore, was to provide gun carriages and caissons and then to distribute the ordnance to best advantage among the many companies and localities that were asking for it.[61] By May 16 the few available gun carriages and caissons were dispatched, and a week later the last of the mounted guns and of the harness had been sent from Richmond.[62] The manufacture of additional gun carriages could not be rapid. Horses were provided by the individual cavalrymen, but they had to be purchased for the artillery. This, too, was slow work, as was the manufacture of harness.[63] However, by June 8 twenty light batteries of four guns were to be put in the field, with horses and harness,[64] though some of the batteries had to use wagon bodies as caissons.[65]

Thanks to the great store at the Norfolk navy yard, the supply of heavy ordnance was ample. The only problem was that of transporting and mounting it. There was some difficulty in procuring the type of carriage desired, and an alarming shortage of ammunition existed, but under the good management of the Virginia navy, 217 guns were soon mounted in 21 heavy batteries in Virginia and more than 300 heavy pieces were sent to other Southern states.[66] Little time, however, was available for tests and none for experimentation.[67]

[58] See *supra*, p. 483 and *O. R.*, 2, 804, 836, 881, 891, 943; *O. R.*, 51, part 2, p. 88; 11 *Calendar Virginia State Papers*, 136, 166; IV *O. R.*, 1, 314; *Cocke MSS.*, April 30, 1861.

[59] Adjutant general's report, IV *O. R.*, 1, 382 ff.; F. H. Smith: *Virginia Military Institute*, 173.

[60] Adjutant general's report, *loc. cit.*

[61] *Cf. O. R.*, 51, part 2, pp. 49, 58–59; Daniel Ruggles to P. St. George Cocke, May 16, 1861, *Cocke MSS.*

[62] *O. R.*, 2, 873; *O. R.*, 51, part 2, pp. 92, 102.

[63] *Cf.* J. B. Magruder to R. E. Lee, April 29, 1861; *O. R.*, 2, 789–90.

[64] Lee report, *O. R.*, 2, 928.   [65] *O. R.*, 2, 100.

[66] These figures are of July 18, 1861; II *N. O. R.*, 2, 77; *cf. O. R.*, 51, part 2, pp. 45–46, 49, 71; *O. R.*, 2, 876, 898, 1008–9; *N. O. R.*, 5, 806; 11 *Calendar Virginia State Papers*, 128.

[67] B. H. Wise; *Henry A. Wise*, 65, 316–17.

In all supplementary equipment, at the time the general calls for volunteers were made, Virginia was dismally lacking. No tentage,[68] no knapsacks, no cartridge boxes, no flags were ready for issue. In the first brush with Federal gunboats, the battery at Sewell's Point, near Norfolk, had to fly the state colors of a Georgia company in the small garrison, as it possessed no others.[69] To avoid the hopeless task of attempting to uniform 51,000 men, Virginia required that the volunteers supply their own clothing, for which an allowance of money was made.[70] Frequently the women of the counties made the uniforms of the first volunteers, and enterprising officers often had the minor equipment for their commands prepared in the towns where they mustered.[71]

The need of a large supply of field transport was in Lee's mind from the first, for despite the mobility that the railroads made possible, he knew the armies must often operate at a distance from tracks.[72] According to the standards adopted by the Federal army, each man required four pounds of transport and each animal twenty-five pounds. To support an army two marches from its base, 2000 wagons were required.[73] Virginia never possessed anything like this quantity and was very slow to accumulate the little she ever had. As late as June, 1861, Colonel Magruder had to complain that his men were in danger of starvation for lack of transportation.[74] In the preliminaries of the Manassas campaign the Confederate army was served largely by hired wagons and teams.[75] Failure to provide adequate transportation was, perhaps, the worst shortcoming of Virginia's preparation, and it was to cost the South dearly. Lack of transportation was one of the chief reasons the Confederates did not pursue the Federals after the first victory at Manassas and it added greatly to the difficulties of Lee's first campaign.[76]

While Lee was working in these and other ways to prepare the

[68] O. R., 2, 839; cf. H. Heth to P. St. George Cocke, May 28, 1861; Cocke MSS.
[69] O. R., 2, 34. [70] O. R., 51, part 2, p. 100.
[71] E.g., W. H. Fry to P. St. George Cocke, June 4, 1861; Cocke MSS. For the specifications for officers' uniforms, see IV O. R., 1, 369.
[72] O. R., 2, 784. [73] Johnston's Bull Run, 9.
[74] O. R., 2, 914; cf. Magruder's G. O. no. 25, Par. 5, June 20, 1861; O. R., 51, part 2, p. 144.
[75] MS. H-15-1, Confederate Museum.
[76] Cf. J. E. Johnston to S. Cooper, July 28, 1861; O. R., 2, 1105; O. R., 5, 768; O. R., 51, part 2, pp. 203–4; cf. ibid., 196; IV O. R., 1, 885.

state forces for the field,[77] the Confederacy was beginning to send Southern volunteer regiments into Virginia to dispute the expected Federal advance. The earliest order for the movement of these troops had been issued without the knowledge of Governor Letcher,[78] and officers holding Confederate commissions had been sent to Lynchburg to prepare for their coming.[79] When Lee's representative arrived in the same town to mobilize Virginia volunteers, there was immediate confusion, which it took much time to straighten out.[80] After some of the Southern troops arrived in Richmond, Letcher directed a Louisiana regiment to report for duty at Harpers Ferry. The colonel of the regiment declined to obey Letcher's order on the ground that the governor of Virginia had no control over him. Letcher, with equal assurance and with the approval of the advisory council, determined to exercise authority over all troops in Virginia until the Confederate States acted.[81] Conflict was in the air, and the personal representative of the Secretary of War began to crowd the wire with suspicions of Lee and of Letcher, intimating that Lee was "troubled about rank." In a personal exchange of telegrams with the President, Lee explained that he was satisfied with his place in Virginia service. The muckraker was then silenced.[82] Friction was definitely relieved on May 10 by an order from the War Department authorizing Lee to "assume control of the forces of the Confederate States in Virginia, and assign them to such duties as you may indicate, until further orders." [83] Four days later Lee was made brigadier general in the regular army of the Confederacy, the highest rank then existing.[84] He continued to discharge all the duties of his Virginia commission, however, for some weeks,[85] and certain of the duties for a much longer time.

---

[77] For the efforts to procure medical supplies, see *O. R.*, 51, part 2, pp. 55–61.

[78] IV *O. R.*, 1, 231, 232, 272.

[79] *O. R.*, 2, 792.

[80] *O. R.*, 51, part 2, pp. 56, 73, 82; *O. R.*, 2, 798; Lee to Cocke, May 7, 1861; *Cocke MSS.*

[81] *O. R.*, 2, 813; *O. R.*, 51, part 2, p. 72.

[82] *O. R.*, 51, part 2, pp. 66–69.

[83] *O. R.*, 2, 827; *Richmond Enquirer*, May 14, 1861, p. 3, col. 6.

[84] M. J. Wright: *General Officers of the Confederate Army*, 46–47.

[85] He used a printed letterhead "Headquarters of the Virginia Forces"; *Cocke MSS.*; *cf.* Lee to Colonel A. Beckley, Aug. 8, Aug. 24, 1861; *Taylor MSS.*; T. T. Fauntleroy to Lee, Aug. 17, 1861; *O. R.*, 51, part 2, p. 239; *O. R.*, 5, 807; *Richmond Examiner*, Aug. 31, 1861, p. 2, col. 5.

Although Lee's new powers were temporarily sufficient for moving Confederate troops,[86] they did not save him from the blunders of inexperience or from overzeal in the War Department. One of the worst instances of this was the action of President Davis in calling on John B. Floyd, former Secretary of War under Buchanan, to raise a brigade of "your mountain rifle-men with their own tried weapons." Floyd accepted the invitation instantly and set about recruiting in the face of the state's own call for men. He subsequently sent an agent South in search of arms, precisely as if he were organizing a separate army.[87]

Floyd's independent command was to have an unhappy influence on operations in western Virginia, concerning which Lee was beginning to be very apprehensive. For that part of the state lying in and beyond the Alleghanies was strategically important and open to the Federals. Its rivers flowed into the Ohio or into the major tributaries of that stream. A Federal force commanding the line of the Baltimore and Ohio Railroad could move up the river valleys, whereas troops from eastern Virginia would have to cross the watersheds. Harpers Ferry was easily turned from western Virginia. United States troops operating from Grafton could advance southeastward and by a shorter march than that to Harpers Ferry could reach Staunton and the upper valley of the Shenandoah. In the larger strategy of a Southern war, railway communications in Kentucky and Tennessee might be interrupted by an armed force based on the westernmost counties of Virginia.

Sentiment was divided in this wide area, which was potentially a source of considerable man-power either for or against Virginia. Many of the settlers had come down from Pennsylvania, were of different racial stock from the people of the eastern part of the state, lacked their long tradition of states' rights, and were inimical to slavery. Their delegates in the convention, with few exceptions, had been Union men and had left Richmond after the ordinance of secession had been passed. Some of these delegates were now agitating for resistance to the state government. Side by side with these politicians and their supporters, especially in the agricultural counties, were groups of slave-holding planters whose in-

[86] Cf. Lee to E. K. Smith, May 14, 1861; O. R., 2, 840; May 21, 1861, ibid., 860.
[87] O. R., 2, 838; IV O. R., 1, 374; O. R., 51, part 2, pp. 152–53, 167.

terests and views were substantially those of Tidewater and Midland Virginia.[88]

Which side was to control, and which army was to occupy this disputed section? Strategically, were the Federals to utilize the B. and O. for troop movements, so that Ohio and New York would march southward to the same drum-beat; or could Virginia hold that railroad and force the East and the West to fight separate campaigns? Would Virginia have to fight on the Rappahannock and the Shenandoah, or could she guard the Potomac and the Ohio? These were heavy questions; in their consequences perhaps the most portentous that arose in Virginia after secession had been determined upon. For it was the loss of military control in the western counties that made possible the separatist movement which dismembered the territory of the Old Dominion and definitely reduced her to a secondary place in a restored Union. Had her western counties been saved, Virginia would today be the twentieth state in area and in population the ninth.

When Lee had first come to Richmond almost all the reports from western Virginia were favorable. Men of standing wrote that the volunteers were mustering, and that if they were supplied with arms promptly they believed they could keep the discontented element in hand.[89] "We are full of the war spirit," one volunteer wrote from Kanawha County, "and are determined to do our duty in defence of the glorious old commonwealth."[90] Finding that nothing had been done to secure western Virginia, except to warn the president of the B. and O. not to permit the Federals to use the line for military purposes,[91] Lee proceeded to rally the doubtful counties before he issued the general call for volunteers. On April 29–30 he designated officers to undertake the organization of troops at Wheeling, in the lower Kanawha Valley, and at Grafton.[92] A few days later Colonel George A. Porterfield, a man of influence in that section, was dispatched to Grafton to take command, with authority to accept five regiments of volunteers. Grafton was strategically most important. Located 175 miles west of Harpers Ferry by rail, on the main line of the

[88] Cf. John Letcher to Geo. W. Summers, May 10, 1861; 1 S. H. S. P., 457–58.
[89] O. R., 51, part 2, pp. 23, 25, 29, 31.
[90] T. L. Broun to Annie Broun, April 24, 1861; MS. B-18-11, Confederate Museum.
[91] Letcher to J. W. Garrett, April 21, 1861; O. R., 51, part 2, p. 21.
[92] O. R., 2, 788, 790–91; cf. Lee to J. M. Mason, May 21, 1861; O. R., 2, 860.

B. and O., it was the junction for the line to Parkersburg and, in addition, was the logical base for an advance southeastward to the head of the Shenandoah Valley. Porterfield was told to co-operate with the officials of the B. and O., who were supposed to be sympathetic, and he was instructed not to interfere with the peaceable operation of the road.[93]

Optimism did not last long. By May 6 the bulk of the news from western Virginia became distinctly unfavorable. Jackson reported much disaffection in that section and urged that troops be sent there.[94] Other information was to the same effect, especially from Grafton, where the people were said to be verging on a state of "actual rebellion" against the authority of Virginia, and were confidently expecting Federal support from Pennsylvania and Ohio.[95] Lee was very much concerned at this, but aside from ordering arms hurried forward, he felt that he could do little. The dispatch of troops from eastern Virginia, in his opinion, would irritate rather than conciliate, and would be accepted as evidence of a purpose to influence the free action of the people in voting on the ratification of secession at the election about a fortnight thereafter. As for throwing troops into western Virginia from Harpers Ferry, he doubtless reasoned, quite apart from the safety of the machinery at the arsenal, that if that position were lost, the northwestern counties would certainly be, but that if Harpers Ferry were held, service on the B. and O. was under control and the northwest might perhaps be recovered.[96] To this view he held in the face of strong appeals for a more aggressive policy, but he began to ponder the possibility of raising troops in the loyal border counties to stimulate the weak-hearted and to silence their disaffected neighbors to the westward.[97] Much importance was attached to what might be accomplished by Colonel Porterfield, who reached Grafton on May 14.[98]

The date of Porterfield's arrival at Grafton was approximately that on which Lee took up in detail the final aspect of Virginia's defensive preparations, that, namely, of disposing the state's enlarged forces to meet the Federal offensive. With Norfolk and

[93] O. R., 2, 802–3.
[94] O. R., 2, 807, 810, 833.
[95] O. R., 2, 827; O. R., 51, part 2, p. 75.
[96] Cf. O. R., 2, 827, 830, 840.
[97] Inferred from Lee to F. M. Boykin, May 13, 1861; O. R., 2, 837–38.
[98] O. R., 2, 843, 848, 849.

Harpers Ferry reasonably well strengthened, he decided he must proceed to concentrate more troops at Manassas Junction,[99] where a small force under General P. Saint George Cocke had been placed by Letcher before Lee took command. He did not believe that Alexandria and the nearby country would speedily be occupied by the Federals, and he was vindicated in this opinion. Despite endless rumors and many fears[100] of a Federal advance, an informal truce had been agreed upon in front of Alexandria and, as late as May 13, was respected by both sides.[101] On May 6, however, Lee had warned General Cocke to prepare for an attack directed from Alexandria,[102] because both he and Cocke reasoned that the Federals would certainly attempt to turn Harpers Ferry by way of Manassas Junction. Such an advance would encounter no large streams, once the undefended Potomac was crossed. It could be made by at least two good roads through a country that presented no serious natural obstacles. And if it reached the line Chantilly-Centreville-Manassas Junction, distant only twenty miles from Washington and Alexandria, it would command the railways and the roads leading to Harpers Ferry and to Winchester. Simple seizure of the Manassas Gap Railroad, leading from Manassas Junction to Strasburg, not only would deprive the Confederate forces at Harpers Ferry of all direct railway connection with Richmond,[103] but would similarly cut off the scant force that was trying to rally the states' rights men in northwestern Virginia. Once Harpers Ferry and the lower valley fell into the enemy's hands the only approach to Grafton would be by road over the mountains from Staunton. This will be apparent from the sketch on the following page.

Lee did not believe that as good a soldier as General Scott would overlook such opportunities, military and political, as the

[99] Lee to P. St. George Cocke, May 15, 1861; O. R., 845.
[100] Cf. O. R., 2, 776, 777, 778, 779, 785, 795, 796, 806; Lee to Cocke, April 29, 1861; Garnett to Cocke, May 3, 1861; Cocke MSS.; O. R., 51, part 2, pp. 50, 66.
[101] O. R., 2, 842–43; cf. O. R., 51, part 2, p. 54.   [102] O. R., 2, 806.
[103] There is, unfortunately, no adequate large-scale contemporary map for all this part of Virginia. Perhaps the best is that on Plates CXXXVI, CXXXVII, and CXLII in the Atlas to Accompany the Official Records of the Union and Confederate Armies (cited hereafter as O. R. Atlas), but for the relative importance of the roads, this has to be supplemented by ibid., Plates V and XXVII. It should be remembered in all studies of these operations (1) that the road via Leesburg was too much exposed in the vicinity of Harpers Ferry to be a safe line of advance, and (2) that the existing (1934) railroad from Winchester to Staunton and Lexington had not then been constructed.

occupation of the Manassas Gap Railroad would offer. As quickly as he could, Lee now began to dispatch additional officers and men to General Cocke for use at Manassas Junction, the point where the Manassas Gap Railroad joined the Orange and Alex-

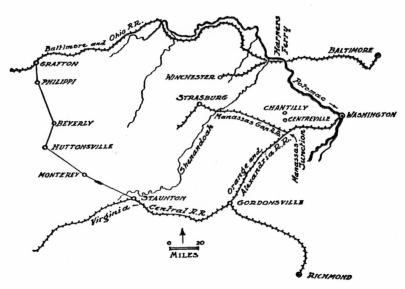

andria. In this effort Lee was vigorously seconded by Cocke, who represented the highest of Virginia traditions.[104] An old West Point graduate, a rich planter of fine character, devoted to Virginia, General Cocke performed a service during the first months of the war for which he has never received just recognition.[105]

Every effort that Lee made to strengthen Virginia's hold on her exposed northern frontier was seconded with the greatest energy by Colonel Jackson at Harpers Ferry. While the machinery was being moved[106] Jackson was collecting troops from the lower

[104] O. R., 2, 806, 817, 819, 821, 824, 826, 828, 831–32, 841, 842, 845, 860; O. R., 51, part 2, pp. 78, 79, 82; Lee to Cocke, May 9, 10, 1861; Garnett to Cocke, May 3, 1861; J. A. Early to Cocke, May 25, June 7, 1861; Cocke MSS. Cocke's first headquarters were at Culpeper Courthouse. Troops were sent there, drilled, and then sent to Manassas. Cf. J. A. Washington to Cocke, May 12, 1861; Cocke MSS.

[105] General Cocke had been named on the staff of Governor Wise on Dec. 2, 1859; and on April 21, 1861, had been made commanding officer on the line of the Potomac. Cocke MSS.; O. R., 51, part 2, p. 21. Cf. C. A. Evans, editor: Confederate Military History (cited hereafter as C. M. H.), 3, 587.

[106] All the machinery and stores at Harpers Ferry, except some seasoned gun stocks, were safely removed before the place was evacuated. For the details and the subsequent

Shenandoah Valley and was drilling them zealously. Reinforced by volunteers from Kentucky and Maryland and by units that Lee sent forward, he had raised his force to 4500 by May 11.[107] Jackson saw a constant threat to Harpers Ferry from Maryland Heights across the Potomac, and without waiting for orders he promptly occupied and fortified that position. Lee was perturbed lest Maryland should take offense at this invasion of her territory, and he cautioned Jackson against inviting an attack he was not strong enough to resist. The question was settled, tacitly, by entrusting the works on Maryland soil to volunteers from that state and to the Kentuckians, who had come to Harpers Ferry without orders and were a quasi-independent force. Jackson carefully omitted from his order-book all instructions for the seizure of the heights.[108] Thanks to his diligence and military judgment, it became apparent that Harpers Ferry not only was measurably safe, as Lee had believed for some days, but that, in certain eventualities, the troops there might be utilized to meet an offensive directed against it by way of Manassas Junction.[109]

From the northern end of the line to the eastern Lee had to turn his attention at this stage of the military preparations, for there had been hints of friction between the army and the navy at Norfolk and some suggestions that the commanding officer, Brigadier General Walter Gwynn, was submerged in detail.[110] To adjust these troubles, and to ascertain the condition of the defenses, Lee left Richmond on May 16, for the first time since he had arrived on April 22, and made a thorough inspection of Norfolk.[111] He found the situation confused and unsatisfactory. Progress on the fortifications was slow.[112] Hastening back to Richmond as soon as he was convinced that he had found the

disposal of the machinery, see *O. R.,* 2, 785–86; *O. R.,* 51, part 2, pp. 34, 53, 98, 99–100, 134, 155; IV *O. R.,* 1, 358, 379, 468 *ff.,* 476, 491; Doc. XL, *Virginia Convention of 1861,* p. 129 *ff.;* 11 *Calendar Virginia State Papers,* 151, 181–82.

[107] *O. R.,* 2, 832–33. For the later arrival of troops from Georgia and of more volunteers from Kentucky, see *O. R.,* 51, part 2, pp. 135, 137.

[108] *Jackson's MS. Order-Book,* Confederate Museum; *O. R.,* 2, 32, 793–94, 797, 806–7, 809, 810, 814, 822, 824, 825, 826, 832–33, 836, 840, 849, 856; *O. R.,* 51, part 2, pp. 66, 71–72, 78, 79, 86, 91, 92.

[109] See *infra,* p. 536. [110] *O. R.,* 2, 808–9; *O. R.,* 51, part 2, p. 64.

[111] Lee to Mrs. Lee, May 16, 1861; *R. E. Lee, Jr.,* 31; *Jones,* 169; *O. R.,* 51, part 2, pp. 92, 96.

[112] On the afternoon of May 18 the Federal steamer *Monticello* bombarded the unfinished works at Sewell's Point. No guns were in position to answer this fire, nor were any placed until the next afternoon. *O. R.,* 2, 33; *O. R.,* 51, part 2, p. 95.

trouble, he relieved General Gwynn, who had not seen regular military service since 1832. In his place Lee put Brigadier General Benjamin Huger, a comrade of Mexican days and, as Lee wrote, "an officer of great merit." [113] Under General Huger's direction, the construction and arming of the batteries went on with less delay.

On May 23 Lee had been in command one month, and that day the voters of Virginia went to the polls to pass on the ordinance of secession.[114] It was conceded that they would ratify it overwhelmingly.[115] And after that, every one believed, invasion would come quickly. Little was known of the mobilization of the United States and in detail that little was not accurate. It was apparent, however, that the greatly superior forces of the North could advance simultaneously from four directions—from the line of the Ohio into western Virginia, from Maryland into the Shenandoah Valley, from Washington to Manassas, and from Hampton Roads on Norfolk or on Richmond. Lee's preparations show that he had all these possibilities in mind, though he perhaps did not believe the attack from the Ohio would materialize so quickly as it did.

Was Virginia ready for the shock? Along the tidal rivers raw earthworks broke the green landscape, and straining men were putting heavy guns in battery. At Norfolk confusion still reigned, though at the navy yard there was great activity. At Gloucester Point the defenders of the York felt secure, while across that beautiful stream sentinels paced the very parapets the British had thrown up at Yorktown in 1781. Between the York and the James, John Bankhead Magruder[116] was busying himself in drawing a defensive line that had previously been decided upon. Jackson at Harpers Ferry and the commanders at Norfolk and

[113] *O. R.,* 51, part 2, pp. 102, 106; *O. R.,* 2, 867.

[114] For Lee's G. O. 17, directing how the vote of the soldiers should be taken, see *Richmond Whig,* May 18, 1861, p. 3, col. 3.

[115] The provision for a referendum is in *Acts of the General Assembly of Virginia of 1861,* pp. 24–25. The geographical distribution of the vote in the election is analyzed in H. T. Shanks: *The Secession Movement in Virginia, 1847–1861,* p. 204 *ff.* The poll, as estimated by Governor Letcher, was: For ratification of the ordinance of secession, 125,-950; against ratification, 20,373. (II *Calendar Virginia State Papers,* 155.)

[116] Magruder had first been assigned to command the artillery around Richmond, *O. R.,* 51, part 2, p. 53, and then had served for a short time in general command of all Virginia forces in and around the capital city. *Richmond Enquirer,* May 10, 1861, p. 3, col. 7.

on the Manassas line saw their numbers increasing daily. In Richmond the crowds overflowed the once-quiet city of John Marshall.[117] The departments were working furiously; the confines of the old fair grounds echoed all day to grounded arms and to sharp orders of command. South Carolinians and French-speaking Creoles from New Orleans swaggered past porches whence Virginia girls observed them with wide, admiring eyes. Munitions were being shipped hourly, cobblers were turning to the manufacture of harness, and feminine fingers were fashioning knapsacks. The state arsenal, expanded quickly, was preparing cartridges, and the mustered wheelwrights of the whole section were preparing gun carriages. Lee's own headquarters were busy, visited by returned officers eager to offer their services to Virginia, and besieged by an army of civilians seeking contracts.[118] Everywhere in Virginia the boys were leaving home or else were chafing under regulations that forbade them to enlist until they were eighteen. Many of the younger married men and not a few in early middle life were volunteering also. New companies met periodically for drill and instruction till their ranks were filled and their orders were received to proceed to one of the rendezvous in the state. Then there would be a day of roses and tears, of farewells and cheers, and General Lee would be notified that another company was available for Manassas Junction or for Harpers Ferry. By the middle of May, preparation, excitement, and confidence were in the air, and from confusion order was gradually emerging. But as yet war was in the picturesque stage, when uniforms were new and hopes were high, when youth saw only the glamour and none of the misery of the conflict that was about to open.

117 *De Leon*, 86–87.　　　　118 *Hood*, 17.

CHAPTER XXX

THE MOBILIZATION COMPLETED

THE day after the people of Virginia ratified the ordinance of secession, Lee received the long-expected news: the Federals that morning, in great strength, had occupied Alexandria and the Virginia side of the Potomac and had captured a small troop of Virginia horse serving as a rearguard there.[1] Lee promptly forwarded to Manassas three regiments of reinforcements and some cavalry[2] and gave orders for dispositions in case the Federals continued their advance.[3] The danger to Manassas Junction was manifestly so acute that he determined to go there and see the situation for himself as soon as he could arrange to leave Richmond.

The occupation of the Virginia side of the Potomac had, of course, a personal aspect that Lee could not wholly overlook, even in the excited hour of the first movements to present an opposing front to the Federals. It meant that the pleasant hill of Arlington was in the hands of those former friends who now were enemies. Lee had anticipated this and was reconciled to it. His concern was for his invalid wife, not for himself. Mrs. Lee had been very loath to leave Arlington, despite the urging of her husband and the imminence of a Federal advance. She had long been unable to decide where to go, and not until about May 14 did she betake herself temporarily to nearby Ravensworth. Even then she left many of the family's possessions and some of the Washington relics within easy reach of marauders. Lee knew that Mrs. Lee could not remain for any length of time at Ravensworth without causing embarrassment to Mrs. Fitzhugh for housing the wife of a "rebel general," but he was unwilling to have her come to Richmond, inasmuch as he expected to take the

[1] O. R., 2, 37–39, 42 ff., 886; O. R., 51, part 2, pp. 104–5; N. O. R., 4, 481; G. Wise: History of the Seventeenth Virginia Infantry (cited hereafter as G. Wise), 11–12.
[2] O. R., 51, part 2, pp. 107–8.   [3] O. R., 2, 872–73; O. R., 51, part 2, p. 108.

field speedily.[4] The daughters went to visit friends in Fauquier County, Virginia. Lee had left his sons free to make their own choice and had most carefully urged Custis not to be influenced by his own example. But all of them sided with the South. Custis resigned, came to Richmond, and soon was working as an officer of engineers; Rooney promptly enlisted and was made a captain of cavalry; Robert was ere long to be chosen to like rank in one of the student companies at the University of Virginia, though, because of his youth, his father was as yet unwilling for him to enter the service.[5] Smith Lee returned his Federal commission early and became a captain in the Virginia navy.[6] Lee took all these changes calmly. "When I reflect," said he, "upon the calamity impending over the country, my own sorrows sink into insignificance." [7]

The impending calamity was brought nearer, three days after the occupation of Alexandria and Arlington, by a report that Federal transports had appeared in Hampton Roads and were unloading troops in large numbers at Newport News, close to Fort Monroe, at the tip of "the Peninsula," as that part of Virginia between the York and the James River is styled.[8] The second of the four probable Federal offensives was taking form. Lee was not unprepared for it. Although the informal truce had continued around Fort Monroe,[9] Lee consolidated the command on the lower Peninsula under Magruder on May 21,[10] and had been strengthening him as steadily as the numerous calls from other quarters had permitted. Embarrassed by lack of cavalry and of wagons, Magruder was making progress on the line intended to link up Jamestown, Williamsburg, and Yorktown.[11]

Lee reasoned that the troops being collected at Newport News might be planning either to turn the position at Yorktown and thus open the York River, or else to cross Hampton Roads,

[4] For Lee's letters, urging her to leave, see *R. E. Lee, Jr.*, 28–32. For correspondence between her and General Irvin McDowell, who promised to protect Arlington, see Jones, *L. and L.*, 143. For the offer of a home by William C. Rives, see Jones, *L. and L.*, 141. For letter from Mrs. Lee to General Scott, enclosing an account of Lee's reception in Richmond, and echoing the old friendship, see *Fitz Lee*, 93.
[5] *R. E. Lee, Jr.*, 32; for Custis, see 11 *Calendar Virginia State Papers*, 133; for Robert, see Jones, *L. and L.*, 143.
[6] Lee to Mrs. Lee, May 16, 1861; *R. E. Lee, Jr.*, 31.
[7] Lee to Mrs. Lee, May 8, 1861; *R. E. Lee, Jr.*, 30.
[8] *O. R.*, 2, 882.
[9] *O. R.*, 2, 870–71; see *supra*, p. 481.
[10] *O. R.*, 2, 865.
[11] *O. R.*, 2, 35, 37, 875, 876, 877, 878, 884, 885, 887.

ascend the Nansemond River, cut the railroad from Norfolk to Petersburg, and mask Norfolk. Both possibilities will be apparent from this sketch:

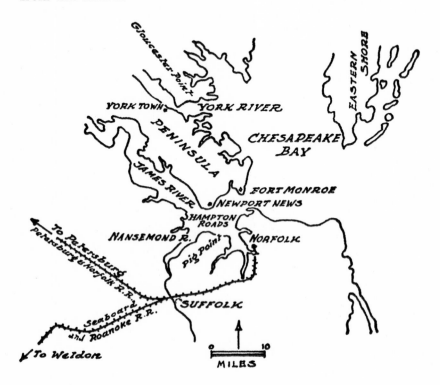

Lee accordingly put both Magruder and Huger on notice.[12] He hastened to send more troops to the Norfolk district and some artillery to defend the approaches to Suffolk.[13] Magruder received a few heavy guns to protect his line from being turned by way of the James, and continued to improve his position.[14]

Before the object of the landing at Newport News had become apparent, Lee felt it necessary to make his proposed visit to Manassas Junction. Leaving Richmond on May 28 he made a hurried inspection of the junction that afternoon, and the next morning

[12] O. R., 2, 882–83.
[13] O. R., 2, 54, 835–36, 839, 863, 875, 884 ff., 889, 911, 919, 993, 997; O. R., 51, part 2, pp. 107, 119, 122.
[14] O. R., 2, 891, 892, 893, 900, 902, 912.

went on to Fairfax Courthouse.[15] The troops, he found, were increasing rapidly in number, but were in every conceivable state of efficiency and the lack of it. Some were ready for action; some of those who had retreated from Alexandria did not even have arms.[16] The officers ranged from wholly inexperienced civilian volunteers to men with West Point training and a solid background of service in the regular army. Lee promptly made new dispositions to cover the flanks and to place a detachment for observation at Fairfax Courthouse. He concluded that the size of the force to be collected at Manassas would make the Federals cautious in any advance against Harpers Ferry along the south bank of the Potomac, and that there consequently would be time for joint operations between the troops at Harpers Ferry and those around Manassas.[17] This was the germ of the strategy subsequently employed in the campaign of First Manassas.

The selection of the best available commander for the force mustering at Manassas Junction had been giving Lee much concern. General Cocke had worked zealously, in the face of many obstacles, but the Virginia convention had concluded that the state had too many general officers and had reduced their number. Letcher had accordingly renominated Cocke, along with others, for rank in the volunteer forces one grade lower than they had previously held. Under another ordinance, officers of the provisional army outranked officers of similar rank among the volunteers. This virtually had displaced Cocke, who for a time had not even had a regiment. Cocke had naturally protested, and Lee had been at pains to explain how the change had come about, but there was no alternative to the selection of an officer of commanding rank to take charge of the Manassas line.[18] Brigadier General M. L. Bonham of South Carolina, the fourth officer to be assigned that rank in the provisional army of the Confederacy,[19] had reported in Richmond with a brigade of South Carolina volunteers,[20] and as these troops were most needed at Ma-

---

[15] R. E. Lee, Jr., 33; O. R., 2, 890–91.
[16] O. R., 2, 43.   [17] O. R., 2, 894, 897.
[18] Cocke's protest, MS., is among the Virginia Executive Papers, May 12, 1861; Lee to Cocke, May 13, 1861; O. R., 2, 836–37; O. R., 51, part 2, p. 109; F. H. Smith to Cocke, May 14, 1861; D. H. Ruggles to Cocke, May 8, 1861; F. G. Skinner to Cocke, May 15, 1861; Cocke MSS.
[19] Wright: General Officers of the Confederate Army, 49.
[20] O. R., 2, 831.

nassas, Bonham was sent there. Being the senior officer he was given command on May 21, with very detailed instructions to hold to the defensive.[21] Lee now concluded that a more experienced soldier than Bonham was needed for Manassas and he began to search about to find him.

On his way back to Richmond from Manassas a crowd surrounded Lee's train at Orange Courthouse, and, after the fashion of the day, demanded a speech. Lee demurred, for he had neither taste nor time for haranguing an idle crowd. The Orangemen persisted until he felt it would seem snobbishness or discourtesy to refuse. He stepped out and told his auditors that he had much more important matters on his mind than speech-making. All those who were in the service should be drilling, and those who for good reason had not joined the army would do well to attend to their own affairs and to avoid the excitement and rumors of crowds. That was all. It was not the utterance of a man currying favor with the multitude, but it made an impression.[22]

When Lee reached the city he found that during his absence President Jefferson Davis had arrived from Montgomery, Ala., to make Richmond the capital of the Confederacy, in accordance with the invitation of the Virginia convention. This invitation had been extended on April 27[23] and had been accepted on May 21,[24] probably because some of President Davis's friends in Virginia had insisted that his presence in Richmond was necessary to a vigorous prosecution of the war.[25] Strategically it was a serious mistake, for it placed almost on the frontier of the Confederacy, in a state whose rivers were open to the warships of the enemy, the capital that was so soon and so surely to become the emblem of the Southern cause that its retention took on a moral significance out of all proportion to the industrial importance of the city, great though that was to the agricultural South.

The preliminaries of this unwise removal of the capital to Richmond had not been wholly cordial, and the separate efforts of the state government and of the Confederacy in Virginia had not been without friction. Governor Letcher had been in no hurry to effect the transfer of the Virginia forces to the Con-

[21] O. R., 2, 865–66, 879. [22] Richmond Whig, June 7, 1861; p. 2, cols. 3–4.
[23] IV O. R., 1, 255. [24] IV O. R., 1, 343.
[25] O. R., 51, part 2, pp. 70, 71, 81, 90, 92.

federacy. An inquiry from Secretary Walker concerning the strength and position of the troops of the Old Dominion had gone unanswered, and when, on May 1, this inquiry had been repeated, Letcher's answer had been a simple statement of Virginia's military resources and plans for mobilization.[26] Later, when Walker had asked whether Virginia desired the Confederate Government to take charge of operations, the governor had contented himself with saying that he would act until the Confederacy assumed the direction of affairs.[27] The Montgomery government had not pursued the subject further, but had gradually asserted its authority thereafter, and on occasion had ignored both Letcher and Lee, though, on May 10, Lee had been given command of all the forces in Virginia. General Joseph E. Johnston had been ordered on May 15 by the War Department to take charge at Harpers Ferry, without reference to Lee, and had been directed to forward from Lynchburg to Harpers Ferry certain Confederate troops that Lee had previously earmarked for Richmond.[28] Subsequently, while Lee had been ordering Confederate forces already in Virginia to points where they were needed,[29] the War Department had dispatched other Southern regiments to Virginia —some to report to Lee and some to move to assigned posts, apparently without regard to Lee's control.[30] Lee had recommended at the very beginning that Johnston be given rank equal his own, and had assigned him to temporary duty around Richmond as a major general on April 26, but in the rebellion of the convention at too many exalted military titles, Johnston had been made brigadier general in the provisional army of Virginia, a position next to that of Lee. Johnston, however, had preferred to accept a commission as brigadier general in the Confederate army, and it was in this capacity that he had been assigned to Harpers Ferry.[31] On his way to that post Johnston had written Lee and had announced to him, "The President intends to

[26] O. R., 2, 783, 792.
[27] O. R., 2, 805; O. R., 51, part 2, p. 74. Relations between Governor Letcher and the Confederate executive were far less cordial than those between Letcher and the governors of the Southern states to whom Virginia supplied arms or from whom she received help. Cf. O. R., 2, 793; MS. N. C., 153, Confederate Museum.
[28] O. R., 2, 844.   [29] E.g., O. R., 51, part 2, p. 107.
[30] O. R., 51, part 2, pp. 104, 107, 119, 120.
[31] O. R., 51, part 2, pp. 36, 60; O. R., 2, 783; Johnston's Narrative, 12–13; 11 Calendar Virginia State Papers, 121.

assemble an army near Harpers Ferry." [32] On Johnston's arrival there Jackson had refused to recognize the new officer's seniority until he had seen documentary evidence of it,[33] but he had then supported him cordially. Johnston had found all the approaches well-guarded and more than 8000 troops at Harpers Ferry, 7000 of them armed. Raw though they were, "a fierce spirit" animated these "rough-looking men," in the words of the inspector, and their only serious deficiency had been in horses for the artillery.[34] The Maryland Heights had been held, plans had been made to block the railroad at Point of Rocks, and conditions generally had been favorable, even if it had been rumored that the Federals had increased to 15,000 the men supposed to be at Chambersburg and Carlisle, Pa.[35] Johnston, however, had been apprehensive from the first, was doubtful of his ability to hold Harpers Ferry, and, though he recognized Lee's authority and even went so far in one letter as to style him "commander in chief," he was only too plainly out of sympathy with Lee's plan to retain Harpers Ferry as long as practicable.[36]

Johnston's attitude, the conflict of authority, the arrival of Davis, and the near approach of the day when the Virginia forces would be taken over by the Confederacy added to the difficulties of Lee's position. There was a feeling of uneasiness and perhaps of jealousy toward the Confederacy on the part of some Virginia officers. They had doubts concerning their future status, despite the purpose of the advisory council to provide for all those capable officers who had resigned from the United States army.[37] However, in this muddle, with a President and a governor, a Confederacy and a state alike to be served, Lee had one asset in his steadfast refusal to be incensed by slights or provoked by the clash of authority. Another asset was the esteem of the President.

Jefferson Davis was then close to his fifty-third birthday, a year and a half younger than Lee. Although his father had been a man of scant schooling, his blood was good, and his instincts, his bearing, and his manners were those of an aristocrat. His well-

[32] O. R., 2, 856.
[34] O. R., 2, 861, 867 ff.
[33] O. R., 2, 871–72, 877.
[35] O. R., 2, 860, 885, 890.
[36] For Johnston's views and the development of the situation at Harpers Ferry, see O. R., 2, 870, 881, 889, 894, 895, 897–98, 899, 904, 908, 910.
[37] IV O. R., 1, 364; 11 Calendar Virginia State Papers, 138, 147; cf. ibid., 147–48, 154, 159.

chiselled features and his fine head bespoke high intelligence; his thin, erect form was commanding and gracious. In his dealings with the public he had dignity without austerity, and his speeches were usually impressive. His experience had been long and varied, as planter, as volunteer in the Mexican War, as senator, and as Secretary of War in the Cabinet of Franklin Pierce. Although not a profound strategist, his understanding of military matters was sound and his viewpoint in war essentially that of the professional soldier. Brief as his service had been in the regular army, he never forgot West Point, or the relations between commanding officer and subordinate. Had he been in the field, as a minor officer, neither Lee nor Jackson would have been more mindful of discipline than he. In his capacity as commander in chief he expected to be obeyed as he would have obeyed. In administration, he was of average capacity or better, occasionally disposed to delay decisions but usually reaching them promptly and reasonably, without permitting himself to be engulfed in detail. He had in him, in fact, some of the qualities essential to the success of a revolution, but these were coupled with serious weaknesses, only a few of which had become apparent in the summer of 1861. His nature was exceedingly sensitive, perhaps because he had received more than his share of applause and had seldom had the tonic of personal criticism. His health, moreover, was uncertain. At intervals—and most inconveniently when he was under the strain of anxious vigils and difficult decisions—he suffered from the inflammation of a facial nerve that caused him agony and prostrating illness. He endured this with fortitude and often discharged his duties when he was almost blinded by suffering and was subjected every few minutes to sharp spasms of the affected nerve, but on occasion his long combat with physical pain made him irritable. His political life had been an endless struggle for a strict and rigid interpretation of legal right, and he was to prove himself too much of a constitutionalist to be a daring revolutionary. He hesitated to exceed the admitted limits of his authority as President, and when he did so he was as unconvincing as he was irritating; but he was instant to claim his full constitutional prerogatives, and in doing so he was often abrupt and sometimes unreasonable. Two things were certain to make him hostile: one was to accuse him of unfairness; the other was to impinge upon his authority as President. In his dealings with men he applied to the fullest the political maxim of loyalty to friends and of hostility to foes. His judgment of men was not exceptional, for he relied too much upon the impressions formed in youth; and impressions once formed he was slow to change. If he named one of his supporters to office, criticism of his appointee he would almost invariably regard as criticism of himself. With a political antagonist he would dispute to the last line of a long correspondence, in as high regard for logical victories in the theoretical points at issue as if he were speaking for *The Congressional Globe.* In the end, if he could not convince he would not attempt to conciliate, but would accept a man as a permanent enemy and would sever relations with him. He had energy, he had a measure of vision, he had patience, patience with everything but contradiction. His stubborn loyalty to friends of mediocre mind was to cost the Confederacy dearly, but in the case of Lee his loyalty was to be, perhaps, his largest service to the South. Davis had not forgotten Lee's superintendency at West Point and his reputation in the old army. At this time, and always, as he subsequently testified, Lee had his "unqualified confidence, both as a man and a patriot, and had the special knowledge of conditions in Virginia that was most useful." [88] From the time of his arrival in Richmond, Davis kept Lee near him and consulted often with him.[39] Together, on Lee's return from Manassas Junction, they conferred on the choice of a commander for that exposed line. The President decided to entrust the post to Lee's friend of earlier days, the "Hero of Charleston," General P. G. T. Beauregard, who was then in Richmond. Beauregard was called in, was given a review of the situation, and was directed to leave the next day for Manassas. His orders, which Lee prepared, were for close vigilance and a strict defensive, a course that Beauregard complained, years afterwards, left him no discretion and no initiative.[40] Had he complained at the time it probably would have made no difference, for Lee had not modified in the slightest his view that Virginia's

[88] I *Davis*, 340. [39] *R. E. Lee, Jr.*, 35.
[40] Alfred Roman: *Military Operations of General Beauregard* (cited hereafter as *Roman*), I, p. 66 ff.; O. R., 2, 896.

safety demanded that she avoid aggression until she was prepared to meet it.

The dispatch of Beauregard to Manassas put three of the four exposed posts in Virginia under the charge of professional soldiers of experience: Huger and Magruder were on opposite sides of Hampton Roads, Johnston was at Harpers Ferry, Beauregard faced the enemy below Washington. Conditions in each of these threatened areas were improving hourly. Very different was the situation in the fourth zone of probable Federal advance, western Virginia. For two weeks the news from that quarter had been bad. Optimistic reports had given place to gloomy intelligence of disaffection, opposition, and open hostility. By May 21 Lee had realized that volunteers would not be raised in adequate numbers in the northwestern counties, and he had adopted the alternative, which he had been maturing, of sending into that section troops from nearby counties in the hope that they would gather strength as they advanced. Commanding officers were enjoined anew to prevent the use of the Baltimore and Ohio by the enemy, though Lee had rejected the proposal of Colonel Jackson that a strong force should be thrown into northwest Virginia as soon as the vote on secession was announced. Lee did not have the men to spare and he could not afford to risk Harpers Ferry or the troops that were garrisoning it.[41]

On June 1 a messenger arrived from General Johnston with dispatches. One of them contained a rumor which had reached Harpers Ferry to the effect that Colonel Porterfield had evacuated Grafton, and that the Federals had occupied it.[42] Lee was loath to believe that this had happened,[43] and still less prepared to learn a few days later that Porterfield had been surprised at Philippi, fifteen miles south of Grafton, and had lost most of his equipment.[44] This was a serious matter, for Philippi was closer by forty miles to Staunton than to Harpers Ferry. If the enemy were permitted to advance unhindered through the mountains to Staunton, a distance of about 120 miles by road, the whole of western Virginia might be cut off.

[41] O. R., 2, 50, 855, 857, 860, 863–64, 864, 873–74, 883, 884, 888; O. R., 51, part 2, pp. 93–94, 103, 109; 11 Calendar Virginia State Papers, 133.
[42] O. R., 2, 895; cf. ibid., 899, 901.   [43] O. R., 2, 897.
[44] For the unopposed occupation of Grafton, see O. R., 2, 44–52; for Philippi, see ibid., 64 ff. See also H. W. Benham: Recollections of the West Virginia Campaign, 677.

A third Federal offensive of unknown strength was thus developing more rapidly and in some respects more ominously than either the threat against Manassas Junction or the concentration in Hampton Roads. Both the state and the Confederate authorities moved quickly to redeem the situation. Porterfield was relieved and brought before a court of inquiry.[45] The militia in seven counties were ordered out.[46] A special expedition was planned to burn the Cheat River bridge on the Baltimore and Ohio.[47] Colonel R. S. Garnett, Lee's adjutant general, was commissioned brigadier general and was hurriedly sent to the Allegheny Mountains. Plans were laid to reinforce him rapidly by way of Staunton.[48]

As soon as these necessary measures of relief had been initiated, Lee paid a visit on June 6–8 to the York and James Rivers,[49] for the Confederate authorities were about to take over the Virginia forces,[50] and Lee wished to satisfy himself that the batteries had been properly placed and armed. He found the work almost completed by the naval officers and by the engineers entrusted with it. Three batteries had been constructed on the York, and nineteen of their thirty heavy guns were already in position. In the two batteries on the lower James, twenty of the thirty-two guns were ready for service. Like progress had been made on the other tidal rivers that time did not permit Lee to visit. Five batteries had been thrown up along the estuaries of the Potomac, one had been dug on the Rappahannock, three were being erected on the Nansemond, though they were not yet armed, and several had risen around Hampton Roads. On the Elizabeth River and in the immediate vicinity of Norfolk there were six batteries, mounting eighty-five guns, most of them already prepared for action. Field works of an elaborate nature had also been con-

[45] The court found him culpable, but Lee, with a reprimand, decided not to proceed further, O. R., 2, 72 ff. See his defence in 16 S. H. S. P., 82 ff.
[46] O. R., 51, part 2, p. 124.
[47] O. R., 51, part 2, p. 124; O. R., 2, 904. For the dispatch of General Henry A. Wise to West Virginia at this time, see infra, p. 579.
[48] O. R., 2, 915; O. R., 51, part 2, pp. 135, 136.
[49] Ryland in Alfred Bagby: King and Queen County, Virginia, 226; Lee to Mrs. Lee, June 9, 1861; R. E. Lee, Jr., 35; cf. O. R., 2, 918.
[50] For the earlier correspondence regarding the transfer, see supra, pp. 470, 501, 515; for the later correspondence, see O. R., 51, part 2, pp. 124, 126, 131, 131–32, 133–34, 134–35.

structed around Norfolk, and the Jamestown-Williamsburg-Yorktown line was taking form.[51]

On his way back to Richmond, Lee was able to stop for a few hours at the White House, though in circumstances far different from those that had formerly attended his visits to that old plantation. His daughter Annie and his daughter-in-law Charlotte were there, together with his little grandson and namesake. Rooney was away, and did not arrive until the coming of the train that carried Lee back to the capital city.[52]

The ceremony of transferring the Virginia forces to the Confederacy was now to be completed. The Confederate Government during the preceding fortnight had been assuming additional parts of the sombre work of defense;[53] the council had tendered all Virginia resources on June 1, reserving only the machinery seized at Harpers Ferry;[54] and on June 5 the Confederate War Department somewhat ostentatiously had called on Virginia to surrender the control of military operations.[55] On Lee's arrival from York River, on June 8, the governor formally issued his proclamation, which Lee incorporated in a general order.[56]

In one sense Lee's immediate task was finished. The rivers were defended by the batteries he had just inspected. The navy yard was operating again, and the frigate *Merrimac,* raised from the bottom, was in dry dock. The old *United States* had been fitted with guns. Arrangements had been made to salvage the sunken *Plymouth* and *Germantown.* As far as practicable, Norfolk had been secured from direct attack and from a turning movement by way of Suffolk. Seven thousand troops, Virginia and Confederate, were on duty there. Magruder had somewhat more than 5100 men on the lower Peninsula. A slightly larger force, approximately 5500, was in Richmond and in Ashland as a reserve. On the Manassas line, 7000 men or more had been assembled, with 2700 around Fredericksburg and on the lower Potomac. At Harpers Ferry the Virginia units mustered 7000 of

---

[51] Captain S. Barron's report, 11 *Calendar Virginia State Papers,* 167–70, gave a much fuller list of these batteries than did Lee's in *O. R.,* 2, 928.

[52] Lee to Mrs. Lee, June 9, 1861; *R. E. Lee, Jr.,* 35.

[53] The commissary and quartermasters' services, for example, on May 31, *O. R.,* 51, part 2, p. 121.

[54] *O. R.,* 51, part 2, p. 124.

[55] *O. R.,* 51, part 2, pp. 134–35.   [56] *O. R.,* 51, part 2, p. 911.

a force that exceeded 8000. All told, approximately 40,000 troops had been enlisted and armed from Virginia and had been supplied with field officers, staff, and partial equipment.[57] Nearly all these soldiers had some lead and powder. A million percussion caps, with 114,400 rounds of infantry ammunition, were to be available in the Virginia laboratory, when delivered to the Confederacy on June 14.[58] One hundred and fifteen field guns had been issued, including twenty batteries of four guns each, harness and caissons complete.[59] The whole mobilization had cost Virginia $3,779,000, including unpaid accounts and claims,[60] and it had been effected in slightly less than eight weeks, during seven of which Lee had been responsible. Thanks largely to Lee's insistence upon a defensive policy, the work had been done without a single major engagement, and with only three brushes, involving some fifty casualties, of whom seven, or thereabouts, had been killed.[61]

The record speaks for itself. "When it is remembered," Lee reported to the governor, "that this body of men were called from a state of profound peace to one of unexpected war, you will have reason to commend the alacrity with which they left their homes and families and prepared themselves for the defense of the State." [62] As an achievement in mobilization it would seem to be without serious error. As a feat in the preparation of a force for service under the conditions of combat prevailing in 1861, it was deficient only in the failure to provide adequate field transportation and in the inability of the state properly to equip the cavalry.

In the larger view of strategy, the disposition of the forces, as

[57] Lee's report, June 15, 1861; O. R., 2, 927–29, and his partial return of troops, May 30, 1861; O. R., 2, 895. To the totals given by Lee in this latter document have been added the troops known to have been dispatched between May 30 and June 8.

[58] Colonel Charles Dimmock's report, 11 Calendar Virginia State Papers, 165–66.

[59] Lee's report, O. R., 2, 928. Governor Letcher continued to have caissons and gun-carriages manufactured after the transfer of Virginia's forces; 11 Calendar Virginia State Papers, 150–51.

[60] 11 Calendar Virginia State Papers, 173; IV O. R., 1, 391–92. Lee's own pay probably was among the unsettled items, for on June 27, 1861, he received a check for $1322.33. This paper is now in the possession of C. S. Hutter of Lynchburg, Va., who gave a photostat of it to Wylie R. Cooke. He in turn presented it to H. R. McIlwaine, former State Librarian of Virginia.

[61] In the evacuation of Alexandria on May 24 (see supra, p. 510), at Fairfax Courthouse on June 1 (O. R., 2, 60), and at Philippi on June 3, 1861 (see supra, p. 519). The casualties cannot be stated with precision, as the number of prisoners taken in Alexandria and at Philippi is nowhere given in exact figures.

[62] O. R., 2, 928.

mobilized, was sound otherwise than as respected western Virginia. Lee doubtless was deceived by the first reassuring reports from that area of disaffection. He probably acted with wisdom in refusing to weaken Harpers Ferry in order to send troops westward along the line of the Baltimore and Ohio, for he might have lost both the column he sent out and Harpers Ferry itself. Limited as his forces were, he had to take chances somewhere. But with the fullest allowance for all these conditions, and with the rough character of the country and the hostility of a large element of the people taken into account, one turns the pages of the correspondence regarding western Virginia with the feeling that the import of the loss of that section was not foreseen, or else that Lee yielded more readily than was his habit to obstacles which were bad enough yet scarcely more serious than others his energy and strategic sense elsewhere overcame.

In effecting the mobilization of Virginia, Lee had hearty encouragement from first to last. Except for the criticisms of Secretary Walker's agent, D. G. Duncan,[63] the records yield no evidence of hostility to Lee or of any lack of co-operation with him. The Richmond press was sympathetic and admiring, or, at worst, refrained at this time from criticism of him. The powerful *Enquirer* and the chatty *Dispatch* were warmly his supporters.[64] "When General Lee assumed the command of affairs here," *The Dispatch* stated editorially, two days before the Virginia forces were transferred to the Confederacy, "everyone knows that our military preparations were in a condition which it makes us shudder to look back upon. But he gave himself, head, heart and soul, to the great work, and so wisely, skillfully and energetically has he used all the resources at his command, that the insolent enemy, notwithstanding his boasted numbers and important possession of the powerful fortress of Old Point, has been held at bay, and compelled to postpone his march of invasion till now we can set him at defiance. We do not pretend that everything has been done which could be done if Gen. Lee had possessed at the start an army of a hundred thousand, or even fifty thousand men; but, bearing in mind the feebleness of our resources, at the beginning,

---

[63] *Cf. supra,* p. 477; *O. R.,* 51, part 2, pp. 39, 54.
[64] *Cf. Richmond Dispatch,* April 30, 1861, p. 2, col. 3, quoting *The Richmond Enquirer. Cf.,* also, *Dispatch,* May 21, 1861, p. 2, col. 1.

in men, arms and munitions of war; remembering that the organization of a large military force is a work of such time and labor that, up to this hour, the Federal government, with all its immense resources of men, means and machinery, has not been able to put itself in position for attack, we may point with honest pride to the position Virginia is now in for defense, and claim that even Gen. Scott with all his boasted military genius and experience, and all the vast resources of his section, has not proved himself as great and efficient a leader as the son of Light Horse Harry, the sagacious, intrepid and high-souled chieftain of Virginia." [65] This was the prevailing opinion and it was expressed formally to the Virginia convention by Governor Letcher in his report on the mobilization. He said: "It is due to truth and justice that I should here record . . . my high appreciation of the industry, judgment and professional skill which has marked the conduct of the distinguished officer who has been called by me, with the unanimous approval of the convention, to conduct the military and naval operations of Virginia." [66] Jubal A. Early, a member of the military committee of the convention, subsequently attested the "active energy and utter abnegation of all personal considerations with which [Lee] devoted himself to the work of organizing and equipping the Virginia troops for the field." [67]

Heavy as were the calls on Lee's energy and patience, during these difficult seven weeks, his strength of body and of character was equal to them. There is a post-bellum tradition that he was something of a "bear" at this time,[68] and it is possible that he did not then have all the imperturbable self-mastery that later elicited the wondering admiration of his subordinates, but there is not an echo in contemporary records of any violent outburst. He arrived early and punctually at his office every morning and methodically transacted business, with a close eye to detail, "but not," Walter Taylor observed, "as is sometimes the concomitant, if not the result of this trait, neglectful of the more important matters dependent upon his decision." He seemed, Colonel Taylor further recorded, "to address himself to the accomplishment of every task that devolved upon him in a conscientious and deliberate

---

[65] *Richmond Dispatch*, June 6, 1861, p. 2, col. 1.
[66] 11 *Calendar Virginia State Papers*, 162.
[67] *Jones*, 2. [68] Gordon in *Riley*, 79.

way, as if he himself was directly accountable to some higher power for the manner in which he performed his duties." [69] Anxious as he was to take the field, and convinced that his stay in Richmond would not be permanent,[70] he met patiently the vexations of office work. Only in his handling of his heavy correspondence was the worry and annoyance of his post manifest to his little staff of aides and clerks. "He did not enjoy writing; indeed, he wrote with labor, and nothing seemed to tax his amiability as much as the necessity for writing a lengthy communication; but he was not satisfied unless at the close of his office hours every matter requiring prompt attention had been disposed of." [71] When the last letter was signed and the last order given in the afternoon, he would take one or two of his official family with him, and would ride out to some camp or fort around Richmond, combining necessary exercise with an inspection. And when he returned it often was to seek out some group of children and to talk with them.[72] No homesickness was discernible in his letters, and there must have been distinct relief for him to know that Mrs. Lee, having left Ravensworth, was at Chantilly, cheerful and reconciled to indefinite absence from Arlington.[73]

He had committed his loved ones, along with his own destiny, his strategy, and his preparations for Virginia's defense, into the hands of a God who was never more personal or more real to him than in those days of a divided nation's insanity. The religious note had become the strongest of his life in the hour when he had cast in his fortune with Virginia and it so remained to his last day. "In God alone must be our trust," he wrote Cassius Lee in a frank avowal that mediation was impossible.[74] Domestic letters contained prayers and self-reproach for ingratitude to God for past mercies.[75] "God's will be done," he said. "We must be resigned." [76] And again: "Be content and resigned to God's will." [77]

[69] Taylor's *General Lee*, 24–25.
[70] Lee to Mrs. Lee, May 25, May 28, 1861; *R. E. Lee, Jr.*, 33, 34.
[71] Taylor's *General Lee*, 25.   [72] Taylor's *General Lee*, 25.
[73] Mrs. Judith McGuire: *Diary of a Southern Refugee* (cited hereafter as *Mrs. McGuire*), 26.
[74] April 25, 1861; *E. J. Lee*, 420.   [75] *R. E. Lee, Jr.*, 29–33, notably 32.
[76] Lee to Mrs. Lee, May 11, 1861; *R. E. Lee, Jr.*, 30.
[77] Lee to Mrs. Lee, May 8, 1861; *R. E. Lee, Jr.*, 30.

"Are you sanguine of results?" a minister asked him in the midst of the intense strain of the first ordeal.

"At present," he answered calmly and with a sincerity that saved his words from any suggestion of cant, "I am not concerned with results. God's will ought to be our aim, and I am quite contented that his designs should be accomplished and not mine." [78]

[78] *Jones,* 143. For his attendance on the opening services of the Episcopal convention, and for his conversation with Bishop Meade, see *R. E. Lee, Jr.,* 31, and Jones, *L. and L.,* 142.

CHAPTER XXXI

THE WAR OPENS ON THREE VIRGINIA FRONTS

AN empty title was left Lee when the Virginia forces were transferred to the Confederate States on June 8, 1861, an empty title and a non-existent command. The regiments raised under his care were now subject to the direction of the War Department. The staff he had called into being with so much labor ceased to function. For the moment he seems almost to have forgotten that he was a brigadier general in the regular army of the Confederacy, subject to call at any time.[1] The distaste for a public life that he occasionally felt in a period of uncertainty showed itself again: "I do not know what my position will be," he confided to Mrs. Lee. "I should like to retire to private life, if I could be with you and the children, but if I can be of any service to the state or her cause, I must continue."[2] He told Maury, in terms less particular, that he did not know "where he was." Maury commented: "You may rely on it, the Confederate States government has come here feeling that there is between it and us something of antagonism." It was Maury's private opinion that Davis did not like Lee.[3]

Considering that inquiry would smack immodestly of place-hunting, Lee had no intention of asking about his status,[4] and the President had not thought to discuss it with him when, on June 10, there came news of something approaching a battle at Big Bethel, eight miles northwest of Newport News. Major General Benjamin F. Butler had planned a surprise attack on a troublesome Confederate outpost of Magruder's command, but one of his regiments, becoming confused, fired into another and

---

[1] *Jones*, 168. There seems to be no foundation for the story, quoted by Jones, that Lee considered enlisting in the cavalry, in the belief that he would not be assigned other duty.

[2] Letter of June 8, 1861; *R. E. Lee, Jr.*, 35.

[3] M. F. Maury to unnamed correspondent, June 11, 1861; C. L. Lewis: *Matthew Fontaine Maury*, 146.

[4] *Cf.* 1 *Davis*, 309.

had given the alarm. A force of some 1400 Confederates met the poorly organized attack of seven Federal regiments and drove them back, inflicting seventy-six casualties, including one major and the youthful Lieutenant Colonel John T. Greble, who had been one of Lee's cadets at West Point. By good chance, some of the Parrott guns purchased by Virginia in 1860 had been sent to Magruder and had been in battery at Big Bethel. They had given the Confederates a definite advantage. Although it could not have happened precisely so anywhere else in Virginia, the hurriedly mobilized Confederate forces at Big Bethel actually had seemed better equipped than had the Union troops whose government had full access to the markets of the world. This little action, involving the loss of only eight Confederate soldiers,[5] naturally encouraged the South, but it was evidence that the Federals were prepared to take the offensive on the lower Peninsula. And as Magruder's position was by no means secure against combined attack by land and water, he had to be strengthened. To this task Lee was assigned immediately. Dispatching congratulations to Magruder,[6] he counselled that officer and the President concerning the defense of the Peninsula and the fortification of the James, precisely as if the responsibility were still Virginia's alone. More troops and more heavy guns were forwarded, defects in the line in front of Williamsburg were corrected, the small steamer *Teazer* was assigned to scout duty on the lower James, and the batteries along that river were improved, somewhat contrary to Magruder's judgment and according to Lee's plans. Magruder, who was wise enough to anticipate a long contest, logically acquiesced, and very industriously prepared his command for emergencies and even embodied some of the militia.[7]

Operations on the Peninsula were closely bound up with those around Norfolk and on the Rappahannock. In the course of a few days, and without any formal written orders, Lee was directing the defense of eastern Virginia, including Richmond, while the War Department and the President in person took over the preparation of the forces at Harpers Ferry and Manassas Junction

---

[5] For the reports, see *O. R.*, 2, 77 ff.   [6] *O. R.*, 2, 925.
[7] *O. R.*, 2, 930, 931, 935, 936, 939, 970–71, 972, 975, 977, 979; *O. R.*, 51, part 2, pp. 139, 141, 144, 149, 174–75, 185–86, 191–92.

for the attacks that manifestly were in the making. Western Virginia remained in some sense a charge both on Davis and on Lee, but the latter was authorized to carry on correspondence with Garnett and to receive that officer's reports.[8]

Much of the now-familiar routine was resumed. Lee expedited the construction of the system of earthworks that Colonel Talcott had designed for Richmond,[9] and he undertook some defenses for the Rappahannock River also, having become a bit more apprehensive of possible offensive movements there.[10] The probability of an attack on Norfolk he kept constantly in mind as he steadily built up its garrison and the forces on the Nansemond.[11] In a short time the Norfolk line, completed and fully armed, was held by six regiments of infantry, one of cavalry, and five companies of artillery, in addition to the naval units.[12] Besides all this, Lee charged himself with equipping and bringing into the field the thousands of Virginia troops who had not been ready for transfer on June 8, and were now to be mustered directly into the Confederate service.[13] As late as the spring of 1862 he occasionally acted as commander of the Virginia forces in matters of enlistment and organization.[14] In the intervals between other assignments Lee drew up his report, as of June 15, on the mobilization of Virginia. Governor Letcher forwarded it to the convention on June 17.[15] There was, of course, no vainglory in this document. It was simple and concise. Its only line of praise was for those who had responded quickly to the call of their state. Its only expression of regret was that the western counties had not supplied their quota of men.

Daily, after June 15, Lee's duties were enlarged, though they were not defined. Jealous as was President Davis of his prerogatives, and instant as was his resentment of all interference, he made the most, in frequent conferences, of Lee's abilities and of his exact knowledge of conditions in Virginia.[16] Soon Lee was in one sense an acting assistant Secretary of War and in another

[8] Lee to Garnett, July 1, 1861; O. R., 2, 239.
[9] O. R., 2, 851, 864, 926; O. R., 51, part 2, pp. 161, 163–64.
[10] O. R., 2, 932, 941, 978–79, 1003.   [11] O. R., 2, 919, 928–29, 993, 997.
[12] O. R., 51, part 2, pp. 164–66. The totals given in the text were reached by July 12.
[13] Lee to Mrs. Lee, July 12, 1861; R. E. Lee, Jr., 36.
[14] Cf. infra (vol. II, p. 27).
[15] O. R., 2, 927–29; Doc. 23, Virginia Convention of 1861.
[16] Taylor's Four Years, 15; R. E. Lee, Jr., 34; cf. Mrs. Chesnut, 83.

sense deputy chief of the general staff, to borrow a later military term, for Davis at this period of the war was his own chief of the general staff. Fortunately for Lee, though his own military family had changed somewhat in personnel, it was still adequate to serve him in the discharge of his miscellaneous duties. Colonel Garnett's Virginia commission had been vacated, but he had been named a brigadier general when sent to western Virginia. Walter Taylor had been retained as a first lieutenant in the regular army of the Confederacy. In Garnett's place had come Lieutenant Colonel R. H. Chilton, with whom Lee had served in Texas. Colonel Deas still worked at Lee's headquarters when not engaged in making inspections, and Colonel Washington remained on duty.[17]

Taken as a whole, the work was both difficult and uncongenial. Although Lee discharged it cheerfully, of course, he desired to be sent on duty with troops and hoped that assignment in Richmond would be brief. "My movements are very uncertain," he wrote Mrs. Lee on June 24, "and I wish to take the field as soon as certain arrangements can be made. I may go at any moment, and to any point where it may be necessary." [18]

There were ample reasons why Lee could not be certain whither he would be sent. Apart from Hampton Roads and Tidewater Virginia, a sudden blow might be struck in northern or in western Virginia by a secret concentration. It had been ascertained that the force which had occupied Grafton and had driven Porterfield from Philippi was part of an army commanded by Major General George B. McClellan, Lee's young associate of the Mexican War. The forces gathering at Chambersburg and manifestly intended for the occupation of the valley of Virginia, were under Major General Robert Patterson, now sixty-nine years of age. Lee remembered him well, of course, as leader of a division of Scott's army at the battle of Cerro Gordo. The largest army of all, mustering in Washington and on the south bank of the Potomac, had at its head Brigadier General Irvin McDowell, who, during the autumn of 1846, had been with Lee in the advance of General

---

[17] *Taylor's General Lee,* 23; *Cocke MSS.,* June 10, 1861. Chilton had resigned as colonel of cavalry in the provisional army of Virginia to accept a commission in the Adjutant General's department, C. S. A.; *O. R.,* 51, part 2, p. 95; 11 *Calendar Virginia State Papers,* 116, 137.

[18] *R. E. Lee, Jr.,* 36.

Wool's column. McClellan could march against Garnett and the head of the Shenandoah Valley, or he could, with equal readiness, reinforce Patterson in front of Harpers Ferry and at the lower end of the valley. Patterson, controlling the central army, could join either McClellan or McDowell. In front of Manassas Junction, McDowell might crush Beauregard or, if bold, might extend his right wing and unite in joint operations with Patterson. The general plan of the Federals, as seen from Richmond, was well conceived and was to be undertaken where the presence of mountains and the absence of railroads would deprive the Confederates of much of the advantage of the inner lines.

The next move on this long northern and western front came at Harpers Ferry, where General Johnston continued as pessimistic as ever of his prospects, though the administration again assured him of its desire to hold the place as long as practicable.[19] On June 13 the Federals made a raid on Romney, fifty-five miles west of Harpers Ferry. The troops engaged in this advance belonged to Patterson's army and they returned quickly into Maryland,[20] but they were assumed by Johnston to be the vanguard of McClellan's forces, moving to a junction with Patterson.[21] Johnston accordingly evacuated Harpers Ferry and took position at Bunker Hill, twelve miles from Winchester on the main road from Hagerstown into the valley. "The want of ammunition," he explained, "has rendered me very timid."[22] From that locality he carried on a lively correspondence with the War Department —he anxious to get more men, more ammunition, additional cavalry support, and better officers, the President very insistent that the valley be not exposed to a Federal advance, and that Johnston remain where he could co-operate quickly with Beauregard in case either his command or the army at Manassas Junction was attacked by superior forces.[23] On July 2, General Patterson crossed the Potomac, and on the 3d drove in Johnston's outposts

---

[19] *O. R.,* 2, 923–25.
[20] Report of Colonel Lew Wallace, *O. R.,* 2, 123.
[21] Johnston's report, *O. R.,* 2, 471.   [22] *O. R.,* 2, 934.
[23] *O. R.,* 2, 935, 937, 940, 945, 948–49, 963. For the promotion of T. J. Jackson to the rank of brigadier general, see *ibid.,* 963. The army on July 4 was styled "The Army of the Shenandoah," *ibid.,* 963. For an ordinance authorizing a loan of $125,000 for the construction of a railroad from Strasburg to Winchester, if Lee deemed it a military necessity, see *Ordinances* [of the Virginia Convention of 1861] *Passed at the Adjourned Session,* 49–50.

and occupied Martinsburg.[24] There he halted, anu there he stayed. Daily expecting an attack, Johnston called out two brigades of militia and asked for the loan of 6000 or 7000 men from Beauregard's army.[25] Johnston was then of opinion that Patterson was receiving 7000 to 8000 reinforcements and he had no intimation of the fact that Patterson actually was threatened with the loss of a large part of his command because of the expiration of the term of enlistment of many ninety-day volunteers.[26] Davis, in reply to Johnston's request for more men, listed the calls being made for troops at Norfolk, on the Peninsula, at Manassas, and in western Virginia, and once more explained to Johnston how the whole of the Shenandoah Valley would be exposed and the army cut off from Richmond if Patterson were not halted.[27] In this correspondence with Johnston, Lee had little part, for Johnston seemed resentful of orders from Lee and was inclined to be censorious in his dealings with him.[28]

Meantime the situation in northwestern Virginia grew ominous. Prior to the surprise of Porterfield's force at Philippi on June 3, Lee had frankly stated that the situation in front of Manassas Gap and elsewhere in Virginia was such that he could not do more to support the force in the northwestern part of the state than to forward arms and to authorize the raising of volunteers.[29] After Porterfield had been driven out and Garnett had been sent to relieve him, Lee forwarded three regiments of infantry for Garnett's immediate reinforcement. Other troops were to be sent as soon as available. Garnett had studied the situation closely and had reported that the enemy showed no disposition to advance beyond Philippi. Beyond that point the Federals were not known to be in great force. In every other respect the situation had been discouraging. On his arrival at Huttonsville, thirty-one miles south of Philippi on June 14, Garnett had found only twenty-three companies of infantry, and these, he had reported, were "in a miserable condition as to arms, clothing, equip-

---

[24] O. R., 2, 157.
[25] O. R., 2, 967, 969.
[26] O. R., 2, 158 ff.
[27] O. R., 2, 974, 977.
[28] O. R., 2, 945, 948, 956, 959–60, 962.
[29] O. R., 2, 254. For various opinions on the situation in northwest Virginia, appeals to its people, and plans for its relief, see 11 Calendar Virginia State Papers, 150, 152–53, 179; O. R., 2, 918, 944, 951, 974–75; O. R., 51, part 2, pp. 142–43, 167–68; Ordinances Passed at the Adjourned Session, 51–52.

ment, instruction and discipline." [80] Still, he had regimented these troops immediately, had pushed forward with them, and, with a single battery, had occupied the passes on Rich Mountain and Laurel Hill. These were considered the most important positions in that part of the commonwealth, because they were crossed by the main highways leading from the Baltimore and Ohio. When Garnett, on June 25, had forwarded his first detailed report to Lee, explaining his difficulties, he had stated that the majority of the people were opposed to the South and that it was almost impossible to get accurate information concerning the position of the enemy. He had discussed, however, the possibilities of attacking and destroying the Cheat River bridge, on the Baltimore and Ohio, fifty miles away, and had seemed in no wise alarmed at the outlook.[31] By July 1 his little force had not mounted above 4500 effectives, and Garnett had felt compelled to ask for further reinforcements. Only twenty-three volunteers had come in, he had said; no hope could be entertained of any real accretion of strength from the country round about. If he was to hold the passes he had to keep 2000 men there, and this reduced his mobile force to 2500. Some help might be afforded, he had thought, if General Wise, who had been in the valley of the Kanawha with a newly formed "Legion," would march against Parkersburg.[32] Before the receipt of this appeal Lee had sent one more regiment to Garnett, and on hearing more fully of the situation he had directed two others to be forwarded under the command of able professional soldiers.[33]

After fortifying the mountain passes Garnett underwent a change of opinion as to the outlook. On July 5 he reported that he did not believe the enemy would attack him, primarily because he supposed the Federals had occupied as much of northwest Virginia as they could want. He questioned whether it was worth while to maintain a large force where its function would inevitably be negative, inasmuch as there was no probability that he would have enough men at his disposal to assume the offensive.[34] Lee did not take this optimistic view. "I do not think it probable," he wrote on receipt of Garnett's dispatch, "that the

[80] O. R., 2, 236. [81] O. R., 2, 237–38. [82] O. R., 2, 239–40.
[83] O. R., 2, 240. [84] O. R., 2, 241–42.

enemy will confine himself to that portion of the northwest country which he now holds, but, if he can drive you back, will endeavor to penetrate as far as Staunton. Your object will be to prevent him, if possible, and to restrict his limits within the narrowest range, which, although outnumbered, it is hoped by skill and boldness you will accomplish." [35]

This warning never reached Garnett. Two days before it was written General McClellan arrived in front of Rich Mountain. His communications were well covered by an ample force, and his dispositions were admirably made. The absence of anything even approaching an intelligence service on the Confederate side enabled McClellan to advance with all the elements of surprise. Rich Mountain pass was defended by a small force under Lieutenant Colonel John Pegram. Garnett held the pass to the northward on Laurel Hill. Deliberately employing the strategy that Lee had helped to develop in Mexico, McClellan planned and executed another Cerro Gordo. [36] General W. S. Rosecrans found an unguarded path to the crest of Rich Mountain, stormed the battery there on July 11 and opened the road for McClellan, who advanced rapidly to Beverly on the 12th. Garnett, finding his flank turned by the capture of Rich Mountain, attempted to withdraw from Laurel Hill, but was pursued. In a rearguard action on the 13th he was cut off and killed at Carrick's Ford, on Shivers fork of Cheat River. Pegram and part of his command were captured the same day. The remainder of his force precipitately withdrew over successive strong positions to Monterey, thirty-five miles southeast of Beverly. [37]

The defeat was complete and might have been serious if McClellan had pursued, for Monterey was only some twenty miles from the railroad that led directly to Staunton, which was itself distant by road about forty miles from Monterey. Three days' hard marching might have carried McClellan to the heart of the Shenandoah Valley. No serious resistance could have been offered. The Confederate casualties had not fallen much short

[35] O. R., 2, 242.

[36] McClellan to E. D. Townsend, July 5; O. R., 2, 198: "If possible, I will repeat the maneuver of Cerro Gordo."

[37] The reports are in O. R., 2, 194 ff. The more important are McClellan, p. 205; Rosecrans, p. 214; H. W. Benham, p. 222; H. R. Jackson, p. 247; J. M. Heck, p. 254; Jed Hotchkiss, p. 261; John Pegram, p. 264; W. C. Scott, p. 273, and W. B. Taliaferro, p. 285. Cf. H. W. Benham: Recollections of the West Virginia Campaign, 683 ff.

of 1000, and most of the survivors were demoralized and scattered.[38] General Scott, however, had been afraid McClellan would outrun his communications and had cautioned him against advancing too far.[39] McClellan obeyed orders.

First news of the disaster reached Richmond on July 14, and created the greater distress because troops from the capital had been engaged in the operations.[40] The extent of the reverse was magnified by McClellan's rhetorical congratulations to his troops. Most Southerners believed the triumph of Northern arms as great as McClellan represented it.[41] Lee's first move was to urge that the strong position at Cheat Mountain, five miles in rear of Beverly, should be held, not knowing that it had already been evacuated.[42] His next step was to order the quasi-independent columns of Wise and Floyd to support the defeated little army.[43] Thereafter he hurried troops forward and placed General W. W. Loring in temporary command, with instructions to cling to the mountain passes, to protect the railroad, and to organize a counter offensive as soon as he thought proper.[44] Lee had overtaxed even his iron endurance during the strains of those difficult July weeks, but he would have gone at once in person to attempt to redeem the evil day had not President Davis desired him to remain in Richmond, in view of the imminence of a hard battle in front of Manassas.[45]

On that sector Beauregard had been receiving further reinforcements, and had organized his forces into brigades, which, unknown to President Davis, he had placed somewhat in advance of the position that Lee had selected for defense.[46] On July 14, the very day that the first reports of Garnett's defeat had reached Richmond, James Chesnut, Jr., a South Carolina member of the Confederate Congress, came down from Manassas with a plan for

---

[38] Cf. H. R. Jackson, O. R., 2, 181–82. [39] O. R., 2, 201–2.
[40] O. R., 2, 245; De Leon, 114–15.
[41] For an early hostile critique of McClellan's campaign, see Charles W. Hill: Comments on Major-General McClellan's Account of His West Virginia Campaign.
[42] O. R., 2, 245, 254. [43] O. R., 2, 981.
[44] Long, 112; O. R., 2, 986. For reports on the situation, troop movements, etc., see ibid., 987, 988–89, 989, 992, 993, 994, 995, 996, 997.
[45] Lee to Mrs. Lee, July 11, July 27, 1861; R. E. Lee, Jr., 36, 37.
[46] O. R., 2, 901, 917, 943–44, 946, 947, 969; O. R., 51, part 2, p. 136. For a controversy between President Davis and Governor Letcher, regarding the appointment of militia officers called out in the emergency, see IV O. R., 1, 419–20; O. R., 51, part 2, p. 169.

the consideration of Mr. Davis. The President was sick with one of the recurring attacks that almost blinded and paralyzed him, but he immediately called a conference to which he summoned General Lee and Adjutant General Cooper. When they came together, in the parlor of the Spotswood Hotel, Mr. Chesnut proceeded to outline, from brief notes, a grandiose strategic plan that Beauregard had directed him to submit for approval. Beauregard, he said, was of opinion that the Federals would have two lines of advance southward from the Washington defenses—one to threaten the force at Manassas, and the other to cut the communications with Johnston. That done, the Federals would be able to force Beauregard to fight at a disadvantage. Consequently, Beauregard proposed that Johnston should lend him 20,000 troops, with which force he would attack and defeat McDowell in front of Fairfax Courthouse. Next, he would detach 10,000 of his men to reinforce Johnston in overwhelming Patterson near Winchester. With Patterson destroyed, Garnett would be given sufficient troops to crush McClellan. Then Johnston and Garnett would march into Maryland and attack Washington from the rear, while Beauregard assailed the capital from the South.[47]

Davis and Lee opposed this plan on obvious grounds: it involved impossible concentration; it assumed Garnett and Johnston were much stronger than they actually were; it took for granted that the enemy would fight a superior force in front of Washington instead of retiring within the fortifications of the city; and, finally, it postulated a continuing offensive power the Confederate forces would not possess after so much marching and fighting.[48] The whole scheme was so impractical that probably neither the President nor Lee would have remembered it had not Beauregard subsequently brought it up in his report on First Manassas.[49] In discussing the situation, however, Davis and Lee again considered the plan previously formulated for co-ordinated action by Beauregard and Johnston. At the time of the conference the President did not consider that McDowell had sufficiently developed his purpose to justify an order for Johnston's withdrawal from the valley. The blow, as he then saw the

[47] O. R., 2, 506–7.   [48] Davis's comment, O. R., 2, 505; Lee's, ibid., 515.
[49] O. R., 2, 485. Beauregard held to the feasibility of this plan. Cf. Roman, 1, 87.

situation, might as readily fall in the valley as at Manassas. The practical and all-important problem was that of so timing the march of Beauregard or of Johnston, as the offensive might require, as not to jeopardize the other.[50]

What followed was under the personal direction of the President, rather than of Lee. On the 17th, Beauregard reported his outposts attacked and called for reinforcements from Johnston and also from General T. H. Holmes, who was commanding at Fredericksburg.[51] Davis promptly ordered Johnston to go to Beauregard's help, if practicable.[52] Receiving this order at 1 A.M. on July 18, Johnston set out as soon as he could dispose of his sick, and at noon on the 20th arrived at Manassas with the van of his army.[53] Meantime, from Richmond and from Lynchburg every company that the railroads could transport was hurried forward by Davis.[54] It was currently believed in the capital that the last disposable troops around the city had been moved to the front where, by this time, the whole South knew the first great battle of the war was about to be fought.[55]

Lee's anxiety over the situation was apparent to all his visitors.[56] He of course wished to go to Manassas, but Davis considered it more important that he remain in Richmond.[57] On Sunday morning, July 21, a very clear and mild day,[58] President Davis found himself unable to endure the inaction he felt compelled to enjoin upon Lee. Taking a special train for the scene of the battle he left Lee to wait and to agonize. Private messages received during the forenoon told of minor advantages on either side. Then came several hours without authentic news, when rumor did its worst with wild tales of a Confederate *débâcle* and a victorious Federal march on Richmond. After dark fell the official dispatches began to trickle in. Presently this one arrived:

Manassas, July 21, 1861.

We have won a glorious though dear-bought victory. Night closed on the enemy in full flight and closely pursued.

JEFFERSON DAVIS.[59]

[50] Lee in *O. R.*, 2, 515.
[52] *O. R.*, 2, 473; text of order, *ibid.*, 478.
[54] *O. R.*, 2, 981, 983.
[56] *D. H. Maury*, 143.
[58] *Miss Brock,* 63.

[51] *O. R.*, 2, 439.
[53] *O. R.*, 2, 473.
[55] *De Leon*, 121.
[57] *R. E. Lee, Jr.*, 37; *Jones*, 384.
[59] *O. R.*, 2, 986.

All the suspense of a frantic city broke into wild rejoicing at this news, only to be checked quickly by consciousness of heavy losses and curiosity for more details.[60] By midnight Lee knew—and all Richmond knew—that after the battle had virtually been lost, the last belated units of Johnston's force had arrived on the overtaxed little railroad, had rushed into action at the right moment on a wavering front, and had precipitated a Federal retreat that soon became a mad rout. The first men to reach Richmond from Manassas, "splashed and muddy hospital stewards and quartermaster's men, who wanted more stretchers and instruments, more torniquets and stimulants," [61] brought wild tales of carnage in the ranks and staggering losses in the high command. Richmond listened, wide-eyed and speechless. Only the sluggish could sleep while apprehension for the safety of sons and joy over the triumph of Southern arms contested for the mastery of excited minds. The next day, rainy and with a heavy, cooling wind, brought more details of the victory, but only a few men came back from Manassas who had shared in the decisive phase of the battle. Not until the 23rd did the tired President return, bringing with him the bodies of the leaders who had been killed in action. He spoke to the crowd from the Spotswood Hotel and described what had happened. An hour later, in a torrential rain, the first ambulance train rolled in with a groan, and Richmond came to herself, at last, in caring for the wounded.[62]

It was the first time in Lee's life that he had experienced the anguish of a battle from afar. His relief was greater, perhaps, and his emotions came more completely to the surface than in any other crisis of the war. "I almost wept for joy," he wrote Johnston, "at the glorious victory achieved by our brave troops. The feeling of my heart could hardly be repressed on learning the brilliant share you had in its achievement." [63] To Beauregard he said, "I cannot express the joy I feel at the brilliant victory of the 21st. The skill, courage, and endurance displayed by yourself excite my highest admiration. You and your troops have the

---

[60] *Long*, 109; *Miss Brock*, 63; *De Leon*, 122.
[61] *De Leon*, 123.
[62] *De Leon*, 125.
[63] Undated letter, quoted in *White*, 113.

gratitude of the whole country." [64] To Mrs. Lee he opened his heart:

"That indeed was a glorious victory and has lightened the pressure upon our front amazingly. Do not grieve for the brave dead. Sorrow for those they left behind—friends, relatives, and families. The former are at rest. The latter must suffer. The battle will be repeated there in greater force. I hope God will again smile on us and strengthen our hearts and arms. I wished to partake in the former struggle, and am mortified at my absence, but the President thought it more important I should be here. I could not have done as well as has been done, but I could have helped, and taken part in the struggle for my home and neighborhood. So the work is done I care not by whom it is done." [65]

His part in the victory was hardly less than if he had been present. The combined forces of Beauregard and Johnston had included forty-one full and two incomplete regiments, and three battalions of infantry; two regiments, one battalion, and ten independent companies of cavalry; one battalion and nine separate batteries of light artillery; and one militia battalion with heavy artillery—a total of 35,207 men.[66] Of this army, eight regiments of infantry, two regiments of cavalry, two incomplete regiments of infantry, six field batteries, the heavy artillery, and an indeterminable part of independent cavalry companies were Virginian. They constituted something more than a fourth of the army, and had, in every instance, been raised and put in the field under Lee's direction, within less than three months. General Early was within the facts, probably, when he stated eleven years afterwards, "but for the capacity and energy displayed by General Lee in organizing and equipping troops to be sent to the front, our army would not have been in a condition to gain the first victory

[64] Letter of July 24, 1861, quoted in *White*, 113.
[65] Letter of July 27, 1861; *R. E. Lee, Jr.*, 37.
[66] These are the figures given in R. M. Johnston: *Bull Run*, 110. He credited Beauregard with 24, 240. Beauregard's return, as of July 21, 1861, though dated Sept. 25, 1861, showed 21,863 (*O. R.*, 2, 568). R. M. Johnston estimated McDowell's strength at around 30,000, exclusive of about 6000 in the Washington defenses (*op. cit.*, 98). In the gross Confederate totals are included all the troops arriving at Manassas during the course of July 21.

at Manassas." [67] Lee was responsible, also, for the selection of the line taken up by Beauregard,[68] and it had been his military judgment, together with that of General Cocke, which had dictated the concentration at Manassas Junction. In large part, also, he fashioned the strategy of a junction between Johnston and Beauregard, though this was a move so manifestly desirable that it must have suggested itself to all who studied the situation in June and July. The doubtful consideration was not *whether* the one force should join the other, but *when;* and here it was the President who made the decision and consequently deserves the credit.

The public, however, did not reflect on the preparation that had made victory possible. It saw only the victory itself, and the men who had achieved it. Beauregard became as popular in Virginia as he had been in South Carolina or in Louisiana. Johnston took the place that Lee had occupied in the affection of Virginia people. The circumstances that had denied Lee a share in the battle of Manassas—the very service that had given him such knowledge of the military situation as to make him indispensable in Richmond prior to the battle—now operated to lower his prestige. The next unlucky turn of the wheel was to destroy that prestige altogether and was to bring him an unpopularity that might readily have ended his military career before his great opportunity came.

[67] Quoted in *Jones,* 2.
[68] *Cf.* Davis, in *O. R.,* 2, 504: "Bull Run, the position previously selected by General Lee."

CHAPTER XXXII

LEE DISCLOSES A WEAKNESS

ON the morning of July 28, 1861, Lee started from Richmond to perform his first field duty for the Confederacy. It was not an impressive departure. No commissaries or quartermasters attended him. His only military companions were Colonel Washington and Captain Taylor. He had no more than two private attendants, Meredith, his cook, a Negro from the White House plantation, and Perry, another Negro, who had been employed in the dining room at Arlington and was now acting as Lee's body servant. Except for his horses, his baggage was of the smallest proportions. The only recorded part of it was a simple mess kit of tin, destined to serve him until after Appomattox.[1] Many a brigadier, starting for the front, had a far larger *entourage* and a more ostentatious leave-taking. If any of the family came to see Lee off, it was Custis, for Mrs. Lee, Robert, and the girls were visiting friends, and Rooney's cavalry was in the Allegheny Mountains.[2]

It was not precisely to the command of an army that Lee was going. He had no written instructions. As the President's confidential military adviser, still in titular command of all the Confederate forces in the Old Dominion, he was being sent to western Virginia, where Garnett had fallen and where small, separate commands were feebly struggling to prevent a Federal advance. His mission was to co-ordinate rather than to command—not to direct operations in person but to see if rivalries could not be suppressed and united effort against the enemy assured.[3] The nature of his assignment had been correctly reported in at least

---

[1] *R. E. Lee, Jr.*, 37, 41, 50; *Taylor's Four Years*, 36.
[2] J. V. Drake: *Life of General Robert Hatton* (cited hereafter as *Drake's Hatton*), 372.
[3] Davis to J. E. Johnston, Aug. 1, 1861; *O. R.*, 5, 767; *ibid.*, 828–29; *Taylor's Four Years*, 16; *Brock*, 194. It was later believed in the Lee family that the command in western Virginia had been offered General Joseph E. Johnston and had been declined by him (*Fitz Lee*, 116). The writer has found no record of this.

one newspaper,[4] but it was not generally understood by the public. The assumption that he was directly in command led the public to expect great achievements of him, but the fact that immediate charge of the troops was not entrusted to him by the President made such achievements almost impossible. Authority and responsibility were divided, with the usual disastrous results. So much trouble could have been avoided if he had temporarily been assigned to command the scattered units in western Virginia that it is difficult to say why this was not done. Perhaps President Davis did not wish Lee formally detached; perhaps he felt that Lee's known tact could best be employed if he appeared on the scene to counsel all the general officers in western Virginia and not to supersede any of the touchy individuals who were exercising semi-independent command in the mountains. The Confederate authorities, in July, 1861, had not developed the courage to deal bluntly with men of this stamp, but proceeded cautiously in an effort to preserve the complete unity of the South. In this instance the welfare of the forces was subordinated to the ambitions of the leaders. It was to prove a costly concession to pride.

As far as Gordonsville, Lee's journey lay along the route he had followed when he had come to Richmond from Alexandria on that memorable 22d of May. West of Gordonsville he continued on the Virginia Central Railroad by way of Charlottesville to Staunton, where he detrained on the evening of July 28. He knew, of course, that he was not making a tour of an army possessed of the proud confidence that Johnston and Beauregard's men felt, now that they had achieved a victory at Bull Run. A measure of demoralization he anticipated. A lack of equipment he was certain to find, because he had learned that some blundering quartermaster had forwarded to General T. J. Jackson at Winchester certain essential supplies intended for General H. R. Jackson at Monterey.[5]

From the hour he arrived at Staunton, however, Lee encountered a state of affairs unlike anything he had ever seen in war. Into the quiet valley town had rolled the backwash of Garnett's

---

[4] *Richmond Examiner,* July 31, 1861, p. 3, cols. 3 and 4: ". . . a tour to the West, looking after the commands of Generals Loring and Wise. . . . His visit is understood to be one of inspection, and consultation on the plan of campaign."
[5] *O. R.,* 2, 993.

little command—men whose zeal for war had been quickly dampened by contact with its dirty, bloody realities, ragged men, hungry men, the sick and the road-worn. One Georgia regiment, shattered in the mountains, had straggled back in such utter despair that its bewildered colonel had granted all its men a furlough without consulting his superiors. General Loring, who had preceded Lee a few days on his way to the army, had countermanded all the furloughs and had put the baffled colonel under arrest, but had been very doubtful of his ability to get the men together again.[6] It was not soldiery that Lee saw at Staunton; it was panic exhausted in paralysis.

With the detachment of mind he always sought to cultivate, Lee did not let himself think solely of these things as, on the morning of July 29, he left Staunton and started on horseback for Monterey. "A part of the road, as far as Buffalo Gap, I passed over in the summer of 1840, on my return to St. Louis, after bringing you home," Lee wrote his wife. "If any one had then told me that the next time I traveled that road would have been on my present errand, I should have supposed him insane. I enjoyed the mountains, as I rode along. The views are magnificent—the valleys so beautiful, the scenery so peaceful. What a glorious world Almighty God has given us. How thankless and ungrateful we are, and how we labour to mar his gifts."[7]

There was rain that first day, but it did not delay him. He regarded it simply as an incident of the journey and not as an omen of what lay ahead. At Monterey, a little village in Highland County, ten miles east of the principal ridge of the Allegheny Mountains, he came to the headquarters of Brigadier General Henry R. Jackson of Georgia, commander on that part of the front. A strange fortune it was that brought such a man into so precipitous a wilderness. For Judge Jackson was a Yale graduate, an art lover, a poet, an ex-judge and former United States minister to Austria. Not long before the war, when still under forty, he had declined the chancellorship of the University of Georgia. The people of Savannah had elected him to the Confederate Congress, but as he had served as the youthful colonel of the First Georgia Volunteers during the Mexican War, he had

---

[6] *O. R.*, 2, 999.   [7] Letter of Aug. 4, 1861; *R. E. Lee, Jr.*, 39.

felt that he should enter the army.[8] With a brigadier's commission, he had brought Georgia troops to western Virginia just before Garnett had been defeated. As the senior officer of the reserve, he had been forced to take charge of operations at a time when the Confederate forces had been in chaos, with every prospect of a quick Federal pursuit to the Virginia Central Railroad. General Jackson would have been far more at ease if he had been asked to translate an obscure passage in an Horatian ode, or if he had been called upon to draft a diplomatic note in the most precise Continental style; but, in a new capacity and in an unfamiliar country, he had kept his head, had used his strong, native intelligence, and had made in the crises what were, all things considered, probably the best dispositions possible with the small force at hand. Although he had acted with decision, Jackson had displayed unusual modesty. He had urged that Lee come in person to western Virginia and he had suggested that a man of greater military experience than himself be placed in direct command.[9] Those of the troops that had not shared in Garnett's campaign— only two regiments at the outset—were in good condition. So were the reinforcements that were now coming up from Staunton, under orders issued after the disaster at Carrick's Ford. But many of the survivors of Garnett's command, as Lee had already seen, were in a pitiable plight, "without tents or camp equipage, and with but the clothing on their backs, the horses of the artillery and cavalry jaded and galled."[10] After their escape from the enemy their recovery of morale was slow. Added to their other miseries was an epidemic of measles, a malady that went hard with the soldiers from the rural districts of the South, most of whom had escaped it in childhood. Fever debilitated many that escaped the measles. Hospital facilities were too crude for classification. The soldiers who kept their health were wet and dejected, for the rain that Lee had encountered on the ride from Staunton had been falling steadily since July 22.[11]

Some of the younger officers, like Rooney Lee and Edward

8 C. M. H., 6, 426 ff.   9 O. R., 51, 2, 182.
10 O. R., 2, 998. Cf. ibid., 989 and O. R., 51, 2, 181.
11 O. R., 2, 989; Taylor's Four Years, 17. Lee stated subsequently that the rains began on July 24, but they started two days earlier. For the effect of the measles on the troops, see Richard Taylor: Destruction and Reconstruction (cited hereafter as R. Taylor), 23, and Surgeon General S. P. Moore's report in IV O. R., 1, 694.

544

Johnson, were already displaying the high promise they later
fulfilled, but many of the others were a shock and perhaps a disillusionment to Lee. Instead of trained soldiers who could be
relied upon to understand orders and to obey them promptly, he
found that the tools of command were zealous and patriotic
enough, but were men to whom everything had to be explained,
men who took their time to follow instructions, apparently unconscious that the very life of the army, much less its military
success, depended upon precision. "It is so difficult," Lee wrote
his wife, "to get our untrained people to comprehend and
promptly execute the measures required for the occasion." [12]

The feebleness of the army seemed all the worse when measured against the assumed strength of the enemy. And the strength
of the enemy was increased by the geographical position he then
occupied in that forbidding land. The Confederates had advanced
westward from the Virginia Central and from the Virginia and
Tennessee Railroads. The Federals had moved to the occupation
of the disputed section of the Old Dominion eastward from the
Kanawha River and southeastward from the line of the Baltimore
and Ohio. The two forces had come together on the watershed
of the Allegheny Mountains, an imposing range that runs northeast and southwest through the whole of Virginia. The contest
was for the mountain passes and the roads that wound through
them.

On the northern part of the front, where Lee then was, the
range was divided, from east to west, into four principal chains
of mountains, the Alleghenies, strictly so-called, Greenbrier Mountain, Cheat Mountain, and Rich Mountain. The distance from the
crest of the Alleghenies to the top of Cheat Mountain was fifteen
miles. These heights were traversed by one of the historic highways
of Virginia, the Staunton-Parkersburg turnpike, which joined the
two towns its name hyphenated. The strongest of the passes through
which this road ran was that on Cheat Mountain, where there was a
long crossing at an elevation in excess of 3500 feet, easily swept
by artillery on the summit. The first conflict had been for Rich
Mountain. Then had come a race for Cheat Mountain. This had
been decided before Lee's arrival. The Federals had occupied the

[12] Letter of Aug. 4, 1861; R. E. Lee, Jr., 38.

eminence while the Confederates were demoralized by the early successes of McClellan. Jackson had been compelled to take second choice, which was the pass over the Alleghenies. Greenbrier Mountain, which did not possess great military strength, could also be occupied by the Southerners as an advanced position, but only because the Federals had not thought it worth taking so long as they held Cheat Mountain. All the advantage of position was on the Northern side.

Fifty miles to the southwest of this sector the James River and Kanawha turnpike ran through the mountains from Covington to the head of light navigation on the Gauley River, one of the two main streams that unite to form the Kanawha River. In that area, where the mountains did not set their parapets so high as in front of Monterey, General Henry A. Wise had been conducting a campaign presently to be described.

It was generally assumed that the Staunton-Parkersburg road and the James River and Kanawha turnpike were the only highways an army could follow across the mountains. That was not the case. West of Cheat Mountain a fairly good road ran from the village of Huttonsville southward up Tygart's Valley and through a cross-range of mountains to a small place known as Huntersville. From that point a difficult but passable road led over the Alleghenies, via Warm Springs, to Millborough,[13] which was close to the Virginia Central Railroad, southwest of Staunton. The essential features of the *terrain* may be seen from the sketch on page 547 on which the Staunton-Parkersburg and the James River-Kanawha roads are marked with double lines and the Huntersville-Millborough road appears as a series of dashes.

If the Federals could push forward up the Kanawha Valley and thence up New River they could reach the Virginia and Tennessee Railroad, which was the only direct line of communication between the two states whose name it bore.

Again, a Federal advance from Huntersville to Millborough would cut off the supplies that were going from Jackson's River, the western terminus of the Virginia Central Railroad, to the Confederate Army in the Kanawha Valley.[14] A Federal advance

---

13 Always spelled thus in war-time dispatches but now shortened to Millboro.

14 The actual terminus at this time was one and one-half miles west of Clifton Forge, according to J. P. Nelson: *The Chesapeake and Ohio Railway*, p. 9. A sketch of the railroad

to Millborough would likewise bring the enemy dangerously close to the rear of the forces in front of Cheat Mountain, who were being supplied in large part from Staunton. Finally, a drive

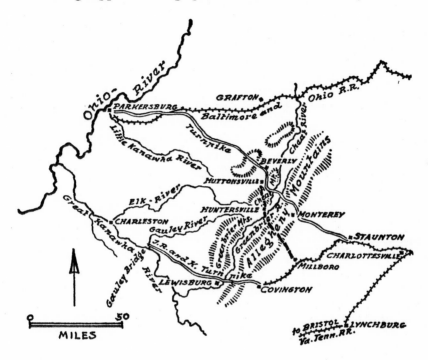

along the Staunton-Parkersburg road, resulting in the occupation of Staunton, would sever all rail communication between eastern and western Virginia and would deprive the South of the rich grain crops of the Shenandoah Valley. In short, any advance of the enemy to the Virginia Central Railroad would be, or would threaten, a major Confederate disaster.

The possibilities of a Confederate offensive were equally great. If Cheat Mountain could be passed there was no insurmountable barrier on the road to the Baltimore and Ohio, at Grafton, some ninety miles from Jackson's outposts at the Greenbrier River. At Grafton, as the Confederates had realized since the beginning of

in the vicinity appears in *O. R., 29*, part 1, p. 947. In February, 1862, J. G. Paxton stated that eight miles of "railroad iron" (rails) were needed to complete the road to Covington. (IV *O. R.*, 1, 944–45.)

the war, they could sever one of the main railways linking the East to the West. If, again, the Confederates could advance down the Kanawha eighty-five miles from Gauley Bridge, while covering their flank against attack from the north, they would reach the Ohio and would effectually free the greater part of western Virginia from the grip of the enemy.

General H. R. Jackson had been quick to sense the importance of the little-known and little-used road from Huntersville to Millborough. Even when his force had been very small he had divided it to protect this route and had urged that reinforcements be sent forward directly from the railroad near Millborough.[15] He had heard, moreover, that from Huntersville a road led northward down Tygart's Valley to the rear of Cheat Mountain, and he had ordered the troops at Huntersville to advance and seize a position that commanded this route.[16]

Leaving out of account, therefore, the units in or adjacent to the Kanawha Valley and those on the march to join Jackson or to strengthen Loring, who had gone to Huntersville before Lee reached Monterey, the disposition of the troops was about as shown on the opposite page.

In this situation, of course, where the strength of the Federals was unknown, the first step had to be defensive. Lee must make certain that the troops were numerous enough, vigilant enough, and well enough fortified in the mountains to keep the Union forces from reaching the Virginia Central Railroad. He had naturally been acutely conscious of this danger before he left Richmond and he had forwarded urgent and explicit orders to hold the mountain passes and to take no chances.[17] It was not until some time after his arrival at the front that he was entirely satisfied the enemy could not break through the defenses and strike the railway.

Offensively, the key position in the campaign manifestly was the high ground north of Huntersville, dominating the road in rear of Cheat Mountain. If the troops that Jackson had sent forward had chosen a good position there was every reason to hope that a quick advance might turn Cheat Mountain before the enemy

[15] O. R., 51, part 2, pp. 187–88; O. R., 2, 988, 991–92.
[16] O. R., 2, 999.   [17] O. R., 2, 996; O. R., 5, 150–51.

was aware of danger from the direction of Huntersville. To ascertain the exact state of affairs Lee bade Jackson adieu on the morning of August 3 and set out for Huntersville with his few

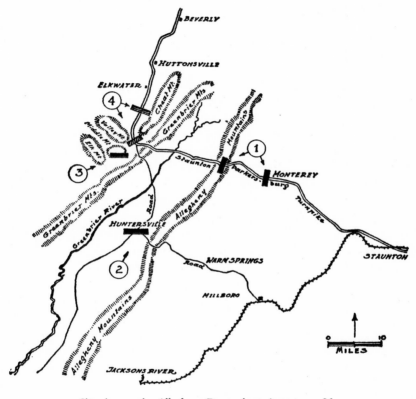

Situation on the Allegheny Front, about August 1, 1861.

1. H. R. Jackson occupying Monterey and Allegheny crest, preparing to advance to Greenbrier River. 2. W. W. Loring at Huntersville with reinforcements coming up from Monterey. 3. Two Confederate regiments in this vicinity, where they might turn Cheat Mountain. 4. United States forces, strength unknown, holding Cheat Mountain and the road to Beverly.

companions. The rain that he had first encountered the day he left Staunton was falling still and was enveloping in damp gloom a country of great natural beauty. The roads, which were bad at best, were becoming very heavy. The return of fair weather began to assume importance as a factor in the campaign.

Lee found Huntersville crowded with sick soldiers, a "most

549

wretched and filthy town," according to a Confederate chaplain.[18]
Situated about twenty-five miles from Monterey, it is on Knapp
Creek within an hour's trot of the Greenbrier River and has an
elevation of 2200 feet. The road from the north in which Lee
was interested had its forks here. One branch was the strategically
important route over the Alleghenies to Millborough. The other
ran southward to the valley of the Kanawha. The place was
worth the risks Jackson had taken when he had divided his little
army in order to dispatch troops thither.

As soon as Lee reached the village he went to call on General
Loring, who, on July 30, had established his headquarters there.[19]
He met with a surprised and distinctly cold reception. Loring
had not expected to see him and was not pleased to greet him.
Not two weeks had passed since Lee had given Loring discre-
tionary orders in Richmond and had sent him forward. And
now, before Loring had developed his plans—here was Lee to see
that he did his duty! Loring did not feel that he needed supervision. A native of South Carolina but a resident of Florida since
boyhood, he had been an Indian fighter while Lee was a headquarters staff lieutenant; and though he was eleven years Lee's
junior and was not a West Pointer, he had seen far more field
service than his commanding officer, thus suddenly descended on
him from the clouds and the mountain top. Had not Loring
been brevetted colonel for gallantry in Mexico? When he had
been entrusted with command of the Department of Oregon had
he not successfully marched a column across the continent? Did
he not have a good record as commander in New Mexico, where
he had whipped Indians more elusive than the raw Federal troops,
and in a country more difficult? It was apparent from the moment of Lee's meeting with Loring that another difficulty had
been added to the inexperience, the demoralization, and the sickness of the Confederates—to endless rains, to roads like bogs, and
to pathless mountains: jealousy had come into the campaign, and
had come at a time when it might cost the army a great opportunity.[20]

For it developed that Colonel William Gilham, whom Jackson

[18] A. H. Noll: *Doctor Quintard* (cited hereafter as *Dr. Quintard*), 17.
[19] *O. R.*, 2, 1009.
[20] *Long*, 120. Long was with Loring and was a witness of virtually all that happened.

had ordered in advance from Huntersville, had gone forward eighteen miles and had come to a ridge known as Valley Mountain, across which the Huttonsville-Huntersville road passed at an elevation of 3460 feet, near the present post office of Mace. From Valley Mountain northward, as reported, the road descended into the lush Tygart's River Valley, in rear of the Federal position in Cheat Mountain pass. Not an enemy had been in sight when Gilham had arrived. If he had been strong enough then he could have swept forward and could have trapped the Federals on Cheat Mountain, opening a way for Jackson on the Greenbrier side. The Federals, however, had quickly learned of Gilham's presence on Valley Mountain and were said to be preparing to fortify a position farther down Tygart's Valley to prevent a Confederate advance. Even now, if Loring would advance with all his forces, the enemy might be driven back and the road could be opened.[21] Everything depended on speed. And Loring showed not the slightest disposition to move fast! Weary teams dragged their loads through the mud of the baffling roads, discharged their boxes and barrels and started protestingly back towards Millborough. Loring's staff officers, some of whom were quite capable, were kept busy in tallying deliveries and in collecting beef cattle, chafing all the while. Loring intended to advance. He confided that much to Lee. But before he went forward he was determined to establish a base at Huntersville and to stock it adequately with supplies brought up from Staunton over the swimming roads.[22] When he would be ready to move, Loring did not say—though the passage of every hour made it more certain that the Federals would realize the full extent of danger and effectually block an advance. The great opportunity was being lost for fear the soldiers might miss their breakfast! Of course, a long offensive could not be sustained without building up a reserve of supplies as Loring proposed, for communications would be difficult to maintain over the execrable roads. To that extent Loring was right. But a brief advance was all that was

[21] The published correspondence of the Federal army shows the opportunity to have been as great as Lee thought it was. General Rosecrans was thinking more about an advance up the Kanawha Valley than about the defense of Reynolds's position. Cf. O. R., 5, 552, 564.
[22] Long, 120.

necessary to seize the key positions, and that was worth the risks, even if the men had to carry their own rations.

Lee's alternatives were plain: he must wait on Loring, smooth down his ruffled feathers, win his confidence, and coax him into action, when and if he could; or else he must disregard Loring's jealousy, overrule his authority, and by virtue of his superior rank order the troops forward. Zachary Taylor would not have hesitated. Neither would Scott. Neither would Lee's hero, Washington. Had Lee employed stern military methods with Loring, as Stonewall Jackson did the following February, when he preferred charges against that officer for neglect of duty,[23] there can be no doubt that President Davis would have sustained him, timid though the administration then was. But Lee could not bring himself to impose his will on Loring. The General was jealous; controversies were to be avoided; Lee's orders were to co-ordinate rather than to command; and, if Loring would not advance, some other way of worsting the enemy must be found. Instead of hurrying Loring to Valley Mountain, he set out to conciliate him and to shape a new plan of campaign in place of the one the Federals had carelessly presented and Loring was negligently letting slip by. So Lee waited on Loring. Dealing most deferentially with his sensitive associate, he issued orders assigning troops to the "Army of the Northwest, under Brigadier General W. W. Loring," [24] and he reminded one of the leaders in the Kanawha Valley that General Loring was "commanding the whole force of the Northwest Army." [25] In a word, he chose the rôle of diplomatist instead of that of army commander and sought to abate Loring's jealousy by magnifying that officer's authority.

All his life Lee had lived with gentle people, where kindly sentiments and consideration for the feelings of others were part of *noblesse oblige*. In that atmosphere he was expansive, cheerful, buoyant even, no matter what happened. During the Mexican campaigns, though his sympathies had been with General Scott, he had largely kept himself apart from the contention and had been a peacemaker. Now that he encountered surliness and jealousy, it repelled him, embarrassed him, and well-nigh bewildered

[23] *O. R.*, 5, 1065–66. [24] *O. R.*, 5, 770.
[25] *O. R.*, 51, part 2, p. 253; *cf. O. R.*, 5, 768.

him. Detesting a quarrel as undignified and unworthy of a gentleman, he showed himself willing, in this new state of affairs, to go to almost any length, within the bounds of honor, to avoid a clash. In others this might have been a virtue; in him it was a positive weakness, the first serious weakness he had ever displayed as a soldier. It was a weakness that was to be apparent more than once and had to be combated, deliberately or subconsciously. His personal humility and his exaggerated sense of his obligations as a man and a Christian were to make him submit to a certain measure of intellectual bullying by those of his associates who were sour and self-opinionated. The more inconsiderate such people were of him, the more considerate he was of them, and the more forbearant, up to the point where his patience failed and his temper broke bounds. Then he would freeze men quickly in the cold depths of his wrath. Prior to this time no man, probably, had guessed it of him, and doubtless he was unconscious of this weakness; but from those days at Huntersville until Longstreet was wounded in the Wilderness on May 6, 1864, there always was a question whether Lee, in any given situation, would conquer his inordinate amiability or would permit his campaigns to be marred or his battles to be lost by it. Of some other commanders in the great American tragedy one might have to ask whether they were drunk or sober on a given day, whether they were indolent or aggressive, whether they lost their heads in the emergency or mastered themselves. Of Lee it became necessary to ask, for two years and more, whether his judgment as a soldier or his consideration as a gentleman dominated his acts.

CHAPTER XXXIII

Lee Conducts His First Campaign

Four days Lee waited on Loring; four days Loring waited on his wagon train. Growing desperate then, Lee set out on August 6 for Valley Mountain, where he arrived the same day. He now found himself in the wilds, surrounded by peaks. Eastward was a mountain of 4775 feet; southeastward was one still higher; southwestward were the twin crests of Middle Mountain. West of the long ridge of Valley Mountain a ravine ran down to Elk River, beyond which loomed the grim barrier of Gauley Mountain Only to the northward, where the heights dropped away to the valley of Tygart's River, was there an open road. The pass itself was directly on the line between Randolph and Pocahontas Counties, at an elevation of 3464 feet. Human habitations were few and rude. The troops found such shelter as they could under the scanty canvas allotted them. Lee had his solitary tent pitched like the others, and in it he, Colonel Washington, and Captain Taylor made their quarters. Primitive as was the life on which they now entered they did not forget the amenities. Every morning and every evening Lee and Washington had their separate private devotions, and they sat down to hard fare, crudely served from Lee's mess-kit of tin, with as much dignity as if they had been dining at Mount Vernon or at Arlington.[1]

A single reconnaissance sufficed to show that the opportunity for a surprise attack on the western side of Cheat Mountain was fading fast. The Federals had their outposts where any advance would be reported promptly, and down Tygart's Valley they were supposed to be throwing up batteries that commanded the approaches. Perhaps at that time, and certainly a few days thereafter, to make a direct, daylight advance down the mountainside into Tygart's Valley would have been to invite destruction even

[1] *Taylor's General Lee*, 30; Lee to Mrs. Lee, Aug. 9, 1861; *R. E. Lee, Jr.*, 39.

if the Confederate force on Valley Mountain had been much larger than the few shivering regiments that Lee found there.

If the best plan of campaign had to be cancelled because of the delay in massing troops on Valley Mountain, what could be substituted for it? This was the first time during the war that Lee had to ask himself that question, but ere the struggle was over he had to put it in many a doubtful hour. To some extent his strategical methods and to a much larger degree his tactics, throughout the war, had to be adjusted to the second-best way of doing things, because an inexperienced subordinate had blundered or a disgruntled commander had sulked.

Here in the fastnesses, hemmed in by mountains that a fox could hardly cross, the solitary alternative to a march down Tygart's Valley, straight into the mouth of the Federal guns, was the discovery of some obscure, unguarded trail to the rear of Cheat Mountain. The only way of finding such a route, if one existed, was to reconnoitre with the greatest care. As Lee had about him scarcely any officers experienced in this difficult work he felt that he should do a part of it. Over night he turned back the wheels of fortune a full fourteen years and once again was a captain of engineers reconnoitring a country not altogether unlike Mexico. The native population was divided in sentiment and as apt to mislead as to aid.[2] Every track had to be followed to the last impassable ravine; every description of the land had to be verified to the last pretended turn of a non-existent road. Early in the morning Lee went out; often wet and weary, it was late before he returned with Washington and Taylor. One day the trio were half a mile in advance of the Confederate pickets, very busily studying the ground ahead of them, when suddenly a Confederate captain and two privates, armed *cap-a-pied*, broke suddenly out of a nearby thicket, stood doubtful for a moment, and then made their embarrassed explanations: from the picket lines they had seen the three figures on the mountain and, mistaking them for Federal scouts, had started out to capture them.[3]

Hourly, as if it were the ally of the North, the rain continued to pour down. By August 10, when twenty successive days of rain had passed, the roads were bottomless in mud. "It was very

[2] *Taylor's Four Years,* 17–18; E. R. Montfort: *From Grafton to McDowell,* 8.
[3] *Long,* 121.

seriously debated whether the army could be fed where it was, and it was feared," Colonel Walter Taylor has recorded, "that it would have to retire to some point nearer the railroad. Time and time again could be seen double teams of horses struggling with six or eight barrels of flour, and the axle of the wagon scraping and leveling the road-bed. . . . The wagons . . . could be moved only step by step, and then with the greatest difficulty." [4] The epidemic of measles that had first appeared among the survivors of Garnett's ill-starred column spread through the other commands, bringing men down by hundreds and provoking fever and a multitude of intestinal ills. One fine, full regiment of 1000 North Carolinians was reduced by sickness to one-third its strength before its men ever heard a hostile gun. Half the army was sick and the other wretched half was ignorant of even the rudiments of personal hygiene in the field. The distress of the soldiers aroused Lee's sympathy, but their negligence provoked his indignation. "Our poor sick, I know, suffer much," he wrote Mrs. Lee a month later. "They bring it on themselves by not doing what they are told. They are worse than children, for the latter can be forced." [5]

While Lee continued his reconnoitring in this unhappy atmosphere, Loring slowly brought the rest of his troops forward from his newly established advance base at Huntersville. By August 12 all of them were at Valley Mountain, but until Lee could find a new line of advance they could do nothing against an adversary now fully alive to the danger on his flank, and aware that Lee was facing him.[6] General McClellan had been recalled to Washington to take charge of the troops on the Potomac.[7] General W. S. Rosecrans, named as his successor, had placed in direct command on the Cheat Mountain sector an able soldier, whom Lee mentioned as "our old friend, J. J. Reynolds of West Point memory," in writing to Mrs. Lee. "He is a brigadier general," Lee continued. "You may recollect him as the Assistant Professor of Philosophy, and lived in the cottage beyond the West gate, with his little, pale-faced wife. . . . He resigned

[4] *Taylor's Four Years,* 17.
[5] Lee to Mrs. Lee, Sept. 17, 1861; *R. E. Lee, Jr.,* 46.
[6] *Long,* 121; *O. R.,* 5, 555; *New York Times,* Aug. 18, 1861, p. 1, col. 5.
[7] He had left on July 23, 1861; *O. R.,* 5, 6.

on being relieved from West Point, and was made professor of some college in the West. Fitzhugh was the bearer of a flag the other day, and he recognized him. He was very polite and made kind inquiries of us all. I am told they feel very safe and are very confident of success." [8]

In these circumstances, while the days dragged on as slowly as the wagons in the mud, Lee tried to be cheerful and gave no outward sign of his inward distress. He drew such comfort as he could from the fact that though the Confederates could not advance, they had at least closed to the Federals the roads leading to Staunton and to Millborough.[9] The wretchedness of the green troops grew deeper daily. "In the subsequent campaigns of the Army of Northern Virginia," Walter Taylor attested, "the troops were subjected to great privations and to many very severe trials—in hunger often; their nakedness scarcely concealed; strength at times almost exhausted—but never did I experience the same heart-sinking emotions as when contemplating the wan faces and the emaciated forms of those hungry, sickly, shivering men of the army at Valley Mountain." [10] The weather gave no promise of change. Ice formed on the night of August 14-15; the soldiers had to huddle around large fires. "A Tennessee hog pen would scarcely be more uncomfortable," one weary officer wrote.[11] "It rains here all the time, literally," Lee told his wife. "There has not been sunshine enough since my arrival to dry my clothes. . . . It is raining now. Has been all day, last night, day before, and day before that, etc., etc. But we must be patient." [12] Supplies were brought forward with increasing difficulty. No more than two or three days' food was ever at hand, never enough to make possible even a short advance had the weather permitted.[13] The horses grew thin and pitiful. While reconnoitring daily in the

[8] Lee to Mrs. Lee, Aug. 9, 1861; R. E. Lee, Jr., 40. The enemy was not so confident as Lee was led to believe. McClellan had been exhorting Rosecrans not to wait for the Confederates to concentrate against him (O. R., 5, 563, 564); John S. Carlile, a leading Unionist politician of western Virginia, was predicting that the Federals would be whipped within ten days unless they were reinforced (O. R., 5, 561); The Cincinnati Commercial credited Lee with 40,000 to 50,000 men (quoted in Richmond Dispatch, Aug. 20, 1861, p. 3, col. 1).

[9] O. R., 5, 768; O. R., 51, part 2, p. 211; Lee to Mrs. Lee, Aug. 9, 29, 1861; R. E. Lee, Jr., 41, 42.

[10] Taylor's Four Years, 17.   [11] Drake's Hatton, 373, 375.

[12] Lee to Mrs. Lee, Aug. 29, 1861; R. E. Lee, Jr., 42.

[13] O. R., 5, 785, 807.

rain and striving to disarm with his diplomacy the jealousy of General Loring, Lee had to guard at long range against a Federal advance up the valley of the Kanawha and had to deal with a continuous controversy between General Floyd and General Wise in that district. He never knew what news of fatal contention the next courier from the south might bring. Nor did he know what the enemy was doing or what Reynolds's numbers were, though every move of the Confederates was quickly reported to the enemy.[14] Disaffection among the militia was as widespread as sickness in the ranks of the volunteers.[15] Still he held tenaciously to the hope of an offensive against the Federals, who had been scattered, as he thought, for the effect their presence might have on the election in western Virginia for the establishment of a "loyal" state government.[16] The press, all the while, was carrying reports of Lee's movements that would have been amusing in their very *naïveté* if there had not been the painful consciousness of doing so little when the newspapers proclaimed so much. Scarcely had Lee arrived at Valley Mountain before he was reported victorious in a skirmish at Rich Spring.[17] A little later there had been exaggerated accounts, quickly corrected, of heavy losses by General Wise in a withdrawal up the valley of the Kanawha, coupled with predictions that Lee would soon drive the enemy back or force his capitulation.[18] Ere long Rosecrans was alleged to be surrounded, with every prospect of being compelled to surrender.[19] A little more and Lee was said to have 37,000 men at Gauley Bridge, which he had not then visited.[20] The next yarn was that "flags of truce" had passed between Lee and Rosecrans. "The first flag," according to this story, "was from Genl. R., requiring an evacuation by Lee, within thirty days. Lee replied, giving Rosecranz ten days in which to leave his encampment. From this evidence, we are inclined to think we will soon receive intelligence of a bloody fight at Big Springs."[21] Not to be out-

14 For his admitted lack of information, see Lee to Floyd, Sept. 4, 1861, *O. R.*, 51, part 2, p. 271. For an example of Rosecrans's knowledge of the Confederate strength, see *O. R.*, 5, 118.
15 *O. R.*, 51, part 2, pp. 231, 244–45.   16 *O. R.*, 5, 782.
17 *Richmond Dispatch*, Aug. 10, 1861, p. 3, col. 1.
18 *Richmond Examiner*, Aug. 19, 1861, p. 3, cols. 2–3; *ibid.*, Aug. 20, 1861, p. 3, col. 3.
19 *Memphis Appeal*, Aug. 25, 1861.
20 *Richmond Dispatch*, Aug. 26, 1861, p. 3, col. 3.
21 *Nashville Banner*, quoted in *Richmond Examiner*, Aug. 30, 1861, p. 2, col. 5.

done by the action of the Southern press in reducing Rosecrans's fictitious ultimatum by twenty days, *The Wheeling Intelligencer* soon had Lee "perfectly surrounded by our Federal troops, 10,000 men with four batteries of 28 cannon in all." More than that, "he sent in a flag of truce the other day to Gen. Reynolds . . . and offered to surrender all his arms if we would only let him through our lines, so that he could go South. He said if we did not accede to his proposition that he would cut his way through. General Reynolds sent back word to cut his way through, as he would never let him out alive" [22]—which sounded exceedingly sanguinary for a man who had been an assistant professor of philosophy! It was not until September, when furloughed officers began to arrive in Richmond from the Army of the Northwest, that the press abandoned its rhodomontade for sober and none-too-cheerful reports of bad weather and worse roads.[23]

Ironically enough, the newspapers grew pessimistic at the very time four things were happening that brought a measure of hope and encouragement to Lee even though the torrential rains still held all operations at a standstill.[24] On August 31 Lee was confirmed as a full general in the regular army of the Confederate States. This had been authorized by Congress on May 16, and Lee had been signing as "General," but now the rank was officially conferred. On the same day Samuel Cooper, the adjutant general, Albert Sidney Johnston, Joseph E. Johnston, and P. G. T. Beauregard received like rank. Their commissions were so dated that Cooper and Albert Sidney Johnston were his seniors. Joseph E. Johnston, his former classmate, and Beauregard were rated his juniors[25]—an arrangement that aroused in Johnston a resentment that colored his views throughout the war. Having outranked all the others in the service of the United States, he took it very hard that three of them were his seniors in the army of the new republic.

[22] Quoted in *Richmond Examiner*, Sept. 4, 1861, p. 2, col. 5.
[23] *Richmond Dispatch*, Sept. 4, 1861, p. 3, col. 1; *ibid.*, Sept. 10, p. 3, col. 1; *ibid.*, Sept. 12, p. 3, col. 1; *Richmond Examiner*, Sept. 6, 1861, p. 2, col. 6; *ibid.*, Sept. 10, p. 2. col. 2.
[24] Lee to Mrs. Lee, Sept. 1, 1861; *R. E. Lee, Jr.*, 43.
[25] M. J. Wright: *General Officers of the Confederate Army*, 9–10; 20 *S. H. S. P.*, 95. For the rediscovery of the original of Lee's commission as a general, see 32 *Confederate Veteran*, 296–97.

Along with the news of his confirmation at the highest grade in the Southern service, Lee received a kind letter from General Cooper, assuring him of the President's approval of his conduct of operations and telling him that Davis wished him to return to his former duties as soon as he felt he could leave western Virginia.[26] It was something, at least, to know that the President understood his difficulties and retained undiminished confidence in him.

As a result of Lee's definite promotion, and as a reward of his patient diplomacy, Loring began to show himself more amenable. His jealousy probably remained, but he interposed no objection as Lee gradually took over the strategy of operations. This was a triumph in itself, unrecorded though it was in the damp annals of the little army in the mountains. "Things are better organized," Lee wrote in a brief period of sunshine. "I feel stronger, we are stronger. . . . Now to drive [the enemy] farther a battle must come off, and I am anxious to begin it. Circumstances beyond human control delay it, I know for good, but I hope the Great Ruler of the Universe will continue to aid and prosper us, and crown at last our feeble efforts with success." [27]

The prospect of a successful offensive was the fourth development of early September. Step by step, literally, a route had been found by which a courageous column could make its way from Valley Mountain along the western ridges of Cheat Mountain to a point two miles west of its crest and directly on the road by which the enemy's force on the top of the mountain was being supplied. Before Lee could ascertain precisely how he might fit this discovery into a plan of attack, General Loring sent to him a civilian engineer, whose name unfortunately does not appear in the records, along with Colonel Albert Rust of the Third Arkansas Regiment. They had ridden over the mountains to Loring's headquarters from General H. R. Jackson's command and they had information that set every ear tingling: hearing that General Lee was most anxious to find a way of turning the Federal position on the top of Cheat Mountain, the engineer had set out from Greenbrier River and, after days of scrambling through thickets

---

[26] O. R., 5, 828–29; cf. Davis to J. E. Johnston, Sept. 5, 1861; ibid., 829.
[27] Letter of Sept. 3, 1861; Jones, L. and L., 147.

and across ravines, had reached a point south of the summit, where the enemy had some trenches and a blockhouse. From this lofty ground, the Federal position on the mountain top could be taken. To prove it, the engineer had taken Colonel Rust with him on a second journey to the position he had discovered, and the two, having made what they said was a careful examination, had returned to Jackson without having aroused the enemy's suspicion.

Rust explained all this to Lee, and was emphatic in his assertion that a column could reach the point he had visited. The enemy's flank was exposed, he insisted. He had seen it for himself. A surprise attack from the height would give Lee Cheat Mountain and would open the way to a general advance against the enemy, who could not hope to find close at hand another such stronghold. All he asked, Rust confidently went on, was that if General Lee decided to attack, he would give him the privilege of leading the assault on the crest. With his usual amiability, and probably without stopping to weigh the matter, Lee assented to this request.[28] It was to prove a most expensive "Yes."

Many considerations had to be weighed before determining to base a plan of attack on Rust's proposal. The ground was very difficult. Besides the steep abysses, the commanding heights and the absence of roads, there was on the face of Cheat Mountain a dense growth of almost impenetrable laurel that was certain to retard, if not to halt, the surprise attack Rust was so anxious to deliver.[29] The strength of the enemy was unknown. Reynolds was assumed to have about 2000 men on Cheat Mountain, and his total force there and at Elkwater, which had now been found to be his principal position down Tygart's River,[30] was believed to be at least equal to that of Loring and Jackson. The Confederates had 15,000 or more, but nearly half of these were sick.[31] Reynolds's men were concentrated; those that Lee would have to employ were separated by the Cheat Mountain, and while they would have

---

[28] *Long,* 122; *Taylor's Four Years,* 23; *Fitz Lee,* 119.

[29] *Taylor's Four Years,* 20.

[30] Reynolds's headquarters were on the farm of Alexander Stalnaker, now owned by A. Z. Hamilton, to whom the writer is much indebted for clearing up the confusion on the maps as to the exact location of Elkwater.

[31] The reports for these early months of the war contain no full returns of the troops in western Virginia. Loring had nineteen regiments, large and small, besides his cavalry and artillery. *Cf. O. R.,* 51, part 2, pp. 283–84.

to attack simultaneously, there was no means of establishing *liaison* between Jackson and Loring. The store of provisions was so scant that a long offensive could not be sustained. Still, there was the possibility of surprise both on the crest of Cheat Mountain and on the western side of the crest. An offensive seemed practicable if pains were taken to meet every contingency and to deliver the attack on the peak and from both sides of the mountain simultaneously. And as an alternative to the attempt, what was there except to remain helpless in the wet, wind-shaken tents on Valley Mountain?

Lee decided to fight the battle, his first battle, and he went about his preparations with an eye to every precaution that his judgment could suggest. By September 8 he had worked out the plan to the point where the order could be issued—tactfully in the name of General Loring.[32] It was a good order, detailed, well-drafted, and very simple in form. Rust was secretly to take a column of about 2000 men to the position he had selected. At the same time, General S. R. Anderson was to move, unobserved by the enemy, along the route Lee had reconnoitred down the western ridge of Cheat Mountain until he reached the road that led to the summit from Tygart's Valley. He was then to occupy the western crest and was to block the road. Jackson, on the eastern side of the mountain, was to take position for a march up the Staunton-Parkersburg turnpike, when Rust had cleared it. General Daniel S. Donelson and Colonel Jesse S. Burks were to be ready to advance down either side of Tygart River toward Elkwater, with Gilham in reserve. Rust was to give the signal by opening fire. When he did so, Jackson was to advance, Anderson was to prevent the dispatch of reinforcements to the stronghold on Cheat Mountain and, if need be, was to support Jackson's attack. Then Anderson was to move down Tygart's Valley. Donelson and Burks were to pursue; the cavalry was to cover the extreme left. Special instructions were given to keep one column from firing into another. Graphically, the plan of advance was to be approximately as indicated on the opposite page, which, however, does not attempt to give the exact routes of advance:

Preparatory to the offensive, Lee issued a supplementary order,

[32] *O. R.*, 51, part 2, pp. 282–83.

over his own signature. He had not yet learned the art of writing papers of this sort in the appealing form he later developed, and

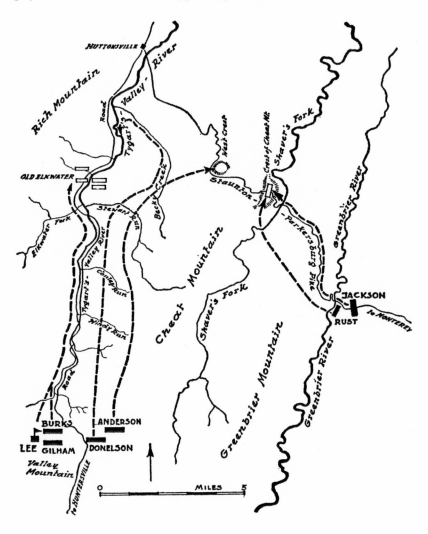

he was not disposed to emulate his old friend McClellan, whose bombastic imitations of Napoleon's addresses to his army had been ridiculed on every key of Southern derision. So Lee followed the traditional style, a style that had not changed greatly since Thucydides had endorsed it as customary more than 2000 years before.

Special Orders ⎱ Headquarters of the Forces,
No. —— ⎰ Valley Mountain, W. Va., September 9, 1861.

The forward movement announced to the Army of the Northwest in Special Orders, No. 28, from its headquarters, of this date, gives the general commanding the opportunity of exhorting the troops to keep steadily in view the great principles for which they contend and to manifest to the world their determination to maintain them. The eyes of the country are upon you. The safety of your homes and the lives of all you hold dear depend upon your courage and exertions. Let every man resolve to be victorious, and that the right of self-government, liberty, and peace shall in him find a defender. The progress of this army must be forward.

R. E. LEE,
General.[38]

The date set for the advance was September 12. Troop movements were to begin on the 9th. As the time approached the weather was quite cold,[34] and the roads, though somewhat better, were still so muddy that wagons sank up to the axles.[35] Gilham and Burks were brought up to the front[36] and seven days' rations were issued the troops that were to operate on the mountains. At 9 o'clock the next morning, September 10, Anderson's brigade started, as it had the longest and most difficult journey to make. The men had no road. In single file they went through the fields and over steep ridges.[37] "It was no uncommon thing," a surgeon wrote, "for a mule to slide twenty feet down a slope, and I could see strong men sink exhausted trying to get up the mountain side." [38] The march continued until 10 P.M., when the

[33] *O. R.*, 5, 192.
[34] As early as Aug. 29, 1861, Lee had written his wife, "I have on all my winter clothes and am writing in my overcoat" (*R. E. Lee, Jr.*, 42).
[35] *O. R.*, 51, part 2, p. 284.
[36] John H. Worsham: *One of Jackson's Foot Cavalry* (cited hereafter as *Worsham*), 44; Charles E. Taylor to his brother, Sept. 14, 1861; *Wake Forest Student*, March, 1916 (cited hereafter as *C. E. Taylor*), 390.
[37] *Dr. Quintard*, 24.
[38] Doctor J. R. Buist to his uncle, *National Intelligencer*, Nov. 22, 1861, p. 2, col. 3. This, the fullest account of Anderson's march, is cited hereafter as *Buist* and has a sombre

column was halted and received the usual inhospitable reception of those grim mountains in the form of a hard rain.[39] Meantime, Donelson had started during the afternoon, as his route was almost as long as Anderson's, though not so uniformly difficult. He was to go down the right bank of the river, then across successive ridges and was at length to descend down Becky Run to the Huntersville-Huttonsville road, in rear of the Federals, who were believed to be concentrated near Elkwater, about six miles up the river from Huttonsville.[40] Donelson soon was compelled to leave his artillery behind, and on some stages of this advance his men had to let themselves down steep declivities by holding to the branches of the trees.[41] Back on Valley Mountain that day there came the disquieting news that the supplies of food at Staunton and Millborough were almost exhausted.[42] This was a very serious matter, for it had been a giant's task to accumulate enough bread, meat, and forage for a few days' advance;[43] but Lee was now confident that his plans would bring success,[44] and he did not hesitate because he might encounter a shortage of provisions after the attack was launched.

Lee himself went forward on the 11th with Burks's and Gilham's troops, who were under the personal direction of Loring. At Conrad's Mill they had a skirmish with a retiring Federal outpost[45]—the first action of any sort that Lee saw during the war. This firing was heard up Cheat Mountain by Anderson. His regiments had started early, but the terrain was so difficult that they had to scramble along until 9 P.M., part of the time at the double-quick, in order to be within striking distance the next morning.[46]

Donelson had an exciting day for green troops. During the forenoon his advance found fresh tracks along the ridges, showing plainly that a Federal column had recently passed down

interest in that it was given in a letter found on the dead body of the addressee when the Federals occupied Fort Walker, at the entrance to Port Royal Sound, S. C.

[39] Dr. Quintard, 24.

[40] It should be noted that the "Old" Elkwater was on the south bank of Hamilton Run, about one mile south of the present Elkwater.

[41] T. A. Head: Campaigns and Battles of the Sixteenth Regiment, Tennessee Volunteers (cited hereafter as Head), 32.

[42] O. R., 5, 846, 851.   [43] O. R., 51, part 2, p. 284.

[44] Lee to Mrs. Lee, Sept. 17, 1861; R. E. Lee, Jr. 45.

[45] Worsham, 44.   [46] Dr. Quintard, 24 ff.

the mountain. Soon Donelson approached the enemy's pickets, but he easily took the men at the first post, four in number, at the Matthews house, and then he bagged the main picket post, some fifty-six in number, at the Simmons house.[47] Up Becky Run, after nightfall, he came upon another picket post, from which the Federals had fled. His approach, evidently, had been observed and reported, but so far as was known, the Federals were not yet aware of Anderson's movements. When his men bivouacked, Donelson reconnoitred and found himself close to still another outpost.[48] The night was cold, but no fires were allowed, and none of the men was permitted to talk above a whisper.[49] His camp was in timber, but on a heavy grade. "Here we tried to sleep," Doctor Buist later wrote, "but the rain poured so, and the torrents ran down the mountain such a flood of water that we would have been drowned had we lain on the ground."

As Loring had advanced on the 11th, dawn of September 12 found Lee where he had every reason to hope for success. The men were hungry, for their rations had been spoiled by the rain. Their muskets were dripping. All were weary. But Anderson was where he could reach the Staunton-Parkersburg pike in a rush; Donelson occupied a position whence he could reinforce either Loring or Anderson. The troops that had marched down the valley under General Loring were close to the enemy. If Rust and Jackson were doing their part of the grim work on the eastern side of Cheat Mountain, that barrier might easily be seized and the enemy driven down Tygart's Valley.

The rain of the night had given place to a fog, and now this lifted, as if in augury. From the eminence where he had taken his stand, Lee could look down the valley and could glimpse the tents of the nearest Federal encampment, "a tempting sight," he termed it.[50] The soldiers, all expectant, withdrew the charges from their wet muskets, and began to clean their arms and to reload with what dry powder could be found. It was a slow task, and it might be interrupted at any minute by the rolling echoes of Rust's triumphant fire.

The attack was to open when a volley from the crest of Cheat

[47] Head, 32 ff.; Nashville Union and American, Dec. 5, 1861.
[48] Head, 23 ff.
[49] Dr. Quintard, 24 ff.   [50] Cf. infra, p. 572.

Mountain announced that Rust was storming the block house and the trenches there. What was delaying the confident colonel? It was long past light, 8 o'clock in fact, and not a sound had come from the summit. Had Rust lost his way? Lee began to ask himself the question, and the minutes passed without an answer. Now a courier reported that Anderson's men were across the Cheat Mountain road and had cut communication between the summit and the Huntersville-Huttonsville road. The Federal pickets had been driven in, with the loss of a few men in Anderson's command. The movement would soon be known to every regiment in the valley: was Rust never going to give the signal?

Presently the expectant silence was shattered by the sound of guns. But it was not a volley. It was more like random firing. And it came from the wrong direction—not from Cheat Mountain, but from up Becky Run. What was afoot there? Lee spurred down the ridge to find out, and made for the main road, which lay on the other side of a wood in the valley. Just as he was about to emerge there was a clanging of sabres, the sharp staccato of horses' hoofs in full career, and a strong Federal cavalry outpost dashed by in the direction of the firing. Lee was within the enemy's position. Before he could decide what to do, there were shouts, bugle-calls, more firing, and the Federals came back the way they had come. They had run into Donelson's pickets and were carrying back the news of his advance. Not one man in the roaring column observed the little group of gray-clad horsemen in the woods. When the Federals had vanished down the muddy road, Lee went into Donelson's lines and learned, to his chagrin, that the firing had been done by impatient soldiers who hoped in this way to clean their guns more quickly.

It did not matter greatly, perhaps. The alarm had been given and the enemy was on the alert by now, for 10 o'clock had come and passed. Something manifestly had gone wrong with Rust. He had to be counted out of the action he was to open. What could be done to reshape the plan to this disheartening development? Nothing, manifestly, except to give battle with the troops west of the mountain, regardless of Rust and of Jackson. Quickly Lee undertook to put the brigades into position to do this. He

567

rode in person to Donelson and directed him to descend into the valley.[51] Anderson he ordered to retire from his exposed position.[52] There was much galloping about and vast confusion. Lee went from regiment to regiment, urging the colonels to get their men in hand. Donelson succeeded to the extent of forcing a small picket across a swollen run, where he captured a few more prisoners. Elsewhere, Lee encountered a curious and invincible passive resistance among the officers. The men were wet and too hungry, he was told, to undertake a battle. Loring could not get into position without crossing the river, and it was too high for fording. Morale was gone. Everywhere there was an excuse, nowhere any zeal for the conflict. By noon it was apparent that nothing could be accomplished. All the high expectations of the morning had evaporated. Lee's elaborate plan could not be executed in any essential. His first battle had ended in utter fiasco.[53]

Not one word did Lee receive from Rust or from Jackson the whole day to explain why the attack on the crest of Cheat Mountain had not been delivered. The morning of September 13 brought no report. As the men had now rested somewhat, Lee determined to see if he could not hold his position in Tygart's Valley and on the ridges and find a new way of reaching the rear of the Federals. It was futile, of course, to attempt anything further on Cheat Mountain, but west of the river, in the direction of Rich Mountain, a turning movement might be possible. Reconnoitring parties were sent out, and Gilham's brigade was put to work cutting a road along the ridge.[54] As a part of the reconnaissance, Colonel Washington and Rooney Lee, with a few men, decided to explore the right branch of Elkwater Fork and duly set out. Late in the afternoon Rooney returned with the sad

[51] *Head, loc. cit.*   [52] *Buist, loc. cit.*

[53] No official reports of this action west of the mountain were written by Confederates. The only accounts of eye-witnesses are already cited; *Long*, 123–24; *Taylor's Four Years*, 28–29; Lee's own in his letter of Sept. 17, to his wife, *R. E. Lee, Jr.*, 45; and M. B. Toney's in his *Privations of a Private*, 22–24. Jefferson Davis (17 *S. H. S. P.*, 367 and 1 *Davis*, 435–36) recorded his memories of Lee's explanation, but his account is manifestly incorrect in several particulars. Davis to W. H. Taylor, Jan. 31, 1878, *Taylor MSS.*, shows that Mr. Davis was hazy concerning the details. For Lee's account of the action, in his letter to Governor Letcher, see *infra*, p. 573. Some items of interest will be found in Reynolds's report, *O. R.*, 5, 185, but this is, on the whole, a singularly vague document.

[54] *C. E. Taylor, loc. cit.*

news that they had suddenly encountered a Federal picket and
had been fired upon. Colonel Washington had fallen at the
first fusillade and his body had not been recovered.[55] Lee's grief
was instant and apparent, for he esteemed Washington both as a
friend and as a gentleman.[56] This was the only incident of consequence during the day, though it is possible that the Confederates in the valley heard some sounds of firing as the Federal
garrison on the summit of Cheat Mountain made a demonstration
against Jackson's outposts on the other side of the ridge.[57] On
the 14th Lee sent a flag of truce to the Federals, with a message
requesting the body of Colonel Washington, if dead, or news of
him, if captured. On the way the bearers of the flag were met by
a party of Federals bringing the remains of the unfortunate
officer.[58] In deep personal grief Lee wrote the first of the many
letters he was doomed to address to those who lost friends known
intimately to him in the army:

Camp on Valley River,
September 16, 1861.

My dear Miss Louisa,

With a heart filled with grief, I have to communicate the saddest tidings you have ever heard.

May "Our Father, Who is in Heaven" enable you to bear it, for
in His inscrutable Providence, abounding in mercy and omnip-
otent in power, He has made you fatherless on earth. Your dear
father, in reconnoitering the enemy's position, came into the
range of fire of his pickets and was instantly killed. He fell in
the cause to which he had devoted all his energies, and in which
his noble heart was warmly enlisted. My intimate association with
him for some months has more fully disclosed to me his great
worth, than double so many years of ordinary intercourse would

---

[55] *National Intelligencer*, Oct. 1, 1861, p. 2, col. 4, citing *The Cincinnati Commercial*,
which quoted a lettter from Elkwater, dated Sept. 16.

[56] *Dr. Quintard*, 30.   [57] *O. R.*, 5, 185.

[58] *National Intelligencer*, Oct. 1, 1861, p. 2, col. 4. The text of the correspondence
is in 34 *Confederate Veteran*, 169. This definitely fixes Sept. 13 as the date of Colonel
Washington's death. Most of the accounts give Sept. 12. For Lee's comments on Washington, see his letter of Sept. 17, 1861, to Mrs. Lee; *R. E. Lee, Jr.*, 45. In the *Taylor MSS.*
is a letter from Joseph Bryan of Richmond, April 27, 1903, giving an account of the
killing of Colonel Washington as related to him by Adam Bell, one of Washington's escort on the reconnaissance. No papers of Colonel Washington, relating to this campaign,
are in the hands of his descendants.

have been sufficient to reveal. We have shared the same tent, and morning and evening has his earnest devotion to Almighty God elicited my grateful admiration. He is now safely in Heaven, I trust with her he so loved on earth. We ought not to wish him back.

May God, in His mercy, my dear child, sustain you, your sisters and brothers under this heavy affliction. My own grief is so great, I will not afflict you further with it.

Faithfully your friend,

R. E. LEE.

Miss Louisa Washington.[59]

Before this letter was penned, Lee learned, through Loring, what had happened east of Cheat Mountain. The information came in the form of a curious and confused report from Rust. His column, it developed, had safely reached the designated position on the morning of September 12, unobserved by the enemy. At the head of his men, Rust in person had captured the first of several pickets who were silently disarmed. These prisoners were costly, however, and served their cause far better with their tongues than with their muskets. They imposed upon the gullible Rust most amazingly. They told him that there were 4000 to 5000 men on Cheat Mountain; that they were strongly fortified; that they knew of his approach; and that they had already telegraphed for reinforcements. After questioning the men, Rust concluded that their capture was nothing short of a providential warning against making the assault, and he looked out on the enemy's position with very different eyes from those he had hopefully turned on it when he had made his reconnaissance. He saw a "fort or blockhouse on the point or elbow of the road," he reported, "intrenchments on the south, and outside the intrenchments and all around up the road heavy and impassable abatis, if the enemy were behind them. . . . We got near enough to see the enemy in the trenches beyond the abatis. . . . I knew the enemy had four times my force; but for the abatis we would have made the assault. We could not get to them to make it." [60]

[59] Southern Churchman, March 14, 1925.
[60] O. R., 5, 191; James H. Wood: The War, 36–38. The Richmond Dispatch of Sept. 18, 1861, p. 3, cols. 1–2, printed the appended description of the Federal works. As there is no account containing approximately so much detail, it is impossible to say how

That was all. Rust simply waited, without firing a gun, and then withdrew as he had come, after he had incautiously let the enemy become aware of his presence.[61] Rust did not know, and it is likely he never learned that instead of "4000 to 5000 men," a force "four times [his] strength," as he reported, the troops on the crest had numbered only 300.[62] Not only so, but their attention had been diverted, at the time Rust was watching them, by the news that the road leading from Elkwater had been cut by Anderson.[63]

At the very time this disheartening news reached him, it became apparent to Lee that nothing could be accomplished on the west side of Tygart's Valley. The enemy was too much on the alert; the *terrain* was too tangled. Supplies were exhausted, and the line of communications via Huntersville, Valley Mountain, and the Huttonsville road was too long and difficult. There was nothing for Lee to do except to order the columns back to Valley Mountain, with absolutely no positive result for all his planning.[64] "Well," said one indignant Tennessean, "at the end of seven days' marching and starvation, we got back to Valley Mountain, the whole affair having proved a failure—in the opinion of our brigade, chiefly from the old fogyism and want of pluck among the Virginians. Never were men more sick of Virginia and Virginians than we are."[65]

Lee's disappointment was profound. Despite a determination not to be influenced one way or another, by an uninformed press, his chagrin must have been sharpened by the comments of the

authentic this may be. It reads as follows: "[The defense] is built on the summit of Cheat Mountain . . . just where the road crosses upon a hill which has no level ground on its top, but suddenly descends on both sides. The forest along the road at this point . . . consists of the white pine, which are tall and stand close together, while the undergrowth is almost wholly mountain laurel, so dense and interlocked as to be almost impenetrable. Here the enemy cleared several acres on each side of the road. On the outer boundary they placed the tall pines they had cut down, partially trimmed and skinned, with their tops outward; presenting to any one approaching a mass of sharp points raised to a considerable height, and strongly interlocked. Inside this they built a wall of logs and cut a deep ditch. In the road they built up, in line with the fortifications, breastworks of great strength and mounted them with pivot guns, while in the centre they erected a blockhouse pierced and armed also with cannon. On the east side from the fort to the Cheat River, one mile and a half distant, they cleared the road for some distance on both sides, and this can be all the way swept by the cannon. The same is the case on the road westwardly for some distance."

[61] Report of Colonel Nathan Kimball, 14th Ind. Vols., *O. R.*, 5, 187.
[62] *O. R.*, 5, 192.   [63] Reynolds's report, *O. R.*, 5, 185; Kimball's report, *ibid.*, 187.
[64] *O. R.*, 5, 192; *Dr. Quintard*, 26; *Head, loc. cit.*; *C. E. Taylor*, 392; *Worsham*, 44.
[65] *Buist, loc. cit.*

newspapers. When news had first come that Rosecrans had detached troops from in front of Lee and was marching on Floyd,
there had been some mild murmurings and some complaints, not
directed against Lee, over what the editors regarded as a poor
disposition of the Confederate troops on the two possible lines of
advance.[66] These misgivings were expressed along with hopes
of a great victory.[67] Then, after the first disconcerting news had
been received, and the difficulties that had been encountered by
Lee had been explained,[68] there came absurd rumors of a great
triumph, culminating in the capture of General Reynolds.[69] *The
Richmond Enquirer,* the most powerful paper in the Confederate
capital, was so confident of the outcome that it indited a laudatory
editorial which concluded with the assertion that if Lee should
force the enemy "to surrender without a blow, it will stand a
monument to his fame of which any professor of the military art,
however gifted or fortunate, might well be proud." [70] Meantime,
in the gossip over a successor to L. Pope Walker, who had resigned as Secretary of War, Lee's name was put forward by
admirers.[71] It was bad enough to have failed; it was worse to
have failure presented as victory and to be lauded for it.

Lee attributed the outcome to the rain and to the will of God.
He had long believed in a daily Providence directing the acts of
man for man's own good, and now that he saw great designs
balanced on a beam that a featherweight of unforeseen circumstances might tip, he recognized the hand of the Almighty in
every happening and found solace in the belief that God had
ordered best. His fullest statement regarding the abortive action
was given in a letter to Governor Letcher, who had addressed
him in terms of high confidence not long before the movement
against Cheat Mountain began. Lee's reply explained his hopes
and, at the same time, exhibited the temper in which he was to
accept throughout the war the reverses that came to him. It is

[66] *Richmond Examiner,* Sept. 14, 1861, p. 2, col. 2; *Richmond Dispatch,* Sept. 17,
1861, p. 2, col. 1.
[67] *Richmond Examiner,* Sept. 14, 1861, p. 2, col. 6; *Richmond Dispatch,* Sept. 16,
1861, p. 3, col. 1.
[68] *Richmond Dispatch,* Sept. 17, 1861, p. 3, col. 1; *ibid.,* Sept. 18, p. 3, cols. 1–2.
[69] *Richmond Dispatch,* Sept. 19, 1861, p. 3, col. 1; *Richmond Examiner,* Sept. 19,
1861, p. 2, col. 5.
[70] Quoted in *Richmond Dispatch,* Sept. 20, 1861, p. 2, col. 4.
[71] *Richmond Dispatch,* Sept. 17, 1861, p. 2, col. 2.

the first of a score of singular letters that Lee was to write, in
varying conditions, during and after the war, to a number of
individuals who made inquiries he felt constrained to answer. All
these letters are penned in the same spirit, characteristic of Lee
the soldier. They are candid and yet reserved; they explain but
they do not clarify. Sometimes they are so difficult to interpret
that one gets the impression Lee was deliberately reticent to the
point of leaving the essential facts obscured. More than once,
where he makes it plain that he is not himself responsible for
failure, he consistently refuses to put the blame on those who
acted under his orders. For these reasons his letter to Governor
Letcher deserves to be quoted in full:

Valley Mountain, September 17, 1861.
My dear Governor: I received your very kind note of the 5th
instant, just as I was about to accompany General Loring's command on an expedition to the enemy's works in front, or I would
have before thanked you for the interest you take in my welfare,
and your too flattering expressions of my ability. Indeed, you
overrate me much, and I feel humbled when I weigh myself by
your standard. I am, however, very grateful for your confidence,
and I can answer for my sincerity in the earnest endeavour I make
to advance the cause I have so much at heart, though conscious
of the slow progress I make. I was very sanguine of taking the
enemy's works on last Thursday morning. I had considered the
subject well. With great effort the troops intended for the surprise had reached their destination, having traversed twenty miles
of steep, rugged mountain paths; and the last day through a
terrible storm, which lasted all night, and in which they had to
stand drenched to the skin in cold rain. Still, their spirits were
good. When morning broke, I could see the enemy's tents on
Valley River, at the point on the Huttonsville road just below me.
It was a tempting sight. We waited for the attack on Cheat
Mountain, which was to be the signal. Till 10 A.M., the men
were cleaning their unserviceable arms. But the signal did not
come. All chance for a surprise was gone. The provisions of the
men had been destroyed the previous day by the storm. They had
nothing to eat that morning, could not hold out another day,

573

and were obliged to be withdrawn. The party sent to Cheat Mountain to take that in rear had also to be withdrawn. The attack to come off from the east side failed from the difficulties in the way; the opportunity was lost, and our plan discovered. It is a grievous disappointment to me, I assure you. But for the rain-storm, I have no doubt it would have succeeded. This, Governor, is for your own eye. Please do not speak of it; we must try again. Our greatest loss is the death of my dear friend, Colonel Washington. . . . Our loss was small besides what I have mentioned. Our greatest difficulty is the roads. It has been raining in these mountains for about six weeks. It is impossible to get along. It is that which has paralyzed all our efforts. With sincere thanks for your good wishes, I am very truly yours,

R. E. LEE.

His Excellency, Governor John Letcher.[72]

"We must try again," he said, but what was left to try? The enemy could not advance. From that fact Lee took such comfort as he might, philosophically affirming that the offensive had left affairs much as they had been, with the routes to the railroad closed.[73] But if the enemy could not advance, neither could Lee. There were no more byways to be followed to the enemy's rear. Every trail was guarded. It was useless to continue to keep on that front more troops than were required to hold the passes. Especially was it wasteful to camp a large force there when Rosecrans was advancing up the valley of the Kanawha against Generals Wise and Floyd, with troops withdrawn from the northern sector. So, three days after he wrote Governor Letcher, Lee struck his tent on Valley Mountain of unhappy memory, ordered Loring to follow him with most of his forces, and started for the headwaters of the Kanawha.

His first campaign had ended ingloriously. He had not been able to hold a foot of ground in advance of the positions occupied by the troops when he arrived. Everything had been against him, to be sure—weather, sickness, and circumstance. It is very doubtful whether any soldier could have succeeded in such weather.[74]

[72] *R. E. Lee, Jr.,* 46–47.   [73] Lee to Mrs. Lee, Sept. 17, 1861; *R. E. Lee, Jr.,* 45.
[74] *Cf. Worsham,* 44–45. "The failure here was owing more to mud than anything else. In all my experience of the war I never saw as much mud. It seemed to rain every

The larger opportunities had been lost before he came. Cheat Mountain had been occupied. The Federals in front of Valley Mountain were being strengthened by the time he reached that position. Loring had been a most difficult person with whom to deal. Rust's conduct on the 12th had been inexcusable.

When all these considerations are given their full weight, Lee's own performance in at least four respects must be adjudged disappointing. The first, already discussed in sufficient detail, was his failure to push Loring forward from Huntersville when, on August 3, he reached that village. The weakness that led Lee to wait on Loring was more than a temporary obstacle to success. It was a threat to his future as a soldier.

Lee's conduct of his first campaign is to be criticised, in the second place, because he consented to let Rust lead the attack against a position that no trained soldier had reconnoitred. Rust had superb troops—they were to prove that in a desperate hour at Sharpsburg—and Rust himself was no coward. He was a thoroughly devoted man, filled with state pride and Southern zeal, but he was a politician, a former member of Congress, with no military experience whatever before 1861. Unacquainted with the whole art of reconnaissance, his report of the situation on Cheat summit should not have gone unchecked. He deserved commendation for having followed the nameless engineer to the crest, but it was a most serious mistake to reward him by entrusting to him the most delicately difficult part of the whole operation. The task called for a trained soldier, not for an unskilled volunteer who, until that day, had never been in action. Yet because Rust was confident the redoubt could be carried, and because he asked the honor of leading the attack, Lee had consented. If he did not weigh the personal factor, he was blamable; if his amiability overrode his judgment, he was no less censurable.

The third question that must be asked regarding Lee's conduct

day and it got to be a saying in our company that you must not halloo loud, for if you should, we would immediately have a hard shower, and when some of the men on their return from picket had to shoot their guns off to get the load out, it brought on a regular flood. Granville Gray always said it rained thirty-*two* days in August. I was told by wagoners that it was hard for them to haul from Millboro, a distance of sixty miles, any more than it took to feed their teams back and forth. I saw dead mules lying in the road, with nothing but their ears showing above the mud."

of his first campaign is whether he should have overridden the objections of the officers who told him during the forenoon of the 12th that their men were in no condition to deliver an attack after Rust failed to surprise the garrison on the mountain top. This may or may not be a valid ground of criticism. Certain it is that in 1863 or in 1864 Lee's officers would not have dared to raise such an objection, and he would not have heeded them if they had. In 1861 it may have been different. The evidence concerning what actually happened is so scanty that no final judgment can be based on it.

Lee's plan for the unfought battle was very elaborate. Five columns were to operate separately and were to attack in specified order on a given signal. Thanks to the extraordinary efforts Lee made with the four small brigades west of the mountains, they were in position to attack on time. So was H. R. Jackson, who had a very short distance to go. Only Rust's change of mind prevented the execution of the plan as Lee had drawn it up. But if the plan had not called for Rust to give the signal, it might have involved some other move equally apt to be upset by unforeseen happenings. In short, the plan of action suggested that Lee was disposed to be overelaborate in his strategy—to attempt too much with the tools he had. Despite hourly warnings and daily disillusionment, he had not yet learned the difference between 1847 and 1861, the difference between the standard of performance of a skilled and of an unskilled staff.

The contemporary criticism of the campaign was more general. It was that Lee was too much of a theorist and that he had been overcautious. The press that had praised him now turned upon him. *The Richmond Examiner,* which was the harshest critic of the Davis administration, reported that Lee had forwarded to the War Department a plan for the action of September 12, adorned with drawings and "said by military men to have been one of the most perfect pieces of strategy in the entire campaign. But," the paper added with a shade of satire, "as [the plan] has been disappointed, it will be useless to canvass its merits." [75] *The Richmond Dispatch* dwelt on Lee's "too great circumspection" and

[75] *Richmond Examiner,* Sept. 24, 1861, p. 2, col. 3. The records show no such paper-plan as *The Examiner* describes.

warned him that "in mountain warfare, the learning of the books and of the strategists is of little value." It went on: "In a country where it is impossible to find enough level land to muster a company of militia, there is very little scope for ingeniously studied military evolutions or consummately arranged plans of campaign on paper." [76]

But Lee had learned much. His excessive consideration for the feelings of others he was not speedily to overcome. Until after the battle of Frayser's Farm he was to employ a strategy much too magnificent. Some of his other mistakes he was never again to repeat. On the positive side, this campaign and the one that was to follow in the valley of the Kanawha disclosed in his dealings with the man in the ranks the aptitude and the understanding that later made it possible for him to build the superb morale of the Army of Northern Virginia.

Numerous instances of this occurred on the rain-wrapped mountains. Dressed simply in an improvised uniform, with a fatigue cap and jacket,[77] he was constantly among the men. Soon he grew a beard, after the military fashion of the time, and as this was gray, it gave him a paternal not to say a patriarchal look in the eyes of his youthful troops.[78] His manner comported with his appearance. Once when a soldier was charged with sleeping on sentry post and pleaded that he had merely sat down and had not heard the approach of the officer because the softness of the ground had deadened the sound of his footsteps, it was Lee who urged leniency.[79] When he saw men drinking from a spring where the horses were watered, he insisted that they use another spring near his quarters.[80] As he was making a reconnaissance near a picket post, and found the soldiers crowding about him curiously, he turned mildly on the most inquisitive of them.

"What regiment do you belong to?" he asked the man.

[76] *Richmond Dispatch*, Sept. 26, 1861, p. 2, col. 1.
[77] M. B. Toney: *Privations of a Private*, 20.
[78] It is impossible to say precisely when he stopped shaving, but he had a beard by October 20, for he quoted some remarks Robert made about it when he saw his son as he passed through Charlottesville that day (letter to Mildred Lee, Nov. 15, 1861; *R. E. Lee, Jr.*, 54–55). After his return to Richmond, when Miss Mary Pegram complained of his changed appearance, Lee laughingly protested: "Why, you would not have a soldier in the field not to look rough, would you? There is little time there for shaving and personal adornment" (Mrs. Mary Pegram Anderson in *Richmond Times-Dispatch*, Jan. 20, 1907).
[79] *Worsham*, 43.
[80] Toney, *op. cit.*, 21.

"First Tennessee, Maury Grays," said the soldier, Walter Akin by name.

"Are you well-drilled?"

"Yes, indeed," the proud private answered.

"Take the position of a soldier."

Akin did so. "Forward, march," said Lee. . . . "By the right flank, march." When Akin's solitary movements headed him for his camp, Lee added: "Double-quick, march." Akin understood; so did his comrades. Lee was troubled no more that day.[81]

Perhaps the most amusing episode of all came on a later reconnaissance. Lee was busy with his field glasses, studying a distant position, when a soldier of the 16th North Carolina Infantry came up to him. Lee made it a rule from the first, at all times and in any circumstances, to hear the requests and complaints of soldiers who sought him out, and he obligingly dropped his glasses and spoke to the man: what did he desire?

Unabashed, the soldier asked if the General could let him have a chew of tobacco, as his supply was out. Lee treated the request as if it were one properly to be made by a lover of the quid, and as he never used or carried tobacco, he referred the Carolinian to a staff officer, who promptly obliged him.[82]

These were small incidents, but they created in the minds of the men a feeling that General Lee understood them, sympathized with them, and was mindful of their wants. Lee was prompted, of course, by his simple interest in his fellow-men, and as he rode unhappily away from Valley Mountain, where some of his officers so signally had failed him, he did not realize that he was creating among the men in the ranks a spirit that in many a bitter hour was to redeem the mistakes of other officers.

[81] 14 *Confederate Veteran,* 521.
[82] Walter Clark, editor: *History of the Several Regiments and Battalions from North Carolina in the Great War,* 1861–65, cited hereafter as *N. C. Regts.,* 1, 753.

CHAPTER XXXIV

POLITICS IN WAR: A SORRY STORY

HENRY A. WISE, Governor of Virginia at the time of the John
Brown raid, had dreamed in 1861 of organizing "an independent
partizan command, subject only to the general laws and orders
of the service," [1] but when the disaffection of western Virginia
became apparent, just before Garnett was sent to the Alleghenies,
Wise was summoned to Richmond by President Davis, was given
a commission as a brigadier general, and was hurried off to the
valley of the Kanawha. He had been the champion of the interests of that section in the great battle over representation in the
Virginia convention of 1850–51, and it was believed that his
presence in that quarter, as the spokesman of Southern rights,
would rally the wavering.[2] With only a few untrained staff
officers and a handful of troops from eastern Virginia, he went
into the disputed territory early in June. By eloquence and personal appeals, he contrived to raise his force during the next seven
weeks to some 2850 men, infantry, cavalry, and artillery, whom
he organized as a "Legion" and mustered into the Confederate
service. Simultaneously, 1800 state volunteers were enlisted or
brought from nearby counties to co-operate with him. Most of
these men were wretchedly equipped and many of the state
volunteers considered that they had entered the ranks solely to
protect their own homes against invaders. Undependable as was
this force, and inexperienced as were the commander and most
of his officers, Wise advanced boldly down the valley of the
Kanawha to Charleston. "Every step," he subsequently reported,
"was amid the rattlesnakes of treason to the South or petty
serpents of jealousy in the disaffection of my own camp." He
went so far that first Adjutant General Cooper and then General
Lee had to warn him of the danger of being cut off.[3] On July 17

[1] *O. R.*, 5, 150–51.
[2] *O. R.*, 2, 908–9; IV *O. R.*, 1, 367; *De Leon*, 107.   [3] *O. R.*, 2, 996.

Wise had a successful brush with a Federal force at Scarey Creek, near Charleston, but a week later he began to fall back in the face of what he believed to be great odds. As some of the state volunteers passed the homes they had enlisted to defend, they began to drop out of ranks, until nearly 500 of them disappeared. The rest of the command held together until it halted, about August 3, ragged and exhausted, to refit at White Sulphur Springs, beyond the reach of the enemy.[4] It had been an unhappy venture, far less the fault of Wise, who had done his best, than of the administration, which had entirely misjudged conditions in the Kanawha Valley. Wise lost none of his confidence or ambition because of this campaign. Regarding his Legion as essentially an independent command, he cherished hopes of faring forth again, as soon as his men were rested and freshly equipped, to fight new battles and win new laurels. His lack of technical knowledge of war did not deter him in the slightest.

While Wise was in the Kanawha Valley, Brigadier General John B. Floyd was completing the enlistment of the "brigade of riflemen" that President Davis had imprudently authorized him to raise, to the great impairment of regular recruiting in southwest Virginia, where Floyd resided.[5] Floyd was as ambitious as Wise. He had been a lawyer, a politician, a member of the Virginia legislature, and, like Wise, Governor of Virginia. Serving as Secretary of War during most of Buchanan's administration, he had been accused of favoring the South by scattering the regular army and by piling up arms of late models in Federal arsenals located in the disaffected states. A darker charge, inspired by politics, of abstracting government bonds, he had, in January, 1861, successfully met. Floyd was not altogether devoid of native military talent. He possessed no little energy and a world of self-reliance, but he was rash and was to disclose a temperament readily confused in action. While Wise hoped to fire the imagination of the country by leading a partizan corps, Floyd believed his immediate destiny was to carry the war triumphantly down the Kanawha Valley and into Ohio. His troops, on the whole, were

---

[4] Wise's reports will be found in *O. R.*, 2, 290–92, 1011, and *O. R.*, 5, 150 *ff.*, 768–70, 771.

[5] See *supra*, p. 502.

much better equipped than those of General Wise, but they lacked good muskets, artillery, and cavalry.[6]

Just at the time Wise was retreating from the Kanawha Valley, Floyd was sending the last of his troops to the western terminus of the Virginia Central Railroad.[7] Floyd himself soon followed his men, prepared for glory and well equipped for publicity, with not less than three newspaper editors on his staff.[8] He was satisfied that Wise's forces had made a failure of their campaign, though, he wrote, "they will not allow it to be a retreat," [9] and he was equally sure that he could redeem the evil hour.[10] "We will," said he, "have stirring work in the West before a great while, I think." [11]

On August 6, at White Sulphur Springs, the two ex-governors met for their first council of war. Each came in the memory of ancient political differences, each in a determination to yield nothing to the other. Floyd was the senior and was intent on asserting his authority over his rival. Wise was resolved, at any cost, to retain the independence of his command, with which he claimed the President had vested him. The two clashed as soon as they began consultation. Floyd was anxious for Wise to move forward in co-operation with the advance he was about to make in the direction of the Kanawha Valley;[12] Wise immediately protested that his tired soldiers would require at least a fortnight in which to refit. The two parted without a final decision. Foreseeing what was certain to follow, Wise appealed to General Lee to separate his command from Floyd's, but Lee was apprehensive of a Federal advance against the Virginia and Tennessee Railroad, and as he could not afford to divide the few regiments covering that line, he rejected Wise's appeal and directed Floyd to assume command of all the troops in that territory unless he had orders to the contrary from Richmond.[13] Floyd had already renewed his call on Wise to advance, without budging him from White

[6] For the conditions of the two commands, see *O. R.*, 5, 775, 776, 778, 780, 786, 788; *O. R.*, 51, part 2, pp. 221, 223–24, 225.

[7] *O. R.*, 51, part 2, pp. 190, 191, 206, 208; cf. *ibid.*, 210.

[8] Lee to Mrs. Lee, Oct. 7, 1861; *White*, 124.

[9] *O. R.*, 51, part 2, p. 210.

[10] *O. R.*, 5, 766; *O. R.*, 51, part 2, pp. 213–14.

[11] *O. R.*, 5, 766.   [12] *O. R.*, 5, 773.

[13] *O. R.*, 5, 773, 774; *O. R.*, 51, part 2, p. 220.

Sulphur,[14] and he promptly availed himself of his new authority from Lee to issue an order assuming command of all the forces intended to operate in the Kanawha Valley.[15]

About that time, word came that the Federals were advancing and were threatening one of the Confederate outposts. Floyd was a bit confused and somewhat self-contradictory in his interpretation of reports of the strength and position of the enemy,[16] but he determined to push forward and directed Wise to send one of his regiments to move with his column. Once more Wise protested, explaining that his men were unready and arguing that his superior's advance was ill-timed. Immediately there was hot contention—new orders from Floyd for Wise to put all his troops in the road, a fresh appeal from Wise to Lee for the separation of his command from Floyd, a vain effort on Lee's part to smooth out the differences, then peremptory orders from Floyd to Wise and grumbling obedience by Wise, who started at length with all except two of his regiments. Lee sided with Wise as to the policy of a general advance, but he could not sustain him, of course, in his defiant insubordination.[17]

The quarrel was already past mending. Wise was satisfied, as he subsequently wrote President Davis, that "General Floyd's design . . . was to destroy my command, and not only transfer to himself the state troops and militia, but by constant detachments of my Legion, to merge it also in his brigade, to be commanded by his field-officers, and be torn to pieces by maladministration, and to sink me, the second in command, even below his majors and captains." [18] Floyd proceeded to take the state troops entirely from under Wise's control, regardless of the General's wrathful protests. In apprising the President of what he deemed to be Wise's failure to co-operate, he showed no disposition to compromise or conciliate. "I know perfectly well how to enforce obedience," he wrote, "and will, without the least hesitation, do it." [19] Again there was an appeal by Wise to Lee for a transfer;

14 O. R., 5, 774, 776.   15 O. R., 5, 781; O. R., 51, part 2, pp. 223, 224.
16 Cf. Reports of Colonel Lucius Davis, O. R., 51, part 2, pp. 228–29, and Floyd's dispatches, ibid., 221, 223, 225, 226.
17 O. R., 5, 778, 779, 781, 782, 783, 785. The measles that had temporarily crippled the other commands in western Virginia had reached Wise's troops by this time (O. R., 5, 787).
18 O. R., 5, 155.   19 O. R., 51, part 2, p. 237.

again Lee had to sustain Floyd and had to explain to Wise that the army of the Kanawha was too small to be divided.[20]

In much contention and excitement, Floyd moved forward after the middle of August to the vicinity of Carnifix Ferry, on the Gauley River.[21] Wise unwillingly followed, his men as dissatisfied as he. Two of his regiments lost half their personnel on the road, through desertion and measles.[22] On August 25, when the cavalry who were covering his advance broke and fled, Wise was forced to halt temporarily. The next day, by a vigorous move, Floyd surprised the 7th Ohio at Cross Lanes and, without any assistance from Wise, routed it and captured many of its men. This initial victory of his career greatly increased Floyd's self-confidence and indirectly led to new friction between him and Wise,[23] who once again renewed his request to be detached. Floyd countered by offering to trade Wise's Legion to any takers in return for three regiments of infantry.[24] There followed a brief season of alarms and rumors, when Floyd had to put aside his dream of an advance to the Ohio, and had, instead, to call up reinforcements in great haste. Disgusted by what he termed Floyd's "vacillating and harassing orders," Wise made a successful demonstration on his own account though his command was still at half its strength because of sickness. This brush salved Wise's pride and served momentarily to offset Floyd's victory at Cross Lanes.[25]

Floyd wrote little about all this to Lee, electing to correspond directly with President Davis. His rival regarded Lee as his defender and rarely indited one of his wrathful notes to Floyd without justifying himself in a letter to Lee. These missives and the condition they disclosed in the upper valley of the Kanawha had added no little to Lee's troubles in the gloom of his mountain camp, but until the second week in September the situation on the scene of the Wise-Floyd war was not alarming. In fact,

[20] O. R., 5, 799–800, 804–5, 810.
[21] O. R., 5, 785, 790, 791, 792, 793, 794, 796, 797, 798, 802, 803, 804, 805, 812 ff.; O. R., 51, part 2, pp. 232, 235, 239, 243, 244, 248. For the Federal view of these operations, see 1 B. and L., 137 ff.
[22] O. R., 5, 803–4.
[23] O. R., 5, 118, 809; O. R., 51, part 2, pp. 254, 257, 257–58.
[24] O. R., 5, 122–23, 802, 812, 819–20, 822, 823, 826, 842; O. R., 51, part 2, pp. 254, 262–63.
[25] O. R., 5, 122, 822, 829, 831, 832.

Floyd's success at Cross Lanes had suggested to Lee a plan by which Floyd might exploit his advantage and perhaps cut communications between the Federals on the northern and southern sectors.[26]

On September 8, however, a new danger developed. Floyd's principal adversary until that time had been Brigadier General Jacob D. Cox, who had been based on the Kanawha River. Now Lee learned that General Rosecrans was preparing to reinforce Cox heavily with troops sent southward from the Huntersville-Elkwater sector. Floyd at that time was on the northern bank of Gauley River, at Carnifix Ferry, with Wise at Hawk's Nest, twelve miles southwest of the ferry, guarding Floyd's flank and rear from a drive up the Kanawha Valley. Lee at once saw that Floyd might be caught between two attacks or overwhelmed from the north. He accordingly warned him to be on the alert against a thrust southward by Rosecrans and advised him to withdraw across the Gauley in case he did not feel strong enough to fight with his back to the river.[27] Floyd did not see fit to take this advice, but remained where he was, writing alternately of being cut to pieces by superior forces and of advancing to the Ohio and laying waste the Federal shore.[28]

On the night of September 8–9, Floyd received positive news of an advance by a force moving down from the north, and he forthwith called on Wise for one regiment of the state volunteers and one from Wise's Legion. Wise sent the state troops but protested hotly against the dispatch of any part of his own small command, on the ground that he was in danger of being attacked by General Cox. A sulphurous exchange was precipitated, in which Wise argued the unwisdom of the course Floyd proposed to follow in meeting the enemy north of the Gauley River. In the midst of this correspondence Wise found space to carry on a quarrel that had been started the previous day by an allegation on Floyd's part that one of Wise's officers had taken a field gun intended for Floyd.[29]

The conclusion of the cross-fire over the dispatch of part of Wise's Legion was a flat announcement by Wise that he would

26 *O. R.*, 51, part 2, pp. 254, 264.   27 *O. R.*, 51, part 2, pp. 281–82.
28 *O. R.*, 51, part 2, pp. 286–87.   29 *O. R.*, 5, 160, 836–37.

exercise his military discretion and decline to send the troops. Before Floyd could answer with a new order, he was attacked, on the afternoon of September 10, by Rosecrans at Carnifix Ferry. He beat off several assaults, but considered the force in his front overwhelming and fell back during the night to the south bank of the river, whence he again ordered Wise to reinforce him. This time Wise obeyed, but ere his men reached Floyd they were told to return, as Floyd was retreating farther to the eastward.[30] Floyd was quick to explain to headquarters that he had less than 2000 men in action and that he would certainly have been victorious if Wise had sent up the regiment he had required, and if fresh troops on the road to him had arrived in time. His retreat across the river, he told the Secretary of War, was in accordance with Lee's orders. He apparently did not think it necessary to add that Lee's recommendation—it was not an order—had been for a withdrawal in case he was threatened, without risking a fight where he might be driven into the stream.[31] Wise, for his part, anticipated all criticism of his course by saying, "I solemnly protest that my force is not safe under his [Floyd's] command."[32]

Floyd had been slightly wounded at Carnifix Ferry and for a time was almost bewildered. On the 11th, when Wise met him, he was so little the master of himself that he admitted in the presence of his rival he did not know what orders to give.[33] The next day he had somewhat recovered his composure, and as the country to the southeast of them was a rugged wilderness that would not sustain his little army, he decided to continue his retreat to Big Sewell Mountain, a distance of something over twenty miles. Wise preceded him, under orders, and halted, at length, on an eminence close to Sewell Creek, near the present post office of Maywood, within a mile of the boundary between Fayette and Greenbrier Counties. Floyd drew up his column a mile and a half west of Wise on the crest of Sewell Mountain. On the late afternoon of the 16th he held a council of war, to which he invited Wise and such of his officers as Wise saw fit to bring.

Up to this point on the retreat he and Wise had staged three

---

[30] O. R., 5, 146 ff., 160–61, 837–38, 838–39, 839–40, 841, 841–42, 843–44. For Rosecrans's report on the action at Carnifix Ferry, see ibid., 129 ff.
[31] O. R., 5, 146 ff.   [32] O. R., 5, 149.   [33] O. R., 5, 161.

distinct controversies—one over Wise's inability to supply Floyd with a cavalry scout, the second over five wagons that Floyd had borrowed from Wise, and the third over fifty-four of Wise's sabres that Floyd's officers were alleged to have taken.[34] At the council, however, nothing was said of this unpleasantness. Everything began amicably. And as Floyd seemed to have no definite plan, Wise proceeded to tell his superior what should be done. Neither he nor Floyd had any definite information as to the strength or position of the enemy, who was supposed to be approaching in two columns, Cox from the west and Rosecrans from the northwest. Wise was satisfied that he had chosen the stronger position and that Floyd held the weaker, and he argued vigorously for a concentration on the high ground his troops then occupied. When Floyd apparently acquiesced, Wise pushed his advantage and asked that certain new troops be incorporated in his command.

The council ended with Wise seemingly in control of the situation. But as Wise left Floyd's camp one of his officers called his attention to activity among the troops, and he had hardly reached his own post before Floyd's column began to pass through, bound across Sewell Creek, on the road toward Lewisburg. Soon there came a dispatch from Floyd, announcing that he had decided to fall back beyond Sewell Mountain to the vicinity of Meadow Bluff, twelve miles away.[35] Wise was instructed to hold himself in readiness to cover the rear.

This was too much for Wise. Outraged at Floyd's change of mind and incensed that his own plan had been rejected, he calmly remained where he was and in answer to repeated inquiries and orders from Floyd contended that he could better co-operate with Floyd and could more readily repulse the enemy where he was than at Meadow Bluff, which was only sixteen miles west of Lewisburg. Privately he intimated to his officers that he would stay where he was and fight, orders or no orders.[36] Very soon the enemy appeared in strength and took the position Floyd had evacuated. Wise had not more than 2200 men and faced at least twice that number.[37] The road between him and

---

[34] O. R., 5, 851–52, 856, 859–60, 861, 863. [35] O. R., 5, 854–55.
[36] O. R., 5, 853, 855, 859–60, 861, 862, 862–63; Taylor's General Lee, 33.
[37] O. R., 5, 868.

Floyd was steep and difficult, crossing many small streams in its twelve miles and liable to be rendered impassable by rains. Friction, rival ambitions, and military insubordination had now reached their climax. Wise seemed in danger of being cut to pieces before Floyd could reinforce him.

Thus matters stood on September 21 when General Lee, accompanied only by Taylor and a small cavalry escort, drew rein in Floyd's camp at Meadow Bluff.[38]

[38] He had come via Frankfort and had camped on the night of Sept. 20 east of Lewisburg. *O. R.*, 51, part 2, p. 304; *Taylor's Four Years*, 35. Taylor in his *General Lee*, 31, would seem to be in error in saying Lee came via White Sulphur, as that was far out of his way.

CHAPTER XXXV

POLITICS, THE RAIN DEMON, AND ANOTHER FAILURE

THE course that Lee from the outset had urged on the senior of the rivals in the Kanawha Valley was simple: Floyd was to advance if he could but was to secure his rear against attack and was not to take any chances whereby the enemy would reach the railroads.[1] As Lee had approached the scene, he had been informed of the imminence of an attack and had directed Floyd to concentrate and fortify in the strongest position west of Lewisburg.[2] Finding on his arrival that Wise had not united with Floyd and that the army had thus far escaped battle, his first determination was, of course, to bring all the troops together. Loring had been ordered to follow Lee to the Kanawha Valley. When he arrived with his troops the Confederates would be strong enough to combat the Federals. Until that time division might mean disaster.

So Lee reasoned. The strain of Valley Mountain, the weariness produced by his long, hurried ride, and his apprehension of a Union attack on scattered forces combined to make him write to Wise, soon after his arrival at Meadow Bluff, a letter that displays a curious touch of heroics. He said:

". . . I know nothing of the relative advantages of the points occupied by yourself and General Floyd, but as far as I can judge our united forces are not more than one-half of the strength of the enemy. Together they may not be able to stand the assault. It would be the height of imprudence to submit them separately to his attack. . . . I beg, therefore, if not too late, that the troops be united, and that we conquer or die together. You have spoken

[1] See *supra*, pp. 519, 547; see also O. R., 5, 768, 771; O. R., 51, part 2, p. 211.
[2] O. R., 51, part 2, p. 304.

to me of want of consultation and concert; let that pass till the enemy is driven back, and then, as far as I can, all shall be arranged. I expect this of your magnanimity. Consult that and the interest of our cause, and all will go well." [3]

Lee's argument did not shake Wise's conviction that he had chosen the better of the two positions. It was his contention, moreover, that for all practical purposes he was united with Floyd. But he had high respect for Lee and apparently was not a little amused at the unwonted rhetoric of Lee's appeal. In answer, he explained at length the advantage of his ground and bade Lee, "Just say . . . where we are to unite and 'conquer or die together.'" [4] Meantime, Lee or no Lee, he held on to the heights in the face of the approach of Rosecrans's army.

The situation called for action. The following day, the 22d, Lee rode forward to Sewell Mountain and made a reconnaissance. The position was naturally as strong as Wise had affirmed. It was stronger, in fact, than that of Floyd, twelve miles to the rear. If the main attack was to be directed along the line of the James River and the Kanawha turnpike, across Sewell Mountain, then it was the course of wisdom to bring up Floyd and to fight where Wise stood. There was but one military argument on the other side: north and south of Wise ran a few inferior roads by which a vigorous enemy might flank his position, cut him off from Floyd, then wipe out both. The reports from the cavalry outposts were not detailed enough to tell whether the enemy was preparing a frontal attack or a flanking movement by these roads. In this uncertainty, Lee left Wise without making a decision or explicitly ordering him to retreat. [5]

On Lee's return to Floyd he found that officer more satisfied than ever that the Federals were outflanking Wise and were moving against him. Floyd, however, had no tangible evidence of this. Consequently, Lee determined to await the development of the enemy's plans. The next morning word came from Wise that the Federals were preparing to attack him and that he could not withdraw. As Floyd still insisted that the enemy was moving around Wise's position, Lee again urged Wise to unite with Floyd

---

[3] O. R., 5, 868; B. H. Wise: *Life of Henry A. Wise*, 302–4.
[4] O. R., 5, 868–69.   [5] O. R., 5, 162.

if possible and, in any case, to send back his wagon train and prepare for a quick retreat on the first evidence of a move against Floyd.[6] On the receipt of this letter, Wise, who had indulged in some heroics of his own earlier in the day, replied that the enemy in his front was not so strong as he had thought.[7] His statements as to the position of the enemy were contradictory and made the situation more involved than ever.

The absence of any large force in front of Wise might mean that the Unionists were turning his flank; but, on the other hand, the lack of positive information of any Federal movement on either side of Wise's position might indicate that the whole Northern army was facing Wise on the mountain though only a part of it was visible. It was a very close question. Once more Lee had to warn Wise of the risks he was taking by remaining in his exposed position, but, at the same time, he had to assume that Wise had correctly stated the case when he said he could not draw away from the enemy without disaster. Lee concluded that the reinforcement of Wise with a part of Floyd's men might make him strong enough to beat off the enemy even if the whole force were in his front. A moderate reduction of Floyd's army might not weaken him past resistance before Loring came up, if it should develop that the Federals, after all, were operating around Wise's flank. It was dangerous, of course, to keep the forces divided, but if they must be divided they could be equalized. On September 24, therefore, Lee started for Wise's position, and had four of Floyd's regiments brought up at once to his support.[8]

When Lee arrived at Sewell Mountain, in no good humor, he found the enemy in sight, a mile and a half from Wise, on the crest that Floyd had first occupied on his withdrawal from Carnifix Ferry. Whether it was Cox or Rosecrans, or both, Lee could not tell, but he had time to look around and to direct a more thorough reconnaissance. The whole of his experience in western Virginia had been a satire on everything he had learned about war, but here, in the very face of the enemy, conditions were worse than any he had yet encountered. Wise's sick troops

[6] O. R., 5, 874. [7] O. R., 5, 874-75.
[8] O. R., 5, 878; O. R., 51, part 2, pp. 312-13.

were wretched and without shelter. Many of the officers were discontented, ignorant of their duties, and bitter toward Floyd and his command.[9] Disorganization and demoralization were widespread. While Lee was examining the situation he was approached by the youthful lieutenant of a command that had been on Sewell Mountain for some days. This officer calmly asked Lee to tell him who his ordnance officer was and where he could find the ordnance depot. Long-taxed patience snapped. Lee eyed him sternly. "I think it very strange, lieutenant," he said, "that an officer of this command, which has been here a week, should come to me, who am just arrived, and ask who his ordnance officer is and where to find his ammunition. This is in keeping with everything else I find here—no order, no organization, nobody knows where anything is, no one understands his duty!"[10] And amid this military chaos, like a stubborn old seneschal in the last hour of a hopeless siege, General Wise strode defiantly. He had already called on those of his soldiers who would stand by him to step forward out of ranks, and he was prepared to make Sewell Mountain a second Thermopylæ, regardless of all the articles of war and every paragraph of the military regulations![11] It was amusing in retrospect, of course, but it was a terrible experience for a man like Lee, who had dealt only with soldiers taught to make discipline their religion.

That night Lee bivouacked on the mountainside covered by his overcoat, for his wagon had not come up,[12] and the next morning he gathered what information he could concerning the alleged operations of the enemy on the roads north and south of Sewell Mountain. All the reports he could collect were that the enemy was not moving in either direction. It was probable, then, that the main force was in front of Wise and might remain there. If that should be the case, then, obviously the thing to do was to bring up Floyd and fight on the ground Wise had chosen. But

---

[9] *Taylor's Four Years,* 33.

[10] T. C. Morton, the lieutenant in question, in 11 *S. H. S. P.,* 519.

[11] Taylor (*General Lee,* 34) told a charming tale how, in one of his brushes in thick woods, Wise ordered an artillerist to open fire. The officer protested that he could not see the enemy and could do no execution. "Damn the execution, sir," Wise was reported to have said, "it's the *noise* that we want."

[12] Lee to Mrs. Lee, Sept. 26, 1861; *R. E. Lee, Jr.,* 49.

to this course there was one objection, political rather than military, but serious none the less: Wise had staked his reputation on Sewell Mountain, Floyd on Meadow Bluff. To order Floyd to come to Wise, after Wise had refused to go to Floyd, would be regarded by Floyd as a distinct rebuff. Not only so, but it would affect the officers and men as well, for they were almost as much the partizans of their respective leaders as if the two veteran politicians had been pitted against each other in a formal military campaign.[13] Two years later, of course, Lee would not have permitted such a consideration to weigh in his decision, but the war was young in 1861, the politicians were powerful, and Lee had been sent out to harmonize differences, not to aggravate them. What, then, should he do? As tactfully as he could, he wrote General Floyd of his conclusion that the enemy was not moving against him, though a rough roundabout road was practicable for an alert enemy and should be watched. Then he added:

"I suppose if we fall back the enemy will follow. This is a strong point if they will fight us here. The advantage is, they can get no position for their artillery, and their men I think will not advance without it. If they do not turn it, how would it do to make a stand here? In that event we shall require provisions and forage. Of the latter there is none, and the horses are suffering. This command is now in movable condition, and can retire or remain at pleasure."[14]

This was not an order, but it hinted very broadly at one. Would Floyd comply or would he be as stubborn as Wise had been? If Floyd acquiesced and swallowed his pride of opinion, would he come forward promptly, before the Federals attacked, or would he emulate his rival's action at the time of the advance from White Sulphur, and march only when he must? And if he came, how would it be possible to reconcile him and Wise or to get their troops to fight side by side?

The answer came most unexpectedly in a dispatch to Lee from Floyd later in the day of the 25th, while the enemy was demonstrating and Wise was at the front. This dispatch contained a

---

[13] *Taylor's Four Years,* 33.   [14] *O. R.,* 51, part 2, p. 312.

copy of an order for General Wise, sent under cover to Floyd. It read as follows:

War Department, C. S. A.,
Richmond, September 20, 1861.

Brig. Gen. Henry A. Wise,
    Gauley River, via Lewisburg, Va.:
    Sir: You are instructed to turn over all the troops heretofore immediately under your command to General Floyd, and report yourself in person to the Adjutant-General in this city with the least delay. In making the transfer to General Floyd you will include everything under your command.
    By order of the President:

J. P. BENJAMIN,
Acting Secretary of War.[15]

Lee forwarded this paper to General Wise without comment. Explicit as were the terms of the order, Wise debated whether to obey or to defy the War Department as he had already defied Floyd, and carry on for the time a war of his own. In his hesitation he wrote Lee, asking his judgment. Lee replied promptly and, of course, urged Wise's immediate compliance with the instructions from Richmond. Wise thereupon drafted a "farewell" to his men, announcing his recall and stoutly affirming that when the President instructed that he be relieved, Davis could not have foreseen that the order would be received when the troops were in the face of the enemy in hourly expectation of attack. Privately, Wise is said to have affirmed that he relinquished command because Lee so advised and not because the War Department so ordered.[16] A few hours afterwards he left for Richmond. In departing from Lee's immediate supervision, he did not pass out of his life. He was to serve with him in after months and was to share the ordeal of Appomattox in precisely the spirit he displayed on Sewell Mountain.
    The conditions that forced President Davis to recall Wise had

[15] O. R., 5, 148–49.
[16] O. R., 5, 163, 164, 879; O. R., 51, part 2, p. 313; Taylor's General Lee, 34. For a partizan defense of Wise's course, as based on better strategy than Floyd's, see Richmond Dispatch, Oct. 1, 1861, p. 1, cols. 5 and 6. Another review appeared in The Richmond Examiner, Sept. 30, 1861. p. 2, col. 6.

been a military scandal for days before the chief executive acted. Wise had made no bones of his distrust of Floyd's judgment, and even in his official correspondence he had indulged in language that no superior could overlook, even on the part of a politician-general. He had actually written Lee of Floyd: "I feel, if we remain together, we will unite in more wars than one."[17] Public men had written Davis warning him that the cause would suffer: "The Kanawha Valley," said one, "is too little to hold two generals. . . . Those who do the fighting and the people through the country have not such confidence in the qualifications of the generals as will cause them to flock to their standard and remain and fight with spirit."[18] Said another: "Wise and Floyd are as inimical to each other as men can be, and from their course and actions, I am fully satisfied that each of them would be highly gratified to see the other annihilated."[19] The President, on September 12, had authorized Lee, if he saw fit, to transfer Wise's command from Floyd and to replace it with other troops.[20] Lee must have thought that this would magnify the evil, for he had taken no action. Colonel Taylor was of opinion that Lee purposely abstained from attempting to pass on the equities of the controversy between Floyd and Wise. The adjutant believed that if Lee did not actually advise such a course, he knew of Mr. Davis's inclination to summon Wise to Richmond.[21] Mr. Davis's growing willingness to take the political risks and to recall Wise as a military necessity was probably quickened into final action by a letter written him on September 15 by Floyd. This was restrained in language, but dwelt on the "peculiar contrariness" of Wise's "character and disposition" and left the matter in Davis's hands with the assertion that Wise's presence was "almost as injurious as if he were in the camp of the enemy with his whole command."[22] After reading that, Davis had to relieve Wise or else supplant Floyd. He could not afford to let Floyd's letter remain unheeded with an offensive by the enemy immediately in prospect.

Three days of uncertainty followed Wise's departure. As the

---

[17] O. R., 5, 127.   [18] John B. I. Logan, in O. R., 51, part 2, p. 252.
[19] Mason Mathews, O. R., 5, 864–65. Cf. W. H. Syme, ibid., 865–66. Mathews's letter probably did not reach Davis until after the order recalling Wise had been issued.
[20] O. R., 5, 848–49.
[21] Taylor's Four Years, 34.   [22] O. R., 51, part 2, pp. 296–97.

enemy gave every indication of attacking at any hour, Lee proceeded to fortify the position. Meantime, he made every preparation for a retreat in case he found it impracticable to hold his
ground.[23] In the midst of this labor Lee had another visitation
from the rain demon that had pursued him from the time he
had left Staunton, two months before. A downpour on the 27th
swept away the bridges, turned the roads into morasses, and cut
off the troops at Sewell Mountain from Floyd's support and from
all supplies. The country furnished nothing.[24] "In some places,"
wrote Chaplain Quintard, "every trace of the road had been so
completely washed away that no one would dream that any had
ever been where were then gullies eight or ten or even fifteen feet
deep."[25]

The situation was relieved in part, but only in part, on the 29th
by the arrival of the vanguard of Loring's little army of 9000.
Thereafter Lee had "great strength," as he wrote Floyd—sufficient
men to meet any attack the enemy was apt to make. He found
it exceedingly difficult, however, to procure food for the men and
provender for the horses, to say nothing of building up a reserve
supply for an offensive. It was the story of Valley Mountain
grimly repeated. Troops and horses lived only from day to day,
the soldiers still dogged by sickness, the animals so thin they
manifestly would break down under heavy duty. Lee looked to
Floyd for supplies; Floyd did what he could to forward them,
still convinced in his own mind that Meadow Bluff was the
proper position for the army. If all the Confederates were gathered at that point, he argued, and the Federals were immediately
in their front, the Union forces would have to negotiate the
twelve wretched miles of mud through which the Southern
teamsters dragged their wagons to Sewell Mountain.[26]

What should Lee do with his enlarged army? Obviously, in a
country that presented such formidable natural barriers, it was
far better to meet an attack than to deliver one. "If they would

23 *O. R.*, 51, part 2, pp. 318–19, 321–22.
24 *O. R.*, 51, part 2, pp. 316–17; *Richmond Dispatch*, Oct. 2, 1861, p. 3, col. 1, Oct.
7. 1861, p. 3, col. 1; Lee to Floyd, Sept. 28, 1861; *Taylor MSS.*
25 *Dr. Quintard*, 32.
26 *Richmond Dispatch*, Sept. 27, 1861, p. 3, col. 1; *Richmond Examiner*, Oct. 18,
1861, p. 2, col. 6, and p. 3, col. 1, quoting *The Lynchburg Republican*, whose editor,
R. H. Class, was acting as one of Floyd's staff officers. *Cf.* Floyd in *O. R.*, 5, 900.

attack us," one newspaper correspondent wrote, "we could whip them without, perhaps, the loss of a man; but, if we have to attack them, the thing will be different." [27]

So thought Lee, who for once was in agreement with the press, and so he explained when Chaplain Quintard stopped to chat with him one day when he came to bring a package from Mrs. Lee.

"Why, General," said Quintard, in the fine disregard of 1861 for the military proprieties, "there are the Federals! Why don't we attack them?"

"Ah," said Lee, gently, "it is sometimes better to wait until you are attacked." [28]

In case the enemy did not assume the offensive, the Confederates could do so by several routes to the rear of Rosecrans,[29] provided the necessary supplies were available. On September 30 Lee wrote Floyd: "I begin to fear the enemy will not attack us. We shall therefore have to attack him." [30] Almost immediately, however, the Federals showed activity, as if they might throw their regiments against Sewell Mountain at any time. From day to day Lee waited for them to do so, and waited with greater resignation, because no reserve of supplies to sustain an offensive was being accumulated at Sewell Mountain. Driving power was lacking somewhere, and the wagon trains were inadequate.

The first few days of October slipped by. The enemy still busied himself as if for an attack, and showed no signs of attempting any turning movement; the staggering teams delivered just enough food to keep the men from actual hunger and just enough forage to save the horses from starvation.

On the night of October 5–6, it seemed as if Lee's decision to await the enemy's attack was to be rewarded. The pickets heard the creaking of wheels on the mountain and concluded that the Federals were moving up their guns, which had been most unfavorably placed. A Federal advance against Lee's strong works meant slaughter for the bluecoats and certain victory for the Southerners. The artillery would mow down the Union troops; the infantry would finish off those that escaped the cannon.

[27] *Richmond Examiner*, Oct. 12, 1861, quoting *Lynchburg Virginian*.
[28] *Dr. Quintard*, 33.   [29] *Cf. O. R.*, 51, part 2, pp. 324, 325–26.
[30] *O. R.*, 51, part 2, pp. 325–26.

POLITICS, RAIN, ANOTHER FAILURE

Lee must have awaited dawn on October 6 in expectancy almost as high as that he had cherished in the mist of September 12, when he rode out on the western ridge above Tygart's Valley in the hope of hearing Rust's opening volley. When day came there was silence. For a time it seemed ominous; then it became suspicious. Presently, when full light came over the ridges and the enemy's trenches could be seen, not a Federal soldier was visible. While Lee had waited for Rosecrans to attack, Rosecrans had reasoned in precisely the same fashion that it was better to receive assaults than to deliver them. Despairing at length of having that advantage, he had decided not to throw away his own men and had prudently chosen to shorten his line of communications for the approaching winter. During the night he had slipped away. The wheels that had been heard were those of a withdrawing wagon train, not those of advancing artillery. Lee immediately organized a pursuit, but the horses were too weak to carry the cavalry far, and the hungry, shivering infantry started without provisions and had no chance of overcoming the lead that Rosecrans's silent retreat had given him. The weather, once again, was on the side of the thickest coat. Dejected, disappointed, and empty-handed, the Confederates had to march back to the wind and cold of Sewell Mountain.[31]

Not unreasonably, the escape of the Federals without the loss of a man was accounted another failure for Lee, but it did not provoke any violent press criticism. "One favorable opportunity to expel the enemy has been lost," said *The Examiner*. "Shall we lose another? General Lee is able and accomplished. In this campaign accidents have baffled his best plans. He has been delayed by incessant rain and unfathomable mud. After two disasters to our arms in that section, he may well have been cautious lest a third should finally ruin our interests there. But excess of caution or malignant chance has wrought, by mere delay, much of the mischief that was dreaded from defeat. The general, we doubt not, now feels the necessity of a more adventurous policy, and he is quite able, we hope, of adapting his plans to the exigency. We look to him and his brave army now for move-

31 *O. R.*, 5, 615; *ibid.*, 51, part 2, p. 335; letter of Oct. 7, 1861, *R. E. Lee, Jr.*, 51; Lee to Rooney Lee, Oct. 12, 1861, *Jones*, 383–84; *Richmond Dispatch*, Oct. 7, 1861, p. 3, col. 1; *Richmond Examiner*, Oct. 10, p. 2, col. 5, Oct. 18, 1861, p. 2, col. 1.

ments and for successes equal to those which have overthrown invasion and treason in Missouri. . . ." [32]

Lee took this and the earlier newspaper criticism as philosophically as he could. "I am sorry, as you say," he confided to Mrs. Lee just after Rosecrans slipped away, "that the movements of our armies cannot keep pace with the expectations of the editors of the papers. I know they can arrange things satisfactory to themselves on paper. I wish they could do so in the field. No one wishes them more success than I do, and would be happy to see them have full swing. General Floyd has three editors on his staff. I hope something will be done to please them." [33]

Without waiting for the approval of the arm-chair strategists, Lee drafted a new plan of advance on the very day of Rosecrans's retreat and delivered the preliminary orders for its execution. The promptness with which he fashioned this plan demonstrated a greater facility than he had thus far exhibited in co-ordinating staff and line to execute his projects. His hope now was to move Floyd quietly from Meadow Bluff to the south of the Kanawha and to have him advance to a point where he could cut the communications of the Federals on the Gauley. Lee was then to press forward to the Gauley, attack the enemy, and, with Floyd's help, drive them out of the Kanawha Valley.[34] Late as the season was, the success of this plan would achieve one main purpose of the campaign in that it would free the more fertile part of western Virginia of the enemy.

Floyd duly set out with all the troops under his immediate command except Wise's Legion, which he told the Secretary of War he found "to be in such a state of insubordination and so ill-disciplined as to be for the moment unfit for military purposes." [35] But no sooner were the soldiers on the march than obstacles to the execution of the strategic plan were encountered. Sickness still thinned the ranks. One North Carolina regiment was reduced to 200 effectives. The departure of Floyd's wagon

[32] *Richmond Examiner*, Oct. 11, 1861, p. 2, cols. 1–2; *cf. ibid.*, Oct. 11, 1861, p. 2, col. 5.
[33] Letter of Oct. 7, 1861, as quoted in *White*, 124.
[34] *O. R.*, 51, part 2, p. 335; *ibid.*, 337.
[35] *O. R.*, 5, 901; *O. R.*, 51, part 2, p. 342; Lee to Floyd, Oct. 10, 1861, *MS.*, regarding a change of troops, a letter courteously placed at the disposal of the writer by J. Ambler Johnston, Esq., of Richmond. Lee had put Wise's command in its entirety under Floyd on Sept. 25; *O. R.*, 51, part 2, p. 326.

train so curtailed the transport that the horses had no forage and the troops on Sewell Mountain lived literally from barrel head to frying pan.[36] The weather was so cold that Lee himself, who usually disregarded both heat and chill, had to propose one night that he and Taylor pool their blankets and sleep together under them.[37] As for the roads, one of the editors on Floyd's staff affirmed that the like of them had never been seen. "Between the two Sewells"—Big Sewell and Little Sewell—he wrote, "they are impassable to any single team. It requires six horses to move a two-horse load, and then it is a slow and tedious business. It is almost impossible for a horse to move out of a walk from General Floyd's to General Lee's camp, and before we could take up our march yesterday, we had to cut a new road nearly four miles long! . . . If a single wagon stalls the whole rear train has to stop until the vehicle is dragged out of the mud, for in many places, the road is so narrow that not even a horse, and sometimes not a footman, can pass a single wagon."[38] Besides all this, General H. R. Jackson, on the Greenbrier, had been attacked by a considerable force on October 3, and though he had very handsomely beaten off the enemy, the movement of the Federals in that quarter might be the first step in a new offensive directed against Staunton and the Virginia Central Railroad.[39] If this were so, Loring would have to return to support H. R. Jackson before Floyd could be in a position to strike at the enemy's communications.[40] And, finally, if all the other difficulties were overcome, there was soon no prospect of surprise. For the newspapers had learned of Lee's plan and were printing the precise details of what was intended to be a secret move.[41]

On October 20, two weeks after the preliminary orders had been issued to Floyd, Lee gave up the idea of an offensive and ordered Loring back to H. R. Jackson.[42] Floyd took this in very bad part, protesting that Lee remained idle when an advance would have made it almost certain that they could have captured the

---

[36] *O. R.*, 51, part 2, pp. 341, 347; Lee to Rooney Lee, Oct. 12, 1861, *Jones*, 384.
[37] *Taylor's General Lee*, 31–32.   [38] *Lynchburg Republican*, Oct. 22, 1861.
[39] *O. R.*, 5, 220–21; Jackson's report, *ibid.*, 224 ff.; *Long*, 130.
[40] *O. R.*, 51, part 2, pp. 338, 347, 348–49.
[41] *Richmond Dispatch*, Oct. 22, 1861, p. 3, col. 1, and Oct. 23, 1861, p. 3, col. 2, quoting *The Lynchburg Virginian*.
[42] *O. R.*, 5, 908; *O. R.*, 51, part 2, p. 361.

whole of the Federal army.[43] Lee, however, was fully satisfied that the Confederates could not and that the Federals would not advance during the few days of open weather that remained,[44] so he completed the evacuation of Sewell Mountain and sent Wise's Legion back to Meadow Mountain, after all. Even the sanguine Floyd began to intersperse his optimistic dispatches with essays on winter quarters.[45]

The campaign in the Kanawha Valley was over--in barrenness and disappointment. There remains but to review it. Lee had been right, from the outset, in reasoning that Rosecrans intended to strike for the railway. On the very day that Lee had reached Huntersville and had cautioned Floyd to be on his guard against a Federal drive on the Virginia and Tennessee Railroad, Rosecrans had announced to Scott his intention of striking for Wytheville on that line.[46] In so far, then, as Lee may have so disposed the forces of Wise and Floyd as to discourage this offensive, he accomplished the negative object of his mission. The same thing may be said, indeed, of the general result of his operations on the Huntersville sector and in the country of the Kanawha: the disaffection of the people, the difficulties of the terrain, the mud, the sickness, the feebleness of the transport, the absence of accurate information of the enemy, the inexperience of the officers, the jealousy of Loring, and the rivalries of Floyd and Wise constituted such an obstacle that Lee is to be credited with some measure of success in that, with negligible losses, he kept the enemy from reaching the railroad. On the other hand, speaking again more strictly of the Kanawha operations, he did little to achieve a positive result. In his plan to meet Rosecrans's anticipated advance on September 24-25, his reasoning was strategically sound. Again, though he may have contributed little to the drastic settlement by President Davis of the controversy between Floyd and Wise, he yielded far less to their pride and peculiarities than he had to Loring's jealousy at Huntersville. He took command with no apologies and with no exaggerated regard for the sensibilities of the two rivals. He soon stopped addressing General

---

[43] *O. R.*, 5, 900, 917, 925, 927; *O. R.*, 51, part 2, p. 360.
[44] *Richmond Examiner*, Oct. 26, 1861, p. 2, col. 2.
[45] *Cf. O. R.*, 5, 901.   [46] *O. R.*, 5, 552; *O. R.*, 51, part 2, p. 211.

Floyd as "commanding Kanawha Army" and wrote to him as "commanding on Meadow Bluff." [47] That was progress for an amiable man.

Lee cannot fairly be criticised for waiting from September 29 to October 6 for Rosecrans to attack. But his operations after October 6, when the launching of an offensive depended on the quick accumulation of supplies, raise a doubt. There is not a line in the dispatches that discloses an energetic effort to overcome the badness of the roads or the feebleness of the transport. If he considered the prospect of an offensive hopeless, there was little point in permitting Floyd to begin his march or to undertake the second advance. If there was a chance of a successful drive, Lee displayed a willingness to wait on the wagon trains that can be given no less a name than inertia. As a strategist, he showed himself facile, but in all that pertained to the commissariat, he seems to have been well-nigh supine at this time. The rains appear to have washed away his initiative.

Whether the difficulties were so great that it was futile to attempt to overcome them is a question not easily decided on the basis of what is now known of the condition of the roads and wagon trains. After October 6 Lee himself believed he could accomplish nothing by assuming the offensive or by continuing the pursuit of Rosecrans. He told General William E. Starke, at a later time, that a battle would have been without substantial result, that the Confederates were seventy miles from their rail base, that the roads were almost impassable, that it would have been difficult to procure two days' food, and that if he had attacked and beaten Rosecrans, he would have been compelled to retire because he could not provision his army.

"But," said Starke, "your reputation was suffering, the press was denouncing you, your own state was losing confidence in you, and the army needed a victory to add to its enthusiasm."

Lee only smiled sadly: "I could not afford to sacrifice the lives of five or six hundred of my people to silence public clamor," he said. And there he left it. [48]

In honor or in discredit, all this was behind Lee after October 20, and nothing was to be gained by remaining in the mountains.

[47] Cf. O. R., 51, part 2, p. 324.   [48] Long, 493–94, quoting Starke.

He had been contemplating a return to Richmond from the time of Rosecrans's retreat on October 6, and he now waited only to visit the hospitals at Lewisburg and White Sulphur, in order to do what he could for the comfort of the sick.[49] On October 30 he turned his horse's head eastward to the Virginia Central Railroad and left western Virginia—left it to the enemy. Failure to drive Rosecrans out had strengthened the Unionists and cowed the secessionists. Already, on October 24, a majority had voted to establish a separate state and West Virginia was lost to the Confederacy and to the Old Dominion.[50] Lee had no further part in the puny, futile efforts made to recover the fringe of the revolted territory, and he saw no more of Loring or of Floyd. Loring served with "Stonewall" Jackson in the winter of 1861–62 and subsequently fought in the far South. Circumstance and an adventurous spirit later carried him to Egypt, where, in 1875–76, he commanded the Khedive's troops in the war with Abyssinia.[51] Not long after Lee's departure General Floyd was transferred to the army of General Albert Sidney Johnston and, at the time of the disaster of February 15, 1862, was in immediate command of Fort Donelson. He later was put in charge of the Virginia State Line in southwest Virginia, but died in August, 1863.[52]

On the afternoon of October 31, accompanied by Taylor, Lee reached the Confederate capital.[53] He had been gone a little more than three months, and during that time he had suffered greatly in prestige, not only in the opinion of the fire-eaters who were perpetually preaching an offensive policy, but also, and equally, in the eyes of the general public. There was little or no new criticism in the press, but cynics began to call him "Granny Lee" and affirmed that his reputation was based on an impressive presence and an historic name rather than on ability as a field commander.[54] Months later, when E. A. Pollard sketched the West Virginia operations in his *First Year of the War*, he contemp-

---

[49] *O. R.*, 51, part 2, pp. 361–62.
[50] For subsequent minor operations in western Virginia in the winter of 1861–62, see *O. R.*, 5, 250–88, 377 ff.; 456 ff.; 494 ff.; 496 ff.; 935–39.
[51] 11 *C. M. H.*, 203. See also W. W. Loring: *A Confederate Soldier in Egypt.*
[52] 3 *C. M. H.*, 594–95.   [53] *Richmond Dispatch*, Nov. 1, 1861, p. 2, col. 2.
[54] McCabe, 48; Long, 130, 195; Fitz Lee, 125; Mrs. Chesnut, 240; *Richmond Dispatch*, July 9, 1862, p. 2, col. 1.

tuously declared: "The most remarkable circumstance of this campaign was, that it was conducted by a general who had never fought a battle, who had a pious horror of guerillas, and whose extreme tenderness of blood induced him to depend exclusively upon the resources of strategy to essay the achievement of victory without the cost of life." [55] This expressed the prevailing opinion, which seemed justified by the poor showing Lee had made. In the atmosphere created by the victory at Manassas, public expectation had outrun achievement, and Lee, along with his campaign, was written down as one of the disappointments of the war. In retrospect, Lee regarded the whole campaign as having been a forlorn hope from the outset,[56] but at the time he made no excuses, offered no apologies, and prepared no report, because any recital of what had happened would of necessity uncover Loring's delay and Rust's mistake and the foolish, well-nigh fatal quarrels between Wise and Floyd. Lee's code of honor did not countenance self-vindication at the expense of others. His sense of duty to the South made him unwilling, besides, to stir up strife where unity was essential to the successful conduct of the war. He might have been named a bureau chief or an assistant Secretary of War; he might have been shelved, as many another officer of early reputation was, at some station where the risks were less than the honors; his first campaign might have been his last, but for the faith President Davis had in him. When Lee called on the President, after his return to Richmond, he was received with the same dignified cordiality Davis had shown before the failure. There was nothing in Davis's manner to indicate that his confidence in Lee had in the least been impaired. Observing that Lee volunteered no report and was disposed to take all the blame without protest, Davis pressed Lee for the details of what had happened. Lee was loath even then to speak, and exacted a promise that nothing would be said publicly in censure of those who had failed. When Davis pledged this, Lee reviewed the campaign verbally.[57] The political experience of the President gave him quick and ready understanding of Lee's difficulties with Wise and

[55] Pollard's *First Year of the War*, 168.
[56] Lee to Mildred Lee, Nov. 15, 1861; *R. E. Lee, Jr.*, 54–55.
[57] Jefferson Davis, quoted in *R. E. Lee, Jr.*, 53; *Jones*, 168; 7 *Rowland*, 283.

Floyd. His knowledge of war made him put full valuation, or more than full valuation, on the other obstacles Lee had encountered. The interview ended with the President as convinced as ever both of the high character and of the high ability of the man at whom the people already were sneering.

CHAPTER XXXVI

An Easy Lesson in Combating Sea-power

His report to the President having been made, the first personal concern of General Lee on his return to Richmond was to visit his wife, whom he had not seen since he had left her at Arlington on April 22, more than six months before. From Ravensworth, Mrs. Lee had gone to visit friends in Loudoun, Fauquier, and Clarke Counties, at Kinloch, Annefield, Meida, and Audley.[1] She had been brave in her separation from the home in which she had spent almost all her life, and after she had moved twice she had humorously declared, greatly to her husband's amusement, that the enemy would have to take her, as she would shift her abode no more.[2] She had changed her mind, however, and with Robert and Mary, about September 15, she had travelled to the Hot Springs.[3] Lee had been anxious for her to reside for the winter with her daughters at some safe and quiet place in North Carolina or Georgia,[4] but having a will of her own in such matters, she had gone instead to Shirley, where she was sojourning when her husband reached Richmond. The girls were scattered—Mary on a round of visits, Agnes and Annie at Clydale, Doctor Richard Stuart's plantation in King George County, and Mildred at school in Winchester.[5] Robert had unwillingly returned to his studies at the University of Virginia, where his father had seen him en route from western Virginia. Custis had been taken from his engineering work on the Richmond defenses to perform temporary duty at Goldsboro, N. C.[6] Rooney was with his command.

It was a delight to Lee to think that his long separation was to be ended in the pleasant atmosphere of his mother's first home,

---

[1] R. E. Lee, Jr., 35, 42–43; Mrs. McGuire, 65.
[2] 2 Letters and Times of the Tylers, 252. [3] R. E. Lee, Jr., 44, 49.
[4] Lee to Mrs. Lee, Oct. 7, 1861; R. E. Lee, Jr., 50.
[5] R. E. Lee, Jr., 55–56.
[6] Lee to Mrs. Lee, June 24, 1861; Fitz Lee, 102; O. R., 51, part 2, pp. 359, 369.

and on November 2 he prepared to go down the river to join Mrs. Lee. Unfortunately, the passenger steamers on the James left in the morning before he could get away, and, as it happened, no government boat was sailing that afternoon. To get to Shirley at all that day, he had to ride, but by the time he got his horse from the stable, darkness was almost upon him and he was unwillingly forced to defer his journey.[7] On Monday, November 4, he conferred at length in the evening with the new Secretary of War, the brilliant Judah P. Benjamin, who had succeeded the overworked and disillusioned L. Pope Walker. The next morning he had an appointment with the President, and before the 5th of November was over, news arrived that postponed to the uncertain future all hope of seeing his wife. A large fleet of Federal warships and transports had been gathering in Hampton Roads in October, and on the 20th it had sailed for an unknown destination.[8] On November 1, Secretary Benjamin had received an intimation that the flotillas were bound for Port Royal Sound, South Carolina.[9] This was soon borne out. Nervous reports from the Palmetto State now told of the arrival of the ships at that destination.[10]

The departure of the fleet was a relief, because it showed that the Federals were not planning an early advance on Norfolk, or up the Peninsula of Virginia. But any offensive in Port Royal Sound was potentially most serious. The Confederate forces in that quarter were weak on land and almost helpless at sea. The blow seemed to be aimed purposely at a point where the authority of Georgia and of South Carolina met, and it was directed against untrained forces, in a rich country that had not yet been inured to the harsher realities of war. Manifestly, the situation would be a difficult one. President Davis for some time had felt that the Southern coast needed additional defenses,[11] and he at once di-

[7] Lee to Mrs. Lee, Nov. 5, 1861; R. E. Lee, Jr., 53.
[8] O. R., 6, 186; cf. O. R., 51, part 2, pp. 354, 360.   [9] O. R., 6, 306, 308.
[10] O. R., 5, 184. The expedition, under Flag-Officer Samuel F. DuPont and Brigadier General Thomas W. Sherman, had been authorized in full on Aug. 2, 1861 (O. R., 6, 168). Instructions had been issued on Oct. 12 and 14 (N. O. R., 12, 214, 220) and the fleet, convoying 12,653 troops (O. R., 6, 185) had arrived off Port Royal Sound on Nov. 4, after a stormy voyage (O. R., 6, 185). The immediate aim of the expedition was to seize two important points on the coast and to hold them for the protection of the blockading fleet, but no definite objectives had been selected (O. R., 6, 202, 203).
[11] O. R., 5: 834.

rected that it be organized as a single military department. By the same order, and to his complete surprise, Lee was named as commander there.[12]

Lee doubtless would have preferred some other assignment, but he was delighted at the prospect of field duty, and he proceeded to make his arrangements for immediate departure. However, his experience in western Virginia had shown him the dangers of divided command and indefinite authority; and, though contention over rank was repulsive to his nature, he overcame his reticence for once and asked the President what his position and authority would be at his new post. He was told *instanter* that he would go to South Carolina as a full general in the regular army of the Confederacy, the senior officer in the department, and with the entire support of the administration. The embarrassment with which he asked the question and the confused modesty with which he received the answer gave Mr. Davis the impression that Lee did not really know what his status was in the Confederate service.[13]

The announcement that Lee had been chosen to command on the threatened southeastern coast of the Confederacy was not received with general favor. "Granny" Lee, whose tenderness of blood had brought failure in western Virginia, was not the man, in the opinion of many, to conduct a vigorous campaign for the defense of Charleston and Savannah. The opposition to him was not voiced in the Richmond press, but it was so strong that Davis deemed it necessary to advise Governor Pickens of South Carolina, and the chief malcontent of the southeastern states, Governor Joseph E. Brown of Georgia, that Lee, in his opinion, was the best soldier available for the duty assigned him. Fortunately, Brown had confidence in Lee and so assured the President.[14] There were others, a minority, who held that Lee would vindicate the President's confidence in him. That invaluable diarist J. B.

---

[12] *O. R.*, 6, 309. For Davis's reasons in creating a single department, see Davis to Governor F. W. Pickens, *ibid.*, 313.

[13] 1 *Davis*, 309.

[14] 1 Davis, 437; Davis at the Richmond memorial meeting of Nov. 3, 1870, quoted in *R. E. Lee, Jr.*, 53; Brown's answer, *O. R.*, 53, 184; Candler: *Confederate Records of Georgia*, 3, 141. Jones (*L. and L.*, 152) quoted a report that nearly all the officers in South Carolina united in a round-robin of protest against Lee's appointment, to which paper Davis is said to have replied: "If Lee is not a general, I have none that I can send you." In available sources, there is no record of such a communication.

Jones, the "rebel war clerk," chronicled Lee's appointment to the defense of Charleston and Savannah, and added with assurance, "those cities are safe!" He continued:

"Gen. Lee in the streets here bore the aspect of a discontented man, for he saw that everything was going wrong; but now his eye flashes with zeal and hope. Give him time and opportunity, and he will hurl back the invader from his native land; yes, and he will commend the challenge of invasion to the lips of the North." [15]

On the morning of November 6, accompanied by a few other officers and attended by Meredith and Perry, Lee left for Charleston, S. C., where he arrived the next day.[16] He did not tarry but hastened by special train to Coosawhatchie,[17] on the Charleston and Savannah Railroad, the station nearest Port Royal Sound. When he arrived he learned that a heavy engagement at the entrance to the sound was in progress between the Federal fleet and the Southern forts, Walker and Beauregard. Excitement was fevered. Nobody at Coosawhatchie knew what had happened or what was to be expected. The commanding officer of the few Confederate troops in that area, Brigadier General R. S. Ripley, had ridden down the river to ascertain the situation. Lee took horse as quickly as possible and hurried in the same direction.

During the evening he met General Ripley. His news was bad: the Confederates at Fort Walker and Fort Beauregard had been overwhelmed during the day by the fire from the enemy's ships.[18] They had been forced to abandon their crippled guns, and as the United States war vessels could readily cut them off from the mainland, they would have to evacuate their island positions at once.[19] It seemed, at the moment, almost another Rich Mountain disaster.

[15] J. B. Jones: A Rebel War Clerk's Diary (cited hereafter as R. W. C. D.), 1, 96. "Challenge" may have been an erroneous transcription of "chalice."

[16] Richmond Examiner, Nov. 7, 1861, p. 3, col. 1; Richmond Dispatch, Nov. 7, 1861, p. 3, col. 1, Nov. 8, 1861, p. 3, col. 6; Charleston Mercury, Nov. 7, 1861. For Perry and Meredith, see R. E. Lee, Jr., 58.

[17] Charleston Mercury, Nov. 8, 1861.

[18] DuPont's report and a good map will be found in N. O. R., 12, 262 ff. An account of the Confederate naval defense, from The Savannah Republican of Nov. 12, 1861, appears in ibid., 295 ff. The military reports are in O. R., 6, 3 ff.

[19] Lee in O. R., 6, 312–13.

Lee took hold at once and gave orders for the withdrawal of the garrisons and of their supports from the two islands on which the captured forts had been located. Then he went back to Coosawhatchie, established his headquarters in an abandoned house there,[20] organized his staff,[21] and proceeded to make his first hurried survey of a problem that the nature of the country and the scantiness of his resources rendered exceedingly complex.

From Georgetown, on Winyan Bay, sixty miles below the boundary line between the two Carolinas, the Atlantic coast is broken by a series of sounds and bays as far south as the mouth of the Saint John's River, a distance of fully 300 miles. The inland waterways cut off from the mainland a multitude of islands, some of them mere mudbanks, some of them the fertile plantations of wealthy rice planters and "sea-island" cotton growers. Down to the sounds flow a number of tidal streams, most of which were then navigable for some miles inland. Near the northern end of the most vulnerable part of this coastline was the city of Charleston, centre and symbol of the secessionist movement. Toward the southern end was the rich seaport of Savannah, whence annually were shipped thousands of bales of the cotton that was the Confederacy's sole basis of credit in the markets of the world. Between these two cities ran the Charleston and Savannah Railroad, 100 miles in length, crossing a number of rivers that could be ascended by light vessels to within a few miles of the railroad bridges.[22] The Federals had complete control of the waterways, with heavy ships for the deeper channels and gunboats for the upper stretches of the rivers; the Confederates had only four converted steamers, armed with two guns each. Of land forces, Lee found not more than 6800 between the Savannah River and the defenses of Charleston. Around Savannah were about 5500, few of whom could be moved, lest Savannah be unduly exposed. All these troops were widely scattered. Some of them were equipped only in part and had scarcely

[20] Lee to Annie Lee, Dec. 8, 1861; *R. E. Lee, Jr.*, 57; *Long*, 141–42. The late Governor D. C. Hayward of South Carolina advised the writer, Oct. 16, 1930, on the authority of A. S. Salley, secretary of the South Carolina Historical Commission, that the house occupied by General Lee, and subsequently destroyed, was probably one that belonged to Mrs. George Chisolm Mackay.

[21] *O. R.*, 6, 312.

[22] Capers in 5 *C. M. H.*, 35–36, and Samuel Jones in *The Siege of Charleston*, 70, list the rivers, the bridges, and the more vulnerable points.

any efficient field artillery.[23] In lower South Carolina was only one battery. The strength of the enemy was as yet undetermined, but the Federal troops were concentrated on well-convoyed transports and could easily be moved to any coastal point selected for attack.

What could Lee do? On the coast were a number of permanent fortifications and new batteries. He did not know how strong these were or how competently garrisoned, but if the fate of Forts Beauregard and Walker was any criterion, they could not, in their existing condition, long withstand the fire of the puissant Federal fleet. Up the rivers he did not have heavy guns to oppose, much less to halt, the approach of the gunboats toward the Charleston and Savannah Railroad.

He determined, in the instant emergency, on three courses of action. The first was to prepare the defenses of Fort Pulaski, of Savannah, and of Charleston for a far more serious bombardment than they had been built to sustain. The second was to obstruct the waterways up which the Federals might send their ships.[24] The third was to assemble the scattered Confederate forces at the most probable points of Federal advance toward the railroad, and, in case of an early attack, to offer such resistance as he could in the field,[25] beyond the range of the gunboats. Orders were issued accordingly, and as a first step toward reinforcing his all-too-feeble army, he asked the War Department if he could utilize temporarily the various units that were passing through Georgia and South Carolina on their way to other fronts. He was promptly given authority to do this, but was reminded that as most of these troops were without arms, they would be of small value to him.[26]

These three measures of immediate defense called for the most intense activity,[27] comparable in many ways to the unrelieved pressure of the mobilization in Virginia. At the outset, fortu-

---

[23] The estimate of Ripley's strength is based on his report of Nov. 18, 1861, O. R., 6, 323–24. For Lawton's strength at Savannah, see O. R., 6, 305. Ripley's September report (O. R., 6, 285) is not clear. On Nov. 19, 1861, Governor Pickens claimed to have 13,100 South Carolina troops from Georgetown to Hardeeville, but his figures were exaggerated. See O. R., 6, 350–51.

[24] O. R., 53, 186–87.

[25] O. R., 6, 312–13; for the warning to Fort Pulaski, see ibid., 6, 32–33.

[26] O. R., 6, 314, 320.   [27] Lee to Mrs. Lee, Nov. 18, 1861; R. E. Lee, Jr., 54.

nately, the Federals showed no signs of leaving their transports or of capitalizing quickly their victory at Port Royal Sound.[28] There were, at the same time, some evidences of encouraging activity and co-operation on the Southern side. Brigadier General A. R. Lawton, commanding at Savannah, assured Lee of his gratification at his arrival and pledged support;[29] a hurried visit to Savannah and to Fort Pulaski on November 10–11[30] showed Lee that Lawton meant what he said. Governor Brown did not interfere in the least, though he had been disposed to assert some authority over the Georgia coast and was even now arguing with the War Department, which he much distrusted, concerning the return of Georgia volunteers then in Virginia.[31] A number of trained naval officers had been sent to the department and were promptly dispatched to Charleston, to Georgia, and to Florida, where they quickly performed admirable service in obstructing the inland waterways.[32] In addition, the blockade-runner *Fingal* came into Savannah on November 13 with a cargo of arms and munitions, from which Lee was authorized to take 4500 Enfield rifles for the use of such new troops as he could collect in Georgia and South Carolina.[33]

As soon as the first defensive measures were under way, Lee determined to make the most of the continued Federal inactivity and personally to inspect the coast defenses. He went first to Charleston, where he wished to see Governor Pickens about the enlistment of South Carolina state troops in Confederate service. He was there November 13–15 and part of November 16.[34] Conditions were better in the Carolina cities than farther south. In the harbor forts Lee found the best-trained artillerists in the department. They were quite capable of giving the Federal naval gunners shell for shell, but unfortunately, were so few in number

[26] They were having much difficulty in getting their supplies ashore (*O. R.*, 6, 188).
[29] *O. R.*, 6, 313–14.
[30] *Charleston Mercury*, Nov. 13, 1861; *Savannah Press*, Jan. 19, 1929, an article by May Wood Cain, quoting Colonel C. H. Olmstead, commanding at Fort Pulaski.
[31] *O. R.*, 6, 307, 315.
[32] *O. R.*, 6, 327; *O. R.*, 53, 186–87. These men, it seems, had been sent at the instance of General James H. Trapier, commanding at Charleston. See *N. O. R.*, 12, 829.
[32] *O. R.*, 6, 318 ff., 320. Cf. 3 *Confederate Records of Georgia*, 145. The *Fingal* was the first ship to reach the Confederacy with supplies sent by Major Caleb Huse, the Southern agent in London. See Caleb Huse: *The Supplies of the Confederate Army*, 32.
[34] *Charleston Mercury*, Nov. 15, 1861, recorded the arrival on the afternoon of Nov. 13.

and entrusted with so vital a defense that it was doubtful whether any of them could be transferred to other endangered points. Officers at Charleston were not in every instance so well-qualified as the enlisted personnel. The work of obstructing the nearby streams was not progressing rapidly enough. Showing none of the hesitancy that had marked his dealings with the sensitive leaders in western Virginia, Lee shifted a few men of doubtful capacity or questionable habits,[35] placed Captain D. N. Ingraham of the navy in general charge of the armament of the batteries, and determined as soon as practicable to name General Ripley to command the Charleston district.[36]

Lee avoided all publicity in the historic old Carolina port and very cautiously refrained from any discussion of his plans;[37] but there was one man, at least, whose inspection he did not escape. Paul Hamilton Hayne was sitting on the parapet of Fort Sumter, observing the sunset—as poets and philosophers should—when Lee arrived to examine the work. "In the midst of the group," wrote Hayne, "topping the tallest by half a head was, perhaps, the most striking figure we had ever encountered, the figure of a man seemingly about 56 or 58 years of age, erect as a poplar, yet lithe and graceful, with broad shoulders well thrown back, a fine justly-proportioned head posed in unconscious dignity, clear, deep, thoughtful eyes, and the quiet, dauntless step of one every inch the gentleman and soldier. Had some old English cathedral crypt or monumental stone in Westminster Abbey been smitten by a magician's wand and made to yield up its knightly tenant restored to his manly vigor . . . we thought that thus would he have appeared, unchanged in aught but costume and surroundings." [38]

In a spirit less romantic, General Lee held a long conference on the night of November 15 with Governor F. W. Pickens, who came down from Columbia to Charleston for that purpose. Lee wanted five additional regiments of South Carolina troops mustered into Confederate service from the state force that Pickens was maintaining.[39] The question to be decided was how the

---

[35] O. R., 53, 191. [36] O. R., 6, 322.

[37] Charleston correspondence of The Richmond Examiner, Nov. 20, 1861, p. 3, col. 1.

[38] Quoted in Jones, 359. Hayne stated this was in the "summer of 1861," but it was probably on this visit.

[39] O. R., 6, 321.

troops were to be armed and for what term they were to be enlisted. These South Carolinians preferred, in the main, the service of their state to that of the Confederacy, but they were anxious to fight. Pickens could arm only a part of them, and the War Department refused to issue rifles to any that did not enlist, as units, for the duration of the war.[40] In a single interview, Lee and Pickens agreed on a compromise: South Carolina was to arm two regiments, or the equivalent, of men willing to serve until peace was declared, and Lee was to issue 2500 of the Enfields received on the *Fingal* to South Carolina commands who pledged a similar period of enlistment. Orders to this effect were issued on November 16,[41] and Lee returned to Coosawhatchie. He waited there only long enough to send Ripley to Charleston and to issue a few necessary instructions.[42] Then he hurried on to Savannah, arriving after midnight on the 17th, and proceeded thence on a two-day inspection of the Brunswick district and the northern part of the east coast of Florida.[43]

The examination of these scattered defenses led to the most important decision of Lee's entire stay in the department. He was satisfied, from what he saw, that it was impracticable to defend all the islands and waterways with the forces he then had or could reasonably hope to muster. He accordingly determined on three related steps: first, to withdraw all the guns and garrisons from the minor, outlying positions; second, to strengthen still further and, if possible, to hold the entrance to Cumberland Sound, the approaches to Brunswick, Fort Pulaski, Savannah, and Charleston; and third, to construct in front of Savannah and the lower end of the Charleston and Savannah Railroad a deep interior line, so drawn that he could concentrate and hold it with the troops at his disposal, while compelling the enemy to fight where the heaviest guns of the warships could not be used.[44]

In making this last decision, Lee may have been influenced to some extent by his father's strategical theories. While Lee was a small boy, "Light-Horse Harry" had once talked with Charles Carter Lee about the defense of the Atlantic seaboard, specifically

---

[40] *O. R.*, 1, 765.   [41] *O. R.*, 6, 322.
[42] *O. R.*, 6, 323; Lee to Mrs. Lee, Nov. 18, 1861; *R. E. Lee, Jr.*, 54.
[43] *Charleston Mercury*, Nov. 20, 23, 1861.
[44] *O. R.*, 6, 327, 332 *ff.*; Long, 140.

of Virginia, against an enemy that controlled the sea. The elder Lee had then said that in case of an attack up the rivers, it would be desirable to withdraw the armed forces from the water front and to take up a line far enough back from the streams to make the guns of the ships useless. Charles Carter Lee doubtless had told his younger brother of his father's views.[45]

The orders for the withdrawal from the more exposed positions General Lee issued on the ground at the time of his inspection, and he appealed to the War Department to supply his greatest immediate need, that of artillerists and qualified instructors in gunnery.[46] For the improvement of the defenses, which he pronounced "poor indeed," he "laid off enough work," as he wrote two of his daughters, "to employ our people for a month." He added: "I hope the enemy will be polite enough to wait for us. It is difficult to get our people to realize their position."[47]

The decision to organize the defense by these successive steps was made about November 19, and was the basis of all that Lee did during the remainder of his service on the southeastern coast. Every day there were new vexations, new developments, new complications, but every day there was effort to speed up the work on the principal forts and obstructions, to further the preparation of the inner line, and to procure and train more troops. It was an unromantic routine of duty, dirt, and drudgery. His ultimate hope, through it all, was that if he built up his force and his fortifications sufficiently, the Federals would be unwilling to leave their ships.[48]

In the arduous work of persuading proud Southern soldiers to bend their backs to pick and shovel, Lee was greatly aided by the singular irresolution of the commander of the Federal land force, Brigadier General Thomas W. Sherman.[49] Until November 24 no movement by the enemy interrupted Lee's preparations. Then

[45] George Taylor Lee, son of Charles Carter Lee, to the writer.
[46] O. R., 6, 327.
[47] R. E. Lee to Annie and Agnes Lee, Nov. 22, 1861; Lee to Annie Lee, Dec. 8, 1861; R. E. Lee, Jr., 56, 57. Cf. Lee to R. F. W. Allston, Nov. 17, 1861, MS.: "[the defense of our coast] will require every exertion on our part to defend our property there exposed."
[48] O. R., 53, 194–95.
[49] This Rhode Islander, with whom Lee had never served in the United States army, was a West Point graduate and was technically proficient, but he underestimated the great advantage that sea power gave him and he consistently magnified his difficulties. Already he had notified Washington that he could not undertake a major operation unless he received twelve additional regiments (O. R., 6, 188, 189, 192).

Flag Officer DuPont landed a force and occupied a part of Tybee Island, at the mouth of the Savannah River, which Lee had evacuated.[50] Lee did not turn aside on this account, nor was he especially alarmed. The work of strengthening Fort Pulaski had not progressed so rapidly as he had wished, to be sure, but the river had been obstructed, and Fort Jackson, close to Savannah, had been armed. Lee did not believe that the passage of the river could be forced[51] and he attached little importance to the seizure of any of the islands, reasoning that the enemy could easily take any of them that the fleet could approach, but that, having pillaged them, the Federals would not find it worth while to hold them.[52] There was, in fact, no certainty in his mind, as yet, that the main attack was to be on Savannah. He sent special warning to General Ripley to be on the alert at Charleston while the Federals were rejoicing over the seizure of Tybee Island.[53]

The digging of the inner line involved close daily inspection. Lee took it upon himself to supervise the work in front of Coosawhatchie, where the enemy could bring his gunboats close to the railroad.[54] When not directly engaged there, he would visit some other part of the line, returning to headquarters for dinner at early candlelight and then working over his official papers until 11 o'clock or midnight.[55] It was a gruelling pace. One day he covered 115 miles, 35 of them on Greenbrier, a young gray horse he had seen in western Virginia and had purchased when his owner's command had joined Lee in Carolina.[56] The strength and endurance of this fine animal won him the reputation of being a "fine traveller" and ere long his old name was dropped and he became simply Traveller. Often Lee rode alone on Traveller to make inspections and, as a lover of horses, frequently visited the stables and examined the animals attached to the batteries.

[50] 12 N. O. R., 325; 6 O. R., 32. General Sherman had no hand in this operation but, on the contrary, argued the very next day that the army should content itself with establishing a firm and secure base on the coast (O. R., 6, 190–91). A little later he was to advise the Secretary of War that his "professional reputation" as a soldier, "to say nothing of the public interest," would not permit him "to make dashes without object and without lasting results" (O. R., 6, 209).

[51] O. R., 6, 33.   [52] O. R., 6, 329.

[53] O. R., 53, 191.   [54] Long, 139.

[55] Lee to Mrs. Lee, Dec. 25, 1861; R. E. Lee, Jr., 59.

[56] R. E. Lee to G. W. C. Lee, Dec. 29, 1861; Jones, L. and L., 157. Traveller became such a figure in the Confederate army that he and General Lee's other mounts deserve a separate note. It appears as Appendix I—5.

His comings and goings were so unostentatious that many of the men did not know him. Once he passed a sergeant and a teamster on his rounds. The sergeant duly saluted him, but the teamster, who happened to be deaf, at once inquired of his companion in a loud voice: "I say, Sergeant, who *is* that durned old fool? He's always a-pokin' round my hosses as if he meant to steal one of 'em." [57]

On December 2, Lee's journey was down Broad River to organize a light force to cope with marauding parties that were doing much damage to the estates of the planters, despite General Sherman's orders to the contrary.[58] Three days later, Lee was at Palmetto Point, where he had a distant view of the fleet, the future movements of which he was hourly pondering. Then, following a futile demonstration by the Federals in the vicinity of Garden's Corner, he went to Charleston again on December 11.[59] That visit gave him a touch of the social life he so much enjoyed, for he put up at the Mills House, where he met a number of ladies, including the wife of Major A. L. Long, formerly of Loring's army, who had been named on the general staff at Lee's headquarters. While Lee was chatting very cheerfully in the parlor of the hotel, a great fire swept swiftly across the city and almost cut off escape from the hotel before Lee was conscious of the proximity of the flames. The members of his party had to make their way down a rear stairs, half-choked with smoke, to reach the open air. Lee insisted on carrying the baby of one of the ladies in his arms, and left his baggage to the flames. Fortunately, the hotel escaped destruction, and Lee and his staff found quarters in the home of Charles Alston on the Battery.[60]

Lee's ready reception at the Alston mansion was typical of the place he had quickly won for himself in South Carolina. His reticence concerning his military plans was generally remarked,[61] but his bearing, his activity, his determination to save Charleston

---

[57] *Eggleston*, 142 ff. [58] *O. R.*, 6, 335; Sherman's orders, *O. R.*, 6, 187–88.

[59] *O. R.*, 5, 195, 196; *O. R.*, 6, 341, 343–44. *Charleston Mercury*, Dec. 14, 1861. Lee remained in Charleston until Dec. 16 or 17, for he dated at Charleston on the 16th a letter acknowledging the gift of a mattress from G. B. Stacy of Richmond (*MS. MO-1*, Confederate Museum; *Calendar Confederate Papers*, 315).

[60] *Long*, 135–36; *Taylor's General Lee*, 40–41. There seems no foundation for the story, quoted by Miss Katherine C. Stiles, in *The Richmond Times Dispatch* of Jan. 20, 1907, that Lee directed the fire fighting and halted the spread of the flames.

[61] *Richmond Examiner*, Dec. 7, 1861, p. 2, col. 6; Dec. 9, 1861, p. 2, col. 6

from the enemy, and the manifest wisdom of his military arrangements, together with the fact that he was the son of a distinguished defender of South Carolina, made a most favorable
impression apparently on every one, with the sole exception of
General Ripley. This officer, a native of Ohio and a graduate
of West Point, had resigned from the army in 1853 and had
entered business in Charleston, the home of his wife. He was
portly, of commanding presence, and, except to his friends, was
of a pompous manner. A sworn enemy of red tape, he was, as
General Beauregard later maintained, of "restless and insubordinate nature," [62] and for some unknown reason took a violent dislike to Lee.[63] With the self-control that always marked his acts,
Lee ignored Ripley's peculiarities and made the most of his
abilities.

For nearly a week Lee studied the city's defenses. He placed
new obstructions in the rivers and he changed batteries without
removing guns from the principal forts, which he insisted on
keeping at full armament in view of the possibility that the
enemy contemplated an attack.[64] Already he had set up Charleston and its environs as one of the five districts into which he had
divided his department.[65] Before he had completed this work at
Charleston, there came a letter from the adjutant general of the
state, with the approval of the governor, placing all the troops of
the state at his disposal, without reservation.[66] This was a triumph
of diplomacy and honest effort. Lee had already received 1400
reinforcements from other states,[67] and soon after he returned to
Coosawhatchie on December 17 he had notice from Richmond
that six regiments of infantry, the Phillips Legion, and two batteries of field artillery were moving to his support. Some of these
troops had already been under his command in western Virginia.[68]

This increment and the pledge of the Carolina state forces
greatly improved his prospects, though he was still embarrassed
by the shortage of artillery and by the rival purchasing of state

---

[62] 2 *Roman*, 276.
[63] See *infra*, p. 630; for Ripley's career see 4 *C. M. H.*, 418–19; *Eggleston*, 164 *ff.*
[64] *O. R.*, 6, 344; *O. R.*, 53, 193, 196.   [65] *O. R.*, 6, 345, 347.
[66] *O. R.*, 6, 345; *O. R.*, 53, 199.   [67] *O. R.*, 53, 190, 192.
[68] *O. R.*, 5, 100; *O. R.*, 6, 347, 348, 349; *O. R.*, 53, 198, 199, 201; *cf. ibid.*, 202.

and Confederate troops in the same territory.[69] Numerical superiority in land forces was shifting, for once, to the Confederate side; but on the rivers and deep estuaries, heavy guns were needed to combat the Federal fleet. Lee accordingly began a series of deferential but continuous appeals to the War Department for more large-caliber ordnance.[70]

Lee was engaged in correspondence on this subject and was pushing hard for the completion of the inner line when he received announcement on December 20 of an event that was later materially to modify his strategic plan. General Ripley telegraphed that Federal warships had convoyed to Charleston more than a dozen old ships loaded with stone and had sunk these in the main ship-channel.[71] It was an act that angered Lee as much as almost any happening of the entire war. "This achievement," he wrote the Secretary of War, "so unworthy of any civilized nation, is the abortive expression of the malice and revenge of a people which it wishes to perpetuate by rendering more memorable a day hateful on their calendar"[72]—the anniversary of the secession of South Carolina.

Fortunately for the port of Charleston, the sinking of the "stone fleet," as it was called, closed only one of the three ship-channels. It served an almost useful purpose in that it indicated to the Confederates that the enemy apparently wished to "bottle up" Charleston and had no immediate intention of attacking there. Lee, however, did not consider that the action of the enemy lessened the necessity of making Charleston as strong as possible. Fearing, rather, that it might result in a relaxation of effort, he prodded Ripley more vigorously than ever to complete the defenses.[73] At the same time, he felt that Ripley would now have opportunity of employing some of his force to protect nearby islands and to break up predatory raids.[74] In a larger strategic view, he made ready to meet an attack farther south.

[69] O. R., 6, 335, 336, 337, 339, 340; O. R., 53, 190, 194. Rumors that his gains were offset by the arrival of 30,000 Federal reinforcements had no foundation in fact. Sherman, on the contrary, was lamenting his weakness and was explaining to Washington that he had to choose "on what point of that extended and well-garrisoned line" he would deliver his attack (O. R., 6, 202; O. R., 53, 197).

[70] O. R., 6, 346, 348.

[71] See DuPont's report, N. O. R., 12, 421 ff.

[72] O. R., 6, 42–43.   [73] O. R., 6, 349, 353, 358, 365.   [74] O. R., 56, 201.

Subsequently, he wavered once or twice in this belief,[75] but increasingly he concentrated his forces and centred his defensive measures on the Savannah sector.[76]

In the midst of these preparations, Lee came to the first Christmas of the war. After distributing a few gifts to the children of his officers, and to his servants, he devoted the greater part of the day to writing a series of characteristic letters to the members of his family, with whom he had not had many opportunities of corresponding since he had come to South Carolina. Mrs. Lee had been to Richmond after he had left and had gone to the White House, where Annie had joined her. Rooney and Charlotte were also there.[77] These four were the only members of the family who could spend Christmas in the old way.

To one of his daughters he enclosed a gift of money and some violets plucked from the garden of his headquarters. "May God guard and preserve you for me, my dear daughter," he wrote. "Among the calamities of war the hardest to bear, perhaps, is the separation of families and friends. Yet all must be endured to accomplish our independence and maintain our self-government. In my absence from you, I have thought of you very often, and regretted I could do nothing for your comfort. Your old home, if not destroyed by our enemies, has been so desecrated that I cannot bear to think of it. I should have preferred it to have been wiped from the earth, its beautiful hill sunk, and its sacred trees buried, rather than to have been degraded by the presence of those who revel in the ill they do for their own selfish purposes."

This was natural resentment, born of loss and separation, but it was no sooner expressed than his old self-control was asserted: "You see what a poor sinner I am," he added at once, "and how unworthy to possess what was given me; for that reason it has been taken away. I pray for a better spirit, and that the hearts of our enemies may be changed." [78]

He must have rebuked himself for his mild outburst, for when he came to write Mrs. Lee, later in the day, it was in complete

[75] O. R., 6, 351, 369, 370–71.
[76] He was quite right in doing so, for at the time the channel at Charleston was being blocked General Sherman was contemplating an offensive against Savannah or against that part of the railroad immediately north of the city (O. R., 6, 203–4, 208).
[77] R. E. Lee, Jr., 56, 58.
[78] Lee to "one of his daughters," Dec. 25, 1861; Jones, L. and L., 156.

mastery of his emotions: "I cannot let this day of grateful re-joicing pass, dear Mary," he began, "without some communication with you. I am thankful for the many among the past that I have passed with you, and the remembrance of them fills me with pleasure. For those on which we have been separated we must not repine. If it will make us more resigned and better prepared for what is in store for us, we should rejoice. Now we must be content with the many blessings we receive. If we can only become sensible of our transgressions, so as to be fully penitent and forgiven, that this heavy punishment under which we labour may with justice be removed from us and the whole nation, what a gracious consummation of all that we have endured it will be."

He wrote next of his daily routine and of Mrs. Lee's visit to Richmond, but he could not keep his mind from the old mansion where they had spent Christmas in so much cheer in other, happier years. "As to our old home," he said, "if not destroyed, it will be difficult ever to be recognized. Even if the enemy had wished to preserve it, it would almost have been impossible. With the number of troops encamped around it, the change of officers, etc., the want of fuel, shelter, etc., and all the dire necessities of war, it is vain to think of its being in a habitable condition. I fear, too, books, furniture, and the relics of Mount Vernon will be gone. It is better to make up our minds to a general loss. They cannot take away the remembrance of the spot, and the memories of those that to us rendered it sacred. That will remain to us as long as life will last, and that we can preserve."

Then, as he wrote, the old instinct of home asserted itself. If Arlington was lost, where could the family hope to reside? He did not think of the rich plantations of White House and Romancock, but of the dilapidated old mansion associated with the names of his ancestors. "In the absence of a home," he went directly on, "I wish I could purchase 'Stratford.' That is the only other place I could go to, now accessible to us, that would inspire me with feelings of pleasure and local love. You and the girls could remain there in quiet. It is a poor place, but we could make enough cornbread and bacon for our support, and the girls could weave us clothes. I wonder if it is for sale and at how much. Ask

Fitzhugh to try to find out, when he gets to Fredericksburg."

Mrs. Lee, it seems, had written to him of the hopes of British intervention that had been aroused by England's quick protest against the action of the Federal navy in seizing, on November 8, 1861, the Confederate commissioners John Slidell and James M. Mason aboard the British steamer *Trent*. "You must not build your hopes [of] peace on account of the United States going into a war with England. She will be very loath to do that, notwithstanding the bluster of the Northern papers. Her rulers are not entirely mad, and if they find England is in earnest, and that war or a restitution of their captives must be the consequence, they will adopt the latter. We must make up our minds to fight our battles and win our independence alone. No one will help us. We require no extraneous aid, if true to ourselves. But we must be patient. It is not a light achievement and cannot be accomplished at once." [79] In this spirit he closed a letter that exhibits many of the prime qualities of the man—his self-restraint, his faith in God, his love of home, his logic, and his sense of realities. As he saw great plantations ruined on the Carolina coast, and women and children forced to flee and live in poverty, his wrath sometimes rose. Once he protested, "No civilized nation within my knowledge has ever carried on wars as the United States government has against us." But this was unusual language for him. The Lee of the long Christmas letter to his wife is the Lee of history.

Almost before these Christmas letters had reached their Virginia destination, the decisive year of Lee's life had opened. Before 1862 ended, the general who had never fought a battle was to have four bloody campaigns to his credit, and the people who had shaken their heads at the mention of his name were to be acclaiming him the savior of the South. There was little at Lee's Carolina headquarters to suggest such an early reversal of fortune, but there was much to indicate that a bitter test awaited the Confederacy. The soldiers in Lee's department had reached nearly 25,000,[80] and General Henry R. Jackson, Lee's associate in

[79] *R. E. Lee, Jr.*, 58–60. These views of the improbability of intervention he elaborated in a letter to Custis, Dec. 29, 1861; Jones, *L. and L.*, 157.

[80] Exclusive of the Fifth District, 22,223, according to IV *O. R.*, 1, 822. *Cf. National Intelligencer*, Jan. 1, 1862, p. 3, col. 3, for information from *The Richmond Enquirer* regarding numbers and dispositions. The Federal force was 14,768 (*O R.*, 6, 217).

western Virginia, had assured him of the whole-hearted co-
operation of the Georgia state troops, the command of which he
had assumed.[81] On the other hand, the terms of the earliest one-
year South Carolina volunteers were expiring, and the failure of
some of them to re-enlist had seriously reduced the strength of the
Confederates in the first military district between Little River
Inlet and the South Santee River.[82] Lee saw in this the possibility
of a ruinous diminution of the Southern armies in the spring of
1862. He had already addressed the president of the South Carolina convention on the subject,[83] and he now wrote Governor
Letcher, urging that Virginia pass a law drafting all one-year
volunteers who did not re-enlist for the war.[84] Even immediately,
what availed 25,000 men on a coast of 300 miles, when the enemy
had it in his power at any time to concentrate all his force against
any one objective by using his fleet? As if in warning of what
might be expected, the Federals landed 3000 men at Port Royal
Ferry on the very first day of the new year.[85] Although they did
no great damage, they demonstrated what Lee pointed out to
Governor Pickens when he said: "[the enemy] can be thrown
with great celerity against any point, and far outnumbers any
force we can bring against it in the field."[86]

In this situation, Lee pressed as vigorously as ever for the completion of the inner line, the obstruction of the rivers, and the
strengthening of the principal forts. At the beginning of the
second week in January, he went to Savannah and thence on a
tour of the east coast of Florida, stopping at Cumberland Island,
where he visited the grave of his father for the first time.[87] He
found much discontent in Florida. General Trapier was in

[81] O. R., 6, 362, 365. It is stated (6 C. M. H., 427) that Lee met H. R. Jackson in a
Savannah hotel on one of his visits to that city and told him he had much regretted
Jackson's resignation from the Confederate service to accept the Georgia command because, at the very time it had been tendered, he had been negotiating with the War Department for Jackson's transfer to his department, as one of two officers he particularly
desired to have.

[82] O. R., 6, 360.   [83] O. R., 6, 349.

[84] 1 S. H. S. P., 462; O. R., 5, 1022.

[85] 5 C. M. H., 39.   [86] O. R., 6, 357.

[87] Lee to Mrs. Lee, Jan. 18, 1861; R. E. Lee, Jr., 61. Long described the visit, op. cit.,
22–23: ". . . we came to a dilapidated wall enclosing a neglected cemetery. The general then, in a voice of emotion, informed me that he was visiting the grave of his father.
He went alone to the tomb, and after a few moments of silence, retraced his steps . . .
we returned in silence to the steamer, and no allusion was ever made to this act of
filial devotion."

controversy with some of the leading men and was anxious to be relieved. The defenses at the south end of Cumberland Island, which Lee thought he should hold, if possible, were inadequately gunned. New ordnance from Virginia had to be solicited for them.[88] "Our defences are growing stronger, but progress slowly," he wrote Custis several days after his return to Coosawhatchie on January 16. "The volunteers dislike work, and there is much sickness among them besides. Guns too are required, ammunition and more men. Still, on the whole, matters are encouraging and if the enemy does not approach in overwhelming numbers, we ought to hold our ground. He is quiescent still. What he is preparing for or when he will strike I cannot discover." [89]

A week later, some of this doubt was cleared up when Lee was called to Charleston by the news that another Federal fleet had appeared off the harbor. On January 23, the number and purpose of the enemy ships could not be determined because of a storm, but on the 25th and 26th, the weather having cleared, Lee witnessed the sinking of a second "stone fleet" consisting of twelve old merchantmen. This time it was the Maffitt channel the enemy sought to obstruct, with no other result, Lee thought, than to deter ships from running the blockade at night.[90] Simultaneously with this second attempt to close Charleston harbor, the Federals began to clear the Confederate obstructions from Wall's Cut on the inland waterway linking Port Royal Sound to the Savannah River. These moves fully convinced Lee that the enemy was preparing for operations somewhere in the vicinity of Savannah.[91] In order that he might be in hourly touch with the preparations for the defense of that city and of Fort Pulaski, Lee went to Savannah on the evening of January 28, and by February 3 he had transferred his headquarters there. He found

[88] O. R., 6, 364–65, 367, 368.

[89] R. E. Lee to G. W. C. Lee, Jan. 19, 1862; Jones, L. and L., 158.

[90] Lee to Mrs. Lee, Jan. 28, 1862; R. E. Lee, Jr., 62. The reports of the sinking are in N. O. R., 12, 512 ff.

[91] O. R., 6, 367, 369, 370–71. For Wall's Cut, see ibid., 6, 85. See also Lee to Mrs. Lee, Jan. 28, 1862; R. E. Lee, Jr., 62; R. E. Lee to G. W. C. Lee, Jan. 19, 1862; Jones, L. and L., 158. Lee was not deceived as to the enemy's plan. Although General Sherman was still undecided whether to attempt a direct advance on Savannah, to cut off Fort Pulaski, or to operate against Fernandina, he had notified the War Department that he had definitely abandoned plans for land operations north of the Savannah River. For the development of Sherman's plan, see O. R., 6, 193 ff., 212, 214, 217, 219–20, 221; 12 N. O. R., 486, 498, 555, 556.

an admiring welcome at the homes of the Mackays,[92] and the
Sorrels, in the hospitality of the Minis family, and in a circle of
cultivated, sympathizing friends; but he also found that work
which should have been finished by this time had "lagged ter-
ribly," to use his own words, and he had to throw himself into
its completion with all his energies. Well it was for him that in
his days as an army engineer he had been forced to give close
personal attention to minutiæ, for now if he wanted them carried
through he had to keep a hundred small projects under his own
eye. Fort Pulaski had been victualled for a siege the day Lee had
left Coosawhatchie;[93] he followed this with changes in the bearing of some of its guns and with new calls on the War Department for the quick delivery of additional heavy ordnance for
nearer batteries;[94] he had to arrange to withdraw all cannon from
the river below the fort;[95] facing attempted profiteering in iron,
he was quick to take what the government required and to pay
for it at the old price;[96] plans had to be made to induce re-enlist-
ment for the war by Georgia troops whose terms were about to
expire;[97] pourparlers had to be opened with Governor Brown
for the destruction of Brunswick, a then deserted resort of rich
planters which Lee did not want the enemy to occupy;[98] an effort
had to be made to get trained artillerists from Charleston in case
General Ripley thought they could be transferred without danger
to the Carolina city.[99] These constituted only a part of the details
to which he had to give his personal attention for a reason he
confided to Mrs. Lee: "It is so very hard to get anything done,"

[92] R. E. Lee to G. W. C. Lee, Jan. 19, 1862; Jones, *L. and L.*, 158. In *The Richmond
Times-Dispatch* of Jan. 20, 1907, Miss Katherine C. Stiles stated that the Mackays put at
Lee's disposal the quarters he had so often used when he had been at Cockspur Island,
more than thirty years before. He usually spent the evenings there, Miss Stiles said, but
would not spend the night for fear he would bring reprisals on the family in case Savannah was captured. This was his practice throughout the war whenever he was close to
the enemy, except in Richmond and in Petersburg. General G. Moxley Sorrel noted in his
charming *Recollections of a Confederate Staff Officer* (cited hereafter as *Sorrel*), 77, that
Lee listened to the music of Miss Sorrel with much pleasure and frequently in later
months inquired about her, always as "my singing bird."

[93] 6 *C. M. H.*, 83.　　　　　　　　　　[94] *O. R.*, 6, 375, 389.

[95] Lee to Mrs. Lee, Feb. 8, 1862, *R. E. Lee, Jr.*, 62–63; *O. R.*, 6, 379.

[96] *O. R.*, 6, 376.　　　　　　　　　　[97] *O. R.*, 6, 376.

[98] *O. R.*, 6, 377, 379, 386–87, 390, 391, 396; 3 *Confederate Records of Georgia*, 151–
52, 152–53, 163–65.

[99] *O. R.*, 6, 385–86, 389.

he wrote, "and while all wish well and mean well, it is so [difficult] to get them to act energetically and promptly." [100]

While Lee was struggling with inertia, incompetence, and a multitude of troublesome duties, the Confederate cause elsewhere had suffered two disasters. On February 6, Fort Henry, on the lower Tennessee River, was captured by a Federal army under a general who then came prominently into the news for the first time, Ulysses S. Grant. A week later, the Union forces, supported by a flotilla of gunboats, invested Fort Donelson, at Dover, Tenn., and on the 15th, after two days' hard fighting, forced 15,000 Confederates to surrender. General Gideon Pillow, whom Lee had known in the Mexican War, and General John B. Floyd, who had been sent from western Virginia to Tennessee, contrived to get away. The cavalry escaped also, thanks to the vigilance of Colonel Nathan B. Forrest. In other respects, the disaster was complete and shook the hold of General Albert Sidney Johnston on Tennessee. Almost at the same time, on February 8, General Henry A. Wise, with 3000 men, was attacked by an overpowering naval and land force at Roanoke Island, N. C., and was driven from the island with the loss or capture of two-thirds of his little command.

The whole South was depressed, but Lee received the reports without flinching. "The news . . . is not favorable," he said before he heard the worst, "but we must make up our minds to meet with reverses and to overcome them. I hope God will at last crown our efforts with success. But the contest must be long and severe, and the whole country must go through much suffering. It is necessary we should be humbled and taught to be less boastful, less selfish and more devoted to right and justice to all the world." [101]

The immediate result on Lee's command of the disasters in Tennessee and in North Carolina was a double call from the War Department—to withdraw all units from the islands to the mainland for a more concentrated defense with a smaller force, and, secondly, to abandon Florida, except for the line of the

---

[100] Lee to Mrs. Lee, Feb. 8, 1862; *R. E. Lee, Jr.*, 63-64.
[101] Lee to Mrs. Lee, Feb. 8, 1862; *cf.* same to same, Feb. 23, 1862; *R. E. Lee, Jr.*, 64.

Apalachicola River, and to send the troops from that state to General Albert Sidney Johnston. The first of these orders Lee had already anticipated, except for Cumberland Island, and the second he executed promptly.[102]

The loss of force amounted to nearly 4000 men,[103] and the change in the situation meant, of course, that Lee could expect no further reinforcements. He would be disadvantaged if the Federals made a descent in force, but he made no complaint to the War Department and continued to press with all his energy for the obstruction of the Savannah River and for the better defense of that sector.[104] It seemed likely that the Federals who had seized Roanoke Island would seek to take Norfolk in reverse rather than turn their attention to Charleston. Their movement, however, was sufficiently doubtful for Lee to hold at Charleston the whole of Ripley's force, 4569 effectives,[105] and to study a further contraction of the lines in that quarter. "I am in favor," he said, "of abandoning all exposed points as far as possible within reach of the enemy's fleet of gunboats, and of taking interior positions, where we can meet on more equal terms. All our resources should be applied to those positions." [106]

Much remained to be done on the Savannah sector, where it was now apparent the enemy was slowly making preparations to deliver his long-delayed offensive.[107] Lee did not believe the troops or the people had been fully aroused to the import of the disaster in Tennessee. In case Savannah were taken, or the railroad were cut, it would be necessary to establish new railroad connections by way of Augusta. Lee urged this strongly on Governor Brown.[108] Obstructions in the Savannah River below Augusta were also desirable as a precautionary measure.[109]

Progress had been substantial but the inner line took form slowly. Anxiety was great as the Federals made ready. When

---

102 *O. R.*, 6, 390, 393–94, 398, 399, 400.

103 This brought Lee's strength down to approximately that of his adversary, who had 17,882. *O. R.*, 6, 237, 371.

104 *O. R.*, 6, 397–98. 105 *O. R.*, 6, 376, 391.

106 *O. R.*, 6, 394; *cf.* to General Evans, *ibid.*, 394.

107 For Sherman's final decision, on orders from McClellan, to reduce Fort Pulaski rather than to attack Savannah, see *O. R.*, 6, 225, 226, 235, 236.

108 *O. R.*, 6, 397. 109 *O. R.*, 6, 384–85.

Lee went to church on February 22, the day set aside by the President for fasting and prayer,[110] it was in a deepened conviction that the Southern cause rested in hands more powerful than his own. Many an hour he spent in prayer, many a midnight found him awake and wondering what the Federals were doing in the river.[111] His messages to his family were blends of hope and doubts, a very complete summary of affairs as he saw them, three months and a half after he had come South. "I am engaged," he said in one of these letters, "in constructing a line of defence at Fort Jackson which if time permits and guns can be obtained, I hope will keep them out." [112] And again: ". . . The enemy seems to be slowly making his way to the Savannah River through the creeks and marshes, and his shells now interrupt its navigation. We have nothing that floats that can contend with him, and it is grating to see his progress unopposed by any resistance we can make. The communication with Fort Pulaski is cut. That may in time be reduced, but I am constructing batteries at Fort Jackson which, if our men will fight, will give him trouble to get to the city. His batteries are so numerous and strong that I know they are hard to resist, but if we have the time and guns they ought if vulnerable to be beaten off. . . . The work progresses slowly and it is with the utmost difficulty that it is pushed ahead. . . . The facilities the arms or branches of these waters afford for approach and investment in all directions make it one of the hardest places to defend I ever saw, against light draft boats." [113]

On March 2, in the same spirit, balancing "buts" and "ifs," he confided to one of his daughters: "I have been doing all I can with our small means and slow workmen to defend the cities and coast here. Against ordinary numbers we are pretty strong, but against the hosts our enemies seem able to bring everywhere, there is no calculating. But if our men will stand to their work, we shall give them trouble and damage them yet." [114]

[110] Lee to Mrs. Lee, Feb. 23, 1862; R. E. Lee, Jr., 65.
[111] Lee to Annie Lee, March 2, 1862; R. E. Lee, Jr., 65.
[112] Lee to Mrs. Lee, Feb. 23, 1862; R. E. Lee, Jr., 64.
[113] R. E. Lee to G. W. C. Lee, Feb. 23, 1862; Jones, L. and L., 161–62.
[114] R. E. Lee to Annie Lee, March 2, 1862; R. E. Lee, Jr., 65–66.

On the evening after he wrote this letter, there was handed to Lee a telegram that read as follows:

General R. E. Lee,   Richmond, Va., March 2, 1862.
  Savannah:
 If circumstances will, in your judgment, warrant your leaving, I wish to see you here with the least delay.

             JEFFERSON DAVIS.[115]

The tone of this message was not that of an order of recall, but in other respects it was as formal and as indefinite as that memorable paper he had received in February, 1861, in Texas. Why did Davis wish to see him? Was it a new command? And why such urgency to have him in Richmond when all signs pointed to an early battle for Savannah? Lee knew no reason for this unexpected summons, but he must have felt it meant his final separation from the coastal command, for he promptly replied that he would leave on the morning of March 4,[116] and he began immediately to make disposition of his staff officers. His chief concern, of course, was for the Savannah defenses, and he gave special and minute instructions to General Lawton concerning the places that remained to be fortified and the measures that should be taken to halt the further progress of the enemy up the Savannah River.[117] In the belief that an emergency in Richmond had inspired the President's telegram, Lee disposed of these details so quickly that he was able to start on the evening of the 3d instead of on the 4th. With Taylor and his servants he took the train to Charleston and thence, after a day, to Richmond.[118]

His mission on the southeastern coast was ended. He never saw Savannah or Cumberland Island or even Charleston again, until he went back, eight years later, prematurely aged and nearing his end, to seek escape from the rigors of a winter in the mountains of Virginia. He had done his work thoroughly. He was fortunate, to be sure, in having as his adversary a man cautious and indecisive, hampered by having to rely for his transport on naval officers who were more interested in maintaining

---

[115] *O. R., 6*, 400.   [116] *O. R., 53*, 221.   [117] *O. R., 6*, 401.
[118] He reached Charleston the 4th and left on the 5th (*Charleston Mercury*, March 5, 1862).

the blockade than in landing an army. He could not have asked a more obliging opponent, one less like the young officer who had used sea-power to the fullest in the Fort Donelson campaign. Making the fullest allowance for Sherman's futility and indecision, Lee nevertheless had prevented the development of an offensive that had threatened serious damage to the Confederate cause. Without the loss of a single soldier from the fire of the enemy, he had held off Sherman from the railroad, and had put so many difficulties in the way of his advance that the Federals had nowhere moved beyond the cover of their warships.

The Unionists battered down Fort Pulaski on April 10–11, 1862, as Lee had anticipated they might, but, on the basis of what Lee had initiated, later commanders so strengthened Savannah that the Federals did not think its occupation worth the losses its capture would entail. The Confederate flag waved there until, on December 21, 1864, an abler Sherman took it in reverse, at the end of his "march to the sea." The credit for the defensive system that balked the combined Federal land-and-sea forces in front of Savannah belongs to Lee more than to any one else. The Charleston defenses, however, which held out until February 17, 1865, were not his work. Lee did little to the forts nearest that city and worked chiefly to obstruct the adjacent streams and estuaries. General Beauregard had done much for the defenses before he left for Virginia and he later rendered the whole of the fortifications more formidable.[119]

Lee's inner line along the coast doubtless was much too elaborate and extended to be held by the limited force subsequently available in the department. This, however, was a virtue at the time the works were thrown up. Having a very small army, but charged with safeguarding a lateral railroad that ran behind the greater part of the line, Lee had to design so strong and so deep a defensive system that it could be held by a few regiments until the arrival of reinforcements by way of the railroad.[120] It is much to be regretted that no complete description of this line exists and that none can be prepared from the records.

Lee departed from South Carolina with the curious distinction

---

[119] 2 *Roman*, 6–8.

[120] For a critique of the system, in answer to Long's excessive claims for Lee, see Thomas Jordan in 1 *S. H. S. P.*, 403 *ff.*

of having been ten months in command of seriously threatened fronts without having fought a single battle. The deaths from wounds during the whole of his direct control of operations in western Virginia and on the southeastern coast could be counted on the fingers of his right hand. It was a period of preparation for action, rather than of action itself, but it was preparation of the most valuable sort. His touch had been more nearly sure. He had not conquered his excessive amiability, as time was to prove, but he had not let it ruin him as a commander. Little of the embarrassment in dealing with grumblers and malcontents that had been shown in western Virginia was apparent in his second command. With Lee as he had been in August, 1861, Ripley might have proved another Loring, for Ripley's language in criticising his commander was so violent that Governor Pickens complained to President Davis.[121] But Lee went ahead as though Ripley were not antagonistic,[122] and Ripley's slurs, whatever their origin, had no material effect on operations. In close dealings with politicians like Pickens and Brown, Lee was as successful as he had been in winning the good opinion of Letcher of Virginia, and vastly more at ease than in dealing with "political-generals" of the Pillow-Floyd-Wise types.

Much was learned, also, by Lee, while on the coast, about handling larger bodies of men. By successive stages he had come from brief command of a few squadrons of cavalry in Texas to the direction of the unhappy forces in western Virginia, and then to the command of 25,000 men, scattered on a line of 300 miles—and all, to repeat, without having to make quick decisions in the midst of action.

He was lucky, moreover, in having an opportunity of studying how a railroad could be utilized for the movement of troops and how it could be defended. He had learned something of new transportation methods, of course, while doing his part in transporting soldiers to Manassas, to Harpers Ferry, and to Norfolk during April–July, 1861; but the responsibility was entirely his in South Carolina and Georgia. It was a useful lesson, well learned, and it convinced him that the proper defense of a railway

[121] *O. R.*, 6, 367.
[122] *Cf.* his contingent approval of Ripley's proposed operations against North Edisto, *O. R.*, 6, 36r

did not consist in scattering small bodies of men along its entire length, but in guarding strategic bridges and crossings and in concentrating his main force where it could be moved rapidly to endangered points.

Finally, this command confirmed Lee's faith in the indispensability of earthworks. Charleston and Fort Pulaski had represented the familiar problems of permanent fortifications, which he had studied for years before the war; the defense of Coosawhatchie and the inner line at Savannah called for stout works quickly constructed from the materials at hand. Such works had been little used in America before that time and were despised by the Confederate volunteers as representing labor no white man should do and cover behind which no Southerner should take refuge. Lee had believed in digging dirt ever since he had constructed the naval battery at Vera Cruz, and though his men complained all along the coast, he persisted in giving them the protection of field fortification. He could hardly have had better training for the task that awaited him at the Confederate capital to which he now returned.

APPENDIX I—1

The Offer of the Union Command to Lee in 1861

Two apparent conflicts of testimony arise in the story of Lee's interview on April 18, 1861, with Francis Preston Blair, Sr. One is whether President Lincoln had actually authorized the tender of command of the Union army to Lee. The other is whether Lee hesitated before declining it.

The first is, in reality, not a conflict but a confusion of testimony. The statement of Nicolay and Hay[1] that Lincoln merely asked Blair to sound out Lee may be accepted as a fact. But Blair had also had a conversation with Secretary Cameron of the War Department, who had apparently empowered him, in plain terms, to tender the command to Lee. Naturally, in talking to Lee, when he found him cold to the proposal, Mr. Blair involved the greater name, that of the President, and left the impression on Lee's mind that the actual offer, which had come from Cameron, had originated with Mr. Lincoln. This was a perfectly natural mistake for which neither Lee, Blair, Cameron, nor Lincoln was to blame. Subsequently, it will appear, Blair was himself confused as to his authorization.

The other conflict is between Lee on one side and Francis P. Blair, Sr., and Montgomery Blair on the other. Lee's statement, made in 1868, has been quoted. "I never intimated to any one," he said, "that I desired the command of the United States Army; nor did I ever have a conversation with but one gentleman, Mr. Francis Preston Blair, on the subject, which was at his invitation, and, as I understood, at the instance of President Lincoln. After listening to his remarks, I declined the offer he made me, to take command of the army that was to be brought into the field; stating, as candidly and as courteously as I could, that, though opposed to secession, and deprecating war, I could take no part in an invasion of the Southern states."[2] This is first-hand evidence and the only first-hand evidence of what occurred. As it is the language of the man who had the best reason to remember the details, and as it was written by one whose reputation for absolute veracity was never questioned, it is not lightly to be put aside.

[1] 4 *Abraham Lincoln*, 98.
[2] Lee to Reverdy Johnson, Feb. 25, 1868; *R. E. Lee, Jr.,* 27.

APPENDIX

Francis Preston Blair made no memorandum at the time of what occurred between him and Lee. His only account of the interview is as follows: "In the beginning of the war Secretary Cameron asked me to sound General Robert E. Lee, to know whether his feelings would justify him in taking command of our army. His cousin, John Lee, sent him a note at my suggestion. Lee came. I told him what President Lincoln wanted him to do. He wanted him to take command of the army. Lee said he was devoted to the Union. He said, among other things, that he would do everything in his power to save it, and that if he owned all the negroes in the South, he would be willing to give them up and make the sacrifices of the value of every one of them to save the Union. We talked several hours on the political question in that vein. Lee said he did not know how he could draw his sword upon his native state. We discussed that matter at some length, and had some hours of conversation. He said he could not decide without seeing his friend, General Scott. He said he could not under any circumstances, consent to supersede his old commander. He asked me if I supposed the President would consider that proper. I said yes. Then we had a long conversation on that subject. He left the house and was soon after met by a committee from Richmond. He went with them, as I understood from some friends afterwards, to consult the Virginia convention as to some mode of settling the difficulty. I never saw him afterwards. The matter was talked over by President Lincoln and myself for some hours on two or three different occasions. The President and Secretary Cameron expressed themselves as anxious to give the command of our army to Robert E. Lee. I considered myself as authorized to inform Lee of that fact." [3]

This statement was not given over Mr. Blair's signature. It was made verbally to Captain James May, who reported it to Chief Justice Chase, by whom, apparently, it was written down, though there is a possibility that May transcribed it for Chase.[4] The report is, therefore, second-hand or third-hand and was made ten years after the event, on the authority of a man who was then eighty years of age. Although there is not the slightest reason for thinking that the senior Blair intended to falsify the facts, his report at fourscore of a conversation that occurred when he was seventy and lasted several hours cannot be accepted as in the same category with Lee's own. At that, it will be observed that the only material conflict between Lee and Blair is in the statement that Blair quoted Lee as saying that "he could not decide without seeing his friend, General Scott." It is quite possible

[3] 3 *Rhodes*, 365 n. [4] *Cf. ibid.*

634

that if anything like this was said, it was *à propos* of Lee's assumption of command in case hostilities did not occur. At that time, it will be remembered, Lee, as he said, still "hoped that peace would have been preserved." [5] Had war been avoided, Lee's ready acceptance of Lincoln's commission as colonel shows that he would unhesitatingly have accepted the command, provided it could have been done without his superseding General Scott. It may have been in connection with just such a contingency that he said he wished to discuss the subject with his old commander.

The only other evidence is that of Montgomery Blair, son of F. P. Blair, Sr. [6] Explaining the Southern point of view, Blair wrote: "General Lee said to my father, when he was sounded by him, at the request of President Lincoln, about taking command of our army against the rebellion, 'Mr. Blair, I look upon secession as anarchy. If I owned the four millions of slaves in the South I would sacrifice them all to the Union but how can I draw my sword upon Virginia, my native State?' He could not determine then; said he would consult with his friend, General Scott, and went on the same day to Richmond, probably to arbitrate difficulties; and we see the result. It is hard for a noble mind to tear itself from home, kindred, friends, and native soil, and go into the opposite ranks to crush them all."

This, of course, was the version the son received from the father, as he was not present himself. His direct quotation of Lee indicates either that the memory of the elder Blair had begun to fade in 1871, or else that Montgomery Blair "dressed up" the story unintentionally in 1865. Further, Montgomery Blair's reference to Lee's departure for Richmond "the same day" shows that he was not familiar with all the facts. Still again, both the Blairs quoted Lee as saying that he could not draw his sword upon Virginia, when, as a matter of fact, Lee did not then know that Virginia had seceded, though he may well have feared that she would.

Without impeaching the honorable, highminded Blairs, except as the memory of the one may have played him false and the information of the other may have been at fault, every law of historical evidence bears out the literal accuracy of Lee's own statement. [7] This would be the conclusion if there were no other evidence than that of the inter-

[5] Lee to Reverdy Johnson, Feb. 25, 1868; *R. E. Lee, Jr.*, 28.
[6] *National Intelligencer*, Aug. 9, 1866; reprinted from *The New York Evening Post*.
[7] It is significant that Doctor William Ernest Smith in his admirable *The Francis Preston Blair Family in Politics* accepts Lee's version without advancing that of the Blairs on the other side, and disposes in this summary fashion of the contention that Lee hesitated: "Certain recent criticisms of the Blair-Lee story," he says, "are not worth refutation." (*Op. cit.*, 2, 18.)

view itself. Behind this evidence, however, stands all that Lee is known to have stated in Texas concerning his intentions. Having determined then, without a mental struggle, to follow the fortunes of Virginia, how can he be reasonably assumed, on the strength of late second-hand testimony, to have hesitated thereafter, except as to the time when honor demanded that he resign?

APPENDIX I—2

TOWNSEND'S ACCOUNT OF LEE'S INTERVIEW WITH SCOTT, APRIL 18, 1861

General Scott knew that he [Lee] was at Arlington Heights, at the house of his father-in-law, Mr. Custis, and one day asked me if I had seen or heard of him lately. I replied in the negative, except that he was on leave and at Arlington Heights. Said the general, "It is time he should show his hand and if he remains loyal should take an important command." I then suggested that I should write a note to Lee and ask him to call at the general's headquarters. "I wish you would," replied the general. The note was written and the next day, April 19, 1861, Colonel Lee came to the office. The general's was the front room of the second story. His round table stood in the centre of the room and I had a desk in one corner. The aides were in an adjoining room with a door opening into the general's. When Lee came in, I was alone in the room with the general and the door to the aides' room was closed. I quietly arose, keeping my eye on the general, for it seemed probable he might wish to be alone with Lee. He, however, secretly motioned me to keep my seat and I sat down without Lee having a chance to notice that I had risen. The general having invited Lee to be seated, the following conversation, as nearly as I can remember, took place. *General Scott:* "You are at present on leave of absence, Colonel Lee?" *Colonel Lee:* "Yes, General, I am staying with my family at Arlington." *General Scott:* "These are times when every officer in the United States service should fully determine what course he will pursue and frankly declare it. No one should continue in government employ without being actively employed." (No response from Lee.) *General Scott* (after a pause): "Some of the Southern officers are resigning, possibly with the intention of taking part with their States. They make a fatal mistake. The contest may be long and severe, but eventually the issue must be in favor of the Union." (Another pause and no reply from Lee.) *General Scott* (seeing evidently that Lee showed no disposition to declare himself loyal or even in doubt): "I suppose you will go with the rest. If you purpose to resign, it is proper you should do so at once; your present attitude is an equivocal one." *Colonel Lee:* "The property belonging to my children, all they possess, lies in Virginia. They will be ruined, if they do not go with their State. I cannot raise my hand against my children." [1]

[1] E. D. Townsend: *Anecdotes of the Civil War*, 29.

APPENDIX I—3

The Summons of Lee to Richmond, April, 1861

On April 17 the Virginia convention had passed an ordinance authorizing the governor to accept the service of volunteers and to invite Virginia officers in the United States army and navy to join the armed forces of Virginia, with rank at least equal to that which they held under the Union.[1] Acting on this authority, Governor Letcher on the 18th, the day of Lee's interview with Blair, sent David Funsten[2] of Alexandria, who was then in Richmond, on a mission to Lee to acquaint him with the action of the convention, and to ask whether he would accept the call of Virginia.[3] Owing to the interruption of traffic, Mr. Funsten was not able to reach Alexandria. After waiting for a day for some word from Funsten, the governor on the 19th dispatched Judge Robertson to interview Colonel Lee, General Scott, and probably some others.[4] Judge Robertson was turned back on the 19th because the Federal authorities had seized the mail boats on the Potomac,[5] but on the 20th he started again by way of Gordonsville, reached Alexandria, learned from Daingerfield that Lee had resigned,

[1] *Journal of the Virginia Convention of 1861;* Ordinances Adopted in Secret Session, p. 6.
[2] David and Oliver R. Funsten were two gallant brothers who are often confused. David, of Alexandria, became colonel of the 11th Virginia Infantry, and Oliver, of Clarke County, held the same rank with the 11th Virginia Cavalry.
[3] John Letcher to the Virginia Convention, *MS.,* April 20, 1861, *Virginia Executive Papers.*
[4] *MS. Journal Virginia Executive Council,* April 19, 1861, Va. State Library; Letcher to Virginia Convention, *MS.,* April 20, 1861, *loc. cit.* Van Horne (*George H. Thomas,* 30–31) intimated that George H. Thomas was one of these, and that influences were at work to give him the supreme command in Virginia. In John Robertson to John Letcher, *MS.,* April 20, 1861, *loc. cit.,* there is a reference to "three others" unnamed. Thomas doubtless was one of these, but there is nothing to indicate that Thomas was considered for the post offered Lee.
[5] John Letcher to the Virginia Convention, *MS.,* April 20, 1861, *loc. cit.*

and so advised Letcher.[6] Meantime, Letcher had received Robertson's telegram. On Sunday, April 21, the governor decided to tender Lee the chief command of the Virginia forces and sent still another messenger to notify him that if he accepted, Letcher would submit his name to the convention for confirmation.[7]

APPENDIX I—4

THE STAFF OF GENERAL LEE

Not infrequently, during the years following the war, General Lee's staff officers were under the embarrassing necessity of having to deny that some men who claimed to have served on the staff of Lee had ever done so. Occasionally, even now, the descendants of some Confederate officers mistakenly aver that their ancestors were members of the "official family" of Lee. In most instances these latter claims are based primarily on a misconception of the organization of the staff.

Occasionally during the war, and especially in a long list of appointments announced on November 2, 1863, the office of the adjutant and inspector general ordered a number of staff officers to "report to General Lee." The usual phrase, "for assignment to duty" seems to have been omitted. As a result, some have assumed that because these men were listed as assistant adjutants general, they were designated for the staff of General Lee. In reality, all of them were assigned to other staffs, most of them to the brigades.

Then, again, in emergencies, or when officers of high rank had been killed, General Lee occasionally attached temporarily to his staff men who had served with the corps staffs. It is difficult in some instances to say whether these men are entitled to be regarded as regular members of his staff.

The chief ground for advancing unfounded claims, however, is a confusion of the personal staff with the general staff. Besides his own immediate adjutants and aides, General Lee had, of course, a force of officers who would now be termed the "general staff." These men, in turn, had a varying number of assistants. In an official phrase, such officers were "attached to the headquarters of the Army of Northern Virginia," but they were not, in any true sense, members of the personal staff of the commanding general.

To make this confusion worse, General Lee himself did not draw

[6] Robertson to Letcher, MS., April 20, 1861, loc. cit.
[7] MS. Journal Virginia Executive Council, April 21, 1861, loc. cit.

any line between his personal staff and the general staff until he assumed charge of the Army of Northern Virginia on June 1, 1862. Further, the general was opposed to large personal staffs as a waste of military material. He kept his own staff strictly within the law, and, on days of battle, pressed the bureau chiefs of the general staff into service as aides, as explained in Vol. II, page 489.

Finally, the assistant inspectors general occupied in some instances a position in Lee's military organization midway between the personal and the general staff, and are difficult to classify.

For these reasons it has seemed best to list the members of his staff separately for the five different periods of his command. The names have been sifted from those given by Long[1] and by Talcott,[2] supplemented by a detailed examination of all the names in the *List of Staff Officers of the Confederate States Army, 1861–1865,* as issued by the editors of the *Official Records* in 1891, and, finally, from the numerous references in the *Official Records* themselves. It has not been possible to assign positive dates for the connection of all officers with his staff, as those in the *List of Staff Officers* are taken, in the main, from military papers signed by the individual officers. In many cases, officers were attached to the staff before and after the date of official documents now extant. Officers who had promotion while on staff duty are here listed with their final or highest rank, unless some special condition makes an explanation necessary.

FIRST PERIOD—THE VIRGINIA COMMAND

Brigadier General R. S. Garnett, assistant adjutant general, who, during the brief period prior to his dispatch to the field, was more nearly a chief of staff to Lee than any other officer ever became.

Colonel John A. Washington, commissioned as aide de camp but soon acting as assistant adjutant general.

Lieutenant Colonel Walter H. Taylor, who ere long was placed in general charge of the "office work."

Colonel George A. Deas, who was assistant adjutant general and, after the departure of Garnett for western Virginia, acted as chief of staff.

Captain F. W. Smith, military secretary for a time in May, 1861.

These might be accounted the immediate personal staff of Lee during April–June, 1861.

In addition, he employed two naval aides for brief periods. They were:

[1] *Op. cit.,* 501–2.   [2] 35 *S. H. S. P.,* 255 *ff.*

Lieutenant John M. Brooke of the Virginia Navy, one of the most brilliant of all Southern naval officers, and

Lieutenant Thomas J. Page, who was temporary "acting aide de camp."

Other officers attached to Lee's headquarters at this time and discharging certain personal staff duties as well as performing general staff work were:

Major Jos. R. Crenshaw, acting commissary general for Virginia.

Colonel, subsequently Major General, Harry Heth, acting quartermaster general for Virginia during May, 1861.

Colonel A. C. Myers, who assumed temporary duty as chief of the quartermaster's department of Virginia, May 31, 1861.

The other members of the incomplete general staff of Virginia were hardly associated enough with General Lee to be reckoned as staff officers.

Besides these, the adjutant general of Virginia, W. H. Richardson, occasionally signed for General Lee as assistant adjutant general.

SECOND PERIOD—THE WEST VIRGINIA CAMPAIGN

Colonel Deas was left in charge of the office in Richmond when General Lee went to West Virginia. The only officers he took with him were Colonel Washington and Colonel Taylor. Colonel Washington was killed on September 13.[3] This left Colonel Taylor as Lee's only personal staff officer. As Lee was not in direct command, he organized no general staff.

THIRD PERIOD—THE SOUTH CAROLINA OPERATIONS

Colonel Walter H. Taylor went with Lee to South Carolina.

After his arrival, Lee named two assistant adjutants general. They were:

Major Thornton A. Washington and

Captain R. W. Memminger.[4]

He had three volunteer aides, as follows:

Captain Joseph Manigault,

Captain John M. Maffitt of the navy, and

Captain J. R. F. Tatnall of the marine corps.

The officers of the general staff, who were in close touch with him because of the smallness of the force were:

Lieutenant Colonel William G. Gill, ordnance officer,

Major, later Brigadier General, A. L. Long, chief of artillery, and

[3] See *supra*, pp. 568–69.   [4] See *O. R.*, 6, 406–7.

APPENDIX

Colonel Jos. C. Ives, chief of engineers, later on the staff of President Davis.[5]

FOURTH PERIOD—ADVISER TO THE PRESIDENT

When General Lee returned from South Carolina in March, 1862, to act as military adviser to the President, a law was enacted[6] providing that he should have a staff of one military secretary with rank of colonel, four aides ranking as major, and not more than four clerks.[7] Lee told Taylor that he could either remain with the adjutant general's department or join him. Taylor chose to take the staff position.[8] Lee thereupon designated this staff.

A. L. Long as military secretary.[9]

As aides:

Walter H. Taylor,

T. M. R. Talcott, son of his old friend Andrew Talcott, and himself an engineer officer,

Charles S. Venable, and

Charles Marshall of Maryland.[10]

Major T. A. Washington was soon brought to Richmond from South Carolina and was assigned from the force of the adjutant general as assistant to Lee.[11]

FIFTH PERIOD—COMMANDER OF THE ARMY OF NORTHERN VIRGINIA

After Lee succeeded General Joseph E. Johnston, June 1, 1862, he offered to retain General Johnston's staff officers. All of them elected to retire with their chief except Captain, later Lieutenant Colonel, A. P. Mason. He remained as an assistant adjutant general. On June 4 the War Department assigned Colonel R. H. Chilton of the regular army of the Confederacy to General Lee, who named him chief of staff.[12] As Lee retained his former staff, his headquarters establishment until March, 1863, was as follows:

R. H. Chilton, chief of staff,

A. L. Long, military secretary, though often discharging many of the duties of chief of artillery,

---

[5] The *List of Staff-Officers* shows that Assistant Surgeon Samuel Muller and Surgeon J. A. Pleasants were assigned to Lee in South Carolina. It is believed that their services were with the troops, rather than at headquarters.

[6] See Vol. II, p. 5.

[7] IV *O. R.*, 1, 997–98, 1021.　　　　　　　[8] *Taylor's General Lee*, 42.

[9] *Long*, 143; *O. R.*, 12, part 3, p. 891; *ibid.*, 51, part 2, p. 548.

[10] Marshall, *op. cit.*, 3, stated that he entered on his duties March 21. The formal announcement from the adjutant general's office bore date of May 10 (*O. R.*, 51, part 2, p. 554).

[11] *Cf. O. R.*, 11, part 3, p. 419.　　　　　　[12] *O. R.*, 11, part 3, p. 574.

Walter H. Taylor, aide de camp but more than aide; after the early spring of 1863, first "acting" and then assistant adjutant general of the army,

Charles S. Venable, aide de camp, and devoting much time to inspections,

Charles Marshall, aide de camp and acting often as military secretary in the preparation of reports,

T. M. R. Talcott, aide de camp, but employed for engineering as well, and

A. P. Mason, assistant adjutant general.

This was the staff with which Lee fought his principal battles of 1862. Taylor, Venable, and Marshall remained with Lee to the end of the war, ate at his mess and rose to the well-deserved rank of lieutenant colonel.

The general staff, as reorganized after Lee assumed command of the Army of Northern Virginia, consisted of the following chiefs:

Lieutenant Colonel, later Brigadier General, E. Porter Alexander, chief of ordnance to November, 1862,

Lieutenant Colonel Briscoe G. Baldwin, chief of ordnance thereafter,

Lieutenant Colonel Robert G. Cole, chief commissary,

Lieutenant Colonel James L. Corley, chief quartermaster,

Surgeon Lafayette Guild, medical director,

Brigadier General W. N. Pendleton, chief of artillery, and

Major H. E. Young, judge advocate general.

All these officers except Alexander served on the general staff to the end of the war. On occasion, they performed duty as if they were members of the personal staff of the commanding general, but they were not regularly at headquarters and did not mess, as a rule, with the commanding general.

Captain Mason retired from Lee's staff in the spring of 1863 to rejoin Johnston. Colonel Chilton, in March, 1864, left the staff to resume service as a brigadier general, with the adjutant and inspector general. Talcott became colonel of the First Regiment of engineer troops, April 4, 1864. Lee did not immediately fill these vacancies. Instead, he used more frequently the members of the general staff already mentioned.

Major H. B. McClellan, after the death of Stuart, whose A. A. G. he had been, served for some months as an aide to General Lee.

Major Giles B. Cooke joined the personal staff in November. 1864, as assistant adjutant general and served regularly thereafter.

APPENDIX

Major H. E. Young, as the war progressed, came increasingly to serve as a member of the personal rather than of the general staff.

Major H. E. Peyton, though engaged much of his time in inspections, had a like distinction.

The following officers, also attached to headquarters, principally as assistant inspectors general, frequently acted in a more personal capacity for General Lee:

Lieutenant Colonel Edwin J. Harvie, June, 1862, subsequently joining General Johnston, with whom he had previously served.

Colonel George W. Lay, March, 1863.

Lieutenant Colonel Edward Murray, December 30, 1862, to August 31, 1863, and again in November, 1864.

General Lee did not always have an engineer officer attached to headquarters. The force of engineers was so small that the chief engineer of the Department of Northern Virginia sometimes had to direct the fortification of Richmond as well as the engineering of the army. When Lee was near Richmond he frequently utilized the services of the officers in the bureau of engineering. The following engineer officers were, however, frequently at headquarters, during the periods indicated:

Lieutenant Colonel William Proctor Smith, who was chief engineer in the summer of 1863.

Captain S. R. Johnston, who was with Lee during the Gettysburg campaign.

Major General M. L. Smith, who officially was chief engineer of the Army of Northern Virginia, from April 16, 1864, to approximately July 20, 1864.

Brigadier General W. H. Stevens, chief engineer during June–July, 1862, and from August, 1864, to the end of the war.

In addition, Major General Jeremy F. Gilmer, then colonel, was chief engineer of the Department of Northern Virginia from August 4, 1862, to October 4, 1862, when he became the brilliant chief of the engineer bureau of the War Department, but his duties kept him in Richmond most of the time.

There were, besides these, numerous assistants in the quartermaster, commissary, ordnance, and medical departments, many of them very efficient men. It is believed, however, that the names contained in this list are those, and all those, of the men who can be accounted either members of the personal staff of Lee or heads of the bureaus of the general staff.

APPENDIX

APPENDIX I—5

GENERAL LEE'S MOUNTS

Soon after General Lee came to Richmond in the spring of 1861, some of his admirers presented him with a bay stallion, whom he named Richmond. This was the mount Lee used when he made his inspections of the camps and fortifications around the capital city before going to western Virginia.[1] Richmond had strong peculiarities. "He is a troublesome fellow," Lee wrote of him, "and dislikes to associate with strange horses. He expresses it more in words than acts, and if firmly treated becomes quiet at last." When with horses he did not know Richmond was prone to squeal.[2] Lee carried Richmond to western Virginia, and as he needed more than one mount there he bought another whom he called simply The Roan or Brown-Roan.

While Lee was engaged in the operations on Sewell Mountain, he saw a young soldier, J. W. Johnston, riding a fine, gray four-year-old. The horse seemed to possess such excellent qualities that Lee inquired about him. He found the horse had been raised by Andrew Johnston near Blue Sulphur Springs and had been given by him to his son, the rider Lee had seen. Originally named Jeff Davis, the horse had won two first prizes at the Greenbrier County fair. Johnston had promised to sell him to Captain Joseph M. Broun, who wanted him for his brother, Major Thomas L. Broun, but he offered to get him for Lee if the general desired him.[3] The horse was delivered to Captain Broun when Johnston, who belonged to the infantry and had been serving on detail, returned to his command. Captain Broun duly turned the horse over to Major Broun, but both brothers used him around Sewell Mountain. Lee saw the animal often, and in asking the Brouns about him, always referred to him as "my colt," saying he would need him later in the war.[4]

When Lee went back to Richmond, he took Richmond and The Roan with him, and when he started to South Carolina, he carried The Roan. Not long after he arrived there, Captain Broun's command arrived and Broun was riding Jeff Davis, who by this time may have been called Greenbrier, for it was by the latter name that Lee referred to him on December 29, 1861.[5] Lee mentioned again the purchase of

[1] 19 S. H. S. P., 333. [2] Jones, L. and L., 161.
[3] Statement of J. W. Johnston to Governor D. C. Hayward of South Carolina, originally printed in The Columbia State and republished in Fairfax Harrison: The Equine F. F. V.'s, 173.
[4] La Bree, 307 ff.: Thomas L. Broun in 35 S. H. S. P., 100.
[5] Jones, L. and L., 157.

the animal, whereupon Broun offered to present the horse to the general. Lee declined the gift, of course, but said that if Broun would willingly sell him, he would gladly try him. Broun promptly sent the horse to Lee, who rode him with much pleasure, but ere long sent him back, saying that he could not use so valuable a horse at such a time unless he owned him. Broun therefore wrote his brother, Major Broun, who was sick in western Virginia. Major Broun replied that if Lee wanted the horse, and would not accept him as a gift, Lee could have him for what Broun had paid for him, $175 in gold. Lee then purchased him for $200, making allowance for depreciation of the currency.[6] The horse was somewhat nervous, had a fast, springy walk, but preferred a "short, high trot," which was hard on riders who had a less good seat than Lee.[7] He never required whips or spur. The general soon dubbed him Traveller and became devoted to him. After the war he wrote this description of his favorite for Markie Williams, who proposed to make a painting of the animal:

"If I were an artist like you, I would draw a true picture of Travel- ler; representing his fine proportions, muscular figure, deep chest, short back, strong haunches, flat legs, small head, broad forehead, delicate ears, quick eye, small feet and black mane and tail. Such a picture would inspire a poet, whose genius could then depict his worth and describe his endurance of toil, hunger, thirst, heat and cold, and the dangers and sufferings through which he passed. He could dilate upon his sagacity and affection, and his invariable response to every wish of his rider. He might even imagine his thoughts through the long night-Marches and days of battle through which he has passed. But I am no artist Markie, and can therefore only say he is a Con- federate grey. I purchased him in the mountains of Virginia in the Fall of 1861,[8] and he has been my patient follower ever since, to Georgia, the Carolinas and back to Virginia. He carried me through the seven days battle around Richmond, the Second Manassas, at Sharpsburg, Fredericksburg, the last day at Chancellorsville, to Penna, at Gettysburg, and back to the Rappahannock. From the commence- ment of the campaign in 1864 at Orange, till its close around Peters- burg, the saddle was scarcely off his back, as he passed through the fire of the Wilderness, Spotsylvania, Cold Harbour, and across the James river. He was almost in daily requisition in the winter of 1864-'65 on the long line of defences from the Chickahominy north

---

[6] La Bree, loc. cit.　　　　[7] 35 S. H. S. P., 99; cf. R. E. Lee, Jr., 84.
[8] Lee, as already explained, was mistaken in this: the purchase was made in South Carolina.

of Richmond, to Hatcher's run south of the Appomattox, 35 miles in length; and in 1865 bore me to the final days at Appomattox Ct. House. You know the comfort he is to me in my present retirement. He is well supplied with equipments— Two sets have been sent to him from England, one by the Ladies in Baltimore and one was made for him in Richmond; but I think his favourite is the American saddle from St. Louis. . . ." [9]

During the Seven Days, when the demands on Lee's mounts were very great, The Roan began to go blind and had to be placed with a farmer who promised to care for him. Richmond died after Malvern Hill.[10] Apparently Lee had no other regular mount than Traveller from that time until after he was thrown to the earth during the Second Manassas campaign, when Traveller became frightened while Lee was standing on the ground, holding the bridle-rein. Stuart then procured for Lee from Stephen Dandridge of "The Bower" a low, quiet, and manageable mare named Lucy Long. About the same time, some friends in southwest Virginia sent the general a fine sorrel horse, whom Lee called Ajax. This horse, however, was too tall for the general, who seldom rode him.

Traveller and Lucy Long served him most of the time until close to the end of the war, when Lucy Long was sent to the rear. The story of her loss and recovery is set forth in the text.[11] Ajax, Traveller, and Lucy Long went with the general to Lexington. Ajax killed himself by running into the iron prong of a gate-latch before the general's death. Traveller and Lucy Long both outlived him. Traveller died of lockjaw after the demise of the general, to the great distress of the Lee household, and was buried on the property of Washington and Lee.[12] Lucy Long injured one of her hind legs and was retired, but lived until 1891.[13] Traveller's bones were disinterred in 1907 and were placed in the museum of Washington and Lee University, where the skeleton now stands. Having shared so much of the fame of the general, his ancestry has been studied. He was variously said by different authorities to be of the Grey Eagle stock and of the stock of an unidentified and perhaps apocryphal imp. Arab. It is thought possible by so eminent an authority as Fairfax Harrison that he was descended from the great Diomed.[14]

The horse furnishings of Traveller are in the Confederate Museum

---

[9] *Markie Letters*, 73–74; incorrectly printed in *R. E. Lee, Jr.*, 83–84.
[10] 19 *S. H. S. P.*, 334.   [11] Volume IV.
[12] See the account of Mrs. Margaret Letcher Showell, *Richmond Times-Dispatch*, Oct. 28, 1929.
[13] 18 *S. H. S. P.*, 39; 19 *S. H. S. P.*, 33–35.   [14] Fairfax Harrison, *op. cit.*, 173.

in Richmond. When Lee rode him, he rarely carried any arms except a pistol, which was in his left holster, where it would be within instant reach when the General was dismounted. Ammunition was kept in the right holster. When the quiet days at Lexington came, this same pistol hung over Lee's bed. After his death, when it was discharged, not a barrel missed fire.[15]

Lee was always exceedingly careful in looking after his horses, in peace as in war. He gave particular attention to their shoeing.[16] The girthing, the throat-band, and the folding of the blanket received Lee's personal attention. When Lee was in open campaigning, he dismounted as often as he could, in order to rest his steed.

[15] *Fitz Lee*, 313.
[16] *Long*, 38; Lee to Major Duffey, MS., May 30, 1863; copy of which was given the writer by Mrs. T. P. Bryan.

Printed in the United States
20041LVS00003B/59